*Publications on Asia
of
the School
of International Studies*

NUMBER 32

This book is sponsored by the China and Inner Asia Program of the School of International Studies (formerly the Institute for Comparative and Foreign Area Studies) of the University of Washington, Seattle.

A Concise Manchu-English Lexicon

JERRY NORMAN

UNIVERSITY OF WASHINGTON PRESS

SEATTLE AND LONDON

Copyright © 1978 University of Washington Press
Printed in the United States of America

Library of Congress Cataloging in Publication Data

Norman, Jerry, 1936-
    A concise Manchu-English lexicon.
    (Publications on Asia of the School of International
Studies ; no. 32)
    Bibliography: p.
    1. Manchu language--Dictionaries--English.
I. Title. II. Series: Washington (State). University.
School of International Studies.
Publications on Asia ; no. 32.
PL477.N67   494'.1   77-14307
ISBN 0-295-95574-0

*Publications on Asia of the School of International Studies is
a continuation of the series formerly entitled Publications on
Asia of the Institute for Comparative and Foreign Area Studies*

Contents

Preface

Manchu was, in theory at least, the official language of the Ch'ing dynasty in China for more than two hundred and fifty years (1644-1911). Because the ruling Manchus were vastly outnumbered by their Chinese subjects, most of the day-to-day business of the empire was undoubtedly carried out in Chinese; nevertheless, an immense number of annals, memorials, edicts, and other official material written in Manchu have survived. Up to the very last days of the dynasty all important documents were bilingual, having both a Manchu and Chinese version. But probably more voluminous than this official, documentary material is the impressive body of translation literature produced by the Manchus beginning even before the official foundation of the dynasty. Classics, commentaries, histories, novels, plays, poetry--in short--Chinese literature of every genre, was translated on an unprecedented scale into the Manchu language. Premodern Sinologists made extensive use of these translations both for learning Chinese and in translating classical works into western languages. Today, it would be foolish to maintain that a knowledge of Manchu is an essential tool for the learning of classical Chinese as some earlier scholars did, but it would be equally rash to claim that the Manchu translations of Chinese literature are totally devoid of interest. So while a knowledge of Manchu is by no means indispensable to the Sinologist or Ch'ing historian, there can be no doubt that it can be a valuable asset in many cases.

Manchu is also of great interest to the linguist. As the best documented member of the Tungusic language family, it has played an important role in the development of the Altaic theory that relates Turkic, Mongolian, and Tungusic together in one of the world's great language families. There is mounting evidence that Japanese and Korean are also related to Altaic, and Manchu, because of its geographical proximity to these two languages, can be expected to play an important role in the further elaboration of this hypothesis.

The aim of the present dictionary is to provide a basic learning tool for the student of Manchu, be he an historian, student of

Chinese literature, or linguist. It is concise in the sense that it does not contain examples of usage (except in rare instances); nor does it contain a complete listing of archaic forms and variant spellings. Place and personal names, names of books, designations of various rare Chinese mythological curiosities and little-known deities have also been omitted. Even so, I believe that the reader of Manchu will find most of the words he encounters in his texts here and will only very occasionally be obliged to consult a more comprehensive lexicon.

A few of the most common spelling variations can be mentioned briefly: Between vowels or between a vowel plus a voiced consonant (but never at the beginning of words) *h* and *g* often interchange; for example, the word for 'to sleep' in some texts is spelled *amhambi*, in others *amgambi*. Final *-n* is sometimes lacking: one may find *daila* for *dailan*, or *maisha* for *maishan*. The simple vowel *o* and the digraph *oo* are sometimes interchanged; for example, *jolambi* may be found for a more usual *joolambi*. After a little experience in reading Manchu texts, the reader will develop a feeling for these graphic variants and they will rarely cause serious problems.

Official titles have, wherever possible, been given according to Brunnert and Hagelstrom's *Present Day Political Organization of China*. Such translations are followed by the abbreviation BH and the number of the relevant section of the book. Translations of titles that do not occur in Brunnert and Hagelstrom are my own. The Chinese for most titles has been given in parentheses following the entry. Certain other difficult terms like the names of Chinese constellations and quaint styles of calligraphy are also followed by their Chinese original for the reader's reference.

Verbs are cited in their *-mbi* form. In this I have merely followed the pattern established by earlier dictionaries. Irregular verbal endings have been given, where feasible, in parentheses following the entry. Since it is expected that the user of this book will have a basic knowledge of Manchu grammar, irregular verb forms generally have not been given separate entries. Derived verbs like the passive, causative, and frequentative have, however, been listed separately.

All entries and subentries are in alphabetical order; *š* follows *s*, and *ū* follows *u*. Entries beginning with *dz* and *ts* have been put in separate sections; *g'* and *k'*, however, have been added to the end of the *g* and *k* sections, respectively.

Acknowledgments

I first began work on this dictionary in 1966 when I was a Fulbright Fellow in Taipei. In 1967 I completed a preliminary draft that was made available to a number of scholars and students for their comments. After I returned to the United States, I began to correct and expand the original draft; the result is the present work.

During the earlier work of compilation I received much aid and encouragement from my two Manchu teachers, James Bosson of the University of California at Berkeley and Kuang Lu of National Taiwan University. It was Professor Bosson who introduced me to Manchu studies and planted in me the seeds of a lasting enthusiasm. The late Professor Kuang was a member of the Sibe minority, probably the last group of native Manchu speakers. I consider myself exceptionally fortunate to have had the opportunity to study with Professor Kuang and to have been able to consult with him regularly during the period when I began work on this dictionary.

The preparation of the final manuscript was greatly expedited by two summer grants. I was supported in the summer of 1974 by a grant from the China Program of the Institute for Comparative and Foreign Area Studies at the University of Washington. A grant from the Committee on Chinese Civilization of the American Council of Learned Societies made it possible for me to devote the summer of 1975 to completing the final draft of the dictionary. I would like to express my gratitude to both of these organizations for their timely and generous support.

Stephen Durrant, now professor of Chinese at Brigham Young University, typed and helped correct the final draft. Without his highly efficient assistance, I would not have been able to finish this work as quickly as I have. Special thanks are due also to Margery Lang, editor of publications for the Institute for Comparative and Foreign Area Studies, and to Felicia Hecker, who skillfully prepared the manuscript for publication.

Of the many people who rendered assistance at the various

stages of this work, the following deserve special mention: Chen Su-chüan, who typed the two earliest drafts; Jerome Cavanaugh, who read through the entire first draft and pointed out many errors to me; Elian Chuaqui-Numan, who helped me with the final proofreading; and Hanson Chase, who is responsible for the Chinese calligraphy.

I owe a special debt of gratitude to my wife, Chen En-chi, who has helped me in countless ways.

Final responsibility for any remaining errors or shortcomings rests solely with me.

Selected Bibliography

Allen Glover M. *The Mammals of China and Mongolia*. 1 vol. in 2. New York: American Museum of Natural History, 1938-1940.

Bailey, L. H. *Manual of Cultivated Plants Most Commonly Grown in the Continental United States and Canada*. New York: Macmillan, 1949.

Brunnert, H. S. and Hagelstrom, V. V. *Present Day Political Organization of China*. Shanghai, 1912.

Chao, Yuen Ren. "Popular Chinese Plant Words: A Descriptive Lexico-grammatical Study." *Language* 29 (1953): 379-414.

Cheng Tso-hsin 鄭作新 , ed. *Chung-kuo ching-chi tung-wu chih, niao-lei* 中國經濟動物誌，鳥類 [The economic animals of China: bird section]. Peking, 1966.

Chou Han-fan 周漢藩 . *Ho-pei hsi-chien yü-lei t'u-shuo* 河北習見魚類圖說 [An illustrated account of the fish in Hopei streams]. Peiping, 1934.

Ch'ing-wen tsung-hui 清文總彙 . Peking, 1897.

Han-i araha manju gisun-i buleku bithe. Peking, 1708.

Haneda, Tōru 羽田亨 . *Manwa jiten* 満和辭典 . Kyoto, 1937.

Hauer, Erich. *Handwörterbuch der Mandschusprache*. Wiesbaden: Otto Harrassowitz, 1952-1955.

K'ung Ch'ing-lai et al. 孔慶萊 . *Chih-wu-hsüeh ta-tz'u-tien* 植物學大辭典 [Botanical dictionary]. Shanghai, 1923.

Shaw Tsen-hwang [Shou Chen-huang] 壽振黃 . *The Birds of Hopei Province.* Peiping: 1936.

——. *Chung-kuo ching-chi tung-wu chih, shou-lei* 中國経濟 動物誌, 獸類 [The economic animals of China: animal section]. Peking, 1964.

Sowerby, Arthur de Carle. "Recent Research upon the Mammalia of North China." *Journal of the North China Branch of the Royal Asiatic Society* 47 (1916): 53-82.

——. *The Naturalist in Manchuria.* 5 vols. in 3. Tientsin, 1922-30.

Ta Ch'ing hui-tien t'u 大清會典圖 1899. Reprint. Taipei, 1965.

von Möllendorff, O. F. "The Vertebrata of the Province of Chih-li with Notes on Chinese Zoological Nomenclature." *Journal of the North China Branch of the Royal Asiatic Society* (n.s.), 11 (1877): 41-111.

Yü-chih wu-t'i Ch'ing-wen chien 御製五體清文鑑 . Reprint. Peking, 1957.

Zakharov, Ivan. *Polnyj Man'čžursko-Russkij Slovar'.* 1875. Reprint. Peking, 1939.

A Concise Manchu-English Lexicon

Abbreviations

BH	Brunnert and Hagelstrom (see bibliography)
caus.	causative
onom.	onomatopoetic
pass.	passive
v.i.	intransitive verb
v.t.	transitive verb

A

A 1. the male or positive principle, yang 2. convex, raised 3. interjection of response 4. interjection of fear 5. vocative particle 6. a tooth in the Manchu script
 A A an interjection of casual response
 A I BUKDAN the outside edge of a piece of folded paper
 A JIJUN I ACANGGA a bronze identification token with raised characters used to gain admittance to a city at night
 A JILGAN a yang tone in music
A FA SERE ONGGOLO see *afanggala*
A SI a sound used for driving chickens or birds
A TA (onom.) the sound of a commotion
ABA 1. hunt, battue 2. where
 ABA BARGIYAMBI to call in a hunt, to call in a battue
 ABA SAHA hunting
 ABA SARAMBI to spread out a battue line
 ABA SINDAMBI to form up a battue
 ABA TUCIMBI to depart on a hunt or battue
ABALABUMBI caus. of *abalambi*
ABALAMBI to participate in a battue, to hunt
ABALANAMBI to go to participate in a battue, to go to hunt
ABALANDUMBI/ABALANUMBI to hunt together, to participate in a battue together
ABALANJIMBI to come to participate in a battue
ABDAHA leaf
 ABDAHA AISIN gold leaf
 ABDAHA EFEN a small cake in the shape of a leaf
ABDAHANAMBI to leaf, to produce leaves
 ABDAHANAME BANJIMBI to produce leaves, to become leafy
ABDALAMBI see *abtalambi*

ABDANGGA 1. having leaves, leafy 2. folded accordion fashion
 ABDANGGA AFAHA a paper folded accordion fashion
 ABDANGGA BITHE a document folded accordion fashion
 ABDANGGA FUNGNEHEN an imperial document on yellow or gold paper
 ABDANGGA MOO the Chinese fan palm
ABDARI tarajò (*Ilex latifolia*)
ABGARI idle, without occupation, retired official
 ABGARI BANJIMBI to be idle, to live in retirement
ABIDA Amida Buddha
ABIDE see *aibide*
ABIMBI see *aibimbi*
ABISHŪN see *aibishūn*
ABIŠAHA DABIŠAHA distantly related, not genuinely related
ABKA 1. sky, heaven 2. weather 3. emperor
 ABKA BE GINGGULERE YAMUN (欽天監) Imperial Board of Astronomy, BH 223
 ABKA BE GINGGULERE YAMUN I ALIHA HAFAN (欽天監監正) Director of the Imperial Board of Astronomy, BH 223
 ABKA BE GINGGULERE YAMUN I ILIHI HAFAN (欽天監監副) Vice-Director of the Imperial Board of Astronomy, BH 223
 ABKA HEYENEHEBI there are a few clouds in the sky
 ABKA SARU by heaven! heaven knows!
 ABKA ŠU NA I GIYAN astronomy and geography
 ABKA TUSIHIYEN OHO the sky has become overcast with mist and clouds
ABKAI by nature, naturally, natural
 ABKAI ARI a demon of the sky, a scoundrel, a thoroughly mischievous person
 ABKAI BANJIBUNGGA ENDURI (天后神) the name of the goddess of the sea

A

ABKAI BUHŪNGGE KIRU a banner having upon it the symbol of the 'heavenly deer'

ABKAI BUTEN the horizon

ABKAI CIRA the emperor's countenance

ABKAI COOHA 'heavenly troops'--an honorific title for the imperial forces

ABKAI DAILAN an imperial punitive expedition

ABKAI DENGJAN a lantern hung on a pole

ABKAI DUKA BE NEIRE MUDAN (啟天門之章) the music used in rites to honor a new Metropolitan Graduate

ABKAI DURUNGGA TETUN (天體儀) a model of the heavenly bodies

ABKAI FEJERGI all under heaven--the world, the universe

ABKAI FULINGGA the T'ien-ming (天命) reign period, 1616-1626

ABKAI HAN the heavenly sovereign--God on high

ABKAI HAN I DEYEN the throne room in the Temple of Heaven in Peking

ABKAI HAN I ORDO the circular altar to Heaven

ABKAI HORGIKŪ (天之樞) the first star of the Great Bear

ABKAI IMIYANGGA GOLOI BOLGOBURE FIYENTEN (奉天清吏司) a section of the Bureau of Justice in Mukden

ABKAI JUI the Son of Heaven, the emperor

ABKAI MORIN a mythical beast--like a horse but with fleshy wings

ABKAI MORINGGA KIRU a banner having the symbol of the 'heavenly horse' upon it

ABKAI SIHIYAKŪ 'the axis of heaven'--the same as *abkai horgikū*

ABKAI SUKDUN weather, air

ABKAI SURE the T'ien-ts'ung (天聰) reign period, 1627-1635

ABKAI ŠU astronomy

ABKAI ŠU I HONTOHO (天文科) Astronomical Section, BH 230

ABKAI ŠURDEJEN USIHA the seven stars of the Big Dipper

ABKAI TAN the altar of heaven

ABKAI TEN I USIHA the North Star

ABKAI TSANG an imperial grain depository

ABKAI WEHIYEHE the Ch'ien-lung (乾隆) reign period, 1736-1796

ABKAI YANG the sun

ABKAMBI an old form of *agambi*--to rain

ABKANA heaven and earth--a great deal, very much (in children's speech)

ABKAWARU cursed by heaven--an oath

ABSA 1. a fishing implement--a board at the end of a boat to which a net was attached 2. a birchbark container

ABSALAN 1. the upper front leg bone of a pig or other domestic animal 2. upper arm bone

ABSAMBI (-ka) to become dry and shriveled, to become skin and bones, to become sickly or emaciated

ABSARI emaciation

ABSI 1. how? 2. where to? whither? 3. what a . . .!, how . . .!

ABSI FECIKI how wonderful!

ABSI GAMARA what is to be done?

ABSI HAIRAKA what a shame

ABSI HIHANAKU how worthless

ABSI OHO what happened?

ABSI OJORO what can one do? what for?

ABSI OJORO BE SARKŪ not knowing how it happened

ABSI SERENGGE what are you saying? nothing of the sort

ABSI YABSI really very . . .

ABSIMBI see *absambi*

ABTAJAMBI to fall off, to come apart

ABTALABUMBI caus. of *abtalambi*

ABTALAMBI to break off (branches), to prune

ABTARAMBI to yell, to scream, to cause a commotion

ABTUKŪLAMBI to miss hitting an animal in a mortal spot (in hunting)

ABU almost, nearly

ABU ABU OHO almost happened

ABUCI ILHA *Lycoris radiata*

ABUHA endive (*Caprella bursa*)

ABUHA HŪLHA accomplice

ABUHA ILHA one type of chrysanthemum

ABULIMBI (-ka) to become exhausted

ABUNA *Draba nemorosa*

ABURAMBI to fight wildly or blindly

ABURAME TANTAMBI to hit and fight wildly

ABURANAMBI to come to blows, to grapple with

ABURI evil, envious, spiteful

ABURI EHE evil, the myriad evils

ACABUBUMBI caus. of *acabumbi*

ACABUKI flatterer, sycophant

ACABUKŪ flatterer, an obsequious person

ACABUMBI 1. caus. of *acambi* 2. to join, to put (back) together, to connect 3. to bring together, to introduce, to recommend 4. to present (to an audience) 5. to mate, to couple 6. to mix, to mingle 7. to come together, to have (sexual) relations 8. to adapt to, to make fit, to attune, to adjust, to match, to

harmonize 9. to wait on, to attend
10. to be obsequious, to flatter
11. to collate, to proofread 12. to
graft (trees)

ACABUFI BODORO FIYENTEN (會計
司) Department of Accounting;
cf. BH 829B

ACABUFI WECERE WECEN a sacrifice
performed in the palace on New
Year's Eve to the imperial
ancestors

ACABUHA JAKDAN I ŠUGI resin, gum

ACABUME ARARA HAFAN (纂修官)
official proofreader, revisor;
cf. BH 94, 139, 177

ACABUME BANJIBUKŪ (編修官)
Compiler of the Second Class,
BH 200B

ACABUME BODOMBI to do accounts

ACABUME BODORO HAFAN (司會)
finance officer

ACABUME BURE HAFAN (供給官)
supply officer

ACABUME HŪLARA FALGANGGA (對
讀所) examination reading
office

ACABUME HŪLARA HAFAN (對讀官)
examination reader

ACABUME TUWARA BITHE a tally consisting of two fitting parts

ACABUME TUWARA BITHEI KUNGGERI (勘
合科) office for issuing
tallies in the Board of War

ACABUN summary, union, adaptation,
harmony, efficacy

ACABUN I FULHUN (應鍾) one of
the six minor pipes in music

ACABUN WECEN offering made to the
earth god on a hill

ACABUNGGA united, harmonized, adapted

ACABUNGGA BOJI contract

ACABUNGGA FUKJINGGA HERGEN (墳書)
an ancient style of Chinese
calligraphy

ACABUNGGA INENGGI a day on which the
yin and yang elements harmonize

ACABUNGGA JUNGKEN chimes

ACALAMBI to act together, to act
mutually

ACALAME SIMNEMBI to assemble all
the candidates in the capital for
the Imperial Examination, to go
for the Imperial Examination

ACAMBI 1. to meet, to get together,
to come together, to combine 2. to
visit (the home of the deceased after
a funeral) 3. to be in agreement,
to be in harmony, to be on friendly
terms, to make up after a quarrel
4. to engage in sexual intercourse,
to copulate, to mate 5. to correspond to, to match, to fit, to be

equal to 6. to be fitting, to be
appropriate 7. (after the conditional converb) should, ought, must

ACARA BE TUWAME in accordance with
what is appropriate

ACARAKŪ inappropriate, unfitting

ACAMJABUMBI 1. caus. of *acamjambi*
2. to put together, to assemble

ACAMJAMBI to come together in one
place, to pool together (money)

ACAMJANGGA composite

ACAMJANGGA BESERGEN a large bed
composed of a number of individual
beds put together

ACAMJANGGA MULAN a large bench
composed of several individual
smaller benches

ACAN 1. harmony, concord, union, meeting, juncture 2. joined 3. domino
piece

ACAN BEIDESI (通判) Second
Class Subprefect, BH 849A

ACAN GIRANGGI shoulder bone

ACANAMBI 1. to go to meet 2. to fit,
to suit, to be to the point, to be
correct

ACANAHA SERE HERGEN I TEMGETU a
tally consisting of two halves
with characters written across it

ACANDUMBI/ACANUMBI to meet together

ACANGGA 1. harmonious, fitting 2. a
tally, an identification token

ACANGGA INENGGI a day that the
heaven's stems, earth's branches,
and the five elements all coincide
favorably

ACANJIMBI (imperative: *acanju*) to come
to meet, to come for an audience

ACANJIME ISANJIRE TULERGI GURUN I
BITHE UBALIYAMBURE KUREN (會同
四譯館) Residence for
Envoys of the Four Tributary
States, BH 392

ACIBUMBI caus. of *acimbi*

ACIHA load, burden

ACIHA FULMIYEN baggage, freight

ACIHI stake, share

ACIHI JAFAMBI to hold a stake or
share in a game of chance

ACIHILABUMBI caus. of *acihilambi*

ACIHILAMBI 1. to divide equally 2. to
form in pairs, to perform in pairs

ACILAMBI in wrestling, to throw by
grabbing the neck

ACIMBI 1. (-ka) to move slightly
2. (-ha) to load

ACIRE KIYOO a baggage litter

ACIN load, burden

ACIN TEMEN pack camel

ACINDUMBI to load together

ACINGGIYABUMBI caus. of *acinggiyambi*

ACINGGIYAMBI to move slightly, to

A

shake

ACU ouch! (said when burned by something hot)

ACU FACU with loving tenderness

ACUHIYADABUMBI caus./pass. of *acuhiyadambi*

ACUHIYADAMBI to slander

ACUHIYAN slander

ACUHŪN harmonious, peaceful, well

  ACUHŪN AKŪ 1. unharmonious 2. out of sorts

ACUN confused

  ACUN CACUN I confused, erratic

  ACUN DE CACUN confused, erratic

ADA 1. plank, board 2. raft

  ADA FICAKŪ musical pipes consisting of sixteen sections

ADABUMBI 1. caus. of *adambi* 2. to attach, to send along with

  ADABUFI WESIMBURE BITHE a copy of a memorial presented to the throne

  ADABUHA AMBAN an accompanying official

  ADABUHA WESIMBURE BITHEI KUNGGERI (副 本 科) archives section

  ADABUME WECEMBI to make an offering in the ancestral temple when the tablet of a newly deceased was placed among the ancestral tablets

ADADA EBEBE an exclamation of surprise

ADADA EDEDE (onom.) the sound of teeth chattering from cold

ADAGE exclamation of affection used when patting an old person or a child on the back

ADAHA a chest or trunk on a wagon

ADAKI 1. neighbor 2. neighboring, adjacent

  ADAKI BOO neighboring house or family

ADAKŪ assistant

ADALI like, same

ADALIKAN somewhat like, rather similar

ADALILIYAN somewhat like

ADALINGGA similar

ADALIŠAMBI to resemble, to be like (used with *de*)

ADAMBI 1. to accompany, to stand by 2. to be attached to, to be close to, to be next to 3. to form the encirclement at a battue 4. to stitch together

  ADAFI KADALARA AMBAN (宗 人) Director of the Imperial Clan Court, BH 60

  ADAFI SIMNERE HAFAN (副 考 官) assistant examiner

  ADAHA BAICARA DOOLI HAFAN (僉 使 道) assistant intendant

  ADAHA BITHEI DA (侍 讀 學 士) Reader of the Academy, BH 194

  ADAHA GIYANGNARA BITHEI DA (侍 講 學 士) Expositor of the

Academy, BH 195

  ADAHA GIYANGNARA HAFAN (侍 講) subexpositor, BH 197

ADAHA HAFAN (輕 車 都 尉) a hereditary title of the sixth grade, BH 944

ADAHA HŪLARA BITHEI DA (侍 讀 學 士) Reader of the Academy, BH 194

ADAHA HŪLARA HAFAN (侍 讀) Subreader of the Academy, BH 196

ADAHA KADALARA DA (參 將) Lieutenant-Colonel, BH 752A, 800

ADAHA TUKIYESI (副 榜) a degree candidate entered on the secondary list, BH 629B

ADAME TEMBI to live next door

ADANAMBI 1. to go to be near, to go to attend 2. to go to form the encirclement at a battue

ADANUMBI to form the encirclement at a battue together

ADARAME how? why? how so? what is to be done?

  ADARAME OHODE SAIN how should one do it?

  ADARAME OHONI how was it?

  ADARAME SECI how might . . . ?

ADASUN lapel

ADASUNGGA having lapels

ADISLAMBI to bless, to pronounce a benediction

  ADISLAME DOBOMBI to read a portion of scriptures at the beginning of a fast period, to fast

ADISTIT blessing

ADU garment

ADUCI herder

ADUHI leather trousers

ADULABUMBI caus. of *adulambi*

ADULAMBI to herd

ADULASI herdsman

ADUN 1. herd 2. swarm

  ADUN BE KADALARA YAMUN (太 僕 寺) Court of the Imperial Stud, BH 936B

  ADUN I AMBAN (上 駟 院 卿) Director of the Palace Stud, BH 88

  ADUN I DA the head of a herd

  ADUN I HIYA (上 駟 院 侍 衛) Guard of the Palace Stud; cf. BH 88

  ADUN UMIYAHA a swarming insect that attacks new grain shoots

ADUNGGIYABUMBI caus./pass. of *adunggiyambi*

ADUNGGIYAMBI to mistreat, to be cruel to

ADURAMBI to rise (of a boil or blister)

AFABUBUMBI caus. of *afabumbi* (2,3)

AFABUMBI 1. caus. of *afambi:* 2. to hand over to, to entrust to 3. to commission, to order, to bid

A

AFABUME UNGGIRE BITHE a document from a higher organ to one of its subordinates

AFAHA list, chapter, page, sheet (of paper)

AFAHANAMBI to form a congealed layer (on the top of a liquid)

AFAHARI a strip of paper, a tally, a label

AFAHARI DAHABURE BA (余票處) letter office of the Grand Secretariat

AFAHASI an agricultural official appointed by the emperor in ancient times

AFAKIYAMBI to run about rapidly, to stumble about

AFAKŪ valiant fighter, hero

AFAMBI 1. to attack, to fight, to do battle, to lay siege to 2. to cause trouble, to be contentious 3. to be restive, to kick off the hobbles, to paw the ground restively (of horses) 4. to encounter, to run into 5. to have charge of, to be charged with, to be assigned to (a post)

AFARA BA battlefield

AFARA CUWAN a warship

AFARA MORIN a horse used in battle

AFARA WAN a siege ladder

AFAN fight, battle, clash

AFAN AMBA quarrelsome

AFANAMBI to go to attack, to strike

AFANDUMBI/AFANUMBI to attack together, to fight together

AFANGGALA beforehand, prematurely

AFANGGALA JABDUMBI to shoot before everyone else on a battue

AFANJIMBI to come to fight or attack

AFARALAME fighting while retreating

AFATAMBI 1. to attack, to fight (of a group) 2. (of horses) to stumble

AFIN the hem of the lining of a fur jacket; cf. *naimisun*

AFIUN opium

AFIYA grass and bean plants cut together while still green

AFIYA TURA a small pillar over the rafters

AGA rain

AGA BAIRE DOROLON a sacrifice offered for rain

AGA BAIRE MUKDEHUN the altar for rain sacrifices

AGA DAMBI to rain

AGA MUKE one of the twenty-four solar divisions of the year falling on February 19 or 20

AGADA the rain deity

AGADA MOO one of the names of the tamarisk, so called because the fluttering of its leaves foretells rain

AGAMBI to rain

AGAHAI NAKARAKŪ to rain incessantly

AGANGGA pertaining to rain

AGANGGA SARA an umbrella

AGE 1. (皇子) Prince, Son of an Emperor, BH 13 2. a polite term of address, master, sir, lord 3. ouch! ow! cf. *ake*

AGELI a swelling found on the larch (*Larix leptolepis*) that is used as a medicine

AGENGGE pertaining to a superior-- your, yours

AGESE plural of *age*

AGU a respectful term of address for men, sir, master

AGUSA plural of *agu*

AGUSE plural of *agu*

AGŪLAMBI to treat another person as senior or leader; cf. *ahūlambi*

AGŪRA 1. vessel, implement, tool, weapon 2. a spear with a panther's tail attached

AGŪRA ENDURI deity of a banner

AGŪRA HAJUN weapons

AGŪRAI HIYA an imperial bodyguard who carried a spear with a panther's tail attached

AG'AJA ether

AHA 1. slave 2. same as *aga*

AHA NEHŪ serving boys and maids

AHA SENGSE lazy slave-girl! a deprecation addressed to a lazy woman

AHADA a slave overseer

AHADA GURJEN katydid

AHADA ŠUSIHA a whip carried by the emperor as he entered the throne room

AHADAN an old badger; cf. *dorgon*

AHANTUMBI to serve as a slave

AHASI plural of *aha*

AHITA a flared slit at the edge of a waist-length jacket

AHŪCILABUMBI caus. of *ahūcilambi*

AHŪCILAMBI to treat as one's senior, to be older than

AHŪLABUMBI caus. of *ahūlambi*

AHŪLAMBI to act as an elder brother

AHŪN 1. elder brother 2. older

AHŪN DEO brothers (collectively)

AHŪN DEO ARAMBI to become bosom friends

AHŪN I BODOME according to the difference of age

AHŪNGGA eldest, of the first rank, eldest son

AHŪNGGA ENEN children of the chief wife

AHŪNGGA JUI eldest son

AHŪRA same as *agūra*

AHŪRAMBI to frighten a reclining animal

A

AHŪRI HŪYARI sound used to frighten
  reclining animals
AHŪŠAMBI to honor as one's senior, to
  treat as an elder brother
AHŪTA plural of *ahūn*
AI 1. what? which? 2. hey!
  AI AI all kinds, various kinds
  AI AI JAKA all sorts of things
  AI AKŪ BANJIMBI to live without
    lacking any necessity
  AI ANIYA in what cyclical year were
    you born?
  AI BAINGGE from where? whence?
  AI BAITA what (matter)? for what
    reason? what use is it?
  AI DALJI of what concern is it?
    of what benefit is it?
  AI DEMUN what manner?
  AI DEREI how can I have the face
    to . . . ? how dare I . . . ?
  AI ERINDE when?
  AI GANAHA why should . . . ? what
    use? *si tede ai ganaha* 'what do
    you want from him?'
  AI GELERAKŪ same as *ai gelhun akū*
  AI GELHUN AKŪ how dare . . . ?
    doesn't dare . . .
  AI GELI how dare I . . . ? how
    dare you! you're welcome
  AI HALA what's the point of doing
    it? (said of frightening things)
  AI HARAN for what reason?
  AI HENDUME GAIMBI how could (I)
    accept it?
  AI HENDURE all the more . . . ,
    not to mention . . . ,
  AI HIHAN what is so unusual about
    that?
  AI JALIN for what reason?
  AI JOBORO what is there to worry
    about? what is bothering you?
  AI JOJIN for what reason, from what
    motive?
  AI MAKTAHAI same as *ai jojin*
  AI OCIBE in any case
  AI OMBINI what can be done? what
    is wrong?
  AI SEME why? for what reason?
  AI SERE says what?
  AI TURGUN why? for what reason?
  AI TURGUN DE why? for what reason?
  AI UTTU GER SEME WAJIRAKŪ what end-
    less prattling
  AI YADARA the same as *ai joboro*
  AI YOKTO to what good purpose?
    for what? how could I be so bold
    to . . . ?
  AI WEI SEME this way and that, in
    an indefinite way
AIBA same as *aibi*
AIBACI whence? from where?
AIBADE where?
AIBI 1. where? 2. what is there?

AIBI HAIBI AKŪ lacking in confidence,
  despondent; cf. *ebi habi akū*
AIBICI whence? from where?
AIBIDE where?
AIBIDERI from where?
AIBIMBI to swell
AIBINGGE from where?
AIBISHŪN slightly swollen
AICI what sort of . . . ?
  AICI JERGI what sort of?
AIDAGAN 1. a four-year-old wild boar
  2. shoulder
  AIDAGAN I KALKA wild boar meat
    cooked with the skin on
AIDAHAN same as *aidagan*
  AIDAHAN I SENCEHE (壁) the name
    of a star
  AIDAHAN SIKA short bristles on a
    horse's tail
AIDAHAŠAMBI 1. to act like a boar 2.
  to be stubborn or obstinate, to use
  force
AIDE where? whither? why? how?
  AIDE UTTU OHO how can it be like
    this?
AIFINI a long time before, much
  earlier, already
AIFUMBI to break one's word
AIGAN archery target
AIGELI what more? same as *ai geli*
AIHA glazed pottery, crockery, porce-
  lain
  AIHA DEIJIRE KŪWARAN a factory for
    making glazed products
  AIHA SIRGEI DENGJAN a lamp or lan-
    tern made of glass fiber and
    mounted on a wooden stand
  AIHA ŠUŠU corn (maize)
AIHADAMBI to leap, to be restive (of
  horses or cattle)
AIHAJI material used for making glazed
  ware
AIHANA glaze
AIHANAMBI to glaze
AIHŪ female sable; cf. *seke*
AIHŪMA 1. (soft-shelled) turtle, tri-
  onyx 2. cuckold
AIHŪME bellows made of leather
AIJIRGAN (金燕) possibly the
  yellow-rumped swallow (*Hirundo
  daurica*)
AIKA 1. if, whether 2. any 3. some-
  thing
  AIKA OHODE every time, always,
    frequently
  AIKA UTTU AIKA TUTTU whether like
    this or like that
AIKABADE if, in the case that
AIKAN cautious, careful
  AIKAN FAIKAN cautious and careful
AIKANAMBI if it is thus, if one does
  thus
  AIKANAHA if it is like that (what

will we do?), like *tuttu ohode ainambi* .

AIKANARAHŪ lest it be like that, I fear it will be like that

AIKTE fruit of the *Prunus japonica*

AILIMBI to avoid the main road, to detour

AILIME GENEHE went by a detour

AILINAMBI to go by a roundabout way

AILUNGGA elegant, elegantly

AIMAKA probably, seemingly

AIMAN tribe

AIMAN HOKI tribe, tribal grouping

AIMAN I ADAHA JORISI (土司指揮僉事); cf. BH 861A

AIMAN I AHŪCILAHA HAFAN (土司長官); cf. BH 861A

AIMAN I ELBIRE DAHABURE HAFAN (土司招討使); cf. BH 861A

AIMAN I ELBIRE HAFAN (土司招討使); cf. BH 861A

AIMAN I HAFAN (土司) chieftain of a native tribe; cf. BH 861A

AIMAN I HAFAN I KUNGGERI (土官科) section on native administrators; cf. BH 861A

AIMAN I MINGGADA (土司千户) chieftain of one thousand, BH 861A

AIMAN I SELGIYERE BILURE HAFAN (土司宣撫使); cf. BH 861A

AIMAN I SELGIYERE TOHOROMBURE HAFAN (土司宣慰使); cf. BH 861A

AIMAN I TANGGŪDA (土司百户) chieftain of one hundred; cf. BH 861A

AIMAN I TOKTOBURE BILURE HAFAN (土司安撫使); cf. BH 861A

AIMIKA CECIKE one name for the wren

AIMIN TAIMIN refractory, contrary to what is proper or natural

AINAMBAHAMBI how to obtain? how can?

AINAMBI to do what? how? how is (are) . . . ? what's up? why?

AINACI AINAKINI so be it

AINACI OJORO what can one do (so that it turns out well)?

AINAHA what happened? what sort of?

AINAHA SEME surely, without fail, categorically

AINAHABI what has happened? what's wrong?

AINAHAI not necessarily, how . . . ?

AINAHAI OMBINI how can it be?

AINAHAI UTTU NI how can it be like this? what an outrage!

AINAHANI what happened?

AINAMBIHE how did it come to be?

AINAME how?

AINAME AINAME for the time being, negligently, carelessly, in a dilatory manner, as one pleases

AINARA what sort of, what is one to do?

AINARAHŪ lest something happen, I fear something will happen

AINARANGGE what is done? *sini ere ainarangge*? 'what is this that you have done?'

AINCI perhaps, probably, apparently, presumably

AINI (the instrumental form of *ai*) wherewith, whereby?

AINU how? why?

AISE (sentence particle) perhaps

AISEMBI say what? is called what?

AISEHE what did (he) say?

AISEME 1. why? 2. same as *ai seme*

AISERENGGE what sort of speech? *sini ere aiserengge* 'what is this you say?'

AISHA Chinese gold-wing (*Chloris sinica*)

AISHA CECIKE same as *aisha*

AISI interest, benefit, profit

AISI OBUMBI to bring benefit to

AISI TEMBI to earn interest

AISILABUKŪ 1. helper 2. prime minister

AISILABUMBI caus. of *aisilambi*

AISILAKŪ helper

AISILAKŪ HAFAN (員外郎) Assistant Department Director, BH 291

AISILAMBI to help, to aid, to reinforce, to provide

AISILAME BAICARA DOOLI HAFAN (副使道) Assistant Superintendent; cf. BH 185E, 835A

AISILAME BENEMBI to dispatch funds for assistance

AISILAME BENERE MENGGUN funds dispatched for assistance

AISILAME BURE MENGGUN grant money

AISILAME DASARA DOOLI HAFAN (參政道) intendant for governmental affairs

AISILAME ICIHIYARA DOOLI HAFAN (參議道) assistant intendant

AISILAME JAFAHA SILGASI (捐貢) a person who obtained a licentiate degree by purchase

AISILAME JAFAHA TACIMSI (捐監) an official of the Imperial Academy

AISILAME JAFARA BAITA BE ICIHIYARA BOO (捐納房) a section of the Board of Revenue concerned with the purchase of official titles

AISILAME KADALARA DA (副將) Colonel, BH 752

AISILAME TACIBURE HAFAN (助教) Assistant Teacher, BH 638

AISILAME TUWARA HAFAN (副總

A

A

裁官) assistant director
AISILAN help, aid, assistance
AISILANDUMBI/AISILANUMBI to help to-
 gether, to help one another
AISILANGGA (副将) colonel of a
 brigade; cf. BH 752, 656D
AISILANJIMBI to come to help
AISILATAMBI to help often
AISIMBI to bless, to uphold, to give
 support to
AISIMU ILHA *Tulipa edulis*
AISIN metal, gold
 AISIN ARGACAN a golden broadax
  carried in processions
 AISIN BADIRI ILHA a sort of red
  flower whose petals overlap one
  another like alms bowls
 AISIN CANGGA a golden signal bell
 AISIN CECIKE ILHA scotch broom
  (*Cytisus scoparius*)
 AISIN CERI ILHA cowherb (*Vaccaria
  vulgaris*)
 AISIN CIFELEKU a golden spittoon
 AISIN DENGJAN ILHA same as *aisimu
  ilha*
 AISIN DERE OBOKŪ a golden basin
  used for face washing
 AISIN DOSIMBURE FAKSI goldsmith
 AISIN GIORO the surname of the
  Ch'ing royal family
 AISIN HIYAN I HOSERI a golden
  incense vessel
 AISIN HOOŠAN gold paper, gold leaf
 AISIN HŪNTAHAN ILHA a type of
  calendula
 AISIN I SESE golden thread
 AISIN ILHANGGA SUKŪ leather deco-
  rated with golden flowers
 AISIN INGGALI 1. golden wagtail
  2. a sort of yellow flower
 AISIN JALASU golden token or
  emblem carried in processions
 AISIN JOFOHORI kumquat
 AISIN KANGGIRI a small golden bell
  worn on hats by officials
 AISIN LAKIYANGGA HIYAN DABUKŪ a
  golden warming pan held in the
  hands
 AISIN LASHANGGA OSE LOHO a gilded
  Japanese sword
 AISIN LUJEN an imperial chariot with
  golden squares on the top, was
  drawn by elephants
 AISIN MALU a golden wine container
  carried in processions
 AISIN MUDURI POO (金龍砲) a
  type of large bronze cannon
 AISIN MULAN a square gilded stool
  carried in processions
 AISIN NENDEN ILHA the Chinese
  Trollius
 AISIN NIKEKUNGGE MULAN a stool with
  carved golden dragon decorations

AISIN NIYANJAN a chariot with
 golden decorations
AISIN SESE NOHO SUJE silk woven
 with golden threads intertwined
AISIN ŠU ILHA nasturtium
AISIN ŠUGIN I ILETU KIYOO a gilded
 or gold-painted sedan chair
AISIN UJIMA another name for the
 chicken
AISIN UJUNGGA GARU a golden-headed
 swan
AISIN UJUNGGA YENGGUHE a yellow-
 headed parrot
AISIN USIHA the planet Venus
AISIN USIHANGGA KIRU a banner of the
 imperial escort with the planet
 Venus depicted upon it
AISINGGA profitable, helpful
AISIRGAN canary
AISIRI TORO ILHA Chinese Hypericum
AISURI a bird resembling a lark, with
 a short tail, white neck, and golden
 eyes
AITUBUBUMBI caus. of *aitubumbi*
AITUBUMBI 1. caus. of *aitumbi* 2. to
 save, to revive, to cure
AITUBUN salvation, revival
AITUMBI to come to, to recover
AITURI a kind of wild kumquat
AIYONGGA ILHA 'golden sandflower'
AJA mother
AJABUMBI caus./pass. of *ajambi*
 AJABUME GISUREMBI to tell from the
  beginning
AJAJA interjection of surprise
AJAMBI to make a small cut, to mar by
 cutting
AJI first-born
 AJI MUYARI dragon's-eye (*Nephelium
  longana*)
AJIDA small, a small bit
 AJIDA JOFOHORI trifoliate orange
AJIGALAMBI to treat as a child
AJIGAN young, small
 AJIGAN TACIN elementary instruction
AJIGE small, little, young
 AJIGE AJIGE a bit, a little
 AJIGE BILERI a small *sona* flute
 AJIGE BUKDARI a small folded book
  used for notices and memorials
 AJIGE BUREN a small brass horn
 AJIGE GIYALAKŪ MOO a small piece of
  wood attached to the front of a
  ship's mast
 AJIGE HALHŪN one of the twenty-four
  solar divisions of the year--the
  seventh or eighth of August
 AJIGE HEFELI the lower belly
 AJIGE HIYA SILMEN sparrow hawk
  (*Accipiter virgatus*)
 AJIGE HOŠO the outside corner of
  the eye
 AJIGE HŪWAŠAN a Buddhist novice

monk

AJIGE JALU one of the twenty-four
  solar divisions of the year--the
  twenty-first or twenty-second of
  May

AJIGE KONGGORO NIONGNIYAHA a small
  yellow wild goose

AJIGE KŪRCAN a small gray crane

AJIGE MAMA the measles

AJIGE MUJILEN care, careful

AJIGE NIMANGGI one of the twenty-
  four solar divisions of the year--
  the twenty-second or twenty-third
  of November

AJIGE NINGGE ERŠEMBI to get the
  measles

AJIGE NIYO COKO a small pewit

AJIGE SURI a type of silk

AJIGE SUSERI *Peucedanum graveolens*

AJIGE ŠAHŪRUN one of the twenty-
  four solar divisions of the year--
  the sixth or seventh of January

AJIGE ŠOŠOBUN (-ᠵ 结) small
  summary--one of the parts of a
  formal essay

AJIGE TACIKŪ elementary school

AJIGE YANGSIMU NIYEHE small sheldrake

AJIGEN 1. young, small 2. a youth

AJIGESI plural of *ajigen*

AJILABUMBI caus. of *ajilambi*

AJILAMBI 1. to remove the chaff 2. to
  tan

AJIN sturgeon

AJIRGALAMBI to cover (as a mare by a
  stallion)

AJIRGAN a male horse, donkey, camel, or
  dog
  AJIRGAN SOGI an edible wild grass
    with prickles on its leaves,
    thistle

AJIRHALAMBI the same as *ajirgalambi*

AJIRHAN the same as *ajirgan*

AJIRKA didn't recognize, confused (an
  acquaintance)

AJISI a fruit in the shape and size of
  the little finger that tastes like
  a persimmon

AK an interjection of sudden surprise

AKA NIYEHE loon, dabchick

AKABUMBI 1. caus. of *akambi* 2. to
  sadden, to bring grief to, to make
  suffer

AKABURU an oath: may grief come upon
  you!

AKACUKA sad, pitiful, grievous

AKACUN sadness, grief

AKAMBI (-ka) to be sad, to grieve
  AKAME GECEHE the ice has frozen all
    the way to the bottom

AKCUHIYAN brittle, sensitive, fragile

AKDABUMBI caus. of *akdambi*

AKDACUKA dependable, trustworthy,

believable

AKDACUN 1. trust, trustworthiness,
  2. what one depends on, livelihood
  AKDACUN AKŪ not dependable,
    doubtful

AKDAMBI to depend on, to trust

AKDAN trust

AKDANDUMBI to trust or depend on one
  another

AKDUKAN rather dependable, reliable,
  firm

AKDULABUMBI caus. of *akdulambi*

AKDULAMBI 1. to protect, to guarantee,
  to defend, to fortify 2. to promise
  3. to recommend
  AKDULARA BITHE a letter of guar-
    antee
  AKDULARA NIYALMA guarantor

AKDULANDUMBI/AKDULANUMBI to fortify
  or defend together, to promise
  together, to recommend together

AKDUN 1. firm, strong, dependable 2.
  trust (for *akdan*)
  AKDUN ACANGGA a pass consisting of
    two matching pieces used for ad-
    mittance to a city at night
  AKDUN GIRDAN a silken pennant on
    which the word *akdun* was embroi-
    dered
  AKDUN JURGANGGA SARGAN JUI a woman
    who after the death of her husband
    does not remarry
  AKDUN SARGAN JUI a woman who does
    not remarry after her husband's
    death
  AKDUN TEMGETU credentials used by
    an imperial envoy

AKDUNGGA firm, solid, enduring
  AKDUNGGA FURDAN solid gateway

AKE interjection used when touching
  something hot

AKIYA river perch; cf. *kiyakū*

AKIYABUMBI 1. caus. of *akiyambi* 2. to
  dry, to smoke

AKIYAMBI to dry up
  AKIYAME GECEHE frozen to the bottom

AKIYAN NIMAHA a fish frozen into the
  ice

AKJABA false hellebore (*Veratrum
  nigrum*)

AKJAMBI (-ka) to thunder

AKJAMBULU flying squirrel

AKJAN thunder
  AKJAN DARIMBI thunder roars
  AKJAN I ADALI DURGIMBI to roar like
    thunder

AKJUHIYAN 1. easy to anger 2. brittle,
  crisp; cf. *akcuhiyan*

AKSABUMBI 1. caus. of *aksambi* 2. to
  frighten (off)

AKSALAMBI to be startled

AKSAMBI (-ka) to be shy, to be retiring, to hide because of fear

A

A

AKSARA SIRGA 'a shy deer'--metaphor for someone who is shy

AKSAMBUMBI see *aksabumbi*

AKSARGAN a belt on which a quiver is fixed

AKŠAMBI (-ka) to become rancid, to become spoiled

AKŠAN water plants left hanging on trees after a flood recedes, branches and plants floating on the surface of water, flotsam, decayed matter
 AKŠAN TAHA GESE like left-behind driftwood

AKŠANTAMBI to smell of decaying matter

AKŠULABUMBI caus./pass. of *akšulambi*

AKŠULAMBI to slander, to revile

AKŠUN 1. slanderous 2. rancid, spoiled
 AKŠUN BE an oath used to revile a person
 AKŠUN DA gullet, throat
 AKŠUN GISUN slanderous words, slander

AKTA gelding
 AKTA UŠE girth

AKTALABUMBI caus. of *aktalambi*

AKTALAKŪ MOO a horizontal wooden support over a door or window

AKTALAMBI 1. to straddle, to span 2. to castrate

AKTALIYAN saddlebag

AKŪ particle of negation: there is not, there are not, doesn't exist, isn't here (there)
 AKŪ OHO died
 AKŪI TEN same as *amba ten*: the great ultimate--the ultimate principle of the universe

AKŪMBI to die

AKŪMBUMBI to endeavor, to exert to the utmost, to do one's best, to fulfill

AKŪMI clothes made of fish skin

AKŪN *akū* plus the interrogative particle *-n*

AKŪNAMBI to reach (the opposite shore), to go to the end
 AKŪNAME everywhere, all over, all around
 AKŪNARAKŪ BA AKŪ utterly complete, there is nothing that isn't reached or completed

AKŪNGGE that which is not, that which doesn't exist

AKŪNJIMBI to arrive at this shore, to come to this side

AKŪTALA until nothing is left

ALA a hill with a level top
 ALA GASHA a name for the pheasant
 ALA ULHŪMA the same as *ala gasha*

ALA ŠALA tenderly, affectionately

ALABUMBI caus. of *alambi*

ALAJAN collarbone, clavicle

ALAKDAHA for *alakdahan*
 ALAKDAHA ASU a net for catching the jerboa

ALAKDAHAN five-toed jerboa (*Allactaga sibirica*)

ALAMBI 1. to tell, to report 2. to wrap with birch bark

ALAMIMBI to carry across the back

ALAN 1. birch bark 2. the shoulder and breast parts of armor
 ALAN EREMBI to peel off birch bark
 ALAN WEIHU birchbark canoe

ALANAMBI to go to report

ALANDUMBI/ALANUMBI to report together

ALANGGIBUMBI caus. of *alanggimbi*

ALANGGIMBI to send to report

ALANJIMBI (imperative *alanju*) to come to report

ALARAME along a low hill

ALARI ILHA mountain vermilion (*Ixora chinensis*)

ALAŠAN 1. a nag 2. a person who uses his strength to no avail

ALBABUN tribute, tribute products

ALBALAMBI to awe, to intimidate

ALBAN 1. public service 2. official, public, fiscal 3. tax, duty, tribute
 ALBAN BOOI TURIGEN I NAMUN (官 房 租 庫) Office for Collecting Rent of Confiscated Property, BH 82
 ALBAN CAGAN official commission, official document
 ALBAN DE YABUMBI to go to an official post
 ALBAN GAIMBI to collect tax or duty
 ALBAN HALAN AKŪ unfortunately
 ALBAN I BUMBI to provide at public expense
 ALBAN I USIN I BOLGOBURE FIYENTEN (屯 田 清 吏 司) a section in the Board of Works concerned with military colonists
 ALBAN JAFAMBI to present tribute
 ALBAN JAFANJIMBI to bring tribute
 ALBAN KAMBI to go out on an official errand
 ALBAN ŠULEHEN duties and taxes
 ALBAN TACIKŪ (官 學) School of the Imperial Household, BH 87
 ALBAN TACIKŪI JUSE students of the above school
 ALBAN WEILEMBI to do official work

ALBANI CECE silken gauze offered as tribute

ALBANI LAMUN HOOŠAN a kind of blue paper used for making borders

ALBANI SUJE silk offered as tribute

ALBASI functionary, the person on duty

ALBATU rough, coarse, common, ordinary

ALBATUKAN rather coarse

ALBATULAMBI to act or speak coarsely

ALCU the concave side of a *gacuha*

ALDA a half-grown pig

ALDAHI AHŪN DEO second cousins

ALDAKŪ a wall placed behind the targets

on an archery field
ALDANGGA distant (in relationship)
   ALDANGGA DALAN a dike built far
     from a shore
   ALDANGGA MUKŪN distant clan
   ALDANGGAI distantly, from a distance
ALDANGGAKAN rather distant
ALDARKAN death before the nineteenth
   year, a premature death
ALDASI halfway, midway, short-lived,
   cut off midway, premature (death)
   ALDASI WAJIMBI to die young
ALDASILAMBI to turn back or stop half-
   way, to be incomplete, to die young
ALDUNGGA strange, queer, uncommon,
   uncanny, ghostly
ALGA same as *alha*
ALGAN a net for catching quail
ALGIDAMBI to praise, to extol
ALGIMBI (-ka) to be famous, to become
   known
ALGIMBUMBI caus. of *algimbi*
ALGIN 1. fame 2. the male otter; cf.
   hailan
ALGINDAMBI to praise, to laud
ALGINGGA famous, well-known
   ALGINGGA JUBENGGE boastful,
     ostentatious
ALGINTU famous
ALGIŠAMBI 1. to be respected, to be
   well known 2. to boast, to put on
   airs
ALGIYABUMBI caus. of *algiyambi*
ALGIYAMBI to skim the fat from the top
   of soup
ALHA 1. many colored, variegated,
   mottled 2. satin in which the woof
   and the warp are of different colors
   3. a horse of more than one color
   4. see *elhe alhai*
   ALHA BULHA many colored, splendid
   ALHA UIHE BERI a bow made from
     spotted buffalo horn
ALHABUMBI 1. caus. of *alhambi* 2. at
   a shamanistic performance, to gather
   a crowd around so that by their
   shouting a trance may be induced in
   the shaman
ALHACAN mottled
   ALHACAN NIYEHE falcated teal
     (*Eunetta falcata*)
   ALHACAN ULHŪMA the small ring-necked
     pheasant
ALHAMBI to go into a trance (of a
   shaman)
ALHANGGA spotted, speckled
   ALHANGGA ANAHŪN MOO spotted *nanmu*
     wood
ALHARI spotted, variegated
   ALHARI COKO a type of variegated
     Fukienese pheasant
   ALHARI NIYEHE a type of white
     spotted duck

ALHATA scattered, dispersed, mixed,
   variegated
   ALHATA SUWALIYATA mixed, variegated
   ALHATA YALI pork in which strips of
     lean and fat alternate
ALHATANAMBI to become spotted or
   mottled
ALHATU spotted, variegated
ALHURU DUDU a dove with a yellow spot-
   ted back
ALHŪDABUMBI caus. of *alhūdambi*
ALHŪDAMBI to imitate, to pattern after
ALHŪDAN pattern, model
ALHŪDANGGA pertaining to a pattern or
   model
ALHŪDANJIMBI to come to imitate
ALHŪDANUMBI to imitate one another
ALHŪJI MAMA an ugly old lady spirit
ALHŪWA membrane (particularly the
   membrane on the heart or liver),
   the cornea of the eye, bamboo mem-
   brane
   ALHŪWA BURIMBI to form a cataract
     on the eye
   ALHŪWA YALI diaphragm
ALIBUMBI 1. caus. of *alimbi* 2. to
   present (a document to a superior),
   to offer
   ALIBUME WESIMBURE BITHE a congrat-
     ulatory letter presented to the
     throne
   ALIBURE BITHE ICIHIYARA KUNGGERI
     (都書科) section concerned
     with handling officials' leave
     permits and other petitions
   ALIBURE BUKDAN a sort of name card
     used by lower officials and
     students
ALIBUN a petition
ALIBUNJIMBI to come to present
ALIGAN support, retainer, base
ALIHAN a strip of lining along the
   hem of an unlined garment
ALIKIYARI a type of small green parrot
ALIKŪ a tray, the tray used for weigh-
   ing on a scale, the lower millstone
ALIKŪLAMBI to put on a scale, to put
   on a millstone
ALIMBAHAMBI to be able to bear
   ALIMBAHARAKŪ 1. intolerable, insup-
     portable 2. greatly, exceedingly
ALIMBI 1. to receive, to accept 2. to
   undertake 3. to endure 4. to sup-
   port, to hold up, to stop up (a leak)
   5. to take a falcon on the hand
   ALIFI BAICARA AMBAN (左都御
     史) Senior President of the
     Censorate, BH 207A
   ALIFI BOŠORO FALGANGGA (督催所)
     Office of Incitement, BH 493.4
   ALIFI DASARA HAFAN (令尹)
     District Magistrate, BH 856
   ALIFI HAFUMBURE HAFAN (通政使)

A

A

Commissioner of the Transmission
Office, BH 928

ALIFI KADALARA AMBAN (宗 令)
Presiding Controller of the Imperial Clan Court, BH 57

ALIFI SIMNERE HAFAN (正 考 官)
Examiner, BH 629B

ALIFI TACIBURE HAFAN (學 正)
Departmental Director of Schools,
BH 851A-6

ALIHA AMBAN (尚 書) President
of a Board, BH 276

ALIHA BITHEI DA (大 學 士)
Grand Secretary, BH 131

ALIHA COOHA a Manchu or Mongol
cavalryman

ALIHA DA (大 學 士) an abbreviation of *aliha bithei da*

ALIHA HAFAN (正 卿) Director;
cf. BH 933, 934

ALIHA NIYALMA steward, manager

ALIHA TACIBURE HAFAN (祭 酒)
Libationer, BH 421A-1

ALIME GAIMBI to accept, to receive

ALIN mountain

ALIN BIRA GIYALABUMBI to be separated by mountains and rivers

ALIN CIBIRGAN mountain swallow

ALIN EFIMBI for a mirage to appear
on a mountain

ALIN I BETHE the foot of a mountain

ALIN I BOSO the shady or north side
of a mountain

ALIN I CAI ILHA sasanqua

ALIN I CECIKE 'mountain sparrow'--
probably *Passer rutilans*

ALIN I EBCI slope of a mountain

ALIN I HISY steep area on a
mountain

ALIN I JUKIDUN Chinese blue magpie
(*Urocissa erythroryncha*)

ALIN I MUDAN curves of a mountain,
a winding mountain road

ALIN I OFORO mountain ridge

ALIN I SAIHA slope under the peak
of a mountain

ALIN I SAKSAHA Asiatic blue magpie
(*Cyanopolius cyaneus*)

ALIN I ULHUMA Reeve's pheasant;
cf. *nikan ulhūma*

ALIN I WAI a hidden spot among the
curves and turns of a mountain

ALIN JAKARAHA the mountains have
become distinct at dawn

ALIN JALGANGGA MOO tree of heaven
(*Ailanthus glandulosa*)

ALIN ULEJEMBI there is a landslide

ALIN YADALI CECIKE thrush (*Garrulax
davidi*)

ALINJIMBI to come to accept

ALIOI the yang tones of the major
scale

ALIOI HŪWALIYASI (協 律 郎)

Chief Musician, BH 389-1

ALIRAME along a mountain

ALISUN grain that has sprouted from
lost or abandoned seeds

ALISABUMBI caus. of *ališambi*

ALISACUKA depressing

ALISAMBI (-ka) to be listless, to be
bored, to be unhappy, to worry

ALISAME KENEHUNJEMBI to tarry, to
be uncertain, to be undecided

ALISATAMBI to be deeply depressed

ALITUN a small table for offerings

ALIYABUMBI caus. of *aliyambi*

ALIYACUN 1. regret 2. waiting

ALIYAKIYAMBI to linger, to pace back
and forth while waiting, to slow
one's pace to allow someone to catch
up

ALIYAMBI 1. to regret 2. to wait

ALIYASUNGGA patient, long-suffering

ALJABUMBI 1. caus. of *aljambi* 2. to
banish, to make leave, to exorcise

ALJAMBI 1. to leave 2. to lose (color)
3. see *angga aljambi*

ALKŪN the gait of a horse or other
livestock

ALKŪN AMBA wide-gaited

ALMIN INDAHŪN a dog with a long muzzle

ALUN INDAHŪN a dog with a short muzzle

AMA father, head of the household

AMAGA afterwards, later, future

AMAGA ENEN descendant

AMAGA INENGGI later, a later day

AMAGA JALAN later generation,
posterity

AMAGANGGE that which is later

AMAHA the same as *amaga*

AMAKA husband's father

AMALA 1. behind 2. after, later

AMALA FIYANJILAMBI to form a rear
guard, to cover the rear

AMALA OBUMBI to set aside

AMALA TUTAMBI to leave behind

AMARGI 1. back, behind 2. north

AMARGI COLHON I KIRU (北 岳 旗)
a banner with Mt. Heng (恒 山)
depicted on it

AMARGI FALGANGGA (後 所) Fifth
Subdepartment of the Imperial
Equipage Department, BH 122

AMARGI FISEMBUHE BOO a building
behind the main house

AMARGI FIYENTEHE (後 股) the
concluding section of the body of
a formal essay

AMARGI JUWERE JEKUI KUNGGERI (北
漕 科) a bureau of the Board
of Revenue concerned with transporting grain from the south (Yunnan) to the north

AMARGI NAHAN the *kang* on the north
side of the room

AMARGINGGE 1. that which comes after

2. afterbirth 3. pertaining to the north

AMARI after, afterwards

AMARIMBI to fall behind

AMASI 1. backward, to the back, toward the back 2. after, henceforth

AMASI BUMBI to sacrifice to the Big Dipper

AMASI DUSHUMBI to draw the right hand back forcefully (in archery)

AMASI JULESI backwards and forwards

AMATA plural of *ama*

AMBA big, great, vast, important

AMBA AJIGE large and small (size)

AMBA BAYARA (護軍營) guard division; cf. BH 734

AMBA BEIKUWEN one of the twenty-four solar divisions of the year falling on January twentieth or twenty-first

AMBA DORO imperial rule

AMBA DULIN a majority

AMBA DUWALINAHA (大簇) one of the six tones of the major scale

AMBA ELHE NIYANJAN (大安輦) an imperial chariot drawn by six men

AMBA ELIOI (大呂) one of the six tones of the minor scale

AMBA ERDEMUNGGE GURUN Germany

AMBA GARMA a large yellow mosquito

AMBA HALHŪN one of the twenty-four divisions of the solar year falling on August twenty-third or twenty-fourth

AMBA HIYOOŠUN the filial piety of the emperor

AMBA HIYOOŠUNGGA supremely filial-- an epithet of the emperor

AMBA HOLBONGGO HOOŠAN paper used for making money that is burned as a sacrifice

AMBA HOŠO the inner corner of the eye

AMBA HŪWALIYAMBURE DEYEN (太和殿) the main throne hall of the Peking palace

AMBA IJA horsefly

AMBA KOOLINGGA HAFAN (太史) Compiler of the Second Class, BH 200B

AMBA KUMUN music played when the emperor retired to his private chambers after a banquet

AMBA LAMPA great chaos

AMBA MUKE a flood

AMBA MURU 1. probably, generally, in outline, approximately 2. sketch, outline

AMBA NIMANGGI one of the twenty-four divisions of the solar year falling on the seventh or eighth of December

AMBA SARGAN the first or chief wife

AMBA SURI a type of rough silk

AMBA ŠAHŪRUN one of the twenty-four divisions of the solar year falling on the twentieth or twenty-first of January

AMBA ŠOGE a fifty-ounce silver ingot

AMBA ŠOŠOBUN (大結) great summary--the last part of a formal essay

AMBA TACIN Mahayana (Buddhism)

AMBA TEN (太極) the great ultimate--the ultimate principle of the universe

AMBA TOOSENGGE ABKA mighty heaven

AMBA YABUNGGA title for a deceased emperor

AMBA YALI meat offered and eaten at a sacrifice

AMBA YOLONGGO JAHŪDAI a type of fast war junk

AMBAKALIYAN rather large, somewhat big

AMBAKAN rather big, a person who is rather large

AMBAKASI plural of *ambakan*

AMBAKI haughty, proud, pompous

AMBAKILAMBI to act haughtily

AMBALINGGŪ 1. huge, imposing, impressive, grand 2. dignified

AMBALINGGŪ ALIN I ALBAN TACIKŪ (景山官學) School at the Red Hill, BH 87B

AMBALINGGŪ MUNGGAN (景陵) the mausoleum of the K'ang-hsi emperor

AMBAN 1. high official, dignitary 2. same as *amba*

AMBAN I MANAMBI 1. to be carried out carelessly 2. (the month) has thirty days

AMBARAMBI to do on a large scale

AMBARAME GIYANGNARA HAFAN (經進講官) an official charged with explaining the classics to the emperor

AMBARAME SIMNEMBI to hold the tri-yearly examination in the capital

AMBARAME WECERE WECEN the sacrifice offered every five years by the emperor to all the imperial ancestors

AMBASA 1. plural of *amban* 2. rather large

AMBASA SAISA (君子) a worthy, wise man, a true gentleman

AMBU mother's elder sister

AMBUHAI AMBUHAI unintentionally

AMBULA greatly, widely, very much

AMBULA ASARARA FIYENTEN (廣儲司) Department of the Privy Purse, BH 77

AMBULA BEIKUWEN extremely cold

AMBULA IKTAMBURE NAMUN (廣積庫) the name of an armory under the

A

A

Board of Works
AMBULAKAN rather greatly, rather much
AMBUMA mother's elder sister's husband
AMBUMBI to overtake and catch
AMBUTA plural of *ambu*
AMCABUMBI caus./pass. of *amcambi*
AMCADAMBI see *amcatambi*
AMCAKŪŠAMBI 1. to follow, to pursue
  2. to interrogate, to question
  3. to investigate
AMCAMBI 1. to pursue, to chase, to
  catch up to 2. to hurry, to rush
  3. to act in retrospect, to act
  posthumously 4. to review (a case)
  5. *dobori be amcame* 'under cover of
  darkness' 6. to take advantage of
  7. to make up for gambling losses
    AMCAME FUNGNEMBI to enfeoff post-
    humously
    AMCAME GEBU BUMBI to give a name
    posthumously
    AMCAME GŪNIMBI to think back in
    retrospect
    AMCARAKŪ can't make it on time,
    unable to meet a deadline
AMCANAMBI to go to pursue, to rush
  (over)
AMCANGGA pertaining to pursuit
    AMCANGGA JAHŪDAI the name of a type
    of large warship
AMCANJIMBI to come to pursue, to come
  pursuing, to catch up with
AMCATAMBI 1. to strive to overtake
  2. to speak before someone else has
  a chance to 3. to overstep one's
  competence
AMDA MUSIHI 1. just sufficient 2.
  lacking in feeling, indifferent
AMDULABUMBI caus. of *amdulambi*
AMDULAMBI to paste, to glue
AMDUN glue, paste, birdlime
    AMDUN BILCAMBI to spread glue
AMGABUMBI 1. caus. of *amgambi* 2. to
  put to bed
AMGACAMBI to sleep together
AMGAMBI to sleep
AMGANAMBI to go to sleep
AMHA wife's father
AMHABUMBI same as *amgabumbi*
AMHACAMBI same as *amgacambi*
AMHAMBI same as *amgambi*
AMHAN same as *amha*
AMHANAMBI same as *amganambi*
AMHŪLAN a whistle
AMIDA aspen tree
    AMIDA NIMALAN sallow
AMIHŪN realgar
AMILA the male of fowl
AMILAMBI 1. to anoint a Buddhist
  icon's eyes with blood and thereby
  impart life to it 2. to grasp the
  cantle of a saddle
    AMILAME CASHŪN FIYELEMBI to vault

backwards grasping the cantle of a
  saddle
AMIN cantle
AMJI father's elder brother
AMJITA plural of *amji*
AMSU food presented to the emperor
    AMSU I DA (尚 膳 正) Chief
    Trencher-Knight, BH 91
    AMSU IBEBUMBI to set food before
    the emperor
AMSULAMBI to dine (used for the
  emperor)
AMSUN wine and food offerings to a
  deity
    AMSUN DAGILARA BOO (神 厨) the
    place where wine and food offer-
    ings were prepared
    AMSUN I DA (司 胙 長) offi-
    cial in charge of preparing of-
    ferings of food and wine
    AMSUN I JANGGIN (司 胙 官)
    an official concerned with the
    preparation of offerings of food
    and wine
    AMSUN I YALI meat used as an offer-
    ing to a deity
    AMSUN JAFAMBI to prepare a food or
    wine offering
AMTALAMBI to test, to try (food), to
  taste
AMTAN 1. taste, smell 2. interest
    AMTAN ACABUMBI to flavor, to add
    seasoning
    AMTAN AKŪ 1. tasteless 2. uninter-
    esting
    AMTAN BAHAMBI to acquire a taste
    AMTAN DOSIMBI to be satisfied with,
    to be pleased with
    AMTAN GAIMBI to take a taste
    AMTAN SIMTEN taste, flavor
    AMTAN SIMTEN AKŪ listless, bored
    AMTAN TUHEMBI to lose taste, to
    lose interest
AMTANGGA 1. tasty, delicious, 2. en-
  joyable, interesting, fun
    AMTANGGAI pleasurably
AMTAŠAMBI to taste continually or
  often
AMTUN (俎) a type of ancient sacrificial vessel
AMU 1. father's elder brother's wife,
  mother's sister 2. sleep 3. the
  pancreas of a pig
    AMU GAIMBI to take a nap
    AMU GETEMBI to awake from sleep
    AMU MANGGA very sleepy
    AMU SEKTU sleeping lightly
    AMU SUREKE wide awake after waking
    up
    AMU SUWALIYAME half asleep, having
    a sleepy aspect
    AMU ŠABURAMBI to become sleepy
AMURAN fond of, intent on, good at,

A

assiduous

AMURANGGA devotee, one who is fond of
  something

AMURGAN a type of fine-grained, yellow
  wood used to make arrow shafts

AMURTU SARLA a swift gray horse

AMUTA plural of *amu*

AN usual, ordinary, common
  AN AKŪ irregular, unusual
  AN BE TUWAKIYAMBI to follow what is
    customary
  AN CIKTAN I TANGGIN a hall where
    the emperor gave instruction or
    lectured
  AN I as usual, as customary
  AN I BAITA an everyday matter
  AN I GISUN saying, proverb
  AN I GU ordinary jade
  AN I JERGI ordinary, usual
  AN I UCURI usually, ordinarily
  AN I WESIMBURE BITHE a memorial
    dealing with a private matter
    that did not have the official
    seal attached
  AN JERGI see *an i jergi*
  AN KEMUN rule, common practice,
    custom
  AN KOOLI custom, usage
  AN WEHE whetstone

ANABUMBI 1. caus./pass. of *anambi*
  2. to yield to, to be defeated
  ANABURE ETERE victory and defeat,
    loss and gain

ANAFU garrison, border garrison
  ANAFU COOHA garrison troops

ANAFULABUMBI caus. of *anafulambi*

ANAFULAMBI to garrison, to guard a
  frontier

ANAGAN 1. excuse, pretext 2. inter-
  calary
  ANAGAN ARAMBI to make an excuse or
    pretext
  ANAGAN I BIYA the intercalary
    month

ANAHŪN MOO nanmu tree (*Machilus nanmu*)

ANAHŪNGGA GURUNG an emperor's coffin

ANAHŪNJAMBI to be yielding, to be
  humble, to be modest, to yield to

ANAHŪNJAN modesty, reticence

ANAHŪNJANGGA modest, humble, reticent

ANAKŪ 1. key 2. pretext
  ANAKŪ ARAMBI to make an excuse, to
    use a pretext
  ANAKŪ FA a sliding window
  ANAKŪ JUI a child born after its
    father is dead
  ANAKŪ SEJEN a one-wheeled pushcart
  ANAKŪI DA (司鑰長) Keeper
    of Palace Keys, BH 108

ANAMBI 1. to push 2. to urge, to
  prompt 3. to extend (a date or a
  deadline) 4. to appoint 5. to make
  excuses, to blame others 6. to push

wider (a battue)

ANAME 1. even: *ama (ci) aname* 'even
  father'; . . . *ci aname* . . . *de
  isitala* 'from . . . to . . .' 2. in
  order, in sequence, one after
  another, one by one

ANAMELIYAN with the chest protruding

ANAMI a grown Manchurian elk; cf.
  kandahan

ANAN 1. an imperial carriage 2. push-
  ing, urging 3. sequence
  ANAN I in turn, successively
  ANAN I SILGASI (挨貢) a grad-
    uate promoted to a position that
    became vacant yearly
  ANAN ŠUKIN obsequious, timid, lack-
    ing in self-confidence

ANANGGA 1. a pretext 2. having a pretext

ANASHŪN flexible, yielding

ANATAMBI 1. to push together or repeatedly 2. to put off (until),
  to procrastinate 3. to refuse

ANCU HIYAN a type of fragrant grass
  burnt at sacrifices

ANCULAN GIYAHŪN hawk

ANCULAN GŪWARA same as *ancun gūwara*

ANCUN earring, ear pendant
  ANCUN GŪWARA probably the North
    China eagle owl (*Bubo bubo*)
  ANCUN I BOHORI decorations of gold,
    coral, or some other precious
    material attached to ear pendants
  ANCUN ILHA a type of jasmine
  ANCUN UMIYAHA cockroach

ANCURAHI gilded leather; cf. *gina*

ANDA a sworn brother, bosom friend,
  friend from childhood
  ANDA JAFAMBI to swear an oath of
    brotherhood
  ANDA SADUN friends and in-laws
  ANDA SAIKAN really good, very good

ANDAHALAMBI to be ashamed, to become
  ashamed

ANDAHAŠAMBI to turn red from embarrassment

ANDALA on the way, midway, halfway
  ANDALA GIYAMUN a post-station along
    the route

ANDAN an instant, a moment
  ANDANDE suddenly, in an instant, at
    once

ANDARAMBI to be shy of strangers (said
  of children)

ANDARGI same as *adaki*

ANDASI halfway, half of the way

ANDUBUMBI to distract a person from
  his worries, to get away from one's
  cares

ANDUHŪRI indifferent, coldhearted,
  unfriendly

ANDUHŪRILAMBI to treat (a person)
  coldly

A

ANFU a garrison, a border post; cf. *anafu*

ANFULAMBI same as *anafulambi*

ANG the sound made by camels and donkeys, a scream used in battle

ANG SEME AFAMBI to attack while shrieking war whoops

ANGGA 1. mouth 2. opening, hole 3. pass, gate

ANGGA ACAMBI to testify in court

ANGGA AIFUMBI to break one's word

ANGGA AKŠUN abusive, slanderous

ANGGA ALJAMBI to promise, to agree to

ANGGA ARAMBI to acknowledge orally

ANGGA BAHAMBI to obtain a confession

ANGGA BAIBI MIOSIRI MIOSIRILAMBI to have a slight smile on one's face constantly

ANGGA BAIMBI to interrogate (a criminal)

ANGGA CAKCAHŪN tight-mouthed, hard to control (of horses)

ANGGA CIRA tight-mouthed (of horses)

ANGGA CUKCUHUN lips protruded--an expression of annoyance

ANGGA DE GAMAHA BA AKŪ (liquor) has never touched his lips

ANGGA DE GAMAMBI to touch the lips-- said of liquor

ANGGA DUYEN weak-mouthed (of horses)

ANGGA FAKSI clever in speech, glib

ANGGA FECUHUN without appetite

ANGGA FODOROMBI to protrude the lips in annoyance

ANGGA GAIMBI to kiss

ANGGA GAKAHŪN with the mouth gaping

ANGGA HETUMBI to make a living, to scrape along, to get by

ANGGA HETUMBUMBI to make a living, to get by

ANGGA HOTOHON having lips that protrude upward

ANGGA I ANAKŪ a pretext for scandal or gossip

ANGGA I HOŠO the corner of the mouth

ANGGA ICI not thinking before speaking, fluently, effortlessly (of speech)

ANGGA ISI please try some (said when offering food to a guest)

ANGGA ISIBUMBI to make or let taste first

ANGGA ISIMBI to taste first

ANGGA JAFAMBI 1. to close the mouth 2. to catch a prisoner of war who is to be used as an informer

ANGGA JOHIMBI the opening (of a boil) shrinks and heals

ANGGA LABDAHŪN having lips that hang downward

ANGGA MENTUHUN without feeling in the mouth (of horses)

ANGGA MIMIMBI to close the mouth

ANGGA OJOMBI to kiss

ANGGA SONJOMBI to have a craving for odd foods when one is pregnant

ANGGA SULA loose-mouthed (of horses)

ANGGA SULFAMBI to migrate to another place because of an insufficiency of food

ANGGA TUCIMBI to come to a head (of a boil)

ANGGAI ANAKŪ pretext for gossip

ANGGAI DAMBI to blow, to puff

ANGGAI JASIMBI to transmit by word of mouth, to deliver an oral communication

ANGGALA 1. population, persons 2. (postposition) in place of, instead of, rather than, not only

ANGGALAMBI to request, to demand

ANGGALINGGŪ fluent, glib

ANGGARA a large jar, a container for water

ANGGARI JANGGARI all mixed up, in disarray

ANGGASI widow

ANGGASI HEHE widow

ANGGASIBUMBI caus. of *anggasimbi*

ANGGASILAMBI to be a widow, to preserve widowhood

ANGGASIMBI to taste, to try

ANGGATU muzzle for domestic animals

ANGGIR NIYEHE the ruddy sheldrake (*Cascara ferruginea*)

ANGGIYAN thornback (a type of seafish)

ANGGŪTA 1. muzzle 2. a piece of iron attached to the end of the hilt of a sword

ANIYA year

ANIYA ALIHA GŪSAI SIDEN YAMUN (值 年 旗 衙 門) General Headquarters of the Banners, BH 718

ANIYA ARAMBI to celebrate New Year's

ANIYA BIYA the first lunar month

ANIYA GOIDAHA old

ANIYA HŪSIME for an entire year, a whole year

ANIYA I FE INENGGI the last day of the year

ANIYA INENGGI New Year's day

ANIYA TOME every year

ANIYADARI every year

ANIYAINGGE pertaining to a (certain) year

ANIYALAME for an entire year, a whole year

ANIYANGGA 1. pertaining to a certain year in the twelve-year cycle 2. aged

ANIYANGGA SAKDA an aged man

ANJA plow

ANJIBUMBI caus. of *anjimbi*

ANJIKŪ hatchet
ANJIMBI to hack, to chop with a hatchet
ANJU meat and fish, animal products, food forbidden to Buddhists
  ANJU BELHERE BA (薀局) a place in the banqueting court where food was prepared for state occasions
ANTA for *antaka*
ANTAHA guest, stranger
  ANTAHA BE BOIGOJILARA BOLGOBURE FIYENTEN (主客清吏司) Reception Department, BH 376 A
  ANTAHA BE TUWAŠATARA BOLGOBURE FIYENTEN (賓客清吏司) department for the reception of foreign guests
  ANTAHA I KUREN hostel for foreign envoys
ANTAHALAMBI to entertain
ANTAHARAMBI to be a guest, to act as a guest, to stand on ceremony
ANTAHASA plural of *antaha*
ANTAHASI a scribe in a military or governmental office
ANTAHAŠAMBI to be a guest
ANTAI same as *antaka*
ANTAKA how is it? what is it like? what about . . . ? how about . . . ?
ANTARHAN CECIKE one of the names of the sparrow; cf. *fiyasha cecike*
ANTU the south side of a mountain, the sunny side of a mountain
ANTUHŪRI cold, indifferent
ANWAN sea perch
AO an interjection expressing doubt
AR the sound of calling or shouting
  AR SEME shouting loudly
ARA 1. chaff 2. interjection of pain or surprise
  ARA FARA an interjection of pain, the sound of expectorating
ARABUMBI caus. of *arambi*
ARAKE same as *ara* (as an interjection)
ARAMBI 1. to do, to make 2. to write 3. to feign, to pretend 4. to celebrate 5. to appoint 6. to recognize as an adopted relation
  ARAHA adopted, appointed
  ARAHA BAYARAI JALAN I JANGGIN (委護軍參領) an appointed Colonel of the Guards Division, BH 734
ARANDUMBI/ARANUMBI to do, write, etc., together
ARANJIMBI to come to do, write, etc.
ARAŠAN propitious, refreshing
  ARAŠAN AGA a seasonable rain, a propitious rain
  ARAŠAN AGANGGA KIRU a gray banner with the symbol of a dragon sewn upon it
ARBUN 1. form, shape, image 2. situation, circumstances

ARBUN BE TUWAME in view of the circumstances, depending upon circumstances
ARBUN DURSUN form, appearance
ARBUN GIRU appearance
ARBUN I ANGGA juncture of two rivers
ARBUN I BA a strategic point
ARBUN MURU situation
ARBUN TACIHIYAN Buddhism
ARBUNGGA possessing form, having good form, pertaining to images
  ARBUNGGA TACIHIYAN Buddhism
ARBUŠAMBI to move, to behave
ARBUŠARANGGE behavior
  ARBUŠARANGGE SAIKAN well-behaved
ARBUTAI in appearance only, for appearance's sake
ARCA BURGA *Salix Urbaniana*; cf. *aršan burga*
ARCAMBI to block, to block the way
ARCAN cream, milk thickened with wine and sugar
ARCILAN BURGA same as *arca burga*
ARDA untried, new, a greenhorn
ARDASHŪN delicate, fragile
ARE an interjection of pain
ARFA barley, grain
  ARFA DIB (Sanskrit *Yavadvīpa* 'Isle of Grain') Java
ARFUKŪ fly swatter, fly whisk
ARGA plan, method, plot
  ARGA AKŪ there is nothing one can do about it
  ARGA BAIMBI to look for a way
  ARGA DERIBUMBI to think up a plan
  ARGA JALI plot, deceit
ARGABUMBI caus. of *argambi*
  ARGABUHA DALAN a dike built in the shape of a crescent moon
ARGACAN a large ax
ARGADABUMBI caus. of *argadambi*
ARGADAMBI to use artifice or cunning (against), to outwit
ARGALI female of Darwin's sheep; cf. *uhūlja*
ARGAMBI to hunt animals in the mountains using a sickle-shaped battue line, to form a crescent or sickle shape
ARGAN 1. sprout 2. crescent 3. fang, tooth of a saw
  ARGAN MUDUN a fine file
  ARGAN OŠOHO fangs and claws
ARGANAMBI 1. to form a crescent 2. to germinate, to sprout
  ARGANAHA formed a crescent moon
ARGANGGA crafty, cunning
ARGAT same as *arhat*
  ARGAT MOO lohan tree
ARGATU male roe, roebuck; cf. *sirga*
  ARGATU SIRGA same as *argatu*
ARGIYABUMBI caus./pass. of *argiyambi*
ARGIYAMBI 1. to peel off, to shave off, to scrape off 2. to graze with a

A

knife or sword

ARGŪMA SARLA an isabella horse

ARHAT an arhat

ARI 1. an evil spirit   2. a good-for-
nothing, a thoroughly mischievous
person

ARJAN liquor made from milk, kumiss

ARKAN scarcely, barely, just, just,
right

ARKAN KARKAN barely, scarcely

ARKAN SEME scarcely, barely, just,
reluctantly

ARKE interjection of pain used when
bumping into something

ARKI distilled liquor, strong liquor

ARSALAN lion

ARSALANGGA pertaining to the lion,
lionlike

ARSARAKŪ strange, out of the ordinary

ARSARI ordinary, common, everyday,
commonplace

ARSARI BANJIMBI to lead an average
life

ARSARI ŠANYAN BELE medium quality
rice

ARSARI ŠARAKA half-white, impure
white

ARSARI TUWABUNGGA HOOŠAN medium-
size paper used for announcements

ARSUMBI (-ka) to sprout, to germinate

ARSUN bud, sprout

ARSUN I CAI tea made of the buds of
tea leaves

ARŠAN BURGA *Salix Urbaniana*--'big leaf
willow'

ARŠU one of the names of the quail;
cf. *mušu*

ARTABUMBI pass. of *artambi*

ARTAMBI to delay, to hold up

ARTU a three-year-old horse

ARUN DURUN AKŪ without a trace

ARUN FURUN news

ARUN FURUN AKŪ without news

ASAHA FASAHA hurried, rushed, busy

ASANGGI 100 quadrillion, countless,
infinite

ASARABUMBI caus. of *asarambi*

ASARAMBI to put away for safekeeping,
to store

ASARI tower, throne room, archive

ASARI I BAITA BE ALIFI KADALARA
AMBAN (領 閣 事) Assistant
Director of the Library, BH 104B

ASARI I BAITA BE DAME KADALARA AMBAN
(提 舉 閣 事) Director
of the Library, BH 104B

ASARI I BAITA BE SIRAME KADALARA
HAFAN (直 閣 事) Officials
on duty at the Library, BH 104B

ASHA 1. wing 2. anything worn hanging
from the belt 3. a piece of iron
placed on the back of armor under
the shoulder piece

ASHABUKŪ a leather clasp for the belt

ASHABUMBI caus. of *ashambi*

ASHAMBI to wear hanging from the belt,
to wear hanging from a button on the
lapel

ASHARA FUNGKU a kerchief carried
from the belt

ASHARA ŠUSIHE a wooden plaque worn
on the belt that served as identification for an official who
wished to enter a walled city
after dark

ASHAN 1. side 2. appendage 3. peripheral, subordinate

ASHAN DA (内 閣 學 士) Sub-
chancellor of the Grand Secretariat, BH 133

ASHAN I AMBAN (侍 郎) Vice-
President of a Board, BH 279

ASHAN I BAICARA AMBAN (副 都 御
史) Vice-President of the Censorate, BH 207B, 208

ASHAN I BITHEI DA (學 士) Sub-
chancellor of the Grand Secretariat, BH 133

ASHAN I DUKA a side entrance to the
palace

ASHAN I HAFAN (男) baron

ASHANAMBI 1. to develop wings 2. to
become distended on two sides

ASHANGGA winged

ASHANGGA MAHALA an old style hat
having long black wings on two
sides

ASHANGGA SINGGERI bat

ASHANGGA YERHUWE a winged ant,
flying ant

ASHARGAN a pendant for the belt

ASHŪBUMBI pass. of *ashŭmbi*

ASHŪLAMBI see *ashŭmbi*

ASHŪMBI 1. to draw the right hand back
to shoot an arrow or throw a spear
2. to resist, to reject, to fend off
(insects)

ASHŪME SINDAMBI to shoot an arrow
by drawing the right hand back

ASI very

ASIHA young, small

ASIHAKI having a youthful appearance
in spite of one's age

ASIHAN young, youth

ASIHAN AISIN HŪNTAHAN ILHA *Adonis
davurica*

ASIHAN SARGAN concubine

ASIHATA plural of *asihan*

ASIHIYABUMBI caus. of *asihiyambi*

ASIHIYAMBI to trim off, to pare off,
to prune

ASIKALIYAN somewhat small

ASIKAN somewhat small

ASIKASI someone or something rather
small

ASU a net (for catching game)

ASU UKSIN   net armor
ASU WEŠEN   net for deer and rabbits
ASUCI   a hunter who uses a net for
    catching game
ASUKI   a small noise
    ASUKI AKŪ   noiseless
    ASUKI WEI AKŪ   without the slightest
    noise
ASUKILABUMBI   caus. of *asukilambi*
    ASUKILABURE FU   a wall that causes
    echoes to rebound
ASUKILAMBI   to make a small noise
ASUKINGGA   noisy, boisterous
ASUMBI   to lift up a garment that is
    too long
ASURI   Asura, a demigod who fights with
    devas in the air
ASURŠAMBI   to threaten one another, to
    provoke one another
ASURU   very, exceedingly
    ASURU ENCU BA AKŪ   not too different
AŠA   elder brother's wife
AŠATA   plural of *aša*
AŠŠABUMBI   caus. of *aššambi*
AŠŠALAMBI   to move slightly, to squirm
AŠŠAMBI   to move, to shake, to vibrate
    AŠŠARA ARBUŠARA   movement
AŠŠAN   1. movement, vibration
    2. behavior
AŠŠANDUMBI   to move together
AŠUMBI (-ka)   to hold in the mouth
AŠUMBUMBI   1. caus. of *ašumbi* 2. to
    stick in the mouth
    AŠUMBUHA FADU JAN   a 'duckbill'
    whistling arrow
ATAN   the point of a fish hook
ATANGGI   when?
    ATANGGI BICIBE   no matter when
    ATANGGI OCIBE   before long, soon
ATARAMBI   to make a commotion, to cause
    a row; cf. *abtarambi*
ATMULA   one of the names for the
    Chinese sweet olive (*Canarium album*)
ATU   a female fish
ATUHA   a male fish
    ATUHA DAFAHA   a male salmon
ATUHŪN   dowry
    ATUHŪN FUDEMBI   to bring the dowry
    to the groom's house
AYA   1. interjection of praise or sur-
    prise 2. see *ai*
AYALAMBI   1. to wax, to cover with a

wax coating 2. to fester
AYALAHA ILHANGGA HOOŠAN   a kind of
    flowered paper covered with a lay-
    er of wax
AYAMBI   to flutter, to struggle (like
    a fish that has taken the hook)
AYAMBUMBI   to captivate, to entice;
    cf. *gisurehei ayambumbi*
AYAN   1. large, great 2. wax, candle
    3. Manchurian wapiti (*Cervus elaphus*)
    AYAN BUHŪ   Manchurian wapiti--see
    above
    AYAN DENGJAN   candle
    AYAN DOBOKŪ   candlestick
    AYAN EDUN   storm wind
    AYAN FODOHO   purple osier (*Salix
    purpurea*)
    AYAN GAHA   a type of large crow with
    a white neck
    AYAN GINTEHE   a tree with green bark,
    small leaves, and fine wood--good
    for bows and knife handles
    AYAN GURJEN   black tree cricket
    AYAN HARSA   beech marten
    AYAN HIYAN   the name of grass burnt
    at sacrifices--rue
    AYAN I CALU (蠟 倉)   wax store-
    house of the imperial household
    AYAN I HAFIRAKŪ   a candle snuffer
    AYAN I NIYAMAN   wick (of a candle)
    AYAN I NIYAMAN TEBUKU   a container
    for burnt wick ends
    AYAN JELKEN   a species of weasel
    AYAN MALANGGŪ   sesame
    AYAN SILMEN   the male of the sparrow
    hawk
    AYAN SUWAYAN   truly precious
    AYAN ŠUGIRI HIYAN   incense made from
    Indian resin
    AYAN TOKTOKŪ   a lantern with a
    candle in it
    AYAN WEHE   a shiny smooth stone
AYANTUMBI   to soar upwards (of hawks
    and eagles)
AYAO   same as *ayoo*
AYARA   sour milk, buttermilk
AYARI   waxlike
    AYARI ILHA   an exotic yellow flower
    similar to a plum blossom
AYOO   a final particle denoting fear
    or doubt

A

B

BA　1. place　2. local　3. *li*--a Chinese mile　4. circumstances, occasion, situation, reason, condition, matter

BA ARAMBI　to make place, to get out of the way

BA BA　everywhere, every place

BA BUMBI　to give a place to, to give a portion to

BA DZUNG（把總）Sublieutenant, BH 752F

BA I GISUN　dialect, local language

BA JIYOO　plantain, banana

BA NA　territory, land, local

BA NA I NIRUGAN　map

BA NA I NIRUGAN NIRURE BOO（輿圖房）department of cartography in the Workshop of the Imperial Household

BA NA TUWARA NIYALMA　a geomancer

BA SIYAN DERE（八仙桌）a large round dining table

BA SULABUMBI　to leave a vacant place

BA WANG　hegemon king

BA WANG ASU　a kind of net for catching fish

BABACI　from everywhere

BABADE　everywhere

BABI　1. same as *ba bi*　2. same as *baibi*

BABUHAN　a five-fingered leather glove for holding falcons

BABUN　1. handle on a bucket or basket　2. crupper

BABUNGGA　having a handle

BACI　same as *ba ci*

BACIHI　married while still a child

BACIHILAMBI　to be married as a child

BADA　dissipation, waste

BADALAMBI　to squander, to dissipate, to waste

BADAN　dish, tray

BADAR　a monk's alms bowl; cf. *badiri*

BADAR SEME　speaking without due deliberation, speaking wildly

BADARAKA　abundant, rich

BADARAMBI　(-ka)　to become wide, to expand, to become larger, to become prosperous

BADARAMBUMBI　1. to enlarge, to expand, to propagate　2. caus./pass. of *badarambi*

BADARAMBUNGGA　magnifying, enlarging

　　BADARAMBUNGGA BULEKU　magnifying glass

BADARAN　enlargement, widening, growth

BADARANGGA DORO　the Kuang-hsü（光緒）reign period, 1875-1908

BADE　(postposition) in the case that, if

BADIRI　a monk's alms bowl

BADUN　a weight measure--ten pecks, a bushel

　　BADUN JAHŪDAI　a ship whose stern had the shape of a bushel measure

BADZUNG（把總）Sublieutenant, BH 752F

BAGIYAMBI　to hold a small child's legs while he urinates or defecates

BAHA　perfect participle of *bahambi*

　　BAHA BAHAI　unintentionally

BAHABUMBI　1. caus./pass. of *bahambi*　2. to dream　3. to get drunk

BAHAMBI　1. to get, to obtain　2. to be able

　　BAHACI　I hope that . . .

　　BAHACI TUTTU　if only it were so!

　　BAHARA SONGKO　tracks that show that the prey has been wounded

　　BAHARAKŪ SONGKO　tracks that show that the prey has escaped

BAHANA　the central pole of a Mongolian yurt

BAHANAMBI　1. to go to get　2. to be able　3. to experience

BAHANASI　connoisseur, expert

BAHANJIMBI　to come to get

BAHIYA　pine cone

BAI　1. plain, simple　2. for nothing, free, in vain　3. at leisure, unemployed　4. only　5. particle of finality

BAI NIYALMA a man without work or position

BAI TEMBI to live in leisure, to live in retirement

BAI TIYEI BITHE visiting card

BAIBI 1. plain, ordinary 2. for nothing, with no purpose, vainly, simply, merely

BAIBULA the paradise flycatcher (*Tersiphone paradisi*)

BAIBULAN see *baibula*

BAIBUMBI 1. caus. of *baimbi* 2. to require, to need, to use

BAIBUNGGA provisions

BAICABUMBI caus. of *baicambi*

BAICABURE TEMGETU a certificate of inspection

BAICAMBI to inspect, to examine, to investigate, to survey

BAICAME BEIDERE HAFAN (提察使) Provincial Judge, BH 830

BAICAME TUWARA HAFAN (監察御使) Censor, BH 213

BAICAME WAKALARA KUNGGERI (糾參科) a section of the Court of State Ceremonial that was in charge of fixing punishments for officials who failed to pay a courtesy visit to the court after receiving an imperial favor

BAICAN inspection, examination

BAICAN I EJEKU (都事) Official of the Censorate Chancery, BH 211

BAICANABUMBI caus. of *baicanambi*

BAICANAMBI to go to inspect

BAICANDUMBI/BAICANUMBI to inspect together

BAICANJIMBI to come to inspect

BAICASI (檢校) Prefectural Police Inspector, BH 850

BAIDALAMBI to punish by beating

BAIHANABUMBI caus. of *baihanambi*

BAIHANAMBI to go to search for

BAIHANJIMBI to come to search for

BAIKŪ whore, lewd woman

BAILI kindness, mercy, tenderness

BAILI ISIBUMBI to repay a kindness

BAILI JAFAMBI to repay a kindness

BAILINGGA merciful, kind

BAILISI 1. beneficiary 2. 'one who seeks happiness,' i.e., a Buddhist, Taoist, or shaman

BAIMBI (imperative *baisu*) to seek, to look for, to wish, to ask for

BAIME SUIMBI to search high and low

BAINDUMBI/BAINUMBI to seek together, to discuss

BAINGGE of a certain place

BAINJIMBI to come to seek, request, etc.

BAISE Chinese cabbage

BAISIN without an official position, at leisure

BAISING settlement, village

BAISU imperative of *baimbi*

BAITA matter, affair, business, event

BAITA AKŪ free, not busy, it doesn't matter, it's no use, useless

BAITA BE ALIHA HAFAN (府丞) Vice-governor of Peking, BH 793

BAITA BE DARA FIYENTEN (經歷司) Registry Office of the Imperial Clan Court, BH 63

BAITA BE KADALARA HAFAN (提調官) Proctor, BH 94, 139, 144, etc.

BAITA BELHEKU (孔目) Junior Archivist, BH 202

BAITA DE AFAHA HAFAN (供事官) Clerk, BH 190, 267

BAITA DE DARA HAFAN (經歷) Commissary of Records, BH 826

BAITA DE HAMIRAKŪ not in conformity with the matter, doesn't correspond to the matter at hand

BAITA EJERE BOO (掛號房) registration office--the police station of the Peking Gendarmerie

BAITA EJERE HAFAN (校理) a secretary of the Wen-yüan-ko (文淵閣)

BAITA HACIN I BOO (業房) business office of the Board of Finance

BAITA I SEKIYEN a quotation from the statutes

BAITA OBURAKŪ does not treat as a matter of consequence

BAITA SITA matters and affairs

BAITA TUŠAHA NIYALMA a person in charge of a matter

BAITA TUWARA NIYALMA someone in charge of a matter

BAITA WESIMBURE BA (奏事處) Chancery of Memorials to the Emperor, BH 105

BAITAI ICIHIYASI (經歷) Registrar, BH 64, 117, 212, etc.; cf. *baita de dara hafan*

BAITAI SARASI (知事) Archivist, BH 830A, etc.; cf. BH 506

BAITAI TURGUN the cause of an event

BAITAKŪ same as *baita akū*; useless

BAITALABUMBI 1. caus./pass. of *baitalambi* 2. to be employed as an official

BAITALABURE HAFAN (騎都尉) a hereditary rank of the seventh grade, BH 944

BAITALAMBI to use, to employ

BAITALAN 1. utilization, use 2. a thing in daily use, a necessity

BAITALAN DE ACABURE NAMUN (供用庫) a storehouse for wax and incense

B

B

BAITANGGA 1. usable, applicable, useful
    2. errand boy, handyman, underling
BAITASI (都 事) official of a
    chancery, BH 211, 212B
BAIŽIN same as *baisin*
BAJAR SEME filled with many and sundry
    things
BAJARGI the far shore, the opposite
    shore
BAJI a little bit (more), a while
    BAJI NONGGIMBI to add a little bit
    more
    BAJI OME in a short while
BAJIKAN just a tiny bit (more)
BAJILA on the opposite shore
BAJIMA a little while more
BAJIMASHŪN a while thereafter
BAJU the dregs from *arki*
BAKALAJI see *bakalji*
BAKALJI a bone above the hoof of a
    horse or cow, pastern
BAKCAMBI see *bakjambi*
BAKCILABUMBI 1. caus./pass. of *bakcil-
    ambi* 2. to put in opposition, to
    make oppose
BAKCILAMBI to oppose, to sit or stand
    opposite
BAKCIN the opposite side, opponent,
    opposite number
    BAKCIN AKŪ without match, peerless
    BAKCIN WAKA is no match (for)
BAKJA BAKJALAME ILIMBI to rear up and
    stop (of horses)
BAKJABUMBI caus. of *bakjambi*
BAKJALAMBI to rear (of horses), to
    come to a sudden stop
    BAKJALAME ILIMBI to come to a sudden
    stop (of a galloping horse)
BAKJAMBI (-ka) to congeal
BAKSALABUMBI caus. of *baksalambi*
BAKSALAMBI 1. to tie into bundles
    2. to divide (troops) into squads
BAKSAN 1. a bundle 2. a squad, a
    small group (of troops)
    BAKSAN MEYEN the ranks, line (of
    soldiers)
BAKSANDA leader of a squad
BAKSANGGA 1. an ancient Chinese grain
    measure equaling eight bushels 2.
    pertaining to a bundle or squad
    BAKSANGGA FICAKŪ a *sheng*, a class-
    ical Chinese wind instrument
BAKSATU (把 總) Sublieutenant,
    BH 752F
BAKSI a scholar, a learned man,
    gentleman
BAKTA the placenta of cattle
BAKTAKŪ the internal organs
BAKTAMBI 1. to contain, to encompass
    2. to bear, to endure
BAKTAMBUMBI 1. to be indulgent
    (toward), to forgive 2. to accept,
    to put up with, to suffer (misfor-

tune)
BAKTAMBUN 1. forgiveness 2. contents
BAKTAN capacity, contents
BAKTANDAMBI to contain, to hold
    BAKTANDARAKŪ doesn't fit, won't go
    in, unforgivable
    BAKTANDARAKŪ ARAHABI put on great
    airs, posed as something great
    BAKTANDARAKŪ BAYAN extremely rich
BAKTANGGA containing, encompassing
    BAKTANGGA BULEKU compass
    BAKTANGGA IKTANGGA implication,
    hidden meaning
BALAI blindly, vainly, carelessly,
    indiscriminately, falsely, unreason-
    ably
    BALAI FEMEN vain talk, useless
    prattling
    BALAI ICI SINDAMBI to put something
    down carelessly, to put just any
    old place
    BALAI ONDOMBI to move blindly, to
    act to no purpose
BALAKTA clots of blood on an afterbirth
BALAMA 1. mad, crazy 2. (sentence
    particle) only, just, however, but
BALAMADAMBI to rave, to act crazily
BALBA having poor eyesight
BALCITAMBI to vouch for
BALDA white on the chest of an animal,
    a pig with white feet; cf. *balta*
BALDARGAN probably the lesser kestrel
    (*Cerchneis naumanni*)
BALDARHAN see *baldargan*
BALDASITAMBI to slip
BALHAMBI to make an offering to the
    gods to escape from smallpox
BALIYA 1. interjection used when
    laughing at someone's ineptitude
    2. an interjection of pity
BALJUN ghost, apparition, goblin
    BALJUN I TUWA ghostly fire, *ignis
    fatuus*
BALTA a dog whose nose ridge is white,
    white hair on an animal's chest,
    a pig with white feet
BALTAHA the hair under the chin of a
    sable
BALU blind; see also *dogo*
BAMBI (-ngka) 1. to be tired, to be
    lazy, to feel too lazy to do some-
    thing 2. to gnaw a hole
BAN 1. a troop 2. half
    BAN ŠI GUWAN HAFAN (辨 事 官)
    attendant in various governmental
    offices
BANAJE TEBUMBI to have evil spirits
    driven out by a shaman
BANAJI the earth god
BANASI myrtle
BANCAN DUHA the rectum of horses,
    donkeys, and mules
BANCUKA tired

BANDA HARA knotweed (*Polygonum aviculare*)
BANDA MAFA the god of hunters
BANDAJIN 1. idler 2. things collected by rodents
BANDAMBI to tire, to become fatigued
BANDAN bench, chair
    BANDAN ASU a large fish net attached to a pole and carried by two men
BANDI learned man, pundit
BANDO the shrub *Pentapetes phoenicea*
BANG bulletin, notice
    BANG YAN number two in the palace examination
BANGGUHE myna bird
BANGNAMBI to accuse someone of doing something wrong
BANGSE night watchman's clapper
BANGTU 1. bracket, support for a rafter 2. a cloud-shaped stirrup
BANIHA thanks, gratitude, thank you!
    BANIHA ARAMBI to thank
    BANIHA BUMBI to thank
BANIHALAMBI to thank
BANIHŪN seriously wounded and sure to be brought down (of game)
BANIHŪNJAMBI to treat kindly
BANILJI wart on a horse's leg
BANIMBI see *banjimbi*
BANIN form, appearance, shape, nature, essence
    BANIN EHE ugly in appearance
    BANIN MAFA paternal grandfather
    BANIN MAMA paternal grandmother
    BANIN SAIN having a good appearance, good-looking
    BANIN WEN appearance, aspect
BANINARAKŪ indefatigable
BANINGGA natural, essential, having form
BANIRKE ENIYE stepmother
BANITAI by nature, inborn
BANITAINGGE that which has a nature, being alike by nature
BANJI a game that uses twenty-four black and white pieces on a chessboard
    BANJI EFIMBI to play the game of *banji*
BANJIBUMBI 1. caus. of *banjimbi* 2. to give birth to, to quicken 3. to compile, to compose, to make up, to form (e.g., a military unit)
    BANJIBUME ARARA HAFAN (纂修官) Proofreader, BH 94, 139
    BANJIBUME DASAKŪ (修撰) Compiler of the First Class, BH 200A
BANJIBUN a compendium, a creation, a product
BANJIBUNGGA productive, creative
BANJIMBI 1. to live, to be born, 2. to form, to come into existence, to become

BANJIHA AHŪN consanguineous elder brother
BANJIHA AMA natural father
BANJIHA DEO consanguineous younger brother
BANJIHA ENIYE natural mother
BANJIHA INENGGI birthday
BANJIRE SAIN get along well together, on good terms with
BANJIRE URSE people of means
BANJIRE WERE life, livelihood
BANJIME the same as *banji*
BANJIN appearance, nature, character, livelihood; cf. *banin*
BANJINAMBI 1. to go to live (at another place) 2. to be reborn 3. to make an appearance, to come about naturally 4. to grow into
BANJINARAKŪ inappropriate (as), unbecoming
BANJINJIMBI to come to live (in a new place)
BANJIRKE step- (as in stepmother, stepfather, etc.)
BANJISHŪN having sufficient money or goods to lead a comfortable life
BANJITAI by nature, inborn, naturally; cf. *banitai*
    BANJITAI DALANGGA a natural dike
BANUHŪN lazy
BANUHŪSAMBI to be lazy
BAR BAR SEME many people talking together
BAR BIR SEME in profusion, in great quantity, many people talking
BARABUMBI 1. caus. of *barambi* 2. to mix, to mix among, to mingle together
BARAG'ALANDA the Sanskrit name for the mandarin duck
BARAMBI to mix together, to soak one's rice with soup, to pour soup on rice
BARAMBUMBI see *barabumbi*
BARAMIDA jack fruit
BARAMIT paramita--the means leading to nirvana
BARAN 1. great number, large quantity, crowd, mass 2. disposition of troops 3. situation, circumstances 4. form, appearance, outline
    BARAN AKŪ without any ado, simply, without ceremony
BARANDZA prajna--transcendental knowledge
BARBEHE a name for the myna
BARDANGGI braggart
BARDANGGILAMBI to brag, to boast
BARGIN see *burgin*
BARGIYABUMBI caus. of *bargiyambi*
BARGIYAMBI 1. to store, to preserve, to protect 2. to take in, to receive, to harvest, to gather, to collect 3. to shave both ends of an arrow shaft

B

B

BARGIYAFI AFABURE KUNGGERI (收發科) Registry, BH 251

BARGIYAHA TEMGETU a confirmation of receipt, a receipt

BARGIYARA ASARARA FALGANGGA (收掌所) Section of Archives, BH 535

BARGIYARA ASARARA HAFAN (收掌官) Collector, BH 652F

BARGIYAN collecting, harvest

BARGIYANAMBI to go to collect

BARGIYARALAMBI same as *bargiyatambi*

BARGIYASHŪN narrowing toward the mouth

BARGIYATAMBI 1. to protect, to take care of 2. to bring together in one place 3. to straighten up, to fix up, to put in order 4. to hold back, to dam up

BARGIYATARA DALANGGA a dam

BARIN female of a beast of prey

BARKIYAMBI to understand, to grasp, to perceive, to notice

BARKIYAKŪ without paying attention, carelessly

BARKIYAME GŪNIHAKŪ without attention, heedlessly, carelessly

BARTANAMBI to become stained by sweat

BARU (postposition) toward

BARUN a full year or month

BASA salary, emolument, recompense

BASA BUMBI to pay a salary to, to give recompense to

BASA WECEMBI to make a thanksgiving offering for rain

BASA WERIMBI to leave a small offering for the gods along the road or in the mountains in thanks for a safe passing

BASAGIYAMBI see *basugiyambi*

BASAN 1. a girth 2. a wickerwork of willow placed on the roof

BASILAMBI to box

BASUBUMBI caus./pass. of *basumbi*

BASUCUN cause for joking or derision

BASUGIYAMBI see *basunggiyambi*

BASUMBI to make fun of, to deride, to mock

BASUNGGIYAMBI to talk in one's sleep

BASUNGGIYARA MANGGA often talks in his sleep

BASUNUMBI to deride together

BAŠA wife's younger sister

BAŠAKŪ a (fly-) whisk

BAŠAMBI 1. to chase away, to drive off 2. to urge, to press 3. to push (a cart), to drive (a vehicle)

BAŠILAMBI to hit with the fists

BATA enemy

BATAK SEME the sound of something metallic striking the ground

BATALABUMBI caus. of *batalambi*

BATALAMBI to be an enemy, to oppose

BATANGGA hostile, inimical

BATKALAMBI to deceive, to cheat, to swindle

BATMAGA ruby

BATUN incompletely thawed--thawed on the surface but still frozen underneath

BATURU 1. brave 2. hero

BATURU KIYANGKIYAN brave and strong

BATURULAMBI to be brave, to act bravely

BATURUNGGA endowed with courage

BAYABUMBI caus. of *bayambi*

BAYALAMBI to be happy, to be glad

BAYAMBI (-ka) to be rich, to become rich

BAYAMBUMBI caus. of *bayambi*

BAYAN 1. rich, rich man 2. having many pocks (from smallpox)

BAYAN ANIYA a bountiful year

BAYAN WESIHUN wealth and honor, wealthy and respected

BAYARA guard, troops on guard duty

BAYARAI JALAN I JANGGIN (護軍參領) Colonel, BH 734

BAYARAI JUWAN I DA (護軍校) Lieutenant, BH 734

BAYARAI KŪWARAN barracks of the banner guard northwest of Peking

BAYARAI TUI JANGGIN (護軍統領) Captain-General, BH 734

BAYASA plural of *bayan*

BE 1. we (exclusive) 2. accusative particle 3. (伯) count (the title) 4. a wooden crossbar in front of a wagon shaft 5. food for birds

BE HIYAN silver pheasant; cf. *šunggin gasha*

BEBELIYEMBI (-ke) to grow stiff from the cold

BEBEREMBI to grow stiff from the cold

BEBU sounds used to lull a baby to sleep, lullaby

BEBUŠEMBI to sing lullabies to

BECEBUMBI caus./pass. of *becembi*

BECEMBI to scold, to reproach, to reprimand

BECEN reprimand, rebuke

BECEN ACAMBI to quarrel

BECEN JAMAN quarrels and arguments

BECUN quarrel, squabble

BECUN COKO fighting cock

BECUN ULHŪMA a fighting pheasant

BECUNUBUMBI caus. of *becunumbi*

BECUNUMBI to fight, to quarrel

BEDERCEKU hesitant, shrinking

BEDERCEMBI to retreat, to withdraw

BEDEREBUMBI 1. caus. of *bederembi* 2. to send back, to withdraw (v.t.), to refuse, to return a courtesy or gift

BEDEREMBI to return, to withdraw (at court or at a ceremony), to die (of a noble personage)

B

BEDEREME KATARAMBI to go slowly (of a horse)

BEDERI stripes or spots on animals or birds

  BEDERI CECIKE a black bird with white spots and a long beak

  BEDERI MOO the tiger-stripe tree of Hainan

BEDERINEME BANJIMBI to form stripes or spots

BEDERINGGE having spots or stripes

BEDU another name for the tiger; cf. *tasha*

BEDUN sturdy, solidly made

BEGING Peking

BEGU pubic bone

BEG'O the ginkgo

BEHE ink, inkstick

  BEHE I HŪCIN a type of spring, so-called because it issues from stones resembling inksticks

  BEHE SUIMBI to grind an inkstone

  BEHEI FOLORO FALGA (墨刻作) a section of the Imperial Library concerned with carving wooden blocks for printing

  BEHEI NAMU a large round ink vessel

  BEHEI TEHE an inkstick holder

BEHELEBUMBI caus. of *behelembi*

BEHELEMBI to grind an inkstick

BEI an inscribed memorial stone

BEIBUN I EFEN sacrificial cakes

BEIDEBUMBI caus./pass. of *beidembi*

BEIDEMBI to examine (a case), to try (a case), to judge

  BEIDERE BOO (刑房) tribunal of the Court of Colonial Affairs

  BEIDERE JURGAN (刑部) Board of Justice, BH 438

  BEIDERE JURGAN I KUNGGE YAMUN (刑科) Department of Criminal Cases, BH 218A

  BEIDERE JURGAN I TOKTOHO GISUN set phrases used by the Board of Justice, legal terms

BEIDEN examination, trial

  BEIDEN BE ALIHA AMBAN (司寇) minister of justice in antiquity

  BEIDEN BE TUWANCIHIYARA YAMUN (大理司) Court of Judicature and Revision, BH 215

BEIDESI judge

BEIDURI sapphire

BEIGUWE root of the mustard plant

BEIGUWEN frost, cold

BEIGUWEREMBI to freeze, to frost

BEIHE an edible seaweed; cf. *kanin*

BEIHUWE scarecrow

BEIKUWEN cold, frigid

BEIKUWEREMBI (-ke) to be cold, to frost

BEILE *beile*, ruler, prince of the third rank

BEILE I FAIDAN I DA (司儀長) Major-Domo of a Prince's Palace, BH 44

BEILE I FUJIN wife of a *beile*

BEILE I JUI DOROI GEGE daughter of a *beile*

BEILE I SARGAN DOROI FUJIN wife of a *beile*

BEILECI a short-haired autumn pelt

BEILECILEMBI 1. to molt, to shed fur 2. to act haughtily

BEILECINEMBI to form a short-haired autumn coat (on animals)

BEISE *beise*, prince, a prince of the fourth rank

  BEISE I FUJIN the wife of a *beise*

BEJE the back of an oven-bed

BEJI a winning combination in the game of *gacuha*

BEJIHIYEBUMBI caus. of *bejihiyembi*

BEJIHIYELE consolation

BEJIHIYEMBI to console

BEJILEMBI to make a hidden allusion

BEKDE BAKDA see *bekte bakta*

BEKDUN debt, loan

  BEKDUN BOŠOMBI to call in a debt

  BEKDUN GAKDUN debts, heavily in debt

  BEKDUN SINDAMBI to make a loan

BEKI firm, strong

BEKIKEN rather firm, somewhat firm

BEKILEBUMBI caus. of *bekilembi*

BEKILEMBI to make fast, to make firm, to strengthen

BEKIN confidence, trust

BEKITU strong, stable, dependable

BEKTE BAKTA dismayed, dumfounded

BEKTELEMBI to cut off the feet as a punishment

BEKTEREMBI (-ke) to be frozen in one's tracks, to be dumfounded by fear

BEKTO fritillary (an herbal medicine)

BEKU pubis of a woman

BELCI madman, deranged

BELCIDEMBI to act like a madman

BELE hulled rice, an edible grain

  BELE BUDA cooked rice

  BELEI SIHABUKŪ a funnel for rice

BELEBUMBI caus./pass. of *belembi*

BELEMBI 1. to harm an innocent person through a false accusation 2. to murder treacherously--especially one's prince

BELEMIMBI to hull rice; cf. *niyelembi*

BELEN 1. false accusation 2. a treacherous murder

BELENDUMBI to accuse one another

BELENI ready-made, already prepared, finished

BELENINGGE something ready-made, that which is already prepared

BELGE a grain of rice, the core of fruit

BELGEMBI to tie things to the saddle

BELGENEMBI to form into grains
BELGERI ILHA the opium poppy
BELHEBUKU (祇候) an official in charge of the needs of foreign emissaries
BELHEBUMBI caus. of *belhembi*
BELHEMBI to prepare
    BELHERE COOHA reserves (troops)
    BELHERE HAFAN (恭奉官) the same as *belhebuku*
BELHEN preparation
BELHENDUMBI/BELHENUMBI to prepare together
BELHENEMBI to go to prepare
BELHENJIMBI to come to prepare
BELHESI (鋪排) preparer--one who prepares everything for a service in a temple
BELHETU (儲將) an official in charge of military supplies
BELI dolt, fool
BELIYEDEMBI to act foolishly, to do in a foolish way
BELIYEKEN somewhat foolish
BELIYEN foolish, doltish
BEMBEREMBI (-ke) to repeat oneself or talk foolishly because of senility
BEN 1. talent, capability 2. a pad or book of paper
BENCAN capital (money)
BENCIYAN the same as *bencan*
BENEBUMBI caus. of *benembi*
    BENEBUME SIMNEMBI to take a preliminary examination for the degree of Metropolitan Graduate
BENEMBI to send (away from the speaker), to deliver, to give as a gift
BENESI messenger; cf. *wesimbure bithei benesi*
BENGNELI suddenly, hastily
BENGNEMBI to be in haste
BENGSEN talent, capability
BENGSENGGE talented (person)
BENJIMBI (imperative: *benju*) to send (hither), to deliver (hither)
    BENJIHE BITHE BARGIYARA BOO (來文房) registry for incoming correspondence in the Workshop of the Imperial Household
BENJU imperative of *benjimbi*
BEO the accusative particle joined to the interrogative particle
BEREBUMBI caus. of *berembi*
BEREMBI (-ke) to be dumfounded by fright or anger, to be lame
BEREN a door or window frame
BERGE a latch or toggle, a small piece of wood or metal to which a rope is attached
BERGELEMBI to attach to a latch or toggle

BERGU see *berhu*
BERHE 1. the bridge of a stringed instrument 2. a small horizontal piece of wood attached to a tiger spear 3. eye discharge caused by the wind
BERHELEMBI 1. to attach a bridge to a stringed instrument 2. the same as *bergelembi*
BERHU term of address used by a wife to her husband's younger sister, or by an elder sister to her younger brother's wife
BERI a bow
    BERI ARAMBI to draw a bow full length (at mounted archery)
    BERI BELHERE BA (備弓處) the place where the emperor's bows were prepared and kept
    BERI CAMBI to draw a bow
    BERI CIRA the bow has a hard pull, the bow is taut
    BERI DOBTON a bow case
    BERI FAKSI 1. a bowmaker 2. a water strider (insect)
    BERI FITHEKU a crossbow
    BERI GIRU the shaft of a bow
    BERI JA the bow has a light pull
    BERI JAFAKŪ the grip of a bow
    BERI NU a crossbow
    BERI TABUMBI to draw a bow
    BERI TATAMBI to draw a bow
    BERI UHUKEN the bow has a weak pull
BERI BERI each one, severally
BERILEKU a drill
BERINGGA USIHA the constellation *hu* (張)
BERINGGE pertaining to archery
    BERINGGE COOHA archers
BERTEBUMBI caus./pass. of *bertembi*
BERTEMBI to dirty
BERTEN dirt, grime
BERTENEMBI to get dirty
BESEREI a mongrel mixture of a *taiha* hunting dog and the common house dog
BESERGEN bed
BESERHEN same as *besergen*
BESERI same as *beserei*
BEŠEHUN stupefied, dazzled, led astray
BEŠEMBI (-ke) to become saturated, to drink to excess
    BEŠEME AGAMBI to rain sufficiently to saturate the ground
BEŠEMBUMBI caus. of *bešembi*
BETE inadequate, useless, ineffective
BETEN earthworm, bait
BETHE foot, (lower) leg
    BETHE BUKDAMBI 1. to bend the knee, to kneel on one knee 2. to draw a tally stick
    BETHE DEMNIYEME CASHŪN FIYELEMBI to do trick riding with the legs

swinging backwards
BETHE GOCIME FIYELEMBI to do trick riding with the legs drawn in
BETHE I FATAN the sole of the foot
BETHE I FATAN I HERGEN plantar lines
BETHE TUKIYEHEI FIYELEMBI to do trick riding with the feet lifted in the air
BETHEI FILEKU a foot warmer
BETHELEKU a trap for entangling the feet of birds
BETHELEMBI 1. to sleep with the legs together 2. to pile grain in small piles to allow it to dry   3. to entangle a bird's feet in a snare
BETHENGGE having legs
BEYE 1. body, self 2. capital
  BEYE ACAMBI to have sexual intercourse
  BEYE BE ARAMBI to commit suicide
  BEYE BE DASAMBI 1. euphemism for to castrate 2. to cultivate oneself
  BEYE CIHAKŪ against one's will
  BEYE DE BIMBI to become pregnant
  BEYE DE GOCIMBI to place near oneself
  BEYE DE OMBI to become pregnant
  BEYE DEKDERELEME KURBUME FIYELEMBI to ride balancing oneself on the hands
  BEYE ILETULEMBI to become incarnate, to appear in bodily form
  BEYE ISIHIMBI to deliver (a baby)
  BEYE JURSU pregnant
  BEYE MEHUMBI to bow
  BEYE NIOHUŠUN naked
  BEYE OSOHON small in stature
  BEYE SISAMBI to exert oneself
  BEYE TEKSIN well built (figure)
  BEYE TOMSOMBI to control oneself
  BEYEBE TUWANCIHIYAMBI to cultivate oneself
BEYEBUMBI caus. of *beyembi*
PᴵYEI by oneself, independently
BEYEINGGE one's own
BEYEMBI to freeze, to be cold
BEYEN freezing, cold
BEYESE plural of *beye*
BI 1. I, me 2. there is, there are, has, have
  BI SINI MEIFEN BE 'I'm going to cut off your head!'--an oath
BIBUMBI 1. caus. of *bimbi* 2. to detain, to retain, to keep back, to leave behind
BIDARUM coral
BIDERE *bi+dere*
BIDURI lapis lazuli
BIGAN wilderness, an uncultivated area, wild
  BIGAN I CAI wild tea
  BIGAN I CIYANLIYANG tax on uncultivated land

BIGAN I COKO pheasant, ring-necked pheasant
BIGAN I GINTALA wild celery
BIGAN I HUKŠEN a hawk that has escaped from captivity
BIGAN I HUTU a ghost or spirit that dwells in the wilderness
BIGAN I IBAGAN a malevolent spirit dwelling in the wilderness
BIGAN I MUCU wild grape (*Vitis Thunbergii*)
BIGAN I NIONGNIYAHA the wild goose
BIGAN I SINGGERI field mouse, vole
BIGAN I ULGIYAN wild pig; cf. *aidagan*
BIGAN I WECEKU the shamanistic god of the wilderness
BIGAN TALA a steppe, the wilds, wilderness
BIGAN URANGGA MOO the wild tung tree (*Calophyllum inophyllum*)
BIGARAMBI to be in the wildernes
BIGARAME through the wilds, across the wilderness
BIGARARA MAHATUN a cap used for distant journeys
BIGATU wild
  BIGATU NIYEHE wild duck, mallard
  BIGATU UNIYEHE wild duck, mallard
BIHA crumb, small piece
BIHAN same as *bigan*
BIHE BIHEI for a long time
BIJABUMBI caus. of *bijambi*
BIJAMBI to break, to snap (v.i.)
BIKCU Buddhist monk
BIKCUNI Buddhist nun
BIKITA (璧) the name of a constellation
  BIKITA TOKDONGGO KIRU a banner with the constellation *bikita* depicted on it
BILA ILHA an exotic white flower that blooms in the autumn
BILABUMBI caus./pass. of *bilambi*
BILAGᴬN period, term, deadline
  BILAGAN I TEMGETU a paper on which a term or deadline is recorded
BILAMBI 1. to break 2. to dull 3. to set a date, to fix a term, to limit
  BILAME GAIMBI to subtract, to take away
BILAN see *bilagan*
BILASI singer
BILCA cake made from bean and millet flour
BILCAMBI to smear, spread a sticky substance on something
BILCI see *bulji*
BILEMBI to lay eggs, to give birth to pigs and dogs
BILERHEN lark
BILERI a wind instrument with eight holes and a metal mouthpiece--a *sona*

B

BILESI a *sona* player, a trumpeter
BILGA same as *bilha*
BILGACUNGGA same as *bilhacungga*
BILGEŠEMBI to brim, to be too full of
    a liquid
BILHA 1. throat 2. a very narrow
    passage 3. a smoke hole
    BILHA BE DASAMBI to clear the throat
    BILHA ILENGGU I GESE AMBAN (元老
    大臣   ) respectful title
    for members of the State Council
BILHACUNGGA a glutton
BILJAMBI (-ka) to soak, to ooze, to
    leak through
BILTEMBI (-ke) to overflow
BILTEN tidal flats, a shallow lake,
    a marsh
BILUBUMBI caus. of *bilumbi*
BILUKAN on the sly, secretly
BILUKŪ one who deceives by using sweet
    talk, a confidence man
BILUMBI 1. to stroke, to rub, to
    nourish, to caress, to fondle 2. to
    cut meat into small pieces
BILUN pacification
BILUNGGA pacified
BILURJAMBI to swindle by pretending to
    be honest
BILUŠAMBI to be affectionate toward,
    to act affectionately
BIMBI (imperfect participle *bisire*,
    imperative *bisu*) 1. to exist, to be
    2. to stay, to remain
BIMSU 1. paralysis 2. quail
BIN DZ betel nut; cf. *merseri*
BING BIYAN camphor
BING BIYANG sound made by the *sona* or
    flute
BINGGIYA water chestnut
BINGHA (畢) the name of a constel-
    lation
    BINGHA TOKTONGGO KIRU a banner
    depicting the constellation *bingha*
BINGSE steelyard
BINGSELEMBI to weigh on a steelyard
BINGSIKU autumn cicada
BINSE see *bin dz*
BIR BIYAR SEME hanging to the floor
    (of clothing)
BIR SEME hanging loose
BIRA river
    BIRA BE KADALARA TINGGIN (河 廳)
    office of river management
    BIRAI CARGI the other side of the
    river
    BIRAI DALIN I FALGANGGA unloading
    area on a riverbank
    BIRAI DENGJAN a paper lantern in
    the form of a lotus used to light
    the way on a river excursion
    BIRAI EBERGI the close bank of the
    river
    BIRAI HŪYA an edible river snail

BIRAI JUGŪN BE UHERI KADALARA AMBAN
(河 道 總 督) Director-
    General of River Conservation, BH
    820D
    BIRAI SEREMŠEN I KUNGGERI (河防
    科) section for river control in
    the Board of Works
    BIRAI WEILEN I FALGA (河 工 甲)
    bureau of river works in the Board
    of Civil Appointments
BIRANGGA having or pertaining to a
    river
    BIRANGGA KIRU (河 旛) a banner
    decorated with the design of a
    flowing river
BIRCA HIYAN MOO the name of an exotic
    tree whose wood is used for making
    scroll rods
BIREBUMBI caus./pass. of *birembi*
BIREGEN a willow palisade built along
    a frontier
BIREKU roller, rolling pin
    BIREKU MOO a wooden roller for
    rolling seed
BIREMBI 1. to rush (into), to attack,
    to breach 2. to roll (dough, seed,
    etc.)
BIREME completely, thoroughly, univer-
    sally
    BIREME HEREME totally and com-
    pletely
    BIREME YABUBURE BITHE IǄIHIYARA BA
    (通 行 書 籍 處) an
    office of the Printing Office and
    Bookbindery charged with the dis-
    tribution of books
BIREN tigress, female leopard
    BIREN I HŪYA an edible river snail
    BIREN TASHA tigress
    BIREN YARHA female leopard
BIRENDUMBI to collide, to run into one
    another
BIRENEMBI to go to run into
BIRETEI totally, universally, com-
    pletely
BIRGA see *birgan*
BIRGAN creek, brook
BIRGEŠEMBI 1. to overeat 2. to hang
    loosely, to dangle
BIRHEŠEMBI the same as *birgešembi*
BIRKU same as *bireku*
BISAMBI (-ka, -ra/ndara) to overflow,
    to flood
BISAN flood
BISANDARA long form of the imperfect
    participle of *bisambi*
BISARAMBI (-pi) to overflow, to pour
    out everywhere
BISARI ILHA an exotic white flower
    that grows along rivers
BISI crab louse, tick
BISIMBI same as *bišumbi*
BISIN a flat iron clasp, a decorative

rivet or tack found on knives, cruppers, bridles, etc.

BISIN DURDUN smooth crepe

BISIN ELDENGGE LOHO a sword with a smooth pommel

BISIN ILHANGGE KOFON SUJE a smooth patterned Soochow silk

BISIRE imperfect participle of *bimbi*

BISIRE EBSIHE one's whole life

BISIRELENGGE all that exists

BISIRENGGE having, existing

BISU imperative of *bimbi*

BISUREMBI to crawl, to creep

BIŠUBUMBI caus. of *bišumbi*

BIŠUKAN 1. somewhat smooth 2. temperate in eating

BIŠUMBI to smooth, to rub, to stroke, to pet, to grope, to feel

BIŠUN 1. smooth, slick, level 2. temperate in eating

BIŠURI MOO coconut palm

BIŠUŠAMBI to keep rubbing, to caress repeatedly

BITA river island, sand bar, eyot

BITHE 1. book 2. letter

BITHE BOO a study

BITHE FUCIHI DOOSE Confucianism, Buddhism, and Taoism

BITHE HŪLAMBI to study

BITHE HŪLARA HAFAN (讀祝官) Reciter of Prayers, BH 79, 382B

BITHE NOHO SUJE silk with writing woven into the pattern

BITHE ŠUWASELARA FALGA (別書作) the court printing office

BITHE YABUBURE BOO (咨文房) office of the palace apothecary

BITHEI AMBAN (文大臣) a high civil dignitary

BITHEI BOO study, studio

BITHEI HAFAN (文官) a civil official

BITHEI HAFAN I FUNGNEHEN I KUNGGERI (文誥科) office in charge of posthumous honors

BITHEI HAFAN I TEMGETU a document sent to a *bithei hafan*

BITHEI HAFAN SINDARA BOLGOBURE FIYENTEN (文選清吏司) department for the selection of civil officials; cf. BH 335

BITHEI JAFAŠAKŪ (掌書) Librarian, BH 639

BITHEI JORINGGA table of contents

BITHEI KUREN library

BITHEI NIYALMA scholar, civil official

BITHEI ŠUNGSI (翰林) Member of the National Academy, BH 191

BITHEI ŠUSAI (文秀才) a baccalaureate of the civil examinations

BITHEI TACIKŪ (儒學) a provincial school for preparing civil and military candidates for the examinations

BITHEI TACIN COOHAI ERDEMU scholarship and military strategy

BITHEI YAMUN (翰林院) the National Academy, BH 191 ff.

BITHELEMBI to notify in writing, to send a letter to

BITHESI scribe, secretary, clerk, BH 293

BITHESI I KUNGGERI (筆貼式科) section of clerks in the Board of Civil Appointments; cf. BH 293

BITUBUMBI 1. caus. of *bitumbi* 2. to see in a dream

BITUHAN border, edging

BITUMBI to edge, to border, to go along the border, to adorn, to decorate

BITUME GAMARA ambiguous, vague

BITURAME along a mountain, via a mountain

BIWANGGIRIT (Sanskrit *vyākaraṇa*) exposition, explanation, grammar

BIYA moon, month

BIYA ALIHA BA (當月處) Record Office, BH 497

BIYA ALIHA FIYENTEN (當月司) Record and Registry Office, BH 455

BIYA AMBA the month has thirty days

BIYA FEKUHE overdue (of a pregnant woman)

BIYA I KIRU moon banner

BIYA I MANASHŪN the end of the month, after the 20th of the month

BIYA JEMBI there is an eclipse of the moon

BIYA KŪWARAHA the moon has a halo

BIYA MANARA ISIKA the moon has almost disappeared

BIYA OSOHON the month has twenty-nine days

BIYAI DAŠURAN USIHA comet

BIYAI HAFAN ILGARA BOO (月官房) a department of the imperial household charged with the monthly rotation of officials

BIYAI HALAN menstruation

BIYAI ICEREME at the beginning of the month

BIYAI MANASHŪN after the 20th of the month

BIYABIYAHŪN pale, wan

BIYABIYASHŪN same as *biyabiyahūn*

BIYADAR SEME speaking recklessly

BIYADARI every month

BIYAHŪN pale, wan

BIYAINGGE of a certain month

BIYALAME months long, lasting for months

B

B

BIYALANGGI blabbermouth, gossiper
BIYALARI ILHA *Rosa indica*--the monthly
  blooming rose
BIYALDASITAMBI to fluctuate greatly
BIYALUMBI to slip away, to flee
    BIYALUME YABUMBI to flee, to escape
BIYAN inscribed tablet above a door
BIYAN SIO (編修) Compiler of the
  Second Class, BH 200B; cf. *acabume
  banjibukū*
BIYANDU lima bean
BIYANGGA moonlike, lunar, round
    BIYANGGA EFEN small round cakes
      filled with sweetened bean paste
      eaten at the moon festival, moon
      cakes
    BIYANGGA FA a window in the shape
      of a full moon
    BIYANGGA INENGGI the 15th of the
      eighth month--the moon festival
    BIYANGGA LONGKON a round gong
    BIYANGGA TUNGKEN a hand drum in the
      form of a moon
BIYANGGIDEI a name for the golden
  pheasant; cf. *junggiri coko*
BIYANGSIKŪ cicada
BIYANGSIRI ILHA an exotic flower--
  'cicada's blossom'
BIYANTAHA a scar on the head, a spot
  on the head where the hair is
  sparse
BIYANTU cudgel
BIYAR SEME brimming (full of water)
BIYARA a type of swallow found in
  Manchuria and Mongolia
BIYARGIYAN faint, pale
BIYARGIYAŠAMBI to be gray, colorless
  (of the weather)
BIYARIŠAMBI to blind (of a strong
  light in the eye)
BIYASHŪMBI the same as *biyalumbi*
BIYATAR SEME the same as *biyadar seme*
BIYOHALAMBI to get away, to escape
BIYOLOKOŠOMBI to tell yarns, to talk
  idly
BIYOLUMBI to shave smooth, to level
  off
BIYOMBI to smooth off a surface
BIYOO a memorial to the throne,
  manifesto
    BIYOO BITHE a memorial to the
      throne
    BIYOO BITHE WESIMBUMBI to present
      a memorial
BIYOO UMIYAHA silkworm
BIYOOHA 1. a horse with a white spot
  on the end of its nose 2. cocoon
    BIYOOHA SUJE satin made from wild
      cocoons
    BIYOOHA SURI silk made from wild
      cocoons
BIYOOHARI ILHA an exotic white flower
  that grows in mountain areas--its

bloom resembles a cocoon
BIYOOLAMBI see *biyolumbi*
BIYOR SEME trickling, slowly, lazily,
  dragging (clothes), slack, limp
    BIYOR SEME ETUMBI to wear clothes
      that are too long or too large
    BIYOR SEME EYEMBI to flow in a
      trickle
    BIYOR SEME UYAN dangling and soft
BIYORAN a cliff of red earth
BIYORONG SEME slowly, languidly
BO HO mint
BO IOI a monk's eating bowl
BOBORŠOMBI to cherish, to dote on
BOCEHE see *bocihe*
BOCERI ILHA *Lychnis senno*
BOCIHE ugly
BOCO 1. color, complexion 2. sex,
  lust
    BOCO DE DOSIMBI to be lustful, to
      be lecherous
    BOCO HACIN I NAMUN (顏料庫)
      a storehouse belonging to the
      Board of Revenue for iron, bronze,
      incense, wax, paper, etc.
BOCONGGO colored, brightly colored,
  colorful
    BOCONGGO ARSALANGGA KIRU (彩獅
      旗) a banner bearing the like-
      ness of a lion
    BOCONGGO NISIHA goldfish
    BOCONGGO ŠUGIN I ILETU KIYOO (彩
      漆亮轎) a ceremonial sedan
      chair painted in many colors
    BOCONGGO ULHŪMANGGA KIRU (華蟲
      旗) a banner bearing the like-
      ness of a pheasant
BODI bodhi--enlightenment
BODISATU bodhisattva
BODISE the hard red fruit of the
  Indian Bodhidharma tree out of which
  rosaries are made
BODISU the same as *bodise*
BODOBUMBI caus./pass. of *bodombi*
BODOGON plan, plot, scheme, strategy
    BODOGON I BITHEI KUREN (方略
      館) Military Archives Office,
      BH 139
BODOHON 1. a small pendant of precious
  stones worn by officials at court
  2. same as *bodogon*
BODOHONGGO good at strategy, full of
  plans and ideas
BODOKŪ abacus
BODOMBI 1. to calculate, to figure
  2. to plan 3. to drive animals to
  a predetermined place
    BODOFI BURE KUNGGERI (支科)
      the name of a section in the Board
      of Revenue
    BODORO BOO (算科) office of
      calculations in the Board of Works
    BODORO TACIKŪ (算學) school

of mathematics
BODOMIMBI to talk to oneself
BODON calculation, plan, policy,
   strategy
BODONGGIYAMBI the same as *bodomimbi*
BODONGGO concerning planning, contain-
   ing plans
BODONOMBI to go to reckon or plan
BODONUMBI to plan or scheme together
BODOR SEME to mumble (through the
   teeth)
BODORI the handle of a plow
BOFULABUMBI caus. of *bofulambi*
BOFULAMBI to wrap
BOFUN a wrapper, a wrapping cloth,
   a bundle
BOHIBUMBI caus. of *bohimbi*
BOHIKŪ wrapping for women's feet
BOHIMBI to bind the feet
BOHOKON somewhat muddy, opaque
BOHOMI 1. a winnowing fan for kaoliang
   and sesame 2. hulls of kaoliang
   and sesame seed
BOHON muddy, opaque, dull, clouded
   over (the pupil)
BOHORI 1. pea 2. a covering for
   lanterns
   BOHORI DEBSE deep-fried pea cakes
BOHOTO a camel's hump
BOIFUKA a clay flute with six holes
BOIGOCILAMBI to come from the earth,
   to glean from the earth
BOIGOJI host, master
BOIGOJILAMBI to act as host or master
BOIGON 1. family, household 2. prop-
   erty
   BOIGON ANGGALA members of a house-
      hold, family
   BOIGON I BOO (戶 房) an office
      in the Court of Colonial Affairs
   BOIGON I JURGAN (戶 部)
      Board of Revenue, BH 349
   BOIGON I JURGAN I TOKTOHO GISUN
      phrases used by the Board of
      Revenue
   BOIGON NAHAN household
   BOIGON NAHAN JAFAMBI to take care
      of the household
   BOIGON SALIMBI to inherit property
BOJHOCILAMBI see *boigocilambi*
BOIHOJI same as *boigoji*
BOIHOJU the god of the earth, the
   shrine of the earth god
BOIHOLOMBI to get free, to get loose
   (from a trap)
BOIHON earth, ground, soil
   BOIHON DALAN an earthen dam
   BOIHON I BUKTAN an earthen mound
      used as a landmark
   BOIHON I HOTON an earthen wall
   BOIHON I KARMAN an earthen fortress
   BOIHON I KEMNEKU an earthen mound
      used like a sundial

BOIHON I MUTUN an earthen mound
   one foot high and ten feet square
   at the base
BOIHON USIHA Saturn
BOIHON USIHANGGA KIRU a yellow
   banner embroidered with a picture
   of Saturn
BOINGGE see *booingge*
BOISILE amber
BOISIRI ILHA 'amber flower'--the name
   of an exotic flower
BOJE an accounting book
BOJI 1. go-between in a business deal,
   witness to a contract 2. contract,
   deed
   BOJI BITHE written contract
   BOJI ILIMBI to make up an agreement
      or contract
   BOJI SEKIYEN a preliminary contract
      or deed
   BOJI UNCEHEN a final contract or
      deed
BOJILAMBI to pawn, to mortgage
BOJINA KEIRE a splendid brown horse
BOJIRI ILHA chrysanthemum
BOKIDA fringe, tassel (often made of
   precious stones)
   BOKIDA ILHA an exotic, pale yellow
      flower that hangs down like the
      weeping willow
BOKIDANGGA having a tassel or fringe
BOKIRSHŪN stiff, unable to move the
   limbs normally
BOKITA an unperforated blunt arrow
BOKORI GAIMBI to kick playfully in
   the rear
BOKSON 1. threshold 2. the curved
   part of the ends of a bow
BOKŠOKON graceful, elegant
BOKŠOLOMBI to be graceful, elegant
BOKŠON the breastbone
BOKTO hunchback
BOLABUMBI caus. of *bolambi*
BOLAMBI to roast, to broil
BOLGO 1. clean, clear 2. honest,
   sincere
   BOLGO DUINGGE HOOŠAN a type of
      paper made from the bark of a tree
   BOLGO HICAN a person who eats
      little
BOLGOBUMBI caus. of *bolgombi*
   BOLGOBURE OBOHON (姑 洗) the
      name of a classical musical note
      corresponding in function to E
BOLGOKON somewhat clean, somewhat
   clear
BOLGOMBI (-ho/ko) 1. to clean 2. to
   make clear, to clarify, to explain
BOLGOMIMBI to abstain, to fast
   BOLGOMI TARGA 'fast and abstain'--
      inscription on a tablet posted on
      fast days
BOLGON clean, cleanliness

B

BOLGOSU see *bolhosu*
BOLHO see *bolgo*
BOLHOMBI the same as *bolgombi*
BOLHOSU a slave of the third generation
BOLI glass
BOLIBUMBI caus. of *bolimbi*
BOLIKŪ 1. bait 2. flag-sign on a shop
BOLIMBI to lure with bait, to entice
BOLIN 1. lure, enticement 2. a dragon
    embroidered on satin
    BOLIN GECUHERI brocade with writhing
       dragons depicted upon it
BOLJOBUMBI caus. of *boljombi*
BOLJOHON agreement, covenant
BOLJOMBI to agree on, to promise, to
    fix (a date), to decide to
    BOLJOCI OJORAKŪ cannot be determined,
       unpredictable, cannot be foreseen
BOLJON wave
    BOLJON COLKON waves
    BOLJON GIDAKŪ bow of a wooden canoe
    BOLJON WEREN waves and ripples
BOLJONGGO conventional, determined by
    custom, customary
BOLMIN incorrupt, sincere
BOLOKON somewhat clean
BOLOMBI (-ko) to be exhausted, used up
BOLORI autumn, fall
    BOLORI BE BODORO HAFAN (秋官正)
       an official of the observatory
    BOLORI BEIDERE BAITA BE UHERI
    ICIHIYARA BA (總辦秋審處)
       central office for the autumn
       assizes
    BOLORI DULIN the autumnal equinox
    BOLORI FORGON I MUKE autumn floods
    BOLORI FULANA ILHA begonia
    BOLORI MUDAN ILHA Japanese anemone
BOLORIKTEN autumn sacrifice to the
    ancestors
BOLOSU glass
    BOLOSU DEIJIRE KŪWARAN imperial
       glass factory
BOMBI (-ngko, -re) to pierce, to bore,
    to make a hole with an awl or pick
BOMBOKON out of humor, annoyed, bored
BOMBON a pile, a wad, a cluster, a
    bunch
BOMBONOMBI to pile up (of clouds), to
    form into layers
BOMBORNOMBI to dodder
BON pick, awl, tool for making holes
    in ice
    BON I BOMBI to break up with a pick
BONCIHIYAN shrill (like the sound of
    a broken cymbal)
BONGCILIHI a fish from the Eastern Sea
    whose flesh and bones resemble those
    of the roe deer
BONGGIBUMBI caus. of *bonggimbi*
BONGGIMBI to send (away from the
    speaker)
BONGGO 1. point, apex 2. first

BONGGO DE GENEMBI to go first, to go
    at the head
BONGGO DOSIKASI (會元) number
    one in the examination for Metro-
    politan Graduate
BONGGO MORIN outrider, lead horse
BONGGO SONJOSI (狀元) number
    one in the palace examination
BONGGO ŠUSAI (案首) number
    one in the baccalaureate examina-
    tion
BONGGO TUKIYESI (解元) number
    one in the provincial examination
BONGJONGGI a coarse, vulgar person, a
    lout
BONGKO 1. bud of a flower 2. a wooden
    cap placed over the point of an arrow
    BONGKO DALANGGA a weir built at a
       fork in a river
    BONGKO SUKIYARA DUKA an ornamental
       gate in which sections of deco-
       rated wood are suspended
BONGKON yellow side ornaments that
    hang down on both sides of an
    official's hat
BONGKONOMBI to form a bud
BONGSIMU NIYEHE one of the names of the
    wild duck
BONIO 1. monkey 2. the ninth earth's
    branch (申)
    BONIO BIYA the seventh month
    BONIO ERIN the double hour from
       four until six in the afternoon
BONME (imperfect converb of *bombi*)
    downward
    BONME GABTAMBI to shoot an arrow
       downward
    BONME WASIMBI to descend from a
       high place
BONO hail
    BONO TORIBUMBI to be hailed upon
BONOMBI to hail
BONTOHO bareback
BONTOHOLOBUMBI caus. of *bontoholombi*
BONTOHOLOMBI to be empty, to be bare,
    to be deprived
BONTU an adze
BOO 1. house, room 2. family
    BOO CIOWAN JIHAI KŪWARAN (寶泉局)
       Coinage Office, BH 366
    BOO GIYA (保甲) constable
    BOO GIYALAN room
    BOO GUWAN (保官) guarantor
    BOO I HOŠO the northwest corner of
       a house
    BOO NAHAN ILIBUMBI to establish a
       family
    BOO NIMAHA whale
    BOO YUWAN JIHAI KŪWARAN (寶源
       局) Coinage Office, BH 460A
BOOCI TUCIKE TEMGETU an official
    certificate allowing a person to
    become a Buddhist monk

BOOCI TUCIMBI to leave one's household, to become a Buddhist monk

BOOI AMBAN (内務府總管) Department Director of the Imperial Household

BOOI DA (管領) officials of the fifth and sixth rank in the Imperial Household

BOOI DURUGAN a family genealogy

BOOI HAFAN the person in charge of the family affairs of a high official

BOOI HEHE housemaid

BOOI ILAN GŪSA (内府三旗) the three banners of the Imperial Household, BH 97

BOOI ILAN GŪSAI ALIHA COOHAI KŪWARAN (内府三旗驍騎營) office in charge of the affairs of the three banners of the Imperial Household; cf. BH 97

BOOI ILAN GŪSAI BAYARA KŪWARAN (内府三旗護軍營) Imperial Guards, BH 97A

BOOI NIRU head of a banner in the household of a prince or in the Imperial Household

BOOI NIRUI BAYARA (包衣擺牙剌) bond-servant guard in the household of a Prince or in the Imperial Household

BOOI NIYALMA member of a household

BOOBAI 1. treasure 2. the state seal

BOOBAI SOORIN throne of the emperor

BOOBAI SUBURGAN pagoda

BOOBAI WEHE precious stone, gem

BOODZ 1. mistress of a brothel 2. see boose

BOOFUN see bofun

BOOHA side dish, a dish served with liquor

BOOHA BELHERE FALGARI (珍饈署) department charged with the preparation of side dishes in the Court of Banqueting

BOOHALABUMBI caus. of boohalambi

BOOHALAMBI 1. to eat side dishes 2. to offer such dishes to the dead on the eighth day after burial

BOOINGE member of the family, belonging or pertaining to a household or family

BOOLABUMBI caus. of boolambi

BOOLAMBI to report

BOOLAN report

BOOLAN HOOŠAN newspaper

BOOLANABUMBI caus. of boolanambi

BOOLANAMBI to go to report

BOONGGA JAHŪDAI houseboat

BOOSE package, bundle

BOOSELAMBI to wrap, to make a package

BOOŠI see boobai wehe

BOR SEME gushing forth

BORBO Achilles tendon

BORBOKI NIYEHE the common teal (Nettion crecca)

BORCILAHA dried beef and mutton cut into squares and used to make soup

BORCILAMBI to hang up to dry

BORCILAHA YALI see borcilaha

BORDOBUMBI caus. of bordombi

BORDOKŪ food used for fattening stock

BORDOMBI to fatten (stock)

BORHOMBI 1. to amass, to heap up 2. to form a circle

BORHOHO NIMAHA fish that come together in a great mass

BORHOME TECEMBI to sit in a circle

BORHON conglomeration, heap, swarm

BORHON BORHON in piles, in heaps

BORHONOMBI to form a heap or swarm

BORHOTO shrub with hard leaves that grows in clumps in damp places

BORIMBI to lull a baby to sleep

BORINAMBI to get stopped up, to stick

BORJIN NIYEHE mallard (Anas platyrhynchos)

BORO 1. gray 2. summer hat

BORO FULAN gray horse

BORO SEBERI black horse with white left hooves

BOROMBI (-ko) to turn (dark) gray

BOROKO MUCU ripe grapes

BORTON dirty (especially the face)

BORTONOMBI to have a dirty face

BOS GURUN Persia

BOSHO kidney, waist

BOSHOLOBUMBI caus. of bosholombi

BOSHOLOMBI to be narrow at the middle

BOSHONGGO having a waist, narrow at the middle, kidney-shaped

BOSO 1. the north side of a mountain 2. cloth

BOSO AIGAN an archery target made of cloth

BOSONGGE made of cloth

BOSORO dates

BOŠI (博士) see taciha hafan

BOŠOBUMBI caus./pass. of bošombi

BOŠOHON a bright yellow dye

BOŠOKŪ 1. a driver, a pusher 2. (領催) corporal, BH 746

BOŠOMBI 1. to urge, to press, to drive, to exhort 2. to expel, to put out

BOŠONDUMBI/BOŠONUMBI to urge or expel together

BOŠONJIMBI to come to urge or expel

BOŠONOMBI to go to urge or expel

BUBU BABA mumbling

BUBUMBI caus. of bumbi

BUBURŠEMBI to delay, to tarry

BUBUYEN 1. grown stiff from the cold 2. unable to get one's words out

BUCA ewe

B

B

BUCEBUMBI caus. of *bucembi*
BUCEHENGGE dead person or thing--an
  oath
BUCELI the spirit of a dead person, a
  ghost
  BUCELI BENEMBI to exorcise a ghost
    that is causing an illness
  BUCELI DOSIKA the spirit of a dead
    person has entered another person
    (and speaks through him)
BUCEMBI to die
  BUCEHE AHA dead slave--an oath
  BUCEME SUSAME dying and perishing--
    used to describe an enemy in dis-
    array
  BUCERE WEILE a capital crime
BUCESHŪN deathly pale
BUCETEI until death, scorning death,
  to the last, desperately
  BUCETEI AFAMBI to fight to the last
BUCETEN despair, desperation
BUCILEBUMBI caus. of *bucilembi*
BUCILEKU a sort of crownless hat with
  earlaps worn by women
BUCILEMBI to put down the earlaps on
  a hat
BUCULIMBI see *bucilembi*
BUDA cooked cereal, cooked rice, food
  BUDA ARAMBI to cook
  BUDA BELHERE BA (飯 局) the
    palace kitchen
  BUDA JEMBI to eat (in general)
  BUDA MUKE WALIYAMBI to pour off
    excess water after boiling rice or
    other cereal
  BUDA NIMEKU jaundice
  BUDAI BOO kitchen
  BUDAI FAKSI cook
  BUDAI MUKE rice broth
BUDALAMBI to eat cooked cereal or
  cooked rice
BUDEMBI to die
BUDUHU loach (*Saurogobio dabryi*)
BUDUHU MOO wild tea--the leaves and
  stems of which are used to make dye
BUDUKAN somewhat useless or inadequate
BUDULIMBI see *buldurimbi*
BUDUN useless, inadequate, incompetent
BUDURHŪNA a type of grass that grows
  on alkaline soil and is eaten by
  camels
BUFALIYAMBI to deny (what has been
  said)
BUFUYEN unclear (of speech)
BUGE 1. gristle 2. same as *buhe*
  BUGE MONGGON windpipe
  BUGE MUKE a solution used for dying
    grass linen, indigo dye
  BUGE YASA an eye disease of cattle
    and horses
BUHA wild buffalo
  BUHA GURGU wild buffalo
  BUHA SINGGERI mole

BUHA UIHE BERI a bow made of wild
  buffalo horn
BUHE indigo
  BUHE MUKE same as *buge muke*
BUHELIYEBUMBI caus. of *buheliyembi*
BUHELIYEMBI to cover
BUHELIYEN a sort of hemp
BUHERE little kingfisher (*Alcedo
  atthis*)
BUHI 1. thigh, lap 2. buckskin, deer-
  skin
  BUHI ADAME knee to knee
  BUHI ARAMBI to sit with one leg
    toward the rear
  BUHI GŪLHA boots made of buckskin
BUHIYEBUMBI caus. of *buhiyembi*
BUHIYECUKE suspicious, suspect
BUHIYECUN suspicion, distrust
BUHIYEMBI to suspect, to surmise, to
  guess
BUHIYEMBUMBI caus. of *buhiyembi*
BUHIYEN a guess, a surmise
  BUHIYEN I EFIN a game of chance
    played with red and black pieces
BUHIYENDUMBI/BUHIYENUMBI to suspect
  one another
BUHŪ deer
BUHŪNGGE deerlike, pertaining to deer
BUJAMBI (-ka) to awake from apparent
  death, to come back to life
BUJAN forest, woods
BUJANTU ULHŪMA one name for a pheasant
BUJENGSY (布 政 司) see *dasan
  be hafumbure yamun*
BUJIHILAMBI to be annoyed, to get mad
BUJU BAJA innumerable, uncountable
BUJUBUMBI caus. of *bujumbi*
BUJUMBI to boil, to cook
BUJUN 100,000
BUKA a ram
BUKDABUMBI 1. caus./pass. of *bukdambi*
  2. to be set back (of the enemy),
  to be routed
BUKDALAMBI to bend, to crease
BUKDAMBI 1. to fold, to bend, to curve
  2. to string a bow by using the
  knees 3. to lose (money)
BUKDAMBUMBI caus./pass. of *bukdambi*
BUKDAN a bend, a fold
BUKDANGGA folded, bent
  BUKDANGGA DENGJAN lantern made of
    folded paper or cloth
BUKDARI a memorial or other paper
  folded accordion fashion
  BUKDARI ACABURE FALGA (摺 配 作)
    a section of the Printing Office
    concerned with memorials
  BUKDARI ARARA KUNGGERI (本 科)
    a section of the Court of Colonial
    Affairs concerned with memorials
  BUKDARI ICIHIYAKŪ (待 詔)
    Compiler, BH 203
  BUKDARI ICIHIYAKŪ I TINGGIN (侍

詔 廳) Office for Compilation of Edicts, BH 203

BUKDARI ICIHIYASI (書 寫) clerk of the Court Chancery

BUKDARUN a folded examination paper

   BUKDARUN BARGIYARA HAFAN (收 卷 官) officer in charge of collecting examination papers

   BUKDARUN DE DORON GIDARA HAFAN (印 卷 官) officer who stamped examination papers

   BUKDARUN I JUMANGGI a bag in which examinations were kept

   BUKDARUN I TALGARI the outside of a folded examination paper

BUKDASHŪN bent, crumpled

BUKDAŠAMBI to press down, to hold down, to force a horse to obey by using the reins

BUKDU BAKDA dragging the foot, stiff-legged

BUKDUHUN elevation, rise

BUKDUN see bekdun

BUKSA an area of ponds and dry land interspersed, a partially cleared field, a field in which some spots have been burned off

   BUKSA BUKSA see buksa

BUKSIBUMBI caus. of buksimbi

BUKSIMBI to ambush, to lie in wait for

   BUKSIHA COOHA troops lying in ambush

BUKSIN ambush

BUKSINAMBI to go to ambush

BUKSINDUMBI/BUKSINUMBI to ambush at several places simultaneously

BUKSU the lumbar region, the loins

BUKSURI unclear, muddled

BUKSURILAMBI to act or do in an unclear or muddled way

BUKTALIMBI to pile up (grain)

   BUKTALIME WAMBI to kill in piles

BUKTAMBI (-ka) to get a stiff neck, to get a crick in the neck

BUKTAN mound, pile

   BUKTAN BUKTAN in piles, in mounds

BUKTU a hunchback, deformed

BUKTULIN sack made of cloth or leather for carrying clothes or bedding

BUKU wrestler

BUKULEMBI to put down the earlaps on a cap

BUKŪN (spelled with a front k) goral (Naemorhedus goral)

BULA thorn, burr

   BULA HAILAN a type of zelkova tree

   BULA ILHA thistle (a kind of flower)

   BULA SOGI spinach

   BULA U HEDEREBUHE was stuck by prickles and thorns

   BULA URANGGA MOO Erythrina indica

BULANGGA having thorns, thorny

   BULANGGA SOGI a type of wild vegetable with prickled leaves

BULARI MOO a type of thorny bush that grows in Szechuan

BULCA YALI the flesh on the arms and legs

BULCAKŪ a person who dislikes and avoids work

BULCAKŪSAMBI to shun work habitually

BULCAMBI to shun work

BULCANDUMBI to shun work together

BULCATAMBI to shun work continually

BULCIN see bulji

BULDU small male pig

BULDURI a type of roe deer that wanders in an area along the coast of North Asia--said to arrive in great herds at certain times and can be killed with clubs

BULDURIMBI to stumble, to trip (of horses and cows)

BULEHEN crane (Grus japonensis)

BULEHENGGE cranelike, pertaining to the crane

   BULEHENGGE KIRU (仙 鶴 纛) a banner bearing an embroidered crane's image

BULEKU 1. mirror 2. a round piece of metal used to protect the heart in combat

   BULEKU BITHE dictionary

   BULEKU DOBTON case for a mirror

BULEKUŠEBUMBI caus. of bulekušembi

BULEKUŠEMBI to look in a mirror, to reflect, to mirror, to perceive clearly

BULEN see bulun

BULERI horn, trumpet

BULGA see bulha

BULGIYAMBI to gild, to plate with gold

BULHA many-colored, polychrome

   BULHA ORHO Spiranthes australis

BULHACAN NIYEHE falcated teal; cf. alhacan niyehe

BULHACAN ULHŪMA one name for a pheasant

BULHŪMBI to bubble up, to swell up

BULI BUTU unclear, muddled

BULIMBI to catch food or bait on the surface of the water (of fish)

BULING SEME startled, dumb-struck

BULINJAMBI 1. to be startled, to be dumb-struck 2. to be lazy

BULIYAMBI to swallow

BULJAN growth on the skin

BULJANAMBI to form a growth on the skin, to scar over, to heal

BULJI of one color, monochrome

BULJIN same as bulji

   BULJIN YACIN completely black

BULTAHŪN prominent, obvious, bulging

   BULTAHŪN TUCINJIMBI to come to the surface, to become prominent

BULTAHŪRI bulging out (especially the eyes)

B

B

BULTARI sticking out, swollen
BULTURIMBI see *buldurimbi*
BULUKAN warm
  BULUKAN ŠERI a warm spring
BULUMBI to stack hay in piles
BULUN 1. a cock (of hay) 2. hub of a
  wheel
  BULUN JAFAMBI to stack in piles
BULUNTUMBI to copulate (of snakes and
  like creatures)
BUMBI (-he) to give
BUMBUKU a leaf bud
BUMBULCAMBI to swell, to distend
BUMBULI a cake made with oil and wheat
  flour
BUNAI 100,000
BUNCUHŪN warm, neither too hot nor too
  cold
BUNG BUNG the sound of a horn, the
  sound made by blowing into a conch
  shell
BUNGGIMBI to give as a present
BUNGJAN a hunchback
BUNGJANAMBI to hump the shoulders,
  to have a hump
BUNGNAMBI to oppress unjustly
BUNJIHA a type of sparrow with large
  head and eyes
BUR BAR SEME in profusion, in great
  quantity
BUR BUR SEME gurgling forth, swelling
  up (of a water spring)
BUR SEME pouring forth, gushing out
BURABUMBI caus. of *burambi*
BURAKI dust
  BURAKI TORON dust
BURAKIŠAMBI to throw up dust (of the
  wind)
BURAMBI 1. to splash with water, to
  pour over 2. to distill
BURAN TARAN in disarray
BURANGGIYAMBI to cook meat quickly in
  boiling water, to parboil
BURAŠAMBI to blow up snow
BURDEBUMBI caus. of *burdembi*
BURDEMBI to blow on a conch, to sound
  advance or retreat on a conch
BURDENUMBI to blow the conch together
BUREN conch horn, brass horn, trumpet
  BUREN UMIYAHA a snail
BURENEMBI to peel off (v.i.), to peel
  and crack (e.g., the surface of a
  dry lake bed)
BURGA willow branch
BURGAMBUMBI to billow up (of incense)
BURGASU NOTHO willow bark
BURGAŠAMBI to hang over, to float
  (smoke or mist)
  BURGAŠAME NIYAMNIYAMBI to have an
    archery contest to see who can
    shoot best at wild game from horse-
    back
BURGIBUMBI caus. of *burgimbi*

BURGIMBI to be in disarray
BURGIN 1. opportunity, favorable
  situation 2. a spell, an interval,
  a sudden burst (of rain) 3. disarray, disorder 4. pommel; cf.
  burgiyen
  BURGIN BURGIN I in sudden bursts,
    in disarray
BURGINDUMBI/BURGINUMBI to be in dis-
  array together
BURGIŠAMBI to be in frequent or con-
  stant disarray
BURGIYELEMBI to grasp the pommel, to
  use the pommel
BURGIYEN 1. the outside surface 2.
  pommel 3. stingy, miserly
BURIBUMBI 1. caus./pass. of *burimbi*
  2. to sink
BURIMBI 1. to stretch over, to cover
  (the surface of an object with
  leather) 2. to put in a lining
BURKIMBI to bury, to inter
BURLAMBI see *burulambi*
BURTEI widespread, common
BURU BARA dim, unclear, hazy, hidden
BURUBUMBI 1. to disappear without a
  trace 2. to die (of a prince)
BURUHUN dim, only partially visible,
  clouded
BURULABUMBI caus. of *burulambi*
BURULAMBI to flee, to take to flight
BURULANDUMBI/BURULANUMBI to flee to-
  gether
BURULU a horse having mixed red and
  white hair
BURUMBI to cover up, to hide
BUSAJAMBI to be blind through injury
BUSALAMBI to blind
BUSANGGIYAMBI to search urgently for
  something lost
BUSE a fortified location
  BUSE DA root of the lily that can
    be boiled and eaten
BUSEHE ILHA lily
BUSEREKU 1. an uncouth person 2.
  pederast, sodomist
BUSEREMBI 1. to act uncouthly 2. to
  commit sodomy or some other un-
  natural sexual act
  BUSERERE BAITA pederasty, sodomy
BUSHENEMBI to get a blister from being
  burnt
BUSU BUSU AGAMBI to rain a fine rain
BUSUBUMBI to suffer a relapse
BUSUMDA lily
BUŠA more
BUŠAKAN a little more
BUŠUHŪN stingy, cheap
BUŠUKU a harmful spirit that bewitches
  children and animals, a fox-sprite
  BUŠUKU DONDON moth
  BUŠUKU YEMJI animal-sprites and
    ghosts

B

BUŠUKUDEMBI to be possessed by a fox-
    sprite
BUŠUKULEMBI to practice ghostly arts,
    to appear as an animal-sprite
BUTABUMBI caus. of *butambi*
BUTALIN clasp for an arrowhead
BUTAMBI to catch (game or fish)
BUTAN HALAN interjection of reproach
    or regret
    BUTAN HALAN AKŪ what a shame!
BUTANAMBI to go to catch
BUTEMJI cunning, deceitful
BUTEN 1. the foot of a mountain 2.
    the hem of a garment
BUTEREMBI 1. to go along the foot of
    a mountain 2. to hem
    BUTEREME along the mountain's foot
BUTHA hunting and fishing
    BUTHAI NIYALMA hunter, fisherman,
        sportsman
BUTHAMBI to hunt, to fish
BUTHASI (虞人) an official of
    ancient times in charge of hunting
    grounds
BUTHAŠABUMBI caus. of *buthašambi*
BUTHAŠAMBI to fish and hunt
    BUTHAŠARA BE KADALARA FIYENTEN
    (都虞司) Department of the
    Household Guard and the Imperial
    Hunt, BH 80
BUTU dark, dim, hidden, secret
    BUTU HALHŪN sultry, hot and humid,
        close
    BUTU HŪLHA thief
    BUTU HŪLHI NIYALMA a stupid person
        who makes no reply when spoken to
    BUTU SABIRGI NOHO SUJE satin woven
        without golden threads
    BUTU SEJEN a closed vehicle used
        for the transport of criminals
    BUTUI secretly
    BUTUI JALAN the underworld
BUTUKEN rather dim, rather secret
BUTULEBUMBI caus. of *butulembi*
BUTULEMBI 1. to cover, to cover up, to
    stop up 2. to act secretly
BUTUMBI to hibernate
    BUTUHA CIBIN a type of hibernating
        swallow
BUTUN hibernation
BUTURI 1. small pustules caused by heat
    2. wine dregs

BUTURINAMBI to form small heat pustules
BUTŪN crock, large jar
BUYA small, insignificant, fragmentary
    BUYA JULEN novel, romance
    BUYA JUSE a child (under ten years
        of age)
    BUYA NIYALMA ordinary person, a
        mean person (as opposed to a
        gentleman), a self-deprecatory
        term used in referring to oneself
    BUYA TUŠAN I HAFAN (小京官)
        officials of the seventh and
        eighth ranks attached to the
        Councils and Secretarial Offices,
        BH 299
BUYAKASI small, minute
BUYARAMBI to be small, to be insig-
    nificant
BUYARAME of small import, insignifi-
    cant, miscellaneous
    BUYARAME BAITA ICIHIYARA BOO (火
    房) an office concerned with
        miscellaneous small dealings
    BUYARAME HACIN I KUNGGERI (雜科)
        section for miscellaneous busi-
        ness in the Board of Works
    BUYARAME HAFAN officials of the
        lower ranks
    BUYARAME JAKA miscellaneous small
        things
    BUYARAME JUJURAME timidly, narrow-
        mindedly, pettily
BUYASI small, petty, tiny, insignifi-
    cant
BUYEBUMBI caus. of *buyembi*
BUYECUKE desirable, precious, enchant-
    ing, amiable
BUYECUN desire, longing, love
BUYEMBI to desire, to long for, to
    admire, to like, to love, to yearn
    for, to do gladly
BUYEN desire
    BUYEN CIHA longing and desire, per-
        sonal desire, greed
    BUYEN CISUI in one's own personal
        interest, according to one's per-
        sonal desires
BUYENDUMBI/BUYENUMBI to desire to-
    gether, to like one another
BUYENIN feeling, desire
BUYERŠEMBI to envy, to covet
BŪRTU KARA a fine black horse

C

CA tendon, sinew
  CA MANGGA stubborn, not easy to deal with, difficult
CA YUWAN YAMUN (察院) bureau of inspection
CAB SEME blindly, recklessly
CABDARA a brown horse with white mane and tail
CABDARI see cabdara
CABGAN SURU a pure white horse
CABI the hair on the breast and stomach (of a horse)
CABIHAN a float on a fish line
CABSIMBI to protect
CABUMBI caus. of cambi
CACARAKŪ a gray grasshopper
CACARI a tent
  CACARI BOO a square tent with cloth sides
CACIHIYAMBI to drip, to run (of the nose)
CACUBUMBI caus. of cacumbi
CACUMBI to sprinkle, to spill, to pour a libation, to drip
CACUN see acun cacun
CACURAMBI to make a racket, to kick up a row
CADABUMBI caus. of cadambi
CADAMBI to wind, to coil around
CADARI (Sanskrit kṣatriya) the warrior caste
CAFUR CIFUR SEME smooth and slippery (said of good-tasting food)
CAGACI (供事) Clerk, BH 190, 267
CAGAN books, documents, papers
CAGATU ULHŪMA the silver pheasant (Gennaeus ycthemerus)
CAHAN buttermilk, sour milk
CAHARA a vessel carried on one's person for drinking water
CAHARNAMBI to clear the throat and nostrils (of a horse)
CAHI hasty, hurried
CAHIMBI to divide, to partition

CAHIN 1. compartment for storing grain, bin, crib 2. a well crib
  CAHIN I USIN a well field (a type of field allotment in ancient times)
CAHŪ a virago, termagant
CAHŪDAMBI see cahūšambi
CAHŪŠAMBI to brawl, to speak sharply, to squabble, to be vituperative (of women)
CAI tea
  CAI ABDAHA tea leaves
  CAI ABDAHA I KUNGGERI (茅茶 科) a section of the Board of Rites concerned with matters relating to tea
  CAI I BOO teahouse
  CAI I DA (尚茶正) Chief Cup-bearer, BH 91
  CAI MORIN BE KADALARA YAMUN (茶 馬司) Office of Tea and Horse Revenue; cf. BH 844 A
  CAI NENDEN ILHA a camellia (Camellia sasanqua)
  CAI TAILI a tea tray
CAIDA tea essence--strong tea to be diluted with water before drinking
CAIDU a type of bean eaten while drinking tea
CAISE 1. hairpin 2. a cake made of fried vermicelli
CAISI see caise
CAK SEME 1. neatly, firmly (wrapped) 2. freezing
  CAK SERE BEIKUWEN a freezing cold
CAKCAHŪN inflexible, unbendable
CAKCIN ten billion
CAKILGATU KULUK a fine horse with whorls of hair on both hind legs
CAKIRI 1. half-cooked, half-done 2. sable or fox pelts speckled with white hair
  CAKIRI DAMIN a white-speckled eagle
  CAKIRI ŠONGKON a white-speckled falcon

CAKJAMBI (-ka) to become crusted over (of snow)
  CAKJAME GECEMBI to freeze hard
CAKSAHA magpie (*Pica pica*)
CAKSIKŪ a small cymbal
  CAKSIKŪ UCUN AMBA KUMUN music accompanied by cymbals and singing used for the emperor, when traveling, when prisoners of war were presented, and when troops were inspected
  CAKSIKŪ UCUN NARHŪN KUMUN music played at banquets given in honor of victorious generals
CAKSIMBI 1. to rattle, to vibrate, to beat a cymbal 2. to make a strike with the *gacuha* 3. to praise 4. to ache (of the bones and joints)
CAKŪ white-necked
CAKŪHA a white-necked magpie
CAKŪLU having white spots or markings
  CAKŪLU CECIKE probably the white chat (*Oenanthe oenanthe*)
  CAKŪLU HONGGON CECIKE a small bird with a light-yellow head and a white speckled neck
  CAKŪLU KIONGGUHE the Fukien myna
  CAKŪLU KUREHU a white-headed woodpecker
CAKŪLUN jackdaw or crow with white ringed neck
CAKŪLUTU CECIKE Chinese bulbul (*Pycnonotus sinensis*)
CAKŪRAN sandalwood (*Santalum album*)
CAKŪRI HIYAN sandalwood incense
CALA 1. over there, on the other side 2. previously, before
CALABUMBI 1. caus. of *calambi* 2. to differ
  CALABURE BA AKŪ there is no difference, almost the same
CALABUN 1. mistake, error 2. difference
CALAMBI 1. to err, to miss 2. to be different
CALANAMBI to go to miss, to go to make an error
CALCIN water that flows on top of ice in the springtime
CALFA incompletely dried birchbark--also called *fulgiyan alan*
CALGABUN disturbance, vexation
CALGARI unorderly, inexperienced in the things of the world, not businesslike
CALGIBUMBI to form waves (as when the wind blows up the water in a river), to overflow, to surge
CALGIN wave, surge, overflowing
CALIHŪN the mealy redpoll (*Acanthis linaria*)
CALIMBI 1. to collapse from fatigue

C

2. to cling, to hold on
CALIYAN pay and provisions (military)
  CALIYAN I BOO (錢糧房) Pay office of the Printing Office and Bookbindery
  CALIYAN I FIYENTEN (經會司) pay office of the Board of Revenues in Mukden
  CALIYAN I KUNGGERI (金科) an office of the Board of Revenues
CALIYANGGA ŠUSAI (廩生) Stipendiary, BH 577C, 629A, 631
CALIYASI tax collector
CALU a granary
  CALU CAHIN I BAITA BE UHERI KADALARA YAMUN (總督倉場衙門) Head Office of Government Granaries at the Capital
  CALU I KUNGGERI (倉科) section on granaries in the Board of Revenues
CALUNGGA 1. pertaining to a granary 2. a grain measure equaling sixteen bushels
  CALUNGGA BELE rice from a granary
CAMANGGA see *ca mangga*
CAMANGGADAMBI to be stubborn
CAMBI (-ngka/ha) 1. to stretch, to pitch (a tent or yurt), to draw (a bow), to build (a bridge) 2. to run away (of a horse)
  CAME GECEHE frozen solid all of a sudden
CAMCI slip (garment worn under a woman's gown)
CAMDA 1. a leather case 2. haze, mist
CAMHAN a temporary arch or structure over a street that carries slogans or holiday greetings
CAMHARI inscribed stone, boundary stone
CAMHATA piebald, speckled
CAMNAMBI to go too far, to miss, to catch after an initial miss
CAMSI a tent erector
CAN 1. a small cymbal 2. a bowl with a narrow bottom 3. meditation, dhyana
  CAN NIMAHA 'dragon liver fish'-- a fresh-water fish much valued for its liver
  CAN TEMBI to sit in meditation
CANANGGI day before yesterday, previously
CANG 1. the autumnal sacrifice 2. sacrificial wine
CANG CANG the sound of bells
CANG CING same as *cang cang*
CANG SEME hard, fast
  CANG SEME GECEMBI to freeze solid
  CANG SEME MANGGA very hard
CANGGA a small gong
CANGGALI impatient
CANGGALIMBI to be exhausted, to get

C

tired, to tire

CANGGI only, scarcely, just

CANGKA 1. perfect participle of *cambi*
2. a white horse with red eyes, nose, and lips

CANGKAI obstinate, stubborn

CANGKAMBI to kill small fish in shallow water with stones

CANKIR NIONGNIYAHA the speckled goose of Chinghai

CANJURABUMBI caus. of *canjurambi*

CANJURAMBI to greet by holding joined hands up at face level and bowing slightly

CAO SEME immediately, straightaway

CAR CIR the sound of meat sizzling--used to describe a painful wound

CAR SEME 1. painful (of a burn) 2. at a breath, at a stroke

CARA 1. a tall wine vessel made of gold, silver, or pewter 2. a horse with red about its eyes, nose, and lips 3. see *cara aniya*
CARA ANIYA the year before last
CARA IHAN a striped cow

CARANAMBI to have white spots or flecks

CARCAN SEME shrieking, screaming

CARCINAMBI 1. to congeal, to begin to freeze, to ice up 2. to heal (of wounds)

CARGI 1. there, over there, that side, beyond 2. formerly
CARGI ANIYA the year after next
CARGI BIYA the month before last

CARGILAKŪ firecracker, fireworks

CARGIMBI to explode

CARKI a wooden clapper
CARKI TŪMBI to hit a wooden clapper

CARKIDAMBI to hit a wooden clapper

CARKIMBI to rattle together (as belt pendants), to create a dissonance, to tinkle

CARNAMBI see *caranambi*

CARUBUMBI caus. of *carumbi*

CARUMBI to fry, to deep-fry
CARURE BOO bakery, place where pastries were prepared

CARUR SEME in an oily manner, smoothly

CAS SEME vaguely, in a fragmentary way
CAS SEME DONJIMBI to hear only bits and pieces

CASHŪLABUMBI caus./pass. of *cashūlambi*

CASHŪLAMBI 1. to turn the back on, to stand or sit with one's back to 2. to be ungrateful
CASHŪLAME TEMBI to sit back to back

CASHŪN backwards, with the back towards
CASHŪN EDUN a tail wind

CASI in that direction, thither, there
CASI AKŪ EBSI AKŪ neither here nor there, without direction, neither coming nor going
CASI FOROMBI to turn in that direc-

tion

CASIBA ILHA a white flower found in Mongolia

CASIKAN a little in that direction

CATA a quadrillion

CE 1. they 2. an imperial document on yellow or gold paper 3. a written answer to a question

CEBKE flat side of the *gacuha*

CEBKE CABKA without appetite

CECE silk gauze
CECE DARDAN a type of silk gauze
CECE GECUHERI silk gauze decorated with dragon patterns; cf. *gecuheri*
CECE UNDURAKŪ silk gauze with dragon patterns on it; cf. *undurakū*

CECEN distention (of the belly)

CECERCUKE annoying, vexing, infuriating

CECEREMBI 1. to press tightly, to embrace tightly 2. to be taut and hard to draw (of a bowstring)

CECERI a type of loose-textured silk, lustring
CECERI ŠOŠONTU an ancient crown-shaped head covering

CECERŠEMBI to exert a great amount of effort, to quiver from exertion

CECIKE a small bird; cf. *gasha*
CECIKE BE FULGIYERE SIHAN a blowpipe for shooting birds
CECIKE BE LATUBURE DARHŪWAN a glued pole for catching small birds
CECIKE FULGIYEKU a blowpipe for shooting small birds
CECIKE MIMI a wild vegetable, the leaves of which can be eaten raw
CECIKE TATARA ASU a net for catching small birds

CECIKELEMBI to notch an arrow holding it between the thumb and forefinger

CEHUN distended, flatulent, overly full (of the belly)

CEJEHEN a piece of wood on the end of a tow rope

CEJELEKU a shirt with a collar

CEJEN the upper part of the chest
CEJEN ANAMBI to expand the chest (as a gesture of pride)
CEJEN TELEBUMBI to have a pain in the chest

CEKCERI a shallow brass cooking vessel

CEKCIHIYAN a small tripod

CEKE 1. a short jacket made of wild animal pelts 2. the side of a *gacuha*

CEKEMU Japanese satin

CEKJEHUN large-chested

CEKU a swing

CEKUDEMBI to swing in a swing

CEKULEMBI see *cekudembi*

CELEBUMBI caus. of *celembi*

CELEHEN a courtyard paved with bricks

CELEHEN I AMBA KUMUN music played
while the emperor returned to the
palace from a banquet and while
officials were thanking him for
favors received

CELEHEN I BOLGONGGO KUMUN music
played during imperial banquets

CELEHEN I HŪWA a courtyard in front
of the throne hall

CELEHERI terrace, platform; cf. *celheri*

CELEKU a ruler, measuring s'ick

CELEMBI 1. to measure (with a ruler)
2. to become tired after a long
journey 3. to pave with bricks or
stone

CELEHE JUGŪN a brick-paved path
through the palace

CELHERI a paved platform before an official building, a terrace, a platform

CELIN a band on the bootleg that is
attached to the trousers to hold
the boot tight

CELMEN nap or pile on cloth

CELMERI thin, well-proportioned (of
a person's figure)

CEMBE accusative of *ce*

CEN one one-hundred millionth

CEN HIYANG agalloch, eaglewood
(*Aquilaria agallocha*)

CENCI ablative of *ce*

CENCILEMBI to examine carefully

CENCILEME TUWAMBI to take a careful
look at

CENDE dative of *ce*

CENDEBUMBI caus. of *cendembi*

CENDEKU inspector, reviewer, tester

CENDEKU SIHAN a pointed pipe used
for extracting samples from grain
sacks

CENDEKUŠEMBI to verify a fact already
known by feigning ignorance and
asking

CENDEMBI to check, to verify, to try
out, to put to the test

CENDENDUMBI/CENDENUMBI to test or
verify together

CENDZ TUBIHE an orange

CENE a peony

CENGME coarse Tibetan wool

CENGMU see *cengme*

CENGSIYANG prime minister

CENI genitive of *ce*

CENINGGE theirs

CENSE same as *cendz tubihe*

CERGUWE roe, fish eggs

CERGUWE WALIYAMBI to lay eggs (of
fish)

CERHUWE see *cerguwe*

CERHUWENEMBI to get a boil or abscess
on the finger

CERI gauze, netting (of silk)

CERI SUJE a satin that resembles

gauze

CERINGGE ILHA a red flower from South
China

CESE register, official record

CESE I NAMUN (冊 庫) storage
room for registers in the Board of
Rites

CI 1. ablative particle: from, by way
of, than 2. rank, military formation
3. paint, lacquer

CIB CAB quiet, still

CIB CIB SEME very quietly

CIB GUKUBUN silence and extinction,
nirvana

CIB SEME 1. quietly 2. swiftly (of
an arrow)

CIBAHANCI a lamaist nun

CIBIHA a white-necked crow that flies
in flocks

CIBIN swallow (*Hirundo rustica*)

CIBINGGA KIONGGUHE a type of myna that
resembles a swallow

CIBIRGAN a small bird resembling a
swallow with reddish head and back

CIBIRI ILHA a yellow flower blooming
in late spring that grows on a vine

CIBSEMBI to be quiet

CIBSEN quietness, stillness

CIBSIDAMBI to lament incessantly

CIBSIMBI to lament, to deplore, to
sigh over

CIBSIN 1. a lament 2. a funeral
notice

CIBSINDUMBI/CIBSINUMBI to lament together

CIBSONGGO 1. harmony, harmonious 2.
the right side of an ancestral
temple

CIBSU HIYAN incense used at sacrifices

CIBTUI repeatedly

CIBUMBI to be squeezed (into a narrow
space)

CICI GOCI timidly, fearfully

CIDAHŪN pelt of a snow rabbit

CIDAHŪN KURUME coat made from a
snow-rabbit pelt

CIFABUMBI caus. of *cifambi*

CIFAHAN viscous mud, mud used as
plaster

CIFAHANGGA AISIN gold paint

CIFAMBI to smear on, to plaster

CIFELEKU a spittoon

CIFELEMBI to spit

CIFENGGU spit, saliva

CIFUN tax, duty

CIFUN ARAMBI to impose a tax

CIFUN GAIMBI to collect tax or duty

CIFUN I BITHE tax receipt

CIFUN I BITHEI MENGGUN property
deeds tax

CIFUN I MENGGUN tax money

CIFURI NIYEHE one name for the common
teal

C

C

CIGE see *cihe*

CIGU NIRU (旗鼓) Captain of the Banner Drum--a Chinese official of the palace

CIHA desire, wish

    CIHAI as one wishes, according to one's desires

    CIHAI CIHAI with great willingness

CIHAKŪ 1. unwilling 2. uncomfortable, ill, not feeling well

CIHALAHAI as one likes, according to one's desire

CIHALAMBI 1. to like, to be fond of, to want 2. to look for shortcomings, to look for others' errors

CIHALAN desire, wish

CIHALŠAMBI 1. to desire ardently 2. to be always looking for others' short-comings

CIHAN desire

    CIHAN BUYEN AKŪ without desire or interest

CIHANGGA willing, eager

    CIHANGGA WAKA unwilling

    CIHANGGAI willing, eager

CIHE louse

CIHETEI wild ass (*Equus hemionus*)

CIK a circle written in texts as a form of punctuation

CIK CAK SEME rustling, making a small noise

CIK CIK suddenly (to think of some-thing)

CIK CIK SEME sadly, morosely, anxiously

    CIK CIK SEME GŪNIMBI to think of constantly, to come to mind sud-denly and often, to be anxious about something

CIK SEME suddenly

    CIK SEME GŪNIMBI to think of sud-denly

CIKEKU a mat of reeds or rice stalks

CIKEŠEMBI to be a little lame (of horses or cows)

CIKIMBI (-ha) to insert or attach snugly, to fit exactly

    CIKIRAKŪ not snugly fitting

CIKIN 1. edge, border 2. the bank of a river

CIKINGGE FU a boundary wall

CIKIRAMBI to go along the edge, border, or bank

    CIKIRAME along the edge, border, or riverbank

CIKIRI 1. wood shavings 2. a dog or horse with white or light blue eyes 3. white hairs or small areas of white on a pelt

    CIKIRI DOBIHI a black fox pelt speckled with white hairs

    CIKIRI NIYEHE a wild duck dappled with white around eyes and bill

CIKIRŠAMBI to act modestly in the presence of older people (of women)

CIKJALAMBI to form a sprout within the ground

CIKSIMBI (-ka) to mature, to grow up, to become tough (of the muscles)

CIKSIN adult, grown-up, mature, able-bodied

CIKTAMBI to take root, to grow up

CIKTAN relationship, natural law, principle

CIKTARAMBI (-ka) 1. to mature, to be-come established in life 2. to be in readiness 3. to flourish, to spread out

CIKTEN 1. trunk, stem, shaft (of an arrow) 2. heaven's stem

CIKTENEMBI to go along the trunk or stem, to form a stem

    CIKTENEME along the trunk or stem

CILBA having the same name

CILBURI a guide rope fastened to a bridle ring to lead beasts of burden, a tether

CILCIMBI (-ka) to swell (as a wave), to come in (for high tide)

CILCIN 1. swelling, boil, bump 2. high tide

    CILCIN AKŪ flawless, clean, efficient

CILCINAMBI to form a boil, swelling, or bump on the skin

CILEBUMBI caus. of *cilembi*

CILEMBI to paint

CILIKŪ choking, difficulty in swallow-ing

    CILIKŪ NIMEKU dysphagia

CILIMBI to choke, to swallow with difficulty

CILIN 1. see *celin* 2. unicorn; cf. *sabintu*

CILME see *celmen*

CIMAHA 1. tomorrow 2. morning

    CIMAHA INENGGI tomorrow

CIMARI 1. tomorrow 2. morning

    CIMARI ERDE tomorrow morning, early in the morning

CIMARIDARI every morning

CIMARILAMBI to be early in the morning, to act early in the morning

CIMCI shirt

CIME a salt-water fish resembling the salmon

CIMEKE GIRANGGI 1. the foot bones of an animal 2. all the small bones in a pig's foot below the ankle bone--used by small girls as toys

CIMIKŪ a 'pacifier'--a nipple-shaped object for babies to suck on

CIMILAN a whistle that functions by sucking rather than blowing air through it

CIMKIŠAMBI to be without appetite, to find food tasteless

CIN 1. chief, principal, main 2.

C

straight, straightforward 3. the
south side 4. a small white heron
CIN I BOO the main house or building
CIN I DIYAN principal palace
CIN I DUKA the main gate
CIN I ERGI place of honor
CIN I GAMAMBI to handle in a
straighforward and honest way
CIN I TEMBI to sit in the place of
honor (at a meal)
CIN I WASIMBI to come straight
down
CINCILABUMBI caus. of *cincilambi*
CINCILAMBI to scrutinize, to examine
CINCILAN an implement used for obser-
vation
CINDAHAN snow rabbit, varying hare
(*Lepus timidus*)
CINDAHAN CABI the fur on the under-
side of a snow rabbit
CING CANG the sound of chipping ice
CING K'O MUJI barley
CING SEME flaming, flashing
CING SEME BANJIMBI to live prosper-
ously
CING SEME DAMBI to flame
CINGGAMBI see *cingkambi*
CINGGILAKŪ a small bell used by Bud-
dhist monks
CINGGIN a three-year-old pig
CINGGIRI ILHA an exotic purple, bell-
shaped flower
CINGGIYA 1. insufficient, short,
narrow 2. narrow-minded, ungenerous
3. near
CINGGIYAKAN somewhat narrow
CINGIRI myna bird (*Gracula religiosa*)
CINGKABUMBI 1. caus./pass. of *cing-
kambi* 2. to gorge oneself, to be
stuffed, to be puffed up, to be
inflated
CINGKAI by far, completely, different,
odd, at variance
CINGKAMBI to stuff, to fill a con-
tainer full, to stuff pelts with
grass or wood
CINGKAME FARGAMBI to pursue to the
end
CINGKAME JEMBI to eat to satiety
CINGKAŠAMBI to stuff full
CINGNEMBI to glue an arrowhead to the
shaft
CINJIRI see *cingiri*
CINUHŪLAMBI to smear with cinnabar
red, to write with red ink
CINUHŪN 1. cinnabar 2. bright red
CINUHŪN I ARAHA BUKDARUN copy of an
examination written in red ink
CINURGAN a small sparrowlike bird
with a black back and vermilion
plumage
CIR SEME gushing out, hurrying
CIR SEME HŪDUN bouncing along

quickly
CIRA 1. hard, solid, fast 2. face,
complexion 3. strict, stern 4.
powerful (of horses)
CIRA ALJAHA the expression (on his
face) changed
CIRA ELHEKEN OHO his face has an
angry look
CIRA MORIN powerful horse
CIRA NIRUGAN portrait
CIRA SINDAHA his face has a happy
look
CIRA TAKAMBI to practice physiognomy
CIRA TAKARA NIYALMA physiognomist
CIRALABUMBI caus. of *ciralambi*
CIRALAMBI to be strict, to act strictly
CIRAN solemnity, seriousness
CIRANGGA colored, having color
CIRASHŪN see *cirgashūn*
CIRCAN a bright yellow pigment
CIRCINAMBI to freeze on the surface
CIRGABUKŪ MIYOOCAN air rifle
CIRGABUMBI to hold back, to block up,
to hold the breath
CIRGASHŪN impeded, blocked, stiff
CIRGEBUMBI caus. of *cirgembi*
CIRGEKU a wooden implement used to
pound earth, a ramrod
CIRGEMBI 1. to ram, to pound (earth)
2. to remove the string of a bow
CIRGEŠEMBI to pound steadily
CIRHASHŪN see *cirgashūn*
CIRHŪBUMBI caus. of *cirhūmbi*
CIRHŪMBI to take back, to let a bow go
lax, to lower a sword after having
brandished it
CIRKU pillow
CIRKU HENGKE winter melon (*Cucumis
melo*)
CIRKU MOO wooden posts on both sides
of a threshold
CIRKU WEHE stone pillars or sup-
ports on both sides of a threshold
CIRUBUMBI caus. of *cirumbi*
CIRUKU see *cirku*
CIRUMBI to support, to pillow, to use
as a pillow
CISE vegetable or flower garden
CISTAN a thin strip of paper placed on
official documents to show places
where corrections were to be made
CISU private, private interest or
profit
CISU AKŪ unselfish
CISU BAITA private matter
CISUI out of one's own interest,
on one's initiative, naturally
(see also *ini cisui*), privately,
on one's own
CISUI BOJI a private contract or
deed (without an official seal)
CISUI HUNGKEREHE JIHA illegal coins
CISUDEMBI to act for one's private

C

interest
CISULEMBI to act in one's own interest,
  to do privately
CITU MORIN a famous swift horse
CIYALIBUMBI caus./pass. of *ciyalimbi*
CIYALIMBI to grab by the hair (in a
  fight)
CIYALINDUMBI to grab one another's
  hair when fighting
CIYAN DZUNG (千總) see *minggatu*
CIYAN HŪ (千户) chief of one
  thousand families in a military
  district
CIYAN ŠI (僉事) secretary
CIYANLIYANG provisions--the same as
  caliyan
CIYANŠI (僉事) secretary
COB SEME appearing suddenly, standing
  out from the crowd
COBALABUMBI caus. of *cobalambi*
COBALAMBI to pry up, to lift with a
  lever
COBAN 1. a lever, a bar for prying
  2. a medical quack
COBANGGA GIN a scale for weighing heavy
  objects
COBDAHA bamboo leaf
  COBDAHA ŠUNGKERI ILHA an orchid
    with bamboolike leaves
COBOLAN an owl-- the same as *yabulan*
COBTO 1. rags, shreds 2. to shreds
  COBTO COBTO in rags, ragged,
    tattered
  COBTO COBTO HŪWAJAHA tore in shreds
COBTOJOMBI to have a piece torn from
  one's clothing
COCARAMBI to act heedlessly or care-
  lessly
COCARI the common snipe; cf. *karka
  cecike*
COCIRAMBI see *cocarambi*
COCO penis
  COCO I DA glans of the penis
  COCO I SEN opening of the urethra
CODOLI haughty, conceited, hard to
  handle (horses)
COHOMBI to do especially, to consider
  as the most important aspect
  COHOME especially, on purpose,
    particularly, exclusively
COHONGGO special
  COHONGGO KINGKEN (特磬) a
    Chinese musical instrument
COHORO piebald, dappled
COHOTO copper or tin forks used in
  playing with a *gacuha*
COHOTOI especially, particularly
COK CAK SEMBI to snap, to click
COKCIHIYAN peak, ridge
COKCOHON jutting up, vertical
  COKCOHON GODOHON towering (height)
COKCOROMBI to rise up vertically, to
  be high

COKI prominent, jutting out
COKIMBI to stick in the ground (arrows
  and like objects)
COKO 1. chicken 2. the tenth of the
  earth's branches (酉)
  COKO BIYA the eighth month
  COKO ILHA a betony (*Stachys aspera*)
  COKO MEGU a mushroom that grows in
    rich soil--it has a white top and
    is black inside
  COKO NAKAMBI to roost
  COKO SENCE the same as *coko megu*
  COKO UMGAN I TOHOLIYO a pastry
    made of chicken eggs, honey,
    sugar, walnuts, and glutinous rice
COKONGGO pertaining to the cyclical
  sign *coko*
  COKONGGO ANIYA year of the chicken
COKTO arrogant, conceited
COKTOLOMBI to act arrogantly
COKŪLU see *cukūlu*
COLARIMBI see of *colambi*
COLAMBI to fry, to stir-fry; cf.
  carumbi
COLGAMBI see *curgimbi*
COLGOGAN FULAN a breed of black horses
  raised by the *Ainugan* tribe
COLGON see *colhon*
COLGOROKO prominent, surpassing, ex-
  celling
COLGOROMBI (-ko) to surpass, to excel
COLGOROPI prominent, imposing
COLHO towering
  COLHO MOO *Catalpa kaempieri*
COLHON peak, high promontory
COLHOROMBI see *colgorombi*
COLHORON a commanding peak
COLIBUMBI caus. of *colimbi*
COLIKŪ an engraving knife
COLIMBI to engrave, to carve
COLKON a wave
  COLKON CECIKE a small, long-beaked
    bird with a black back that eats
    pine cones
COLO courtesy name, nickname, title
  COLO BUMBI to grant a title
COMAN goblet, large cup for wine
COMARI ILHA gardenia (*Gardenia jasmin-
  oides*)
COMBOLI the groin
COMCOK bunch, cluster
  COMCOK ERIHE one style of rosary
COMGOMBI to stamp, to tread on
COMKO MORIN dapple-gray horse
COMLIMBI to make an incision
COMNOMBI to tread down, to stamp on
COMO see *coman*
CONGGAI spotted kingfisher (*Ceryle
  lugubris*); cf. *cunggai*
CONGGALABUMBI see *tunggalabumbi*
CONGGIMBI see *congkimbi*
CONGGIRI a type of cymbal
CONGGIŠAMBI see *congkišambi*

CONGKIBUMBI caus. of *congkimbi*

CONGKIMBI 1. to peck 2. to fight (of quails) 3. to pound grain to remove the husk

CONGKIRI GŪWASIHIYA one name for the eastern egret; cf. *gūwasihiya*

CONGKIŠAKŪ a pestle

CONGKIŠAMBI 1. to peck 2. to thresh grain

CONTOHO a hole or gap in a wall or dike

CONTOHOJOMBI to form a hole or gap

COO a spade

COO BITHE paper money

COOCARAMBI see *cocarambi*

COOCIYANLI sand lark (*Calandrella rufescens*)

COOGAN little egret (*Egretta garzetta*)

COOHA 1. army, troops 2. soldier 3. military, martial

COOHA BARGIYAMBI to reassemble troops

COOHA BE ALIHA AMBAN (司 馬) minister of war (in antiquity)

COOHA BE KADALARA TINGGIN (清 軍 廳) bureau of military affairs-- an organ for dealing with military offenses in each province

COOHA BEDEREMBI troops return (victoriously)

COOHA DAIN troops, armies

COOHA GOCIMBI to withdraw troops

COOHA HUWEKIYEBURE TEMGETU a silver placard given to a soldier as a commendation

COOHA MORINGGA FIYENTEN office of a military commander

COOHA OBUME BANJIBURE KUNGGERI (編 軍 科) section in charge of military banishment in the Board of War

COOHA OBURE WEILE an offense punished with military banishment

COOHA UREBURE TINGGIN (演 武 廳) bureau concerned with drilling troops

COOHAI AGŪRA I KUNGGERI I BAITA ALIRE BOO (軍 器 科 值 房) arsenal of the weapons office in the Board of Works

COOHAI AGŪRA I KUNGGERI I BAITA HACIN I BOO (軍 器 科 案 房) chancery of the weapons office in the Board of Works

COOHAI AGŪRA I KUNGGERI I BODORO BOO (軍 器 科 算 房) accounting office of the weapons office of the Board of Works

COOHAI AMBAN (武 大 臣) a high military dignitary

COOHAI BAITAI KUNGGERI (軍 務 科) military affairs bureau in the Board of War

COOHAI BAITALAN I KŪWARAN (軍 需 局) military supplies depot

COOHAI BAITALAN I NAMUN (軍 需 庫) commissary warehouse; cf. BH 656A

COOHAI BELHEN I BOLGOBURE FIYENTEN (武 庫 清 吏 司) a department in the Board of War; cf. BH 415A

COOHAI BOO (兵 房) war office of the Bureau of Colonial Affairs

COOHAI DASAN I SIMNEMBI to take an examination in the military arts

COOHAI ERDEMUNGGE I KUNGGERI (將 材 科) a section of the Board of War concerned with the promotion of officers

COOHAI FAFUN military law, martial law, military discipline

COOHAI FIYAN the disposition of an army

COOHAI FIYAN BE NONGGIBURE MUDAN music played while the emperor inspected the troops

COOHAI FIYENTEN (兵 司) the military bureau in Mukden

COOHAI HAFAN a military officer

COOHAI HAFAN I FUNGNEHEN I KUNGGERI (武 誥 科) a section concerned with posthumous enfeoffment of military officers

COOHAI HAFAN I TEMGETU credentials of a military officer

COOHAI HAFAN SINDARA BOLGOBURE FIYENTEN (武 選 清 吏 司) Department of Selection, BH 415A

COOHAI JURGAN (兵 部) Board of War, BH 415

COOHAI JURGAN I KUNGGE YAMUN (兵 科) war section of the Grand Secretariat

COOHAI MORINGGA FIYENTEN (兵 馬 司) police office; cf. BH 796

COOHAI NASHŪN important military matters

COOHAI NASHŪN I AMBAN (軍 機 大 臣) Grand Councillor, BH 129

COOHAI NASHŪN I BA (軍 機 處) Council of State, BH 128

COOHAI NIYALMA soldier, warrior

COOHAI TUSANGGA INENGGI favorable days for military undertakings

COOHALAMBI to go to war, to send troops

COOHALAHA MORIN war horses

COOHAN see *coogan*

COOHIYAN Korea; cf. *solho*

COOLAMBI see *colambi*

COOLAN GAHA a red-beaked bird resembling a raven

COOLGON see *colgon*

COOMAN see *coman*

COR SEME gushing forth uninterruptedly

C

CORBOKŪ a device used to hold open the mouth of a horse (or other domestic animal)

CORBOMBI to pry the mouth open (of domestic animals)

CORBOHO TURA a post or stump to which animals are tied while given medicine

CORDOMBI to play (Mongolian instruments such as the *coron* and *mekeni*)

CORHO 1. an iron tube on a helmet for holding a tassel 2. a wooden tube used in the brewing of liquor

CORHON another name for the woodpecker; cf. *fiyorhon*

CORO the day after tomorrow

CORODAI one name for the phoenix; cf. *garudai*

CORON a four-holed wooden flute

CORON GOCIKA the belly has fallen (of horses and cattle)

CORON TATAN a small, temporary, wooden, tent-shaped structure

COS the sound of ricocheting or rebounding

COSHO an attached iron nail or hook for hanging or attaching objects

COTHO eggshell

COTOLI see *codoli*

CU 1. interjection used to set a dog on someone or thing 2. get out!

CU CA the sound of whispering or murmuring

CU NIRU a fire arrow

CUBA a woman's sleeveless court garment decorated with dragon patterns

CUBA SIJIGIYAN a woman's court garment--a cape decorated with dragon patterns

CUBUMBI to be squeezed into a narrow space; cf. *cibumbi*

CUBUME TEMBI to sit tightly together

CUCU CACA the sound of whispering or talking in a low voice

CUDU one ten billionth

CUIKEN golden plover

CUIKENGGE MAHATUN a hat worn by astrologers in ancient times

CUK CAK SEME bitterly, viciously (of fighting)

CUKCAMBI to protrude

CUKCAHA WEIHE bucktooth

CUKCUHUN protruding forward

CUKCUREMBI to face forward, to protrude

CUKU a kind of gelatinous dessert eaten out of a bowl

CUKULEMBI to stir up, to incite, to set a dog on prey

CUKUMBI to become tired, to be spent

CUKŪLU 1. nearsighted 2. a horse that goes about hanging his head

CUKŪMBI to hang down (the head), to look down, to bow down, to lie prostrate

CUKŪRŠEMBI to bow down profoundly

CUKŪŠAMBI to rush about blindly

CULASUN MOO a kind of cedar with bamboolike leaves

CULGAMBI 1. to inspect troops, to hold an inspection 2. to hold an assembly

CULGAN 1. inspection of troops (especially by the emperor) 2. an assembly, a league

CULGAN ACAMBI 1. to inspect troops 2. to hold an assembly

CULIN CECIKE one name for the oriole; cf. *gūlin cecike*

CULUK SEME coming and going all the time, suddenly coming and going

CUMCUMBI to squat holding one's arms about the knees

CUMCURAMBI 1. to pass quickly in front of a superior with the body bowed 2. to dart away, to disappear (of animals frightened by the approach of an enemy)

CUN CUN I gradually, by degrees

CUNCEO a fine silk

CUNG SEME directly, straight

CUNG YANG INENGGI the ninth day of the ninth month--a festival

CUNGGAI spotted kingfisher (*Ceryle lugubris*); cf. *conggai*

CUNGGUR NIYEHE Chinese little grebe (*Podiceps ruficollis*)

CUNGGURU navel

CUNGGŪŠAMBI to butt, to beat the head on something, to shove

CUNU GASHA black-capped kingfisher (*Halcyon pileata*)

CUR CAR SEME the sound of firecrackers and rockets

CUR SEME 1. the sound of a rocket flying 2. slipping, sneaking

CUR SEME GENEHE slipped out

CURBI GASHA turquoise kingfisher (*Halcyon smyrnensis*)

CURGIMBI to chatter, to make lots of noise

CURGIN chattering, noise, commotion

CURGINDUMBI to make a commotion (of a group), to prattle, to prate

CURHŪ the young of the pike

CURHŪMBI to go a stretch (of road)

CURHŪN length, stage (of a trip)

CURUN a measure of length equal to thirty Chinese feet

CUS SEME see *cur seme*

CUSE 1. bamboo 2. silk 3. a cook

CUSE MOO bamboo

CUSE MOO I ARSUN bamboo shoots

CUSE MOO I ITU bamboo partridge (*Bambusicola thoracica*)

CUSE MOO I UNDEHEN a bamboo stave
used for whipping
CUSE SINGGERI a small catlike
animal that eats bamboo roots
CUSEINGGE HOOŠAN paper made of bamboo
fiber
CUSENGGE NICUHE a pearl-like product
growing on bamboo
CUSERI made of bamboo, pertaining to
bamboo, bamboolike
CUSERI CECIKE a small gray-bodied
bird with red feet
CUSERI DUINGGE HOOŠAN a paper made
from bamboo
CUSERI HOOŠAN a white paper made
from bamboo
CUSERI TORO ILHA a red, five-petaled
flower with bamboolike leaves
CUSILE crystal

CUWAN boat, ship
CUWAN FEKUMBI to board a boat (in a
battle)
CUWANGNAMBI to seize by force, to
pillage, to rob
CŪN MOO Chinese cedar (*Cedrela sinen-
sis*)
CŪN ŠA a flowered light silk used for
making summer clothing
CY 1. a five-holed flute 2. a Chinese
foot measure 3. a bamboo rod used
for flogging
CYLEBUMBI caus./pass. of *cylembi*
CYLEMBI to flog with a bamboo rod
CYMING an imperial order of posthumous
enfeoffment
CYSE 1. pool, pond 2. garden; cf.
cise

C

D

DA 1. root, stock, base, foundation, source 2. leader, chief 3. a measure--five Chinese feet, two cubits 4. trunk of a tree 5. a measure for fish

DA AN I as usual, as always, as before

DA ARAMBI to lay a foundation

DA BEYE BAHAMBI to recuperate

DA DUBE stock and branches, beginning and end

DA FUJURI curriculum vitae

DA FUTA the main rope attached to a net used for trapping; cf. *dangdali*

DA GIN DZ a wife of wife's elder brother

DA GIO elder brother of one's wife

DA JIHA model for copper coins

DA JOKSON the starting line for mounted archers

DA MAFA great-great-grandfather

DA MAMA great-great-grandmother

DA MURU in broad outline, in general

DA SARGAN the chief wife

DA SEKIYEN MAFA progenitor

DA SUNTO the model for the dry measure *sunto*

DA SUSU birthplace, place, or origin

DA ŠU father's younger brother

DA TOLOMBI to count the hits at archery

DA UJUI USIHA the name of the brightest star in the constellation *abkai ujui usiha*

DA UŠE a line from the reins that passes through the bit of a bridle

DABABUMBI 1. caus. of *dabambi* 2. to go too far, to overstep, to go across 3. to waste, to squander 3. to boast, to exaggerate

DABABURAKŪ thrifty

DABAGAN a mountain pass

DABAKŪ wedges of wood on both sides of a gate that allow wheeled vehicles to enter

DABALA 1. (sentence particle) only, merely 2. (postposition) besides

DABALI 1. excessively, exceeding, too 2. (postposition) beyond, across, through

DABALI DULEKE passed beyond

DABALI FEKUHE jumped across

DABALI FIYELEMBI to jump across (equestrian trick)

DABALI UŠE a strap on the wagon-saddle that is attached to the shaft of the cart

DABALI WESIKE rose beyond

DABALIKAN somewhat excessive

DABAMBI to cross, to surpass, to go beyond, to climb over

DABAHA NIMEKU consumption

DABARA OLORO crossing and fording

DABANAMBI to surpass, to cross over, to go to cross

DABARGAN a bag carried on the body--used like a pocket

DABAŠAKŪ 1. presumptuous, extravagant 2. a person who tries to live beyond his means or station

DABAŠAMBI to act presumptuously

DABATALA excessively, presumptuously

DABCI having one's eyes askew, suffering exotropia

DABCIKŪ a double-edged sword

DABCILAKŪ a small hunting knife, dagger

DABCILAMBI to go askew, to run crooked

DABDALI headstrong, unruly, agitated

DABDURI quick-tempered, excitable

DABDURŠAMBI to flare up, to go into a rage

DABGIBUMBI caus. of *dabgimbi*

DABGIMBI to weed, to pull weeds with the hands

DABGIYAMBI see *dabkimbi*

DABKAMBI to haunt, to torment, to

bring harm to (of ghosts)

DABKIMBI   1. to repair with glue or plaster   2. to whip on (a horse)

DABKŪRI   double, having layers, storied (building)

DABKŪRI DALAN   a doubled dike or dam

DABKŪRI DORGI HOTON   the Forbidden City

DABKŪRI DUKA   a double gate

DABKŪRI KOTOLI   a double sail

DABKŪRI LEOSE   a storied building

DABKŪRI OMOLO   great-grandchild

DABKŪRI TAILI   a double blossom

DABKŪRILAMBI   to double

DABSI   upper arm

DABSIMBI   to incline, to wane

DABSULABUMBI   caus. of *dabsulambi*

DABSULAMBI   to preserve in brine, to salt, to pickle

DABSUN   salt

DABSUN BE GIYARIRE YAMUN (巡 盐 司)   department of salt control; cf. BH 835B

DABSUN BE YABUBURE BITHE BE PILERE BAICARA FALGANGGA (批 验 盐 引 所)   office of the salt examiner; cf. BH 835A

DABSUN CIFUN I MENGGUN   salt gabelle

DABSUN FUIFURE HAHA   salt worker

DABSUN I BAITA BE BAICARA HAFAN (盐 政)   controller of salt affairs; cf. BH 369, 369A

DABSU I CIFUN   salt tax

DABSUN I KŪWARAN   salt factory

DABSUN I URSE   salt smugglers

DABSUN JUWERE BAITA BE KADALARA HAFAN (盐 运 使)   Salt Controller, BH 835

DABSUN JUWERE BEIDESI (运 判)   Sub-Assistant Salt Controller, BH 835A

DABSUN JUWERE ILHICI (运 副)   Deputy Assistant Salt Controller, BH 835A

DABSUN JUWERE KADALASI (提 举)   Salt Inspector, BH 835A

DABSUN JUWERE UHECI (运 同)   Assistant Salt Controller, BH 835A

DABSUN TUCIRE BA   an area where salt is produced, a salt mine

DABSUN TUYEKU YONGGAN   ammonium chloride

DABTA   a gluepot

DABTABUMBI   caus. of *dabtambi*

DABTAMBI   1. to do repeatedly, to do over a long period of time   2. to pile up (v.i.)   3. to repeat over and over in order to instill, to din into   4. to beat metal thin

DABTARA FOLHO   a hammer for beating metal

DABTAN   again, repeatedly--see *dahūn dabtan i*

DABUBUMBI   caus. of *dabumbi*

DABUKŪ   fire lighter, small stove, burner

DABUMBI   1. caus. of *dambi*   2. to light (a fire or lamp)   3. to figure in with, to take into account, to include, to consider   4. to be injured

DABUME   including, comprising

DABURAKŪ   not included, not taken into account

DACAKŪ   a wide hair ornament worn in the chignon of Sibe women

DACI   1. from the beginning, once upon a time, formerly, hitherto   2. by itself, by nature

DACI DUBEDE ISITALA   from beginning to end

DACILABUMBI   caus. of *dacilambi*

DACILAMBI   to inquire, to seek information, to find out

DACILANJIMBI   to come to inquire

DACUKAN   rather sharp

DACUN   sharp, shrewd, decisive, resolute

DACUN JEYENGGE AMBA JANGKŪ   a very sharp large sword

DACUN SUKDUN   spirit, high morale (especially of troops)

DACUNGGA   sharp

DADAGE   interjection of affection used when patting an old person or a child on the back

DADARAMBI   to open (the mouth), to open wide, to expand

DADARI   a trap for weasels and marmots

DADE   1. originally, at first, in the beginning   2. (postposition) in addition to

DADU MOO   gangplank

DADUN   1. lame   2. without hands or feet

DAFAHA   chum salmon(*Oncorhynchus keta*)

DAFUN   an arrow wound

DAFUN EHE   the arrow wound is too shallow (not deep enough to kill)

DAFUN SAIN   the arrow wound is deep (deep enough to kill)

DAGILABUMBI   caus. of *dagilambi*

DAGILAMBI   to prepare, to get ready, to set out wine or food

DAHABUMBI   1. caus. of *dahambi*   2. to subdue, to subjugate   3. to recommend a person possessing a special talent or merit for a high post, without the official examination   4. to paint, to decorate with

DAHABURE AFAHA   receipt, bill, list of merchandise

DAHABURE AFAHARI   a note containing an order of the emperor inserted into a memorial to the throne

DAHABURE GISUN TUCIBUMBI   to give a

D

grade on the official examination

DAHACAMBI   1. to follow together   2. to receive, to meet   3. to obey

DAHALABUMBI   caus. of *dahalambi*

DAHALAMBI   1. to follow, to pursue, to run down   2. to bring a countersuit against

DAHALANJIMBI   to come following

DAHALASI   follower, servant

DAHALI   1. the second, the next   2. in playing with the *gacuha*, the second bone thrown

   DAHALI SONJOSI (榜 眼) number two in the imperial examination, BH 629C

DAHALJI   a manservant under a life contract

DAHALTU   orderly, manservant

DAHAMBI   (perfect participle *daha*) 1. to follow   2. to submit, to surrender   3. to obey

   DAHAME (postposition) because, since

DAHAN   a horse from two to five years old

DAHANCAMBI   to follow together, to obey together

DAHANDUHAI   1. before long, in a while, shortly, subsequently   2. one after another, in succession

DAHANDUMBI/DAHANUMBI   to follow after one another

DAHANJIMBI   to come following, to come to surrender

DAHARALAME   following, attending

DAHASHŪN   1. obedient   2. posthumous title for the wife of an official of the seventh order

DAHASI   a granary attendant

DAHASU   obedient, docile

DAHATA   a leather bag affixed inside a quiver to hold arrowheads

DAHIBUMBI   caus. of *dahimbi*

DAHIMBI   to repeat, to do again

   DAHIME   again, same as *dahin, dahūme*

DAHIN   again

   DAHIN DAHIN   repeatedly, again and again

DAHŪ   a fur coat worn with the fur outside

DAHŪBUMBI   caus. of *dahūmbi*

DAHŪLAMBI   to wear a *dahū*

DAHŪMBI   1. to repeat, to do again   2. to repair a torn mat

   DAHŪME   again

DAHŪN   again, repeatedly

   DAHŪN DABTAN I   repeatedly

   DAHŪN DAHŪN I   repeatedly, time after time

DAI JOO (待 詔)   clerk of the Court Chancery

DAI MEI   tortoise shell

DAI ŠENG   the hoopoe; cf. *indahūn cecike*

DAI TUNG DOOHAN I TUWAME KADALARA HAFAN I YAMUN (大 通 橋 監 督 衙 門)   the office of the grain transport inspector at Ta-t'ung bridge

DAIBIHAN   1. frame, casement   2. border or edging on quivers and bags

DAICILAMBI   to run at an angle, to run askew

DAICING   the Manchu dynasty

DAIDAN DOHOLON   a type of sour-tasting wild vegetable with willowlike leaves

DAIFAHA   a fence made of reeds and willow branches

DAIFAN (大 夫)   a high official in ancient times

DAIFASA   plural of *daifan*

DAIFU   medical doctor

   DAIFU I DORO   medicine (the study)

DAIFULAMBI   see *daifurambi*

DAIFURABUMBI   caus. of *daifurambi*

DAIFURAMBI   to treat, to practice medicine

   DAIFURARA BITHE   a medicine book

DAIFUSA   plural of *daifu*

DAIHAN   a fish weir

DAILABUMBI   caus./pass. of *dailambi*

DAILAMBI   1. to make war against, to undertake a punitive expedition against   2. to be mad, to be possessed

   DAILAHA INDAHŪN   a mad dog

DAILAN   a military campaign, a punitive expedition

DAILANABUMBI   caus. of *dailanambi*

DAILANAMBI   to go to make war against, to go to make a punitive expedition against

DAILANDUMBI/DAILANUMBI   to make war against one another

DAILANJIMBI   to come on a punitive expedition against

DAIN   1. troops, army   2. war, battle

   DAIN COOHA   troops, army

   DAIN I HAHA   a warrior, soldier

DAIPUN   a mythical great bird, the roc

DAISELABUMBI   caus. of *daiselambi*

DAISELAMBI   to substitute for someone, to take over a post temporarily

DAIŠAMBI   to act like a madman, to rave, to rage

DAKDA DAKDA   in great leaps

DAKDA DIKDI   the same as *dakda dakda*

DAKDAHŪN   1. curled upward, suspended upward   2. too short (of clothes that have curled upward)

DAKDARI   suddenly, unexpectedly, first

DAKDARŠAMBI   1. to jump (up on)   2. to act in an aggressive manner

DAKSA   a misdeed

DAKSIN   see *daksa*

DAKŪ   see *uhe dakū*

DAKŪLA   the skin on the belly of a fish or animal

DALABUMBI caus. of *dalambi*
DALACI foreman, leader
DALAMBI 1. to be leader, to be at the head 2. to measure in cubits
DALAN 1. withers 2. dam, dike
DALANGGA dam, dike, pertaining to a dam or dike
DALBA side
  DALBAI BOO side wings of a house
  DALBAI MOO running boards on the outside of the railing of a ship
DALBAKI on the side, located at the side(s)
DALBARAME along the side
DALBASHŪN on the side, lying on its side
  DALBASHŪN DEDUMBI to lie on the side
DALBU dart, pin, peg
DALDA secluded, hidden spot
DALDABUMBI caus. of *daldambi*
DALDAHAN 1. a leather cover for a football (*mumuhu*) 2. a flat piece of bone used as a falcon's perch
DALDAKŪ 1. a screen, a veil 2. a curtain hung over the entrance of houses when the emperor passed
DALDAMBI to hide from view, to screen, to cover
DALDANGGA a protective wall erected in back of a door
DALDASHŪN covered, hidden
DALGAN piece, lump, fragment
  DALGAN BOIHON clod of earth
  DALGAN DALGAN I piece by piece, in pieces
DALGANAMBI to form a lump, to form pieces
DALGIYAN WEHE red ocher
DALHAN see *dalgan*
DALHI repetitious, annoying, tedious
DALHIDAMBI to be repetitious, to be tedious
DALHIHANAMBI to become crumbly, to harden (of fat)
DALHŪDAMBI to prattle on and on
DALHŪKAN rather sticky, bothersome, annoying
DALHŪN 1. sticky 2. annoying, bothersome, too talkative
  DALHŪN CIFENGGU sputum
DALHŪWAN a sticky pole used for catching birds
DALIBUMBI 1. caus. of *dalimbi* 2. to cover over
DALIBUN 1. shelter, refuge 2. obstacle
DALIKŪ screen, covering, a protective screen by a doorway, a protective covering, a shelter
  DALIKŪ UCE a storm door
DALIMBI 1. to block off, to obstruct, to screen off, to seal, to cover up, to conceal, to protect 2. to force an animal back into a battue 3. to

drive (a wagon)
DALIN shore, riverbank, limit
  DALIN AKŪ limitless
DALIRAME along the shore, along a riverbank
DALITUNGGA MAHATUN a hat worn by military officials in ancient times
DALIYAN 1. a kind of folding pouch worn over the girdle, a satchel 2. a wrestler's garment woven from coarse heavy fiber
DALJAKŪ unconnected with, unrelated
DALJI relation, bearing, connection
  DALJI AKŪ unconnected, unrelated; cf. *daljakū*
DALJINGGA related to, concerned with
DALUKAN bothersome, annoying
DALUMBI to adhere tightly--as bark to a tree or hair to the skin of a scalded slaughtered animal
DAMBAGU tobacco
  DAMBAGU GOCIKŪ a pipe (for smoking)
  DAMBAGU GOCIMBI to smoke (tobacco)
  DAMBAGU OMIMBI same as *dambagu gocimbi*
  DAMBAGU TEBUMBI to put tobacco (in a pipe)
DAMBI 1. to burn (v.i.) 2. to blow (of the wind), to rain, to snow 3. to take care of, to care about 4. to mind someone else's business, to interfere 5. to operate, to work (v.i.) 6. to help
DAMBUMBI 1. caus. of *dambi* 2. to add, to apply (medicine)
DAMDAN a trillion
DAMIN eagle, vulture
DAMJALABUMBI caus. of *damjalambi*
DAMJALAMBI 1. to carry on a pole 2. to pierce through with an arrow
DAMJAN a carrying pole, a carrying-pole load
  DAMJAN SEBSEHE an insect resembling a grasshopper with a fat body and long wings
  DAMJAN SELE a window or door latch
DAMJATALA clear through, clean through (of an arrow)
DAMNAMBI to sift, to strain
DAMTULABUMBI caus. of *damtulambi*
DAMTULAMBI to pawn
  DAMTULARA PUSELI pawnshop
  DAMTULARA PUSELI I CIFUN pawnbroker's tax
DAMTUN an article for pawning, a hostage
  DAMTUN WERIMBI to leave behind as a hostage
DAMU only, but
DAN a snare for wild fowl, wolves, and foxes
DAN DABURAKŪ without noticing someone,

to pay no attention (to other
people)

DAN BI AMBA KUMUN musical compositions
played while foreign dignitaries
and emissaries ascended the steps to
the throne room

DAN MU sandalwood; see *cakūran*

DANAHŪN CECIKE one name for the hoopoe; cf. *indahūn cecike*

DANAMBI to go to take care of, to go
to aid

DANARA HAFAN (都 司) First
Captain BH 752C

DANCALAMBI for a bride to visit her
parents' home for the first time
after marriage

DANCAN the wife's family

DANCAN I BOO the wife's family

DANCARAMBI see *dancalambi*

DANG only, just

DANG SEME only

DANGDAKA stretched out, with legs extended

DANGDALI a dragnet used for catching
fish

DANGDALILAMBI to use a *dangdali* in
fishing

DANGGA elder, belonging to the older
generation

DANGGASA plural of *dangga*

DANGGI at least, a little bit

DANGGIRI a small brass gong hung from
a crook--used by Buddhist monks

DANGKAN a hereditary house slave

DANGNABUMBI caus. of *dangnambi*

DANGNAHAN the soles of shoes and boots

DANGNAMBI 1. to substitute, to replace
2. to oppose, to pit against

DANGNACI OJORAKŪ irreplaceable

DANGNIYABUMBI caus. of *dangniyambi*

DANGNIYAMBI to kick a football (*mumuhu*)

DANGPULI a pawnshop

DANGSAHA an open-topped birchbark basket

DANGSE records, document, register,
archive, the census register

DANGSE ASARARA KUNGGERI (檔 科)
archives office of the Board of
Works

DANGSE BAITAI BOO (檔 案 房)
office of documentary affairs

DANGSE BARGIYARA HAFAN (典 籍)
Sub-Archivist, BH 412A, 413A

DANGSE BARGIYARA TINGGIN (典 籍
廳) archives office, records
office

DANGSE CI HŪWAKIYAMBI to expunge
from the banner roll

DANGSE EFULERE BA (註 銷 處)
section for the disposal of records

DANGSE EJERE HAFAN (典 簿)
Archivist, BH 412A, 413A

DANGSE EJERE TINGGIN (典 籍 廳)
Record Office, BH 202 etc.

DANGSE FAKSALAMBI to remove from the
family register, to expunge from
the census register

DANGSE JAFAŠAKŪ (主 簿) Registrar, BH 220, etc.

DANGSE JAFAŠARA HAFAN (主 簿)
Registrar, BH 220, etc.

DANGSE JAFAŠARA KUNGGERI (司 業
科) registry section of the Office of the Gendarmerie

DANGSE JAFAŠARA TINGGIN (主 簿
廳) registry office

DANGSIBUMBI caus. of *dangsimbi*

DANGSIMBI to reprove, to censure

DANGŠAN blade of grass, chaff, thread
ends

DANIYALABUMBI caus. of *daniyalambi*

DANIYALABUHA WAI I BA a curve or
recess offering protection

DANIYALAMBI to seek cover from, to go
to for protection

DANIYAMBI see *daniyalambi*

DANIYAN cover, refuge, safe place,
protection

DANJIMBI to come to take care of, to
come to aid

DANOSG'A ILHA *Achyranthes aspera*

DANUMBI to care for one another, to
aid one another

DAR SEME shivering

DAR SEME ŠURGEMBI to shake from
cold or fright

DARA waist, lower back

DARA COOHA reserves (troops), relief troops

DARA GOLOMBI to have an ache in the
lower back

DARABUBUMBI caus. of *darabumbi*

DARABUMBI to invite to drink, to offer
a toast, to serve (wine)

DARAMA waist, midsection

DARAMBI (-ka) 1. to draw taut (a bow)
2. to train (falcons, dogs, etc.),
to tame 3. to tease, to taunt

DARAMBUMBI to train (falcons, dogs,
etc.)

DARANAMBI to go to draw a bow

DARANG SEME long and straight, outstretched

DARANG SEME DEDUMBI to lie
stretched out full length

DARANUMBI to invite one another to
drink, to toast one another

DARASU an undistilled Mongolian
liquor

DARAŠAMBI to stretch a bow fully taut

DARBAHŪN lying straight on the back

DARBALJI sparrow hawk (*Accipiter
nisus*)

DARDAHA ephemerid

D

DARDAN satin with golden threads interwoven

DARDAN SEME trembling
DARDAN SEME ŠURGEMBI to shiver from cold

DARGALABUMBI caus./pass. of *dargalambi*

DARGALAMBI to grant privileges
DARGALAHA AMBAN a dignitary who has retired with full pay

DARGIMBI to shake, to tremble

DARGIYA jugular veins

DARGIYAMBI to hold up the fists, to brandish (a sword or staff)

DARGŪWAN a wooden hoe
DARGŪWAN YANGSAMBI to hoe with a wooden hoe

DARHA CECIKE North China wren (*Troglodytes troglodytes*)

DARHŪWA reed
DARHŪWA CECIKE see *darha cecike*

DARHŪWAN 1. pole, staff 2. plowing stick 3. the beam of a balance 4. the same as *dargūwan*

DARI (postposition) each, every

DARIBUMBI caus. of *darimbi*

DARIMBI (-ka/ha) 1. to scrape against, to rub a sore (of horses) 2. to pass through, to drop by, to perform an errand or other action on one's way somewhere else or while doing something else 3. to make fun of, to mock 4. to roar (of thunder)

DARIMBUMBI to develop a sore by rubbing; cf. *darubumbi*

DARIN a sore caused by rubbing, a saddle sore

DARINAMBI to drop in on, to pay a casual visit

DARKA CECIKE snipe; cf. *karka cecike*

DARMALAME along the back

DARTAI 1. suddenly 2. temporarily
DARTAI ANDANDE suddenly, in a moment
DARTAI DE suddenly

DARUBUMBI 1. caus. of *darumbi* 2. to be obligated 3. to develop friction sores 4. to be prone to frequent illnesses

DARUDAI one name for the phoenix

DARUGAN see *darhūwan*

DARUHAI often, continually, regularly
DARUHAI HŪSUN a person engaged for long-term labor

DARUMBI 1. to buy on credit 2. to last, to endure 3. to recognize mistakenly
DARUHA URUN a daughter-in-law taken into the home as a child

DARUN 1. a watering spot 2. a landing spot for canoes

DASA plural of *da*

DASABUMBI caus. of *dasambi*

DASAKŪ corrector, something used to

repair another thing

DASAMBI 1. to rule 2. to correct 3. to cure 4. to repair
DASAHA JUGŪN a road prepared for the emperor

DASAME again

DASAN rule, government, control
DASAN BE HAFUMBURE YAMUN (通政使司) Transmission Office, BH 928
DASAN BE SELGIYERE HAFAN (布政使) Lieutenant-Governor or Financial Commissioner, BH 825, etc.

DASANGGA keeping order, having talent for government

DASARGAN a prescription, a formula

DASARHAN see *dasargan*

DASARTUNGGA pertaining to a reformer

DASATAMBI to put in order, to arrange

DASHŪWAN a bow case
DASHŪWAN DUBE (五甲刺) the fifth *jalan*
DASHŪWAN GALA (東四旗) the left wing of the eight banners
DASHŪWAN I MUHEREN a ring on a bow case
DASHŪWAN MEIREN (四甲刺) the fourth *jalan*

DASHŪWATU (左軍) adjutant of the left battalion

DASIBUMBI caus./pass. of *dasimbi*

DASIHI dust, dirt

DASIHIKŪ GASHA a bird of prey

DASIHIMBI 1. to swoop down and seize (of birds of prey) 2. to immolate
DASIHIRE HAFAN (遊擊) Major, BH 752B

DASIHIYABUMBI caus. of *dasihiyambi*

DASIHIYAKŪ a feather duster

DASIHIYAMBI to dust with a feather duster

DASIKŪ a cover, a top

DASIMBI to cover, to shut

DASIN handle, grip

DASITAMBI to conceal, to gloss over

DASU children
DASU MAKTAMBI to use felled trees as a defense against enemy arrows

DASUKŪ fish hawk, osprey; cf. *suksuhu*

DASUMBI to lead a dissolute life

DAŠOSE boy, lad, servant boy

DAŠURAMBI to harm, to damage

DAŠURAN damage, harm

DATA plural of *da*

DATSAI FAKSI one who decorated houses on festivals

DATSAILAMBI to decorate houses during a festival

DAYABUMBI 1. caus./pass. of *dayambi* 2. to execute

DAYACAMBI to depend on together

DAYAMBI to be dependent on, to rely on (someone else's power or influence),

D

to attach oneself to someone for gain

DAYANAMBI to go to depend on

DAYANCAMBI to shake the head (of horses)

DAYANDUMBI/DAYANUMBI to depend on one another

DAYANJIMBI to come to rely on

DE the dative-locative particle

DEB SEME everywhere

DEBDEREMBI to beat, to flap (wings)

DEBDERŠEMBI to beat the wings vigorously

DEBE DABA swarming (of insects)

DEBEMBI (-ke) to overflow, to run over
DEBERE BE GIDARA JAHŪDAI a boat used at flood time

DEBEN overflowing, flooding

DEBEREN the young of animals
DEBEREN GŪLIN CECIKE a small Chinese oriole; cf. *gūlin cecike*

DEBEYE ORHO moss, lichen

DEBKEBUMBI caus. of *debkembi*

DEBKEJEMBI to come loose, to come unraveled; cf. *subhejembi*

DEBKELEBUMBI caus. of *debkelembi*

DEBKELEMBI to untwist, to unravel

DEBKEMBI to bring up again, to take up again

DEBSE 1. a cake made of fruit 2. a ceremonial arrow used by shamans

DEBSEHUN drooping (eyelids), sleepy-looking

DEBSEREMBI to droop (of the eyelids)

DEBSIBUKU cloth of a flag or banner; cf. *wadan*

DEBSIKU fan (made of feathers)

DEBSILEMBI to tower above, to go before

DEBSIMBI to fan, to flap, to flutter
DEBSIRE GARUNGGŪ KIRU a banner depicting a soaring phoenix

DEBSIN fanning, flapping

DEBSITEMBI to fan continually, to flutter continually

DEBŠIMBI see *debsimbi*

DEBTELEBUMBI caus. of *debtelembi*

DEBTELEMBI to untangle, to unravel

DEBTELIN a volume (of an old-style book), a book, a notebook
DEBTELIN I BURGIYEN cover of a book

DEBUMBI caus. of *dembi*

DEDE DADA restless

DEDENGGI frivolous, loose in behavior (of women)

DEDUBUMBI 1. caus. of *dedumbi* 2. to let lie, to put to rest 3. to put to bed 4. to rise (of dough), to leaven

DEDUCEMBI to lie down together, to sleep together

DEDUMBI 1. to lie down, to lie 2. to spend the night (with) 3. (v.t.) to bed, to take to bed (a woman)

DEDURE BIYA month of confinement after parturition

DEDURE BOO bedroom

DEDUN 1. an overnight stopping place, a post station 2. one day of a journey

DEDUNEBUMBI caus. of *dedunembi*

DEDUNEMBI to go to spend the night

DEDUNGGE HENGKETU an insignia of a reclining melon on wood (used by the imperial guard)

DEFE 1. a measure for cloth, a bolt (of cloth) 2. border, hem

DEFELINGGU bolt (of cloth)

DEFELIYEMBI (-ke) to lie in strips

DEFERE an edible fernlike wild plant (*Dryopteris crassirhizoma*)

DEFU bean curd; cf. *turi miyehu*

DEHE fishhook

DEHEBUMBI caus. of *dehembi*

DEHELE a short sleeveless jacket, a fur riding jacket

DEHELEMBI (-ke), to catch with a hook

DEHELEN a short sleeveless jacket

DEHELI SONJOSI (探花) third in the court examination

DEHEMA husband of mother's sister--uncle

DEHEMATA plural of *dehema*

DEHEMBI 1. to refine, to smelt, to temper 2. to cure (tobacco)
DEHEHE AISIN refined gold

DEHEME mother's younger sister--aunt

DEHEMETE plural of *deheme*

DEHEN refining, smelting, curing

DEHENGGE ŠURUKŪ a boat hook

DEHEREMBI to stir up, to rouse

DEHI forty

DEHICI fortieth

DEHIMBI see *dehembi*

DEHITE forty each

DEHUREMBI to search everywhere

DEIDE black buckwheat flour, whole buckwheat flour

DEIJIBUMBI caus./pass. of *deijimbi*

DEIJIKU firewood
DEIJIKU BE KEMNERE KŪWARAN (惜薪廠) storage place for fuel in the Board of Works

DEIJIMBI to burn

DEIJIN burning
DEIJIN I HIJA a vessel used for burning offerings (e.g., paper money)
DEIJIN I UKDUN a kiln for tile and bricks

DEISUN waistband (of skirts and trousers)

DEJI 1. choicest (part), the cream, the best part 2. the first portion offered as a sacrifice to the deities or to the guest of honor

DEJI BUMBI to offer the choicest part to one's elders or superiors

DEJI JAFAMBI to take the best or choice part

DEK SEME rising, beginning

DEKDE DAKDA up and down, uneven

DEKDEBUMBI 1. caus. of *dekdembi* 2. to reappear, to rise again

DEKDEHUN 1. somewhat high, rather high 2. upward

DEKDEKU float on a fishing pole, float for an oil lamp

DEKDEKU DOOHAN a pontoon bridge, a floating bridge

DEKDELEMBI to get up, to spring up

DEKDELJEMBI to start (from fright while sleeping)

DEKDEMBI to float, to rise

DEKDEN floating, rising

DEKDEN I GISUN 1. everyday saying 2. baseless talk, gossip

DEKDEN I HENDUHENGGE as the saying goes . . .

DEKDENGGE exalted

DEKDENGGI the fat that floats to the surface of water in which meat is boiled

DEKDENI GISUN see *dekden i gisun*

DEKDERHŪN one name for the seagull; cf. *kilahūn*

DEKDERILEMBI to rise high

DEKDERŠEMBI to be deluded, to be carried away over something, to be crazy

DEKE see *deken*

DEKEN 1. rather high 2. a *mu*--approximately one sixth of an acre 3. a rise, a high place

DEKIMBI see *deijimbi*

DEKJIMBI (-ke) 1. to develop, to improve, to prosper 2. to burn

DEKJIRE JALUNGGA NAMUN (將盈庫) depository for the salt and post administration

DEKJIN developing, prospering

DEKJIN TUWA prairie fire, forest fire

DEKSITEMBI to be uneasy

DELBIN brim of a hat

DELE 1. top, on top 2. the emperor

DELE HARGAŠAMBI to have an audience with the emperor

DELEJEN a courtyard without walls or moats

DELEKEN rather high or superior, somewhat over

DELEMBI to catch in a noose

DELEN udder, teat

DELEREMBI to come apart at the joints (of wooden objects)

DELERI 1. top, surface 2. superficial,

careless 3. uppermost

DELESI superficial

DELFERI rash, hasty, careless

DELFIN see *delfiyen*

DELFIYEN too wide, loose, baggy (of clothes and hats)

DELGE see *delhe*

DELHE one hundred *ch'ing* (頃)

DELHEBUMBI 1. caus. of *delhembi* 2. to cut up (a slaughtered animal)

DELHEMBI to divide, to separate

DELHEN 1. the same as *delhe* 2. dividing, separation

DELHENTUMBI to make one's last will and testament

DELHENTUHE GISUN will, testament

DELHETU NIRU the same as *booi niru*

DELI WEHE a large stone, a boulder in a stream

DELIHUN spleen

DELIHUN MADAMBI to swell (the belly of a horse)

DELIŠEMBI to overflow, to be overabundant

DELIYEHUN see *delihun*

DELIYEMBI to burn

DELMECEMBI to warn

DELULEMBI to grab the mane of a horse

DELULEME FIYELEMBI to trick ride while grabbing the mane

DELUN mane

DELUN GIDAME FIYELEMBI to trick ride while pressing down on the horse's mane

DEMBEI greatly, in high degree, exceedingly

DEMBI 1. to calculate, to reckon 2. to take one's turn at duty

DEMESI braggart, boaster

DEMESIKU boasting

DEMESILEMBI to swagger, to act boastfully

DEMNIYEBUMBI caus. of *demniyembi*

DEMNIYECEMBI to shake, to rock (of a sedan chair)

DEMNIYELEMBI to stretch one's self

DEMNIYEMBI to estimate the weight of an object by weighing it in the hand

DEMSI see *demesi*

DEMTU (斗) the Big Dipper

DEMTU TOKDONGGO KIRU (斗宿旗) a banner depicting the Big Dipper

DEMULEMBI to be strange, to act strangely

DEMUN 1. odd, peculiar, heretical 2. trick

DEMUNGGE 1. strange, peculiar, heretical 2. monster, odd creature

DEMUNGGE FEKSIN trick riding

DEN 1. high, tall 2. loud

DEN BOJIRI ILHA sunflower

D

DEN JILGAN I in a loud voice
DEN I ICI upward
DEN TU direction pennant
DENDEBUMBI caus. of *dendembi*
DENDECEMBI to divide with one another, to share with one another
DENDEMBI to divide, to share
DENDEME KADALARA YAMUN (分司) a suboffice of some larger unit
DENDEME TACIBURE HAFAN (學錄) Sub-Registrar, BH 412A
DENDEN DANDAN step by step
DENDENUMBI to share together
DENG lamp, lantern
DENG LUNG lantern
DENG TSOO wick
DENG DENG SEME gagging, choking
DENG SEME stuck (for a word), exhausted, at wit's end
DENG SEME ILIMBI to stop from exhaustion (of horses)
DENG SEME OHO stuck for words, at wit's end
DENGGE glorious
DENGGEBUMBI caus. of *denggembi*
DENGGELJEMBI to shake, to reel
DENGGEMBI to throw far, to fling, to send flying, to throw (in wrestling)
DENGJAN lamp, light
DENGJAN DABUMBI to light a lamp, to turn on a light
DENGJAN I SINDAKŪ a lampstand
DENGJANGGA pertaining to lamps or lights
DENGJI ORHO bulrush
DENGLU lantern; cf. *deng, deng lung*
DENGLUNG see *denglu*
DENGNEBUMBI caus. of *dengnembi*
DENGNEHEN the leg of a boot
DENGNEKU a small steelyard
DENGNEMBI to weigh on a small steelyard, to balance, to compete with
DENGNIYEMBI to play with the football (*mumuhu*)
DENGSE a small steelyard
DENGSE I ILGA a steelyard weight
DENGSELEBUMBI caus. of *dengselembi*
DENGSELEMBI to weigh on a small steelyard; cf. *dengnembi*
DENGSIBUMBI caus. of *dengsimbi*
DENGSIMBI to rattle, to vibrate, to bump along (of a carriage)
DENGSITEMBI to tremble (from fright), to shake, to vibrate up and down
DENGTSOO wick
DEO 1. younger brother 2. younger (of males)
DEOCILEBUMBI caus. of *deocilembi*
DEOCILEMBI to perform the duties proper to a younger brother, to show fraternal deference
DEOCIN duty of a younger brother, fraternal deference

DEOCINGGE one who is assiduous in performing the duties of a younger brother
DEOCY fermented bean paste
DEONE a four-year-old bovine
DEOTE plural of *deo*
DEOTELEMBI to behave like a younger brother
DER DAR SEME many, very
DER SEME 1. in profusion, many 2. snow-white
DERAKŪ without shame, without face, shameless
DERAKŪLAMBI to act shamelessly, to insult
DERAKŪNGGE shameless
DERBEBUMBI caus. of *derbembi*
DERBEHUN damp, moist
DERBEHUN SUKDUN damp air
DERBEMBI to be damp, to become damp
DERBEMBUMBI to become wet or damp
DERCILEMBI to lay out a corpse, to prepare a corpse for burial
DERDEN DARDAN shaking, vibrating
DERDEN DARDAN AŠŠAMBI to shake, to vibrate
DERDEN SEME shaking, trembling
DERDU a bib worn next to the skin over the breasts
DERDU CECIKE a small bird resembling a thrush
DERDUHI camphor
DERE 1. face 2. 'face,' reputation, honor 3. table 4. surface 5. direction, area 6. a measure word for flat objects 7. (sentence particle) probably, likely
DERE ACAMBI to meet
DERE BANIMBI see *dere banjimbi*
DERE BANJIMBI to take 'face' into account, to have a regard for personal friendship, to act from personal motives
DERE EFULEMBI to have a falling out with, to quarrel with a friend
DERE FAN DASAMBI to set out a table (of food or delicacies)
DERE FELEMBI to disregard 'face,' to act without shame
DERE FUNCEBURAKŪ to have no way to save face
DERE FUSIMBI to shave (the whiskers)
DERE GAIMBI to act for motives of honor, to stand up for one's honor
DERE MANGGA shameless, bold
DERE SILEMIN the face looks silly
DERE ŠEHUN thick-skinned, impervious to embarrassment
DERE ŠEHUN GIRURAKŪ same as *dere mangga*
DERE TOKOME in the presence of, facing, in person, personally

E

DERE WALIYABUMBI to lose face
DERE WALIYATAMBI to lose face, to
  form a grudge against
DEREI genitive/instrumental of *dere*,
  see *emu derei*, *ai derei*
DEREI BANGTU ornaments on the cor-
  ners of a table
DEREI BETHE a table leg
DEREI HAŠAHAN tablecloth, table
  cover
DEREI SIDEHUN table support
DEREI TALGARI table top
DERECUKE see *derencuke*
DERENCUKE decorous, proper
DERENCUMBI to treat with partiality
  because of a personal relationship
DERENG DARANG sanctimonious, feigning
  propriety, barely able to behave
  properly
DERENGGE decorous, proper, noble (in
  one's actions)
  DERENGGE JAN a square hunting
    arrow having a hole on each of its
    four sides
DERENGTU portrait
DERESU feather grass, broom grass
  (*Lasiagrostis splendens*)
DERETU long table, long desk
DERGE erect, straight
  DERGE SIMHUN the index finger
DERGI 1. top, above, over 2. upper
  3. east, eastern 4. emperor
  DERGI ABKA heaven above
  DERGI ADUN I JURGAN (上駟院)
    the Palace Stud, BH 88
  DERGI AMBA FUKJINGGA HERGEN (上
    方大篆) a type of seal
    script
  DERGI AMSU CAI I BOO BE UHERI KADAL-
    ARA BA (總管御膳房茶
    房處) office in charge of
    the Imperial Buttery; cf. BH 91
  DERGI ASARI eastern tower, another
    name for the *Dorgi Yamun*
  DERGI ASHAN BOO the eastern side
    room
  DERGI BITHE FOLORO BA (御書處)
    the Imperial Library, BH 94A
  DERGI BITHEI BOO (尚書房)
    study room for the young princes
    (the emperor's sons)
  DERGI BITHEI TAKTU (御書樓)
    imperial library
  DERGI BUTHAI HACIN BELHERE BA (上
    虞備用處) the Imperial
    Hunting Department, BH 733
  DERGI COLHON I KIRU (東嶽處)
    a blue banner depicting the form
    of a mountain
  DERGI EJEN emperor
  DERGI ERGI the east, eastern direc-
    tion
  DERGI ERGI MUNGGAN I BAITA BE ALIFI

  ICIHIYARA YAMUN (東陵承辦
    事務衙門) adminis-
    tration of the Eastern Tombs
  DERGI ERGI MUNGGAN I BOOI AMBAN I
    YAMUN (東陵内務府總
    管衙門) office of
    the superintendent of the Eastern
    Tombs
  DERGI ERGI MUNGGAN I WEILERE JURGAN
    (東陵工部) board of
    works of the Eastern Tombs
  DERGI ERGI SIMNERE BITHEI KŪWARAN
    name of a small gatehouse to the
    left of the Ming-Yüan tower in the
    examination Hall
  DERGI FEMEN the upper lip
  DERGI FIYENTEN (更司) Eastern
    Section of the Imperial Equipage
    Department, BH 122
  DERGI GURUNG NI BAITA BE ALIHA YAMUN
    (詹事府) Supervisorate of
    Imperial Instruction, BH 929
  DERGI GURUNG NI BAITA BE ALIHA YAMUN
    I ALIHA HAFAN (詹事府詹
    事) Chief Supervisor of Instruc-
    tion, BH 929
  DERGI GURUNG NI BAITA BE ALIHA YAMUN
    I ILHI HAFAN (詹事府少詹
    事) Supervisor of Instruc-
    tion, BH 929
  DERGI HESE imperial edict
  DERGI HESE BE GINGGULEME DAHARA
  BAITA HACIN BE KIMCIME BAICARA BA
    (稽察欽奉上諭事件
    處) Chancery for the publi-
    cation of Imperial Edicts, BH 105A
  DERGI HORON BE BADARAMBURE MUDAN a
    musical piece played after the
    emperor had inspected the troops
  DERGI HOŠO the east
  DERGI NAHAN the eastern *kang* (oven-
    bed), located against the west wall
    of a house; this was considered
    the *kang* of honor
  DERGI OKTOI BOO (御藥房)
    the Imperial Dispensary, BH 92
  DERGI ŠONGGE INENGGI the first day
    of the month
DERGIKEN somewhat upper, superior, or
  high
DERGINGGE eastern, upper
DERGIŠEMBI see *derkišembi*
DERGUWE see *derhuwe*
DERHI a straw or rush mat
  DERHI ORHO moss
DERHUWE a fly
  DERHUWE BAŠAKŪ fly whisk, fly swat-
    ter
  DERHUWE IJA horse fly
DERI (ablative particle) from, than
DERIBUMBI 1. caus. of *derimbi* 2. to
  begin, to let begin 3. to conjure
  up, to think up (a plan) 4. to play

D

D

(music)

DERIBUME ILIBURE KUNGGERI (開 設 科) bureau concerned with promotions and discharges in the Board of Civil Appointments

DERIBURE FIYENTEHE (起 股) the section following the introduction in a formal essay

DERIBURE GIYANGNAN (起 講) the third part of a formal essay

DERIBUN beginning

DERIBUN DUBEN beginning and end

DERIBUNGGILEMBI to make a beginning

DERIBUŠEMBI to begin, to originate

DERIMBI (-ke) 1. to dim (of the eyesight) 2. to have a change of heart 3. to enter

DERISHUN 1. changed (in heart) 2. cruel

DERKIMBI to soar high, to hover over

DERKIŠEMBI to flutter in the wind

DERSEN pure, genuine, unmixed

DERSEN GABSIHIYARI a type of swift dog

DERSEN HOOŠAN a type of pure white paper--'white crane paper'

DERTU CECIKE a small bird resembling a starling; named *dertu* from its note

DESEREKE overflowing, expansive

DESEREMBI (-ke, -pi) to overflow (in great quantity)

DESEREPI overflowing, superabundant

DESI upward

DESI WASI up and down, all around

DESIHI a snare for sable and similar animals

DESIHIMBI to throw down with both hands (at wrestling)

DESIKU a shamanistic arrow with a tuft of flowering maple (*Abutilon avicennae*) tied to it

DESUNGGIYEMBI 1. to scream in a loud voice 2. to stir up dust

DETHE 1. pinion 2. arrow feathers

DETHENGGE KILTAN (羽 葆 幢) a pennant having five red tassels

DETU marsh, swamp

DETU DAMBI the swampland is being burned off (in preparation for cultivation)

DEYEBUMBI caus. of *deyembi*

DEYEMBI to fly

DEYERE CUWAN an airplane

DEYERE DOBI 1. flying squirrel (genus *Sciuropterus*) 2. a bat

DEYERE GÜWASIHIYANGGA KIRU (振 鷺 旗) a banner embroidered with the image of a heron

DEYERE SINGGERI a flying squirrel (genus *Sciuropterus*)

DEYERE ŠANYANGGA FUKJINGGA HERGEN (飛 白 書) a style of calligraphy

DEYEN palace, great hall, throne room

DEYEN BOO main hall of a temple

DEYEN DE SIMNEMBI to take the palace examination

DEYEN DE TEMBI to take one's place in the throne room (for an audience)

DEYENGGE flying, airborne

DEYENGGU 1. a kite (toy) 2. choral singing

DEYENGGULEMBI to sing in unison

DI (帝) god

DIGI a hairnet

DILBIHE (氐) the name of a constellation

DILBIHE TOKDONGGO KIRU (氐 宿 旗) a banner of the escort having the constellation *dilbihe* depicted upon it

DING HIYANG lilac (*Syringa vulgaris*)

DINGSE ORHO a grass that grows in clumps, has narrow leaves and yellow blossoms; flour made from its dried roots mixed with wheat flour and egg white serves as a foot salve

DISE draft (of a document or essay)

DISELAMBI to make a draft

DIYAN 1. palace, throne room, great hall 2. hostel, inn

DIYAN DE TEMBI to take one's place in the throne room (for an audience)

DIYANDZ 1. the spots on dice or dominoes 2. ornament of filigree

DIYANLAMBI 1. to mortgage 2. to take a trick (at cards)

DIYANŠI (典 史) Prison Warder, BH 766A

DO 1. the internal organs 2. the filling of pastries, *giyose*, and so forth

DOBI fox

DOBI YASHA a net for catching fox

DOBIHI a fox pelt

DOBIRI an animal resembling a fox that can climb trees

DOBKE one name for the screech owl; cf. *hūšahū*

DOBOMBI to offer (in a ceremony)

DOBON 1. offering 2. night

DOBON DULIN midnight

DOBON I ŠU ILHA a gilded wooden lotus flower

DOBONIO all night

DOBONOMBI to go to offer

DOBORI night

DOBORI ABKAI TAMPIN the second vessel of a water clock

DOBORI DULIME the whole night through

DOBORI DULIME JIMBI to come (unexpectedly) at night

DOBORI DULIN   midnight
DOBORI JETERE GIYAHŪN   one name for
   the horned owl; cf. *fu gūwara*
DOBTOKŪ   a sheath, a covering (for small
   objects)
DOBTOLOBUMBI   caus. of *dobtolombi*
DOBTOLOKŪ   a sheath or covering for
   large things
DOBTOLOMBI   to sheathe, to cover
DOBTOLON   doubled sack for a corpse
DOBTON   1. a small sheath, a small bag
   (for a seal), a container for tal-
   lies   2. a cover, cover for Chinese-
   style books   3. scabbard
DOBTONGGŪ   pertaining to a cover or
   sheath
DOBUKŪ   a falcon's perch
DOBUMBI   1. caus. of *dombi*   2. to place
   a falcon on its perch
DODANGGA   1. monster   2. sorcerer   3.
   a blind man
DODO   fetus, embryo
DODOBUMBI   1. caus. of *dodombi*   2. to
   force into a squat (at wrestling)
   3. to crouch
DODOMBI   to squat
DODORI   a hat with a wide brim
DOGO   blind
   DOGO IJA   a gadfly with a colored
      head
DOGON   a ford, a ferry (place where
   people are ferried across streams)
   DOGON ANGGA   a ford, a ferry, a
      place where people are ferried
      across streams
   DOGON JAFAHA   the ford has frozen--
      the river is frozen sufficiently
      hard to cross
DOHA   a tick
DOHO   1. lime   2. blind; cf. *dogo*
   DOHO MUKE HUNGKEREMBI   to pour
      mortar (a mixture of lime, sand,
      and water) into the crevices of
      brickwork
DOHODOMBI   to hop on one foot
DOHOLOBUMBI   caus. of *doholombi*
DOHOLOMBI   1. to cover with lime   2.
   to hold between the legs (at wrest-
   ling)
DOHOLON   lame
   DOHOLON YOO   a sore on a horse's
      hoof
DOHON   see *dogon*
DOHOŠOMBI   to limp, to be lame
DOIDON   lame
DOIGOMŠOLOMBI   to go before, to precede
DOIGOMŠOMBI   to prepare beforehand,
   to make precautions
DOIGON   beforehand, previously
   DOIGONDE   beforehand, previously
DOINGGE LEKE   a flat cake with a ju-
   jube filling
DOJIHIYAN   one name for the black bear;

cf. *mojihiyan*
DOKDO DAKDA   by leaps and bounds, to and
   fro
DOKDOHON   protruding
   DOKDOHON FURGI   a breakwater jutting
      out diagonally from a dike
DOKDOHORI   in rows on a high place
DOKDOLAMBI   to start (from fright), to
   spring up
DOKDOLOMBI   to protrude upward
DOKDORI   suddenly (to stand up)
   DOKDORI ILIHA   sprang up
DOKDORILAMBI   the same as *dokdolambi*
DOKDORJAMBI   to act unsettled, to be
   erratic, to jump about
DOKDORŠOMBI   the same as *dokdorjambi*
DOKDOSLAMBI   to be startled
DOKITA   a wild boar; cf. *kitari*
DOKJIHIYAN   the high spots on both sides
   of the skull
   DOKJIHIYAN NIRU (犬 批 箭)   a
      small arrow with a flattened head
DOKO   1. inside, lining of a garment
   2. path, short cut
   DOKO JUGŪN   path, short cut
DOKOLOMBI   1. to take a short cut   2. to
   take a liking to   3. to wrap both
   legs around the opponent's legs (in
   wrestling)
DOKOMIMBI   to line (a garment)
DOKSIDAMBI   to be cruel, to act vio-
   lently
DOKSIN   cruel, violent, fierce, wild,
   bad-tempered (of livestock)
DOKSIRAMBI   to act cruelly, to mistreat
DOKSOHON   protruding, sticking out
DOKSOMBI   to jut out, to protrude
   DOKSOHO WEIHE   protruding tooth
DOLA   barren land
DOLBI NIRU   a type of arrow somewhat
   smaller than a *keifu*
DOLCIN   1. ford   2. waves
DOLI   1. the pulp of fruit   2. unsteady
   pace (of a horse)
DOLMOBUMBI   caus. of *dolmombi*
DOLMOMBI   to add liquor to a cup
DOLO   inside, the inside, inner
   DOLO GOSIMBI   to be very hungry
   DOLO ILIMBI   not to yield easily (of
      a bowstring)
   DOLO PING SEMBI   to have eaten to
      satiety
   DOLO TATABUMBI   to be worried, to be
      concerned
   DOLO TOKOBUMBI   to have sharp pains
      in the belly
DOLORI   1. inside, inner   2. secretly
DOMBI   to alight (of birds and insects)
DOMNOBUMBI   caus. of *domnombi*
DOMNOMBI   1. to pay respects in the
   Manchu manner (of women)   2. to play
   on the water (of dragonflies)
DOMNON   obeisance made by Manchu women

D

DOMNON SINGGERI   ground squirrel
DOMO 1. female undergarment 2. teapot
  DOMO ETUKU female undergarment
DON fluttering of birds from one place to another, alighting (of birds)
  DON HADAMBI to be caught in a net stretched across a river (of fish swimming upstream)
DONAMBI to alight in a swarm
DONDOBA wasp
DONDON a small butterfly
DONGJIHIYAN lower jaw of a sheep
DONGMO a round pot for holding milked tea
DONGNIYOROMBI to raise the head high (of horses)
DONJIBUMBI 1. caus. of *donjimbi* 2. to notify
DONJIMBI to listen, to hear
  DONJICI I have heard that . . .
DONJIN what has been heard, hearsay
DONJINAMBI 1. to go to hear 2. to be generally known
DONJINDUMBI/DONJINUMBI to listen together
DONJINJIMBI to come to listen
DONO see *tono*
DOOBUMBI caus. of *doombi*
  DOOBURE HŪSUN a ferryboat man
DOOCAN a Buddhist or Taoist rite offered for a dead soul
DOOCANG same as *doocan*
  DOOCANG ARAMBI to perform a religious ceremony, especially one for the dead
DOODZ a bully, a rowdy
DOOHAN bridge
  DOOHAN JUGŪN I KUNGGERI (橋道 科) office of bridges and roads in the Board of Works
DOOLABUMBI caus. of *doolambi*
DOOLAMBI 1. to pour 2. to make a clean copy
DOOLI (道) Circuit, BH 213
  DOOLI HAFAN (道) Intendant, BH 838
  DOOLI YAMUN (道) Office of the Provincial Censor, BH 213
DOOMBI to cross (a river)
DOONAMBI to go to cross
DOONJIMBI to come to cross
DOORAMBI to imitate
DOORAN 1. unexploited land, virgin land 2. land spared from a prairie fire 3. a person spared from smallpox 4. old grass remaining among new grass
DOORIN gangplank, a plank used to board and to disembark from a vessel
  DOORIN I HŪSUN caretaker of a gangplank
DOOSE a Taoist priest
  DOOSE BE KADALARA FIYENTEN (道

錄 司) bureau for Taoist affairs
DOOSEDA a Taoist abbot, an official in charge of Taoist affairs
DOOSI greedy, covetous
DOOSIDAMBI to covet, to be covetous
  DOOSIDAHA WEILE ARAHA ULIN I NAMUN (職 罰 庫) Treasury (where fines were deposited), BH 456
DORAKŪ unreasonable, wrong
DORAKŪLAMBI to be unreasonable, to act wrongly, to be impolite to
DORAN 1. a row of armored scales (on a suit of armor) 2. see *dooran*
DORDON DARDAN SEME shivering, shaking
DORGI 1. inside, inner, the inner part 2. imperial, the court
  DORGI AMBAN (内 大 臣) Senior Assistant Chamberlain of the Imperial Bodyguard, BH 98
  DORGI AMSU I BOO (内 膳 房) the palace pantry
  DORGI BA 1. inland area 2. the palace
  DORGI BADE BOLGOMIMBI to observe the major fast in the palace
  DORGI BAITA BE UHERI KADALARA YAMUN (内 務 府) the Imperial Household, BH 75
  DORGI BELHERE YAMUN (奉 宸 苑) Bureau of Imperial Gardens and Hunting Parks, BH 90
  DORGI BITHE UBALIYAMBURE BOO (内 繙 書 房) Manchu-Chinese Translation Office, BH 140
  DORGI BITHESI (中 書) Secretary of the Grand Secretariat, BH 137
  DORGI BODOGON strategy, military planning
  DORGI CALU Imperial Granaries, BH 567
  DORGI CALU BE KADALARA YAMUN (内 倉 監 督 衙 門) Office of the Inspector of Imperial Granaries, BH 567
  DORGI EFEN I BOO (内 餑 餑 房) the palace bakery
  DORGI FAIDAN BE KADALARA YAMUN (鑾 儀 衛) the Imperial Equipage Department, BH 109
  DORGI FAIDAN SINDARA NAMUN (内 駕 庫) storage place for the imperial escort
  DORGI HANCIKI HAFAN court officials
  DORGI HOBO an inner coffin
  DORGI HOTON the imperial city
  DORGI KADALAN I YAMUN (内 關 防 衙 門) Chancery of the Imperial Household, BH 85
  DORGI KOOLINGGA HAFAN (内 史) Secretary of the Grand Secretariat, BH S. 137
  DORGI OKTOSI (御 醫) Imperial

Physician, BH 238

DORGI SIMNENGGE KUNGGERI (内 考 科) office concerned with examinations and civil appointments in the capital

DORGI SURI a type of silk thinner and coarser than satin

DORGI TANGGINGGE BOO (内 堂 房) the name of an office in the Board of Civil Appointments

DORGI YAMUN (内 閣) Grand Secretariat, BH 130

DORGICI ablative of *dorgi:* from inside

DORGICI GOHOLOMBI at wrestling, to catch on the inside of the thigh with the foot

DORGICI HALGIMBI to wrap one's legs around an opponent's thigh while holding his head

DORGIDERI 1. from inside 2. in private, secretly

DORGOLOMBI to be stunted, to shrivel up

DORGON badger (*Meles meles, Arctonyx collaris*)

DORGON I UNCEHEN 'badger's tail'-- the inflorescence of the sorrel

DORGORI one name for the wild boar; cf. *kitari*

DORIMBI to gallop

DORO 1. doctrine, precept, morality, Tao, way, rule, rite, ritual 2. gift

DORO ARAMBI to salute, to greet, to perform a ritual

DORO BE ALJAMBI to act contrary to proper behavior

DORO BE DASARA TANGGIN (修 道 堂) the name of the first hall of the west wing of the Imperial Academy

DORO BE SONGKOLORO MUDAN music performed during a wine-drinking ceremony at court

DORO BENEMBI to give a gift

DORO DE AISILAHA AMBAN (光 禄 大 夫) honorary title of the first rank class one, BH 945

DORO DE HŪSUN AKŪMBUHA AMBAN (通 議 大 夫) honorary title of the third rank class one, BH 945

DORO DE HŪSUN BUHE AMBAN (中 議 大 夫) honorary title of the third rank class two, BH 945

DORO DE TUSA ARAHA AMBAN (資 政 大 夫) honorary title of the second rank class one, BH 945

DORO DE TUSA OBUHA AMBAN (通 奉 大 夫) honorary title of the second rank class two, BH 945

DORO DE WEHIYEHE AMBAN (榮 禄 大 夫) honorary title of the first rank class two, BH 945

DORO ELDENGGE the Tao-kuang (道 光) reign period, 1821-1850

DORO JAFAMBI to be in power, to hold the reins of government

DORO JORIRE YAMUN (鴻 臚 寺) Court of Banqueting, BH 934

DORO ŠAJIN the administration and the law

DORO YANGSE 1. veining, grain (of wood) 2. form, proper form

DORO YOSO rites and customs, norm, form

DOROI AMBA KIYOO a large golden imperial sedan chair carried by sixteen men

DOROI BEILE (多 羅 貝 勒) Prince of the Blood of the third degree, BH 18

DOROI BEILE I EFU (郡 君 儀 賓) the son-in-law of a *doroi beile*

DOROI DENGJAN lanterns hung on both sides of the gate of the palace during important ceremonies

DOROI EFU (縣 主 儀 賓) son-in-law of a prince of the second degree

DOROI ETUKU court dress, ceremonial garments

DOROI FAIDAN vehicular procession of a noble personage

DOROI FAIDAN I KIYOO an imperial sedan chair carried by sixteen men

DOROI FUJIN (郡 主 福 晉) wife of a prince of the blood of the second degree (*doroi giyūn wang*)

DOROI GEBU a monk's religious name

DOROI GEGE (縣 主) Daughter of a Prince of the Blood of the second degree, GH 31

DOROI GIYŪN WANG (郡 王) Prince of the Blood of the second degree, BH 17

DOROI JAKA gift

DOROI MAHATUN a hat worn during the Shang dynasty

DOROI SARA I FIYENTEN (擎 蓋 司) Umbrella Section (of the Equipage Department), BH 119

DOROI SUHEN GIRDANGGA (儀 鍠 氅) an emblem used on the banner of the imperial guards

DOROI UMIYESUN a belt for a court dress or ceremonial garment

DOROI YORO a ceremonial arrow

DOROHON small in stature (of children)

DOROLOBUMBI caus. of *dorolombi*

DOROLOMBI 1. to salute, to greet with the hands joined in front of the face, to pay one's respects 2. to perform a rite

D

D

DOROLORO SEKTEFUN a kneeling cushion
DOROLORO TEMGETU a placard showing
    where one should kneel during a
    ceremony
DOROLON 1. rite, ceremony 2. propriety
    DOROLON AMBA FAIDAN a procession in
        which the empress took part
    DOROLON BE JORIRE ŠUSAI master of
        ceremonies
    DOROLON BE KADALARA FIYENTEN (掌
        儀司) Department of Cere-
        monial, BH 79
    DOROLON FAIDAN a procession in which
        the imperial concubines took part
    DOROLON I AMBA KIYOO a golden sedan
        chair employed by the empress that
        was carried by sixteen men
    DOROLON I BOO (禮房) office of
        rites in the Court of Colonial Af-
        fairs
    DOROLON I EJEHEN rules for the per-
        formance of ceremonies
    DOROLON I JURGAN (禮部) Board
        of Rites, BH 376
    DOROLON I JURGAN I KUNGGE YAMUN (禮
        科) Section of Ceremonies, BH 822
    DOROLON I JURGAN I TOKTOHO GISUN
        phrases used by the Board of Rites
    DOROLON I TETUN I BITHEI KUREN (禮
        器庫) depository for ritual
        books and paraphernalia
    DOROLON KOOLI I KUNGGERI (禮儀
        科) section concerned with ritual
        in the Court of Banqueting
    DOROLON KUMUN GABTAN JAFAN BITHE TON
        the six arts--rites, music, arch-
        ery, chariot driving, writing, and
        mathematics
DOROLONJIMBI to come to salute
DOROLONOMBI to go to salute
DORON a seal, a stamp
    DORON BE DARA BA (印管處)
        office of the seal in the Board of
        Civil Appointments
    DORON BE TUWAKIYARA KUNGGERI (知
        印科) office of the seal in
        the Court of Colonial Affairs
    DORON BE TUWAŠARA BA (監印處)
        office of the seal in the Board of
        Finance
    DORON GAIMBI to confiscate an of-
        ficial's seal
    DORON GIDAMBI to put one's seal on
    DORON GIDAHA BOJI a contract or bill
        of sale with an official seal on it
    DORON HUNGKERERE KŪWARAN (鑄印
        司) seal-casting section of the
        Board of Rites
    DORON I BOCO a seal stamp pad
    DORON I BOO (印房) the office
        of the seal in a government bank;
        cf. GH 549
    DORON I HOOŠAN plain paper stamped

with a seal
    DORON I TUWAKIYASI (知印)
        keeper of the seal
    DORON I UNCEHEN the last stroke of
        a Chinese character or the last
        flourish in a Manchu or Mongolian
        word
    DORON I WESIMBURE BITHE a memorial
        stamped with a seal that dealt
        with official business
    DORON TEMGETU I KUNGGERI (印信
        科) office of the seal in the
        Board of Rites
DORONGGO 1. moral, honest, possessing
    proper principles 2. Taoist-like
    3. gentle (of horses)
DOSHOLOBUMBI caus./pass. of *dosholombi*
DOSHOLOMBI to love, to favor
DOSHON 1. favor, love 2. favorite,
    favored person
    DOSHON HAHA homosexual friend
    DOSHON HAHA JUI catamite
    DOSHON HEHE paramour, mistress
DOSI 1. to the inside, into 2. (with
    de) addicted to
    DOSI GOCIMBI to inhale
    DOSI GOCIME GUWEMBUMBI to make a
        sound while inhaling
    DOSI TULESI inward and outward
DOSIDAMBI see *doosidambi*
DOSIKAN a little inward, a little bit
    into
DOSIKASI (進士) Metropolitan
    Graduate--a holder of the highest
    degree in the imperial examination
    system, BH 629C
DOSILA a narrow lapel underneath a
    larger lapel on a garment
DOSIMBI (-ka) 1. to enter, to advance
    2. to succeed in an examination, to
    pass an examination 3. to become
    addicted to
    DOSIRE DE ILIBURE KIRU (入躍
        旗) a yellow banner used to
        signal courtiers to rise as the
        emperor returned to his palace
DOSIMBUMBI 1. caus. of *dosimbi* 2. to
    put into, to insert, to inlay, to
    admit a guest
DOSINAMBI to go in, to go to enter, to
    accede
DOSINAN 1. going in 2. form of appear-
    ance in the rebirth cycle (Sanskrit
    gati)
DOSINDUMBI/DOSINUMBI to enter together
DOSINJIMBI to come in, to come to
    enter
DOSOBUMBI caus. of *dosombi*
DOSOMBI to bear, to tolerate
    DOSORAKŪ unbearable
DOSOMBUMBI caus. of *dosombi*
DOTORI perseverance, profundity,
    stability

DOTORI AKŪ indecisive, lacking per-
  severance
DOYOLJOMBI to get sprained (of a
  horse's or mule's hind leg)
DOYONGGO satin with brocaded dragons
DU thigh, thighbone, femur
  DU DE GAIMBI to grab by the thigh
    (in wrestling)
  DU ERGI a side flap on a Chinese
    garment
  DU GIRANGGI pelvis
  DU SELE iron objects worn on both
    thighs for hanging bow cases and
    quivers
DU GIOWAN ILHA azalea
DUBE end, extremity
  DUBE AKŪ endless, limitless
  DUBE BELE sprouted grain
  DUBE TUCIKE has come to an end
  DUBEI JECEN outer limit, farthest
    boundary
  DUBEI SUKŪ the foreskin
  DUBEI TOLDOHON a clasp at the end of
    a scabbard
DUBEDE at the end, at last, finally
DUBEGERI see *dubeheri*
DUBEHERI at the end, at last, finally,
  scarcely; cf. *dubede*
DUBEINGGE the end one, the last one
DUBEMBI to terminate, to end, to die
DUBEMBUMBI caus. of *dubembi*
DUBEN end, termination
  DUBEN DERIBUN the beginning and end
DUBENGGE pointed, sharp
DUBENTELE up until the end
DUBERI toward the end, just before the
  end
DUBESILEMBI to terminate, to be at an
  end
DUBI bean flour
DUBIBUMBI caus. of *dubimbi*
DUBIMBI (-ke/he) to get accustomed, to
  become domesticated, to get ac-
  quainted with
DUBISE a cake made from bean flour
  DUBISE EFEN same as *dubise*
DUBUMBI see *tūbumbi*
DUDU 1. eastern turtledove (*Strepto-
  pelia orientalis*) 2. (都 督)
  a military governor
  DUDU NIYEHE the teal; cf. *borboki*
DUDU DADA the sound children make when
  first learning to speak
DUDUNGGE CECIKE one name for the myna
DUDURI the crown of a hat
DUFE dissolute, lascivious, loose,
  lacking restraint
DUFEDEMBI to act dissolutely, to
  carouse, to indulge in sexual ex-
  cesses
DUGŪI a narrow bridge, a plank
  DUGŪI COHORO a horse with zebralike
    stripes

DUHA intestine, gut
  DUHA DO innards, inner organs
DUHAN see *duha*
  DUHAN SINGGERI a small black rat-
    like animal that has a gutlike
    growth on its stomach
DUHEMBI (-ke) to be finished, to be
  completed
DUHEMBUMBI caus. of *duhembi*
  DUHEMBUME UJIMBI to care for one's
    parents until death
DUHEN scrotum
DUHENTELE until the end
DUIBULEBUMBI caus. of *duibulembi*
DUIBULEMBI to compare, to give as an
  example
DUIBULEN comparison
DUIBUMBI to arrange, to put into order
DUICI fourth
DUIDZ a pair, a couplet
DUILEBUMBI caus. of *duilembi*
DUILEMBI to judge, to try, to examine,
  to determine the truth
DUILEN judicial hearing, interrogation
  DUILEN I EJEKU (評 事) Assis-
    tant Secretary of the Court of
    Judicature and Revision, BH 216
DUIN four
  DUIN ARBUN the four forms of man:
    youth, old age, masculine, fem-
    inine
  DUIN BILTEN the Yangtze, the Yellow
    River, the Huai River, the Chi
    River
  DUIN BIYA the fourth month of the
    lunar calendar
  DUIN DERE the four directions
  DUIN DURBEJEN I MONGGO BOO a four-
    sided Mongolian yurt
  DUIN ERGI the four corners of the
    world
  DUIN ERGI AIMAN I KUNGGERI (四
    夷 科) office of the peoples
    of the four directions in the
    Board of Rites
  DUIN ERIN the four seasons
  DUIN ERIN I ILHANGGA TUMIN LAMUN
  SARA a dark blue processional
    umbrella embroidered with the
    flowers of the four seasons
  DUIN FORGON the four seasons
  DUIN HOŠO the four oblique direc-
    tions: SE, NE, SW, NW
  DUIN ICI in the four directions
  DUIN IRUNGGE MAHATUN a hat with
    four tufts on top, worn by of-
    ficials in antiquity
DUINA one hundred-sextillionths, an
  infinitesimal amount
DUINGGE folded in four, in fours, four
  times
  DUINGGE HOOŠAN a sheet of paper
    four times as large as an ordi-

D

nary sheet

DUINGGERI   four times

DUISE   an antithetical couplet

DUITE   four each

DUKA   gate

    DUKA BE KADALARA HAFAN (監門官) gatekeeper at the examination hall

    DUKAI BONGKO   an adornment over a gate

    DUKAI ENDURI   god of the gate

    DUKAI ENDURI NAMUN (門神庫) a depository in the Board of Works where images of the gate god were stored

    DUKAI KIRU (門旗) a red banner embroidered with the word for gate

    DUKAI SENGGELE   board placed on each side of a gate

DUKDUHUN   raised, elevated, piled up

DUKDUREMBI (-ke)   to rise, to swell

DUKDURHUN   unlevel, lumpy, raised,

DUKDURŠEMBI   to rise up, to form a lump

DUKJIMBI   to talk loudly

    DUKJIME DURGIMBI   to talk loudly

DUKSEMBI (-ke)   to blush, to turn red

DUKSI   a fruit resembling the wild grape

DUKSUMBI   see *duksembi*

DUKSURSEHUN   rough (of terrain)

DULAN NIMAHA   shark

DULBA   careless, inexperienced, foolish (because of a lack of experience)

DULBADAMBI   to act carelessly or foolishly

DULBAKAN   rather careless, somewhat inexperienced or foolish

DULDURI   a pilgrim's staff with nine rings around it

DULE   really, in fact, when you come right down to it

DULEBUMBI   see *dulembumbi*

DULEFUN   degree of an angle

    DULEFUN SANDALABURE DURUNGGA TETUN (距度儀) a sextant of the Peking observatory

DULEMBI (-ke, -ndere/re)   1. to pass, to go by   2. to burn

    DULEKE ANIYA   last year

    DULEKE BIYA   last month

DULEMBUMBI   1. caus. of *dulembi*   2. to endure, to pass through, to experience   3. to set on fire   4. to cure

DULEMŠEKU   negligent, careless, rough

DULEMŠEMBI   to act negligently, to act carelessly

DULENUMBI   to pass together

DULGA   half, half-filled

DULGAKAN   a little less than half (filled)

DULIBUMBI   caus. of *dulimbi*

DULIMBA   middle, center

    DULIMBA BE ALIHA USIHA   the stars *lambda* and *mu* in the Big Dipper

DULIMBA BE BODORO HAFAN (中官正) Astronomer for the Mid-year, BH 229

DULIMBA HŪWALIYASUN BOLGONGGO KUMUN   music played while food was brought in for a palace banquet

DULIMBA HŪWALIYASUN SIRABUNGGA KUMUN   music played while the emperor returned to the palace from a congratulatory ceremony

DULIMBA HŪWALIYASUN ŠOO KUMUN   same as the preceding entry

DULIMBA HŪWALIYASUN ŠUNGGIYA KUMUN   music played during the offerings at the altars of heaven, earth, and millet, and the Ancestral Temple, and Temple of Confucius

DULIMBA HŪWALIYASUN YA KUMUN   the same as the preceding

DULIMBA I GURUN   China

DULIMBA I TU   a banner carried in the center of a battle line

DULIMBA JUGŪN   the path leading from the main part of a residence to the main gate

DULIMBA SELE   a metal clasp in the middle of a quiver or bow case

DULIMBADE   in the midst of

DULIMBAI ELIOI (仲呂) one of the six minor pipes

DULIMBAI FALANGGA (中所) central office of the Imperial Equipage Department; cf. BH 109

DULIMBAI FIYENTEHE   the central section of a classical essay

DULIMBAI FULHUN (黃鐘) one of the six major pipes

DULIMBAI GURUN   China

DULIMBAI HECEN I BAICARA YAMUN (中城察院) censorate office of the middle city (Peking)

DULIMBAI HECEN I COOHA MORINGGA FIYENTEN (中城兵馬司) police office of the central city

DULIMBAI IRGEN GURUN   the Chinese Republic

DULIMBAI SIMHUN   the middle finger

DULIMBAINGGE   the middle one

DULIMBANGGE   same as *dulimbaingge*

DULIMBI   to stay up all night, to watch, to keep a vigil

DULIN   half, middle

DUMBI   (for *tumbi*) to hit, to strike

DUMIN CECIKE   a cuckoo nestling

DUNA   chalcedony

DUNCIHIYA   see *dunjihiyana*

DUNDABUMBI   caus. of *dundambi*

DUNDAMBI   to feed pigs, to raise pigs

DUNDAN   pig food

DUNEN   a four-year-old ox

DUNG   a cave

DUNG GUWA   see *dungga*

DUNGGA watermelon
   DUNGGA USE watermelon seed
DUNGGAMI of the same age
DUNGGU cave, grotto
DUNGKI tired, exhausted, weak in judg-
   ment
DUNGŠUN one hundred million
DUNJIHIYANA former, earlier
DUR DAR SEME shaking, trembling
DUR SEME the sound of many people
   talking or laughing, the sound of
   drums, with a commotion
   DUR SEME INJEMBI to burst out
     laughing, to laugh uproariously
DURAHŪN staring, fixed (of the eyes)
DURAMBI to stare
DURANGGI muddy, murky, given to exces-
   sive drinking
DURANGGILAMBI to drink excessively
DURBE a dog with two spots on its
   forehead
DURBEJEN 1. square, four-cornered 2.
   corner, angle
   DURBEJEN DERE a square table at
     which eight people can sit
   DURBEJEN SIMELEN a square pond at
     the Altar of Earth
DURBEJENGGE square, having corners
   DURBEJENGGE ŠUFATU a square turban
     used in antiquity
DURBEJITU carpenter's square
DURBEMBI to shake, to tremble
DURDUN crepe
   DURDUN SA crepe
DURGEBUMBI caus./pass. of *durgembi*
DURGECEMBI to shake violently, to be
   convulsed
DURGEMBI to shake, to tremble
   DURGEME AKJAMBI the thunder rolls
DURGEŠEMBI same as *durgecembi*
DURGIMBI to coo, to warble
   DURGIRE DUTU a person who, through
     deafness, makes silly or irrele-
     vant remarks
DURGIYA the morning star
   DURGIYA USIHA the same as preceding
     word
DURHA four short wooden teeth attached
   to a flail
DURHUN see *durahūn*
DURI a swinging cradle
   DURI DE DEDUBUMBI to place a baby in
     a cradle
DURIBUMBI caus./pass. of *durimbi*
   DURIBUHE EJEN a dispossessed owner
DURILEMBI to rock in a cradle
DURIMBI 1. to seize, to rob 2. to
   sleep in a cradle
DURINDUMBI/DURINUMBI to seize together
DURSUKI similar, looking alike
DURSUKILEBUMBI caus. of *dursukilembi*
DURSUKILEMBI to make alike, to use as
   a model, to copy

DURSULEBUKŪ an interpreter in ancient
   South China
DURSULEMBI 1. same as *dursukilembi*
   2. to resemble, to be like 3. to
   act in accordance with
DURSULEN I WECEN a sacrifice made dur-
   ing times of war
DURSUN likeness, form, shape, model,
   pattern, appearance
DURSUNGGA having form, material
DURUGAN list, chart, register, diagram
   DURUGAN FISEN genealogical register
DURUJUN one name for the stork; cf.
   weijun
DURULAMBI to provide a model
DURULEMBI to form, to model
DURUN 1. form, shape, figure 2. model,
   mold 3. rule, norm
   DURUN ARAMBI to pretend, to put on
     airs
   DURUN HIYAN incense pressed into
     blocks
   DURUN I EFEN molded cakes
   DURUN I HIYAN cake of incense
   DURUN I MATAN candies molded in
     various shapes
   DURUN I YAHA charcoal bricks
   DURUN KEMUN rule, regulation, prac-
     tice, custom
   DURUN MURU shape, form
   DURUN SINDAMBI to pretend, to feign
   DURUN TUWAKŪ model, example
DURUNGGA 1. exemplary, model 2. hav-
   ing form, representational
   DURUNGGA DOBTOLON an animal or
     devil mask worn over the head dur-
     ing certain games
   DURUNGGA TETUN instrument--espe-
     cially an astronomical instrument
DURUNGGE exemplary
DURUSGA MOO Indian palm (*Corypha um-
   braculifera*), a plant whose leaves
   were used for paper
DUSHUBUMBI caus. of *dushumbi*
DUSHUMBI 1. to sling, to hurl 2. to
   emboss
DUSHUN dark in color, dull, slow-wit-
   ted, muddled
DUSHUTEMBI to fling around
DUSIHI 1. a two-piece man's skirt, a
   mail skirt 2. a front lapel
DUSIHILEBUMBI caus. of *dusihilembi*
DUSIHILEMBI to hold (as in a sack or
   pocket), to hold in an upturned
   garment
DUSIHIYEN 1. unclear, misty, blurred
   2. muddle-headed, stupid
DUSY (都 司) captain; cf. *danara
   hafan*
DUTE on the inside, inner
   DUTE TALU a short cut
   DUTE YALI meat adhering to skin
DUTELEMBI to go by a short cut

D

D

DUTELEME YABUMBI   to go by a short cut

DUTHE   1. the vertical wooden support of a window lattice   2. a fish with scales spotted with red

DUTHENGGE   having a grate or lattice work

DUTU   deaf, a deaf person

DUTUNG (都 統) lieutenant general; cf. *gūsai i ejen*

DUTUREMBI   to feign deafness

DUWALI   category, kind, type, party, clique

DUWALI ACABUMBI   to match up

DUWALIBUN   a book arranged according to categories, an encyclopedia

DUWALINAMBI   to categorize

DUWALINGGA   of the same type or category

DUWAN   1. satin   2. weeds   3. a pock still not broken out

DUWANSE   satin

DUWARA   mayfish, sweetfish

DUWARGIYA   see *durgiya*

DUWARGIYAN   bright, brilliant

   DUWARGIYAN USIHA   Venus, Orion

DUYEMBUMBI   to attack an unprepared enemy, to make a surprise attack

DUYEN   1. cold, indifferent, distant (of people)   2. stubborn, restive (of horses)

DUYUN CECIKE   one of the names of the goatsucker; cf. *simari cecike*

DZ

DZ

DZ (子) viscount

DZAI SIYANG (宰 相) prime minister

DZAMBAG'A   the champac tree (*Michelia champaca*)

DZANDAN   sandalwood; cf. *cakūran, dan mu*

DZANDZ   see *dzanse*

DZANSE   a finger presser, a torture device used in interrogating women

DZANSELABUMBI   caus. of *dzanselambi*

DZANSELAMBI   to apply the finger presser

DZENGSE   an orange

DZOGUWAN   workshop foreman

DZOOLI (皂 隸) petty attendant in a *yamun*, lictor

DZUN HŪWA MAJAN (遵 化 長 披 箭)

a long slender arrow

DZUNG BING GUWAN (總 兵 官) the commander of Chinese troops in a province

DZUNG GIYA (總 甲) superintendent of block wardens

DZUNG NI DUKA   a religious sect

DZUNG ŠIKA   palm fronds

DZUNG ŽIN FU (宗 人 府) the Imperial Clan Court; cf. *uksun be kadalara yamun*

DZUNGDU (總 督) governor general; cf. *uheri kadalara amban*

DZUNGSE   glutinous rice filled with meat or sweet bean paste and wrapped in bamboo leaves

DZUŠI   Buddhist patriarch

E

E 1. yin, the female or negative principle 2. an exclamation used to call
someone's attention, an exclamation
of surprise or exasperation
  E I BUKDAN the inside of a crease
  or fold
  E JIJUN I ACANGGA an identification
  token cast in bronze with indented
  characters used to gain entrance
  to a city at night after the gates
  have been closed

EBCI 1. rib 2. framing timbers (of a
ship) 3. (steep) side of a hill

EBCILEME along the (steep) side of a
hill

EBDEREKU destroyer

EBDEREMBI to harm, to destroy, to ruin

EBDEREN destruction, havoc, harm
  EDBEREN I DERIBUN (速 別) a
  classical pitch corresponding in
  function to G sharp

EBEBE interjection of surprise

EBEBUMBI caus. of *ebembi*

EBECI see *ebci*

EBEGEI if only, oh that . . .

EBELE this side

EBEMBI (-ke) to become soaked through,
to become soggy

EBENEMBI see *ebeniyembi*

EBENIYEBUMBI caus. of *ebeniyembi*

EBENIYEMBI to soak, to steep (tea)

EBEREGI see *ebergi*

EBEREHUN see *eberhun*

EBEREMBI (-ke) to diminish, to decrease, to decline, to subside

EBEREMBUMBI caus. of *eberembi*

EBERGI 1. this side, this place 2.
after

EBERHUKEN rather weak

EBERHUN weak

EBERI weak, deficient, inadequate, inferior

EBERIKEN somewhat deficient

EBERINGGE not up to par, inferior

EBETUHUN hollow, empty
  EBETUHUN HOLO empty, lacking substance, false

EBI HABI AKŪ not feeling well, without
energy, listless, in bad humor

EBIBUMBI caus. of *ebimbi*

EBILUN a delicate, sickly child

EBIMBI to be full (after eating), to
be sated

EBIŠEBUMBI caus. of *ebišembi*

EBIŠEMBI to bathe, to swim
  EBIŠERE OTON bathtub

EBIŠENEMBI to go to bathe or swim

EBIŠENUMBI to bathe or swim together
or in a group

EBSI hither, up till now, since
  EBSI CASI AKŪ hither and yon, back
  and forth
  EBSI CASI DE back and forth,
  hesitant
  EBSI FOROMBI to turn and face in
  this direction
  EBSI JIO come here
  EBSI OSO like this!

EBSIHE (postposition) exhausting, ex-
erting, up to the last, to the extent of: *mutere ebsihe* 'to the best
of one's ability'

EBSIHIYAN hither, up till now

EBSIKEN a little in this direction

EBSINGGE what has been up until now,
existing until now, long-lasting

EBŠEMBI to hurry, to hasten, to be
busy

EBŠU a newly hatched quail

EBTE a young hawk taken from the nest
and raised at home

EBUBUMBI 1. caus. of *ebumbi* 1. to
dismantle a tent, to unpack, to un-
load
  EBUBURE BA I CIFUN a duty imposed
  at the place of unloading
  EBUBURE CAMHARI a notice ordering
  riders to dismount at the gates of

E

the palace

EBUBUN 1. stopover on a journey 2.
provisions for traveling officials
EBUBUN I KUNGGERI (下程科) office in charge of caring for
emissaries to the court

EBUHU quick, urgent
EBUHU SABUHŪ in a rush, in a flurry,
agitated

EBUMBI to dismount, to get off a vehicle, to stop (at an inn), to get
down

EBUNDUMBI/EBUNUMBI to stop or stay
(of a group), to get off (of a
group)

EBUNEMBI to go to stop, to go to dismount

EBUNJIMBI 1. to come to stop or stay,
to come to dismount 2. to descend
(of a deity)

EBURGI the confluence of two rivers

ECI surely, indeed, really
ECI AI of course, certainly
ECI AINARA what else is one to do?
of course

ECIKE father's younger brother--uncle

ECIKESE plural of *ecike*

ECIMARI this morning

ECINE secretly, behind one's back

EDE dative/locative of *ere*, to this,
here, then, and then, in this (matter)
EDE AIBI what difference does this
make?
EDE AINAMBI what is one to do in
this matter?

EDEDEI brrr--the sound of teeth chattering from cold

EDEKIRAKŪ an incorrigible person

EDELEMBI to be lacking, to be deficient, not to be enough, to owe a
debt
EDELEHE NIMEKU deformity, disability

EDEMBI (-ke) to go bad (of food and
milk)

EDEN 1. lack, deficiency 2. lacking,
deficient, blemished 3. a scrap
of cloth
EDEN DADAN deficiency, lack, incomplete
EDEN DADUN see *eden dadan*

EDENG a sawfish (*Pristis pectinatus*)

EDERI this time, this way, by here
EDERI TEDERI here and there, this
way and that
EDERI TEDERI BULCATAMBI to look for
ways to avoid things

EDULEBUMBI caus. of *edulembi*

EDULEMBI 1. to be paralyzed 2. to
catch cold
EDULEHE NIMEKU cold, grippe,
rheumatism

EDUMBI to blow (of the wind)

EDUN 1. wind 2. a cold
EDUN BIYAI BAITA sexual intercourse
EDUN DAMBI the wind blows
EDUN DASIHIKŪ the two largest
pinions on birds of prey
EDUN DE ŠASIHALABUMBI to be toppled
by the wind
EDUN DEKDEHE 1. a wind has arisen
2. has caught cold
EDUN FAITAKŪ a board nailed upright
on a rafter
EDUN FAITAMBI to sail crosswind
EDUN FAITAME YABURE JAHŪDAI one
type of large seagoing warship
EDUN FUR SEMBI the wind blows
softly--said of the south wind in
the summer
EDUN GOIMBI to catch cold
EDUN I TEMGETU a flag that shows
the direction of the wind, wind
pennant
EDUN NESUKEN OHO the wind has
calmed
EDUN NESUKEN ŠUN GENGGIYEN I MUDAN
a musical composition played at
the banquet after the plowing
ceremony
EDUN NIMEKU a cold, rheumatism
EDUN TUWAMBI to relieve oneself,
to go to the toilet

EDUNGGE pertaining to the wind
EDUNGGE GASHA a type of sparrow
hawk
EDUNGGE HIYEBELE a type of buzzard
EDUNGGE ŠUNGKERI ILHA wind orchid
(*Angraecum falcatum*)

EDUNGGIYEBUMBI caus. of *edunggiyembi*

EDUNGGIYEMBI to winnow

EFEBUMBI to lose one's sight, to blind

EFEHEN a large hand ax

EFEMBI to be blind

EFEN bread, pastry, cake, any sort of
of breadlike product made from flour
EFEN BELHERE BA (點心局)
kitchen where pastries were prepared for the palace

EFIBUMBI caus. of *efimbi*

EFICEMBI to play together

EFIKU toy, game, fun
EFIKU INJEKU fun and laughing, a
good time

EFIMBI to play, to enjoy oneself, to
act
EFIRE HEHE actress
EFIRE JAKA toy, plaything
EFIRE URSE actors

EFIN game, play

EFISI buffoon, clown, jester
EFISI INJESI clowns and merrymakers

EFIYECEMBI see *eficembi*

EFIYEMBI see *efimbi*

EFIYEN see *efin*

EFU 1. the husband of one's elder

sister 2. wife's elder brother
3. the husband of wife's elder sister 4. the husband of an imperial
princess

EFUJEBUMBI 1. caus. of *efujembi* 2. to
ruin, to destroy, to overthrow

EFUJEMBI 1. to be ruined, to be
spoiled, to be defeated 2. to be
dismissed from a position

EFUJEN destruction, ruin, downfall

EFULEBUMBI caus. of *efulembi*

EFULEMBI 1. to destroy, to ruin, to
break 2. to remove from office,
to dismiss

EFULEHE DABSUN denatured salt

EFULEN destruction, ruin

EFUTE plural of *efu*

EGULETU ALHA a horse with cloudlike
markings

EHE bad, evil, inauspicious

EHE ACABUN bad omen, bad sign

EHE BA destiny, fate

EHE BOCO MENGGUN poor quality sil-
ver_ (containing impurities)

EHE GŪNIMBI to take something amiss

EHE HAFAN an evil official

EHE INENGGI an inauspicious day,
a day on which there is bad weather

EHE SUI sin

EHE SUKDUN miasma, evil vapors

EHE WA a bad smell, a stink

EHE WEILENGGE NIYALMA criminal
charged with homicide

EHECUBUMBI caus./pass. of *ehecumbi*

EHECUMBI to slander, to defame, to
accuse falsely

EHECUN slander, abuse

EHELINGGU bad, wicked, incompetent

EHELIYAN stupid, simple

EHELIYANGGŪ stupid, incompetent

EHEMBI see *eherembi*

EHEREBUMBI caus. of *eherembi*

EHEREMBI 1. to become evil or fierce
2. to have a falling out with, to
be on bad terms with someone

EHERENDUMBI 1. to become evil (of a
number of people) 2. to be on bad
terms with each other

EHURHEN a lark with a yellow beak,
black head, yellow eyes, red back,
and spotted wings

EI 1. an interjection for calling attention 2. an interjection of derision

EI EI 1. the sound of crying 2. the
sound of derisive laughter

EIBI HAIBI AKŪ see *ebi habi akū*

EICI 1. or 2. perhaps

EICI . . . EICI . . . now . . .
now . . , either . . . . or . . .

EICIBE no matter, be it as it may,
in any case

EIFU grave

EIFU KŪWARAN cemetery

EIFUN a boil, a pimple, a swelling

EIFUNEMBI to develop a boil or a swelling, to get goose flesh

EIGEN husband

EIGEN GAIMBI to take a husband, to
get married

EIGETE plural of *eigen*

EIHEN donkey, ass

EIHEN BOCO brown

EIHEN CUSE brown silk

EIHERI 1. brown 2. the name of a
fabulous ratlike beast.

EIHUME the hard-shelled turtle

EIHUME USIHA the name of a star in
the Milky Way

EIHUMENGGE FUKJINGGA HERGEN (龜
書) a style of calligraphy

EIHUMENGGE USIHA see *eihume usiha*

EIHUN stupid, foolish

EIHUTU the same as *eihun*

EIKTE a type of red sour fruit (*Crataegus pinnatifida*), a hawthorn

EIMEBUMBI pass. of *eimembi*

EIMEBURU you hateful thing!

EIMECUKE hateful, loathsome, repugnant

EIMECUN repugnance, antipathy

EIMEDE 1. repugnant (person) 2. smart,
lovable (of children)

EIMEDEMBI to feel aversion or repugnance

EIMEDERE JAKA a repulsive thing

EIMEDESE plural of *eimede*

EIMEMBI (-ke, -re/ndere) to abhor, to
detest, to find unpleasant

EIMEMBUMBI caus./pass. of *eimembi*

EIMEMBURU see *eimeburu*

EIMERCUKE abominable, detestable; cf.
eimecuke

EIMERECUKE see *eimercuke*

EIMPE a type of edible wormwood; cf.
empi

EITE halter, bridle

EITEN all (in attributive position),
every

EITEN BAITA everything, every matter

EITEN JAKA everything, every object

EITEREBUMBI caus. of *eiterembi*

EITEREKU deception, fraud, deceptive,
fraudulent

EITEREMBI 1. to deceive, to defraud
2. to do thoroughly, to do repeatedly

EITERECI in general, for the most
part, thoroughly

EITERECIBE in any case, all in all,
on the whole

EITEREME thoroughly, generally, in
any case

EITEREME YABUMBI to act deceitfully

EITERŠEMBI to cheat on the sly

E

E

EJE a castrated bovine, ox
EJEBUKŪ annalist, chronicler
EJEBUMBI caus. of *ejembi*
EJEBUN record, notes
EJEHE an imperial rescript, edict, decree
EJEHEN commentary, gloss, note
EJEKE industrious, assiduous, diligent
EJEKU 1. secretary 2. (侍讀) Reader, BH 135, 196
    EJEKU HAFAN (主事) Second Class Secretary of a Board, BH 292
    EJEKU I TINGGIN (都事廳) Chancery of the Censorate, BH 211
EJELEBUMBI caus. of *ejelembi*
EJELEMBI to be master of, to rule, to occupy by force, to establish control over
EJELENDUMBI/EJELENUMBI to occupy together, to occupy (of a group)
EJELESI owner, possessor
EJELTU one having authority
EJEMBI to remember, to take account of, to record, to note down
EJEN ruler, lord, master, host, emperor
    EJEN ILIMBI to be one's guide, to be leader, to be master
EJERGEN governance
EJESU having a good memory
EJETE plural of *ejen*
EJETUN record, description, gazetteer
    EJETUN BITHEI KUREN (志書館) office for the compilation of dynastic records
EJETUNGGE pertaining to records
EJIHE a food made from dried cream
EK SEMBI to be tired of, to be annoyed with
EK TAK SEME overbearingly, arrogantly
    EK TAK SEME ESUKIYEMBI to reprove arrogantly
EKCIN 1. bank (of a river) 2. an evil spirit
    EKCIN JOLO ugly, hideous
EKCUMBI to slander someone behind his back
EKE 1. a pause particle used when one cannot think of what to say next 2. you there!
    EKE EKE SEMBI to stutter, to stammer
    EKE YA who was it now?--said when one can't think of a person's name
EKEHE see *eke*
EKIDUN CECIKE another name for the crow tit; cf. *kidun cecike*
EKIMBI see *ekiyembi*
EKISAKA still, quiet, calm
EKIYEHUN 1. too little, lacking 2. empty, unoccupied
EKIYEMBI 1. to diminish, to be deficient, to be too little, to be lacking 2. to be vacant, to be unoccupied

    3. to go away (a boil or swelling)
    4. to subside (floodwaters)
EKIYEMBUMBI caus. of *ekiyembi*
    EKIYEMBURE DALANGGA a dam used to regulate the flow of water in a river
EKIYEN lacking, decrease, vacancy
EKIYENDEMBI see *ekiyembi*
    EKIYENDERE GUCU a false friend, a dangerous friend
    EKIYENDERE JALIN I MENGGUN meltage fee
EKIYENIYEBUMBI caus. of *ekiyeniyembi*
EKIYENIYEMBI to lessen, to diminish
    EKIYENIYERE NONGGIRE CESE population register
EKŠEMBI to hurry, to hasten
    EKŠEME SAKSIME rushing, hurrying, in a rush
EKŠENDUMBI/EKŠENUMBI to hurry (of a group)
EKŠUN 1. bothersome, troublesome (of a person) 2. the dregs of yellow rice wine
EKTEMBI to stamp the front hoof on the ground, to paw the ground
EKTERŠEMBI to distinguish oneself, to excel
ELBEBUMBI caus. of *elbembi*
ELBEFEMBI to talk carelessly, not giving sufficient heed to what one is saying
ELBEKU a cover, a shelter put up as a protection against the sun
ELBEMBI 1. to cover 2. to thatch
ELBEN covering, thatch
    ELBEN FEMBI to cut thatch with a sickle; cf. *elbefembi*
    ELBEN GŪWARA a type of owl
    ELBEN I BOO a thatched house, a humble cottage
    ELBEN I JEOFI a thatched hut with a round roof
ELBENFEMBI to speak nonsense
ELBESU a person rash in speech and actions
ELBETU 1. coarse (of workmanship) 2. a sacrificial hat worn during the Shang dynasty
ELBIBUMBI caus. of *elbimbi*
ELBIHE raccoon-dog (*Nyctereutes procyonoides*)
ELBIHENGGE pertaining to the raccoon-dog
ELBIMBI to summon, to call together, to invite, to win over to one's own side
ELBINDUMBI/ELBINUMBI to bring over to one's own side (of a group)
ELBINEMBI to go to summon
ELBIŠEBUMBI caus. of *elbišembi*
ELBIŠEMBI to bathe in a river
ELBIŠENEMBI to go to take a bath in a

river

ELBIŠENUMBI   to bathe together in a
   river

ELCIN   emissary, messenger
   ELCIN CECIKE   one of the names of
      the *mejin cecike*

ELDEDEI   one name for the lark; cf.
   wenderhen

ELDEMBI (-ke, -pi)   1. to shine, to
   glow   2. to shine forth, to be well-
   known

ELDEMBUMBI   1. caus. of *eldembi*   2. to
   glorify, to extol
   ELDEMBUME ENGGELENEMBI   to go to,
      to visit (honorific)

ELDEN   light, glory, resplendence

ELDENEMBI   to go to shine, to shine
   there

ELDENGGE   shining, glowing, resplendent,
   glorious
   ELDENGGE AMBALINGGŪ   glorious and
      grand
   ELDENGGE SARACAN USIHA (華 蓋)
      the name of a constellation
   ELDENGGE WEHE   a (funerary) inscrip-
      tion, stele

ELDENJIMBI   to come to shine, to grace
   a place with one's presence

ELDERHEN   one name for the lark; cf.
   wenderhen

ELDERI USIHA   the seventh star of the
   Great Dipper

ELDEŠEMBI   to shine incessantly

ELE   1. (used after a participle) all
   2. still more, especially
   ELE . . . ELE . . .   the more . . .
      the more . . .
   ELE ELEI   1. still more, to an even
      greater degree   2. continuous

ELE MILA   free and easy, casual, at
   ease

ELEBUMBI   caus. of *elembi*

ELECUN   satisfied, content, pleased
   ELECUN AKŪ   unsatisfied, covetous

ELEHUDEMBI   to be satisfied, to be
   content

ELEHUN .content, generous, satisfied
   with one's lot, tolerant, content
   in adversity
   ELEHUN SULA   free and easy, unre-
      strained, content

ELEI   1. still more, more   2. almost
   ELEI ELEI   still more, much more,
      more and more
   ELEI ELEKEI   almost, hardly

ELEKEI   almost, hardly

ELEMANGGA   1. on the other hand, on the
   contrary, in spite of that   2. still
   more, especially

ELEMBI   to suffice, to be enough

ELEMIMBI   to tow (a boat)

ELEN   1. sufficiency   2. a goal
   ELEN DE   sufficiently

ELEN DE ISIMBI   to reach a suffi-
   cient level, to be enough
   ELEN DE ISINAMBI   to reach a goal
   ELEN OMBI   to be sufficient
   ELEN TELEN AKŪ   matched in strength,
      evenly matched

ELENGGE   everything

ELENGGI   slovenly, lazy (of women)

ELEREMBI (-ke)   1. to bare the chest
   2. to become exhausted from running,
   to be out of breath

ELERI   1. sufficient, self-satisfied
   2. disorderly (of clothing)

ELETELE   until (it is) enough, in sufficient quantity
   ELETELE BUMBI   to give in sufficient
      quantity

ELGEBUMBI   caus. of *elgembi*

ELGEMBI   to lead an animal by the reins

ELGIN   see *elgiyen*

ELGIYEKEN   somewhat rich, somewhat prosperous

ELGIYEN   prosperous, rich, plentiful,
   abundant
   ELGIYEN ANIYA   a good year (of a
      harvest)
   ELGIYEN I FUSEMBURE FIYENTEN (慶
      豐 司)   Pasturage Department,
      BH 83
   ELGIYEN ICE CALU   a granary in the
      city of Peking
   ELGIYEN JALUNGGA CALU   a granary
      located in Chihli
   ELGIYEN TESUHE NAMUN   a silver de-
      pository in Shansi
   ELGIYEN TUMIN   rich and abundant
   ELGIYEN TUMIN CALU   a granary just
      outside Peking
   ELGIYEN TUSANGGA CALU   a granary by
      An-ho bridge

ELGIYENGGE   richly endowed, lavish

ELHE   1. peace, calm, well-being   2.
   peaceful, well, healthy, easy, slow
   ELHE AKŪ   not well, not feeling well
   ELHE ALHAI   slowly, easily, calmly,
      easygoing
   ELHE BE BAIMBI   to ask after a per-
      son's health
   ELHE BE FONJIMBI   to inquire after
      a person's health
   ELHE NUHAN   at ease, not rushed,
      casual
   ELHE SAIN   well, in good health
   ELHE TAIFIN   1. peace   2. the K'ang-
      hsi (康 熙) reign period,
      1662--1721

ELHEBUMBI   to calm, to let rest
   ELHEBURE HIYAN MOO   the tree *Styrax
      benzoin* from which gum benzoin is
      obtained

ELHEKEN   rather well, gentle, rather
   slow

ELHEKŪ   contraction of *elhe akū*

E

E

ELHENGGE peaceful, pacific
ELHEO how are you?
ELHERHEN one name for the lark; cf.
    wenderhen
ELHEŠEBUMBI caus. of *elhešembi*
ELHEŠEMBI to take it easy, to act
    leisurely, to slow down, to slacken
ELI one-thousandth of a Chinese foot
ELIN storeroom under the roof, loft
ELINTU a large black ape (*Cynopithecus*)
ELINTUMBI to observe from afar
ELIOI the six lower pipes of the an-
    cient Chinese music scale
ELJE jawbone of a whale
    ELJE BERI a bow made from the jaw-
        bone of a whale
ELJEMBI to oppose, to resist, to defy
ELJENDUMBI/ELJENUMBI to oppose one
    another
ELJENJIMBI to come to oppose
ELKIBUMBI caus. of *elkimbi*
ELKIMBI 1. to summon by waving the
    hand, to signal to, to greet 2. to
    brandish a sword in preparation for
    entering combat
ELKINDUMBI/ELKINUMBI 1. to wave (of a
    group) 2. to brandish (of a group)
ELMIN an unbroken horse
ELMIYEN see *elmin*
ELU onion, scallion
ELURI prodigy, prodigious
EMBICI 1. or 2. perhaps 3. in the
    first place
EMDE together
EMDUBEI continually, persistently,
    steadily, frequently, earnestly,
    keep on . . .
EME mother
EMEKE husband's mother--mother-in-law
EMEKEI how frightful!
EMEMBIHEDE sometimes, now and then,
    at times
EMEMU some
    EMEMU ERINDE sometimes
    EMEMU FONDE sometimes, at certain
        times
    EMEMU URSE some people
EMEMUNGGE some (as substantive)
EMETE plural of *eme*
EMGEI see *emgeri*
EMGERI 1. once 2. already
EMGI together
    EMGI SIMNERE HAFAN assistant to
        the examination proctor
EMGILEMBI to act together, to act
    mutually
EMHE wife's mother--mother-in-law
    (in some early texts it may also
    refer to a husband's mother)
EMHULEMBI to take for oneself, to take
    for one's own use
EMHUN alone, sole, lonely
EMILE the female of birds

EMILEBUMBI caus. of *emilembi*
EMILEMBI to cover, to screen off, to
    block out
EMKE one (as substantive)
    EMKE EMKEN I one by one, little by
        little
EMKECI once, point by point, in detail
EMKEN see *emke*
EMPI the name of a number of low herbs
    of the *Artemisia* or *Chenopodium*
    families; cf. *eremu*
EMPIREMBI to talk nonsense, to talk
    foolishly
EMTE one each
EMTELEMBI to receive one each
EMTELI alone, sole, single
EMTENGGERI once each
EMTUN see *amtun*
EMTUNGGE JODON plain hemp cloth, sack-
    cloth
EMU one
    EMU ADALI the same
    EMU AKŪ not the same
    EMU ANAN one after another, in turn
    EMU BADE OBUME SINDAMBI to stake
        all on a single bet
    EMU BIHA a small bit, a small seg-
        ment
    EMU BUKDAN one sheet of folded paper
    EMU BURGIN one spell of confusion
    EMU CIMARI the amount of land that
        can be plowed in a single day--
        approximately six *mu*
    EMU DE OCI in the first instance
    EMU DEREI at the same time
        that . . . , while . . . , on the
        one hand
    EMU DEREI . . . EMU DEREI . . . on
        the one hand . . . on the other
        hand . . .
    EMU ERGEN I in one breath, in one
        swallow, in one burst of effort
    EMU ERGUWEN one period of twelve
        years
    EMU ERIN one (meal) time
    EMU ERINDE for a moment
    EMU FALAN a little while, a while
    EMU FEHUN one pace (five Chinese
        feet)
    EMU FIYEN one set of feathers on an
        arrow
    EMU FUTA 1. one *sheng* (180 Chinese
        feet) 2. one string of cash
    EMU FUTA JIHA one string of cash
    EMU GALA one hand's length
    EMU GIRIN I BA one district, one
        region
    EMU GŪNIN I intently, wholeheart-
        edly, with singleness of mind
    EMU HAHA one man's measure (thirty
        mu)
    EMU HUNGKEN JIHA 5662 strings of
        cash and 369 pieces

EMU HŪFAN a joint business venture, partnership

EMU I GINGGULERE ORDO a pavilion housing inscribed stone tablets

EMU I HAFURE consistently

EMU ICI consistent, hitherto, up to now

EMU IKIRI in succession, in a row

EMU INDEME one stage of a journey

EMU JEMIN I OKTO one dose of medicine

EMU JUKTE one large slice (of meat)

EMU JULEHEN I with one's whole attention, with singleness of purpose, directly

EMU JUWE GIYAN one or two items

EMU KIYA one cell of a honeycomb

EMU MARI once, one time

EMU OCI at first, in the first place

EMU OKSON one pace

EMU SEFERE SALIYAN one handful exactly

EMU SIRAN I in a row, successively

EMU SUIHEN I BANJIMBI to live keeping one's mind on what is truly important

EMU ŠURU SALIYAN I CIKTEN a stick or rod exactly one span long

EMU TALGAN one surface, one flat object

EMU TEMUHEN one round or cylindrical object, a spool

EMU UDU several, a series of, successively

EMU UFUHI SULABUMBI to leave an extra portion of cloth in a seam to be used for letting out garments when they become outgrown

EMU UHUN one parcel, one bundle

EMU YABUN EMU AŠŠAN every action and motion

EMU YOHI one complete set (of a book)

EMUCI first

EMUDE in the first place

EMURSU having one layer, simple, unlined

EMURSU ETUKU an unlined garment

EMUSE one year old

EN yes--interjection used to answer affirmatively

EN EN SEME saying yes, yes . . .

EN JE SEME same as *en en seme*

EN JEN ready, finished, complete

EN JEN I BELHEMBI to make ready

ENCEBUMBI caus. of *encembi*

ENCEHEDEMBI to be capable, to be talented

ENCEHEN capable, adept, talented

ENCEHEN AKŪ inadept, not talented

ENCEHENGGE a capable person, an adept one

ENCEHEŠEMBI to be capable, to be talented

ENCEHUN see *encehen*

ENCEMBI to apportion food and drink to guests at a meal

ENCINA suddenly, all at once

ENCU different, other, strange

ENCU DEMUN heterodoxy

ENCU FACU doting (on a child)

ENCU FALGA country estate

ENCU HACIN I extraordinarily

ENCU INENGGI another day

ENCU TEMBI to live separately

ENCUHEN livelihood, property

ENCULEBUMBI caus. of *enculembi*

ENCULEMBI to be different, to do differently, to go one's separate way

ENCULEME separately, in addition

ENCUMBI see *encembi*

ENCUNGGE that which is different

ENDEBUKU error, mistake

ENDEBUKU BE MISHALARA TINGGIN (緼 挺 廞) the name of a section of the Imperial Academy

ENDEBUKU UFARACUN errors and mistakes

ENDEBUMBI 1. caus. of *endembi* 2. to go astray, to err, to lose one's grip, to do by accident 3. to choke by getting food caught in the windpipe

ENDEBUFI WAMBI to kill by accident

ENDEMBI 1. to err, to be mistaken about 2. euphemism for 'to die'

ENDEREO am I not right?

ENDERI SENDERI uneven, battered, in bad shape

ENDESLAMBI to make a small error

ENDUHEN one name for the crane; cf. *bulehen*

ENDURI spirit, god, deity

ENDURI CECIKENGGE LOHO a sword with the image of a divine bird on its blade

ENDURI GIRDAN a banner hung before holy images

ENDURI HUTU spirits and ghosts

ENDURI NAMUN a storehouse for religious vessels and paraphernalia

ENDURI NIKEBUN painted icon of a god or a plaque with a god's name written on it

ENDURI NIYALMA an immortal, a Taoist deity

ENDURI URGUNJEBURE KUMUN a piece of music played at minor sacrifices

ENDURI WECEKU spirits and gods

ENDURIN a Taoist immortal

ENDURINGGE divine, holy, sacred

ENDURINGGE EJEN the divine lord-- the emperor

ENDURINGGE ERDEMU AMBULA SELGIYERE MUDAN a musical piece played at banquets given in honor of meri-

E

torious generals and officials

ENDURINGGE NIYALMA a holy man, a
sage, a saint

ENEN descendants, progeny

ENENGGI today

ENENGGI CIMARI this morning

ENESE plural of *enen*

ENESHUKEN somewhat sloping

ENESHUN gently sloping

ENESHUN TAFUKŪ steps in front of
the platform in a temple

ENETKEK India, the valley of the
Ganges, Indian, Sanskrit

ENETKEK HERGENGGE LOHO a sword with
Sanskrit written on the blade

ENG 1. interjection of pain 2. interjection of disapproval

ENG SEME drawling (an answer), groan-
ing

ENGGE a bird's beak

ENGGE FULGIYAN ITU Chinese Chukar
partridge (*Alectoris graeca*)

ENGGECI see *enggici*

ENGGELCEMBI to act in an excessive
way

ENGGELE SENGGELE AKŪ unaffectionate,
indifferent (to relatives or friends)

ENGGELEBUMBI caus. of *enggelembi*

ENGGELEKU a ledge or projection on a
cliff

ENGGELEMBI 1. to jut out, to project
2. to rise (of prices) 3. to lean
forward (to look) 4. to border on,
to overlook, to command a view of

ENGGELEME TUWAMBI to lean out to
look

ENGGELENEMBI to go to watch, to approach, to pay a visit (honorific),
to go (honorific)

ENGGELENJIMBI to come near, to come to
pay a visit (honorific), to come
(honorific)

ENGGELENJIRE BE YARURE GIRDAN (降
引 幡) a banner used by the
imperial escort

ENGGELESHUN projecting outward

ENGGELJEMBI see *enggelcembi*

ENGGEMU saddle

ENGGEMU FAKSI a saddler

ENGGEMU GAIMBI to unsaddle

ENGGEMU HŪWAITAMBI to put on a
saddle

ENGGERHEN a towering projection

ENGGETE MOO an alder

ENGGETU CECIKE brown bush warbler
(*Phylloscopus fuscatus*)

ENGGICI secret, secretly, privately

ENGGULE a type of onion that grows in
sandy soil (*Allium victorialis*)

ENGKI CONGKI just enough

ENIHEN bitch

ENIHUN loosely wound (of fibers)

ENIRHEN wisteria

ENIYE mother

ENIYEHEN see *enihen*

ENIYEHUN see *enihun*

ENIYEINGGE pertaining to motherhood,
maternal

ENIYEN female moose (*Alces alces*)

ENIYEN BUHŪ doe

ENIYENIYE hibernating (of snakes)

ENJI vegetable dishes, vegetarian

ENJI BELHERE BA (素 局)
kitchen for the preparation of
vegetarian dishes for the emperor

ENTEHEME eternally, always

ENTEHEME ASARARA CALU a granary
located in Heilungkiang

ENTEHEME ELGIYEN CALU a granary in
Ilan Hala

ENTEHEME ELGIYENGGE CALU a granary
in Shantung

ENTEHEME ELHE CALU a granary in
Kwangtung

ENTEHEME GINGGUN CALU granaries in
the provinces

ENTEHEME IKTAMBURE CALU a granary
in Heilungkiang

ENTEHEME JALUNGGA NAMUN a silver
depository in Kiangsu

ENTEHEME JULGE high antiquity

ENTEHEME TAIFIN CALU a granary in
Kilin

ENTEHEME TUSA ARARA NAMUN the
treasury of Tungling

ENTEHEME TUSANGGA CALU emergency
granaries

ENTEHEN regular, fixed, long-term

ENTEHEN HETHE fixed property, real
property

ENTEHETEI forever

ENTEKE this sort of

ENTEKENGGE one like this

EO lotus root

ERDE early, early in the morning

ERDE BAICARA DANGSE yamen em-
ployee's attendance record

ERDE BUDA breakfast

ERDEDARI every morning

ERDEKEN rather early, nice and early

ERDELEMBI to be early, to do early

ERDEMU capability, virtue, power

ERDEMU BE NEILEKU (諭 德) an
official one step lower in rank
than *tuwancihiyakū* in the Supervisorate of Imperial Instruction

ERDEMU ETEHE POO (德 勝 礮)
the name of a large cannon

ERDEMU GASHA a name for the chicken

ERDEMU MUTEN talent, capability

ERDEMUNGGE virtuous, talented, moral

ERE this

ERE AI DEMUN what is this all
about?

ERE ANIYA this year

ERE BIYA this month

ERE CIMARI this morning
ERE DURUN I   in this fashion
ERE FONI this time
ERE MINI NIMEKU this is my weakness
ERE NIYALMA DE DOTORI BI this man
  has hidden talents
ERE NIYALMA FISIKAN this man just
  gets by
ERE UCURI of late, recently
ERE UJU BE TONGKI cut off this
  head!--an expression of abuse
EREBE AINAMBI how should (we) handle
  this?
ERECI AMASI after this, hereafter
EREI JALIN because of this
EREBUMBI caus. of *erembi*
ERECUKE hopeful
ERECUN hope, expectation
  ERECUN AKŪ hopeless
EREHUNJEBUMBI caus. of *erehunjembi*
EREHUNJEMBI to hope constantly, to
  hope earnestly
EREINGGE this person's
EREMBI 1. to hope 2. to peel birch-
  bark off a tree
EREMU yellow artemisia (*Artemisia
  annua*)
ERENI by this, through this, from this,
  therefore
ERETELE up till now, up to this point
ERGECE NIYEHE the mandarin duck; cf.
  ijifun niyehe
ERGECUN at leisure, free, leisure
ERGELEBUMBI caus./pass. of *ergelembi*
ERGELEMBI 1. to force, to coerce 2.
  to torment 3. to carry (one's arm)
  in a sling
ERGELEN force, coercion
ERGELETEI by force, obligatory
ERGEMBI (-he/ke) to rest, to pause
  ERGERAKŪ indefatigable
ERGEMBUMBI caus. of *ergembi*
ERGEN 1. breath, life 2. penis
  ERGEN BEYE body and life
  ERGEN DEN breathing is difficult
  ERGEN GAIMBI to breathe
  ERGEN HETUMBI to manage to get by
  ERGEN HETUMBUMBI to make one's
    livelihood
  ERGEN I SEN the opening of the
    urethra
  ERGEN JAKA penis
  ERGEN JOCIMBI to be murdered, to
    perish
  ERGEN SUMBI breathing stops
  ERGEN ŠELEMBI to stake one's life,
    to be desperate
  ERGEN TAMBI life hangs on a thread
  ERGEN TEMŠEMBI to struggle to live
    (of an ill person), to gasp for
    breath
  ERGEN YADAMBI to stop breathing,
    to die

ERGENDEMBI to rest
  ERGENDERAKŪ never rests, without
    rest
ERGENDUMBI/ERGENUMBI to rest (of a
  group)
ERGENGGE living, living creature
  ERGENGGE JAKA living creature
ERGEŠEMBI to breathe hard from fatigue
  or overeating, to pant
ERGI 1. direction, side 2. this side
ERGINGGE pertaining to direction
ERGULE self-willed
  ERGULE OHO departed from the pat-
    tern
ERGUME court dress
ERGUWE see *erhuwe*
ERGUWEJITU compasses
ERGUWEMBI to go around, to circle
  around
  ERGUWERE GARUNGGŪ FUKJINGGA HERGEN
  (迴 鸞 書) a style of cal-
    ligraphy
ERGUWEN 1. perimeter, circumference
  2. a period of twelve years, a cycle
  ERGUWEN ANIYA the cyclical year of
    one's birth
  ERGUWEN DE TORHOMBI to go around in
    a circle
ERHE 1. a green frog 2. see *erihe*
ERHEMBI see *ergembi*
ERHUWE a piece of red felt used to
  cover the hole on the top of a yurt
ERI isn't it like this? isn't it
  here?
ERIBUMBI caus. of *erimbi*
ERIDARI see *erindari*
ERIHE a Buddhist rosary (with 108
  beads)
  ERIHE BE TOLOMBI to recite the
    rosary
ERIKU broom
  ERIKU ŠUŠU broom straw
  ERIKU USIHA comet
ERILEMBI to act at the right time,
  to keep the proper time, to do often
  ERILEME at the right time, on time,
    from time to time
  ERILEME GUWENDERE JUNGKEN a chiming
    clock
  ERILERE NIONGNIYAHA one name for
    the wild goose; cf. *bigan i
    niongniyaha*
ERIMBI to sweep
ERIMBU a gem, precious stone
  ERIMBU ILHA a bright red exotic
    flower
  ERIMBU WEHE a precious stone, gem,
    jewel
ERIN 1. time, season 2. one of the
  two-hour divisions of the day
  ERIN AKŪ often
  ERIN BE AMCAME punctually
  ERIN FONJIRE JUNGKEN alarm clock

E

E

ERIN FORGON propitious time, the
  right moment
ERIN FORGON I TON I BITHE a calendar
  book
ERIN FORGON I TON I BITHE DE AFAHA
HAFAN (司 書) Compiler in the
  Calendar Section, BH 229
ERIN FORGON I TON I BITHE KUNGGERI
  (時 憲 科) a section of the
  Board of Rites concerned with cal-
  endrical matters
ERIN FORGON I TON I BITHE WEILERE
TINGGIN (司 書 廳) a bureau
  concerned with the compilation of
  the calendar in the Imperial Board
  of Astronomy
ERIN FORGON I TON I HONTOHO (時
  憲 科) Calendar Section in the
  Imperial Board of Astronomy, BH
  229
ERIN HŪDA current price
ERIN I KEMNEKU a small sundial
ERIN I KEMUN clock, watch
ERIN JAFAFI on time, punctually
ERIN NIMAHA shad
ERIN SONJORO TACIKŪ a school at
  which astronomy was taught
ERIN TUTAMBI   to exceed a deadline
ERIN TUWARA HAFAN (司 晨) As-
  sistant Keeper of the Clepsydra,
  BH 231
ERIN TUWARA HONTOHO (漏 刻 科)
  Section of the Clepsydra, BH 231
ERINDARI every time, on every occasion
ERINGGE pertaining to time
  ERINGGE GASHA one name for the
    chicken
  ERINGGE NIONGNIYAHA one name for the
    wild goose; cf. bigan i niongni-
    yaha
ERITUN soapberry
ERKE powerful, strong, bold
ERKEN TERKEN this way and that, in
  various ways, faltering, stalling
ERKI 1. willful, self-willed, despotic
  2. leaning on a parent in order to
  walk (of a child)
ERKILEMBI to use force, to act despot-
  ically
ERKU see eriku
ERPE a growth on the lip
ERPENEMBI to form a growth on the lip
ERSE plural of ere; cf. ese
ERSELEN a lion
ERSULEN a type of willow whose bran-
  ches were used to make cages
ERSUN ugly, repulsive
ERŠE MAMA midwife
ERŠEBUMBI caus. of eršembi
ERŠEKU an attendant in a local official
  office
ERŠEMBI 1. to serve, to wait on, to
  attend 2. to take care of (children)

  3. to get smallpox
ERTELE up till now
ERTUMBI to depend on, to rely on
ERTUN dependence, reliance
ERU fearless, intrepid, brave
ERUKEN rather fearless, rather intre-
  pid
ERULEBUMBI caus. of erulembi
ERULEMBI to torture, to punish
ERUMBI see erulembi
ERUN torture, punishment
  ERUN BE GETUKELERE TACIHIYAN DE
    AISILARA TEMGETUN (明 刑 弼
    教 旌) an inscribed banner of
    the imperial escort
  ERUN BE GINGGULERE FIYENTEN (慎
    刑 司) Judicial Department
    (of the Imperial Household), BH 81
  ERUN KORO torture and punishment,
    penalty
  ERUN NIKEBUMBI to apply torture, to
    inflict punishment
  ERUN SUI torture and crime!--a term
    of abuse
ERUWEDEBUMBI caus. of eruwedembi
ERUWEDEMBI to drill (a hole), to make
  a hole with an auger
ERUWEN drill, auger
ESE plural of ere--these people, these
ESEINGGE these people's
ESHEN father's younger brother--uncle
ESHETE plural of eshen
ESHUKEN somewhat raw
ESHUN 1. raw 2. untried, untamed,
  unfamiliar, strange
  ESHUN CECERI raw silk of one color
  ESHUN GIOWANSE same as eshun ceceri
  ESHUN LINGSE fine-figured raw silk
  ESHUN SELE raw iron, pig iron
  ESHUN SUBERI white raw silk
ESHUREBUMBI caus. of eshurembi
ESHUREMBI to become wilted, to become
  bad
ESHURUMBI see eshurembi
ESI certainly, of course (usually fol-
  lowed by the conditional converb)
  ESI SECI OJORAKŪ involuntarily
ESIHE scale (of a fish)
ESIHENGGE scaled, having scales
ESIKE interjection--I'm full, I've had
  enough to eat
ESUKIYEBUMBI caus. of esukiyembi
ESUKIYEMBI to scream, to screech, to
  shout, to rail at, to reprove, to
  bawl out
ESUNGGIYEMBI to shout, to yell (an-
  grily)
EŠE husband's younger brother--brother-
  in-law
EŠEBUMBI caus. of ešembi
EŠEMBI 1. to scale (a fish) 2. to be
  slanting or oblique
  EŠEME ACABUHA HERGEN (切 音 字)

E

a device for recording the pronunciation of Chinese characters by using two other characters

EŠEMELIYAN somewhat slanting

EŠEN slanting, oblique

    EŠEN I BOO a side hall in the palace

EŠENGGE slanting, oblique, diagonal

    EŠENGGE FU a diagonal wall

    EŠENGGE MOO diagonal planking outboard of a ship

    EŠENGGE MUDAN oblique tones

EŠENJU BOO an obliquely built house

EŠENJU JUGŪN a diagonal road

EŠERGE MOO a tree that grows in the mountains and has deep graining

EŠETE plural of *eše*

ETEHEN victory

ETEMBI 1. to overcome, to win, to be victorious 2. to be hard on one end (a bow)

    ETEME HALAMBI to surmount, to make a change for the better

    ETERE BE TOKTOBURE POO (制 勝 礮) the name of a large bronze cannon

ETEN force, resistance

ETENGGI hardy, strong, powerful

ETENGGILEBUMBI caus. of *etenggilembi*

ETENGGILEMBI to use force, to resort to force

ETERI ILHA the name of a dark red exotic flower

ETUBUMBI caus. of *etumbi*

ETUHUKEN rather strong, rather powerful

ETUHUN 1. strong, powerful, vigorous 2. bridegroom

    ETUHUN DAHABUMBI to accompany the bride to the house of the bridegroom

ETUHUŠEBUMBI caus. of *etuhušembi*

ETUHUŠEMBI to use force

ETUKU clothing, garment

    ETUKU ADU clothing

    ETUKU DUSIHI clothes

    ETUKU HALAMBI euphemism for 'to menstruate'

ETUKULEMBI to dress

    ETUKULERE BULEKU a dressing mirror

ETUKUNGGE pertaining to clothing

ETUMBI to put on (clothing), to wear

EU JEU Europe

EYE 1. pit for storing grain, vegetables, etc. 2. pitfall 3. dungeon

EYEBUKU see *mukei eyebuku*

    EYEBUKU ASU a fish net used to catch fish swimming close to the surface

EYEBUMBI caus. of *eyembi*

EYEMBI 1. to flow 2. to sink (of a steelyard)

    EYEFI SEKIYEFI laggard, dallying, lazy

    EYEHE SOHIN a moving ice floe

    EYERE USIHA meteor, falling star

EYEMELIYAN a bit sinking (of a steelyard)

EYEMPE see *eimpe*

EYEN flow, current

    EYEN SEYEN AKŪ indifferent, unaffected

EYENEMBI to flow in that direction

EYER HAYAR sauntering pleasantly (strolling)

EYERI HAYARI see *eyer hayar*

EYERJEMBI to have a fresh appearance, to look nice and fresh

EYERŠEBUMBI caus./pass. of *eyeršembi*

EYERŠECUKE despicable, hateful, disgusting

EYERŠEMBI 1. to feel sick at the stomach 2. to be disgusted

EYUN 1. elder sister 2. elder (of girls)

EYUNGGE elder (of girls)

EYUTE plural of *eyun*

F

FA 1. window 2. magic 3. dharma
 FA BE FEKUMBI to jump out the window
 FA CIKIN window sill
 FA I GEBU religious name
 FA I OROLOKŪ window screen
 FA I SANGGA an opening in the lat-
  ticework of a window
 FA ULHŪMA black grouse (*Lyrurus
  tetrix*)
FABUMBI 1. caus. of *fambi* 2. to
 chase down (a defeated opponent)
FACABUMBI caus. of *facambi*
FACAMBI to disperse, to scatter
FACIHIN see *facuhūn*
FACIHIYAŠABUMBI caus. of *facihiyašambi*
FACIHIYAŠAMBI to worry, to be upset
FACIHIYAŠANDUMBI/FACIHIYAŠANUMBI to
 worry (of a group)
FACUHŪN 1. confused, in disarray, con-
 fusion, disorder 2. rebellion
 FACUHŪN I BA diaphragm, midriff
FACUHŪRABUMBI caus. of *facuhūrambi*
FACUHŪRAMBI 1. to be in disorder, to
 rebel 2. to feel confused and dis-
 oriented (of a sick person)
FADAGAN magic
 FADAGAN DERIBUMBI to perform magic
FADAKU venom, poison
FADAMBI to employ magic (in order to
 harm someone)
FADARHŪN one name for the woodpecker;
 cf. *fiyorhon*
FADU bag, pouch
 FADU JAN a whistling arrow with a
  square head
FADULABUMBI caus. of *fadulambi*
FADULAMBI to pack in a bag
FAFAHA a type of sour cherry
FAFULABUMBI caus. of *fafulambi*
FAFULAMBI to fix by law, to hand
 down a decree, to prohibit
FAFUN law, decree, prohibition
 FAFUN I BITHE the code of law

FAFUN I GAMAMBI to handle by law--
 to put to death
FAFUN JAFAHA HAFAN judge
FAFUN KOOLI laws and statutes
FAFUN KOOLI BITHEI KUREN (律例
 館) Commission of Laws, BH 439
FAFUN SELGIYEN decree, promulgation
 of a law
FAFUN ŠAJIN regulations and prohi-
 bitions
FAFUNGGA 1. having legal force, legal
 2. worthy of respect
 FAFUNGGA BAIBULA paradise fly-
  catcher; cf. *baibula*
 FAFUNGGA INENGGI holiday, festival
FAFURI brave, courageous, fierce
FAFURŠAMBI to act bravely, to act
 fiercely
FAFUSHŪLAMBI 1. to make an oath, to
 swear 2. to make an appeal to
 troops before battle
FAFUSHŪN 1. oath, vow 2. a declara-
 tion or oath made to troops before
 battle
FAHA 1. kernel, grain, seed, the pit
 of a fruit 2. eyeball
 FAHA SINDAMBI to mature (of grain
  or fruit)
FAHABUMBI caus./pass. of *fahambi*
FAHALA 1. the dregs of a liquid
 (suspension) 2. dark purple 3.
 opaque, cloudy
 FAHALA NURE heavy, opaque liquor
 FAHALA SURAN slops, water left over
  from cooking or washing rice
FAHAMBI 1. to throw, to throw down
 (at wrestling) 2. to stamp (the
 foot)
 FAHAME GISUREMBI to attack someone
  verbally
 FAHAME INJEMBI to be convulsed with
  laughter
 FAHAME TEMBI to throw oneself into
  a chair from fatigue

FAHARA GIDA a throwing spear
FAHANAMBI to ripen (of grains and
  fruits)
FAHARAMBI to remove the seeds from
  hazel and pine nuts
FAHATAMBI to stamp (the foot)
FAHI inner thigh, perineum
FAHŪN 1. liver 2. courage 3. wheel
  rim
    FAHŪN AKŪ without courage
    FAHŪN AMBA brave, daring
    FAHŪN I ALHŪWA membrane that grows
      on the liver of animals
    FAHŪN SILHI close friend
FAIDABUMBI caus. of *faidambi*
FAIDAMBI to line up, to arrange in
  order
FAIDAN 1. row, rank, formation 2.
  escort 3. procession
    FAIDAN BE DASARA HAFAN (治 儀
      正) Assistant Section Chief (of
      the Equipage Department), BH 123,
      125
    FAIDAN BE JORIRE HAFAN (雲 麾
      使) Assistant Marshal, BH 125
    FAIDAN BE KADALARA HAFAN (冠 軍
      使) various officials of the
      Equipage Department; cf. BH 115,
      123
    FAIDAN BE TUWANCIHIYARA HAFAN 整
      儀 尉) Controller of the Sixth
      Class, BH 125
    FAIDAN BE TUWARA HAFAN (鑾 儀
      使) Commissioner of the Imperial
      Equipage Department, BH 111
    FAIDAN I DA (王 府 長 史   )
      Commandant of a Prince's Palace,
      BH 43
    FAIDAN I DABCIKŪ I FIYENTEN (班
      劍 司) Sword Section (of the
      Imperial Equipage Department),
      BH 122
    FAIDAN I ETUKU clothing worn by the
      imperial escort 典 儀
    FAIDAN I HAFAN (典 儀) Assist-
      ant Major-domo of a Prince's Pal-
      ace, BH 46
    FAIDAN I JANGGIN general term for
      officials in the Imperial Equipage
      Department
    FAIDAN I KIYOO a sedan chair car-
      ried by eight porters that was
      used by the empress in processions
    FAIDAN I NIYALMA porters and in-
      signia bearers of the imperial
      escort
    FAIDAN I SEJEN a carriage used by
      the empress
    FAIDAN I TUNGKEN a large drum used
      by the imperial escort
    FAIDAN I YAMUN (鑾 儀 衞)
      Imperial Equipage Department, BH
      109

FAIDANDUMBI/FAIDANUMBI to line up
  (of a group)
FAIDANGGA ordered, ranked
    FAIDANGGA DENGJAN a pair of lamps
      placed on the altar at state sac-
      rifices
FAIDASI (序 班) Usher (in the
  Board of Rites), BH 382B
    FAIDASI MAHATUN a hat worn by of-
      ficials in ancient times
FAIFAN clapping
FAIFUHALAMBI to dye blue with indigo
FAIHACAMBI to worry, to be upset, to
  fret
FAIJIMA see *faijuma*
FAIJUMA 1. malformed 2. odd, suspi-
  cious, fishy 3. worse (of an ill-
  ness)
FAISHA palisade
FAISHALABUMBI caus. of *faishalambi*
FAISHALAMBI to build a palisade
FAITABUMBI caus. of *faitambi*
FAITABURU may you be cut to pieces!--
  an expletive
FAITAKŪ a small saw (used to cut bones)
FAITAMBI 1. to cut, to slice 2. to
  cut off, to shorten   3. to cut out
  clothing
FAITAN 1. eyebrow 2. a cut
    FAITAN FEHEREMBI to knit the brow
FAITANUMBI to cut together
FAITARABUMBI caus. of *faitarambi*
FAITARAMBI to cut into pieces, to
  mince
    FAITARAME WAMBI to kill by cutting
      to pieces--an extreme form of
      capital punishment
    FAITARAME WARA WEILE a crime pun-
      ishable by delimbing and execu-
      tion
FAJAMBI 1. to defecate (of birds and
  animals) 2. to fade (of stars)
FAJAN feces (of animals and birds),
  dung
    FAJAN FUHEŠEMBI to roll dung into
      balls
    FAJAN ONGGOMBI to become consti-
      pated (of animals)
FAJIRAN wall, an outside wall sur-
  rounding a building
FAJU a fork, forking
FAJUHŪ anus
FAJUHŪRAMBI to perform anal coitus
FAJUKŪ see *fajuhū*
FAK FIK (onom.) the sound of fruit
  falling
FAK SEME 1. sturdily, vigorously 2.
  with a plump, with a thud
    FAK SEME BANJIMBI to grow up to be
      sturdy
    FAK SEME FARAKA fell into a faint
    FAK SEME TEHE sat down with a plump
    FAK SEME TUHEKE fell with a thud

F

F

FAKA a wooden pole with a fork at one
   end
FAKACA short in stature
FAKADAMBI to hit a ball with a stick
   (a type of game)
FAKARI short-legged
FAKAŠAMBI see *fakadambi*
FAKCABUMBI caus. of *fakcambi*
FAKCAMBI 1. to come apart, to divide
   (v.i.), to split, to separate 2. to
   part, to leave
FAKCAN splitting, separation
FAKCANGGA distinct, separated
FAKCASHŪN estranged, alienated
FAKDANGGA CECIKE one name for the myna;
   cf. *kūbulin ilenggu cecike, guwen-
   dehen*
FAKIRI GASHA one name for the chicken
FAKJILAMBI to hold onto, to cling to,
   to support oneself on
   FAKJILAME MARAMBI to refuse stub-
      bornly
FAKJIN 1. support, purchase 2. spur
   on a male fowl
   FAKJIN AKŪ without support, helpless
   FAKJIN BAHARAKŪ without getting a
      hold
   FAKJIN NIKEKU dependence, support
      and reliance
FAKSA 1. straight into, deep into
   2. violently (angry), wholeheartedly,
   greatly
FAKSABUN see *joringga i fakcabun*
FAKSALABUMBI 1. caus. of *faksalambi*
   2. to separate, to remove
FAKSALAMBI to separate, to part
FAKSALAN separation, division
FAKSI 1. craftsman, workman 2. skilled
   3. clever, shrewd
   FAKSI BOŠORO DA (司 匠) Over-
      seer, Inspector of Works, Clerk
      of Works, Overseer of Works, BH 77,
      82, 96, 460A
   FAKSI CECIKE one name for the wren;
      cf. *darha cecike*
   FAKSI DA chief artisan
   FAKSI JURGAN (武 備 院) Im-
      perial Armory, BH 89
FAKSIDAMBI to act shrewdly, to act
   cleverly, to argue cleverly
FAKSIKAN rather clever, shrewd, or
   skilled
   FAKSIKAN I FORGOŠOME FIYELEMBI to
      do a skillful turn at trick riding
   FAKSIKAN I GAMAMBI to handle
      cleverly
FAKSINGGA endowed with skill, skillful
FAKSISA plural of *faksi*
   FAKSISAI KUNGGERI (匠 科) a
      section of the Board of Works con-
      cerned with artisans
FAKŪ a stone dam in a river--used for
   catching fish

FAKŪRI pants, trousers
   FAKŪRI FERGE the seam in the seat
      of trousers
FALABUMBI 1. to exile, to banish, to
   expel 2. see *gūnin falabumbi*
   FALABURE WEILE crime punished by
      exile
FALABUN exile, banishment
FALAN 1. floor 2. threshing floor
   3. quarter of a town 4. sacrificial
   site 5. a while, a short period
   FALAN SOMBI to offer bread on the
      threshing floor after the autumn
      harvest
FALANGGA pertaining to the floor or
   earth
   FALANGGA DENGJAN a lantern hung on
      a pole that is stuck in the earth
   FALANGGA NAHAN an earthen floor
      with a passage under it through
      which hot air from an outside fire
      passes--a type of central heating
FALANGGŪ the palm of the hand
   FALANGGŪ DUMBI to clap the hands
   FALANGGŪ FAIFAN applause
   FALANGGŪ FORIMBI to clap the hands
   FALANGGŪ USIHA a sweet fruit in the
      shape of a man's palm that comes
      from Yunnan
FALASU enamel, enamelware
FALGA 1. clan, tribe 2. all the peo-
   ple living on one street, quarter of
   a town 3. office, bureau 4. group,
   clump, grove 5. measure word for
   buildings 6. gust (of wind)
   FALGA FALGA in clumps, in groves,
      in gusts
FALGANGGA 1. office, subsection 2.
   Second Class Transport Station (on
   the Grand Canal) (所), BH 834
FALGARI bureau, office
   FALGARI I AISILAKŪ (置 丞)
      Director of an Office, BH 389, 391
   FALGARI I ICIHIYAKŪ (置 正)
      Assistant Director of an Office
FALHA see *falga*
FALI 1. measure word for solid objects,
   a lump 2. a unit of money
FALIBUMBI caus. of *falimbi*
FALIMBI 1. to tie, to bind 2. to con-
   clude (a treaty or agreement)
FALIN tying, binding
FALINDUMBI to be bound to one another
FALINGGA having connection, connected,
   bound
FALINTAMBI to trip, to stumble
FALINTU MONIO one name for the monkey
FALISHŪN intermittent
FALMAHŪN (房) the name of a constel-
   lation
FALU Manchurian bream (*Megalobrama
   terminalis*)
FAMAMBI to lose one's way, to get lost

FAMBI 1. to dry up, to become very
thirsty 2. to become tired
FAMBUMBI see *famambi*
FAMHA spindle, a stick or board for
winding thread or yarn
FAN 1. pan, dish, tray 2. barbarian,
foreign
    FAN DASAFI TUKIYEMBI to put assorted
    delicacies on a tray and offer
    them to guests
    FAN FERE a small gulch or canyon,
    the course of a creek or a spring
FANCABUMBI caus./pass. of *fancambi*
FANCACUKA vexing, annoying, stifling,
causing despair
FANCAKŪ NIMEKU epilepsy
FANCAMBI 1. to get angry, to be sti-
fled 2. to spring (of a lock)
    FANCAME HALHŪN stifling hot
    FANCAME INJEMBI to be convulsed
    with laughter
FANDI a wooden grip on an oar or on a
mast
FANDZ 1. foreigner, (western) barbar-
ian 2. see *fanse*
FANG square (as in 'square feet')
FANG JANG Buddhist abbot
FANG SEME solidly, immovably
FANGDZ prescription, recipe
FANGGA magic, possessed of magic
powers
    FANGGA BITHE amulet, fetish, charm
    FANGGA NIYALMA magician
FANGKABUMBI 1. caus. of *fangkambi*
2. to repay a debt with an object of
equivalent value, to make restitu-
tion, to compensate for
FANGKAKŪ an earth packer--usually a
large flat stone
FANGKALA low, short
FANGKAMBI to throw down, to drive, to
beat
    FANGKAME TEMBI to sit in a rigid,
    unnatural manner
FANGNAI sure, firm, determined, resolute, stubborn
    FANGNAI OJORAKŪ unsure, irresolute
FANGNAMBI to deny, to go back on what
one has said
    FANGNAME LAIDAMBI to deny what one
    has said
FANGSE 1. pongee, a light raw silk;
cf. *sirgeri* 2. banner
FANGSIKŪ racks on both sides of a
stove used for drying noodles
FANGŠAKŪ a device used for smoking
fox, rabbits, badgers, etc. from
their holes
FANGŠAMBI 1. to smoke (v.t.), to fu-
migate, to smoke out 2. to deny,
to lie
FANGŠANGGA TUBI a smoking rack for
meat and fish

FANIHIYAN a chopping board
FANIYAHIYAN see *fanihiyan*
FANIYAN see *fanihiyan*
FANSE 1. bailiff, policeman 2. trader
FAR SEME in profusion, in large
quantity
FARA 1. an ox-drawn sleigh used for
carrying hay or wood 2. horn strips
on both sides of a grip 3. the
edges or shafts of a wagon
FARADAMBI to get stuck in the mire
(of wheels)
FARAMBI 1. to spread freshly harvested
grain out to dry 2. (-ka, -pi) to
faint, to lose consciousness
FARAMBUMBI caus. of *farambi*
FARANG SEME solidly, immovably
FARANGGA having shafts
    FARANGGA DUKA the outer door of an
    official office
    FARANGGA DUKAI TAKŪRSI bailiff of
    the outer door
FARFABUMBI 1. caus. of *farfambi* 2. to
be confused
FARFAMBI 1. to be in disarray, to be
confused, to be unclear 2. to throw
swiftly (at the game of *gacuha*)
FARGABUMBI caus./pass. of *fargambi*
FARGAMBI to pursue
    FARGARA COOHA pursuit troops
FARGANAMBI to go to pursue
FARGI a perch for chickens
FARHA CECIKE one name for the wren;
cf. *darha cecike*
FARHŪDAMBI to act in a foolish or
muddled way
FARHŪKAN rather dark
FARHŪN dark, obscure, unclear, con-
fused, muddled
    FARHŪN SUWALIYAME in the period
    just before dawn
FARHŪŠAMBI to act blindly
FARI see *geri fari*
FARILAMBI 1. to become dark 2. to be
upset, to be worried
FARINGGIYAMBI to cut with a sickle and
lay out to dry
FARSA 1. mint 2. a very small fresh-
water fish of little value
    FARSA GIRANGGI lower bones of the
    rib cage, asternal or floating
    ribs
FARSI 1. piece, strip 2. a unit of
currency
    FARSI FARSI in pieces, in strips
FARSILABUMBI caus. of *farsilambi*
FARSILAMBI to cut or make in pieces
    FARSILAHA CINUHŪN cinnabar in
    pieces
    FARSILAHA HIYAN incense in pieces
    FARSILAHA OKTO medicinal pellets or
    pills
FARSINAMBI to be in pieces

F

F

FARŠAMBI to risk one's life, to act
carelessly
FARŠATAI fearlessly, recklessly, with-
out heed for life
FARTAHŪN protruding, thick at the end
FARUDAI the phoenix of the south
FASAK SEME the sound made by a beast
or bird suddenly emerging from a
thicket
FASAN fish weir
FASAN FEKUMBI to become disloyal,
to rebel
FASAN IREN fish weir
FASAR SEME in many pieces, scattered,
in great numbers
FASAR SEME GENEHE crumbled, became
undone
FASAR SEME HŪWAJAHA broke into
many pieces
FASAR SEME LABDU in great quantity
FASE 1. raft 2. the weights used on
a scale or steelyard
FASILAN 1. fork, forking 2. discord
FASILAN NIRU a forked arrow
FASILAN SALJA a road with a three-
way forking
FASILANGGA forked
FASIMBI 1. to hang (oneself) 2. to
cling to, to climb
FASIME BUCEMBI to die by hanging
FAŠŠABUMBI caus. of faššambi
FAŠŠAMBI to exert effort, to go to a
lot of trouble
FAŠŠAN exertion, effort, zeal
FAŠŠAN BE BAICARA BOLGOBURE FIYENTEN
(稽 動 清 吏 司) a
section of the Board of Civil Ap-
pointments; cf. BH 337
FAŠŠANDUMBI/FAŠŠANUMBI to exert effort
together
FAŠŠANGGA expending effort, meritori-
ous
FAŠU one name for the quail; cf. mušu
FATABUMBI caus. of fatambi
FATAK (onom.) the sound of falling
objects
FATAKŪ the name of a dark red flower
FATAMBI to pinch, to pick (fruit)
FATAN 1. the sole of the foot or a
shoe--also used as a term of con-
tempt 2. a comblike tool used for
working silk on a loom
FATANAMBI to go to pinch or pick
FATANJIMBI to come to pinch or pick
FATANUMBI to pick together
FATAR SEME to the best of one's
ability, with all one's might
FATAR SEME AŠŠAMBI to wiggle with
all its might (a fish)
FATARAMBI 1. to pinch repeatedly 2.
to use things sparingly
FATARI ILHA a flower resembling the
gardenia with small leaves

FATARŠABUMBI caus. of fataršambi
FATARŠAMBI 1. to pinch repeatedly
2. to be in the habit of using
things sparingly
FATHA hoof, foot (of fowl), claw
FATHA BERI a bow with cow's hooves
mounted on it
FATHAÇAMBI see fathašambi
FATHAŠAMBI to be discouraged, to be
dejected, to be despondent
FAYABUN expense, consumption
FAYAMBI 1. to spend, to squander, to
consume 2. to sell
FAYANGGA soul, the yang soul
FAYANGGA GAIMBI to call the soul
(said of shamans)
FAYANGGA HŪLAMBI the same as
fayangga gaimbi
FAYANGGA ORON the yang soul and
the yin soul
FAYANGGA TUCIMBI the soul departs
from the body
FE old, not new
FE AMBA CALU a granary in Peking
FE AN I in the old, customary way
FE DURUN old-fashioned
FE GUCU old friend
FE KOOLI old regulations
FE SUSU one's native place
FEBGIYEMBI to talk while in a delir-
ium, to talk in one's sleep
FEBHI see febigi
FEBIGI an insect that lives in damp
places, has a white body and a red
head
FEBSEHE cockroach
FEBUMBI to be stopped by a head wind
FECECUHUN see fecuhun
FECIKI strange, odd, wonderful
FECUHUN low, base, devious, unfaithful
(wife)
FEDE advance! work hard!
FEFE vulva, female pudenda
FEHEREMBI (-ke) to calm down, to be-
come placated
FEHEREN the area between the eyebrows
FEHI 1. brain, brains 2. memory
FEHI AKŪ without memory
FEHUBUMBI caus./pass. of fehumbi
FEHUHEN a footrest, a foot rail
FEHUMBI to step on, to tread on, to
trample
FEHUN a pace
FEHUNEMBI to go to tread on
FEHUNJIMBI to come to tread on
FEHUTEMBI to trample
FEHUTENUMBI to trample together, to
trample (of a group)
FEI (妃) an Imperial Concubine (of
the third rank), BH 8
FEI DZ nut of the tree Torreya nuci-
fera, torreya nut; cf. fisha
FEI DZOO soap

FEI GIN gold leaf
FEIBIHE see *febigi*
FEIDZ see *fei dz*
FEIFUMBI to boil, to brew
FEIGIN see *fei gin*
FEIHE see *fehi*
FEINGGE an old thing
FEISE brick, tile
    FEISE MOOI KUNGGERI (磚木科)
      a section of the Board of Works
    FEISE WEHE brick
    FEISEI DUKA the name of the left or
      right gates before the main gate
      of the examination hall
FEJERGI under, underneath
    FEJERGI FEMEN the lower lip
FEJERGINGGE that which is below
FEJILE under, underneath
    FEFILE BAHA became pregnant
    FEJILE BI is pregnant
FEJILEBUMBI caus. of *fejilembi*
FEJILEMBI to catch with a *fejilen*
FEJILEN a noose made of hair from a
    horse's tail--used for catching wild
    fowl
FEJUN base, vile
FEKCEHUN see *fekcuhun*
FEKCEKU a drug used for poisoning
    fish--it is made from the leaves and
    bark of a tree resembling the walnut
FEKCEMBI 1. to jump, to hop 2. to
    beat, to pulse
FEKCUHUKEN somewhat astringent
FEKCUHUN astringent, puckery (like the
    taste of an unripe persimmon)
FEKSIBUMBI 1. caus. of *feksimbi* 2. to
    gallop (a horse) 3. to set dogs on
    game at night
FEKSIKU a pole with hooks that is
    placed at the bottom of a body of
    water to catch carp
FEKSIMBI to run, to gallop
FEKSIMBUMBI caus. of *feksimbi*
FEKSIN gallop
FEKSINDUMBI/FEKSINUMBI to run together
FEKŠULEMBI to treat with alum
    FEKŠULEHE DUINGGE HOOŠAN paper
      treated with alum to be used for
      painting
FEKŠUN alum
FEKUBUMBI caus. of *fekumbi*
FEKUCEMBI to leap up, to jump (rope),
    to hop, to skip
FEKUCENUMBI to leap up in a group
FEKUMBI 1. to jump, to leap 2. to
    wrinkle up (of cloth that has been
    wet)
FEKUMBUMBI caus. of *fekumbi*
FEKUN a leap, a jump
    FEKUN WALIYABUMBI to have a fright
FEKUNEMBI to jump across (away from
    the speaker), to jump to the other
    side

FEKUNJIMBI to jump across (toward the
    speaker)
FEKURI an ox-drawn wooden sledge used
    for carrying wood and hay
FELEBUMBI caus. of *felembi*
FELEHUDEMBI to act brashly, to do
    accidentally, to encounter
FELEHUN 1. brash, brazen 2. brashly,
    recklessly, accidentally
FELEKU tassel or ornament on a bridle
FELEMBI 1. to act recklessly 2. to
    assassinate 3. to roll the hair
    into a chignon
    FELEFI YABUMBI to act recklessly
    FELERE ANTAHA assassin
FELHEN 1. a shelter for cattle 2.
    trellis
FELHERI ILHA a raspberry (*Rubus rosi-*
    folius)
FELIYEBUMBI caus. of *feliyembi*
FELIYEMBI 1. to walk, to take steps
    2. to frequent (a place) 3. to
    discuss marriage
    FELIYEME YABUMBI to go for a walk
FELIYEN walking
FEMBI 1. to lay out new-mown hay or
    other grass to dry 2. to talk
    heedlessly
    FEHE GISUN careless talk
FEMEN lip
    FEMEN ACABUMBI to sew together
    FEMEN KAMNIMBI to close the lips
      tightly
FEMPI a paper seal used on envelopes
    and on doors
    FEMPI DOBTON I KUNGGERI (封筒
    科) a section in the Court of
    Colonial Affairs
FEMPILEBUMBI caus. of *fempilembi*
FEMPILEMBI to seal
    FEMPILEHE DOBTON a sealed paper
      pouch for official reports
    FEMPILEHE DOBTONOHO BITHE a docu-
      ment sealed in a pouch
FEN a square piece, a slice
FENDZ portion, share, contribution
FENEHE tinder, kindling
    FENEHE CECIKE pseudo goldcrest
      (*Phylloscopus inornatus*)
FENEHIN see *fenehe*
FENEMBI to go to lay out new-mown hay
FENG bee, wasp
FENGSE pan, jug
    FENGSE I TUWABUN an artificial
      landscape or scene placed in a
      bowl
FENGSEKU a small porcelain pan or bowl
FENGSI a practitioner of geomancy
FENGŠEN prosperity, good fortune
    FENGŠEN BE ALIHA USIHA two of the
      stars in the Great Dipper
FENGŠENGGE prosperous, fortunate
FENIHE swarm, flock

F

F

FENIHE ULHŪMA a type of pheasant that flies in flocks

FENIHIYEN a small table for burning incense

FENINGGE something old

FENIYEKU one member of a swarm or flock

FENIYEKU WEIJUN one name for the stork; cf. *weijun*

FENIYELEMBI to form a flock, to swarm, to flock

FENIYEMBI to smelt

FENIYEN flock, swarm, drove, herd, crowd

FENIYEN FENIYEN I in flocks, in swarms

FENIYENGGE forming flocks, swarming

FEO IO ephemerid

FEPI cutting board for fodder

FER FAR SEME weakly, fluttering slowly like a butterfly in flight

FER FER (onom.) the sound of yelping dogs

FER SEME fluttering, floating, wafting

FERE 1. bottom, base, floor 2. the central banner in a battue

FERE HECEME completely, exhaustively

FERE JALAN the first *jalan* of a banner

FERE SELE a piece of iron in the bottom of a quiver

FEREI BELE rice on the floor of a granary

FEREI BOO the building behind the main house

FEREI MOO crosspiece between the legs of a table or bed

FEREHE SINGGERI bat

FEREMBI (-ke) 1. to become old, to become worn out 2. to become deaf, to be deafened 3. to become giddy, to become dizzy

FEREMBUMBI caus. of *ferembi*

FERENEMBI to become worn out, to become decayed

FEREŠEBUMBI caus. of *fereŝembi*

FEREŠEMBI to take a sample

FERETU adjutant, assistant

FERGE 1. the back claw of a fowl 2. the seam joining the two halves of a pair of trousers 3. see *ferhe*

FERGETUN a thumb ring used on the right hand in archery

FERGIMBI to become numb, to sting

FERGIME NIMEMBI to suffer from a sting

FERGUWEBUMBI caus. of *ferguwembi*

FERGUWECUKE strange, wonderful, astonishing

FERGUWECUKE FUKJINGGA HERGEN (奇 字 篆) a style of calligraphy

FERGUWECUKE GUNGGE POO (神 功 礮) the name of a large cannon that weighed a thousand catties

FERGUWECUKE HORONGGO BAKCIN AKŪ POO (神 威 無 敵 礮) the name of a large cannon that weighed three thousand catties

FERGUWECUKE HORONGGO ENDURI the name of a deity

FERGUWECUKE HORONGGO KIRU the name of a banner embroidered with dragons or serpents on a dark background used by the imperial escort

FERGUWECUKE HORONGGO POO (神 威 礮) the name of a large brass cannon weighing four hundred catties

FERGUWECUKE KARAN the Peking observatory

FERGUWECUKE SABINGGA SENCE I FUKJINGGA HERGEN (芝 英 篆) a style of calligraphy

FERGUWECUN wonder, marvel

FERGUWEMBI to be astonished, to wonder at, to admire

FERGUWEN 1. wonder 2. understanding, intellect

FERGUWENDUMBI/FERGUWENUMBI to wonder at (of a group)

FERHE 1. the thumb, the big toe 2. see *ferge*

FERHE GIDAMBI in dividing up objects, to take the best for oneself

FERHE SIRGE the thickest string on a stringed instrument

FERHELEMBI to grasp with the thumb (a bowstring)

FERI horse, donkey, or mule hide with the hair removed

FERIMBI to strive

FERKINGGE experienced, knowledgeable, learned

FERTEN vomer, the thin bone separating the nostrils

FESEN see *fesin*

FESER SEME 1. broken in small pieces 2. frightened, stunned, astonished

FESER SEME HŪWAJAHA broke into small pieces, shattered

FESER SEME MEIJEHE broke into small fragments (of porcelain)

FESHEBUMBI caus. of *feshembi*

FESHEKU see *fesheleku*

FESHELEBUMBI caus./pass. of *feshelembi*

FESHELEKU shuttlecock

FESHELEMBI 1. to kick 2. to open up (border regions)

FESHELEME TABUMBI to string a bow by placing the foot on one end

FESHEMBI to suffer

FESHEN a tiered bamboo or wooden rack

used for steaming various foods
    FESHEN EFEN steamed bread, *mantou*
FESHEŠEMBI to kick repeatedly
FESIN handle, stock, grip
    FESIN I TOLDOHON hilt of a sword
FESINGGE having a handle
FESKU see *fesheleku*
FEŠŠEMBI see *feshešembi*
FETEBUMBI caus. of *fetembi*
FETECUN criticism, gossip, backbiting
FETEKU an ear-pick
FETEMBI 1. to dig, to dig out, to dig up 2. to criticize 3. to analyze, to scrutinize
    FETEME NIYAMNIYAMBI to shoot under the target (at mounted archery)
FETEN 1. digging, excavation 2. fate 3. element
FETENUMBI to criticize one another's weak points
FETEREKU overly critical, prone to criticism
FETEREMBI 1. to dig, to dig out 2. to criticize (faults) 3. to investigate, to go into
FETEREN investigation
FETERI opening, small hole
    FETERI FETERILEMBI to flare the nostrils while laughing
FETERILAMBI see *feteri feterilembi*
FETHE the dorsal fins of a fish
FETHEKU oar
FETHEKULEMBI to row
FETHEŠEMBI to paddle in water
FETHI see *huwethi*
FEYE 1. nest 2. wound 2. the eye of a needle
    FEYE DE EDUN DOSIMBI a draft penetrates the wound
    FEYE FIYARTUN scars of wounds
    FEYE TUCIKE an injury resulted
    FEYE TUWARA HEHE woman coroner
    FEYE YEBE OHO the wound has healed
FEYELEMBI 1. to build a nest, to nest 2. to get wounded
FEYENGGE wounded, pertaining to a wound
FEYESI coroner
    FEYESI TUWARA NIYALMA coroner
FI writing instrument, writing brush, pen
    FI I DUBE the tip of a writing brush
    FI I HOMHON a cover for a writing brush
    FI I KITALA the shaft of a writing brush
    FI I NENGGELEKU a stand for writing brushes
    FI I OBOKŪ a washing basin for writing brushes
    FI I SIHAN a vessel for holding writing brushes
    FI I ULGAKŪ a vessel for wetting

writing brushes
    FI ŠURGEBUHENGGE FUKJINGGA HERGEN (戰筆書) a style of calligraphy
FIB SEME wavering, unsteady
FICAKŪ a six-holed flute blown from one end
    FICAKŪ ORHO a short reed that grows in mountainous areas
FICAKŪNGGE pertaining to the flute
FICAMBI 1. to pipe, to blow (a flute) 2. to decoy game with a horn or flute
FICAN blowing, piping
FICARI an eight-holed bamboo flute
FIDEMBI 1. to dispatch (troops), to transfer (troops) 2. to intrigue
    FIDEME ICIHIYAMBI to dispatch (troops)
    FIDEME KADALARA AMBAN (提督) Provincial Commander-in-Chief, BH 750
FIDENEMBI to go to transfer
FIFAKA FOSOKO in all directions, helter-skelter
FIFAMBI (-ka) 1. to ricochet, to rebound 2. to stray
FIFAN a four-stringed, plucked instrument with frets, a lute
FIFANGGA pertaining to the lute
    FIFANGGA NIYEHE a type of duck
FIFARI a two-stringed instrument similar to a *fifan*
FIHA YOO a blister
FIHALI foolish, idiotic
FIHALIKAN rather foolish
FIHANAMBI to develop a blister
FIHAŠAMBI to be stuck for words
FIHATA glans penis
FIHE the upper part of the foreleg of a quadruped, the flesh on the aforementioned part
FIHEBUMBI caus. of *fihembi*
FIHEMBI (-ke) to fill, to stuff
    FIHEME LABDU abundantly full
FIHENEMBI to go to fill
FIHENJIMBI to come to fill
FIHETE foolish, silly
FIHETEMBI to weep, to sob
FIHIN BIYA the second month of winter
FIJIREMBI to scrape along the ground (arrows and birds)
FIJIRHI one name for the wildcat; cf. *ujirhi*
FIJIRI hemp seeds
FIK FIK SEME see *fik seme*
FIK SEME in profusion, thickly, heavily, closely
    FIK SEME BANJIMBI to grow thickly
    FIK SEME JALUKABI packed in tightly
FIKA Chinese olive (*Canarium album*)
    FIKA DENGJAN a lantern made in the

F

F

shape of a Chinese olive

FIKA JAHŪDAI a boat pointed at both ends

FIKA JINGGERI a nail pointed at both ends

FIKA NIMEKU a swelling of the abdomen from constipation

FIKA ŠORO a bamboo basket narrow at both ends

FIKA TUNGKEN a drum narrow at both ends and bulging in the middle

FIKACI an olive-shaped, exotic fruit with a seven-layered skin

FIKANAMBI to have a bulging belly

FIKATALA extremely far (a road)

FIKSEMBI to be in profusion; cf. *fik seme*

FIKTAN FIKTU discordant, cracked

FIKTE dim, obscure, foolish

FIKTEMBI to be dim, to feel giddy

FIKTU 1. crack, fissure 2. dissension, discord, grudge 3. pretext

FIKTU BAIMBI to seek a pretext, to seek dissension

FILA a plate

FILAINGGE pertaining to plates

FILAN a wood used in the manufacture of bows

FILEBUMBI caus. of *filembi*

FILEKU a pan for burning charcoal, a brazier, stove

FILEKU I TUBI a grate cover for a brazier

FILEMBI to warm oneself by a fire

FILFIN barren, vacant, empty

FILI 1. solid, filled 2. resolute, persevering

FILI FEISE a type of very hard brick

FILI FEISEI KŪWARAN a factory for making a very hard variety of brick

FILI FIKTU AKŪ without a solid reason

FILIKAN rather solid

FILINGGA MOO red sandalwood; cf. *cakūran; dan mu*

FILITAHŪN see *filtahūn*

FILTAHŪN empty (place), unoccupied, vacant

FIMEBUMBI caus. of *fimembi*

FIMEMBI 1. to put forth, to bring near, to present 2. to sew together, to sew a seam 3. to test, to try 4. to occur

FIMERAKŪ cannot happen

FINA ring at the end of the crupper

FING SEME firmly, resolutely, faithfully

FINGGE resolute, serene

FINGKABUMBI to have colic, to get abdominal pains

FINTAHA bag, satchel

FINTAMBI 1. to ache 2. to shy (of

wild animals), to be frightened (wild animals)

FINTEMBI see *fintambi*

FIO SEME directly, plainly

FIOHA pullet, young tender chicken

FIOR SEME slurping, eating noisily

FIOSE see *fiyoose*

FIOTA fart

FIOTAMBI to fart; cf. *fiyotombi*

FIR FIR SEME see *fir fiyar seme*

FIR FIYAR SEME elegantly, gracefully

FIR SEME quietly, calmly, imposingly, fluently

FIR SEME ARAMBI to write fluently

FIRFIN FIYARFIN with tears flowing

FIRGEMBI (-ke) to leak out, to be revealed

FIRGEMBUMBI caus. of *firgembi*

FIRUBUMBI caus. of *firumbi*

FIRUMBI 1. to curse 2. to implore, to pray

FISA the back

FISA WAŠAKŪ back scratcher

FISAI NIKEKU a back rest, a back support

FISAI ŠURDEN a twirl of the sword over the back when performing a sword dance

FISEKU the upturned eaves at the corners of Chinese buildings

FISEKU BORO an ancient-style summer hat with a wide brim

FISEKULEMBI to shield with the hand

FISEKULEME TUWAMBI to look shielding the eyes with the hand

FISEMBI (-ke) 1. to project, to jut out 2. to fork, to branch 3. to spurt

FISEKE FASILAN a forked branch

FISEME AGAMBI to rain in torrents

FISEMBUMBI 1. caus. of *fisembi* 2. to relate 3. to leave a wide margin when sewing

FISEMBUHE JUGŪN a suspended roadway built in mountainous areas

FISEN relation, offspring, progeny

FISENGGE projecting, jutting out

FISENGGE SIHIN the upward projecting eaves of a Chinese building; cf. *fiseku*

FISHA the nut of the tree *Torreya nucifera*, torreya nut; cf. *fei dz*

FISHACI an exotic fruit resembling the *fisha*

FISIHE panicled millet (*Panicum miliaceum*)

FISIHIBUMBI caus. of *fisihimbi*

FISIHIMBI to shake, to scatter

FISIKAN somewhat thick, somewhat dense, of rather good quality (meat)

FISIKU slow, negligent, sluggish

FISIN 1. thick, dense 2. good quality

(meat)

FISIN BOSO   finely woven linen

FISIN CECE   finely woven silk crepe

FISIN HALFIYAN SESE GILTASIKŪ   silk
with thick gold thread woven into
it

FISIN HOOŠAN   a coarse paper produced in Peking

FISIN MUHELIYEN SESE GILTASIKŪ   silk
with thick round gold threads
woven into it

FISITUN   a ritual vessel for offering
millet

FIŠUR SEME   sluggishly, slowly

FITA   fast, tight, taut

FITHEBUMBI   1. caus. of *fithembi*   2. to
set off (firecrackers)

FITHEJEMBI   to explode (of firecrackers), to crackle

FITHEKU BERI   crossbow

FITHEMBI   1. to snap, to spring, to
pluck, to flip   2. to explode, to go
off   3. to play (a stringed instrument)

FITHEME ACANAMBI   to correspond
exactly

FITHEN   a spark that flies out from a
fire

FITHENEMBI   to bloom

FITHENGGE YAHA   charcoal that bursts
while it is being burned

FITUHAN   a round stringed instrument
resembling a Chinese zither

FIYA   birch

FIYAB SEME   shying (of livestock)

FIYABKŪ   thrush, a bird of the genus
Turdus

FIYACUMBI   to cry out from pain, to
groan, to moan

FIYADA   1. jawbone   2. term of abuse
used toward persons of no ability

FIYAFIKŪ   see *fiyabkū*

FIYAGAMBI   to harden, to dry up, to
form a crust, to heal (of a sore)

FIYAGAN   see *fiyahan*

FIYAGANJABUMBI   caus. of *fiyaganjambi*

FIYAGANJAMBI   to exchange with one
another, to make a compromise

FIYAHAN   1. callus, hard skin   2. the
sole of the foot   3. agate, jade,
tortoise shell, and other such
precious objects

FIYAHANAMBI   to harden, to form a callus

FIYAJUMBI   1. to be anxious about something beforehand   2. to be turbulent
(of clouds before a storm breaks)

FIYAK FIK SEME   suddenly, with sudden
movements, without deliberation

FIYAK SEME   suddenly, with a start

FIYAKIYAMBI   to be hot from the sun

FIYAKIYAME HALHŪN   hot from being
exposed to the sun

FIYAKIYAN   burning hot, the sun's heat

FIYAKIYAN I DALIKŪ   a shelter from
the sun

FIYAKSA   Manchurian yew (*Taxus cuspidata*)

FIYAKŪBUMBI   caus. of *fiyakūmbi*

FIYAKŪMBI   1. to heat, to dry by a fire,
to dry in the sun   2. to bake

FIYAKŪNGGA TUBI   a bamboo implement
used for drying things by a fire

FIYALANGGI   a loose talker

FIYALAR SEME   loosely, wildly (of
speech)

FIYALHŪ   evasive, fond of shirking work

FIYAN   1. color, complexion   2. appearance   3. light (of a lamp)   4. rouge,
makeup   5. colored, bright

FIYAN ILHA   colored flowers used to
decorate bowls of vegetables or
fruit

FIYAN NEMEBUMBI   to have a nice
appearance

FIYAN TUWABUMBI   to show off one's
military prowess before a battle

FIYAN TUWARA JEBELE   a quiver used
during a demonstration of prowess
before a battle

FIYANA   a frame used for carrying
things on the back

FIYANARAKŪ   an iron

FIYANARAMBI   1. to pretend, to feign
2. to iron, to press   3. to act in
an artificial, put-on manner

FIYANCIHIYAN   abstemious, not fond of
eating

FIYANGGA   1. colored, polychrome, mot-
ley, multicolored   2. decorated,
fresh, good looking

FIYANGGA FAIDAN   cortege of the imperial concubines of the sixth and
seventh rank

FIYANGGA LAKIYAN   decorative hangings made of colored cloth or
paper

FIYANGGA ORDO   a pavilion-shaped
object made of colored silk that
was placed on a high table and
used at the presentation of imperial awards and rescripts

FIYANGGA TUHEBUKU   colored hangings
at the top of drapes or curtains,
valance

FIYANGGA ULHŪMA   a brightly colored
pheasant

FIYANGGŪ   youngest, least, smallest

FIYANGGŪ SIMHUN   the little finger

FIYANGGŪ SIRGE   the thinnest string
on a stringed instrument

FIYANGGŪŠAMBI   to behave like a spoiled
child

FIYANGTAHŪN   large and strong, able-
bodied

FIYANGTAHŪRI   large and robust

F

F

FIYANGTANAMBI to become large and strong

FIYANJI 1. support, assurance, guarantee 2. rear guard, the rear
FIYANJI COOHA the rear guard, reserves
FIYANJI ERTUN support and trust

FIYANJILAMBI to protect, to shield, to serve as the rear guard

FIYANTORO ILHA a pink flower resembling the peach blossom

FIYAR FIR SEME right away, quickly

FIYAR SEME right away, immediately

FIYARATALA in great quantity, very much, very many

FIYARINGGIYABUMBI caus. of *fiyaringgiyambi*

FIYARINGGIYAMBI to dry in the sun, to bleach in the sun

FIYARTUN scar, blemish, spot
FIYARTUN GIYALU crack in a bone or horn

FIYARTUNAMBI to form a scar

FIYARU maggot, larva

FIYARUNAMBI to get maggots
FIYARUNAHANGGE maggoty--used as a term of abuse
FIYARUNARANGGE see *fiyarunahangge*

FIYARUNARU see *fiyarunahangge*

FIYASAMBI to dry out (firewood)

FIYASHA the wall of a house
FIYASHA CECIKE sparrow

FIYATAR SEME foolishly, absurdly

FIYATARAKŪ a bush resembling the wild grape, the wood of which is used to make wild animal calls

FIYE kudzu vine (*Pueraria thunbergiana*)

FIYEGU MOO a tree that has been scratched by tigers to the point of bleeding sap

FIYEHU MAMA the goddess of mountain roads

FIYELEBUKU a saddle used for practicing equestrian tricks

FIYELEKU 1. a steep slope, a cliff 2. brazier, a small stove; cf. *fileku*
FIYELEKU HADA a steep cliff

FIYELEMBI 1. to do equestrian tricks 2. to fly in circles, to hover (of falcons) 3. to warm oneself by the fire

FIYELEN 1. chapter, section of a book 2. amaranth (*Amarantus mangostanus*) 3. yellow-beaked young birds

FIYELENGGU capercaillie; cf. *horki*

FIYELESU a shrub of the pokeweed family (*Phytolacca acinosa*)

FIYELFE a level area between high mountains or on the shore of a river

FIYEN 1. powder 2. the feathers on the arrow shaft
FIYEN AKŪ without direction, unstable

FIYEN FIYAN complexion, makeup
FIYEN I IJUKŪ powder puff

FIYENE frame for carrying a saddle

FIYENGGU a thick spot on a bear's belly

FIYENGSERI an exotic yellow fruit with a white, powdery interior

FIYENTEHE 1. petal, clove (of garlic), a section, a slice, a strand 2. one row of feathers on an arrow 3. one of the parts of a cloven hoof

FIYENTEHEJEMBI to crack, to fissure

FIYENTEMBI 1. to section 2. to spread rumors

FIYENTEN section of an official organization
FIYENTEN I AISILAKŪ (寺副) the name of an official of the Court of Judicature and Revision
FIYENTEN I ICIHIYAKŪ (寺丞) the name of an official of the Court of Judicature and Revision

FIYEOLEHE a type of sea fish with large scales

FIYEREMBI see *fiyentehejembi*

FIYEREN fissure, fault (in the earth)

FIYERENEMBI to form a crack or fissure

FIYEREREN see *fiyeren*

FIYO fart; cf. *fiyoo*; *fiota*

FIYOHA see *fioha*

FIYOHOMBI to toss the *gacuha*, using the thumb as a catapult

FIYOKOCOMBI to rear (of a horse), to kick (of horses and mules)

FIYOKOROMBI to talk foolishly, to act foolishly

FIYOLOR SEME untruthfully

FIYOO 1. dustpan 2. winnowing fan 3. a dancing mask made from willow branches and painted with animal figures 4. see *fiyo*

FIYOOKOROMBI see *fiyokorombi*

FIYOOSE a gourd dipper, a ladle

FIYOOTAMBI see *fiyotombi*

FIYOOTOMBI see *fiyotombi*

FIYOR SEME see *fior seme*

FIYORHON woodpecker (*Dryocopus martius*)

FIYORHŪN see *fiyorhon*

FIYOTOKŪ black beetle

FIYOTOMBI 1. to fart 2. to brag
FIYOTOHO GISUN bragging, boasting

FO a small net attached to a pole-- used to fish things out of ice floes

FO SANG HŪWA ILHA hibiscus

FO ULEBUMBI to feed a child pre-chewed food

FODO 1. a willow branch used at shamanistic ceremonies 2. a pole hung with a quantity of various colored paper money that is placed beside a grave
FODO WECEMBI to offer sacrifice in the presence of an erected willow

branch

FODOBA   a type of small bird

FODOHO   willow

 FODOHO ABDAHA I FUKJINGGA HERGEN (柳葉篆) a style of calligraphy

 FODOHO INGGARI   the fuzz or down
from a willow tree

FODOMBI (-ko)   to pant, to gasp for
breath

FODOR FOSOK SEME   raging, violently
angry

FODOR SEME   seething, furious

FODOROMBI (-ko)   1. to pant, to gasp
2. to go against the grain, to
bristle

FOHODOMBI   to anger, to incite

FOHOLOKON   rather short

FOHOLON   short

FOIFOBUMBI   caus. of *foifombi*

FOIFOKŪ   sharpener, strop for sharpen-
ing knives

FOIFOMBI   to sharpen

FOIHORI   careless, light, superficial

FOIHORILAMBI   to do carelessly, to
neglect, to treat indifferently

FOJI   a skin covering for boots and
shoes (worn in cold weather)

FOKJIHIYADAMBI   to act in a coarse or
boorish manner

FOKJIHIYAN   boorish, coarse

FOKTO   jacket made of grass linen

FOLGO   see *folho*

FOLHO   a small iron hammer

FOLKOLOMBI   to leave a space, to make
an interval, to make a pause

 FOLKOLOME   here and there, interspersed, at intervals

FOLOBUMBI   caus. of *folombi*

FOLOMBI   to carve, to engrave, to print

 FOLOHO ACANGGA FUKJINGGA HERGEN (刻
符書)   a style of calligraphy

 FOLOHO HITHA   engraved metal decorations on a horse's bridle

 FOLORO FAKSI   engraver, carver,
printer

FOLON   a carved inscription

FOMBI (-ha)   to chap

FOMCI   see *fomoci*

FOMILAMBI   to tuck the clothing in

FOMOCI   stockings, socks

FOMON   one name for the wren; cf.
darha cecike

FOMOROMBI   to get tangled up

FOMPI   chapped

FON   time, season

FONDO   through, thorough, completely

 FONDO GEHUN   transparent, translucent

 FONDO TUCIKE   went through and came
out the other side

FONDOJOMBI   to be broken or torn through

FONDOLOBUMBI   caus. of *fondolombi*

FONDOLOMBI   to penetrate, to go through

FONDOMBI   see *fondolombi*

FONGKO   a small brass drum

FONGSOMBI   to become black from smoke

FONGSON   soot, dirt

FONGSONGGI   1. soot, dirt   2. a turbot-
like fish found in the Sunggari
River

FONIYO   female roe deer

FONJIBUMBI   caus. of *fonjimbi*

FONJIMBI   to ask

FONJIN   question, questioning

FONJINAMBI   to go to ask

FONJINDUMBI/FONJINUMBI   to ask (of a
group)

FONJINGGIMBI   to send to ask

FONJINJIMBI   to come to ask

FONJISI   1. questioner, interrogator
2. (理問) Law Secretary, BH
826

FONTOHO   1. small hole in an object   2.
a type of bottomless vessel

FONTOMBI   see *fondolombi*

FOR   (onom.)   1. the sound of slurping
2. the sound of a loom   3. the
sound of neighing

FOR FOR   (onom.) the same as *for*

FORFOI   orangutan

FORGON   1. season, the course of the
year   2. fate

 FORGON I YARGIYAN TON   the official
calendar

FORGORI ILHA   *Rosa indica*

FORGOŠOBUMBI   caus. of *forgošombi*

FORGOŠOMBI   1. to revolve, to rotate
2. to transfer, to change

 FORGOŠOME FIYELEMBI   to turn in the
saddle while trick riding

 FORGOŠOME NIYAMNIYAMBI   to suddenly
reverse direction while shooting
from horseback

FORIBUMBI   caus./pass. of *forimbi*

FORIKŪ   a wooden clapper

FORIMBI   to strike, to knock

FORINGGA HŪSUN   a man who goes about at
night striking the hours on a gong
or clapper

FORINGGIYAMBI   to test an arrow shaft
by turning it between the fingers

FORIŠAMBI   to strike hard

FORITU   a stick with small bells attached to it--used by Buddhist monks

FORJIN   a small knot or excrescence on
a tree

 FORJIN MOO   a tree with very hard
wood that grows on riverbanks

FORKO   spinning wheel

 FORKO I SABKA SELE   pivot on a spinning wheel

FOROBUMBI   1. caus. of *forombi*   2. to
pray, to chant incantations

FOROBUN   rotation, chanting of incantations

FOROHON CECIKE   one name for the hoopoe;

F

cf. *indahūn cecike*

FOROMBI 1. to spin 2. to turn, to turn around, to face, to turn toward

FOROMIMBI see *foringgiyambi*

FORON 1. swirl, curl, whirl 2. rotation (of an arrow between the fingers)

    FORON SAIN the rotation of the arrow shaft is right, i.e., it is straight

FORONOMBI to turn (in that direction)

FORONTU curly, having curly hair

    FORONTU KARA a black horse with curly hair on the belly

    FORONTU MORIN a horse with curly hair on the breast

FORTOHON having a turned-up nose (of animals)

FOSKIYAMBI see *fosokiyambi*

FOSOBA reflection, ray

FOSOBUMBI caus./pass. of *fosombi*

FOSOK (onom.) the sound of a wild beast leaping from cover

FOSOKIYAMBI to get upset because of impatience

FOSOLHON warm (of the sun)

FOSOMBI 1. (-ko) to shine, to light up 2. to splash, to splatter

FOSOMIKŪ TOHON a button for securing the hem while one is riding

FOSOMIMBI to tuck in the hem

FOSON sunlight, sun's rays, the glow of a fire

FOSONGGI see *fongsonggi*

FOSONJIMBI to come shining, to shine in here

FOSONOMBI to go shining, to shine in there

FOSOPI illuminated

FOSOR SEME many, in great quantity (of wild animals)

FOSOROMBI (-ko) to shrink

FOŠOR SEME seething (used to describe anger), foaming

    FOŠOR SEME OBONGGI DEKDEHE produced white foam

FOTOR SEME 1. bubbling (of water), foaming 2. furiously

    FOTOR SEME FUYEMBI to boil furiously

FOYO 1. *ula* grass--a soft grass used as padding in shoes 2. cloth woven from horsehair

    FOYO ORHO *ula* grass

FOYODOMBI to divine

FOYODON divination

FOYONOMBI to become matted (of hair)

FOYORI an exotic plumlike fruit

FOYORO plum

    FOYORO ORHO see *foyo orho*

FU 1. an outside wall 2. prefecture 3. residence, mansion

    FU I AISILARA HAFAN (治中) Sub-Prefect of the Metropolitan Prefecture, BH 793

    FU I ALIHA HAFAN (府尹) Prefect of the Metropolitan Prefectures, BH 793

    FU I ILHI HAFAN (府丞) Vice-Governor of Peking, BH 793

    FU I SARACI (知府) Prefect, BH 848

FU FA SEME panting, feverish

FU GŪWARA eared owl (*Asio otus*)

FU NIMAHA back carp

FUBIHŪN CECIKE the Korean hoopoe

FUBISE an exotic fruit from Tonkin

FUBUMBI caus. of *fumbi*

FUCEBUMBI caus. of *fucembi*

FUCEMBI to get angry, to get mad

FUCENDUMBI/FUCENUMBI to get angry (of a group)

FUCENG see *fu i ilhi hafan*

FUCIHI Buddha

    FUCIHI DORO the way of Buddha, Buddhism

    FUCIHI DZUŠI Buddhist patriarch

    FUCIHI ERHUWEKU niche for a Buddha image

    FUCIHI HUWEJEKU the brightly ornamented background of a Buddha image

    FUCIHI I NOMUN Buddhist sutra

    FUCIHI IKTAN scriptures and valuables kept inside a Buddha image

    FUCIHI MIYOO Buddhist temple

FUCIHINGGE pertaining to Buddha, Buddhist

    FUCIHINGGE MAHALA a liturgical hat surmounted with the images of the five Dhyāni-Buddhas that is worn by monks during services

FUCIHIYALABUMBI caus. of *fucihiyalambi*

FUCIHIYALAMBI to singe (off)

FUCIHIYAMBI to cough

FUCIHIYAŠAMBI to heat in a flame

FUCU FACA (onom.) whispering

FUDAMBI to vomit

FUDANGGA with the hair going the wrong way, bristly, unkempt

FUDARAMBI (-ka) 1. to go against, to rebel 2. to be bristly, to be unkempt (of hair) 3. to oppose, to resist

FUDARAN opposition, rebellion

FUDASI recalcitrant, rebellious, obstinate

    FUDASI GŪWARA a type of owl

    FUDASI HALAI recalcitrant and perverse

FUDASIHŪLAMBI to go mad, to lose one's mind

FUDASIHŪN rebellious, disloyal, recalcitrant, obstinate

FUDEBUMBI caus. of *fudembi*

FUDEHUN see *fundehun*

FUDEJEMBI to develop a flaw, to crack,

to rip

FUDELEBUMBI caus. of *fudelembi*

FUDELEMBI to rip out a seam, to tear apart, to take apart

FUDEMBI 1. to see off, to accompany 2. to accompany a trousseau 3. to give a gift on departure

FUDEHE JAKA dowry, trousseau

FUDENEMBI to go to see off

FUDENJIMBI to come to see off

FUDEŠEBUMBI caus. of *fudešembi*

FUDEŠEMBI to dance in order to drive away evil spirits (to cure an illness)--specifically to dance in honor of the tiger god

FUDEŠERE SAMAN a shaman who dances in honor of the tiger god

FUDZ master, respectful term for teachers and elders

FUFA (onom.) the sound of panting

FUFEN 1. one thousandth 2. a tenth of an inch

FUFUBUMBI caus. of *fufumbi*

FUFUMBI (-ha) to saw

FUFUN a saw

FUFUTAMBI to torment oneself, to slave away (at a job)

FUGU see *fuhu*

FUHALI completely, totally, really, actually

FUHAŠABUMBI caus. of *fuhašambi*

FUHAŠAMBI 1. to exchange, to barter 2. to read carefully, to study

FUHAŠAME KIMCEMBI to study, to devote oneself to the study of

FUHEN the mold on the surface of fermenting substances

FUHEŠEBUMBI caus. of *fuhešembi*

FUHEŠEKU ORHO tumbleweed

FUHEŠEMBI to roll, to roll over, to somersault, to tumble

FUHEŠEME INJEMBI to double up with laughter

FUHIYEMBI to get angry, to get mad

FUHU wart

FUHU BANJIMBI a wart appears

FUHUN the appearance of anger or rage, enraged, angry

FUIFUBUMBI caus. of *fuifumbi*

FUIFUKŪ kettle, pot for boiling liquids

FUIFUMBI to boil, to stew, to boil down (as salt)

FUJIN wife of a feudal lord, wife of a *beile*, lady

FUJISA plural of *fujin*

FUJIYANG (副 将) Colonel, Regimental Commander, BH 752

FUJULAMBI see *fujurulambi*

FUJUN gracious, refined

FUJURAKŪ indecorous, dishonorable, dishonest, tactless, unrefined

FUJURI 1. foundation, basis, origin 2. hereditary

FURJURI AMBAN a hereditary dignitary

FUJURI BOO a family in which men frequently followed official careers, a gentry family

FUJURI NIRU hereditary banner chief

FUJURULABUMBI caus. of *fujurulambi*

FUJURULAMBI to probe deeply, to get to the bottom of something, to make inquiries, to investigate

FUJURULAME FONJIMBI to make inquiries, to get to the bottom of something

FUJURUN prose poem, a *fu* (賦)

FUJURUNGGA fine, elegant

FUJURUNGGA YANGSANGGA alluring, elegant and noble

FUKA 1. bubble, blister, pustule 2. circle, a circle in the Manchu writing system 3. enceinte in front of a city gate, bastion on a city wall 4. wild-animal cage

FUKANAMBI to bubble, to form bubbles

FUKCIHIYAN see *fukjihiyan*

FUKCIN see *fukjin*

FUKDEJEMBI to open up again (a wound)

FUKDEREMBI to have a relapse (of illness), to reopen (of a wound)

FUKIYAMBI see *fuyakiyambi*

FUKJIHIYADAMBI to hurry

FUKJIHIYAN common, ordinary, despicable

FUKJIN beginning, origin, foundation

FUKJIN ILIBUMBI to lay a foundation

FUKJINGGA original, ancient, primitive

FUKJINGGA HERGEN (篆 書) a style of calligraphy--seal characters

FUKJINGGA HERGEN I KUREN (篆 字 館) an office in Peking charged with developing a pseudo 'seal script' for Manchu

FUKJINGGA MAHATUN a style of hat worn in ancient times

FUKJIŠAMBI to be restrained, to hold back

FUKSUHU large excrescence on a tree

FUKTALA bracken fern (*Pteridum aquilinum*)

FULABURU dark blue or black with a slightly reddish tinge, blue flecked with red or pink

FULABURU GASHA Chinese blue and white flycatcher (*Cyanoptila cyanomelana*)

FULACAN a bag for storing flint

FULAHŪKAN light pink

FULAHŪN 1. pink, reddish 2. the fourth of the heaven's stems (丁) 3. naked, bare, impoverished, barren

FULAHŪN YADAMBI to be impoverished

FULAHŪRI deep red, fire red

FULAHŪRI KAMTUN a deep red head

F

scarf used during the Han dynasty

FULAKCAN pouch for carrying a flint

FULAN a light-colored horse with a dark mane and tail

FULANA *Prunus humilis*; cf. *ulana*

    FULANA ILHA crab-apple blossom

FULARAMBI (-ka) to become red, to blush

FULARGAN a rust-colored swallow

FULARI of a red shade

    FULARI CECIKE the same as *fulgiyan sišargan*

    FULARI ILHA an exotic red flower that blooms in autumn

FULARILAMBI to flash red, to lighten

FULARJAMBI to have a red appearance

FULARŠAMBI see *fularjambi*

FULATA red-eyed, having red circles about the eyes

    FULATA NISIHA a type of small, red-eyed fish

FULCA an exotic sweet purple fruit, about the size of a man's finger

FULCENGGE ILHA rainbow pink (*Dianthus chinensis*)

FULCIN cheekbone, cheek

FULCU an exotic fruit resembling the wild grape

FULCUHŪN ŠULHE a type of pear (*Pyrus betulaefolia*)

FULCUN a large exotic red fruit shaped like a man's finger

FULDUN grove, thicket, clump

    FULDUN FULDUN I in clumps, in thickets

FULEFUN for his sake (used in prayers)

FULEHE root

    FULEHE SUWALIYAME together with the roots, including the roots

FULEHENGGE pertaining to or having roots

FULEHU alms given to monks

FULEHUN alms, good deed, kind act (Sanskrit, *dāna*)

    FULEHUN BAIMBI to beg for alms

    FULEHUN I HAFAN (廩生) Honorary Licentiate, BH 958

    FULEHUN I SILGASI (恩貢) Senior Licentiate by Imperial Favor, BH 629A

    FULEHUN I TACIMSI (廩監) an Honorary Licentiate conferred upon certain joyous occasions, BH 959

FULEHUNGGE gracious, kind

FULEHUSI almsgiver, benefactor

FULENGGI ashes

    FULENGGI BOCO ash-colored

    FULENGGI NIYANCIHA tender grass shoots

FULENGGINGGE NAMU KUWECIHE a gray dove with black neck and red feet

FULFINTU CECIKE Japanese waxwing (*Bombycilla japonica*)

FULGAMBI see *fulhambi*

FULGIDEI golden pheasant (*Chrysolophus pictus*)

FULGIKE rubythroat (*Calliope calliope*)

FULGIYACI short-haired summer pelts of deer

FULGIYAKAN light red, reddish

FULGIYAN 1. red, purple 2. the third of the heaven's stems (丙)

    FULGIYAN AFAHA voucher given for the use of a public horse, receipt for tax or toll

    FULGIYAN ALAN red birchbark that still has not dried out

    FULGIYAN CAISE a thin fried cake made from flour and honey

    FULGIYAN CIBIRGAN a type of red swallow

    FULGIYAN ENGGETU KERU a type of a crow with red feet and beak

    FULGIYAN FULAN a dark brown horse with dark mane and tail

    FULGIYAN GAHANGGA KIRU (赤鳥旗) a banner of the imperial escort depicting a red crow

    FULGIYAN GASHA one name for the wild goose; cf. *bigan i niongniyaha*

    FULGIYAN GASHANGGA KIRU (朱雀旗) a banner of the imperial escort depicting a small red bird

    FULGIYAN HAFUKA broke out with the measles

    FULGIYAN HAKSANGGA EFEN a type of crunchy red cake

    FULGIYAN ILETUNGGE GU a round jade object with a hole in the center used for sacrifices at the altar of the sun

    FULGIYAN JAMURI ILHA a variety of red rose

    FULGIYAN JIYOO BING a type of hard brown cake

    FULGIYAN JUGŪN equator

    FULGIYAN JUGŪN I HETU UNDU I DURUNGGA TETUN an astronomical instrument used for observing the position of heavenly bodies in relation to the equator

    FULGIYAN JUI baby, newborn babe

    FULGIYAN LEFUNGGE KIRU (赤熊旗) a banner of the imperial escort depicting a red bear

    FULGIYAN MURSA carrot, beet

    FULGIYAN NUNGGASUN red felt

    FULGIYAN SELBETE the name of a wild grass

    FULGIYAN SISA small red beans

    FULGIYAN SIŠARGAN Pallas's rose finch (*Carpodacus roseus*)

    FULGIYAN SUIHETU COKO red-crested pheasant

    FULGIYAN SURU bay (color of a horse)

    FULGIYAN ŠUNGKERI ILHA red Chinese orchid (*Bletilla chinensis*)

FULGIYAN TOSI the red crest of a crane

FULGIYAN TOSINGGA FIYORHON red-crested woodpecker

FULGIYAN UJIRHI red wildcat

FULGIYAN UMIYESUN 'red sash'--the descendants of the six *Ningguta beile*

FULGIYAN URANGGA MOO a tree of the *Clerodendrum* family

FULGIYAN YARHA red leopard

FULGIYAN YASA trachoma

FULGIYANGGA pertaining to red, red-haired

FULGIYARI COKO rooster with very red feathers

FULGIYEBUMBI caus./pass. of *fulgiyembi*

FULGIYEKU 1. whistle, pipe 2. blow-gun, blowpipe

FULGIYEMBI to blow

FULHA poplar

FULHAMBI to produce pus, to flow (of pus); cf. *ki fulhambi*

FULHERI a round red exotic fruit

FULHUMBI to put out shoots, to sprout

FULHUNTU see *fulhutu*

FULHUREMBI (-ke) to sprout, to germinate, to grow, to develop

FULHUREMBUMBI caus. of *fulhurembi*

FULHUREN 1. sprout 2. beginning, inception

FULHUTU a type of ritual cap worn during the Chou dynasty

FULHŪ bag, sack

FULHŪCA small sack

FULHŪMA a type of southern pheasant

FULHŪSUN satchel, carrying bag

FULHŪTU HŪWAŠAN a mendicant monk

FULI jerky, dried meat or fish

FULIBUMBI to take form, to take shape

    FULIBURAKŪ doesn't take shape--used to describe a person grasping for words as he sobs or pants

FULIMBUMBI see *fulibumbi*

FULIN 1. form, shape 2. luck, lucky fate

FULINGGA lucky, having good fortune

FULIYAMBI 1. to forgive, to pardon 2. to mend an arrow shaft

FULKŪRAN MOO a type of hawthorn

FULMAI ILHA an exotic flower the plant of which resembles wheat

FULMIN see *fulmiyen*

FULMIYEBUMBI caus. of *fulmiyembi*

FULMIYEMBI to bind, to tie up, to tie together

FULMIYEN bundle, package

FULMUN BOIHON a bluish clay used for making molds used in casting bronze

FULNACI ILHA *Pyrus halliana*, the red blossom of the Japanese cherry

FULNIYERI ILHA a fragrant red exotic flower

FULSURI ILHA an exotic creeping plant with red blossoms

FULU 1. surplus, excess, left over, extra 2. excelling, surpassing, better 3. a sacklike protector for a wounded finger

FULU JEKU early grain

FULU LEN a great deal larger

FULUKAN somewhat excessive, somewhat better

FULUN salary, emolument

    FULUN BE KIMCIRE TINGGIN (稽俸廳) salary office of the eight banners

    FULUN CALIYAN I KUNGGERI (俸糧科) salary section of the Board of War and the Court of Banqueting

    FULUN CALIYAN ICIHIYARA BA (俸餉處) salary office of the Board of Finance

    FULUN FAITAMBI to cut off one's salary as a punishment

FULUNGGA grand, majestic

FULUNGGE excessive, extra, left over

FUMA imperial son-in-law; cf. *efu*

FUMBI (1) (-ha/he) to wipe, to wipe off

FUMBI (2) (-ngke, -mpi) to become numb

FUMEREBUMBI caus. of *fumerembi*

FUMEREMBI 1. to mix up, to confuse, to stir together 2. to fight in a confused manner

    FUMEREME AFAMBI to fight a fierce battle

FUMERENUMBI to be mixed together

FUN 1. one-hundredth (of a Chinese foot) 2. powder 3. fragrant odor

    FUN BEYE identical, homogeneous

FUNCEBUMBI caus. of *funcembi*

FUNCEMBI to be left over, to be in excess

    FUNCEME over, in excess

FUNCEN excess, left over

    FUNCEN DABAN extra and excess

FUNCETELE to the point of excess

FUNDE (postposition) in place of, instead of, for

    FUNDE BOŠOKŪ (驍騎校) Lieutenant, BH 727

    FUNDE OROLOHAKŪ without having a substitute

    FUNDE WEILEMBI to substitute for someone

FUNDEHUN 1. desolate, forsaken 2. pallid

FUNDESI animals and birds that have been released

FUNEMBI to become numb

FUNFULAMBI 1. to order, to forbid 2. to get ready beforehand, to prepare

FUNG ŠUI geomancy

FUNG TIYAN GOLOI BOLGOBURE FIYENTEN (奉天清吏司) branch

of the Board of Punishments in Mukden

FUNGGAHA feather, down

FUNGGALA tail feather, feather in an official's hat

FUNGGIN 1. an old boar 2. the thick skin of a pig

FUNGHŪWANG phoenix

FUNGKERI HIYAN *Coumarouna odorata*
    FUNGKERI ILHA a type of Chinese orchid found in marshes

FUNGKU towel, cloth for wiping, kerchief

FUNGKŪ log, block of wood

FUNGLU salary

FUNGNEBUMBI to be enfeoffed

FUNGNEHEN a document conferring enfeoffment, grant
    FUNGNEHEN BE KIMCIRE BOLGOBURE FIYENTEN (驗封清吏司　　　) Department of Grants, BH 338
    FUNGNEHEN EJEHE I KUNGGERI (誥勅科) a section of the Board of War in charge of edicts, grants, and rescripts
    FUNGNEHEN EJEHE ICIHIYARA BA (誥勅房) a section of the Grand Secretariat in charge of edicts, grants, and rescripts
    FUNGNEHEN ICIHIYARA KUNGGE YAMUN (中書科) Imperial Patent Office, BH 137A

FUNGNEMBI to enfeoff

FUNGSAN 1. rank (the taste of mutton or beef) 2. impoverished 3. the oil gland at the base of a bird's tail, uropygial gland
    FUNGSAN YADAHŪN destitute, impoverished

FUNGSE 1. flour, meal 2. basin, pan

FUNGŠUN smelling of urine

FUNGTO see *fungtoo*

FUNGTOO envelope

FUNIMA a poisonous sand fly

FUNIYAGAN power of judgment, understanding

FUNIYAGANGGA endowed with good judgment

FUNIYAHA a parasitic worm that lives in the hair on the backs of horses and cattle

FUNIYAHAN see *funiyagan*

FUNIYANGGA see *funiyagangga*

FUNIYEHE hair, fur, nap
    FUNIYEHE DASITU bangs worn by young boys in ancient times
    FUNIYEHE DEN CEKEMU a type of velvet with a thick surface
    FUNIYEHE I ŠOŠON an artificial lock of hair worn by women over their natural hair
    FUNIYEHE SEN pore
    FUNIYEHE SULABUMBI to let the hair grow long

FUNIYEHELEMBI to pull the hair (while fighting)

FUNIYEHENGGE hairy, hirsute

FUNIYESEN see *funiyesun*

FUNIYESUN a kind of coarse woolen, felt

FUNJIMA sand fly, gnat

FUNTAMBI (-ka) to become moldy

FUNTAN mold

FUNTANAMBI to form mold

FUNTU deer horn in velvet--used in medicine

FUNTUHU gap, empty space, interval, lacuna

FUNTUHULEMBI 1. to make a gap, to leave a space 2. to be absent from one's post

FUNTUHUN see *funtuhu*

FUNTUMBI 1. to brave (the rain, a storm, etc.) 2. to cross a river (of livestock) 3. to charge bravely (enemy troops)

FUNTURABUMBI caus. of *funturambi*

FUNTURAMBI to root, to dig with the snout

FUNTUREMBI see *funtumbi*

FUNTURŠAMBI to root persistently

FUR SEME gently, easily, lightly, nicely, smoothly
    FUR SEME SAIKAN fresh and pretty
    FUR SEME TUCIKE flowed lightly (sweat)

FURANAHA dust, fine dirt, ashes

FURCAN a small, red-billed crane

FURDAN 1. scar, wound 2. pass, gateway 3. eye of a needle 4. a twisted root
    FURDAN DOGON I KUNGGERI (關津科) office concerned with passes and fords in the Board of War
    FURDAN DUKA gate at a pass
    FURDAN I TEMGETU BITHEI KUNGGERI (關引科) a section of the Board of War concerned with issuing pass permits
    FURDAN KAMNI narrow pass

FURDEHE pelt, fur, fur jacket
    FURDEHE KURUME a fur jacket
    FURDEHE SOFORO a saddle cushion made of fur

FURFU ape, orangutan

FURFUN FARFAN in streams (tears)

FURGI 1. a bundle of willow branches or reeds used to repair dams or dikes 2. a stick with a tuft of grass attached to the end--used in shamanistic rites 3. collar for draft animals
    FURGI COKO one name for the turkey
    FURGI TAI dike terrace

FURGIBUMBI caus./pass. of *furgimbi*

FURGIMBI 1. to drift, to wash up (of sand and dust) 2. to foment, to

bathe with a warm medicated liquid
3. to come in (of the tide) 4. to
be hot (of taste)

FURGIN 1. tide 2. hot (in taste)

FURGISI a man who lays out *furgi* when
the river level is low

FURGISU ginger

FURHŪN CECIKE one name for the hoopoe;
cf. *indahūn cecike*

FURIMBI to dive, to swim under water,
to plunge

FURITAN one name for the pelican; cf.
kūtan

FURITU NIYEHE diving duck

FURNA a bondman of the second generation

FURSUN 1. shoots, sprouts (especially
of a grain) 2. sawdust
FURSUN SAIN growth is good (said of
domestic animals)

FURSUNGGA NIYEHE one name for the wild
duck

FURU 1. excrescence in wood 2. canker
sore 3. tangled branches 4. cruel,
violent

FURUBUMBI caus. of *furumbi*

FURUDAMBI to act in a cruel or violent
way

FURUKŪ a grater

FURUMBI to slice, to grate, to cut into
fine pieces

FURUN meat scraped from a bone

FURUNAMBI to develop a canker sore in
the mouth

FURUNGGA HANGSE finely cut noodles

FURUNUMBI to slice together

FURUSUN TASHARI one name for the eagle

FUSA Bodhisattva

FUSE unintentionally
FUSE INJEHE laughed unintentionally

FUSEJEMBI 1. to burst (of bubbles and
boils) 2. to break through 3. to
break up (of ice)

FUSELEMBI to break open, to make a hole
in

FUSELI an inedible freshwater fish
resembling the black carp whose gall
is used as a medicine

FUSEMBI (-ke, -ndere) to propagate, to
reproduce, to breed

FUSEMBUMBI caus. of *fusembi*

FUSEN propagation

FUSENGGE FULANA ILHA a type of wild
red cherry blossom

FUSEREBUMBI caus. of *fuserembi*

FUSEREMBI to trim, to edge, to put on
a fur trimming
FUSEREHE MAHALA a hat with a fur-
trimmed brim

FUSEREMBUMBI see *fuserebumbi*

FUSERI Szechuan pepper (*Zanthoxylum
piperitum*)
FUSERI MOO Szechuan pepper tree

FUSHAMBI to lose everything, to be
wiped out

FUSHEBUMBI caus. of *fushembi*

FUSHEKU a fan
FUSHEKU I HERU the frame of a fan
FUSHEKU I TALGARI a fan's covering
FUSHEKU I TEMUN handle of a fan
FUSHEKU I TUHEBUKU an ornament at-
tached to the handle of a fan

FUSHEMBI to fan
FUSHEHE BONGKO cotton still in the
boll, raw cotton

FUSHU 1. stand for cooking pot 2. ex-
crescence on a tree
FUSHU GURJEN hearth cricket
FUSHU NAHAN a *kang* near the stove

FUSHUBUMBI 1. caus. of *fushumbi* 2.
to set off (firecrackers)

FUSHUMBI 1. to burst open (of flower
buds) 2. to go off (of firecrackers), to crack from overheating

FUSI abominable, loathsome, frightful,
monstrous
FUSI BAHAFI BANJIHANGGE a term of
abuse
FUSI BAHAMBI to give birth to a
monstrosity as a result of ridicul-
ing a person or thing
FUSI BAHARAHŪ afraid of giving birth
to a monstrosity

FUSIBUMBI caus./pass. of *fusimbi*

FUSIHEN an erasable lacquer board used
for writing

FUSIHŪLABUMBI caus./pass. of *fusihūlambi*

FUSIHŪLAMBI to look down upon, to
despise

FUSIHŪN 1. down, downward 2. westward
3. humble, low, cheap 4. junior,
subordinate

FUSIHŪSABUMBI caus./pass. of *fusihū-
šambi*

FUSIHŪSAMBI to look down upon, to
despise

FUSILARU a term of abuse--misbegotten,
cretin

FUSIMBI (-ha) 1. to shave, to shave
off, to cut the hair 2. to trim the
feathers on an arrow shaft

FUSKU see *fushu*

FUSU FASA flustered, in great rush

FUSUBUMBI caus. of *fusumbi*

FUSUKU sprinkling can

FUSUMBI to sprinkle (water)
FUSURE TAMPIN a sprinkling can

FUSUR SEME 1. flaky and soft 2.
steadily (of a horse's gait)
FUSUR SERE BOIHON loose earth

FUSURI GUNGGULU a parrot's crest

FUSURI ILHA the cotton rose (*Hibiscus
mutabilis*)

FUSURI NIYEHE the same as *alhari
niyehe*

FUSURJEMBI   to crack, to become worn
FUŠAHŪ   one name for the scops owl; cf.
   hŭšahŭ
FUŠARCAN   a red-headed crane
FUŠARGAN   one name for the rose finch;
   cf. *fulgiyan sišargan*
FUTA   1. rope, line, string   2. one
   sheng (180 Chinese feet)
   FUTA FEKUCEMBI   to jump rope
   FUTA MISHAN   a line for measuring
     the depth of water
   FUTAI KŪWARAN   rope factory
FUTAHI   a first-generation bondman
FUTALABUMBI   caus. of *futalambi*
FUTALAMBI   to measure in *sheng*
   FUTALAHA USIN   extended land

FUWEN   1. minute   2. one-tenth of a
   Chinese inch   3. candareen
FUYAKIYAMBI   to become nauseous, to
   become sickening
FUYAMBI   to feel like vomiting, to feel
   nauseated
FUYAN   Curcuma, turmeric
FUYARI NIYEHE   a type of duck whose
   flesh has a nauseating smell--the
   same as *aka niyehe*
FUYEBUMBI   caus. of *fuyembi*
   FUYEBURE TAMPIN   a pot for preparing
     boiling water
FUYEMBI   1. to come to a boil, to boil
   2. to skin (an animal)
FUYENDUMBI/FUYENUMBI   to skin together

F

G

GABA   three iron backpieces affixed to the épaulière on a suit of armor

GABSIHIYALABUMBI   caus. of *gabsihiyalambi*

GABSIHIYALAMBI   1. to be swift   2. to march with light baggage, to make a forced march   3. to form the vanguard

GABSIHIYAN   1. quick, clever, alert   2. vanguard

GABSIHIYAN I HIYA (前 鋒 侍 衛)   Imperial Guardsman of the Vanguard Division, BH 735

GABSIHIYAN I JANGGIN (前 鋒 参 領)   Colonel of the Vanguard Division, BH 735

GABSIHIYAN I JUWAN I DA (前 鋒 校)   Sergeant of the Vanguard Division, BH 735

GABSIHIYARI   see *dersen gabsihiyari*

GABSIYAN   see *gabsihiyan*

GABŠAMBI   see *gabtašambi*

GABTABUMBI   1. caus. of *gabtambi*   2. to shine (forth)

GABTAKŪ ORHO   bramblebush (*Bidens bipinnata*)

GABTAMA   nettles, brier, a sort of thorny plant

GABTAMBI   1. to shoot an arrow   2. to shine, to radiate

GABTARA NIYAMNIYARA   dismounted and mounted archery

GABTARA ORDO   archery pavilion

GABTARA TUNGKEN   a small ball of felt used as a target

GABTAN   archery

GABTANAMBI   to go to shoot

GABTANDUMBI/GABTANUMBI   to shoot together

GABTANJIMBI   to come to shoot, to shoot hither

GABTAŠAMBI   to shoot a great number of arrows, to shoot repeatedly

GABULA   glutton, gluttonous

GACILABUMBI   caus./pass. of *gacilambi*

GACILAMBI   1. to injure, to harm   2. to deprive

GACUHA   a toy or die made from the ankle bone of a sheep or other animal

GACUHA GIRANGGI   the anklebone

GADAHŪN   grown tall or long, bulging (of the eyes)

GADANA BEYE   all alone, on one's own

GADAR SEME   incessantly (of talking)

GADARAMBI (-ka)   to become long, to grow stiff

GAFA   having gnarled or twisted hands

GAHA   crow, raven, rook, jackdaw, general name of birds of the genus *Corvus*

GAHA CECIKE   black drongo (*Dicrurus macrocercus*)

GAHA GARIRE BERI   a type of ancient bow

GAHA HENGKE   a type of gourd used as a medicine against dysentery (*Trichosanthes cucumeroides*)

GAHA OTON   bitter melon (*Momordica charantia*)

GAHA POO   puffball (a type of mushroom)

GAHA YASA   *Euryale ferox*--an aquatic plant with edible fruit

GAHACIN   one name for the cormorant; cf. *suwan*

GAHANGGA   pertaining to the crow

GAHARI   shirt, blouse

GAHARI UKSIN   a shirt of armor, hauberk

GAHŪ   curved toward the front, extended forward

GAHŪ FIHA   with the mouth gaping

GAHŪMBI   to jut foward, to curve toward the front

GAHŪNGGA   jutting forward, curved toward the front

GAHŪRILAMBI   to lean forward, to jut

G

forward

GAHŪŠAMBI 1. to stand with the mouth gaping 2. to be so hungry that one is reduced to begging 3. to be unable to swallow 4. to remain speechless, to be unable to get the words out
GAHŪŠAME BAIMBI to beg with the mouth gaping, to beg pitifully

GAHŪŠATAMBI intensive form of *gahūšambi*

GAI 1. hey! 2. impediment, obstacle

GAIBUMBI 1. caus./pass. of *gaimbi* 2. to be defeated

GAIBUŠAMBI 1. to be defeated due to lack of strength (at wrestling) 2. to fear cold, to be unable to stand the cold

GAIHAHŪ KONGGORO a swift, dun-colored horse

GAIHAMSITU wonderful, marvelous
GAIHAMSITU KONGGORO a wonderful dun-colored horse

GAIHARI suddenly

GAIHARILAMBI to be sudden, to act suddenly, to realize something suddenly

GAIHASU suddenly changed, unexpectedly better

GAIHŪ for *gaihao*?

GAIJAMBI 1. to receive (goods) 2. to pass (an examination) 3. to confess
GAIJARA BITHE receipt for receiving government goods

GAIKABUMBI caus. of *gaikambi*

GAIKAMBI to broadcast, to spread abroad, to praise

GAILAMBI (-ka) to be possessed, to be hexed

GAIMBI (imperative: *gaisu*) 1. to take, to take away, to take off 2. to marry (a wife)
GAIHA GEBUI BITHE a list of successful candidates in the examination for Metropolitan Graduate

GAINDUMBI/GAINUMBI to take together, to contend

GAIRALAME taking steadily

GAIRELEME see *gairalame*

GAISILABUMBI caus./pass. of *gaisilambi*

GAISILAMBI to entangle, to catch up

GAISILAN entanglement, involvement

GAISILANDUMBI/GAISILANUMBI to entangle one another

GAISIN see *gaisilan*

GAITAI 1. suddenly 2. by chance
GAITAI . . . GAITAI . . . now . . . then . . .
GAITAI GAITAI all of a sudden

GAJARACI see *gajarci*

GAJARCI a guide

GAJARCILAMBI to lead the way

GAJI see *gaju*

GAJIBUMBI caus. of *gajimbi*

GAJIMBI (imperative: *gaju*) to bring, to bring along

GAJIRACI see *gajarci*

GAJIRTAI guide

GAJU imperative of *gajimbi*

GAJUNGGA ORHO aconite, wolfsbane

GAKAHŪN with gaping mouth, gaping (crack)

GAKARABUMBI caus. of *gakarambi*

GAKARAMBI 1. to crack open, to form a fissure 2. to become distant from one another (friends and relatives)

GAKARASHŪN separated, estranged

GAKDA 1. single, sole 2. crippled in one leg 3. blind in one eye
GAKDA BETHE lame in one leg, one-legged
GAKDA BEYE alone, on one's own
GAKDA YASA one-eyed, blind in one eye

GAKDAHŪN tall and lean

GAKDAHŪRI tall and skinny man

GAKDUN debt, liability

GAKSI partner

GALA 1. hand, arm 2. one of the sides of the encirclement in a battue 3. a measure equaling two Chinese feet and five inches
GALA BETHE HIYAHALAME FIYELEMBI at trick riding, to ride with the arms and legs crossed
GALA BUKDAMBI to bend the forearm
GALA DACUN quick-handed, dexterous
GALA ENDUBUMBI to lose one's grip
GALA FUTA a lasso for catching falcons
GALA GIDAŠAMBI to wave the hand
GALA ISIMBI to set the hand to, to take action
GALA JOOLAMBI to place the hands in the sleeves
GALA MONJIMBI to rub the hands from exasperation or regret
GALA SIDAHIYAMBI to turn the sleeves back and uncover the arms
GALA UNUMBI to put the hands behind the back
GALAI AMBAN (前鋒統領) Commandant of the Vanguard Division, BH 735
GALAI AMBAN I SIDEN YAMUN (前鋒 統領衙門) office of the Commandant of the Vanguard Division
GALAI DA (翼長) Brigadier, BH 571, 737
GALAI FALANGGŪ palm of the hand
GALAI FALANGGŪ BE JORIRE ADALI like pointing at the palm of the hand--very easy
GALAI FALANGGŪ I HERGEN the lines on the palm of the hand

GALAI FILEKU a small stove for
warming the hands
GALAI HURU the back of the hand
GALAI MAYAN armpit
GALAI SUJAKŪ an armrest
GALAI TEYEKU a railing, a hand sup-
port
GALADAMBI to set the hand to, to begin
work; cf. *gala isimbi*
GALAKTUN a protective sleeve made of
mail
GALAMBI (-ka) to clear up (of the wea-
ther)
GALAMU a shuttle used in weaving
GALANGGA TAMPIN a teapot with handles
GALBI good at hearing, possessing
keen hearing
GALBINGGA a person with good hearing
GALGA clear (of weather)
GALGAN see *galga*
GALGIRAKŪ no match for (at wrestling)
GALGIYARAKŪ see *galgirakū*
GALI precocious, smart for one's age
GALIN CECIKE one name for the oriole;
cf. *gūlin cecike*
GALIRAKŪ below par, not up to standard,
not comparable, inferior
GALJU 1. slippery ice 2. a quick and
accurate archer
GALMAN mosquito
GALMAN HEREKU Amur nuthatch (*Sitta
europaea*)
GAMABUMBI caus. of *gamambi*
GAMAMBI 1. to take (to another place)
2. to manage, to look after, to
deal with, to execute (an order),
to regulate, to dispatch
GAMAN managing, method of dealing with
something
GAMJI covetous
GAMJIDAMBI to be covetous
GAMJILAMBI see *gamjidambi*
GANABUMBI caus. of *ganambi*
GANAD an arrow with a head resem-
bling a duck's bill
GANAMBI 1. to fetch, to go to get 2.
to gather
GANCUHA BEYE all on one's own, alone
GANCURGAN see *ganjuhan*
GANG GANG (onom.) the sound of a flock
of wild geese calling
GANG SEME like wild geese crying
GANGGADA a tall person
GANGGADABUMBI caus. of *ganggadambi*
GANGGADAMBI to be tall
GANGGAHŪN tall and skinny; cf. *gakdahūn*
GANGGAN hard, tough, strong
GANGGARI 1. hard 2. the cry of the
wild goose
GANGGARI NIONGNIYAHA one name for
the goose
GANGGARI TUHEMBI to fall down hard
GANGGATA tall in stature; cf. *ganggada*

GANGGI ten quadrillion
GANIO strange, odd, extraordinary,
inauspicious
GANIONGGA 1. monster, monstrosity 2.
ominous, menacing, weird, uncanny
GANIONGGA GASHA a type of owl, the
same as *yabulan*
GANIONGGA GISUN a magic oath
GANIONGGA HŪSAHŪ the same as *hūsahū*
GANIONGGA JAKA monster, uncanny
thing
GANJI completely, all
GANJIMBI see *gajimbi*
GANJUHALAMBI to fix on a saddle
GANJUHAN thongs attached to a saddle
for carrying gear, saddle rigging
GANJURGA see *ganjuhan*
GAOWA UMIYAHA a type of worm found
in fish's stomachs
GAR (onom.) a sound made when one is
under pressure, the sound of shout-
ing
GAR GAR (onom.) sound made by a small
baby
GAR GIR (onom.) the sound made by a
flock of crows, the sound made by a
group of people arguing
GAR MIYAR (onom.) the sound of many
people shouting
GAR SEME loudly
GAR SEME JABUMBI to answer loud and
clear
GAR SEME SUREMBI to scream loudly
GARBAHŪN sparse, thin (of branches
in a tree)
GARDAMBI to rush, to walk fast
GARDAŠAMBI to walk vigorously, to walk
swiftly, to walk in a race
GARGALABUMBI caus. of *gargalambi*
GARGALAMBI to be single, to be odd
(of a number)
GARGAN 1. branch 2. the earth's
branches 3. single, odd 4. branch
of a river 5. leaf of a door 6.
comrade, friend
GARGAN BIRA branch river or stream
GARGANAMBI to branch (of a river)
GARGANGGA branching, having branches
GARGATA single, alone, odd
GARGATA HERGEN a single letter (of
the alphabet)
GARGITAI single and alone
GARGIYAN sparse, skimpy (of branches
on a tree); cf. *garbahūn*
GARHATA see *gargata*
GARHATALAMBI see *gargalambi*
GARI MARI asunder, in two, in twain,
split
GARICI one name for the cormorant
GARILAMBI to split asunder
GARIMBI 1. to caw 2. to copulate (of
dogs)
GARIMIMBI see *garilambi*

G

GARIN 1. guard of a sword, pommel 2. extra, supernumerary
　GARIN KUTULE an extra or superfluous house slave
　GARIN MORIN an extra horse (led by rope behind a rider)
GARINGGA lewd, bawdy, lustful, whore
　GARINGGA HEHE lewd woman, whore
　GARINGGA MAMA mistress of a brothel
GARJA see *garjihūn*
GARJABUMBI 1. caus. of *garjambi* 2. to split, to crush
GARJAMBI to split (v.i.), to break (v.i.)
GARJASHŪN 1. broken, split 2. debilitated (of a horse)
GARJIHŪN a large fierce dog
GARLABUMBI caus. of *garlambi*
GARLAMBI to break, to ruin, to destroy, to take apart
GARLAN ruin, destruction
GARMA a four-pointed arrow used for shooting small game
GARMIBUMBI caus. of *garmimbi*
GARMIMBI to cut into small pieces, to tear into pieces, to break up
GARSA precocious, smart, intelligent, dexterous; cf. *gali*
　GARSA JAHŪDAI a swift ocean-going vessel
GARSAKAN rather precocious, rather intelligent, rather dexterous
GARŠA a monk's habit
GARTAŠAMBI see *gardašambi*
GARU swan
GARU TURU with combined effort
GARUDAI phoenix (male)
GARUDANGGA like the phoenix
　GARUDANGGA ILHA an exotic, white, autumn-blooming flower with a short stem
　GARUDANGGA SEJEN the carriage used by the empress and dowager empress
　GARUDANGGA YENGGUHE a brightly colored type of parrot
GARUKIYARI a type of small green parrot
GARUN long leggings used for mountain climbing
GARUNGGŪ a mythical bird resembling a phoenix whose appearance is an omen of peace, the kalavinka bird
　GARUNGGŪ GARUDAI FULGIYAN HOŠONGGO ŠUN DALIKŪ a square red fan with kalavinka birds depicted on it
　GARUNGGŪ GARUDANGGA FUKJINGGA HERGEN (鸞凰書) a style of calligraphy
GASABUMBI caus./pass. of *gasambi*
GASACUN grudge, complaint
GASAMBI 1. to complain, to hold a grudge 2. to grieve, to lament
GASAN 1. grief, baneful influence, woe

2. the meat remaining after a bird of prey or predatory animal has killed and eaten
　GASAN DULEBUMBI to offer a young pig as a sacrifice at dusk outside the west wall of the house in order to drive off evil influences
GASANDUMBI/GASANUMBI to hold a grudge against one another, to complain to one another
GASHA large bird
　GASHAI SONGKONGGO FUKJINGGA HERGEN (鳥蹟書) a style of calligraphy
GASHAN calamity, disaster
GASHANGGA pertaining to large birds
　GASHANGGA FUKJINGGA HERGEN (鳥書篆) a style of calligraphy
GASHATU a military standard with birds depicted on it
GASHŪBUMBI caus. of *gashūmbi*
GASHŪMBI to swear, to take an oath
GASHŪN an oath
GASHŪNGGA pursuant to an oath, sworn
　GASHŪNGGA AHŪN DEO sworn brothers
GASIHIYABUMBI caus. of *gasihiyambi*
GASIHIYAMBI 1. to seize someone's goods by force, to ravage 2. to harm someone for one's own profit
GASIHIYANDUMBI/GASIHIYANUMBI to ravage together
GAŠAN village, country (as opposed to the city)
　GAŠAN FALAN the people of a village, community
　GAŠAN HARANGGA the inhabitants of a village
　GAŠAN I AHA village slave--a term of abuse
　GAŠAN I CALIYASI village tax collector
　GAŠAN I DA village chief
　GAŠAN I SAISA the notables of a village
　GAŠAN TOKSO villages and hamlets
GATHŪWA a jacket made of weasel or sable fur
GE 1. husband's elder brother 2. elder brother
GE GA SEME quarreling, wrangling
GEBGE GABGA tottering, wavering (of a small child walking)
GEBKELJEMBI 1. to glisten, to shine, to have a fresh oily appearance 2. to be abundant
GEBSEHUN very skinny, emaciated
GEBSEREMBI (-ke) to become very skinny
GEBU name, repute, fame
　GEBU AKŪ SIMHUN the ring finger, the fourth finger
　GEBU ALGIMBI to become famous
　GEBU ALGIN fame, renown

GEBU ARAMBI to name, to sign one's name

GEBU BAHA became famous

GEBU BITHE name card

GEBU BUMBI to name, to bestow an honorary name on

GEBU GAIMBI to gain fame, to obtain repute

GEBU HALA name and surname

GEBU HALA I DANGSE labor service roster

GEBU ISINAHA his name is established

GEBU JERGI name and rank

GEBU JERGI BE TUCIBUME ARAHA BITHE personal manifest

GEBU KOOLI general laws

GEBU SINDAMBI to sign one's name

GEBU TUCIKE became famous, famous

GEBUI AFAHA calling card

GEBUKŪ nameless

GEBUKŪ ŠUMHUN the ring finger

GEBULEMBI to name, to call by name

GEBUNGGE 1. named, bearing the name . . . 2. well-known, famous

GEBUNGGE TACIHIYAN a well-known teaching

GECEMBI to freeze, to frost

GECEN frost

GECEN GECEMBI there is a frost

GECERI ILHA the name of an exotic flower that purportedly blooms in the depths of winter

GECETU NIONGNIYAHA one name for the wild goose

GECUHERI brocade, satin with dragons or flowers depicted on it

GECUHERI SIJIGIYAN a gown made of brocade

GECUHUN a frost, a freeze

GECUHUN ERIN a period sufficiently cold to freeze water

GEDACU raw silk

GEDEHUN staring, gaping, unable to sleep

GEDUBUMBI caus. of gedumbi

GEDUMBI to gnaw

GEDUREBUMBI caus. of gedurembi

GEDUREMBI to graze, to munch on grass

GEFEHE butterfly

GEFEHE ILHA pansy

GEFERI ILHA an exotic pink flower in the shape of a butterfly

GEGE elder sister, young lady, respectful term of address to young ladies

GEGESE plural of gege

GEHENAKŪ petty, obnoxious

GEHEŠEMBI to nod (the head)

GEHU GEHULEMBI to extend the neck (of a bird while running)

GEHUKEN rather bright, somewhat bright

GEHULEMBI to nod (of birds)

GEHUMBI to bend the body forward, to bow

GEHUN 1. bright, shining, clear 2. openly

GEHUN GAHŪN brightly shining (of the sun)

GEHUN GEREKE (the sky) became very bright

GEHUN HOLTOMBI to deceive openly

GEHUN ŠEHUN brilliantly white, dazzling white

GEHUNGGE YOSO the Hsüan-t'ung (宣 統) reign period, 1909--1912

GEI SEME very thin (of silk)

GEIGEHUN weakly, feeble

GEIGEN 1. a gacuha lying on edge 2. see geihen

GEIGEREMBI (-ke) to be weakly

GEIHEN the shaft of the penis

GEJE GAJA petty, small

GEJENGGI irksome, obtrusive

GEJI a snare for birds

GEJI SINDAMBI to set a bird snare

GEJIHEŠEBUMBI caus./pass. of gejihe-šembi

GEJIHEŠEMBI to tickle under the arm

GEJING GEJING SEME the same as gejing seme

GEJING SEME chattering, persistent, obnoxious

GEJUN halberd, spear

GEJUN GIJUN I FIYENTEN (戈戟司) Spear Section, BH 122

GEJUNGGE DEJI a small amount of money taken from the winner at gambling games

GEJUREBUMBI caus. of gejurembi

GEJUREKU 1. cruel, tyrannical 2. mischievous

GEJUREMBI to mistreat, to act cruelly toward

GEKDE GAKDA see kekde kakda

GEKDEHUN skinny, skin and bones

GEKU uvula

GELAMBI to come to, to wake up

GELEBUMBI caus. of gelembi

GELECUKE frightful

GELECUN same as gelecuke

GELEKU something frightful

GELEMBI to fear

GELENDUMBI/GELENUMBI to fear together, to fear one another

GELERJEMBI to brim (with tears)

GELERŠEMBI see gelerjembi

GELEŠU timid, shrinking

GELEŠEMBI see gelerjembi

GELFIYEKEN rather light (of color)

GELFIYEN light, faint (of color)

GELFIYEN FAHALA rose-colored

GELFIYEN FULAHŪN pink, light red

GELFIYEN LAMUN light blue

GELFIYEN SOHON light yellow

GELFIYEN SUWAYAN CECIKE one name for the hawfinch; cf. turi cecike

GELFIYEN ŠANYAN CECIKE one name for

G

the bullfinch; cf. *ūn cecike*

GELFIYEN YACIN CECIKE the same as *yacin ūn cecike*

GELGUN same as *gelhun*

GELHUN timid, fainthearted

GELHUN AKŪ dare to . . ., fearlessly

GELHUN AKŪ GISUREMBI dares to speak, speaks without fear

GELI also, still, again

GELMERJEMBI to shine, to glitter

GEMBI to give a girl in marriage

GEMU 1. all, in every case 2. even (adverb)

GEMULEMBI to make the capital

GEMULEHE BA the place of imperial residence, imperial capital

GEMUN the imperial capital, the capital

GEMUN HECEN 1. the capital city, Peking 2. Urga

GEMUN HECEN I DOOLI (京畿道) Metropolitan Circuit, BH 213

GEMUN HECEN I HAFAN I KUNGGERI (京官科) office of metropolitan officials in charge of hereditary appointments and enfeoffments

GEMUN I HAFASAI SIMNEN the examination for the officials of the capital given every three years

GEMUNGGE pertaining to the capital

GEMUNGGE HECEN the capital city; cf. *gemun*

GEN the slightly protruding bone at the base of the back of the neck, the first thoracic vertebra

GEN GAN AKŪ perplexed, muddled, mixed up

GENCEHELEBUMBI caus./pass. of *gencehelembi*

GENCEHELEMBI 1. to strike with the back of a sword or like object 2. to land on the back (of the *gacuha*)

GENCEHEN 1. the back of a sword or like object 2. undersurface (of a shoe) 3. the base of a wall 4. the edge of a field

GENCEHEN MUKŠANGGA FUKJINGGA HERGEN (殳篆) a style of calligraphy

GENCEHENGGE having a back or under side

GENCEHENGGE HENGKE carambola (*Averrhoa carambola*)

GENCEHEŠEMBI to strike repeatedly with the back of a sword or like object

GENCIHELEMBI see *gencehelembi*

GENEBUMBI caus. of *genembi*

GENEMBI to go

GENE OSO get going!

GENE OSO AKŪ haven't you gone yet?

GENGGE GANGGA all alone, on one's own, wandering about alone, vagrant

GENGGECEMBI to wander from place to place, to lead the life of a vaga-

bond

GENGGEDEMBI to be weak, to be feeble, to walk unsteadily

GENGGEHUN bent forward, stooped

GENGGELE COKO one name for the hoki pheasant; cf. *gūnggala coko*

GENGGEN soft

GENGGEREMBI (-ke) to become weak and stooped

GENGGERI wavering, staggering

GENGGITUNGGA illustrious, manifest

GENGGIYEKEN rather clear

GENGGIYELEBUMBI caus. of *genggiyelembi*

GENGGIYELEMBI to make clear, to make bright, to elucidate

GENGGIYEN 1. bright, clear 2. enlightened

GENGGIYEN ABKA clear sky, blue sky, heaven

GENGGIYEN ABKA GEHUN ŠUN in broad daylight

GENGGIYEN BIYA bright moon

GENGGIYEN CAI green tea

GENGGIYEN CAI I BOO (清茶房) room in the palace used for the preparation of green tea

GENGGIYEN CUKŪLU night blind

GENGGIYEN DUWANSE bright blue satin

GENGGIYEN EJEN an enlightened ruler

GENGGIYEN MISUN soy sauce

GENGGIYEN TUGI a light cloud

GENGGIYENAKŪ paltry, petty, unreasonable

GENGGIYENGGE bright, illuminated, clear

GENGGIYESAKA rather bright, rather clear

GENGGIYESU a fourth-generation house slave

GENGGUMBI to stand with the head inclined slightly forward, to incline forward (of a wagon overladen in the front)

GEO a mare

GEODEBUMBI caus./pass. of *geodembi*

GEODEHEN GASHA a poetic name for the pheasant

GEODEMBI to lead astray, to seduce, to lure

GEODEN seduction, luring away

GEOGE presumptuous, pretentious, haughty

GEOGEDEMBI to be presumptuous, to be haughty

GEOHE see *geoge*

GEOHEDEMBI see *geogedembi*

GEOLEMBI to sneak up on (game), to hunt from concealment

GEOŠEN pike (*Esox reicherti*)

GEOŠERI beaver

GER (onom.) the sound made by snarling dogs, the sound of many people talking together

GER GAR (onom.) the sound of shouting and quarreling

GER SEME incessantly (of speaking)
GER SEME WAJIRAKŪ the same as *ger seme*

GERBEN GARBAN crawling spiderlike, scraggly, walking in an irregular manner

GERCI accuser, one who brings suit, plaintiff

GERCILEBUMBI caus./pass. of *gercilembi*

GERCILEMBI to bring suit, to accuse, to bring a charge

GEREKEN rather many, quite a few

GEREMBI (-ke, -ndere) to become bright, to dawn
GERENDERE GING the last watch (just before dawn)

GEREMBUMBI 1. caus. of *gerembi* 2. to await the dawn

GEREN 1. a crowd, a troup 2. numerous, many, the various . . . 3. of common origin, common, general 4. issue of a concubine
GEREN EME father's concubine
GEREN FILA a percussion instrument comprising ten small brass gongs
GEREN GILTUSI (庶吉士) Bachelor, graduate of the lowest degree, BH 201
GEREN GILTUSI BE TACIBURE KUREN (教習庶常馆) Department of Study of the National Academy, BH 201
GEREN GOLOI BAITA BE ICIHIYARA BOLGOBURE FIYENTEN (職方清吏司) Department of Discipline, BH 415A
GEREN I TACIN custom, habit
GEREN JUI son of a concubine
GEREN KANGGIRI a percussion instrument comprising sixteen small metal gongs on a frame
GEREN LEOLEN public opinion

GERETELE until dawn

GERGEMBI to dawn

GERGEN 1. yellowish tree cricket (*Oecanthus rufescens*) 2. see *gerhen*

GERGEN GARGAN SEME continuously arguing and wrangling

GERGEN SEMBI to prattle

GERGUWENGGE COKO one name for the hoki pheasant; cf. *gūnggala coko*

GERHEN 1. twilight 2. grain with small ears
GERHEN MUKIYEME at twilight

GERI 1. time, number of times 2. epidemic 3. dim, indistinct, unclear
GERI FARI 1. indistinct, dim, unstable 2. worried, flustered
GERI GARI indistinct, unclear, dim
GERI GARILAME faintly, indistinctly
GERI GERI flashing, twinkling

GERI GOIHA died in an epidemic (livestock)

GERI SEME indistinctly

GERI SUKDUN pestilential vapors, unhealthy weather

GERILAMBI 1. to flash 2. to catch a glimpse of

GERILARALAMBI to flash, to shine

GERINJEMBI to move back and forth (of the eyeballs)

GERIŞIKU see *gerišeku*

GERIŠEKU oscillating, wavering, irresolute

GERIŠEMBI to waver, to oscillate, to twinkle

GERKUŠEMBI to wink at, to make eyes at

GERSI FERSI dawn, daybreak

GERTELE see *geretele*

GERUDEI the female phoenix

GERUDENGGE pertaining to the female phoenix

GESE (postposition) like, same
GESE TUŠAN same post, same official position

GESEJEMBI to unravel, to break from wear (of a rope)

GESER NIYEHE one name for the little grebe; cf. *cunggur niyehe*

GESUMBI to come to, to regain consciousness, to wake up

GEŠAN balustrade, bannister

GETE plural of *ge*

GETEBUMBI 1. caus. of *getembi* 2. to wake up (v.t.)

GETEHUN see *getuhun*

GETEHURI CECIKE one name for the sparrow

GETEMBI to awaken
GETERAKŪ not to make any progress in one's studies

GETEREMBI (-ke) to be swept clean, to be washed clean, to be eliminated, to be rooted out

GETEREMBUMBI 1. caus. of *geterembi* 2. to sweep clean, to wash clean 3. to eliminate, to root out 4. to drive out (evil spirits)

GETERILAMBI to beam with joy (the eyes)

GETUHUN awake

GETUKELEBUMBI caus. of *getukelembi*

GETUKELEMBI to make clear, to elucidate, to explain; cf. *genggiyelembi*

GETUKEN clear, lucid, understandable
GETUKEN ŠETUKEN clear, lucid

GEYE gāthā--a Buddhist verse

GEYEBUMBI caus. of *geyembi*

GEYEMBI to carve, to engrave
GEYEME GAYAME uneven, serrated

GEYEN carving, serration

GI BITHE see *geye*

GI BUHŪ muntjac, barking deer (*Muntiacus muntjac*)

GI DZUI FURGI rock-point dike

GIB SEME   deafened (temporarily by a
loud noise)

GIBAGAN 1. crust 2. crust formed on
the sides of a pot in which rice is
cooked

GIBAGANAMBI   to form a crust, to become
encrusted

GIBALABUMBI   caus. of *gibalambi*

GIBALAMBI   to paste on, to mount (pictures or calligraphy)

GIBAN   pasting, mounting

GICUKE   shameful, disgraceful
GICUKE MANGGI   shamefaced, embarrassed

GIDA   spear, lance
GIDA MUKŠAN   a long pointed wooden
lance

GIDABUMBI   caus./pass. of *gidambi*

GIDABUN   suppression, defeat

GIDACAN 1. ornament, decoration (on
saddles, helmets, armor, bow cases,
belts, and rosaries) 2. the two
middle feathers in a falcon's tail

GIDACUN   see *gidacan*

GIDAKŪ 1. a press for metal 2. a
decorative headband worn by Manchu
women 3. a paperweight

GIDALABUMBI   caus./pass. of *gidalambi*

GIDALAMBI   to pierce with a spear

GIDAMBI 1. to press, to crush, to roll
flat 2. to stamp (a seal) 3. to
force, to press (to do something)
4. to quell, to crush, to defeat
5. to raid, to plunder 6. to
suppress, to hold back (laughter)
7. to close, to shut, to turn off
8. to hide, to deceive, to put on
9. to salt, to preserve in brine or
soy sauce 10. to brood, to hatch
GIDAME ARAMBI   to write in the semicursive script
GIDARA HERGEN   the semicursive script

GIDANAMBI   to go to raid, to go to force

GIDANJIMBI   to come to raid, to come to
force

GIDARAKŪ   without concealment, out in
the open, frankly

GIDASHŪN   somewhat bent forward, bent
over

GIDAŠABUMBI   caus./pass. of *gidašambi*

GIDAŠAMBI 1. to beckon to come, to
wave to 2. to take unfair advantage
of, to wrong, to oppress

GIDU USIHA   one of the stars of Ursa
Minor

GIDZ   a clapper

GIHI   deer hide
GIHI JIBCA   a jacket made of deer
hide

GIHINTU LORIN   a mule born from a mare

GIHŪ ŠAKDAMBI   to be stored away for
too long (of edibles)

GIHŪŠAMBI   to beg

GIHŪŠAME BAIMBI   to beg persistently

GIJAN   fragments of meat left over
after slicing

GIJIRI   rice straw used for weaving
mats

GIJUN   a long three-pointed spear

GIKIBUMBI   caus. of *gikimbi*

GIKIHANGGE   a term of abuse used toward
an incompetent, greedy person

GIKIMBI   to fill up

GILACAMBI   to have a fever

GILAHŪN INENGGI   cloudy day

GILAJAN 1. bare, desiccated 2. an old
desiccated tree without bark
GILAJAN HOTO   a bald-headed man

GILAJIN 1. sharp and clear (of a voice)
2. see *gilajan*

GILBAR KEIRE   a horse with a reddish
body and black tail and mane

GILEMBI   to advance in pairs to offer
wine to a deceased person

GILERJEMBI   to feign ignorance, to be
secretive about something

GILERŠEMBI   see *gilerjembi*

GILGAMBI   to burn down to ashes, to
come to the very end

GILHA INENGGI   a clear windless day

GILHAMBI   see *gilgambi*

GILI   the base of an animal's horn; cf.
jili

GILJABUMBI   caus./pass. of *giljambi*

GILJACUKA   forgivable, pardonable

GILJAMBI   to pardon, to forgive
GILJAME GAMAMBI   the same as
giljambi
GILJAME GAMARAO   please excuse me!

GILJAN   pardon, forgiveness

GILJANGGA   compassionate, merciful,
clement

GILMAHŪN   shining, glistening

GILMARI ILHA   sunflower

GILMARJAMBI   to shine, to glow, to
flash

GILTA GILTA   shining, glowing

GILTA GILTI   glittering, gleaming

GILTAHŪN   glittering, shining, clean

GILTARI   shining, glittering
GILTARI AMIHŪN   flowers of sulphur,
sublimed sulphur
GILTARI NIOWERI   shiny, colorful,
bright
GILTARI SIŠARGAN   one name for the
rose finch; cf. *fulgiyan sišargan*

GILTARILAMBI   to shine, to glitter

GILTARŠAMBI   to shine brightly, to
gleam

GILTASIKŪ   silk brocade

GILTUKAN   attractive, nice-looking,
handsome

GILTUNGGA   refined, talented

GILTUSI (廪吉士)   Bachelor
(of the National Academy), BH 201

GILUK   a good horse that can traverse

a great distance in one day

GIMDA (角) a Chinese constellation
  GIMDA TOKDONGGO KIRU (角 宿 旗) a banner of the imperial escort depicting the constellation *gimda*

GIMŠU the male quail

GIN 1. scale, steelyard 2. catty
  GIN I ILHA the scale of a steelyard
  GIN I TON number of catties

GIN ALHA colorful flower-patterned satin

GIN CIYAN GI a variety of pheasant-- probably the North China ring-necked pheasant; cf. *jihana coko*

GINA 1. a trap for sable and squirrels, a deadfall 2. sheepskin decorated with gold leaf
  GINA ILHA Chinese balsam

GINCIHI shiny through continued long use

GINCIHINEMBI to become shiny through wear

GINCIHIYAN 1. fair, beautiful 2. bright, shining
  GINCIHIYAN LEKE a thin smooth cake made of honey, flour, and sesame oil
  GINCIHIYAN ŠOBIN flat baked wheat cakes with a smooth, shiny surface
  GINCIHIYAN TUWABUNGGA HOOŠAN a type of slick paper used for public announcements

GINCIHIYARI TAIHA a type of dog with long smooth hair

GINCIRI MOO China fir (*Cunninghamia sinensis*)

GINCITU MOO a tall palm found in the Tonkin region (*Caryota ochlandra*)

GINDANA prison, jail
  GINDANA BE KADALARA HAFAN (提牢) Inspector of Prisons, BH 457
  GINDANA BE KADALARA TINGGIN (提牢廳) Prison Office, BH 457

GINDERHEN one name for the crested lark; cf. *wenderhen*

GING 1. watch (of the night) 2. scripture, sutra 3. capital (city)
  GING BITHE Buddhist scripture
  GING FORIMBI to strike the watch (with a wooden clapper)
  GING FORIRE NIYALMA a night watch-man
  GING FORISI watchman who strikes the night watches
  GING HECEN capital city; cf. *gemun hecen*

GINGGACUN sad, depressing

GINGGAMBI see *gingkambi*

GINGGE clean, pure

GINGGEN a catty

GINGGIN 1. a piece of wood attached to a dog's neck to keep him from biting 2. see *ginggen*

GINGGUHE one name for the parrot

GINGGUJI respectful, chaste
  GINGGUJI HEHE the wife of an enfeoffed official of the fourth rank

GINGGULEBUMBI caus./pass. of *ginggu-lembi*

GINGGULEMBI 1. to respect, to honor, to act respectfully 2. to write the standard form of the script
  GINGGULEME ARAMBI to write the standard form (楷書) of the script
  GINGGULERE HERGEN (楷書) the standard form of the script

GINGGULEN respectful, attentive, care-ful

GINGGUN respect, honor
  GINGGUN AKŪ without respect or honor, improper
  GINGGUN HOOŠAN a type of thick paper made in Peking
  GINGGUN KUNDU respect and honor

GINGKABUMBI caus./pass. of *gingkambi*

GINGKACUKA sad, depressing, depressed

GINGKAMBI to feel depressed, to feel downcast

GINGLI (經歷) registrar, proctor
  GINGLI JERGI HAFAN official advisor

GINGNEBUMBI caus. of *gingnembi*

GINGNEHEN picul (120 catties)

GINGNEMBI 1. to weigh on a steelyard 2. to offer a cup with both hands at a sacrifice or shamanistic rite

GINGSIMBI 1. to mumble 2. to growl while sleeping (of a dog) 3. to recite in a singsong fashion

GINJI golden pheasant; cf. *junggiri coko*

GINJULE BURGA white willow (*Salix alba*)

GINTALA Chinese tubular celery (*Oenanthe stolonifera*)

GINTEHE see *ayan gintehe, indahūn gintehe*

GINTOHO a unit of weight equivalent to twenty-four Chinese ounces

GINTU a wooden frame for holding straw in place (in a yurt)

GIO 1. roe deer (*Capreolus capreolus*) 2. mother's brother
  GIO HOLHON *Atractylis ovata*
  GIO URA *Agaricus quercus*

GIODOHON quick, alert, lively

GIOGIN the palm of the hand
  GIOGIN ARAMBI to place the palms of the hands together (for prayer)

GIOGIYAN well formed, fine
  GIOGIYAN EFEN small stuffed dump-lings--usually boiled

GIOGIYANGGA KIYOO an open imperial sedan chair carried by sixteen peo-ple

GIOHAMBI to beg (for alms)

G

GIOHOMBI see *giohambi*

GIOHOŠOMBI to beg persistently

GIOHOTO beggar

GIOI DZ tangerine

GIOI ILHA chrysanthemum

GIOI ŽIN (舉 人) Provincial Graduate, BH 629B

GIOINGGE JAHŪDAI a warship with a flat keel

GIOISE tangerine; cf. *jofohori*

GIOLU skull

GIOSE 1. pongee (silk) 2. see *giyose*

GIOWAN 1. copper 2. section of an old-style Chinese book--*chüan*

GIOWANSE coarsely woven raw silk (used for painting) 2. a scroll

GIRAN corpse

   GIRAN BE TUWAMBI to examine a corpse

   GIRAN JAFAMBI to cremate a corpse

   GIRAN TUCIBUMBI to take a corpse to the place of burial

   GIRAN TUWARA NIYALMA coroner

GIRANGGI bone

   GIRANGGI JALAN joint

   GIRANGGI PAI domino

   GIRANGGI SASUKŪ same as *giranggi pai*

   GIRANGGI YALI relatives, relations

GIRANGGILAMBI to be wounded to the bone

GIRATU big-boned (of livestock)

GIRATUNGGA big-boned, stocky

GIRDAN 1. cloth or strips of pelts cut with scissors 2. evenly cut slices of meat 3. pennant 4. border trim on a banner

   GIRDAN KILTAN I FIYENTEN (旛 幢 司) Flags and Signals Section, BH 120

GIRDANGGA outfitted with strips of pelt or cloth

GIRDU CECIKE see *derdu cecike*

GIRHA (箕) the name of a constellation

   GIRHA TOKDONGGO KIRU (箕 宿 旗) a banner depicting the constellation *girha*

GIRI CECIKE one name for the myna

GIRIBUMBI caus. of *girimbi*

GIRIKŪ a small knife for trimming skin, paper, and cloth

GIRIMBI to trim with a knife or scissors, to cut evenly, to cut a strip

GIRIN 1. strip 2. section, area

   GIRIN EFULEMBI to break the ice on a river in the autumn to catch fish

   GIRIN I BOO house facing the street

GIRINJAMBI to exert oneself

GIRKŪMBI to act intently, to act with a single purpose, to concentrate

GIRU 1. appearance, aspect, form 2. a wooden bow before it is laminated with horn

   GIRU SACIMBI to cut out the wooden shaft of a bow

   GIRU SAIN good looking

GIRUBUMBI 1. caus./pass. of *girumbi* 2. to shame, to bring shame to, to be disgraced

GIRUCUN shame, disgrace, disgraced

GIRUDAI the phoenix of the south

GIRUMBI (-ha) to be ashamed, to feel ashamed, to be embarrassed

GIRUTU ashamed, embarrassed; cf. *gicuke manggi*

GISABUMBI 1. caus. of *gisambi* 2. to wipe out, to annihilate

GISAMBI (-ka) to be wiped out, to perish utterly

GISAN 1. perishing, annihilation 2. hair that falls out

   GISAN HALAMBI to have the hair fall out and be replaced by new

GISE prostitute, whore

   GISE HEHE whore

   GISE HEHE I FALAN house of prostitution, brothel

GISHE vine of a cucurbitaceous plant; cf. *jushe*

GISIHA hazelnut tree; cf. *jisiha*

GISTA 1. end of a tendon 2. devious, cunning

GISUHE see *gishe*

GISUN 1. speech, word, language 2. drumstick

   GISUN AIFUMBI to break one's word

   GISUN ANABURAKŪ obstinate, unyielding in speech

   GISUN BANJINARAKŪ not to have the words (to express one's anger or indignation)

   GISUN BE GAIJARA TEMGETUN (納 言 旌) one of the pennants of the imperial escort

   GISUN BEDEREBUMBI to take back news

   GISUN BUMBI to give one's word, to assent

   GISUN DAHAMBI to obey

   GISUN FULIBURAKŪ can't get the words out, remains speechless

   GISUN FULU NIYALMA busybody

   GISUN GAIMBI to obey

   GISUN GOICUKA what was said is to the point

   GISUN HESE speech

   GISUN I FESIN an object of talk (criticism or gossip)

   GISUN MUDAN language

GISUREBUMBI caus. of *gisurembi*

GISURECEMBI to talk together, to discuss

GISUREMBI to speak, to talk

   GISUREHEI AYAMBUMBI to persuade, to move with words

   GISURERE HAFAN (給 事 中)

Junior Metropolitan Censor, BH 210

GISUREMBUMBI see *gisurebumbi*

GISUREN talk, discussion

GISURENDUMBI/GISURENUMBI to talk to one
another

GISURENEMBI to go to talk

GISURENJIMBI to come to talk

GITA LOODAN very small

GITALA see *gintala*

GITARILAMBI see *giltarilambi*

GITUHAN a zitherlike instrument with
twelve strings

GITUKU name of the bamboo partridge in
southwest China

GIYA see *giyai*

GIYA SIYAN LEKE a steamed cake with a
sugar and jujube filling

GIYA ŠA ETUKU a monk's habit

GIYA ŠE DZUN Kāsyapa Buddha; cf.
g'asib

GIYAB (onom.) the sound made by the
Pekingese dog

GIYABALABUMBI caus. of *giyabalambi*

GIYABALAMBI 1. to press, to hold between two objects 2. to punish by
applying a press to the feet

GIYABAN a foot-press used for punishing
criminals, pressing sticks

GIYABAN GIDAMBI to apply the pressing sticks

GIYABAN GŪLHA boots made from the
skin of the thighs of horses,
mules, or donkeys

GIYABSAHŪN emaciated, thin and weak

GIYABSARAMBI (-ka) to be emaciated

GIYABUMBI caus. of *giyambi*

GIYADURAKA chaotic, in every direction

GIYAHA leaves that have fallen from
a tree

GIYAHA SIHAMBI leaves fall

GIYAHALCAMBI to move agilely (of
horses)

GIYAHŪHA CECIKE one name for the wren;
cf. *jirha cecike*

GIYAHŪN accipitrine birds--hawks,
falcons, etc.

GIYAHŪN BAKSI falconer

GIYAHŪN CECIKE shrike; cf. *mergen
cecike*

GIYAHŪN I OŠOHO a hawk's claws

GIYAHŪN MAKTAMBI to launch a falcon

GIYAHŪN UJIRE BA a place where falcons are kept

GIYAHŪN YASA a mosslike plant
(*Lycopodium clavata*)

GIYAI street

GIYAI GIRIN the street front

GIYAI YUWAN (解元) number one in
the provincial examination

GIYAJALAMBI to serve as an attendant

GIYAJAN 1. attendant of a *beile*,
beise, or prince 2. large shears

GIYAJI fragile, attractive but not
sturdy

GIYAJILAMBI see *giyajalambi*

GIYAKDA a small curved knife

GIYAKDALAMBI to cut with a small
curved knife

GIYAKTA leaves that have fallen from
a tree; cf. *giyaha*

GIYAKTU CECIKE brown bush warbler; cf.
enggetu cecike

GIYALABUMBI caus. of *giyalambi*

GIYALABUN interval, space, pause

GIYALAGANJAMBI see *giyalganjambi*

GIYALAHABUMBI see *giyalgabumbi*

GIYALAKŪ 1. separation, compartment,
section 2. divider, separator
3. interval, space

GIYALAMAHA headband, diadem

GIYALAMBI to make a space or pause
between, to separate, to be separated (by an interval), to be intermittent, to be in between

GIYALAMTUN in the Chou dynasty, the
name of a small table on which flesh
was offered

GIYALAN 1. space between, interval,
interstice 2. measure word for
rooms and houses

GIYALANAMBI to form a divider, to form
an interval

GIYALGABUMBI caus. of *giyalgambi*

GIYALGAMBI to neglect to give something due, to omit, to delete

GIYALGANJAMBI to do by turns

GIYALHŪHA dry wood split up for burning

GIYALIN GAHA jackdaw

GIYALTU a type of sea fish

GIYALU crack, fissure, defect

GIYALU BAIMBI to look for defects

GIYALUNAMBI to crack, to develop a
defect

GIYAMBI to pare, to whittle

GIYARA MOO split firewood

GIYAMULABUMBI caus. of *giyamulambi*

GIYAMULAMBI to go by the relay-post
system

GIYAMUN relay station, relay post,
military post station

GIYAMUN BE KADALARA HAFAN (驛站
官) official in charge of a post
station

GIYAMUN BE KADALARA YAMUN (驛站
監督衙門) office of an
Inspector of Military Post Stations, BH 754

GIYAMUN I CALIYAN BODORO KUNGGERI
(驛傳科) Military Posts
Section, BH 425

GIYAMUN I FALGANGGA (館所)
an office of the Board of War in
charge of matters relating to post
stations

GIYAMUN I HAHA manservant at a post

G

G

station
GIYAMUN I HŪSUN post-station worker
GIYAMUN I MORIN post horse
GIYAMUN TEBUMBI to establish a
    string of relay posts
GIYAMUSI (驛 丞) Inspector of a
    Post Station, BH 754
GIYAN 1. reason, right, principle,
    order 2. reasonable, right, in
    order, proper 3. measure word for
    rooms and buildings
    GIYAN BE JORIKŪ (中 允) an
        official in the Supervisorate of
        Imperial Instruction just under
        the *erdemu be neileku*
    GIYAN BE MURIMBI to be unfair
    GIYAN DE ACANAMBI to be reasonable
    GIYAN DE ACANARAKŪ unreasonable
    GIYAN FIYAN reasonable, orderly
    GIYAN GIYAN I in proper order, in
        an orderly and reasonable manner,
        in detail
    GIYAN I on principle, by right
    GIYAN I . . . CI ACAMBI must,
        ought to
GIYANAKŪ limited
    GIYANAKŪ UDU how short, how limited,
        how few
GIYANCEO raw silk
GIYANCIHIYAN HOOŠAN a type of thin
    shiny paper
GIYANDU (監 督) inspector
GIYANG 1. river 2. ginger 3. (onom.)
    the sound of a dog barking
GIYANGDU cowpeas (*Virga sinensis*), a
    pastry made of cowpeas
GIYANGGA reasonable, moral
GIYANGGIYAN reasonable
GIYANGGUHE one name for the myna
GIYANGKA BERI a gripless bow made from
    the horns of the water buffalo
GIYANGKŪ a shirker
GIYANGKŪŠAMBI to be always shirking
    one's duty or work
GIYANGNABUMBI caus. of *giyangnambi*
GIYANGNAKŪ one who insists that he
    is always right, an arguer
GIYANGNAKŪŠAMBI to be always insisting
    on one's own views
GIYANGNAMBI to explain, to comment on
GIYANGNAN Kiangnan, the areas south of
    the Yangtse
    GIYANGNAN GOLOI BOLGOBURE FIYENTEN
        (江 南 清 吏 司) a sec-
        tion of the Board of Finance con-
        cerned with Kiangnan
    GIYANGNAN GOLOI FALGA (江 南 甲)
        office of the Board of Civil Ap-
        pointments concerned with Kiangnan
GIYANGNANDUMBI/GIYANGNANUMBI to explain
    (of a group)
GIYANGSIMBI to yelp (of dogs that are
    tied up and want to escape)

GIYANSI spy, enemy agent
GIYANTU a whiplike weapon with a four-
    cornered iron tip
GIYAPI peeled, having a raised crust
    GIYAPI ŠOBIN a type of baked
        cake with a raised crust
GIYAPINAMBI to shed a layer of skin,
    to peel (v.i.)
GIYAR GIR (onom.) the sound made by
    monkeys and birds
GIYAR GIYAR (onom.) the same as *giyar
    gir*
GIYARGIYAN SEME scolding constantly
GIYARIBUMBI caus. of *giyarimbi*
GIYARICI patrolman, policeman
GIYARIMBI 1. to patrol, to make an
    inspection tour 2. to go away from
    home to fast
    GIYARIME DASARA AMBAN (巡 撫)
        Governor, BH 821
    GIYARIME KEDEREMBI to make a tour
        of inspection
    GIYARIME KEDERERE HAFAN (巡 視
        官) guard officer
GIYARIMSI (巡 檢) Sub-district
    Magistrate, BH 857
GIYARINAMBI to go to patrol, to go to
    inspect
GIYARINJIMBI to come to patrol, to
    come to inspect
GIYASE stand, frame
GIYATARABUMBI caus./pass. of *giyatar-
    ambi*
GIYATARAMBI 1. to reduce, to deduct
    2. to appropriate in an irregular
    manner, to extort
GIYEI TIYEI announcement
GIYEI UCURI Kalpa; cf. *g'alab*
GIYEN indigo
    GIYEN GASHA Chinese blue and white
        flycatcher (*Cyanoptila cyanomelana*)
    GIYEN LAMUN indigo blue
GIYENGGE see *cunggur niyehe*
    GIYENGGE CECIKE see *jirha cecike*
GIYOB SEME (onom.) the sound of an
    arrow flying close by
GIYOGIYAN see *giogiyan*
GIYOHOLOMBI to rage, to rave
GIYOHOMBI see *giohombi*
GIYOK SEME with a bang, with a crash
GIYOLO the crown of the head
    GIYOLO I ŠURDEN the swirling of a
        sword above the head while dancing
GIYOMO (角) the third note in the
    classical pentatonic scale
GIYONG SEME (onom.) the sound made by
    the wings of a phoenix in flight
GIYOO a type of dragon
GIYOOCAN a practice field for archery
GIYOOSE see *giyose*
GIYOOSI teacher, instructor
GIYOR SEME (onom.) the sound made by
    the belly growling when one is

G

hungry, borborygmus

GIYOROBUMBI to be beaten into unconsciousness

GIYOROMBI (-ko) to lapse into unconsciousness (from a beating)

GIYOS SEME with a bang

GIYOSE a type of meat pastry, a meat-filled dumpling

GIYUN a measure of weight equivalent to thirty catties

GO a golden neck ornament worn by married women at court ceremonies

GOBI desert, wasteland

GOBIMBI to hew, to chop

GOBOLOBUMBI caus. of *gobolombi*

GOBOLOMBI 1. to fail, to be unsuccessful, to miss, to lack 2. to alight on a tree (of pheasants)

GOCI MOO the Chinese scholar tree (*Sophora japonica*)

GOCI TATA restless, unsettled

GOCIHIYAŠAMBI see *guwacihiyašambi*

GOCIKA pertaining to the imperial bodyguard

  GOCIKA AMBAN (御 前 大 臣) Adjutant General, BH 101

  GOCIKA BAYARA (親 軍) Imperial Bodyguard, GH 98, 100

  GOCIKA BAYARAI JUWAN I DA (親 軍 校) Lieutenant of the Imperial Bodyguard, BH 100

  GOCIKA HIYA (御 前 侍 衛) Guard of the Antechamber, BH 99

GOCIKANGGA pertaining to the Imperial Bodyguard

  GOCIKANGGA MUKŠAN a mace carried by the Imperial Bodyguard

GOCIKŪ 1. an apron or shirt of armor 2. leggings

GOCIMA drawer

  GOCIMA DERE a table with drawers, a chest of drawers

GOCIMBI (-ka) 1. to draw, to pull, 2. to play a stringed instrument 3. to withdraw (troops) 4. to extract, to press out (oil) 5. to fall, to recede (of water), to draw back 6. to become skinny (of horses) 7. to appear, to come out (of a rainbow)

GOCIMBUMBI 1. caus. of *gocimbi* 2. to suffer cramps 3. to freeze solid

  GOCIMBURE NIMEKU cramps

GOCINGGA BUREN a long horn made from wood, a wood-wind instrument

GOCINGGA MUDAN the entering tone of Chinese

GOCISHŪDAMBI to be modest, to act modestly

GOCISHŪN modest, humble

GOCIŠAMBI to shrink back, to draw back

GODOHON erect, tall and straight

  GODOHON ILIBUMBI to set up straight

GODOMBI to leap high out of the water (of fish)

GODOMIMBI to mumble to oneself

GODONDUMBI/GODONUMBI to leap high out of the water (of many fish)

GODOR SEME mumbling, chattering

GODORI leaping up suddenly, all at once

GODORILAMBI to leap up, to spring up

GOFOHO a snare for catching small birds in trees

GOFOHOLOMBI to be intertwined, to be entangled

GOFOLOKO a wooden lantern holder placed on a rafter

GOHO 1. elegant, dainty, adorned 2. fop, dandy

GOHODOMBI to adorn oneself, to make up

GOHOLOBUMBI caus. of *goholombi*

GOHOLOMBI to hook, to put on a hook

GOHON a hook

  GOHON I JIHA SELE three iron rings on the leather strap of a quiver

GOHONGGO having a hook, provided with hooks, hook-shaped

  GOHONGGO SUJAHAN a hook for holding a window or a plaque

  GOHONGGO WASE a hook-shaped tile at the corners of a roof

GOHOROMBI (-ko) to bend (v.i.), to form the shape of a hook, to curl (v.i.)

GOHOŠOMBI 1. to hook in 2. to take amiss, to get entangled in an argument

GOHOTO a wooden cylinder used for rolling or pounding grain

GOHŪ see *goho*

GOIBUMBI caus./pass. of *goimbi*

GOICUKA 1. hindering, in the way 2. attention drawing, out of the ordinary 3. to the point, appropriate

  GOICUKA AKŪ unhindered, without obstacle

  GOICUKA BA hindrance, obstacle

GOIDABUMBI caus. of *goidambi*

GOIDAMBI to last for a long time, to endure

  GOIDAHAKŪ before long, in a short while

  GOIDAME ELGIYEN CALU a granary located in Shantung

GOIDANAMBI to decay

GOIHOROMBI (-ko) to be weak in determination, to lack courage

GOIMAN charming, enticing, elegant

GOIMANGGA possessing enticements or charm

GOIMARAMBI to adorn oneself, to make oneself attractive, to entice with one's charms

GOIMBI (-ha) 1. to hit the mark, to strike the target 2. to be struck

G

(by an arrow) 3. to be hit upon, to become one's turn to do something

GOITO a calk placed on the bottom of snowshoes to prevent slipping

GOITOBUMBI to do in vain

GOJI a crooked finger

GOJIME (sentence particle) only, solely

GOJINGGA see *gojinggi*

GOJINGGI fast-talking

GOJONG SEME fast and unclear (of speech)

GOJONGGI the same as *gojong seme*

GOJOR SEME see *gojong seme*

GOKCI the handle of a plow

GOKJI a molting bird

GOKJIBUMBI caus. of *gokjimbi*

GOKJIMBI to knot up, to plait, to plait with silk thread

GOKO (onom.) the sound of chickens cackling

GOKSI ceremonial court dress without flared shoulder pieces

GOLAFUNGGA MOO yew tree

GOLAMBI to shoot off an arrow with a flourish of the hand

GOLBON a clothes rack

GOLCEHEN COKO a long-tailed chicken

GOLDEREN a long table used for trans- acting official business

GOLIN copper, bronze

GOLMIKAN rather long

GOLMIN long

 GOLMIN ASARI DE TUGI FISIN I MUDAN music played in the Hanlin Academy during banquets

 GOLMIN FUNGKU a long towel or wiping cloth

 GOLMIN JAN a type of long whistling arrow

 GOLMIN TEMGETU a small, long, of- ficial seal used by petty provin- cial officials

 GOLMIN UNCEHENGGE ŠANYAN BAIBULA the paradise flycatcher; cf. *baibula*

GOLMISHŪN rather long, longish

GOLO 1. river bed 2. province, dis- trict 3. saddlebow

 GOLOI AMBAN (外省大臣) provincial officials of high rank

 GOLOI BEISE feudal prince

 GOLOI HAFAN (外省官員) provincial official

GOLOBUMBI caus. of *golombi*

GOLOCUN frightful

GOLOHOI in a frightened manner

GOLOHON fright

 GOLOHON GAIMBI to douse a fright- ened child with water

GOLOHONJOMBI 1. to be exceedingly frightened 2. to wake up trembling (of children)

GOLOMBI to be startled, to be scared

GOLON TUWA a fire that starts on a

cloudy night and causes birds to land

GOLONDUMBI/GOLONUMBI to be startled (of a group)

GOLONGGO pertaining to a province or district

GOLONOMBI to freeze along the banks of a river

GOLOROMBI to go to another province

GOLOTOME SIMNEMBI to take the examina- tion for the degree of provincial graduate

GOLTON the charred remains of a tree after it has been burnt

GOMBI (-ha) to go back on one's word, to break a promise, to renege

GON GAN (onom.) the cry of a goose or swan

GONDOBA see *hondoba*

GONGGIBUMBI caus. of *gonggimbi*

GONGGIMBI to send to get

GONGGOHON listless, restless, bored, a listless person

GONGGOHORI plural of *gonggohon*

GONGGON standing upright (of the *gacuha*)

GONGGORI with a start

 GONGGORI ILIMBI to stand up sud- denly with a start

GONJAMBI 1. to take a turn for the worse 2. to regret what one has promised

GORBI MOO sandalwood tree

GORGI clasp on the girth of a horse

GORGIN MOO Amur cork tree (*Phelloden- dron amurense*)

GORO 1. far 2. a tree of the *Sophora* family

 GORO AIGAN GABTARA KACILAN an arrow used for long range target shoot- ing

 GORO MAFA maternal grandfather

 GORO MAMA maternal grandmother

 GORO OMOLO daughter's child

 GORO YASAI BULEKU telescope

GOROKI distant, distant place

 GOROKI BE BILURE BOLGOBURE FIYENTEN (柔遠清吏司) Depart- ment for Receiving Princes of Outer Mongolia, BH 495

GOROKIN a southern barbarian

GOROKINGGE a person from a distant place, a distant place

 GOROKINGGE BE TOHOROMBURE BOLGOBURE FIYENTEN (徠遠清吏司) Department of Eastern Turkestan, BH 495

GOROKON rather far

GOROMILAMBI see *goromimbi*

GOROMIMBI to do from afar, to go a long distance

 GOROMIME BODOMBI to plan from afar

 GOROMIME GŪNIMBI to think of from

afar
GOROMIME YABUMBI to go a long dis-
   tance
GOSIBUMBI caus./pass. of *gosimbi*
GOSICUKA 1. pitiful 2. lovable
   GOSICUKA KENEHUNJECUKE pitiful and
   suspicious
GOSICUNGGA merciful, compassionate
GOSIHOLOMBI 1. to be bitter 2. to act
   in a miserable or distressed manner,
   to be miserable or distressed
GOSIHON 1. bitter 2. miserable, suf-
   fering
   GOSIHON DUHA the small intestine of
   a sheep
GOSIHORI a large bitter exotic fruit
GOSIHŪN see *gosihon*
GOSIMBI 1. to pity, to have mercy
   2. to love, to cherish 3. to hurt
   (of an abrasion)
   GOSIHABI few pocks have appeared
GOSIN pity, mercy, love
GOSINDUMBI to love one another
GOSINGGA loving, compassionate,
   cherished, beloved
   GOSINGGA GUCU a cherished friend
GOSITAMBI to like, to love
GOSLAMBI to release the hand upward
   after shooting an arrow
GOTOR SEME fast and unclear (of
   speech); cf. *gojong seme*
GU 1. father's sister 2. jadeite,
   nephrite, precious stone
   GU DENGJAN ILHA a fragrant red
   exotic flower that blooms at night
   GU DZUNG a type of thin woolen
   GU FILEKU ILHA an exotic white
   flower that resembles a hand
   warmer
   GU FIYAHAN gems and tortoise shell,
   jewels and precious stones
   GU HONGGO ILHA a white, bell-shaped,
   exotic flower
   GU I CIKTENGGE FUKJINGGA HERGEN
   (玉 筋 篆) a style of calligraphy
   GU I CINCILAN a jade tube used in
   antiquity for observing the
   heavens
   GU I DEYEN TUGI JEKSENGGE MUDAN
   music played while wine was offered during great banquets in the
   palace
   GU I YAMUN DE YEBKEN URSE BE ISABURE
   MUDAN music played while food was
   served during a banquet at the
   Hanlin Academy
   GU LUJEN the name of one of the
   imperial chariots
   GU NIYANJAN the name of one of the
   imperial coaches
   GU ORHO a type of henbane found in
   Vietnam and Kwangtung (*Hyoscyamus*

agrestia)
   GU SIFIKŪ ILHA short-cluster plan-
   tain lily (*Hosta glauca*)
   GU SUJE I HITHEN a ritual vessel
   for holding jade and silk at sacri-
   fices
   GU WEHE unrefined jade, raw jade
GUBCI universal, all, entire
   GUBCI ABKAI MUHELIYEN DURUNGGA TETUN
   a global map of the heavens at the
   Peking observatory
   GUBCI ELGIYENGGE the Hsien-feng
   (咸 豐) reign period, 1851-1861
GUBCINGGE universal, whole
GUBSU bud (of a flower), measure word
   for flowers
GUBULEMBI to grow entangled, to be
   intertwined
GUCENG jewels worn at the girdle
GUCIHI rival (female)
GUCIHIYEREKU rival, a person who is
   jealous of another
GUCIHIYEREMBI to be jealous, to be a
   rival
GUCIHIYERENDUMBI/GUCIHIYERENUMBI to be
   jealous of one another
GUCU friend, comrade, companion
   GUCU ARAMBI to treat as a friend, to
   become friends
   GUCU DUWALI a group of friends, a
   clique
   GUCU FALIMBI to make friends
   GUCU GARGAN friends and acquaint-
   ances, friends
   GUCU GIYAJAN (王 府 隨 侍)
   attendant in the palace of a prince
GUCULEMBI to make friends, to be
   friends with
GUCUNG SEME see *gojong seme*
GUCUSE plural of *gucu*
GUDEŠEMBI to strike repeatedly with the
   fist
GUDZ the frame of a fan
GUFAN a precious stone from the state
   of Lu
GUFU husband of father's sister
GUFUTE plural of *gufu*
GUGIO black jade
GUGIOI a jade girdle ornament
GUGU GUGU sound used to call chickens
GUGUI see *gugioi*
GUGUN GASHA a Fukienese bird having a
   gray head, green wings, blue tail,
   and red and black feet--possibly a
   cuckoo
GUGUR SEME stooped, bent over
GUGUREMBI (-ke) to stoop, to be bent
   over from old age, to shrink up from
   cold
GUGURŠEMBI to bow before superiors
GUG'AN red jasper
GUHE saltpeter
GUHEREN ILHA an exotic flower with

G

G

large leaves, a purple stalk, and sacklike blossoms

GUHŪTUN　the name of a sacrificial jade of the Hsia dynasty

GUH'ANG　the same as *guceng*

GUI　turtle, tortoise

GUI HŪWA　osmanthus (a small fragrant white flower)

GUIFEI　an imperial concubine of the second rank

GUIFUN　a ring (for the finger)

GUIGU　vigorous, healthy (of an old person)

GUIKERI　Japanese raisin tree (*Hovenia dulcis*)

GUILEBUMBI　caus. of *guilembi*

GUILEHE　apricot

　　GUILEHE BOCO　apricot-colored

GUILEMBI　to invite, to make an appointment, to arrange a meeting

GUILENDUMBI　to invite one another

GUILENEMBI　to go to invite

GUILENJIMBI　to come to invite

GUILERI　a type of apple (*Malus prunifolia*)

GUINI (兔)　the name of a constellation

　　GUINI TOKDONGGO KIRU (兔宿旗) a banner depicting the constellation *guini*

GUIOI　a high quality nephrite

GUISE　cabinet, chest, counter

GUJEHE　the name of the cuckoo in Kiangtung

GUJIRI ILHA　the passion flower

GUJUNG SEME　assiduously, concentrated, diligently

GUKDU GAKDA　with ups and downs, uneven, unlevel

GUKDUHUN　a rise, a high place

GUKDUN JOFOHORI　tangerine (*Citrus nobilis*)

GUKDUREMBI　to rise up, to tower

GUKI MOO　an exotic tree resembling the weeping willow

GUKIO　a type of precious stone

GUKIONG　hyacinth (a gem)

GUKJUREMBI　(-ke)　to become crooked

GUKSEN　a short burst of rain, a blast of wind, a measure word for clouds

　　GUKSEN GUKSEN　in bursts, in spells, one by one (clouds)

　　GUKSEN GUKSEN AGAMBI　to rain in bursts or spells

GUKSU　see *guksen*

GUKUBUMBI　caus. of *gukumbi*

GUKUBUN　annihilation, extinction

GUKUMBI　to be annihilated, to be wiped out, to perish, to be extinguished

GUKUNG　a jadelike stone

GULAN　a pearl-like stone

GULBU　a white bug that falls into rivers on autumn days

GULEJEMBI　to come loose (of a knot)

GULHUKEN　rather complete

GULHUN　complete, intact, entire

　　GULHUN DUBENGGE SUIHE　a tassel untrimmed at the end

　　GULHUN EMU INENGGI　all day

　　GULHUN FUNGLU JETERE HAFAN　full-salaried official

　　GULHUN SUWANDA　a clove of garlic

　　GULHUN ŠOGE　whole ingots

　　GULHUN TEKSIN　neat, orderly

GULI JUŠEN HALANGGA NIYALMA　the same as *jušen*

GULIN CECIKE　one name for the oriole; cf. *gūlin cecike*

GULIYATUN　the name of an ancient ritual vessel

GULU　1. simple, pure, unadulterated, unrefined, in its natural state 2. white, plain in color

　　GULU FULGIYAN　one of the eight banners--the pure red banner

　　GULU FULGIYAN SUJE KIRU　a pure red banner used by the escort of an imperial concubine of the first rank

　　GULU HAKSAN BOCOI SUJE SARA　a pure gold-colored silk parasol used by the escort of an imperial concubine of the third rank

　　GULU HAKSAN BOCOI SUJE ŠUN DALIKŪ　a pure gold-colored silk fan-parasol used by the escort of an imperial concubine of the first rank

　　GULU HOŠONGGO ŠUŠU BOCOI SARA　a pure purple square umbrella

　　GULU LAMUN　one of the eight banners--the pure blue banner

　　GULU SUJE　plain silk

　　GULU SUWAYAN　one of the eight banners--the pure yellow banner

　　GULU ŠANYAN　one of the eight banners--the pure white banner

GULUKEN　rather plain, rather unadorned

GULUNG SEME　chattering, idly (of talking)

GULUR SEME　stuttering

GULURJEMBI　to stutter

GUMEN　a type of red gem

GUN ETUKU　the official dress of the Chou king

GUNDA ILHA　an exotic flower said to bloom in the moonlight

GUNG　1. duke　2. palace　3. merit 4. a mine

　　GUNG DE WESIMBI　to return to the palace

　　GUNG ILGAMBI　to judge merit

　　GUNG NI GEGE I EFU　the daughter-in-law of a duke

　　GUNG NI JUI GEGE　the daughter of a duke

G

GUNG ŠENG a scholar recommended by the local government on the basis of accomplishment and virtue

GUNGCEO silk prepared by the imperial factory

GUNGCU see *gungceo*

GUNGCUN see *gungceo*

GUNGDZ young master

GUNGGE merit, accomplishment

GUNGGE AMBAN a meritorious official

GUNGGE AMBAN I ULABUN ICIHIYARA KUREN (功臣館) an office charged with compiling the biographies of meritorious officials

GUNGGE BE SAIŠARA GOROKI BE BILURE TEMGETUN a banner of the imperial escort on which *gungge be saišara goroki be bilure* was written

GUNGGE ILGAMBI to judge merit

GUNGGU the back of the head

GUNGGUCEME GENGGECEME irresolute, shrinking from decision or responsibility, apprehensive

GUNGGUHUN CECIKE one of the names of the hoopoe; cf. *indahūn cecike*

GUNGGULEMBI to shoot upward (an arrow)

GUNGGULU crest on a bird's head

GUNGGULUN COKO a crested chicken

GUNGGULUNGGE crested

GUNGGULUNGGE NIONGNIYAHA a crested goose

GUNGGULUNGGE SAMAN CECIKE a crested lark

GUNGGULUNGGE ŠE a crested eagle

GUNGGUMBI 1. to feel apprehension 2. to be overwhelmed (with sadness) 3. to cower, to shrink away

GUNGGUME TEMBI to sit cowering

GUNGGUN GANGGAN indecisive, shrinking from decision or responsibility, apprehensive

GUNGHUN (宫) one of the musical notes of the pentatonic scale

GUNGJU princess

GUNGKERI ILHA magnolia

GUNGMIN honest, sincere, fair

GUNGNEBUMBI caus. of *gungnembi*

GUNGNECUKE respectful

GUNGNEMBI to show respect to

GUNGNENEMBI to go to show respect

GUNGŠI (供事) clerk; cf. *baita de afaha hafan*

GUNIREMBI (-ke) 1. to loosen, to come loose 2. to calm down, to be relieved 3. to slam

GUNIYEREMBI see *gunirembi*

GUPAI mah-jongg piece, domino

GUR SEME 1. snarling, growling 2. talking too much

GUREHE 1. the broad tendons on a cow's throat 2. lazy but crafty, given to shirking work

GUREHEDEMBI to be always shirking one's duty

GUREHELEBUMBI caus. of *gurehelembi*

GUREHELEMBI to wrap with the tendons from a cow's neck

GUREHELEHE BERI a bow that has been wrapped with a cow's neck tendons

GURELJI a type of large cricket

GUREMBI see *gurumbi*

GURGU wild animal, beast

GURGU DARIMBI the animals pass very close (at a battue)

GURGUNGGE decorated with animal figures

GURGUŠEMBI to hunt wild animals

GURGUTU animal heads carved on the four corners of a building

GURHU see *gurgu*

GURIBUMBI 1. caus. of *gurimbi* 2. to move (v.t.), to transfer

GURIBUME FUNGNEMBI to transfer a title of enfeoffment to one's father or grandfather

GURIBURE BITHE a document circulated among all the subdivisions of a governmental organ

GURIMBI to move, to transfer

GURINEMBI to go to move, to move to another place

GURINJIMBI to come to move, to move here

GURIWA ILHA an exotic flower whose leaves and stalk resemble bamboo

GURJEN a cricket

GURJENDUMBI to chirp

GURLUN GŪWARA eared owl; cf. *fu gūwara*

GURUBUMBI caus. of *gurumbi*

GURUMBI (1) to dig up, to dig out (vegetables, herbs)

GURUMBI (2) (-ke) to redden, to become inflamed

GURUN 1. country, tribe, people 2. ruling house, dynasty

GURUN BE DALIRE GUNG (鎮國公) Prince of the Blood of the fifth degree, BH 20

GURUN BE DALIRE JANGGIN (鎮國將軍) Noble of the Imperial lineage of the ninth rank, BH 24

GURUN BE TUWAKIYARA JANGGIN (泰國將軍) Noble of the Imperial lineage of the eleventh rank, BH 26

GURUN BOO the Court

GURUN DE AISILARA GUNG (輔國公) Prince of the Blood of the sixth degree, BH 21

GURUN DE AISILARA JANGGIN (輔國將軍) Noble of the Imperial lineage of the tenth rank, BH 25

GURUN GŪWA an outsider

GURUN I BODOGON statecraft, national strategy

G

GURUN I EFU (囯倫額駙)
husband of a *gurun i gungju*
GURUN I EJEN   monarch, ruler, king,
emperor
GURUN I GUNGJU (囯倫公主)
Princess born to an Empress, BH 14
GURUN I JUSE BE HŪWAŠABURE YAMUN
(國子監) Imperial Academy
of Learning, BH 412
GURUN I SUDURI BE ASARARA YAMUN
(皇史宬) the storage place
for the national historical ar-
chives
GURUN I SUDURI KUREN (國史館)
State Historiographer's Office,
BH 205
GURUN I TACIKŪ (太學) the
literary designation of the Im-
perial Academy of Learning, BH 412
GURUNEMBI   to go to dig out
GURUNG   1. palace   2. constellation
GURUNG DEYEN   palace
GURUNG DE WESIMBI   to return to the
palace
GURUNUMBI   to dig out (of a group)
GURUTUN   a sacrificial vessel of Emperor
Shun
GUSE   1. a Buddhist nun   2. see *gudz*
GUSHEMBI   1. to develop (into some-
thing), to succeed   2. to be of use,
to be of value
GUSHUMBI   see *gushembi*
GUSIO   a sort of precious stone
GUSUCUKE   out of humor, annoyed, dull,
annoying
GUSUCUMBI   to be out of humor, to feel
bored, to be annoyed
GUSUCUN   annoyance, dejection, sadness
GUSUI   a precious stone worn at the
girdle; cf. *guceng*
GUTE   plural of *gu*
GUTI   a type of precious stone
GUWA   the eight trigrams used for
divination
GUWA MAKTAMBI   to cast the trigrams
GUWA TUWAMBI   to consult the trigrams
GUWAFU   1. crutch   2. oars
GUWAFU MOO   a short pole with a piece
of wood attached at right angles
to one end that was used as a wea-
pon
GUWAIDZ   crutch, walking stick
GUWAIGE   the same as *guwafu*
GUWALASE   a wild sour-tasting plant
similar to shepherd's purse
GUWALASUN   a short sleeveless jacket
worn by women
GUWALI   dwellings located on both sides
of the city gates outside of a city,
outskirts, suburb
GUWAN   Taoist monastery
GUWAN DZ   pot, jar
GUWAN IN PUSA   the bodhisattva

Avalokiteśvara
GUWANDZ   a short nine-holed bamboo
flute
GUWANG MUCEN   a type of iron cooking
pot made in Kwangtung
GUWANGGA ILHA   poet's jessamine (*Jas-
minum grandiflorum*)
GUWANGGUN   undependable person, villain,
rascal
GUWANGGUSA   plural of *guwanggun*
GUWANGGUŠAMBI   to behave like a rascal,
to act villainously
GUWANGLAMBI   to stroll, to walk about
GUWANGSE   1. leg-irons, manacles   2. a
crossbar of a fence with holes pro-
vided for the vertical poles
GUWANGSE SANGSE ETUBUMBI   to put on
leg-irons and handcuffs
GUWANGSI   banquet attendant
GUWANGSI TEBUMBI   to station a ban-
quet attendant
GUWANGŠA   fine silk from Canton
GUWANNI   lazy, indolent, prone to shun
work
GUWASE   long thin cakes
GUWATALAMBI   to divide into equal por-
tions
GUWEBUHEN   amnesty, pardon
GUWEBUMBI   to remit, to pardon, to
grant amnesty, to spare
GUWEBURE HESE   a writ of amnesty
GUWECEHE   pale
GUWECIHERI   bluish gray
GUWEI DZ ŠEO   executioner
GUWEJIHE   stomach
GUWEJIHE DA   the opening of the
stomach, appetite
GUWEKE   careful, attentive
GUWELE GALA   on the lookout, furtive,
stealthy
GUWELECEMBI   to act furtively, to peek,
to spy on
GUWELEKU   concubine
GUWELEMBI   to act stealthily
GUWELKE   1. careful, attentive to de-
tail   2. (interjection) pay heed to
GUWEMBI (1)   1. to forgive, to pardon
2. to avoid, to escape
GUWEMBI (2)   (-ngke, -ndere)   to chirp,
to tweet, to quack, to clang, to
make a noise (like a drum), to sound
GUWENDERE ŠE I KIRU (鳴鳶旗)
a banner of the imperial escort
with a kite depicted on it
GUWEMBUMBI   caus. of *guwembi* (2)
GUWENCI   chirping, tweeting, quacking,
cackling
GUWENDEHEN   one name for the myna
GUWENDEMBI   1. to chirp, to tweet, to
quack, to cackle   2. to make a con-
tinual clanging or drumming sound
GUWENDEN CECIKE   a type of small red
bird with yellow feet

GUWENDENGGE ITU one name for the
partridge; cf. *itu*

GUWENDERHEN the lesser skylark (*Alauda
arvensis*)

GUWEŠEMBI 1. to lead astray 2. to
bruise

GUYE 1. the heel of the foot 2. a
piece of iron at the end of a sword's
handle

GUYE SELE an ornamental iron cor-
nerpiece on bow cases and quivers

GUYOO green jasper

GŪBADAMBI to struggle, to squirm, to
resist (when tied up or penned in)

GŪBCIBUMBI caus. of *gūbcimbi*

GŪBCIMBI to put a load on an animal's
back

GŪBIMBI to tie down objects with a
rope

GŪBIRI old-world arrowhead (*Sagittaria
sagittifolia*)

GŪCA female goat, nanny

GŪCIHIYALAMBI to be startled, to flinch

GŪCIHIYAŠAMBI to be astounded

GŪCILA a partially burnt tree

GŪDU GADA prattling, chattering,
chatting

GŪDUMBI to spawn

GŪI GŪI 1. (onom.) a sound made by
hunters chasing game 2. a sound used
to call the saker falcon

GŪJE a sound used to call a falcon

GŪJU see *gūsu*

GŪLA BEYE oneself, one's own person

GŪLABUMBI caus. of *gūlambi*

GŪLAKŪ precipice, deep canyon

GŪLAMBI 1. to back up, to come back
into the pipe (of smoke) 2. to
roll down, to precipitate

GŪLAME TUHENJIHE rolled down from
a high place

GŪLDARAKŪLAMBI to get colic

GŪLDARGAN eastern house swallow
(*Hirundo rustica*)

GŪLDARHAN see *gūldargan*

GŪLDUN arch, tunnel

GŪLDURAKŪ YOO a sunken boil from which
great quantities of blood and pus
flow forth

GŪLDURAMBI 1. to pass through, to penetrate 2. to sink inward (of a boil)
3. to arch 4. to dig a tunnel, to
undermine

GŪLDURAME EYEMBI to flow under-
ground, to flow through a tunnel

GŪLDURI a passage for water at the
foot of a dike, a drain, a discharge
duct

GŪLDUSI spy, agent

GŪLGA see *gūlha*

GŪLGANAMBI to grow upward (a defect in
an animal's hoof)

GŪLGI see *gūrgi*

GŪLGIRAKŪ unrelenting, refusing to
forget

GŪLHA boot

GŪLHA FOYO *ula* grass

GŪLHA ŠUSEN a leather strap attached across the heel of a boot

GŪLHI WEHE CINUHŪN the best quality
cinnabar

GŪLI GALI (onom.) the call of the
oriole

GŪLI GALI SEMBI to cry like an
oriole

GŪLIBUMBI caus. of *gūlimbi*

GŪLIMBI (-ka) to be on good terms

GŪLIN CECIKE oriole (*Oriolus chinensis*)

GŪLINDUMBI to be on mutually good
terms

GŪLJAMBI to refloat a grounded boat
downstream by pulling from behind
with a tow rope

GŪLJARGAN see *gūljarhan*

GŪLJARHAN the grip of a whip or other
similar article that has been wrapped with cord or thongs

GŪLMAHŪN 1. rabbit, hare 2. the
fourth of the earth's branches (卯)

GŪLMAHŪN BIYA the second month

GŪLMAHŪN I ASU a net for catching
rabbits

GŪLMAHŪNGGA ANIYA the year of the
rabbit

GŪLTURAKŪLAMBI see *gūldarakūlambi*

GŪLU GALA (onom.) the sound of
whispering

GŪMBI 1. to growl 2. to cut out
(meat)

GŪN HALAMBI to molt, to shed the skin
(of snakes)

GŪNA three-year-old cow

GŪNAN see *gūna*

GŪNG GANG (onom.) the sound made by
a wild goose

GŪNGGALA COKO the hoki pheasant
(*Crossoptilon mantchuricum*)

GŪNGGARI NIONGNIYAHA a type of wild
goose found in the Koko Nor region

GŪNGKALI a recessed area at the foot
of a riverbank

GŪNGKAMBI to be hot and humid, to be
sultry

GŪNGKAN Adam's apple

GŪNGKANAMBI to have a protruding
Adam's apple

GŪNIBUMBI caus./pass. of *gūnimbi*

GŪNICUN mindful, remembering

GŪNIGAN thought, opinion, feeling

GŪNIGANGGA thoughtful

GŪNIHAKŪ unexpectedly

GŪNIJAN reflection, meditation

GŪNIMBI to think, to reflect, to consider, to intend

GŪNIN 1. intention, thought, opinion,
feeling, sense 2. mind, spirit

G

G

3. token (of one's feelings or intention)

GŪNIN ACABUMBI to set forth one's views

GŪNIN ACAMBI to have similar views

GŪNIN AKŪ unintentional

GŪNIN AKŪMBUMBI to do one's very best, to exhaust all effort

GŪNIN BAHAMBI to be pleased, to get an idea

GŪNIN BAIBUMBI to have one's plans upset, to be upset

GŪNIN BAIMBI to ask for an opinion

GŪNIN BE UJIMBI to cultivate one's thoughts or intentions (especially towards one's parents)

GŪNIN CINGGIYA indecisive, vacillating

GŪNIN DE ACAMBI to correspond to one's views

GŪNIN DE TEBUMBI to be concerned about, to keep in mind, to pay attention to

GŪNIN DE TEBURAKŪ unconcerned, unperturbed about something

GŪNIN DEN proud, haughty

GŪNIN EFULEMBI to be deeply hurt, to be very sad

GŪNIN ELEHUN content, satisfied

GŪNIN FALABUMBI to have confused thoughts, to be confused

GŪNIN FAYAMBI to go to a lot of trouble

GŪNIN HIRI OHO became disappointed

GŪNIN I CIHAI as one likes, in accordance with one's wishes

GŪNIN I SALIGAN arbitrary action

GŪNIN ISIBUMBI to announce one's intentions

GŪNIN ISIKA one's intention is realized, satisfied

GŪNIN ISINAHA BA hope, wish, intention

GŪNIN ISINAMBI to hope for

GŪNIN JAFAMBI to have a firm intention

GŪNIN SAHA GUCU a bosom friend

GŪNIN SINDAMBI the mind is at ease, to be calm, not to worry

GŪNIN TARHŪN overbearing, domineering

GŪNIN UNENGGI sincere

GŪNIN USAMBI to be disappointed

GŪNIN WALIYABUMBI to be confused, to be bewildered

GŪNIN WEREŠEMBI to pay attention, to be careful

GŪNINAMBI to have a thought come to mind, to recall

GŪNINGGA full of ideas, reflective

GŪNINJAMBI to consider, to think over carefully, to reflect upon

GŪR GAR (onom.) the sound made by a flock of flying birds

GŪR GŪR SEME sound of flying birds

GŪRAKŪŠAMBI to peer, to leer

GŪRAN 1. cord for tying a bundle 2. a male roe deer, roebuck; cf. *gio*

GŪRBAMBI to shun, to shy

GŪRBI cattail, reed

GŪRGI a clasp

GŪRGI FOYO a type of swamp-growing reed that is somewhat taller than *ula* grass

GŪRGILABUMBI caus./pass. of *gūrgilambi*

GŪRGILAMBI 1. to flame, to burn 2. to clasp, to buckle

GŪRGIMBI see *gūrgilambi*

GŪRGIN flame

GŪRGIN DALIKŪ the lid of a stove or heater

GŪRGIN MUDURI DARDAN satin with a pattern of flames and dragons

GŪSA banner

GŪSA BE KADALARA AMBAN (都統) Lieutenant-General (of a banner), BH 719

GŪSA I EJEN (都統) Lieutenant-General (of a banner), BH 719

GŪSAI BAITAI KUNGGERI (都統科) office of banner affairs in the Board of War

GŪSAI BEISE (固山貝子) Prince of the blood of the fourth degree, BH 19

GŪSAI DA (協領) Colonel of a Regiment of the Provincial Manchu Garrisons, BH 746

GŪSAI EFU (縂統儀賓) husband of a Princess of the eighth rank

GŪSAI FUJIN the wife of a *beise*

GŪSAI GEGE the daughter of a *beise*

GŪSAI YAMUN (都統衙門) headquarters of a banner

GŪSICI thirtieth

GŪSIHIYA border, boundary

GŪSIN thirty

GŪSINGGERI thirty times

GŪSITA thirty each

GŪSU thick, heavy rope

GŪSULAMBI to tie up with heavy rope

GŪTUBUMBI 1. to be contaminated, to be spoiled 2. to shame, to spoil

GŪTUCUN shame, insult, shameful

GŪWA other, another

GŪWABSI to another place, elsewhere

GŪWACIHIYA with a start, with a wince

GŪWACIHIYA GŪWACIHIYA AŠŠAMBI to wake up with a start

GŪWACIHIYA TATA with a start

GŪWACIHIYALAMBI to be startled, to startle

GŪWACIHIYAŠAMBI to feel jittery, to feel unsettled, to have the flesh creep

GŪWAHIYAN 1. a hole for cooking used by soldiers in the field 2. a tripod used for supporting a cooking pot over a hole 3. a constellation in Lyra
  GŪWAHIYAN ARAME ILIHABI have set up camp
GŪWAIDABUMBI caus. of *gūwaidambi*
GŪWAIDAMBI to lean on, to lean to one side
GŪWAIDANAMBI to walk swaying from side to side, to stagger
GŪWAIMARAMBI see *goimarambi*
GŪWAIMBI see *goimbi*
GŪWAINGGE someone else's
GŪWAISUNTUMBI to pretend not to notice, to slight a person
GŪWALIYABUMBI caus. of *gūwaliyambi*
GŪWALIYAMBI (-ka, -ndara) 1. to change (v.i.) 2. to spoil (of food) 3. to fade (of colors)
GŪWALIYAMBUMBI see *gūwaliyabumbi*
GŪWALIYANDARAKŪ unchangeable, constant
GŪWALIYAŠAKŪ changeable
GŪWALIYAŠAMBI to have frequent internal disorders
GŪWAMBI to bark
GŪWAMBUMBI caus. of *gūwambi*
GŪWANCIHIYAN unappetizing
GŪWANG GŪWANG (onom.) the sound of barking
GŪWANUMBI to bark (of a group of dogs)
GŪWAR GŪWAR (onom.) the cry of ducks, frogs, or doves
GŪWAR SEMBI to quack, to croak
GŪWARIMBI to croak (of frogs)
GŪWAŠIHIYA eastern egret (*Egretta alba*)
GŪWAŠABUMBI to be blamed or rejected (by spirits and demons)
GŪWAŠAMBI (-ka) to spoil (of sour things)

GŪWAŠŠABUMBI caus. of *gūwaššambi*
GŪWAŠŠAMBI 1. to cut meat into strips 2. to throb
GŪWAŠŠAN thin strips of meat
GŪYAMBI 1. to brush against trees during the mating season (of deer) 2. to roar (of dragons)
GŪYANDUMBI to mate, to jump about (of mating deer)
G'ABIŠARA one name for the pheasant
G'ACI one tenth to the seventeenth power
G'ALAB 1. Kalpa, world period 2. disaster, ruin
G'AMULIYANG chameleon
G'AN steel
  G'AN I SIREN steel wire
G'ANG see *g'an*
G'ANGG'A the Ganges
G'ANJE sugar cane
G'ANGSE a carrying-pole carried by two men
G'ANJUR NOMUN the Kanjur
G'ANSE tangerine
G'AODZ salve, ointment
G'AOMING document of posthumous enfeoffment for officials above the fifth rank
G'AOSY proclamation, announcement
  G'AOSY BITHE proclamation, announcement
G'AOŠI BITHE see *g'aosy bithe*
G'AOYOO salve, ointment
G'ASIB Kāśyapa Buddha
G'O one tenth of a *sheng*
G'ODARG'A chicken (a word of Sanskrit origin)
G'OGIN widower
G'ONA ILHA an exotic light red flower
G'ONGG'ON a *gacuha* that is standing upright

G
G G'

H

HA 1. a small net for catching pheasants 2. (onom.) a sound made by breathing on frozen objects 3. (onom.) a sound made when eating something hot or salty 4. (onom.) the cry of a bird of prey when it sees a man

HABCIHIYADAMBI to treat affectionately or warmly, to show sympathy to

HABCIHIYAN affection, warmth, sympathy

HABGIYAMBI to yawn

HABŠABUMBI caus./pass. of *habšambi*

HABŠABUHA NIYALMA the accused, defendant

HABŠAMBI 1. to accuse, to bring to court 2. to report to, to be responsible to

HABŠAHA NIYALMA accuser, plaintiff

HABŠARA BAITA grievance

HABŠARA BITHE letter of accusation

HABŠAN accusation, complaint

HABŠANAMBI to go to accuse, to go to report

HABŠANDUMBI/HABŠANUMBI to accuse together, to accuse one another

HABŠANJIMBI to come to accuse, to come to report

HABTA the wing of a saddle

HABTA HABTALAMBI to soar, to glide (of large birds)

HABTAHA a wide girdle used to protect a man's midsection in battle

HABTALAMBI to squint, to wink, to blink

HABTAŠAMBI 1. to wink or blink repeatedly 2. to soar, to glide

HACA handful, skein

HACIHIYABUMBI caus. of *hacihiyambi*

HACIHIYAMBI 1. to urge, to press, to force 2. to rush, to hurry 3. to entreat to eat or drink

HACIHIYAN compulsion, urging, pressing

HACIHIYANAMBI to go to urge, to go to force

HACIHIYANDUMBI/HACIHIYANUMBI to press or urge together

HACIHIYANJIMBI to come to urge, to come to force

HACIKA see *hacuka*

HACILAMBI 1. to separate according to types, to classify 2. to itemize, to recount point by point

HACILAHA DARDAN silk with many kinds of flowers woven in it

HACILAME point by point, item by item, every kind

HACILAME WESIMBURE KUNGGERI (達言科) office concerned with preparing itemized reports for the emperor

HACIN 1. kind, sort, class, item 2. article, paragraph 3. condition, intention 4. the fifteenth day of the first month (the lantern festival)

HACIN GEREN people with unorthodox views

HACIN HACIN I all kinds of, various kinds of

HACIN I UCURI the lantern festival

HACIN I YAMJI the evening of the lantern festival

HACIN INENGGI 1. the fifteenth day of the first month 2. various auspicious days such as the fifteenth of the first month and the second day of the second month

HACIN MEYEN I DANGSE land record books

HACIN TOME each kind, every item, item by item, altogether

HACINGGA all kinds of

HACUHAN 1. a small cooking pot 2. see *huwešere hacuhan*

HACUHIYAN a large three-legged vessel of ancient times, a tripod

HACUKA dirty, disgraceful, shameful

HACUKADAMBI to commit dirty acts, to commit lewd acts

HACUMBI (-ka) to become dirty, to become defiled

HADA crag, a small cliff
  HADA CIBIN rock-martin (*Ptyono-progne rupestris*)
  HADA WEHE gravel, broken stones

HADABUMBI caus. of *hadambi*

HADAFUN see *hadufun*

HADAGAN see *hadahan*

HADAHA see *hadahan*
  HADAHA USIHA the North Star

HADAHAN a nail or peg of iron, bamboo, or wood
  HADAHAN NISIHA a small fish shaped like a tent peg

HADAI plug, wedge, tap

HADALA horse's bridle
  HADALA MULTULEMBI to remove a horse's bridle
  HADALA ŠABAN cleats--four iron teeth placed on a round frame and attached to the soles of shoes to prevent slipping on a slippery or steep surface
  HADALA YOO a sore on a horse's mouth caused by a bridle

HADAMA BURGA a type of willow that grows alone--it has white bark and its wood is good for making arrows

HADAMBI 1. to nail, to tack 2. to sting (of insects) 3. to sole (shoes or boots) 4. to fix the eyes on
  HADAHAI fixedly (of looking)
  HADAHAI FEKSIMBI to run with an arrow stuck in the body

HADANAMBI to fix the eyes on, to stare

HADARA grayling--a small fish that lives in clear cold water (*Salmo thymallus*)

HADUBUMBI caus. of *hadumbi*

HADUFUN scythe, sickle

HADUHŪN salty

HADUMBI to cut with a sickle, to reap

HADUNAMBI to go to cut with a sickle, to go to reap

HADUNJIMBI to come to cut with a sickle, to come to reap

HADUNUMBI to reap together

HAFA shallow
  HAFA ŠORO a shallow basket

HAFAN official, officer
  HAFAN BAHAMBI to obtain an official position
  HAFAN EFULEMBI to be dismissed from office
  HAFAN HALI an official
  HAFAN HERGEN official rank
  HAFAN I BOO (吏房) office of personnel of the Court of Colonial Affairs
  HAFAN I JURGAN (吏部) Board of Civil Appointments, BH 333
  HAFAN I JURGAN I KUNGGE YAMUN

(吏科) section of Personnel of the Censorate

HAFAN I TANGKAN an official grade or rank

HAFAN I TEMGETU I KUNGGERI (遇科) an office of the Board of Civil Appointments charged with issuing orders to local officials who were appointed monthly and with checking on the terms of those previously appointed

HAFAN JERGI rank and title

HAFAN SINDAMBI to appoint an official

HAFAN SINDARA BOLGOBURE FIYENTEN (録勳清吏司) Department of Inner Mongols, later *jasak dangsei bolgobure fiyenten*

HAFASA plural of *hafan*

HAFASI scholar, official
  HAFASI ŠUFATU a head wrapping worn by *hafasi*

HAFIN clamp, vise
  HAFIN MOO the two pieces of wood that hold a ship's mast in place

HAFIRABUMBI 1. caus./pass. of *hafirambi* 2. to be embarrassed, to find oneself in difficult circumstances

HAFIRAHŪN pressed, pinched, forced between two objects, narrow

HAFIRAKŪ pincers, pliers
  HAFIRAKŪ SIBIYA metal fasteners that secure an axle to a cart
  HAFIRAKŪ SIMHUN a sixth finger

HAFIRAMBI 1. to pinch, to press or hold between two objects 2. to hold under the arm 3. to press a seam together 4. to put pressure on, to compel 5. to put in a difficult situation 6. to threaten
  HAFIRAHA AFAHA a memorandum pressed between the leaves of a document

HAFIRAN seam on a boot

HAFIRHŪN see *hafirahūn*

HAFIRŠAMBUMBI caus. of *hafiršambi*

HAFIRŠAMBI to use economically

HAFIRŠANUMBI to use economically (of a group)

HAFIŠAMBI to pat affectionately, to flatter

HAFIŠANGGA obsequious, flattering

HAFITAMBI 1. to press or hold on both sides of an object, to pinch 2. to inlay
  HAFITAME AFAMBI to attack from two sides, to mount a pincer attack
  HAFITAME GEYEMBI to engrave on two sides
  HAFITARA FULHUN one of the six minor scale pipes

HAFU 1. penetrating, going through 2. thorough, comprehensive 3. enlightened, possessing understanding

HAFU HAFU penetrating, thorough, throughout, total, comprehensive

HAFU HIYOOŠUNGGA thoroughly filial

HAFUKIYAMBI to inform in detail, to give a thorough rundown on

HAFULAMBI 1. to penetrate, to go through 2. to forbid

HAFUMBI (-ka, -re/ndara) 1. to penetrate, to go through, to soak through, to pierce 2. to understand thoroughly, to comprehend 3. to communicate, to have relations with

HAFUNDARAKŪ impenetrable

HAFUMBUBUMBI caus. of *hafumbumbi*

HAFUMBUKŪ interpreter, translator

HAFUMBUKŪ HAFAN an official translator

HAFUMBUKŪ KAMCIHABI accompanied by a translator

HAFUMBUMBI 1. caus. of *hafumbi* 2. to translate, to interpret 3. to inform in detail, to give a thorough account of

HAFUN transparent, permeable

HAFUN CECE smooth transparent silk gauze

HAFUNAMBI to connect with another place, to form a free passage to another place

HAFUNGGA thorough, constant

HAFUNGGA BOO in a house, a central room that connects with both front and back rooms

HAFUNGGA MAHATUN a hat with openings on both sides

HAFUNGGA OMOLO a descendant of the sixth generation

HAFUNGGA TALU a thoroughfare

HAFUNJIBUMBI caus. of *hafunjimbi*

HAFUNJIMBI to come through (in this direction), to come straight through

HAGA fish bone

HAGABUKŪ a four-inch wooden hook with an iron tip used to catch black carp

HAGAMBI 1. to get something caught in the throat 2. to form a hard abscess in the breast

HAHA male, man

HAHA I DEJI a superior man, champion

HAHA JUI boy

HAHABUKŪ the same as *hagabukū*

HAHAMA ANCUN an earring with a single pearl

HAHANGGE male, masculine

HAHARAMBI to act like a man, to act in a manly way

HAHARDAMBI to become a man

HAHASI plural of *haha*

HAHI urgent, hurried

HAHI CAHI hurried, agitated, urgent

HAHIBA quick, nimble

HAHIKAN rather urgent

HAHILAMBI to act quickly or urgently, to hurry

HAHŪBUMBI caus. of *hahūmbi*

HAHŪMBI to grow (of feathers on a bird)

HAHŪRABUMBI caus. of *hahūrambi*

HAHŪRAKŪ choker used for restraining a dog

HAHŪRAMBI 1. to grab by the throat, to choke 2. to occupy a militarily strategic point

HAHŪRŠAMBI 1. to hold by the throat continually, to throttle 2. to accuse obstinately

HAICING the peregrine falcon; cf. *šongkon*

HAIDAN a large hook on which frogs and small fish were used as bait

HAIDAN SISIMBI to fish with a *haidan*

HAIDARABUMBI caus. of *haidarambi*

HAIDARAMBI to lean, to lean to one side, to droop, to hang the head

HAIDARŠAMBI to lean to one side while walking

HAIDU lopsided, leaning to one side

HAIFIRAMBI see *hafirambi*

HAIFIRŠAMBI see *hafiršambi*

HAIGARI see *haihàri*

HAIGŪ see *haihū*

HAIHA 1. mountain slope 2. spool for yarn or thread

HAIHABUMBI caus. of *haihambi*

HAIHAMBI to tumble over, to fall to one side

HAIHAN 1. welt of a shoe or boot 2. bone, feathers, hemp stalks, and hair fed to falcons to clean out their stomachs

HAIHARAMBI to lean to one side, to topple, to incline

HAIHARAME along the slope of a hill

HAIHARI see *heiheri haihari*

HAIHARILAMBI to reel from side to side

HAIHARŠAMBI to stagger, to reel, to sway

HAIHAŠHŪN inclined, leaning, awry

HAIHŪ 1. soft 2. staggering, weaving from side to side

HAIHŪLJAMBI to flutter (in the wind)

HAIHŪN one name for the otter; cf. *hailun*

HAIHŪNA Mongolian lark (*Melanocorypha mongolica*)

HAIHŪNGGA soft, supple

HAIHŪNGGA ŠUFA a new-style handkerchief

HAIHŪWA bream

HAIJAN a mode of Manchu singing during which the singer imitates the movements of a snake

HAIJUNG SEME reeling under a heavy load

HAILAMBI to scorn an offering

HAILAMI   see *hailambi*
HAILAN 1. elm tree 2. vexation, scorn
   HAILAN GAIBUMBI to be vexed, to be
     distressed
   HAILAN GAIMBI to vex, to distress
   HAILAN SENCE a type of yellow
     fungus that grows on elms
HAILASHŪN precipitous, steep
HAILUN otter (*Lutra lutra*)
   HAILUN CECIKE turquoise kingfisher
     (*Halcyon smyrnensis*)
HAIRACUKA 1. pitiable, pitiful 2. too
   bad, what a shame!
HAIRACUN regrettable, pitiable
HAIRAKAN 1. regrettable 2. what a
   shame!
HAIRAMBI (-ka, -ndara) 1. to regret,
   to begrudge, to be unwilling to part
   with 2. to love tenderly
HAIRAN regret, begrudging, compassion,
   tenderness
   HAIRAN JAKA an object that one is
     loath to part with
   HAIRAN NIYALMA a person that one is
     very fond of
HAIRANDAMBI to begrudge
HAISANDA wild garlic
HAITA a large wild pig
HAITANG crab apple
HAJAN wooden palisade surrounding a
   fortress
HAJI 1. dear, beloved 2. affection
   3. scarce, lean (year), famine
   HAJI ANIYA a famine year, a lean
     year
   HAJI GUCU a dear friend
   HAJI HAIRAN tender love
HAJILAMBI 1. to love, to fall in love
   2. to fish with a net stretched
   across a stream
HAJILAN love
HAJIN affection
HAJINGGA BAIBULA one of the names of
   the paradise flycatcher; cf. *baibula*
HAJUN 1. weapon, tool 2. a sicklelike
   knife used in tiger traps
HAK (onom.) the sound of clearing
   one's throat
HAKCIN quick-tempered, rash, brusque
HAKDA old grass left over from the previous year, a spot of grass remaining in an area that has been burnt
   over
HAKSABUMBI 1. caus./pass. of *haksambi*
   2. to scorch, to become scorched
HAKSAMBI (-ka) 1. to become scorched,
   to get dark from contact with sunlight or fire 2. to turn red in the
   rising or setting sun (clouds) 3.
   to have a burning sensation in the
   stomach
   HAKSAHA TUGI reddish clouds
HAKSAN 1. steep, precipitous 2. cruel,

brutal 3. golden, reddish brown
HAKSAN BOCOI JUNGGIDEI KIYOO a
   yellow sedan chair carried by
   eight men that was used by concubines of the second rank
HAKSAN BOCOI SUJE DE AISIN DAMBUHA
   GARUDANGGA KIRU a banner used by
   the escort of concubines of the
   second class--it had a phoenix
   embroidered upon a yellow back-
   ground
   HAKSAN HAKCIN precipitous, high and
     steep
   HAKSAN UMIYESUN a yellow sash worn
     by members of the imperial clan
HAKSANGGA EFEN a type of baked wheat
   cake
HAKŠABUMBI caus. of *hakšambi*
HAKŠAMBI 1. to fry in fat 2. to
   render fat or oil 3. to become
   scorched
HAKŠAN scorched
HALA clan, family, family name
   HALA HACIN all sorts of
   HALA UMIYAHA a small red insect
     found in wells
HALABUMBI caus./pass. of *halambi*
HALAHAI nettle
HALAI FUDASI in confusion
HALAMBI 1. to exchange, to change
   (clothing), to take the place of
   2. to burn (of a hot object)
   HALAME JURUME ETUMBI to change
     clothes a number of times
HALAN 1. menstruation 2. exchanging
HALANAMBI to go to exchange, to go
   closer to
HALANDUMBI/HALANUMBI to exchange to-
   gether
HALANGGA belonging to the same clan or
   family
HALANJAMBI to exchange in turn, to
   take turns
HALANJIMBI to come to exchange
HALAR (onom.) the sound made by jade
   pendants hitting together, tinkling
HALAR HILIR (onom.) the sound of bells
   on the girdle, the sound made by a
   shaman's sword
HALAŠAKŪ a pampered child
HALAŠAMBI 1. to act spoiled, to act up,
   to pout 2. to wiggle and squirm
   about, to act unsettled before the
   onset of a fever or smallpox
HALBA the shoulder blade
HALBAHA 1. a small knob on a helmet,
   the decoration on the top of a
   banner pole, a finial 2. the wide
   part of an arrowhead 3. a spoon
   HALBAHA MOO a three-holed wooden
     plank two feet long used in cere-
     monies in the shamanistic shrine
HALBAHAN spoon-bill pelican

H

H

HALBIŠAMBI to curry favor, to fawn
HALBUBUMBI caus. of *halbumbi*
HALBULHA one who gives shelter to ban-
  dits and thieves
HALBUMBI to give entrance to, to take
  into one's home, to give shelter to
HALDA sturgeon's spleen--used as a
  medicine for boils
    HALDA YOO a boil between the
      shoulder blades
HALDABA flatterer, an obsequious per-
  son, sycophant
HALDABAŠAMBI to be obsequious
HALDARAMBI to slip and fall
HALFIRI a flat hollow fruit about the
  size of a tangerine
HALFIYAKAN somewhat flat
HALFIYAN flat, thin
    HALFIYAN NIMAHA flatfish, flounder
    HALFIYAN TURI flat bean (*Dolichos
      lablab*)
HALFIYANGGA flat in form
    HALFIYANGGA JAHŪDAI a type of flat-
      boat used on the Yangtze
    HALFIYANGGA TUNGKEN a flat drum
      used in religious services
HALGIBUMBI caus. of *halgimbi*
HALGIMBI to wrap around, to wind, to
  entwine
HALHAN plowshare
HALHIMBI see *halgimbi*
HALHŪKAN rather hot
HALHŪN hot
    HALHŪN BEDEREMBI one of the divi-
      sions of the solar year--falling
      on the 23rd or 24th of August
    HALHŪN ŠAHŪRUN BULUKAN NECIN hot,
      cold, warm, even--used to describe
      the nature of medicines
    HALHŪN ŠERI a hot spring
HALHŪRI pepper
HALI 1. untillable marshland, swamp,
  untilled land, virgin land 2. of-
  ficial
    HALI ULHŪ marsh grass
HALMAN face soap
HALMARI a sword used by shamans
HALMUN an iron ring placed in the hub
  of a wheel into which an axle is
  inserted, a bushing
HALTAN YOO see *halda yoo*
HALU fine flour or meal
HALUKAN warm
    HALUKAN EDUN a warm wind
HALUKŪ thick cotton trousers
HALUNGGA GŪLHA fur-lined boots
HAMGIYA 1. skullcap 2. plants re-
  sembling sagebrush or mugwort
    HAMGIYA SUIHA dry brush, overgrowth
HAMGIYARI one of the names for the
  wild pig
HAMIBUMBI caus. of *hamimbi*
HAMIMBI (-ka) 1. to approach, to be

close to, to almost reach 2. to
  suffice 3. to be within reach 4.
  to bear, to tolerate
HAMIKA almost, within reach
HAMIME about to, on the point of
HAMIRAKŪ 1. unbearable 2. insuf-
  ficient 3. unattainable 4. un-
  successful
HAMINAMBI to go near to, to approach
HAMINJIMBI to come near to, to approach
HAMIŠAMBI to go right up to, to ap-
  proach closely
HAMTAKŪ a child who defecates where
  he ought not
HAMTAMBI to defecate
HAMTANAMBI to go to defecate
HAMTU felt hat
HAMU excrement
HAMUTAMBI see *hamtambi*
HAN emperor, khan
    HAN I UKSUN I EJEHE the genealogy
      of the imperial clan
    HAN I UKSUN I EJEHE KUREN (玉牒
      館) bureau for the compilation
      of the genealogical record of the
      imperial clan
    HAN USIHA the second star of the
      Great Dipper
HAN DUNG reservoir, tank
HANA a section of lattice wall of a
  yurt
HANCI near
    HANCI FIMEMBI to approach, to come
      near to
HANCIKAN rather near
HANCIKI near, near place, vicinity
HANCIKINGGE that which is near, one
  who is nearby
HANCUHA MUCEN a three-legged cooking
  pot, tripod
HANDA a pock mark, a scar
HANDU 1. the rice plant 2. leaven for
  making soy sauce
    HANDU BELE late maturing rice
    HANDU BOIHON mud in a rice paddy
    HANDU CISE a rice paddy
    HANDU IRI the same as *handu cise*
    HANDU ORHO rice stalks, rice straw
    HANDU TARIRE KŪWARAN (稻田廠)
      Imperial Agricultural Office, BH
      90A
    HANDU UMIYAHA the rice worm
HANDUCUN a song of the rice harvest
HANDUMBI to plant in a paddy field
HANDUTUN a round vessel for holding
  grain offerings at sacrifices
HANGGABUMBI 1. caus. of *hanggambi*
  2. to impede, to hinder, to obstruct,
  to occlude 3. to spoil
HANGGAI packsaddle
    HANGGAI ENGGEMU the same as *hanggai*
    HANGGAI NIRU an unpolished, rusty
      arrowhead

HANGGAMBI to moisten by sprinkling
HANGGI see *hangki*
HANGGIR HINGGIR (onom.) the tinkle of
  bracelets and anklets
HANGGIR SEME tinkling, jingling
HANGGISUN a long silk cloth fringed at
  both ends
HANGKI China-berry tree (*Melia japon-
  ica*)
HANGNABUMBI caus. of *hangnambi*
HANGNAMBI to solder, to weld, to re-
  pair metal pots
  HANGNARA FAKSI a repairer of pots
  HANGNARA OKTO solder
HANGNAN solder
HANGNASI borax
HANGSE noodles
HANGSI 1. a type of very thin silk
  2. the spring festival falling on
  the 5th or 6th of April
HANI MAJIGE see *hani tani*
HANI TANI tiny, little; cf. *heni tani*
HANJA incorrupt, honest, clean, pure
  HANJA BOLGO incorrupt and clean
  HANJA GIRUTU incorrupt and possess-
  ing a sense of shame
HANJADAMBI to act honestly, to act
  incorruptly
HANJAMBI to be covetous, to be greedy
HAO one ten-thousandth of a Chinese
  foot
HAR SEME pungent, having a sharp odor
HARA 1. the short autumn coat of
  sable or lynx 2. *Setaria viridis*--
  a common weed, foxtail 3. black (of
  horses)
HARAMBI to watch, to observe
HARAN reason, cause
HARANAMBI to produce foxtails, to
  produce weeds
HARANGGA 1. subordinate, subject,
  belonging to, vassal to . . . (the
  one) in question, the said . . . ,
  the appropriate . . .
  HARANGGA AIMAN BE ALIHA BOLGOBURE
  FIYENTEN (典屬清吏司   )
  Department of the Outer Mongols,
  BH 495
  HARANGGA BA a dependent or sub-
  ordinate area
  HARANGGA HAFAN subordinate (of-
  ficial)
HARATU subordinate, underling, subject
HARDAKŪ carp
HARDAME see *herdeme hardame*
HARGA see *harha*
HARGASI see *harkasi*
HARGAŠABUMBI caus. of *hargašambi*
HARGAŠAMBI 1. to look up, to look up
  to, to look into the distance from
  a high place 2. to go to court, to
  have an audience at court
  HARGAŠAME GOIDAHA I have longed to

meet you
  HARGAŠAME TUWAMBI to look up, to
  look into the distance
  HARGAŠARA DOROLONGGO KUNGGERI (朝
  儀科) a bureau charged with
  checking the credentials of those
  granted imperial audiences
HARGAŠAN the court
  HARGAŠAN DE HENGKILENJIRE BOLGOBURE
  FIYENTEN (王會清吏司   )
  Department for Receiving Princes
  of Inner Mongolia, BH 495
HARGAŠANAMBI to go to court
HARGAŠANDUMBI/HARGAŠANUMBI to look up
  together
HARGAŠANJIMBI to come to court
  HARGAŠANJIRE ACANJIRE KUNGGERI (朝
  參科) a bureau of the Imperial
  Patent Office that was concerned
  with imperial audiences
HARGI 1. a place where water flows
  very swiftly, rapids 2. mustard
  HARGI SOGI mustard (the plant)
  HARGI ŠURDEKU whirlpool, eddy
HARHA the leather between the sole and
  the leg of a boot
HARHŪ mire, mud
  HARHŪ BOIHON the mud at the bottom
  of a body of water, slime, mire
  HARHŪ UMIYAHA *Cicindela chinensis*--
  a small worm with black and yellow
  spots that is used to cure the
  bite of a mad dog
HARHŪDAMBI to stir up the mud on the
  bottom of a river or lake in order
  to stifle fish
HARI 1. crooked, bent, curved, awry,
  inclining 2. cross-eyed 3. a net
  bag for holding deer's innards
HARIBUMBI caus./pass. of *harimbi*
HARIKŪ an iron (for pressing clothing),
  a cauterizing iron
HARIMA EFEN a type of baked cake
HARIMBI 1. to iron, to press (clothing)
  2. to cauterize sores on cattle 3.
  to conceal, to hide
  HARIHA EFEN baked cakes used as
  offerings
  HARIHA GESE NIMEMBI to hurt like hell
HARINGGA see *garingga*
HARKASI influenza
HARSA yellow-throated marten (*Martes
  flavigula*)
HARŠAKŪ protector, guardian
HARŠAMBI 1. to protect, to defend 2.
  to cover up for 3. to be partial to
HARŠANDUMBI/HARŠANUMBI to cover up for
  one another, to protect one another
HARTUNGGA 1. subordinates, subjects
  2. (標) Chinese banner troops in
  the provinces
HASAHA scissors, shears
  HASAHA UMIYAHA centipede

H

H

HASAHALAMBI to cut with scissors or
  shears
HASAHANGGA FUKJINGGA HERGEN (剪刀
  家) a style of calligraphy
HASALA a fast-running cow
HASALABUMBI caus. of *hasalambi*
HASALAKŪ shears for cutting metal
HASALAMBI to cut with scissors, to
  shear
HASAMBI to hurry, to be in a rush
HASAN mange, itch, scabies
HASANAMBI to get the mange or scabies
HASHALABUMBI caus. of *hashalambi*
HASHALAMBI to erect a fence or pali-
  sade, to mark off
HASHAN a fence of wood or kaoliang
  stalks, a palisade
  HASHAN UMIYAHA millipede
HASHŪ 1. left 2. erroneous, improper,
  depraved
  HASHŪ ERGI FIYENTEN (左司)
    first department (of a governmental
    organ)
  HASHŪ TONGGO TABUMBI to fasten the
    thread on the left side
HASHŪTAI heterodox, depraved
  HASHŪTAI DORO heterodoxy, black
    magic
HASI 1. persimmon 2. eggplant
  HASI FUNTA the white powder on the
    surface of dried persimmons
  HASI ŠATAN large dried persimmons
HASIBA 1. protection, care 2. speed
HASIHIMBI to go hurriedly, to scurry
HASIMA Manchurian crayfish
HASINGGA pertaining to the persimmon,
  persimmon-shaped
  HASINGGA TAMPIN a persimmon-shaped
    container
HASIRI the color of eggplant, dark
  purple
HASRUN SIRGA a white horse with red
  spots about the nose and eyes
HASTAI see *hashūtai*
HASU ORHO a type of climbing plant
  whose melonlike fruit can be salted
  and eaten
HASURALAMBI see *hasurgalambi*
HASURAN the bark of the peach tree
  HASURAN MOO the tree from which
    hasuran is taken
HASURGALAMBI to cover with the bark
  of the peach tree (arrows)
HASUTAI 1. left-handed, with the left
  hand 2. heterodox, depraved
  HASUTAI DORO the same as *hashūtai
    doro*
HAŠA a small storage house
  HAŠA BOO the same as *haša*
HAŠABUMBI caus. of *hašambi*
HAŠAHAN 1. a cloth covering (for
  vehicles) 2. a container for grain
  made of mats sewn together 3. the

felt covering for a section of a
  Mongolian yurt 4. a device for
  catching fish 5. tablecloth, table
  covering
HAŠAKŪ a scrubbing brush made from
  kaoliang stalks or the stalks of
  other grains
  HAŠAKŪ DENGJAN lanterns placed on
    the four corners of the yellow
    tent in temples and at altars on
    days of sacrifice
HAŠAMBI 1. to scrub 2. to surround,
  to encompass 3. to cover, to pro-
  tect
HAŠAN drapery, curtain, hangings
HAŠATAMBI to protect carefully
HATA a thin belt or strip of cloth
HATABUMBI caus./pass. of *hatambi*
HATABURU hateful--an expletive
HATACUKA hateful, detestable
HATAKAN rather strong, somewhat hard
HATAMBI 1. to loath, to find repug-
  nant, to hate 2. to immerse red-hot
  metals into water to harden them,
  to temper 3. to fire (ceramics or
  pottery)
  HATAME DEIJIMBI to temper (metals)
HATAN 1. hard, strong 2. strong (of
  liquor) 3. pungent, strong tast-
  ing 4. violent, fiery
HATARAMBI to fall ill suddenly, to
  have a sudden pain, to have a fit
  of temper
HATUHŪN salty
  HATUHŪN MUKE brackish water
  HATUHŪN USIHA a type of fruit from
    the South
HAYABUMBI caus. of *hayambi*
HAYADAMBI to act licentiously
HAYAHAN border, trim (on clothing)
  HAYAHAN DAHŪ a court garment
    trimmed with sable, lynx, or black
    fox
  HAYAHAN I ERGUME a fur-trimmed
    court dress
  HAYAHAN I ULHUN a sable-trimmed
    shoulder piece
  HAYAHAN UNDURAKŪ trimmed dragon
    satin
HAYAKTA a wild pig with upturned tusks
HAYALJAMBI to wind, to twist, to
  slither
HAYAMBI 1. to coil, to twist, to twine
  2. to hem, to trim, to edge
  HAYAHA HIYAN coiled incense
  HAYAHA MEIHE USIHA (螣蛇) the
    name of a Chinese constellation
    that has the appearance of a
    coiled snake
HAYAN licentious, loose, dissolute
HE stretcher, litter
HE FA SEME gasping, panting
HE GI the hoki pheasant; cf. *gūnggala*

coko

HEBDEBUMBI caus. of *hebdembi*

HEBDEMBI to discuss, to talk over, to consult

HEBDENEMBI to go to talk over

HEBDENJIMBI to come to talk over

HEBDEŠEMBI to talk over carefully or thoroughly

HEBE 1. consultation, deliberation, planning 2. plan, plot, intrigue

   HEBE ACAMBI to hold a consultation, to come together to deliberate

   HEBEI with forethought, deliberately

   HEBEI AMBAN (參贊大臣) Councillor, BH 867, 880

   HEBEI BA (議政處) an office in charge of receiving and handling memorials concerning affairs of state

   HEBEI LATUMBI to have an adulterous affair

HEBENGGE 1. of one mind, in agreement 2. obedient to the pull of the reins

HEBEREMBI to investigate, to inquire into

HEBEŠEBUMBI caus. of *hebešembi*

HEBEŠEMBI to discuss, to talk over, to consult about

HEBEŠENJIMBI to come to discuss

HEBTE IHAN a cow with white hair on both sides of the belly

HEBTEHE a wide waistband (worn by women)

HEBTEŠEMBI 1. to struggle for breath, to gasp 2. to greet someone with bows and raised hands

HEBU the end of a thread, a snag

HEBUNEMBI to form thread ends or snags

HECEBUMBI caus. of *hecembi*

HECEMBI 1. to scoop out completely 2. to use up

   HECEME GAMAME completely, thoroughly

HECEN city, city wall

HECERI ILHA an exotic yellow flower that blooms in spring

HEDE 1. stump 2. the scar of a boil 3. remainder, leftover

HEDEI a bunghole, a mortise

HEDEREBUMBI caus./pass. of *hederembi*

HEDEREKU a rake

   HEDEREKU ORHO ivy

HEDEREMBI to rake, to rake in, to scratch (of thorns)

HEDERENUMBI to rake together

HEDU itch, scabies

HEFA SEME see *he fa seme*

HEFELI belly

   HEFELI HŪWAITAKŪ a maternity girdle

   HEFELI NIMEMBI to have a belly ache

   HEFELI WAKJAHŪN the belly hangs down in a paunch

HEFELIYEBUMBI caus. of *hefeliyembi*

HEFELIYEMBI to carry at the bosom, to

cherish

HEFELIYEN 1. bosom 2. see *hefeli*

HEFELIYENEMBI to have diarrhea

HEHE woman, female

   HEHE DETHE the smaller feathers on a bird's wing

   HEHE DOOSE a Taoist nun

   HEHE FEYESI female undertaker, female coroner

   HEHE KELI husband's brother's wife

   HEHE NAKCU wife of mother's brother

   HEHE TOHON loop for a button

   HEHEI LANG young girl

HEHENGGE female, pertaining to women, feminine

HEHERDEMBI to become a woman, to become nubile

HEHEREKU old-womanish, possessing feminine pettiness

HEREREMBI to act in a feminine way

HEHERI 1. palate 2. indentation, groove, crevasse

   HEHERI FAITAME cutting across a crevasse

   HEHERI MADAHA the palate has swollen (a sign of sickness in cattle)

HEHESI plural of *hehe*

HEI HAI (onom.) the sound of crying

HEIHEDEMBI to stagger, to reel (of a drunk person)

HEIHERI HAIHARI staggering, reeling

HEIHERI HAIHARILAMBI to reel, to stagger

HEIHULE a small round fish with a small mouth

HEIHUWE *Nasus dauricus*--a type of fish resembling the salmon

HEJEMBI 1. to mend by stitching threads in a crisscross pattern 2. to have difficulty in breathing, to gasp 3. to make a betrothal

HEJEN FIYAKA a dog sled

HEJIHE 1. a steep area on the side of a mountain 2. the horizontal wooden bar on a pounder or pestle (for rice)

HEJIHELEME along the steep part of the side of a mountain

HEJIMBI see *hejembi*

HEKCEHUN falling of the flood waters in autumn

HEKCEMBI to ebb, to go out

HEKDEREHUN see *hekderhen*

HEKDEREMBI to go across a steep area on a mountainside

HEKDERHEN a steep slope

HEKDERHUN see *hekderhen*

HEKTEREMBI (-ke) to lose consciousness

HELE 1. mute, dumb 2. see *helen*

   HELE HEMPE stuttering

   HELE HEMPE AKŪ speechless, without talent for speaking

HELEDEMBI to stutter

HELEN 1. a spy, an informer, an enemy
captive who gives information 2.
see *hele*
  HELEN AKŪ speechless, inarticulate;
cf. *hele hempe akū*
  HELEN BURUBUMBI to lose one's
speech due to illness
  HELEN HEMPE stuttering; cf. *hele
hempe*
  HELEN HEMPE AKŪ see *hele hempe akū*
  HELEN JAFAMBI to catch an enemy in
order to extract information from
him
HELERI HALARI careless, neglectful,
sluggish
HELIYEN 1. pounder for grain, pestle
2. praying mantis
  HELIYEN SEBSEHE praying mantis
HELME see *helmen*
HELMEHEN spider
  HELMEHEN I ASU spider web
HELMEKU spider; cf. *helmehen*
HELMEMBI to spin a web
HELMEN 1. shadow, shade 2. reflection
  HELMEN URAN echo, reaction
HELMENEMBI to cast shadows
HELMEŠEMBI to reflect light, to cast
a shadow
HELNEBUMBI caus. of *helnembi*
HELNEMBI to invite, to go to invite
  HELNERE ŠUSIHE a silver identifica-
tion plaque carried by dignitaries
while on an inspection
HEMHIMBI to grope one's way along
HEMILEMBI to gather up (the hem of a
garment)
HEMPE stuttering, stutterer
HEN a small portable chair made of
wood or bamboo
  HEN TAN I needy, in need
HENCEBUMBI caus. of *hencembi*
HENCEHEN a small hoe-shaped implement
(for scraping the sides of cooking
pots)
HENCEKU mortar for pounding grain
HENCEMBI to pound in a mortar
HENDEN see *hente*
HENDUBUMBI caus. of *hendumbi*
HENDUMBI to say, to speak
HENG O ENDURI the moon goddess Heng O
HENGGE see *hengke*
HENGGENEMBI to have an unkempt appear-
ance, to be uncombed and dirty
HENGGILEMBI see *hengkilembi*
HENGKE melon, cucurbitaceous plants
HENGKERI a type of small melon
  HENGKERI FULANA ILHA *Pirus spec-
tabilis*
HENGKI shortened imperative of *heng-
kilembi*
HENGKILEBUMBI 1. caus. of *hengkilembi*
2. to have shares equally apportioned
according to the number of people

HENGKILEKU 1. a clamp for holding
together broken objects 2. the
hammer on a musket 3. one who
kowtows
  HENGKILEKU UMIYAHA a 'kowtow bug'--
a small black beetlelike bug that
makes a kowtowing motion
HENGKILEMBI to kowtow, to prostrate
oneself
HENGKILENDUMBI/HENGKILENUMBI to kowtow
together
HENGKILENEMBI to go to kowtow, to go
to court
HENGKILENJIMBI to come to kowtow, to
come to court
HENGKIN a kowtow, a prostration
  HENGKIN I TUWABUN name list of
officials granted audiences at
court
  HENGKIN I TUWABUN I KUNGGERI (啟
疏科) an office of the Court
of Banqueting concerned with the
above-mentioned list
HENGKIŠEMBI to kowtow repeatedly
HENI 1. a little, a bit 2. a pinch
(the amount one can pick up with
four fingers) 3. at all (with
negative expressions)
  HENI AKŪ not in the slightest
  HENI SEREME BAHAKŪ did not foresee
at all
  HENI TANI a bit, a little, only
HENJEMBI see *hencembi*
HENJIMBI to come to invite
HENTE 1. full-grown wild pig 2.
pitchfork
  HENTE NIRU a forked arrow
HENTELEMBI to use a pitchfork
HEO marquis
HEO SEME passable, sufficient but not
perfect, fairly well
  HEO SEME BANJIMBI to get by fairly
well
  HEO SEME ISIKA sufficient
HEOLEDEMBI to be careless, to be
negligent, to be idle
HEOLEKEN rather negligent
HEOLEN negligent, lazy, slovenly
HEOŠEMBI to be hesitant, to be unde-
cided
HEPEREMBI (1) (-ke) to dodder from
old age
  HEPEREME SAKDAHA has become a dod-
dering old man
HEPEREMBI (2) 1. to rake in greedily,
to grab up greedily 2. to drink to
excess
HER HAR (onom.) the sound of clearing
one's throat
HER HAR SERAKŪ doesn't speak to any-
one, doesn't pay attention to any-
one, haughty, snobbish
HERCIBUMBI caus. of *hercimbi*

HERCIMBI to wind thread onto a spool

HERCUN aforethought, attention

HERCUN AKŪ inattentive, not paying attention

HERCUN AKŪ DE without realizing it

HERDEMBI 1. to wander about begging, to be in dire straits 2. to pick up from the ground, to pick up from horseback

HERDEME HARDAME roaming about begging

HEREBUMBI caus. of *herembi*

HEREKU a ladle for lifting things from water

HEREKU MAŠA a perforated spoon for lifting things from water

HEREMBI 1. to ladle out, to fish for, to drag for, to take out of water with a net 2. to produce (paper)

HEREN corral, stable

HERESU a grass growing along the edges of salt marshes that is eaten by camels

HERGEBUMBI caus. of *hergembi*

HERGEMBI 1. to skim the top of a liquid 2. to produce (paper)

HERGEN 1. writing, written characters, letter 2. design, lines on the palm 3. rank, title

HERGEN ARAMBI to write

HERGEN DASAKŪ (正字) a clerk in the Supervisorate of Imperial Instruction

HERGEN FOLORO FALGA (刻字處) engraving office in the Imperial Library

HERGEN I KEMUN lined paper, paper with cells for characters

HERGENEMBI to form designs or characters

HERGENEHE CECE silken gauze with inwoven characters

HERGENEHE SUJE silk with inwoven characters

HERGESI (儒士) a clerk of the Board of Rites

HERGIBUMBI caus. of *hergimbi*

HERGICE thread wound onto a spool from a hank, spindle

HERGIMBI 1. to wind (thread) 2. to wander, to vagabond 3. to circle (of predatory birds)

HERGIME HEJEME winding and crisscrossing

HERGIN 1. the border or margin of a net 2. an outline 3. tie, bond 4. orderer, leader 5. cycle 6. order

HERGIN BE TEKSILERE HASHŪ ERGI FIYENTEN (肅紀左司) the name of a section of the Board of Punishments in Mukden

HERGIN ŠOŠOHON outline, general account

HERGINEMBI see *hergenembi*

HERGITU spindle

HERIN a high spot in the bed of a body of shallow water

HERSEMBI to be attentive

HERSERAKŪ inattentive, paying no attention to others

HERŠEMBI see *hersembi*

HERSU see *kersu*

HERU spokes of a wheel

HESE 1. imperial order, edict 2. divine decree, fate

HESE WASIMBUMBI to issue an edict

HESEI by imperial order, by decree

HESEI BUHENGGE ordained by decree

HESEI KIRU TEMGETU a banner sent by the emperor to dignitaries in the border regions

HESEBUMBI to ordain, to determine

HESEBUN fate, determination

HESEBUN BE ALIHA USIHA the stars *iota*, *kappa*, *lambda*, *mu*, *nu*, and *ksi* in the Big Bear

HESIHEŠEMBI to saunter along

HESIHETEMBI to stumble along

HESITEMBI the same as *hesihetembi*

HEŠELEMBI to pull in a fishnet

HEŠEMILAMBI see *hešemimbi*

HEŠEMIMBI to close a bag with a drawstring

HEŠEN 1. cord or rope along the edge of a net, selvage 2. guiding principle, fundamental principle, rule of conduct 3. boundary, border, shore, margin

HEŠEN BE FESHELEMBI to extend the border

HEŠEN HERGIN guiding principles

HEŠEN I CAMHARI a boundary marker, a boundary stone

HEŠEN ULHUN basic principles, leading principle, outline

HEŠENEMBI to wear tattered or dirty clothes

HEŠU HAŠU trifling, petty, annoying

HEŠU HAŠU NIYALMA a petty man

HEŠUREBUMBI caus. of *hešurembi*

HEŠUREKU rake

HEŠUREMBI 1. to rake in, to rake up 2. to do completely, to do thoroughly

HETEBUMBI caus. of *hetembi*

HETEHEN a nail or hook used for hanging objects

HETEMBI 1. to roll up, to turn back (the sleeves of a garment), to lift up (the hem of a garment) 2. to fold, to fold up 3. to perform a half kowtow in the Manchu fashion (of women) 4. to recede (of fog)

HETEME GOHOLOMBI to grab one leg and pull up on it (at wrestling)

H

HETEME ILHA a cup-shaped piece of
iron atop a helmet
HETEME ŠUFATU a type of rolled turban
HETEME TASIHIMBI to grab after the
sole of the foot and push (at
wrestling)
HETEREMBI see *hederembi*
HETHE 1. property, possessions, wealth
2. occupation, undertaking 3. stalk,
stubble 4. bridle without a metal
buckle 5. line on the crupper 6.
pressed cuff on a court garment
HETHEBUMBI caus. of *hethembi*
HETHEMBI 1. to pluck out (grass) 2.
to pull vegetables out of boiling
water
HETU 1. horizontal 2. stocky, broad
(of a person's build) 3. located
at the side, peripheral 4. woof
(in cloth)
HETU BAITA gossip, scandal
HETU BOO wings lying to both sides
of the main house, side rooms
HETU DALANGGA dam on a river
HETU FICAKŪ a horizontal flute
HETU HITHA ornament on the girth of
horse
HETU NIYALMA a third party, a third
person, an outsider, someone else
HETU ŠAMBI to look at askance
HETU TUWAMBI the same as *hetu
šambi*
HETU ULIN a sudden windfall
HETU UNDU horizontal and vertical,
warp and woof
HETU UNDU SARKŪ doesn't know any-
thing, doesn't know up from down
HETUKEN rather stocky
HETULIYAN rather horizontal
HETUMBI (-he/ke) to transverse, to pass
across, to cross, to spend (a
period of time)
HETUMBUMBI 1. caus. of *hetumbi* 2. to
manage to get by 3. to raise
through the winter
HETUREBUMBI caus. of *heturembi*
HETUREMBI 1. to cut off, to block, to
intercept, to interrupt 2. to
intercept and rob, to ambush
HETUREN a horizontal beam or rafter
HETURHEN hobby (*Falco subbuteo*)
HETURI 1. ordinary, commonplace 2.
unofficial, private 3. unexpected,
sudden
HETURI BADE in private life, in
one's unofficial life
HETURI BAITA private matter, pe-
ripheral matter
HETURI DASARGAN a popular remedy,
an unauthorized prescription
HETURI FAIDAN an ordinary escort
HETURI FAIDAN I KIYOO a sedan chair

with gold-colored curtains that
was carried by eight men
HEYE discharge from the eyes
HEYENEMBI to discharge matter from
the eyes
HI CY one name for the mandarin duck;
cf. *ijifun niyehe*
HIB SEME striking solidly (of an arrow
shot at an animal)
HIBCAN 1. scarce, needy, meager 2.
frugal
HIBCARABUMBI caus. of *hibcarambi*
HIBCARAMBI to be frugal, to act
frugally
HIBCARANDUMBI/HIBCARANUMBI to be
frugal together
HIBCILAKŪ frugal person, miser
HIBSA see *hiyabsa*
HIBSU honey
HIBSU EJEN honeybee
HIBSUNGGE pertaining to honey
HIBSUNGGE USIHA a chestnutlike
fruit
HIBTA 1. a protective shoulder pad of
felt for carrying 2. a type of
shawl
HICAN frugal, abstemious, simple in
one's way of life, uncorrupted
HICUMBI to look for faults in someone,
to find fault
HIDA curtain made of bamboo or reeds
HIDAKŪ a curtain in front of a door
or window to protect from rain
HIDAMBI to wind yarn onto a wooden
spindle
HIFE barnyard grass (*Panicum crus-
galli*)
HIFE BELE a type of millet
HIFE HARA a type of millet with
spreading ears
HIHAJAMBI see *hiyahanjambi*
HIHALAMBI 1. to be rare, to be pre-
cious 2. to value, to esteem
HIHAN rare, precious
HIHANAKŪ not precious, worthless, not
worthy
HIHŪN BUDUN listless, lacking enthu-
siasm, depressed, uninterested,
desultory
HIJA a stove for melting silver and
other metals
HIJA I NUHALIYAN a heated oven-
bed
HIJA I TUKDA grate on a smelting
stove
HIJADA a person in charge of smelting
stoves
HIJUHŪN blind
HILTERI armor scales worn visibly on
the outside of a mail skirt
HILTERILEMBI to attach *hilteri* to
a mail skirt
HIMCI in two, asunder

HIN GIRANGGI the tibia

HINA one ten-thousandth of a Chinese foot

HINCEO silk woven from twisted thread, worsted silk

HINCI see *himci*

HINCU see *hinceo*

HING JE mendicant monk

HING SEME 1. honest, sincere, earnest 2. serious (of an illness)

HING TSAI see *hinggari*

HINGGARI floating heart (*Nymphoides peltatum*)

HINGGE school of fish, swarm of fish

HINGGERI (虛) the name of a constellation

    HINGGERI TOKDONGGO KIRU (虛宿旗) a banner depicting the constellation *hinggeri*

HINGKE land not suitable for agriculture

HINGNECI mallow

    HINGNECI ŠU ILHA water lily

HINGSENGGE sincere, honest

HIO SEME sighing deeply

HIOHŪN see *hihūn*

HIONG SEME (onom.) the sound of wings flapping

HIONGHIOI GASHA the Chinese great shrike (*Lanius sphenocercus*)

HIONGHŪWANG realgar

HIR SEME sad, bereaved

HIRACAMBI to keep looking askance, to spy on intently

HIRAMBI to look askance at, to spy on

HIRANDUMBI to spy on one another

HIRGA see *hirha*

HIRGAMBI see *hirhambi*

HIRGEN the dried bed of a creek or river

HIRHA flint

HIRHABUMBI caus. of *hirhambi*

HIRHAMBI to cut off, to shear off

HIRHELEMBI to flow along

HIRHO corsac; cf. *kirsa*

HIRHŪBUMBI caus./pass. of *hirhūmbi*

HIRHŪMBI 1. to scrape 2. to irritate, to provoke 3. to scrape against a wall or tree to stop itching (of animals)

HIRI 1. firmly, fast (asleep) 2. disappointed

    HIRI AKDAMBI to trust firmly

    HIRI OHO became disappointed

    HIRI ONGGOHO completely forgot

HIRIHŪN thick-skinned

HIRSA corsac; cf. *kirsa*

HISALABUMBI caus. of *hisalambi*

HISALAMBI to pour a libation of liquor in honor of the dead

HISDAKŪ cymbals

HISE actor, actress

HISHABUMBI caus. of *hishambi*

HISHAKŪ a brush

HISHAMBI 1. to brush, to brush against, to scrape 2. to strike (a flint) 3. to sharpen, to whet

HISHAN dirty spot, dirt adhering to something

HISHANAMBI to form a dirty spot, to become dirty

HISHŪN shy, modest, restrained

HISY a very steep and dangerous spot on a mountainside

HITAHA see *hitha*

HITAHŪN 1. nail (of the finger or toe) 2. pick for a stringed instrument

HITAHŪSAMBI to press firmly with a fingernail

HITARHŪN wrinkled

HITARŠAMBI to wrinkle

HITEREMBI (-ke) to knit the brow, to frown

HITERENEMBI to bunch up in wrinkles-- said of clouds that are piled one atop another like fish scales

HITHA 1. ornament on a horse's bridle or crupper 2. a scale of armor 3. dividing wall in a beehive 4. see *šu ilhai hitha*

HITHALAMBI to make a beehive

    HITHALAME GIYALAMBI to make cells in a beehive

HITHARI an exotic red fruit with a skin resembling armor scales

HITHEMBI 1. to sprinkle water 2. to sprinkle chopsticks with wine at shamanistic rites

HITHEN chest, trunk

HITHŪN see *hitahūn*

HIYA 1. guard, page, specifically an imperial guard who wore peacock feathers (cf. BH 99) 2. drought 3. spindle for winding thread

    HIYA GURUN I SIRDAN a type of ancient arrow

    HIYA KADALARA DORGI AMBAN (領侍衛內大臣) Chamberlain of the Imperial Bodyguard, BH 98

    HIYA KADALARA DORGI AMBAN I BA (領侍衛內大臣處) office of the above officer

    HIYA SILMEN female sparrow hawk (*Accipiter virgatus*)

    HIYAI IDUI JANGGIN (侍衛班領) Commander of a Relief of the Bodyguard, BH 99

    HIYAI JUWAN I DA (侍衛什長) Sergeant of the Imperial Bodyguard, BH 99

HIYABAN coarse hempen cloth

HIYABSA 1. a press 2. two boards bound by cords used as a cover for books or documents 3. a halter made of two pieces of board

    HIYABSA ENGGEMU a yoke for beasts

H

of burden

HIYABSA JAHŪDAI a type of large
   seagoing vessel

HIYABSALABUMBI caus. of *hiyabsalambi*

HIYABSALAMBI to splint a broken limb

HIYABSAMBI to lick (as a mother cow
   its young)

HIYABULAKŪ a lantern rack

HIYABULE see *hiyebele*

HIYABUN lantern

HIYADABUMBI caus. of *hiyadambi*

HIYADAMBI 1. to plait, to weave (a net
   or basket) 2. to darn, to mend

HIYADAN 1. a rack of shelves 2. com-
   partments in a closet or chest

HIYADANGGA KUNGGERI (架 閣 科)
   a section of the Office of Discipline
   in the Board of War

HIYAGANJAMBI see *hiyahanjambi*

   HIYAGANJAME TUHEKE fell in heaps--
   said of the corpses of bandits
   that have been executed

HIYAHABUMBI caus. of *hiyahambi*

HIYAHALABUMBI caus. of *hiyahalambi*

HIYAHALAMBI to cross one another, to
   cross back and forth

   HIYAHALAME TABUMBI to string a bow
   by bending it with the knees

HIYAHALI CECIKE crossbill (*Loxia
   curvirostra*)

HIYAHALJAMBI see *hiyahalambi*

HIYAHAMBI to cross, to crisscross

HIYAHAN 1. an abatis--a means of
   military defense consisting of
   pointed stakes jutting outward from
   a central shaft 2. crosspiece on a
   crupper

   HIYAHAN I ENGGEMU a saddle with a
   support on it for holding a child

   HIYAHAN MULAN 1. chair with a back
   2. folding chair

   HIYAHAN MULAN I ILETU KIYOO an
   open litter with a folding chair

   HIYAHAN SILTANGGA JAHŪDAI a ship
   with crossing masts

HIYAHANJAMBI to be piled up, to lie in
   a confused heap

   HIYAHANJAME TUHEKE see *hiyaganjame
   tuheke*

HIYAHŪ wheezing, a rattling sound in
   the throat, asthma

HIYAIJAI see *tontu*

HIYAK SEME furious, in a rage

HIYALAMBI to carry a child on the back

HIYALAR SEME the sound of metal or
   porcelain falling

HIYALHŪWA hemp stalks

HIYALHŪWARI a match (made from hemp
   stalks)

HIYALU a net carrying bag

HIYALURI ILHA an exotic small white
   flower that resembles a net made
   from silk thread

HIYAMTUN the name of a small sacrificial vessel of the Hsia dynasty

HIYAN 1. incense, perfume 2. *hsien*,
   county, district

   HIYAN CENG (縣 丞) assistant
   district magistrate

   HIYAN DABUKŪ incense burner

   HIYAN DABUKŪ I SINDAKŪ a table on
   which an incense burner is placed

   HIYAN DERE a table used for burning
   incense

   HIYAN FILA a dish on which incense
   is burned

   HIYAN I CALIYASI (縣 總) district tax clerk

   HIYAN I EJESI (典 史) Jail
   Warden, BH 857

   HIYAN I FANGŠAKŪ a bag in which incense is placed

   HIYAN I HOSERI a box for incense

   HIYAN I JUMANGGI a small bag for
   holding incense

   HIYAN I SIRACI (知 縣) District Magistrate, BH 855

   HIYAN I SIHAN a cylindrical container used for burning incense

   HIYAN I SIRAMSI (縣 丞) Assistant District Magistrate, BH 857

   HIYAN I TACIBUKŪ HAFAN (教 諭)
   District Director of Schools, BH
   857

   HIYAN SISIKŪ a flat wooden or clay
   vessel for incense

HIYANCI a hunting rifle with a long
   thin barrel

HIYANCILAMBI to form a herd (of deer
   in summer)

HIYANCUHU NIMAHA salted fish

HIYANG BE eunuch

HIYANG BING cake of incense

HIYANG CA jasmine tea

HIYANG CUN MOO *Cedrela sinensis*

HIYANG HING SEME energetically,
   vigorously

HIYANG SEME vociferously, energetically

HIYANGCI chess

   HIYANGCI SINDAMBI to play chess

HIYANGCILAMBI the same as *hiyangci
   sindambi*

HIYANGLU an incense burner; cf. *hiyan
   dabukū*

HIYANGTARŠAMBI to act overbearingly,
   to be arrogant

HIYANGTU somewhat squint-eyed

HIYANJUHŪ NIMAHA see *hiyancuhu nimaha*

HIYARI squint-eyed

HIYARIBUMBI to wither up from a
   drought

HIYARŠAMBI to get up and leave, to
   evade

HIYASA plural of *hiya*

   HIYASAI BUDAI BOO (侍 衞 飯

局) kitchen of the Imperial
Bodyguard

HIYASE 1. box 2. a box containing
offerings attached to the top of a
pole (used by shamans) 3. a Chinese
peck

HIYASEKU a person who watches over
weights in a market place

HIYATAHAN a bejeweled goblet of the
Hsia dynasty

HIYATAN railing

HIYATARI railing on a street

HIYATU fringe of warp threads left on
cloth after it is removed from the
loom, thrum

HIYEBELE black-eared kite (*Milvus
lineatus*)

HIYEDZ see *hiyese*

HIYEKDEN MOO see *fiyatarakū*

HIYENA hyena

HIYENAKŪ unfit, incompetent, unstable

HIYESE scorpion

HIYO ŠENG student

HIYOB SEME (onom.) the sound of a bone-
headed arrow striking

HIYOK SEME (onom.) the sound of sighing

HIYONG SEME (onom.) the sound of an
arrow flying through the air

HIYOOŠULABUMBI caus. of *hiyoošulambi*

HIYOOŠULAMBI to be filial, to act
filially

HIYOOŠUN filial

HIYOOŠUNDUMBI see *hiyoošuntumbi*

HIYOOŠUNGGA filial, a filial person

HIYOOŠUNTUMBI to show one's filial
piety through offerings to one's
deceased parents and grandparents

HIYOOŠURI GAHA one name for the crow

HIYOR HIYAR (onom.) the sound of a
horse neighing
HIYOR HIYAR SEME 1. neighing 2.
strongly, obstinately

HIYOR HIYOR SEMBI to be robust

HIYOR SEME (onom.) the sound of the
feathers on a flying arrow

HIYOTOHON curved up at both ends,
arched
HIYOTOHON DERETU a table with
curved ends

HIYOTONGGO SON curved eaves on a house

HIYOTONGGO ULHŪMA a poetic name for
the pheasant

HIYOTOROBUMBI caus. of *hiyotorombi*

HIYOTOROMBI (-ko) to curve up at the
ends, to turn up at the ends

HIYOTORŠOMBI to walk erratically due
to a lack of strength

HO GI a turkey

HO HA (onom.) the sound of sighing;
cf. *hiyok seme*

HO HOI the sound made by hunters to
scare animals out of hiding

HO HŪWA ILHA lotus

HO LAN GURUN Holland

HOB SEME 1. shoving, pushing 2.
(onom.) the sound of an arrow
striking

HOBAI printed calico or chintz

HOBO coffin
HOBO MUSEN bier

HOBOLON elder (tree)

HOBORHO the outer coffin (in ancient
times)

HOCIKON beautiful, attractive, talented

HOCIKOSAKA 1. attractive 2. in good
health, in good condition

HODAN GASHA the name of a bird that
resembles a chicken and cries both
day and night--possibly the hoki
pheasant

HODE perhaps, maybe, possibly

HODORI the fry of the Siberian salmon

HODZ a gold medallion worn about the
neck by women on their court attire

HOFIN a small porcelain vase

HOFIYAN dexterous, talented, capable

HOFUN bubbles or foam on the surface
of muddy water

HOGI turkey

HOHAN see *hoohan*

HOHO 1. pod, peapod 2. earlobe
HOHO EFEN boiled meat pastries made
in the shape of a peapod; cf.
giyose

HOHOCO ILHA a flower that resembles
the flower of the bamboo and produces seeds in a pod

HOHOCU an exotic cherrylike fruit
that grows on a vine

HOHODOKŪ a speaking tube

HOHODOMBI to cup the hands and call
through them to someone far away

HOHON 1. a barrel for holding liquor
2. hollow tree in which a bear
spends the winter

HOHONGGO MOO pagoda tree, Chinese
yellow-berry (*Sophora japonica*)
HOHONGGO MOOI USE the seed of the
yellow-berry tree used for making
yellow dye

HOHONOMBI 1. to form pods, to hang
down in podlike fashion 2. to form
icicles

HOHORI the soft cartilage jutting out
at the side of the aural cavity
HOHORI JAN a whistling arrow made
from a cow's horn

HOI see *hūi*

HOIDZ see *hoise*

HOIFALABUMBI caus. of *hoifalambi*

HOIFALAMBI to dye black with a con-
coction of the leaves and stems of
the wild tea plant *wence moo*

HOIFAN a dye made from the leaves and
stems of the wild tea plant *wence*

H

moo

HOIHALAMBI   to go on the winter hunt

HOIHAN   the area of a battue

   HOIHAN SINDAMBI   to form a battue
     formation

HOIHO   a tailless chick

HOILABUMBI   caus. of *hoilambi*

HOILACAMBI   to look to both sides, to
   glance to both sides

HOILALAMBI   to glance backward

HOILAMBI (-ka)   to be dirty, to be
   soiled

HOILAMBUMBI   caus. of *hoilambi*

HOILANTU   a type of monkey indigenous to
   west China

HOILASHŪN   1. soiled, faded   2. wretched

HOILEMBI   to apply lime or mortar

HOISE   Moslem, Uighur

   HOISE I TACIHIYAN   Islam

   HOISE NIRU   chief of a Moslem banner

   HOISE TACIKŪ   a Moslem school

HOJI   coriander

HOJIGON   see *hojihon*

HOJIHON   son-in-law

HOJIHOSI   plural of *hojihon*

HOJIKO   one name for the chicken; cf.
   coko

HOJIRI ILHA   a white or violet aster

HOJO   beautiful, attractive, pleasing

   HOJO FAHA   pupil of the eye

HOJON ILHA   corn poppy (*Papaver Rhoeas*)

HOJU   see *hojo*

HOKCI   a wild edible plant with thin
   stems and pointed leaves

HOKI   1. companion, comrade, partner,
   accomplice   2. clerk in a store

HOKILAMBI   to form a group of friends,
   to form a clique, to work as part-
   ners, to form a partnership

HOKOBUMBI   caus. of *hokombi*

   HOKOBURAKŪ   without cease

HOKOMBI   1. to part, to take leave
   from   2. to abandon, to reject   3.
   to divorce   4. to resign from

HOKOTOI   divorced (of a woman)

HOKSOMBI   to be depressed, to be melancholy

HOKTON   1. cork   2. float   (on a fishing
   line or net)

   HOKTON MOO   a cork tree

HOKTOSŌMBI   to hunt on high ground during a flood

HOLBOBUMBI   1. caus./pass. of *holbombi*
   2. to be connected with, to get
   joined

HOLBOHON   1. one person of a pair   2.
   connection, link

HOLBOKŪ   fastener, clamp

HOLBOMBI   1. to connect, to join   2. to
   pair, to mate, to get married   3. to
   implicate

   HOLBOME ACABUMBI   to get married

HOLBON   1. pairing, a pair   2. mate

   3. marriage   4. agreement

   HOLBON I HITHAN   joint, hinge

HOLBONGGO   connected, paired

   HOLBONGGO FUKJINGGA HERGEN （填篆）
     a style of calligraphy

   HOLBONGGE HOOŠAN   paper produced
     from two or four layers of bamboo

HOLBOTO ILHA   bindweed

HOLDON   1. signal fire, beacon   2.
   falling star, meteor   3. Siberian
   cedar

   HOLDON I KARAN   the same as *holdon
     tai*

   HOLDON MOO   Siberian cedar

   HOLDON TAI   beacon tower

   HOLDON TUHEKE   a star fell

   HOLDON TUWA   beacon fire

HOLHOCI   *Atractylis ovata*

HOLHON   the lower part of the leg

   HOLHON GIRANGGI   the bone of the
     lower part of the leg, the shin,
     tibia

   HOLHON GOCIMBUMBI   to pull a muscle
     in the calf

HOLIMPA   a grain resembling maize

HOLIN   the inside of the cheek

HOLKON   moment, instant

   HOLKONDE   suddenly, in an instant

HOLO   1. valley   2. ravine, furrow, a
   tile drain, ditch   3. false, spurious, not genuine   4. aurochs

   HOLO CILBURI   martingale

   HOLO JIBCA   a jacket of artificial
     fur

   HOLO KŪDARHAN   a cloth crupper

HOLOKON   rather false, somewhat spurious

   HOLOKON ULUKEN   rather false and
     spurious

HOLON GAHA   jackdaw, general name for
   birds of the genus *Corvus*

   HOLON WEIJUN   stork; cf. *weijun*

HOLOR (onom.)   sound of a bell

   HOLOR HALAR   (onom.) the sound of
     many bells

HOLTOBUMBI   caus./pass. of *holtombi*

HOLTOMBI   to deceive, to lie

HOLTON   see *holdon*

HOLTONUMBI   to deceive one another, to
   lie to one another

HOLTOŠOMBI   to deceive often

HOLTU CECIKE   the name of a small bird

HOMHOLOMBI   to stick in a scabbard, to
   sheath

HOMHON   scabbard, top for a writing
   brush

HOMIDA CECIKE   one name for the goatsucker; cf. *indahūn cecike*

HOMIN   hoe

HOMITU GŪWASIHIYA   one name for the
   egret; cf. *gūwasihiya*

HOMSO   a shuttle

   HOMSO MAKTAMBI   to pass a shuttle
     back and forth

HOMSORI BELE rice that has turned red from long storage

HON very, most, too

HONCI sheepskin

HONCUN see *huncun*

HONDOBA a kind of foxtaillike grass that can be eaten by horses

HONGGOCO small white-bellied fish that have been frozen in the ice of a stream

HONGGOCON willow herb

HONGGOLON NIYEHE the same as *honggon niyehe*

HONGGON small bell
  HONGGON CECIKE a small bird with a bell-like voice
  HONGGON NIYEHE a type of wild duck

HONGGONO CECIKE the same as *honggon cecike*

HONGGONOMBI 1. to form bubbles, to form small bells 2. to crumble, to come apart, to shatter
  HONGGONOME GECEHE has frozen into small pieces

HONGGORI a bell-shaped fruit from Szechuan used as a medicine
  HONGGORI ILHA the flower of the bead tree

HONGKO 1. end 2. spur of a mountain 3. a place where level land ends 4. head of a pestle 5. the forward part of a boat 6. small footbridge over a mountain stream
  HONGKO CECIKE a small, yellow-breasted black bird whose cry resembles that of the swallow

HONGKOLO GALMAN a large yellow mosquitolike insect

HONGKŪ see *hongko*

HONIKA the young of fish, fry

HONIKI a small bear with short front legs

HONIN 1. sheep 2. the eighth of the earth's branches (未)
  HONIN BIYA the sixth month

HONINGGA pertaining to the sheep
  HONINGGA ANIYA the year of the sheep

HONO still, yet

HONOKTA see *honggoco*

HONTOHO 1. half 2. a bannerman with half salary 3. section of an organization
  HONTOHO MOO an identification plaque in two pieces that can be fitted together for verification

HONTOHOLOBUMBI caus./pass. of *hontoholombi*

HONTOHOLOMBI to divide into halves, to halve

HONTOHON see *hontoho*

HONTOHOTO half each, a half for each person

HOO one ten-thousandth of a Chinese foot

HOO HIO SEME bravely, decisively, powerfully, intrepidly

HOO HOO SEME torrentially

HOO SEME surging, flooding, torrential, mightily
  HOO SEME DAMBI to blow violently (of the wind)
  HOO SEME YABUMBI to go in an elated manner

HOOCANG ETUKU coat made of feathers

HOOHAN blue heron

HOOHO see *hoo hoo seme*

HOOŠAN paper
  HOOŠAN DAHABUMBI to burn paper on which charms have been written-- done by a shaman for a sick person
  HOOŠAN HEREMBI to produce paper
  HOOŠAN HERGEMBI the same as *hoošan herembi*
  HOOŠAN I PAI paper playing cards
  HOOŠAN I TUKU the surface of a paper fan
  HOOŠAN JIHA paper money
  HOOŠAN SASUKŪ the same as *hoošan i pai*

HOOŠANG see *hūwašan*

HOOŠARI MOO paper mulberry (*Broussonetia papyrifera*)

HOPAI a tally used by official post riders for drawing provisions

HOPEN fire basin, small charcoal stove

HOR SEME neighing, whinnying

HORGIKŪ 1. pivot, fulcrum 2. socket, socket of the hip joint 3. a pole with a wheel on top to which swings are attached

HORHO 1. closet, upright chest 2. pen for pigs or sheep 3. cage 4. outer coffin

HORHODOMBI to take shelter, to seek refuge

HORHOTU a large wooden cage for catching tigers and leopards

HORHŪ outer coffin; cf. *horho*

HORIBUMBI caus./pass. of *horimbi*

HORIGAN pen, corral

HORILAKŪ ASU a long net cast from two boats into still water

HORIMBI to enclose, to put in a pen, to imprison

HORIN 1. cage 2. see *horho*

HORKI the Siberian capercaillie (*Tettao parvirostris*)

HORO eel; cf. *hūwara*

HOROKI having a senile aspect

HOROLAMBI see *horolombi*

HOROLOMBI to show severity, to intimidate, to frighten

HORON 1. majesty, authority, awe, power 2. poison, especially that of bees, wasps, hornets, and scorpions

H

HORON AISILAHA DAIFAN (武翼大夫) an honorary military title of the third rank second class

HORON AKDUN AISILAHA HAFAN (武信佐郎) an honorary military title of the sixth rank second class

HORON AKDUN HAFAN (武信郎) an honorary military title of the sixth rank first class

HORON BE ALGIMBUHA AMBAN (達威大夫) honorary military title of the first rank first class

HORON BE BADARAMBUHA AMBAN (振威大夫) honorary military title of the first rank second class

HORON BE ILETULEHE DAIFAN (昭威大夫) honorary military title of the fourth rank first class

HORON BE SELGIYEHE AMBAN (武顯大夫) honorary military title of the second rank first class

HORON BE SELGIYERE TEMGETUN an insignia of the imperial escort

HORON BE TUCIBUHE DAIFAN (宣武大夫) honorary military title of the fourth rank second class

HORON BODOHONGGO HAFAN (武略郎) honorary military title of the fifth rank second class

HORON DUBE the tongue of a snake

HORON ERDEMUNGGE HAFAN (武德郎) honorary military title of the fifth rank first class

HORON FAFURINGGA AISILAHA HAFAN (奮武佐郎) honorary military title of the seventh rank second class

HORON FAFURINGGA HAFAN (奮武郎) honorary military title of the seventh rank first class

HORON GIRANGGI small curved bones from the breast of a tiger used as medicine

HORON GUNGGE AMBAN (武功大夫) honorary military title of the second rank second class

HORON HŪSUN BISIRE SULA HAFAN powerful gentry

HORON I OKTO poison

HORON TOOSE authority, power

HORON TUWANCIHIYANGGA AISILAHA HAFAN (修武佐郎) honorary military title of the eighth rank second class

HORON TUWANCIHIYANGGA HAFAN (修武郎) honorary military title of the eighth rank first class

HORONGGO 1. powerful, terrible, awe-inspiring, possessing great authority, majestic, regal 2. poisonous

HORONGGO CECIKE a mythical bird that was supposed to drive off evil influences--its carved image was often attached to the end of a pole

HORONGGO CECIKENGGE MUKŠAN a pole with an image of the horonggo cecike attached to the end

HORONGGO GURGU a fabulous beast with a long tail and two horns

HORONGGO GURGUNGGE KIRU (辟邪旗) a banner of the imperial escort with the image of the horonggo gurgu embroidered on it

HORONGGO YANGSANGGA DEYEN I BITHE WEILERE BA (武英殿修書處) Printing Office and Bookbindery at the Throne Hall, BH 94

HORONTU MAHATUN a hat used by the bodyguard of a ruler in ancient times

HOSAN ILHA an exotic flower resembling the osmanthus that blooms monthly throughout the year

HOSE box

HOSERI the same as hose

HOSERI DENGJAN a fireworks box

HOSHORI curly (hair)

HOSHORI INDAHŪN a curly-haired dog

HOSHORILABUMBI caus. of hoshorilambi

HOSHORILAMBI to curl, to crinkle

HOSHORINAMBI to be disheveled, to be unkempt

HOSO HASA (onom.) the sound of shaking paper

HOSORI 1. dandruff, flakes of skin 2. soot 3. earwax 4. crust, filings

HOŠO 1. corner 2. area, region 3. direction 4. edge 5. square

HOŠO BAIMBI to present hoho efen, liquor, cattle, etc. before a wedding

HOŠO MUHELIYEN square and round

HOŠO SAHAMBI the same as hošo baimbi

HOŠO TAKTU a four-cornered observation tower of the examination hall

HOŠOI CIN WANG (親王) Prince of the Blood of the first degree, BH 15

HOŠOI DUKA a side door, a corner door

HOŠOI EFU (郡主儀賓) the son-in-law of a hošoi cin wang

HOŠOI FUJIN (親王福晉) the wife of a hošoi cin wang

HOŠOI GEGE (郡主) the daughter of a hošoi cin wang

HOŠOI GUNGJU (和碩公主) the Daughter of the Emperor by an Imperial Concubine, BH 14

HOŠOI GUNGJU I HOŠOI EFU (和碩 額駙) the husband of a *hošoi gungju*

HOŠON 1. quarter, precinct 2. square

HOŠONGGO square, four-sided

HOŠOTOLOBUMBI caus. of *hošotolombi*

HOŠOTOLOMBI 1. to let a corner protrude 2. to make into a square

HOŠOTONGGO having corners, angular
  HOŠOTONGGO ŠUFATU a square-shaped turban

HOŠŠOBUMBI caus./pass. of *hoššombi*

HOŠŠOMBI to deceive, to entice, to mislead
  HOŠŠOME GAMAMBI to abduct, to kidnap

HOTO 1. gourd 2. cranium, baldhead 3. a piece of iron over the shoulder piece of a suit of armor
  HOTO CEKEMU flowery Japanese satin
  HOTO GUWEJIHE the third stomach of a ruminant
  HOTO HENGKE squash
  HOTO YOO scald-head--a disease in which parts of the scalp become bald

HOTOCI coconut
  HOTOCI MAHATUN an ancient-style hat made of a coconut

HOTOHO see *hotohon*

HOTOHON turned up, bulging (of the lips)

HOTON walled city, city wall
  HOTON FEKUMBI to assault a city wall
  HOTON I DA (城守尉) Military Commandant of a Minor Manchu Garrison in the Provinces, BH 746
  HOTON MANDAL a small shelter in which Buddhist monks recite the scriptures

HOTOROMBI (-ko) to curve up at one end

HU see *hū*

HUBTU a long cotton padded gown

HUDE the stern of a ship
  HUDE JAFAMBI to guide the rudder, to steer

HUFUMBI see *hūfumbi*

HUHU leaven for making liquor
  HUHU I SUWALIYAN a mixture of millet and oat bran

HUHUCU *Adenophora*--a medicinal herb

HUHUN 1. breast 2. milk
  HUHUN I ENIYE wet nurse
  HUHUN I TUMIHA teat, nipple
  HUHUN JEMBI to suck the breast
  HUHUN SIDAKABI milk has filled the breasts
  HUHUN SIMIMBI to suck the breast

HUHURI unweaned, suckling
  HUHURI JUI a child still not weaned
  HUHURI GEBU a baby name

HUIDZ see *hoise*

HUJENGGE GASHA one name for the owl;

cf. *yabulan*

HUJU 1. trough 2. a hollowed-out piece of wood held together with rings that was used for transporting silver

HUJUBUMBI caus. of *hujumbi*

HUJUKU bellows

HUJUMBI 1. to operate a bellows 2. to prostrate oneself, to bow deeply, to cower, to crouch

HUJUREBUMBI caus. of *hujurembi*

HUJUREKU a small mortar for sesame seeds, bean curd, etc.
  HUJUREKU CIFUN milling tax

HUJUREMBI to grind, to mill

HUJURI a wind tube used for making fires in the open

HUJURUKŪ see *hujuku*

HUKSA see *hukšen*

HUKSIDEMBI to rain violently

HUKSUMBI see *hukšumbi*

HUKŠEBUMBI caus. of *hukšembi*

HUKŠEMBI 1. to carry on the head, to wear on the head 2. to pile earth around the roots of a young plant 3. to appreciate, to thank, to be thankful to 4. to swell; cf. *hukšumbi*
  HUKŠEME ŠUFATU a head covering consisting of a flat board with cloth hanging down on both sides

HUKŠEMBUMBI to put a hood on a falcon

HUKŠEN 1. falcon's hood 2. a falcon kept in the house
  HUKŠEN GARUDAI an old phoenix

HUKŠENUMBI 1. to carry on the head (of a group) 2. to pile earth around the roots of a young plant (of a group)

HUKŠERI BELE rice that has turned brown from long storage

HUKŠUMBI (-ke) to swell

HUKTAMBI see *hūktambi*

HUKTU a long cotton padded gown; cf. *hubtu*

HUKTURI see *kukduri*

HUKUN dirt, dust, manure

HULE a measure of volume equaling ten lesser pecks, a bushel

HULUN MURAKŪ a whistle used for luring deer

HULUR SEME squeaking

HUMSUHUN craw of a bird

HUMSUN 1. craw of a bird 2. eyelid
  HUMSUN I TEILE 'with only the eyelid'--with little effort

HUMŠE Manchurian wood owl (*Strix alucona*)

HUMTU hunchbacked

HUMUDU bustard (*Otis tarda*)

HUNCU sleigh, sled

HUNDU the same as *humtu*

HUNGGIYANGLAMBI to play cards

HUNGKEN see *emu hungken jiha*
HUNGKEREBUMBI caus. of *hungkerembi*
HUNGKEREMBI 1. to pour 2. to cast
  (metal)
    HUNGKEREME in profusion, copiously
    HUNGKEREME AGAMBI to rain cats and
      dogs
    HUNGKEREME FEKSIMBI to run at break-
      neck speed
HUNGKIMBI to become soft, to become
  pulverized (of dry things)
HUNIO water bucket
HURCEMBI to find fault with, to criti-
  cize
HUREN 1. the ridge of the nose 2. an
  arch on the hearth for placing cook-
  ing pots 3. a badger trap
    HUREN WASE arched tile used on the
      roofs of temples and palaces
HURENEMBI to arch, to form a vault
HURGEN team and plow--used as a measure
  of a person's wealth
HURHU see *hurku*
HURHUI CECIKE one name for the goat-
  sucker; cf. *indahūn cecike*
HURKU sulphur
HURKUN GŪWARA one name for the eared
  owl; cf. *fu gūwara*
HURSE an earthen cooking pot
HURU 1. turtle or tortoise shell 2.
  the back of a bird 3. the back of
  the hand 4. a rise, a high place;
  cf. *kuru*
HURUGAN tortoise shell
HURUNEMBI see *hurenembi*
HURUNGGE having a shell
HUTEREMBI (-ke) to wrinkle
HUTHE scab
HUTHENEMBI to form a scab
HUTHUBUMBI caus./pass. of *huthumbi*
HUTHUMBI to tie up, to bind
HUTU 1. ghost, devil, disembodied
  spirit 2. an ugly man
    HUTU ENDURI ghosts and deities
    HUTU GELEKU an exotic fruit that
      can be made into rosaries
HUTUCEMBI to curve up at the ends
HUTUNGGE 1. devilish, demonic 2. hate-
  ful, deceitful
HUTURCEMBI see *kuturcembi*
HUWACA hole through which an oven-bed
  is lighted
HUWEJEBUMBI caus. of *huwejembi*
HUWEJEHEN a screen
HUWEJEHENGGE TOJIN a peacock with its
  tail feathers spread
HUWEJEMBI 1. to screen off, to cover
  2. to set up a screen
HUWEJEN 1. a board covering for the top
  of an oven-bed 2. a board covering
  for a cooking pot 3. a weir for
  catching fish in fast water 4. see
  huwejehen

HUWEJENGGE DUKA a screen placed by a
  door
HUWEKI fertile, fruitful, luxuriant
HUWEKIYEBUBUMBI caus. of *huwekiyebumbi*
HUWEKIYEBUMBI 1. caus. of *huwekiyembi*
  2. to admonish, to guide, to incite
  zeal
HUWEKIYEBUN encouragement, advice,
  admonition
HUWEKIYEMBI to be enthusiastic, to do
  zealously, to expend great effort,
  to rouse oneself, to be happy
HUWEKIYEN enthusiasm, happy mood, zeal
HUWEKIYENDUMBI/HUWEKIYENUMBI to be
  enthusiastic together
HUWELEN see *heolen*
HUWENGGE luxuriant, abundant
HUWENGKIYEMBI to peck out of a shell
  (of chicks)
HUWENJI a wooden cup or bowl with a
  handle
HUWERKE a shutter over a window made
  from wood or matting
HUWESI knife
HUWESIKU see *huwešeku*
HUWESILEMBI to stab or pierce with a
  knife
HUWESIŠEMBI to stab repeatedly with a
  knife
HUWEŠEBUMBI caus. of *huwešembi*
HUWEŠEKU iron (for pressing clothing)
HUWEŠEMBI to iron, to press (clothing)
    HUWEŠERE HACUHAN a flatiron
HUWEŠEN Buddhist nun
HUWETEN upland buzzard (*Buteo hemi-
  lasius*)
HUWETHI seal (a sea mammal)
HUYE a pit dug close by a riverbank
  from which a hunter shoots birds of
  prey that come to take the bait he
  has put out
    HUYE TEMBI to sit in a pit in order
      to catch quail
HŪ 1. a paste made of boiled rice or
  other grain, paste 2. the back of
  the neck 3. one-millionth of a
  Chinese foot 4. a unit of measure
  equaling five small pecks
    HŪ I DA the base of the back of the
      neck, the first thoracic vertebra;
      cf. *gen*
HŪBA amber
HŪBALABUMBI caus. of *hūbalambi*
HŪBALAMBI to paste, to mount, to paste
  paper over a window
    HŪBALARA FAKSI a person who mounts
      paintings and calligraphy
HŪBAN 1. a tablet carried in the hand
  during audiences in ancient times
  2. a jade implement pointed at one
  end and square at the other--used
  during important ceremonies in ancient times

HŪBARAK clergy, clerical
HŪBERI a fur neckpiece worn by women
   in winter
HŪBILABUMBI caus./pass. of *hūbilambi*
HŪBILAMBI to trap, to trick, to snare
HŪBIN trap, snare
   HŪBIN DE DOSIKA fell into a trap
HŪBIŠABUMBI caus. of *hūbišambi*
HŪBIŠAMBI to trap, to snare
HŪBUMBI caus. of *hūmbi*
HŪCIN a well
   HŪCIN ŠODOMBI to clean out a well
HŪCINGGA pertaining to a well
HŪDA 1. business 2. price, value 3.
   goods
   HŪDA ARAMBI to convert to cash, to
      sell off
   HŪDA MAIMAN business
   HŪDA MANGGA expensive
   HŪDA TOKTOSI dealer, broker, middle-
      man
   HŪDAI BA market, marketplace
   HŪDAI JAKA merchandise
   HŪDAI NIYALMA merchant
HŪDAŠABUMBI caus. of *hūdašambi*
HŪDAŠAMBI to engage in business, to
   trade
   HŪDAŠARA NIYALMA businessman, mer-
      chant
HŪDUKALA fast! hurry!
HŪDUKAN rather fast
HŪDULABUMBI caus. of *hūdulambi*
HŪDULAMBI to hurry, to hasten
HŪDUN 1. fast, quick 2. boil, car-
   buncle
   HŪDUN FUIFUKŪ a vessel for heating
      up tea or liquor
   HŪDUN HAFUKA a boil having red lines
      in it
   HŪDUN YOO boil, carbuncle
HŪDUNGGA speedy, swift
HŪFAN company, partnership, troupe
HŪFUBUMBI 1. caus. of *hūfumbi* 2. to
   run aground
HŪFUMBI to run aground
HŪFUN gruel used to feed domestic
   animals
   HŪFUN ULEBUMBI to prepare gruel for
      feeding to livestock
HŪHA 1. a knot of cotton at the end of
   a whip 2. a cotton rope
HŪHŪBA a long gown without slits at
   the side
HŪHŪCAN see *huhucu*
HŪHŪLI one name for the scops owl; cf.
   hūšahū
HŪI 1. red felt edging on the lower
   part of a saddle blanket 2. an
   exclamation--now, then 3. meeting,
   assembly, association
HŪI HAI SEME dizzy, unsteady
HŪI HIYANG fennel
HŪI HŪWA ILHA a type of fragrant orchid

HŪI KUI (會 魁) a title bestowed
   on those who placed between sixth
   and thirteenth on the imperial
   examination, BH 629C
HŪI SEME 1. dizzy 2. surging; cf.
   hūwai seme
HŪI ŠORO a matted basket used for
   pressing oil
HŪI TAI frivolous, dawdling
HŪI YUWAN (會 元) those who
   placed second to fifth in the im-
   perial examination, BH 629C
HŪIFAN see *hoifan*
HŪISE Moslem; cf. *hoise*
HŪJACI constable, policeman
   HŪJACI BE KADALARA BA (菅 轄
   番 投 處) office of the Control-
      ler of the Police Bureau, BH 81
   HŪJACI BE KADALARA FIYENTEN (番
   子 司) police division of the
      office of the Banner General of
      Mukden
HŪJIBUMBI caus. of *hūjimbi*
HŪJIMBI to rouse a recumbent tiger by
   shouting
   HŪJIME DAMBI to sough (of the wind),
      to blow so as to set the leaves of
      trees in motion
HŪJIRI alkaline, alkali, soda
   HŪJIRI BA an alkaline place
HŪJU a Central Asiatic pearl
HŪK SEME unaware (of fatigue)
HŪKCUMBI to surprise, to catch unaware
HŪKJUN one name for the stork; cf.
   weijun
HŪKTAMBI 1. to be hot and moist, to
   be steaming 2. to ferment
HŪKTAMBUMBI caus. of *hūktambi*
HŪLABUMBI caus. of *hūlambi*
HŪLAMBI 1. to shout, to call 2. to
   read aloud 3. to crow
   HŪLARA HAFAN (贊 禮 郎)
      Herald, Ceremonial Usher, BH 79,
      382B, 391
HŪLAN chimney, smoke hole
HŪLANABUMBI caus. of *hūlanambi*
HŪLANAMBI to go to call, to go to read
HŪLANDUMBI/HŪLANUMBI to call together,
   to read together
HŪLANGGA COKO one name for the chicken;
   cf. *coko*
HŪLANGGA GASHA see *hūlangga coko*
HŪLANJIMBI to come to call, to come to
   read
HŪLAŠABUMBI caus. of *hūlašambi*
HŪLAŠAMBI to exchange, to barter, to
   trade, to exchange places with
HŪLAŠANDUMBI to exchange with one
   another
HŪLDURAMBI see *gūldurambi*
HŪLGA see *hūlha*
HŪLGI see *hūlhi*
HŪLGICAN NIYEHE one name for the wild

H

duck known as *yargican niyehe*

HŪLHA 1. bandit, robber, thief 2. rebel 3. secret, on the sly

    HŪLHA BE JAFARA TINGGIN (捕盜廳) Bureau of Police Affairs, BH 795A-D

    HŪLHA HOLO robbers and thieves, bandits

    HŪLHAI FEYE den of bandits

HŪLHABUMBI caus./pass. of *hūlhambi*

HŪLHAMBI 1. to rob, to steal 2. to act secretly, to act furtively, to act on the sly

HŪLHANAMBI to go to steal

HŪLHANDUMBI/HŪLHANUMBI to steal (of a group)

HŪLHANJIMBI to come to steal

HŪLHATU swindler, thief

HŪLHI muddleheaded, confused, mixed up, blurred

    HŪLHI LAMPA primeval chaos

HŪLHIBUN deception, delusion

HŪLHIDAMBI to act in a confused manner, to be in a daze

HŪLHIKAN somewhat confused

HŪLHIMBUMBI 1. to be led astray, to be deluded, to be deceived 2. to lead astray, to delude

HŪLHITU a muddleheaded person

HŪLURI MALARI careless, lax, hasty

HŪMAN talent, capability

HŪMARABUMBI caus. of *hūmarambi*

HŪMARAMBI (-ka) to have a dirty face, to be soiled

HŪMBI to plait, to braid

HŪMBUR SEME in great quantity, profusely, frequently

HŪMSU see *humsun*

HŪNAMBI to form a paste, to form a mess, to become all tangled up

HŪNCIHIN relative, of the same clan or family

HŪNCUN the name of a Manchu tribe

HŪNG HIYONG (onom.) 1. the sound of the tide 2. the sound of running horses

HŪNG I POO a European cannon

HŪNG SEME (onom.) the sound of a fire

HŪNGKO the front part of a ship, the bow

HŪNGNIYOOLAMBI to rain while the sun is shining

HŪNGSI 1. pebble 2. Chinese little grebe (*Poliocephalus rufficollis*)

HŪNGSIBUMBI caus. of *hūngsimbi*

HŪNGSIMBI 1. to fling, to hurl, to hurl to the ground, to throw away, to discard 2. to talk nonsense, to talk wildly

HŪNGSITU GASHA the same as *kuringge gasha*

HŪNOOLAMBI to cause an uproar

HŪNTA hemp

HŪNTAHAN cup, mug, glass

    HŪNTAHAN I TOKTON rack for cups used at offerings

    HŪNTAHAN TAILI I CARGILAKŪ cup and plate rocket--a type of fireworks

HŪR HAR SEME shying (of horses)

HŪR HŪR SEME flaming, blazing

HŪR SEME blazing, flaming

    HŪR SEHE became a bit tipsy

HŪRFU orangutan

HŪRGA see *hūrha*

HŪRGA SOGI watercress

HŪRGADAMBI see *hūrhadambi*

HŪRGIBUMBI caus./pass. of *hūrgimbi*

HŪRGIKŪ whirlpool, vortex, eddy

HŪRGIMBI to spin, to turn around

    HŪRGIME DAMBI to blow in whirls

    HŪRGIME YABUMBI to go for a stroll

HŪRHA a large fishing net; cf. *hūrhan*

HŪRHADAMBI to catch fish in a large net

HŪRHAN a large fishing net

    HŪRHAN I WEIHE protruding teeth

HŪRI pine nut

    HŪRI BAHIYA pinecone

    HŪRI FAHA pine nut

    HŪRI FAHA I ŠOBIN baked cake with pine nuts

HŪRKA a horsehair snare used to catch small birds

HŪRU a mouth harp made of cow's horn and bamboo

HŪRUDAMBI to play the mouth harp

HŪSE beard

HŪSETAI bearded

HŪSHA MONGGON windpipe

HŪSHŪRI COKO a chicken with curly feathers

HŪSIBA ORHO ivy

HŪSIBUMBI 1. caus. of *hūsimbi* 2. to be beset by (illness)

HŪSIHA MOO wild walnut

HŪSIHAN woman's skirt

HŪSIKŪ see *monggon hūsikū*

HŪSIMBI to wrap, to wrap up, to envelope

    HŪSIME entirely, completely, whole

    HŪSIME ŠUFATU a linen hat worn in ancient times

HŪSINGGA SIJIGIYAN a broad-sleeved habit worn by Buddhist and Taoist monks

HŪSIRI MOO a type of oak (*Quercus dentata*)

HŪSITUN foot-binding, especially the type worn by men

HŪSUBURE HAFAN see *hūsun bure hafan*

HŪSUN 1. strength, power, might 2. laborer, worker

    HŪSUN BUMBI to expend effort, to be diligent

    HŪSUN BURE HAFAN a diligent official

    HŪSUN ETUHUN powerful, healthy

    HŪSUN FAKSI I KUNGGERI (夫匠

科) section concerned with laborers and artisans in the Board of Works

HŪSUN HAMIRAKŪ not within one's power

HŪSUN I DURIMBI to carry away by force

HŪSUN I EBSIHE with all one's might

HŪSUN I HOJIHON a son-in-law who lives in the house of his wife's parents

HŪSUN TUCIMBI to perform labor, to render service

HŪSUN YABUMBI to work, to do physical labor

HŪSUNGGE powerful, mighty

HŪSUNGGE BOO a powerful rich family

HŪSURI earwax; cf. *hosori*

HŪSUTULEBUMBI caus. of *hūsutulembi*

HŪSUTULEMBI to do with power, to use strength, to strain

HŪŠA kudzu-vine (*Pueraria Thunbergiana*)--a plant used for making a type of coarse linen

HŪŠA SIREN a vine with three-pronged leaves that grows on pine and cypress trees

HŪŠAHŪ scops owl (*Otus scops*)

HŪŠAJU taro

HŪTHŪMBI see *kūthūmbi*

HŪTHŪRI see *kūthūri*

HŪTUNG alley, lane

HŪTURI good luck, good fortune

HŪTURI BAIMBI to pray for good fortune

HŪTURI FENGŠEN AISIMBI to bestow good fortune and prosperity

HŪTURI FENGŠEN JALAFUN good fortune, prosperity (many sons), and long life

HŪTURI IMIYAMBI good fortune arrives in abundance

HŪTURI ISIBUMBI to bring good fortune

HŪTURI ISIMBI good fortune arrives

HŪTURI NURE wine offered by the emperor at state sacrifices

HŪTURINGGA possessing good fortune, fortunate

HŪWA 1. courtyard, yard, garden 2. in two, asunder, apart

HŪWA HŪWA SEME in two, asunder

HŪWACARAMBI to snore

HŪWACIHIYAN ENGGEMU a saddle with a horn-shaped saddle horn

HŪWAFIHIYA 1. a wooden tool in the shape of a halved bamboo used for smoothing arrow shafts 2. a pastry of flour, honey, and sesame made in the shape of the tool described above

HŪWAFIHIYABUMBI caus. of *hūwafihiyambi*

HŪWAFIHIYAMBI to shave an arrow shaft smooth

HŪWAI MUKENGGE KIRU (准 旗) a blue banner of the imperial escort depicting waves on a green background

HŪWAI SEME 1. surging, in great quantity (of water), billowing 2. boundless, limitless

HŪWAI TOLON a bonfire lit to announce some important event to the people

HŪWAIDANAMBI to dry up, to wither

HŪWAISE pagoda tree, the Chinese yellow-berry (*Sophora japonica*); cf. *hohonggo moo*

HŪWAITABUMBI caus. of *hūwaitambi*

HŪWAITAKŪ something that is tied on; cf. *tobgiya hūwaitakū*, *hefeli hūwaitakū*

HŪWAITAMBI to tie, to tie up

HŪWAJALAMBI to sign a contract or agreement

HŪWAJAMBI to break (v.i.), to tear, to crack

HŪWAJAN painter, artist

HŪWAJIYOO MOO Szechuan pepper tree (*Zanthoxylum piperitum*)

HŪWAKIYABUMBI caus. of *hūwakiyambi*

HŪWAKIYAMBI 1. to peel, to peel off 2. to take away, to revoke, to abrogate

HŪWAKŠAHALABUMBI caus. of *hūwakšahalambi*

HŪWAKŠAHALAMBI to erect a wooden railing or fence

HŪWAKŠAHAN stave in a wooden railing or fence

HŪWAKŠAN a small stave used in card playing to show whose turn it is

HŪWAKŠIHA see *hūwakšaha*

HŪWALA IHAN an isabella cow

HŪWALABUMBI caus. of *hūwalambi*

HŪWALAMA USIHA wild walnut

HŪWALAMBI 1. to break up, to cut up, to split 2. to rip up 3. to cut (the hair) 4. to gouge out 5. to play the finger game

HŪWALAR (onom.) the sound of wading in water, the sound of splashing

HŪWALAR HILIR (onom.) the sound of fishnets in water

HŪWALAR SEME (onom.) the sound of flowing water, the sound of splashing

HŪWALIYAMBI to harmonize, to unite, to reconcile, to conciliate

HŪWALIYAMBUMBI caus. of *hūwaliyambi*

HŪWALIYAN see *hūwaliyasun*

HŪWALIYANDUMBI to harmonize with one another

HŪWALIYAPI in full concord

HŪWALIYASUN 1. harmony, concord, union 2. harmonious, in concord, united 3. gentle

HŪWALIYASUN EDUN a gentle wind

HŪWALIYASUN NECIN harmony and peace

H

H

HŪWALIYASUN TOB   the Yung-cheng (雍正) reign period, 1723-1735

HŪWALIYASUN TUGI KUMUN BE HALANJAME DERIBURE MUDAN   a piece of music played during the offering of wine at the end of the plowing ceremony

HŪWAMIYAMBI   to peel, to shell

HŪWANG BE   *Phellodendron amurense*--a kind of oak whose bark is used in Chinese medicine

HŪWANG DOO   the ecliptic

HŪWANG GUIFEI (皇貴妃)   Imperial Concubine of the First Rank, BH 6

HŪWANG LI   see *huwangli*

HŪWANG TAIDZ (皇太子)   the Heir Apparent, BH 12

> HŪWANG TAIDZ I FEI (皇太子妃)   concubine of the Heir Apparent

HŪWANGDAN   yellow lead ore

HŪWANGDANA   yellow-breasted bunting (*Embereza aureola*)

HŪWANGDI   emperor

HŪWANGGA   on good terms with, in concord

HŪWANGGAR SEME   surging and roaring

> HŪWANGGAR SEME AGAMBI   to rain copiously

HŪWANGGAR HŪWALAR   roaring and splashing

HŪWANGGIYAMBI   to prevent, to stand in the way

> HŪWANGGIYARAKŪ   there is no harm, it does not stand in the way, it makes no difference

HŪWANGGIYAN   a quiver worn on the back

HŪWANGHEO   empress

HŪWANGLI   calendar, almanac

HŪWANGSE   orpiment

HŪWANTA   a bald mountain

> HŪWANTA SEBSEHE   a yellow locustlike insect with small wings

HŪWANTAHŪN   bald (of mountains)

HŪWANTANAMBI   to become bald

HŪWAR   (onom.) the sound of a thing being dragged on the ground

HŪWAR HIR   1. (onom.) the sound of clothing rubbing together   2. profuse (of tears)

HŪWAR HIR SEME   see *huwar hir*

HŪWAR SEME   see *huwar hir*

HŪWARA   1. file   2. eel; cf. *horo*

HŪWARABUMBI   caus. of *huwarambi*

HŪWARADAMBI   to file, to plane

HŪWARAKA   a window shutter made of willow twigs

HŪWARAMBI   to file

HŪWASA HISA   (onom.) the sound of stepping on dry leaves

HŪWASAR   1. (onom.) the sound made by desiccated plants in the wind   2. coarse, rough

HŪWASAR SEME   coarse, rough

HŪWAŠABUKŪ   a kind of local school in ancient times

HŪWAŠABUMBI   1. caus./pass. of *huwašambi*   2. to raise, to bring up, to nourish, to bring to maturity or fruition, to accomplish

> HŪWAŠABURE COOHA   a young man brought up at state expense who was destined for military service; as such, exempt from the corveé

HŪWAŠADA (僧官)   abbot, Buddhist superior

HŪWAŠAMBI   1. to grow up, to mature, to develop   2. to raise, to bring up

HŪWAŠAN   a Buddhist monk

> HŪWAŠAN BE KADALARA FIYENTEN (僧錄司)   section on monastic affairs

> HŪWAŠAN DOOSE I KUNGGERI (僧道科)   office of Buddhist and Taoist affairs in the Board of Rites

HŪWAŠASA   plural of *huwašan*

HŪWAYAMBI   to sign a contract or agreement

HŪYA   1. a sea snail   2. cup made from a sea-snail's shell   3. a half-grown roe deer

> HŪYA EFEN   a wheat cake made in the form of a sea snail

HŪYAMBI   to cry (of eagles, falcons, etc.)

HŪYAN   rheumatism in the shoulder

HŪYANAMBI   to form a crust of dirt on the face

HŪYASUN   foot fetters (for hawks and falcons)

HŪYUKŪ ŠORO   a basket that is lowered into a soy vat to press out the clear soy sauce

HŪYUŠEMBI   to exchange temporarily

> HŪYUŠEME BOJILAMBI   to remit (money)

I

I 1. he, she 2. the genitive particle 3. an interjection used to get the attention of subordinates

I CI an interjection of regret

I I 1. (onom.) the sound of sobbing 2. an interjection of derision

IBADAN mountain elm, the wood of which was used for making spears

IBAGAN 1. monster, apparition, phantom 2. a madman

    IBAGAN DAILAHA went stark raving mad

    IBAGAN GAILAKA see *ibagan dailaha*

    IBAGAN HIYABUN 1. the spadix of reeds 2. the seed-bearing part of a reed

    IBAGAN I HALMARI the pod of the honey locust tree, used as soap

IBAGASA the plural of *ibagan*

IBAGAŠAMBI to act strangely while possessed by a spirit or phantom, to act like one possessed

IBAHAN see *ibagan*

IBAHAŠAMBI see *ibagašambi*

IBAKABUMBI caus. of *ibakambi*

IBAKAMBI to shorten

IBAKCI a thorny bush resembling the wild grape that bears an inedible fruit

IBAŠEN MUKE water from melting snow

IBEBUMBI 1. caus. of *ibembi* 2. to offer, to present

    IBEBUME WESIMBURE KUNGGERI (進呈科) an office in the Grand Secretariat in charge of petitions and memorials

IBEDEMBI to advance gradually

IBEDEN gradual advance

IBEHEN the end of a bow

IBELEMBI to advance slowly

IBEMBI 1. to advance, to go forward 2. to give an increase of feed to

IBENEMBI to go forward, to advance

IBENJIMBI to come forward

IBENUMBI to advance together

IBERELEMBI to advance

IBERI the back part of a helmet

IBEŠEMBI to advance gradually

IBETE rotten tree, rotten wood

IBGE see *ibehen*

IBIRI see *iberi*

IBIYABURU loathsome creature!

IBIYACUKA loathsome, disgusting

IBIYACUN 1. loathing, disgust 2. disgusting person

IBIYADA the same as *ibiyacuka*

IBIYAHA well-developed ears of grain

    IBIYAHA JAFAMBI to select good ears of grain to lay aside for use as seed

IBIYAHALAMBI to select choice ears of grain for seed

IBIYAMBI to loathe, to detest

IBIYON detestable, hateful

IBKABUMBI caus. of *ibkambi*

IBKAMBI (-ka/ha) to shorten, to diminish

IBKAŠAMBI to advance step by step

IBTE an outgrowth on a tree that has begun to rot; cf. *ibete*

IBTENEMBI to rot, to decay (of trees)

    IBTENEHE OFORO a nose that has turned red because of drinking

IBURŠAMBI to crawl, to creep

ICA a type of long white ocean fish with no fins--called the 'noodle fish' in Chinese

ICABUMBI see *acabumbi*

ICAKŪ unpleasant, unfitting, uncomfortable, uneasy, not feeling well

ICAKŪLIYAN rather unpleasant

ICAKŪSAMBI to find unpleasant, to find odious, to dislike

ICAMBI 1. to neigh 2. see *acambi* 3. see *isambi*

ICANGGA 1. suitable, fitting, proper 2. good tasting 3. comfortable

ICE 1. new 2. the first ten days of

the month 3. beginning, at the be-
ginning, the first day of a lunar
month 4. fresh
ICE BIYA new moon
ICE CAI bud tea
ICE CALU a granary near Mukden
ICE HAFAN new (inexperienced) of-
ficial
ICE HOJIHON bridegroom
ICE ILHANGGA SUJE new-style flow-
ered silk
ICE NIMAHA fresh fish
ICE TUŠAN new incumbent
ICEBUMBI caus. of *icembi*
ICEBURAKŪ uncontaminated
ICEBUN contamination, smearing
ICEKEN rather new
ICEMBI 1. to dye 2. to bleach 3. to
contaminate
ICEMLEBUMBI caus. of *icemlembi*
ICEMLEMBI 1. to make new, to renew 2.
to do anew, to do over
ICEREME during the first ten days of
the month; cf. *ice*
ICI 1. right (as opposed to left) 2.
direction, dimension 3. in accord-
ance with, along with, after, ac-
cording to, facing, on the side of,
toward
ICI ACABUMBI to conform to
ICI ACABUME GISUREMBI to speak in
conformity
ICI ACABUME WEILEMBI to act in
conformity
ICI AKŪ see *icakū*
ICI BAHARAKŪ not following a de-
finite course of action, not setting a goal
ICI ERGI the right-hand side
ICI ERGI FIYENTEN (右 司)
second department of a governmental
organ
ICI KANI AKŪ at variance, disagree-
ing
ICIHI spot, blemish, flaw
ICIHI AKŪ spotless, without blemish
ICIHI DASIHI spot, blemish
ICIHIYABUMBI caus. of *icihiyambi*
ICIHIYAMBI 1. to arrange, to manage,
to take care of 2. to put in order,
to tidy up 3. to get oneself ready,
to grooom 4. to prepare a corpse
for burial
ICIHIYARA ETUKU shroud, clothing
for the dead
ICIHIYARA HAFAN (郎 中) De-
partmental Director, BH 290
ICIHIYANDUMBI/ICIHIYANUMBI to manage
together
ICIHIYANJAMBI to put in order care-
fully, to order reasonably
ICIHIYASI (更 目) Departmental
Police-master and Jail Warden, BH

851A
ICIKŪŠAMBI see *icakūšambi*
ICINGGA 1. having direction, purpose-
ful 2. experienced, competent,
skilled
ICINGGA AKŪ inexperienced, incom-
petent, unskilled
ICIŠAMBI to aim at, to strive for, to
incline to
ICITAI right-handed (especially at
archery)
ICU a fur coat or jacket without an
outer covering
ICUHIYAN see *acuhiyan*
IDARAMBI to gasp for breath, to feel
pain while breathing
IDARŠAMBI to have a pain in the chest
or belly
IDU a turn at duty, shift, turn
IDU ALIBUMBI to pass on one's duty
to the next shift
IDU ARAMBI to take one's turn
IDU DOSIMBI to go on duty, to take
up one's turn
IDU FEKUMBI to skip one's turn
IDU GAIMBI the same as *idu arambi*
IDU I BOO a guardroom
IDU ILIBUMBI to pass on one's turn
to another
IDUKAN rather coarse
IDUMBI to glue feathers onto an arrow
shaft
IDUN coarse, rough, uneven
IDURABUMBI caus. of *idurambi*
IDURAMBI to do duty in turn, to serve
in turn
IDURAME KEDEREMBI to patrol at
fixed intervals
IFIBUMBI caus. of *ifimbi*
IFIMBI to sew
IFIN sewing, needlework
IGAN see *ihan*
IGEHE the stem of fruits and melons
IGEN the two ends of a bow
IGEN ŠUKUMBI to attach the ends of
a bow
IGERI USIHA the herd boy--the star
Altair
IHACI cowhide
IHAN 1. bovine, cow, ox, bull 2. the
second of the earth's branches (丑)
IHAN BIYA the twelfth month
IHAN BULA the honey locust tree
IHAN BUREN a signal horn made of
brass
IHAN HONIN I ADUN I BAITA BE KADA-
LAME ICIHIYARA UHERI DA (牛羊
館 總 監) superintendent of
livestock in the Board of Rites
IHAN MORIN I CIFUN BE KADALARA
YAMUN (牛馬稅務監督
衙門) office in charge of
taxes on horses and cows in the

Mukden Board of Revenue

IHAN MUŠU a type of small yellow quail

IHAN NIMAHA sea cow--a type of scaleless fish about a yard long that bears some resemblance to a cow

IHAN TUWA bonfire

IHAN UNCEHEN a scaleless fish somewhat larger than a perch with a round tail and sharp stickers on its back

IHAN YAKSARGAN reed warbler (*Phragomaticola aedon*)

IHANGGA pertaining to the cow

IHANGGA ANIYA the year of the cow

IHASI rhinoceros

IHASINGGA KIRU a banner embroidered with the image of a rhinoceros

IHIDA the bits of meat left over after an animal has been butchered

II see *i i*

IJA gadfly

IJA CECIKE great titmouse (*Parus parus*)

IJA NIYEHE little grebe (*Podiceps ruficollis*)

IJARI ILHA banana shrub (*Magnolia fuscata*)

IJARLAMBI to smile

IJARŠAMBI 1. to smile cheerfully 2. to polish

IJASHA MAHALA a hat topped with a chrysanthemum-shaped ornament--used by high officials

IJIBUMBI caus. of *ijimbi*

IJIFUN comb

IJIFUN NIRU an arrow with a shaft shaped like the back of a comb

IJIFUN NIYEHE mandarin duck (*Aix galericulata*)

IJILABUMBI caus. of *ijilambi*

IJILAMBI to become accustomed to one another (livestock)

IJIMBI (-ha) 1. to comb 2. to put the vertical threads on a loom 3. to put in proper order, to regulate

IJIMBI WEKJIMBI to straighten out something tangled, to put in order

IJIRE WEKJIN basic principle

IJIN 1. warp 2. taut, tight

IJIN WEKJIN 1. warp and woof 2. order and rule

IJISHŪN obedient, submissive, docile, filial

IJISHŪN DASAN the Shun-chih (順治) reign title, 1644-1662

IJISHŪN HEHE posthumous title given to the main wife of an official of the fifth rank

IJU stunted, undersized

IJUBUMBI caus. of *ijumbi*

IJUMBI (-ha) to smear, to spread

IJUME DARIME GISUREMBI to speak sarcastically, to intimate something bad about a person

IJURABUMBI caus./pass. of *ijurambi*

IJURAMBI to rub

IJURŠAMBI to rub vigorously

IKDAKI the white hair on the sides of a roe's tail

IKENGGE 1. original 2. chief, great, large

IKIRI 1. pair, twins 2. in pairs, in succession, one after another 3. along the way, on the road

IKIRI AFAHA a book in which records of official money transactions were kept that was divided into two parts, one of which was given to the payee as a receipt and the other kept by the government

IKIRI COKO one name for the chicken; see *coko*

IKIRI JUNGKEN a set of sixteen bronze bells hung in pairs, each producing a different tone

IKIRI KINGKEN a set of sixteen L-shaped stones hung in pairs, each producing a different tone

IKIRI MULU a ridgepole that extends through two different buildings

IKIRILAME forming a pair

IKTABUMBI caus. of *iktambi*

IKTAMBI (-ka) to accumulate, to pile up, to collect, to gather

IKTAMBUMBI caus. of *iktambi*

IKTAN 1. accumulation, piling up 2. in Buddhist writings *skandha*

IKTANGGA implicit, hidden

IKŪBUMBI caus. of *ikūmbi*

IKŪMBI to shrink, to contract

IKŪN contraction, shrinking

IKŪRSUN marrow of the spine

IKŪRŠAMBI to crawl (like a snake or worm), to creep along

IKŪRULAMBI to get up, to stand up (of horses)

ILACI third

ILACI DE OCI in the third place

ILACI JALAN I OMOLO great-great-grandchild

ILADALA unstable, inconstant

ILADAMBI 1. to jump forward with the legs crossed (a kind of game) 2. to be unstable, to be inconstant, to act irresolutely

ILADAME FAITAMBI in cutting out clothes, to cut down the dimensions so that one part is smaller

ILAFIBUMBI caus. of *ilafimbi*

ILAFIMBI to turn back, to curl back

ILAGI vapor from dew

ILAHA the green bark of the willow

ILAMBI (-ka) to bloom

ILAN three

ILAN ACANGGA HERGEN three Chinese
  characters used to represent the
  sound of a Manchu word
ILAN BETHENGGE HŪNTAHAN a three-
  legged gold or jade wine vessel
  used for sacrificial purposes
ILAN BIYA the third month
ILAN DEDUME FUDEMBI to accompany to
  the third stage of a journey
ILAN DOROLON I BITHEI KUREN (三
  禮館) office in charge of
  editing the classics of ritual
ILAN ERDEMU the three powers--
  heaven, earth, and man
ILAN FAFUN I YAMUN (三法司)
  Three High Courts of Judicature,
  BH 215
ILAN FU the hottest period of the
  summer occurring right after the
  summer solstice
ILAN GŪSAI MENGGUN AFABURE TOKSOI DA
SABE KADALARA BA (管理三旗
  銀兩莊頭處   )
  Office for collecting rents on
  Imperial lands, BH 78A
ILAN HAFU BITHEI KUREN (三通
  館) office in charge of compiling the San-t'ung
ILAN HEŠEN the three moral relation-
  ships: prince-subject, father-son,
  husband-wife
ILAN IRUNGGE MAHATUN an ancient-
  style hat with three high ridges
  on top
ILAN JAIFAN three bones that join
  together in the croup of a horse
ILAN MULFIYEN I SUJE silk having a
  three-tier round pattern
ILAN NAMUN I DANGSE BOO (三庫檔
  房) business office of the three
  palace storehouses (for silver,
  textiles, and pigments)
ILAN NIYAKŪN the ceremony of kneel-
  ing thrice
ILAN SIDEN I CALU the three grana-
  ries of the Imperial Household
ILAN TACIHIYAN the three teachings:
  Confucianism, Buddhism, Taoism
ILAN TUHEBUKU I MAHATU an ancient-
  style hat topped with three
  jeweled pendants
ILAN UNGGALA MIYOOCAN a three-
  barreled musket
ILANGGERI three times
ILARI BOSO a type of very wide white
  cloth
ILARSU three-tiered, three-leveled,
  three-storied
ILASE three years old
ILATA three each
ILBABUMBI caus. of *ilbambi*
ILBAKŪ trowel for applying plaster
ILBAMBI to plaster (a wall)

ILBAN 1. plaster 2. the plastered
  surface of an oven-bed
ILBARILAMBI to smile
ILBAŠAMBI to laugh while putting
  pressure against the lips with the
  tongue
ILBEKE fond of eating fatty foods
ILCAMBI see *incambi*
ILDAMBI to be quick-witted, to be
  agile, to be bright
ILDAMU 1. elegant, refined 2. agile,
  quick-witted, bright
ILDAMUNGGA elegant, graceful, tasteful
ILDEDEI one name for the turkey
ILDEFUN the back of the head, the
  juncture of the neck and the cranium
ILDEHE the bark of the linden tree
ILDUBI one name for the *yabulan* (a
  type of owl)
ILDUBUMBI caus. of *ildumbi*
ILDUFUN GIRANGGI see *ildefun*
ILDUMBI (-ka) to be well acquainted
  with, to be friends with
ILDUN 1. convenient, comfortable 2.
  convenience, opportunity
  ILDUN DE taking advantage of,
    according to one's convenience
ILDUNGGA acquainted, on good terms
  ILDUNGGA AFAHA a summary of of-
    ficial documents
  ILDUNGGA DUKA side door, service
    door
ILDUŠAMBI to take advantage of an
  opportunity
ILE a type of hunting net
ILEBUMBI caus. of *ilembi*
ILEKESAKA rather clear
ILEMBI 1. to lick 2. to remove the
  stems from hemp
ILENGGU 1. tongue 2. the trigger of
  a trap 3. a wooden stick hanging
  from the nose ring of a domestic
  beast 4. the clapper of a bell
  ILENGGU DASAKU tongue scraper
  ILENGGU DUBE the tip of the tongue
ILEREBUMBI caus./pass. of *ilerembi*
ILEREMBI to tether with a long rope,
  as for grazing
ILETU 1. clear, open, out in the open,
  obvious, manifest, distinct 2.
  neat, clean 3. not shy, open
  ILETU COOHA troops in the open
  ILETU HŪLHA bandit who operates in
    the open
  ILETU KIYOO an open sedan chair
  ILETU YABUMBI to act openly
ILETUKEN rather clear, rather open
ILETULEBUMBI caus. of *iletulembi*
ILETULEHEN a horizontal tablet over a
  door or gate
ILETULEMBI 1. to be clear, to be
  obvious, to become clear, to become
  obvious 2. to develop 3. to re-

veal, to expose

ILETULEME WESIMBURE BITHE a memorial presented to the throne on festive occasions

ILETUN 1. elucidation, clearing up 2. chart, table 3. see *iletu*

ILETUNGGE bright, clear

ILETUNGGE GU a jade ornament, symbol of a male child, used in ceremonies in ancient times

ILGABUMBI caus./pass. of *ilgambi*

ILGABUN 1. discernment, judgment 2. difference

ILGACUN difference, differentiation

ILGACUN AKŪ without difference

ILGAMBI to distinguish, to differentiate

ILGANAMBI see *ilhanambi*

ILGANDUMBI to distinguish (of a group)

ILGANGGA see *ilhangga*

ILGARI paper strips attached to a willow branch--used as an offering to spirits

ILGARI TUCIBUMBI to hang out willow branches with paper streamers on them--used by shamans for driving off evil spirits

ILGAŠAMBI to visit friends or relatives

ILGAŠANAMBI to go to visit

ILGIN skin from which the hair has been removed, leather

ILGIN I ŠOŠONGGO MAHALA an ancient-style leather hat used during wartime

ILGIRI NIYEHE a small diving duck with oily flesh, the same as *aka niyehe*

ILHA 1. flower, blossom 2. patterned, colored, polychrome 3. gradations on a scale

ILHA AKŪ SIRGERI plain white silk yarn

ILHA AKŪ TURTUN plain thin pongee

ILHA CECIKENGGE LOHO a sword decorated with colored bird patterns

ILHA I FELHEN a flower stand

ILHA I FENGSE a vessel with a miniature landscape in it

ILHA I SIMEN nectar

ILHA NOHO DARDAN satin with large patterns on it

ILHAI DOBOKŪ flower vase

ILHAI HUNGKEREKU a watering can for flowers

ILHAI NIYAMAN calyx

ILHAI SUKU a clump of flowers

ILHAI TEBUKU a sack used for carrying flowers

ILHAI TUBI a protective cover placed over flowers

ILHAI UKDUN a warm pit used for forcing plants

ILHAI YAFAN flower garden

ILHAKŪ TUBIHE fig

ILHAMUKE wild strawberry

ILHANAMBI 1. to bloom 2. to grow dim (of the eyes)

ILHANGGA colored, patterned, flowery

ILHANGGA CUSE MOO golden bamboo

ILHANGGA FUNGKŪ a brightly colored carved or embroidered stool

ILHANGGA MOO rosewood

ILHANGGA SIRGERI thin silk having a brightly colored pattern

ILHANGGA ŠOBIN cakes with colored patterns stamped on them

ILHANGGA TURTUN brightly patterned thin silk

ILHANGGA WEHEI NIOWARIKŪ malachite green

ILHANGGA YABIHAN coffered ceiling

ILHARI see *ilgari*

ILHI 1. next, subsequent 2. vice-, sub-, assistant 3. dysentery

ILHI ANAMBI to ascend to the next step in rank

ILHI ANAME in order, one after another

ILHI BAYARAI JALAN I JANGGIN (副護軍參領) Lieutenant-Colonel, BH 734

ILHI HAFAN (少卿) subdirector, vice-president

ILHI HAFUMBURE HAFAN (通政副使) Deputy Commissioner of the Transmission Office, BH 928

ILHI HEFELIYENEMBI to have dysentery

ILHI JALAN I JANGGIN (副參領) Lieutenant-Colonel, BH 658

ILHI JORISI (副指揮) Assistant Police Magistrate, BH 796A

ILHI KADALARA DA (副管) assistant director of the Imperial Clan School; cf. BH 717

ILHI TACIBUKŪ HAFAN (訓導) Subdirector of Schools, BH 857

ILHI TACIBURE HAFAN (司業) assistant director of the National Academy of Learning

ILHI TAKŪRAKŪ (副使) assistant overseer, assistant inspector; cf. *takūraku*

ILHI TUŠAN I HAFAN assistant magistrate

ILHI UJU I JERGI grade one-B

ILHIN see *ilgin*

ILHINEMBI to have dysentery

ILHO see *ilhū*

ILHO MOO the tree *Idesia polycarpa*

ILHURU the name of a small colorful bird

ILHURU DUDU a multicolored dove

ILHURU GIYAHŪN CECIKE a type of shrike

ILHŪ 1. upright, vertical 2. appropriate, suitable

I

ILHŪNGGA lying straight (of hair on an animal)

ILIBUMBI 1. caus. of *ilimbi* 2. to erect, to set up 3. to stop, to end, to bring to an end
  ILIBUCI OJORAKŪ without being able to stop

ILICAMBI to stand together

ILIHAI immediately, on the spot
  ILIHAI ANDANDE immediately
  ILIHAI WAHA killed him on the spot

ILIHANGGA strong, durable (of silk products)

ILIMBAHABUMBI caus. of *ilimbahambi*

ILIMBAHAMBI (-baha) 1. to become accustomed, to get used to 2. to be at peace with, to be calm

ILIMBI (-ha) 1. to stand 2. to stop
  ILIRE TERE BE EJERE YAMUN (起居注衙門) office for compiling the records of the emperor's daily activities

ILIMELIYAN in a standing position

ILIN standing, standing position

ILINAMBI to go to stand on, to settle down, to stop (on)

ILINGGA HENGKETU a wooden emblem carved in the shape of a melon
  ILINGGA HIYAN incense in the form of long sticks

ILINJAMBI to stand unsurely (of a small child), to loiter, to stand around

ILINJIMBI to come to stand (on)

ILKIDUN one name for the partridge; cf. *jukidun*

ILMAHA uvula

ILMAHŪ shuttle used in weaving

ILMEN lead or stone weights placed on the bottom of nets

ILMEREMBI (-ke) to break loose

ILMOHO USIHA (戍星) one of the stars in the constellation of Orion

ILMUN HAN the ruler of the underworld

ILTEN a high shoulder piece or collar on court garments

IMAHŪ goral (*Naemorhedus goral*)

IMALAN the tree *Cudrania Cochinchinensis*

IMARI *mu*--a Chinese measure of land area

IMATA completely, all, totally, thoroughly

IMBE accusative form of *i*

IMCI see *imcin*

IMCIN a type of drum used by shamans

IMCIŠAMBI to beat an *imcin*

IMENGGE MOO Chinese tallow tree

IMENGGI vegetable oil
  IMENGGI DABUKŪ oil lamp

IMENGGILEMBI to oil, to rub with oil

IMETE a small snail

IMETEN ILHA lilac

IMHE (翼) the name of a constellation

IMHE TOKDONGGO KIRU (翼宿旗) a banner depicting the constellation *imhe*

IMISUN see *imiyesun*

IMIYAHA insect, bug; cf. *umiyaha*

IMIYAHANAMBI to get worms; cf. *umiyahanambi*

IMIYAMBI to assemble, to gather
  IMIYARA SABINTUNGGE KIRU (遊麒旗) a banner with the image of a unicorn on it

IMIYAN assembly, gathering

IMIYANTU a sacrificial hat of the Hsia dynasty

IMIYELEMBI to gird oneself; cf. *umiyelembi*

IMIYESUN belt, girdle; cf. *umiyesun*

IMSEKE the young of the otter

IN the female or negative principle-- Chinese yin
  IN I SIMEN vaginal discharge, menstrual discharge
  IN YANG the male (positive) and female (negative) principles

IN DU GURUN India

INA the son of one's sister--nephew

INCAMBI to neigh

INCI ablative of *i*

INDAHŪLAMBI to fall simultaneously (in wrestling)

INDAHŪN 1. dog 2. the eleventh of the earth's branches (戌)
  INDAHŪN BIYA the ninth month
  INDAHŪN CECIKE the hoopoe (*Upupa epops*)
  INDAHŪN FEKUN 'dog gallop'--a type of gallop that resembles a dog running
  INDAHŪN GINTEHE a type of tree that grows near rivers with colored bark and red and white flowers
  INDAHŪN HOLDON Siberian cedar
  INDAHŪN I DERHUWE a dog-fly
  INDAHŪN MANGGISU one name for the badger; cf. *dorgon*
  INDAHŪN MUCU wild grape
  INDAHŪN NACIN a type of falcon
  INDAHŪN SINDAMBI to set dogs (on game)
  INDAHŪN SORO sour jujube
  INDAHŪN SORO DEBSE cake made of sour jujubes
  INDAHŪN UJIRE BA kennel

INDAHŪNGGA pertaining to the dog
  INDAHŪNGGA ANIYA the year of the dog

INDAN an arrow lacking an arrowhead

INDE dative/locative of *i*

INDEBUMBI caus. of *indembi*

INDEHEN malaria

INDEMBI to rest (on a journey), to spend the night, to halt, to spend time

INDEN stopover (on a journey)

INDERI a mare or cow that gives birth to young after a year's gap

INE MENE at will, willingly, as one pleases, may just as well

INEKU 1. same, this (day, month, year) 2. still, as before
  INEKU ANIYA this year
  INEKU BIYA this month
  INEKU INENGGI today
  INEKU JIHE FUCIHI Tathāgata
  INEKU OMOLO a descendant of the sixth generation
  INEKU SILE broth, water in which meat has been cooked

INEMENE see *ine mene*

INENGGI 1. day 2. a type of sea fish resembling the sea bream
  INENGGI ABKAI TAMPIN the upper part of a water clock
  INENGGI DOBORI AKŪ both day and night, ceaselessly
  INENGGI DULIN midday, noon
  INENGGI HETUMBUMBI to live, to get by
  INENGGI ŠUN DE in the daytime
  INENGGI TOME every day

INENGGIDARI every day

INENGGISHŪN around noon, close to midday

ING 1. camp, military encampment 2. battalion
  ING ILIMBI for a camp to be set up

ING CING sapphire

ING GASHA eagle

ING HŪNG ruby

ING LO tassel

INGGA MOO a type of camphor tree

INGGAHA 1. down, fluff 2. the fuzz on the bloom of a cattail
  INGGAHA CECE a type of very light fabric made of down
  INGGAHA CEKEMU velvet
  INGGAHA SUJE a type of tightly woven thick woolen that resembles satin
  INGGAHA ŠUFANAHA SURI a sort of silk crepe

INGGALA 1. down, fluff 2. the mealy redpoll

INGGALI wagtail, a bird of the genus *Motacilla*

INGGARI the down or fuzz from the bloom of the willow tree
  INGGARI ORHO duckweed

INGGIRI GURUN England

INGGUHE see *yengguhe*

INGTORI cherry

INGTURI see *ingtori*

INGYANG SEME buzzing (of flies)

INI genitive of *i*
  INI CISUI on his own initiative, by itself, of its own accord

ININGGE his, her

INIYAHA looper, measuring worm

INJAHA the young of the gazelle; cf. *jeren*

INJAHAN see *injaha*

INJEBUMBI caus. of *injembi*

INJECEMBI to laugh together

INJECUKE funny, humorous, amusing

INJEKU 1. joke 2. funny, amusing
  INJEKU ARAMBI to joke

INJEKUNGGE comical, gay, jovial

INJEKUŠEMBI to ridicule, to laugh at

INJEMBI to laugh

INJEMELIYAN smiling

INJENDUMBI/INJENUMBI to laugh (of a group)

INJESI joker, clown

INJIRI veil on a woman's hat used to protect her face from the sun

INTU CECIKE the name of a small brown bird that chatters incessantly

INU 1. also, too 2. even (adverb) 3. so, yes 4. correct

IO oil, paint, lacquer

IO G'ANG CING a kind of brown cloth

IODAN an oilcloth raincoat

IOGI (遊擊) Major; cf. *dasihire hafan*

IOI 1. a musical instrument made in the shape of a lying tiger--the toothed ridge down the back is stroked with a wooden stick at the conclusion of a musical selection 2. one of the five tones; cf. *yumk'a*

IOIMTUN a ritual vessel used by king Shun

IOJAN a painter

IOLEBUMBI caus. of *iolembi*

IOLEMBI to oil, to paint, to lacquer
  IOLEHE HOOŠAN oil paper
  IOLERE FAKSI a lacquer worker, a painter

IOSE pomelo

IOWAN see *yuwan*

IOWANBOO see *yuwamboo*

IOWEI see *yuwei*

IRA glutinous millet

IRAHI 1. ripple 2. a shaft of light coming through a crack in a door or window

IREN 1. ripples and foam caused by swimming fish 2. wild reindeer (*Rangifer tarandus*)

IRENEMBI to cause ripples (of fish)

IRESHŪN sunken, sloping down towards the front (of animals)

IRGA see *irha*

IRGAŠAMBI to flirt with the eyes, to wink at

IRGE HONIN a castrated ram, a wether

IRGEBUMBI to compose verse

IRGEBUN poem, verse

I

IRGECE MOO   the name of a black and
   deep-red colored tree that grows in
   Tibet
     IRGECE NIYEHE   one name for the
       mandarin duck; cf. *ijifun niyehe*
IRGEN   people, the common people
     IRGEN I KUNGGERI (民科) sec-
       tion of civil affairs (of various
       governmental organs)
     IRGEN SERE TEMGETU   pass used at
       local examinations by nonofficial
       participants
IRGESE   plural of *irgen*
IRHA   remnants of cloth
IRI   1. fifty *mu*; cf. *imari*   2. vege-
   table garden
IRKIMBI   to provoke a person to anger
IRKINJIMBI   to come to provoke
IRMU   one name for the quail; cf. *mušu*
IRUBUMBI   caus./pass. of *imimbi*
IRUDAI   the phoenix of the north
IRUKŪ   lead sinker on a net
IRUMBI (-ha)   to sink, to drown
IRUN   1. a row of tiles   2. rows between
   furrows in a field   3. raised path
   between fields   4. the inside part
   of an oven-bed
IRUNGGE MAHATUN   an ancient-style hat
   that indicates rank by the number of
   ridges on top
IRUSHŪN   sunken, submerged, secret,
   hidden
IRUSU HIYAN   incense made from the plant
   Aquilaria Agallocha
ISABUMBI   1. caus. of *isambi*   2. to
   gather, to assemble, to collect to-
   gether
ISABUN   gathering, assembly, collection
ISAKŪ   meeting, congregation
ISAMBI   to come together, to gather, to
   assemble
ISAMJAMBI   to accumulate, to collect
ISAN   gathering, assembly, meeting
     ISAN NEIMBI   to hold a meeting
ISANAMBI   to go to assemble
ISANDUMBI/ISANUMBI   to gather together
ISANGGA MEKTEN   a game of chance in
   which a number of people make bets
   on a monthly drawing of tallies
ISANJIMBI   to come to assemble
ISANJINGGA BOO   the antechamber of the
   throne room where those who awaited
   audiences assembled
ISARLAMBI   to be assembled
ISE   chair
     ISE I SEKTEFUN   a chair cushion
ISEBUMBI   1. caus. of *isembi*   2. to
   punish, to reprimand   3. to intimi-
   date
ISEBUN   1. punishment, reprimand   2.
   intimidation
ISECUN   intimidated, frightened, over-
   awed

ISEKU   frightened, worried
     ISEKU AKŪ   unafraid
ISELEBUMBI   caus. of *iselembi*
ISELEKU ILHA   an exotic flower that
   grows in the mountains of Kweichow
     ISELEKU UMIYAHA   scorpion
ISELEMBI   to oppose steadfastly
ISEMBI   to fear, to lack courage,
   to be timid
ISHA   1. Siberian jay (*Garrulus
   glandarius*)   2. greedy and covetous
   person
ISHELIYEKEN   rather narrow
ISHELIYEN   narrow
ISHU   reel or skein of thread
ISHUN   1. towards, facing, opposite
   2. next   3. cf. *ishunde*
     ISHUN ANIYA   next year
     ISHUN BIYA   next month
     ISHUN CASHŪN   facing and back to
       back, in two directions at once,
       with a wringing motion
     ISHUN EDUN   head wind
     ISHUN JABUMBI   to contradict, to
       take an unyielding position in an
       argument
     ISHUN MUDURI   facing dragons (on
       satin)
     ISHUN SEFERE   the two hands joined
       exactly together, thumb to thumb,
       forefinger to forefinger
ISHUNDE   mutually, to one another
ISI   Japanese larch
ISIBUBUMBI   caus. of *isibumbi*
ISIBUMBI   1. caus. of *isimbi* (1, 2)
   2. to send, to take to, to deliver,
   to pass to (someone)   3. to bestow
   4. to accompany to   5. to repay, to
   give back   6. to inflict   7. to
   obtain, to get into one's possession
   8. to begin the training of falcons
   and hunting dogs
ISIHIBUMBI   caus. of *isihimbi*
ISIHIDABUMBI   caus./pass. of *isihidambi*
ISIHIDAMBI   to grab hold of and shake
ISIHIMBI   to shake, to wave
ISIMBI (1) (-ka, -pi)   1. to reach, to
   arrive   2. to approach, to come up
   to   3. to suffice   4. (with *de*) to
   be as good as   5. to be about to
   (with the imperfect participle:
   jetere isika)
     ISIKA (with imperfect participle)
       almost, about to
     ISIME   approximately
     ISIMELIYAN   approximately (with
       numbers)
     ISIRAKŪ (with *de*) not as good an
       alternative as . . . ,
       it's better to . . . , not as
       good as
     ISIREI   imminent, approaching, im-
       pending

ISĪMBI (2) (-ha) to pull up (grass), to pluck

ISIMBUMBI caus. of *isimbi* (1)

ISINAMBI 1. to reach, to arrive (at that place) 2. to go so far as to . . .

ISINGGA sufficient, adequate

ISINJIMBI (imperative: *isinju*) to arrive (at this place), to reach (here)

  ISINJIHA BE EJEMBI to record incoming documents

ISITAI see *icitai*

ISITALA up to, until

ISOHON bezoar--concretions found in the bellies of ruminant animals that are used as medicine

ISU plain black satin

ISUHE see *ishu*

ISUHŪN weak, delicate, sickly (of children)

ISUKA golden eagle

ISUNGGE ŠUFATU a military head covering of ancient times made from black satin

ITELE one hundred-trillionth (of a Chinese foot)

ITEN a two-year-old cow

ITU Chinese partridge (*Perdix barbata*)

ITULHEN saker, Shanhan falcon (*Falco cherrug*)

ITURHEN see *itulhen*

ITURI a nestling cuckoo; cf. *dumin cecike*

  ITURI KEKUHE one name for the cuckoo; cf. *kekuhe*

I

J

JA 1. cheap, inexpensive 2. easy
>JA AKŪ 1. wonderful, marvelous 2. not easy 3. not cheap
>JA BE BODOMBI to do the easy way, to save trouble or work
>JA DE BAHARAKŪ not easy to obtain
>JA TUWAMBI to seem easy, to look down on

JA FU BITHE see *jafu bithe*

JA JA 1. a sound used to scare off children or animals 2. (onom.) the sound made by a bird when it is caught

JA JI (onom.) the sound of many people screaming

JABARHAN an iron hoop

JABCACUN regret, regrettable

JABCAMBI 1. to regret 2. to blame, to reproach 3. to swarm (of insects)

JABCANDUMBI/JABCANUMBI to regret (of a group)

JABDUBUMBI caus. of *jabdumbi*

JABDUGAN 1. interval, pause 2. free time

JABDUHANGGA at leisure, relaxed, natural, leisurely

JABDUMBI 1. to be at leisure, to have the time to 2. to complete (successfully), to hit the mark, to make a successful attempt 3. to strike a blow
>JABDUHAI TEILE as time permits, as opportunity allows
>JABDUHAKŪ didn't have time to, didn't succeed in
>JABDURAKŪ 1. doesn't have time to 2. taken unawares, taken by surprise

JABDUNGGA leisurely

JABHŪ (張) the name of a constellation
>JABHŪ TOKDONGGO KIRU (張宿旗) a banner on which the constellation *jabhū* was depicted

JABJAN python, large snake

JABKŪ a small bag of arrows carried at the side

JABSUN a hundred billion

JABŠABUMBI caus. of *jabšambi*

JABŠAKI good fortune, advantage
>JABŠAKI BE YABUMBI to live depending or hoping for good fortune

JABŠAMBI 1. to obtain an advantage, to derive benefit from 2. to be by good luck, to be a matter of chance 3. to be inexpensive

JABŠAN good luck, good fortune, advantage
>JABŠAN BAIMBI to seek good luck, to look for an advantage, to depend on good fortune
>JABŠANDE fortunately, by good luck

JABTUNDUMBI to regret mutually, to regret (of a group)

JABUBUMBI caus. of *jabumbi*

JABUMBI to answer, to respond

JABUN 1. answer 2. deposition (at law)
>JABUN GAIMBI to take a deposition

JACI 1. too, very 2. frequently, apt to, susceptible to
>JACI ELEHUN too aloof (to one's relations)
>JACI FAHŪN AMBA too bold (used to scold people)
>JACI OHODE all the time, often, no matter what

JACIN second, other

JACINGGE second born

JADAHA crippled, disabled, paralyzed

JADAHALAMBI to be disabled, to be crippled

JADAHAN see *jadaha*

JAFABUMBI caus. of *jafambi*

JAFAKŪ handle, grip
>JAFAKŪ HADAMBI to nail a grip on (a bow)
>JAFAKŪ URHUBUHE BERI a bow with a

beveled grip
JAFAKŪNGGA having a handle
 JAFAKŪNGGA DENGJAN a lantern with
  a handle
 JAFAKŪNGGA TUNGKEN a large drum with
  a handle
JAFAMBI 1. to take in the hand, to
 grasp, to seize, to hold, to grip,
 to take hold of one's opponent (at
 wrestling) 2. to offer 3. to pick
 (fruit) 4. to collect (taxes) 5.
 to drive (a chariot or wagon) 6. to
 freeze 7. to cremate
JAFAN 1. bridal gift, dowry 2. driv-
 ing of chariots or wagons
JAFANAMBI to go to seize, to go to
 offer
JAFANGGA pertaining to holding
JAFANJIMBI to come to seize, to come
 to offer
JAFANUMBI to grasp one another
JAFAŠAMBI to hold continually, to
 keep groping for
JAFATA a hawk that leaves the nest of
 its own free will
JAFATAMBI to keep in rein, to restrain
JAFU 1. felt, wool blanket 2. direc-
 tive, decree
 JAFU BITHE directive, decree
 JAFU FOMOCI wool socks, socks made
  of felt
 JAFU SEKTEFUN a felt cushion or pad
JAFUKŪNGGA economical, thrifty
JAFUNAMBI to become like felt, to form
 felt
JAFUNUBUMBI caus. of *jafunumbi*
JAFUNUMBI to grasp one another, to
 wrestle
JAFUTA see *jafata*
JAGURI TUNGKEN a foot-long drum used
 by the imperial escort
JAHA a dugout with a sharp front end
 and straight stern
JAHALA a horse with red or brown
 stripes around the neck
JAHALTU SIRGA a horse with silver
 stripes on its neck
JAHARA 1. see *jahari* 2. multicolored
JAHARI pebbles and stones found along
 a river bed
 JAHARI DALANGGA a dam of pebbles
  and river stones
 JAHARI WEHE pebble, rock
JAHŪDAI boat, ship
 JAHŪDAI FEKUMBI to jump aboard a
  boat
 JAHŪDAI GIYALAN cabin on a boat
 JAHŪDAI I FALGARI DA (船署長)
  chief of the river constabulary
JAI 1. next, following, second 2.
 still, again, more 3. later 4. and
 JAI INENGGI the following day
 JAI JALAN I OMOLO great-grandchild

JAI JERGI second class
JAI JERGI DOSIKASI second-class
 metropolitan graduate
JAI JIDERE ANIYA year after next
JAICI second
JAIDA kitchen knife, cleaver
JAIDAKŪ 1. small knife 2. bronze
 cymbals
JAIDALAMBI to cut with a cleaver
JAIDAMBI to exorcise, to drive out
 (demons)
JAIDARI a type of small cymbal
JAIDE in the second place
JAIFAN confluence of the sources
 (small streams) of a river
JAILABUMBI 1. caus. of *jailambi*
 2. to move aside, to ward off, to
 parry
 JAILABUME BALHAMBI to try to get
  rid of smallpox by offering a
  pig and cakes
JAILAMBI to avoid, to get out of the
 way of, to shun, to hide
JAILANAMBI to go to hide
JAILANDUMBI/JAILANUMBI to hide to-
 gether, to avoid together
JAILATAMBI to shun continually
JAIRA female black bear (*Euarctos
 thibetanus*)
JAJABUMBI caus. of *jajambi*
JAJAMBI to carry on the back
JAJANAMBI 1. to go carrying on the
 back 2. to swarm, to be in great
 numbers
JAJI an interjection of praise used
 toward small children
JAJIGI turbot
JAJIHI see *jajigi*
JAJILABUMBI caus. of *jajilambi*
JAJILAMBI to stack sorghum stalks,
 grass, or wood into a large pile
JAJIMBI see *jajilambi*
JAJIN a big pile or heap of stalks,
 grass, or wood
 JAJIN YALI meat from the face of
  a pig
JAJURI thicket, dense grove
JAJURINAMBI to form a thicket
JAK JIK (onom.) the sound of birds
 screaming in flight
JAK MOO *Haloxylon ammodendron*--a low
 bush that can be used as fuel even
 when it's green
JAKA 1. thing, object 2. material,
 stuff 3. side, edge, border 4.
 crack, fissure 5. interval, fault
 6. particle used after the imper-
 fect converb: just, as soon as,
 about to
 JAKA BAIMBI to look for faults
 JAKA ŠOLO free time, free interval
 JAKADE see separate entry below
JAKACI from oneself

J

J

JAKADE 1. (after the imperfect participle) because of, when   2. (postposition) to the presence of, up to,
by, in front of
JAKALABUMBI to make a space between
two things
JAKAMBI to fit joints together in the
framework of a house
JAKAN 1. just, just now, not long (in
duration), recently   2. see *jaka*
JAKANABUMBI caus. of *jakanambi*
JAKANAMBI to crack, to split, to form
a fissure, to divide (v.i.)
JAKANJAMBI to investigate carefully,
to study assiduously, to research
JAKANJAME FONJIMBI to interrogate,
to question carefully
JAKARABUMBI caus. of *jakarambi*
JAKARAKŪ the crack between the high
end wall of a house and the roof
JAKARAMBI 1. to crack, to form a fis-
sure 2. to break up with (friends
or relatives) 3. to get a little
better (of an illness)
JAKARAME (postposition) along, along
the side of
JAKDAN pine
JAKDAN I ŠUGI resin
JAKDU one one-hundred billionth
JAKJAHŪN crack, fissure, break, hole
JAKJARAMBI (-ka) to form a crack
JAKSAMBI (-ka, -pi) to turn bright red
JAKSAN colored clouds (at dawn or dusk)
JAKSANGGA dusk-colored
JAKSANGGA GURUNG (紫宮) the
name of a constellation
JAKSANGGA ILHA crape-myrtle
JAKSANGGA TEN (紫極) the name
of a constellation, also called
dergi bikita
JAKSARI MOO a tree with red branches
and purple blossoms that reportedly
grows in the South Sea islands
JAKSUN fir, momi fir (*Abies firma*)
JAKTAHAN ILHA an exotic purple cup-
shaped flower
JAKŪCI eighth
JAKŪN eight
JAKŪN BIYA the eighth month
JAKŪN EDUNGGE KIRU the eight-wind
banners
JAKŪN FAFUN the eight proscriptions
JAKŪN FAIDAN eight rows (of dancers)
JAKŪN GŪSA the eight banners of the
Manchus
JAKŪN GŪSAI KUNGGERI (八旗科)
office in charge of the eight ban-
ners' affairs in the Board of
Civil Appointments in Mukden
JAKŪN GŪSAI NE BEIDERE BAITA
ICIHIYARA BA (八旗現審
所) summary court for banner
affairs

JAKŪN GŪSAI TURUN (八旗大
纛) the great standard of the
eight banners--a banner in the
colors of the eight banners
JAKŪN GŪSAI UHERI EJETUN BITHEI
KUREN (八旗通志館   )
office in charge of compiling the
jakūn gūsai uheri ejetun bithe
(called the *Pa-ch'i t'ung-chih*
in Chinese)
JAKŪN KULUK the eight valiant
steeds
JAKŪN MUDAN the tones of the eight
materials--metal, stone, silk,
bamboo, gourd, earth, rawhide, and
wool
JAKŪN NIYALMA TUKIYERE HAKSAN BOCOI
KIYOO a golden sedan chair carried
by eight porters and used by im-
perial concubines
JAKŪN UBU DE DOSIKA GUNG a duke who
possessed the eight privileges
JAKŪN UBU DE DOSIMBUHAKŪ GURUN BE
DALIRE GUNG (不入八分鎮
國公   ) Prince of the
Blood of the seventh degree, BH 22
JAKŪN UBU DE DOSIMBUHAKŪ GURUN DE
AISILARA GUNG (不入八分輔
國公   ) Prince of the
Blood of the eighth degree, BH 23
JAKŪN UBUI NARHŪNGGA FUKJINGGA HER-
GEN (八分書) a style of
calligraphy
JAKŪNGGERI eight times
JAKŪNJU eighty
JAKŪNJUCI eightieth
JAKŪNJUTE eighty each
JAKŪRI SUJE silk woven from eight dif-
ferent types of thread
JAKŪRU a measure equaling eight Chi-
nese feet
JAKŪTA eight each
JALA 1. a marriage go-between, match-
maker 2. measure word for fences or
walls
JALA NIYALMA matchmaker
JALA YABUMBI to act as a go-between
JALAFUN long life
JALAFUN HERGENGGE ŠUN DALIKŪ a
parasol of the escort with the
word *jalafun* written upon it
JALAFUNGGA possessing long life,
long-lived
JALAFUNGGA ILHA the flower *Tupistra
chinensis*
JALAFUNGGA KILTAN a pennant of the
imperial escort bearing the word
jalafungga
JALAFURI ILHA an exotic white flower
from an evergreen plant
JALAHI cousin or nephew of the same
surname
JALAHI AHŪN DEO male cousins on the

paternal side

JALAHI JUI nephew (son of one's brother)

JALAHI SARGAN JUI niece (daughter of one's brother)

JALAHI URUN the wife of a nephew

JALAKTALAMBI to leave a space, to make a pause (in music)

JALAKTAN pause, space

JALAKŪ a bird lure

JALAMBI (-ka, -ra/ndara, -pi) to let up (of an illness), to pause, to desist

JALANDARAKŪ without pause, uninterrupted

JALAPI after a pause, after a while

JALARAKŪ the same as *jalandarakū*

JALAN 1. a section (of bamboo, grass, etc.), a joint 2. generation, age 3. world 4. subdivision of a banner, ranks 5. measure word for walls and fences

JALAN BAITA affairs of the world

JALAN GURUN the world

JALAN HALAME generation after generation

JALAN HALAME BOŠORO NIRU hereditary banner chief

JALAN I JANGGIN (參 領) Colonel, BH 658, 659 R-222

JALAN JALAN I in turn, in succession, section by section, generation after generation

JALAN JECEN the world

JALAN SI a *jalan*, subdivision of a banner, ranks

JALAN SIRAMBI to continue for generations, to be hereditary

JALAN SIRARA HAFAN (世 襲 官) hereditary official

JALANGGA 1. measured, temperate, economical 2. chaste 3. pertaining to a generation

JALANGGA HEHE chaste woman--usually refers to a widow who remained unmarried

JALAPI after a while, after a pause; cf. *jalambi*

JALARI one-quintillionth (of a Chinese foot)

JALASU 1. an emblem or token carried by emissaries 2. an imperial document conferring enfeoffment

JALASU ILHA the flower *Stachyuras praecox*

JALBARILAMBI see *jalbarimbi*

JALBARIMBI to pray

JALDAMBI to deceive, to cheat

JALDAŠAMBI to deceive thoroughly

JALGAMBI to put back together (broken things), to rejoin, attach

JALGAN 1. length of life, span 2. fate, destiny, lot

JALGANGGA pertaining to long life

JALGARI MONIO see *jalhari monio*

JALGARI MOO 1. a bamboolike tree growing eight or nine feet tall 2. tamarisk

JALGASU MOO *Cedrela chinensis*

JALGIYABUMBI caus. of *jalgiyambi*

JALGIYAMBI 1. to fill out by taking from an abundance and adding to a scarcity, to add, to make even, to share one's abundance 2. to compromise

JALGIYANJABUMBI caus. of *jalgiyanjambi*

JALGIYANJAMBI 1. to make even, to balance out 2. to come to an understanding, to compromise, to break a precedent in order to accommodate

JALHAMBI the same as *jalgambi*

JALHARI MONIO a type of monkey that has an extremely long life span

JALI 1. a red inedible fruit resembling the hawthorn 2. wicked, traitorous 3. plot, intrigue

JALIDAMBI to plot against, to intrigue against

JALIMI see *jalmin*

JALIN 1. reason, motive, occasion 2. (postposition) because of, in order to, on account of: *mini jalin* 'on my account'

JALINDE (postposition) for the sake of

JALINGGA traitorous, wicked, crafty

JALINGGA KIYANGKIYAN wicked and violent

JALINGGA KOIMALI wicked and deceitful

JALINGGA ŠUBAN a wicked official, subordinate

JALIYUN for (his) account

JALMIN knotweed

JALU full, fullness

JALU ELDEMBURE DENGJAN a hanging lantern in which a number of candles burn

JALU GURUN the entire nation

JALUKAN somewhat full

JALUKIYABUMBI caus. of *jalukiyambi*

JALUKIYAMBI to fill out, to fill up, to fill a quota

JALUMBI (-ka, -ndara, -pi) 1. to be full, to be fulfilled 2. to fulfill

JALUMBUMBI caus. of *jalumbi*

JALUN fullness

JAMAN quarrel, row

JAMARAMBI to quarrel, to have a row

JAMARANDUMBI/JAMARANUMBI to wrangle with one another

JAMARŠAMBI to be continually quarreling

JAMBI to exorcise an illness by the burning of charms and the recitation of incantations

J

J

JAMDAN HIYAN MOO   sandalwood tree

JAMPAN   curtain, net (for mosquitoes)

JAMPANGGA CECE   fine gauze used for curtains

JAMPIN   1. see *jampan*   2. see *jempin*

JAMU   1. pink, peach-colored   2. the name of a sweet red fruit
    JAMU ILHA   an exotic red rose without odor

JAMURI   one hundred-quadrillionth (of a Chinese foot)
    JAMURI ILHA   hedgerose
    JAMURI ORHO   gromwell (*Lithospermum officinale*)

JAN   a whistling arrow with a bone head with holes in it

JANAMBI   to exorcise an illness by burning paper charms and by reciting incantations

JANCUHŪKAN   rather sweet

JANCUHŪN   sweet, pleasant, agreeable
    JANCUHŪN HENGKE   sweet melon (*Cucumis melo*)
    JANCUHŪN JOFOHORI   tangerine
    JANCUHŪN MURSA   carrot
    JANCUHŪN SILENGGI   sweet dew
    JANCUHŪN USIHA   chestnut
    JANCUHŪN YOO   a small boil or pustule on the skin

JANCUHŪNJE   sugar cane

JANCUHŪRI ORHO   licorice

JANG   1. ten Chinese feet; cf. *jušuru*   2. a pole used for beating criminals

JANG BITHE   accounts books

JANG JING   (onom.) the sound made by birds looking for one another

JANG LOO   elder

JANG LOO HŪWAŠAN   Buddhist abbot

JANGCI   a felt cape worn during snow or rain

JANGCIN   see *jangci*

JANGDZ   the son of a prince of the second class

JANGGA MOO   camphor tree

JANGGA NIRU   a whistling arrow with a bone head

JANGGALCAMBI   to amble (of horses)

JANGGALIBUMBI   caus. of *janggalimbi*

JANGGALIMBI   to be in dire straits, to be hard pressed

JANGGIN (章京)   1. secretary in various government organs   2. Adjutant (of a banner), BH 724, 874
    JANGGIN DELI   a large stone used to bar a gate
    JANGGIN HADAHAN   linchpin on a cart
    JANGGIN ŠUFATU   a type of turban worn by military officers in ancient times

JANGGISA   plural of *janggin*

JANGGŪWAN   pickled or preserved vegetables, melons, etc.

JANGJU   chess
    JANGJU CEKEMU   a type of velvet produced in Changchow

JANGKIRI COKO   one name for the peewit; cf. *niyo coko*

JANGKŪ   a long-handled sword

JANGLABUMBI   caus. of *janglambi*

JANGLAMBI   to beat with a pole (as a punishment)

JANGNAMBI   to take hold of

JANGTURI   a village head

JANJURI   strawberry

JANUMBI   to be spiteful, to harbor enmity

JAR   (onom.) 1. the sound made by men working hard   2. the sound made by crickets   3. the sound made by a bone-headed arrow
    JAR JAR   (onom.) the sound made by crickets
    JAR JIR   (onom.) the sound made by birds early in the morning

JARGIMA   locust, grasshopper

JARGISU   ginger produced in Fukien

JARGIYALAKŪ ASU   a type of large fishnet

JARHŪ   red wolf (*Cuon alpinus*)

JARHŪN   same as *jarhū*

JARI   a shaman's helper

JARIMBI   to chant prayers (of a shaman)

JARIN   musk
    JARIN MOO   musk tree--grows in the valleys in the region south of the Yangtze

JARJI CECIKE   one name for the oriole; cf. *gūlin cecike*

JARKIN COKO   one name for the peewit; cf. *niyo coko*

JASAK   chief of a Mongol banner
    JASAK I DANGSEI BOLGOBURE FIYENTEN (旗籍清吏司) Department of the Inner Mongols, BH 495

JASE   1. border, boundary, frontier   2. border region   3. water gate   4. palisade, barricade
    JASE JAFAMBI   to erect a barricade
    JASE JECEN   frontier, border region
    JASEI AMARGI FIYELENGGU   the Mongolian *Tetrastes bonasia*
    JASEI DUKAI JANGGIN (關口守尉) banner-chief of a frontier gate
    JASEI HAFAN   frontier official

JASELAMBI   to establish a frontier, to secure a border

JASIBUMBI   caus. of *jasimbi*

JASIGAN   1. letter, mail   2. things posted to a distant place

JASIHIYA   one name for the eastern egret; cf. *gūwasihiya*

JASIMBI   to post, to mail, to send (a letter

JASINDUMBI   to write to one another, to

correspond

JAŠU the name of the quail in early autumn; cf. *muša*

JATA mediocre (person), untalented, good-for-nothing

JAYA a birchbark canoe (with a turned-up front)

JAYABUMBI caus. of *jayambi*

JAYAMBI 1. to cut the jaw off a slaughtered animal 2. to stutter

JAYAN the termination of the dentary bone, the joint of the jaws
  JAYAN I HŪSUN with clenched teeth, obstinate

JE 1. affirmative interjection--yes 2. (short) millet (*Setaria italica*) 3. grain in general
  JE FALAN threshing floor

JE JA (onom.) the sound made by men working

JE JA SEME screaming, shouting loudly

JEBELE 1. quiver 2. right wing, right side
  JEBELE DASHŪWAN I FIYENTEN (弓矢司) Bow and Arrow Section, BH 119
  JEBELE DUBE the third *jalan* of a banner
  JEBELE GALA the right wing--i.e., the Plain Blue, Plain Red, Bordered Red and Bordered Blue
  JEBELE MEIREN the second *jalan* of a banner

JEBELETU designation of the third adjutant of a camp or battalion

JEBKELEBUMBI caus. of *jebkelembi*

JEBKELEMBI to be careful or cautious

JEBKEŠEMBI to be very cautious

JEBSEHE an insect that eats the joints on the stalks of grain

JEBUMBI caus. of *jembi*

JECEN border, frontier
  JECEN AKŪ borderless, limitless
  JECEN DALIN shore, shoreline

JECUHERI see *jecuhuri*

JECUHUNJEMBI to hesitate, to be hesitant

JECUHURI 1. hesitant, in doubt, undecided, vacillating 2. askew, crooked

JEDEBULE a meaningless word occuring at the beginning of verses of Manchu songs

JEDZ see *bukdari*

JEFOHON an exotic fruit resembling the pomelo

JEFU imperative of *jembi*

JEJA see *je ja*

JEJE father

JEKDE MOO a tree resembling the pear tree whose dark reddish bark is used for decorative purposes

JEKDUN chaste, pure, chastity, purity
  JEKDUN BE TUWAKIYAMBI to guard one's purity

JEKDUN MOO Manchurian privet (*Ligustrum lucidum*)

JEKDUN SARGAN JUI a chaste maiden

JEKDUNGGE chaste, pure; cf. *jekdun*

JEKENEMBI to go to eat

JEKENJIMBI to come to eat

JEKSE 1. a burnt over place on the steppe 2. a place not touched by rain 3. an empty place among red clouds at sunset or at dawn

JEKSIMBI 1. to dislike 2. to be timid, to be anxious, to be frightened

JEKSITEMBI to be frightened often, to be constantly anxious

JEKŠEMBI the same as *jeksimbi*

JEKŠUN sharp-tongued, caustic

JEKU grain, provisions
  JEKU AGA one of the twenty-four divisions of the solar year--falling on April twentieth or twenty-first
  JEKU BE BAICARA TINGGIN (盤糧廳) grain control office along the waterways used for grain transport
  JEKU BE FARINGGIYAMBI to cut grain and lay it out to dry
  JEKU BE KADALARA TINGGIN (糧廳) grain administration bureau
  JEKU HARA see *hara*, definition (2)
  JEKU I DOOLI (糧道台) grain intendant
  JEKU I FIYENTEN (糧儲司) office of grain matters of the Board of Revenue in Mukden
  JEKU JUWERE HAFAN BE ILGARA KUNGGERI (督糧科) office of grain administration in the Board of War
  JEKU TEKSILEHE the grain has become even--i.e., is near maturity
  JEKUI BAITA BE TEFI ICIHIYARA YAMUN (坐糧廳衙門) office of the Supervisor of Government granaries in the Capital
  JEKUI KUNGGERI (糧科) grain section in the Board of Revenues in Shensi

JEKUJU the god of millet, the shrine to the god of millet

JEKUNEMBI to swell and form pus

JELAMBI to stop (of rain), to clear up

JELBE young of the salmon trout

JELE see *jelen*

JELEME CECIKE a gray sparrow with blackish spots

JELEN hesitant, in doubt, vacillating

JELGIN see *jelgiyen*

JELGIYEN a chin strap of a hat

JELKEN a type of weasel

JELMIN rape (a vegetable), rape-seed oil--used as a hair dressing by women

JELU salmon trout (*Hucho taimen*)

J

JEMBI (1) (imperative *jefu*, -ke, -tere)
to eat
  JEKE BERI a bow on which the horn
   facing doesn't reach to the notches
   for the bowstring
  JEKE YADAHA contesting the original
   owner's right to something
  JEKE YADAHA GENEHE left without pay-
   ing attention to others
  JEKE YADAHA I BURULAHA fled without
   regard to others
  JETERE FIYANCIHIYAN NIYALMA a person
   who eats little
JEMBI (2) (-ngke, -ndere, -mpi) to
bear, to put up with, to tolerate
JEMDELEMBI to mismanage, to be corrupt,
to abuse one's responsibility
JEMDEN corruption, malpractice, mis-
management
JEME wet nurse
JEMENGGE food, foodstuffs
JEMETU LORIN mule born from a jenny ass
JEMGETU sign of misfeasance, fraud,
falsification
JEMIN a dose
JEMPI 1. patient, long-suffering 2.
perfect converb of *jembi* (2)
JEMPILEMBI to fry cakes
JEMPIN fried cakes of buckwheat or
wheat filled with meat or vegetables
  JEMPIN INENGGI the second day of
   the second month when pan-fried
   cakes are eaten
JEN ŽIN a Taoist immortal
JENDERAKŪ cannot bear, unbearable; cf.
jembi (2)
JENDERE imperfect participle of *jembi*
(2)
JENDU secretly, softly
  JENDU ALHŪDAMBI to imitate on the
   sly
  JENDU GISUREMBI to talk softly
JENDUKEN secretly on the sly, quietly
JENDUKESAKA secretly, in secret
JENDUMBI 1. to secrete, to keep secret
2. to eat one another
JENDUN secrecy, secret
JENGDZ (正字) title of one of
the heir apparent's tutors
JENGGE 1. food, provisions 2. pure,
incorruptible
JENGKE perfect participle of *jembi* (2)
JENUMBI to eat together
JEO department (a political subdivi-
sion)
  JEO I BEIDESI (州判) Second
   Class Assistant Department Magis-
   trate, BH 851A
  JEO I DOOSEDA (道正) Superior
   of the Taoist Priesthood in a
   Department, BH 573B
  JEO I ERIN SONJOSI (典術)
   Departmental Inspector of Petty

Professions, BH 851A
  JEO I HŪWAŠADA (僧正) Super-
   ior of the Buddhist Priesthood in
   a Department, BH 573A
  JEO I SARACI (知州) Department
   Magistrate, BH 855
  JEO I TACIBUKŪ HAFAN (學正)
   Departmental Director of Schools,
   BH 851A
  JEO I UHECI (州同) First
   Class Assistant Department Magis-
   trate, BH 851A
  JEO PAN (州判) Second Class
   Assistant Department Magistrate,
   BH 851A
JEOFI a hut with a round roof made of
birchbark
JEOFINGGE BOO a hermit's hut
JERDE sorrel horse
JEREMPE see *jerpe*
JEREN Mongolian gazelle, zeren (*Pro-
capra gutturosa*)
JERGI 1. rank, step, grade 2. order,
sequence 3. layer, level 4. time
5. and so forth, et cetera
  JERGI ILHI sequence, succession
  JERGI TANGKAN I ALIN a small bronze
   monument in the courtyard before
   the main throne room in Peking on
   which the ranks of officials were
   inscribed
JERGICELEMBI to rank, to put in order
JERGILEBUMBI caus. of *jergilembi*
JERGILEMBI 1. to be in order, to be
arranged according to rank 2. to
be equal to
JERGILEN ranking, ordering
JERGINGGE of the same rank, of the
same sort, of the same layer, consisting of layers
  JERGINGGE DALANGGA a dam built in
   layers resembling fish scales
  JERGINNGE HOSERI boxes containing
   food arranged layerlike on a rack
JERGIŠEMBI see *jerkišembi*
JERGUNA see *jerguwen*
JERGUWELEBUMBI caus. of *jerguwelembi*
JERGUWELEMBI to make a railing or
fence
JERGUWEN 1. railing, fence 2. the
horizontal posts of a railing 3.
the horizontal stones of a stone
railing 4. horizontal stones on the
steps to the palace
  JERGUWEN I BONGKO a railing post
   knob
  JERGUWEN I DENGJAN red lantern hung
   on the post knobs of a railing at
   New Year's
JERIN 1. edge, border 2. anvil
JERINGGE WASE tile with decorative
borders
JERKIN dazzling light

J

JERKIN ILHA   Kousa (*Cornus kousa*)

JERKINGGE ILHANGGA LOHO   a sword made of highly polished steel

JERKISEMBI   to blind (of light), to dazzle, to be dazzled

JERPE   a growth on the lip

JERUN   a measure equaling eight Chinese feet

JESERI   arrow with a bone head used for hunting birds

JETEN (軫)   the name of a constellation

    JETEN TOKDONGGO KIRU (軫 宿 旗) a banner depicting the constellation *jeten*

JEYEN   blade, sword

    JEYEN I DUBE   point (of a knife's blade)

JEYENGGE   having a blade, sword

JI GIDA   halberd

JI ILHA   safflower

JIBCA   a short fur jacket or coat

JIBCALAMBI   to wear a fur jacket or coat

JIBCAN   see *jibca*

JIBCI   pincushion, needle-cushion

JIBEGUN   having narrow eyes

JIBEHUN   1. cover, quilt   2. same as *jibegun*

JIBEREMBI (-ke)   to squint the eyes, to narrow the eyes

JIBGE   1. stingy   2. slow, negligent

JIBGEHUN   close, dense, impenetrable

JIBGESEMBI   1. to be stingy   2. to be slow, to tarry, to loiter   3. to begrudge, to keep for oneself

JIBIN   fine-meshed

    JIBIN ASU   a fine-meshed net

JIBSIBUMBI   caus. of *jibsimbi*

JIBSIGAN   see *sektefun i jibsigan*

JIBSIMBI   to lie in layers or folds, to pull over (clothes)

    JIBSIME FUSEMBI   to increase many-fold

JIBSINUMBI   to be folded over one another

JIBSIRGE   gold and silver filigree

JIBUMBI   caus. of *jimbi*

JIDERE   imperfect participle of *jimbi*: coming, future, next

    JIDERE ANIYA   next year, the coming year

    JIDERE BIYA   next month, the coming month

    JIDERE OMOLO   great-great-great-grandchild

JIDUJI   after all, finally, in fact, really, surely

JIDUN   the back side of a mountain

JIDURAMBI   to be jealous

JIFEBUMBI   caus. of *jifembi*

JIFEMBI   to fill in cracks in the hull of a boat or in a tub, to calk

JIFERE FAKSI   a calker

JIFU NUNGGELE   *Mallotopus japonicus*

JIFUBUMBI   to get stuck in wood (of saws and awls)

JIFUN   pliant, yielding, elastic

JIFUNUMBI   to be elastic, to be extendable

JIFUNURE SUKDUN   mirage

JIGANAMBI   see *jihanambi*

JIGEYEN   1. hard of hearing (because of old age)   2. slow

JIGIYEN   see *jigeyen*

JIHA   1. money, copper coin   2. a tenth of a tael

    JIHA EFIMBI   to gamble

    JIHA EFIRE FALAN   gambling hall

    JIHA FAFUN I YAMUN (錢 法 堂) Coinage Office, BH 460A

    JIHA FESHELEKU   shuttlecock made from a copper coin and feathers

    JIHA FESKU   the same as *jiha fesheleku*

    JIHA FILA   a small plate

    JIHA HUNGKERERE KŪWARAN I TAKŪRAKŪ I YAMUN (作 廠 大 使 衙 門) operations office of the mint

    JIHA I KEMNEKU   a board with a depression in it into which a certain number of coins will fit-- used for counting large numbers of coins

    JIHA ILHA   a flower of the genus *Inula*, the buds of which resemble coins

    JIHA TEKDEBUMBI   to burn sacrificial paper money

JIHANA BOJIRI ILHA   *Inula britanica*-- the same as *jiha ilha*

JIHANA COKO   Mongolian ring-necked pheasant

JIHANA YARHA   a spotted leopard

JIHANAMBI   to bloom (of grains)

JIHARI YANGGALI   the name of a small bird--the feathers around the neck resemble a string of cash

JIJI JAJA   twittering

JIJIRGAN   a poetic name for the house swallow

JIJIRI   a mat woven from fine straw-- used in summer

    JIJIRI ORHO   a type of grass (*Anthistiria ciliata*) that is used for weaving mats and shoes

JIJUBUMBI   caus. of *jijumbi*

JIJUGAN   see *jijuhan*

JIJUHAN   digram, trigram, or hexagram of the *Book of Changes*

    JIJUHAN I KUBULIN   changes of the digrams

JIJUMBI   to draw lines, to draw, to write, to cast lots

JIJUN   stroke, line, lines of a divination figure

J

JIJUNGGE pertaining to divination
JILABUMBI caus. of *jilambi*
JILABURU pitiful person
JILACUKA pitiful
JILAKAN pitiable, pitiful, poor
JILAMBI to pity, to have compassion
  for, to love
    JILAHABI "has been merciful to-
      ward"--i.e., has formed only a
      few pockmarks
JILAN 1. compassion, pity, love 2. a
  place where water doesn't freeze
  because of a fast current
    JILAN MUKENGGE KIRU (濟旗) a
      banner of the imperial escort with
      a design of flowing water depicted
      on a green background
JILANGGA compassionate, gentle
JILARI GAHA the same as *holon gaha*
JILBI see *jilbin*
JILBIMBI to sew a gold border on
  clothing
JILBIN a thin gold border
JILEHUN unabashed, audacious
JILEKUN see *jilehun*
JILERŠEMBI 1. to ignore (someone)
  deliberately, to feign ignorance
  2. to brim with tears
JILGAMBI to sound, to shout, to sing
  (of birds)
JILGAN sound, noise, voice
    JILGAN I BULEKUŠERE TOOSENGGE FUSA
      Bodhisattva Avalokiteśvara
JILGANDUMBI to shout together
JILGANGGA GASHA the name of a bird
  that sings at night--its voice can
  be heard, but its form is never
  seen
JILGIBUMBI caus. of *jilgimbi*
JILGIMBI to remove the hair from a
  hide
JILHA stamen and pistil of a flower
JILHAMBI to burn to ashes; cf. *gilgambi*
JILHANGGA ILHA the name of an exotic
  flower--its stem and leaves resemble
  the camellia, has large buds, and is
  very fragrant
JILI 1. anger, temper 2. the base of
  the horn on deer, roe, etc.
    JILI BANJICUKA annnoying, vexing
    JILI BANJIMBI to get angry
    JILI DOSOMBI to hold back one's
      anger
    JILI HATAN irascible
    JILI NUKIBUMBI to get fed up, to
      become angry
JILIDAMBI to get angry, to become mad
    JILIDAME FACIHIYAŠAMBI to become
      angry and agitated
JILIHANGGA 1. excitable 2. ardent,
  intense 3. virtuous, chaste (of
  women)

JILIHANGGA HEHE a widow who remains
  unmarried after her husband's
  death
JILIHANGGA SARGAN JUI a betrothed
  girl who commits suicide upon
  hearing of the death of her fiancé
JILINAMBI 1. for a hole to form in
  river ice 2. see *jili banjimbi*
JILKIN skein, hank, tuft, lock, strand
JILUN pitiable, poor; cf. *jilakan*
JIMA sesame
    JIMA MALANGGŪ white sesame
    JIMA ŠOBIN a baked wheaten cake
      filled with red bean paste and
      sprinkled with sesame seeds
JIMALAMBI to attach a spearhead to
  the shaft
JIMBI (imperative: *jio*, -he, -dere) to
  come, see also *jidere*
JIN see *jing*
JIN ŠI the same as *dosikasi*
JING 1. just, just at the time when,
  on the point of 2. often, fre-
  quently, all the time, keep on . . .
    JING SEME all the time, keep
      on . . .
JING JIYANG (onom.) the sound of flutes
  and stone bells
JING YANG (onom.) the sound of birds
  singing harmoniously
JINGGERI 1. a small nail with a large
  head 2. a nail on armor
    JINGGERI FANGKAMBI to drive in an
      armor nail
JINGGIYA a sty on the eye
JINGJAN small and colorless
JINGJANAMBI to be very small or short
JINGJARA 1. yellow-browed bunting
  (*Emberiza chrysophrys*) 2. the
  common sparrow
JINGJI 1. heavy, steady, firm 2.
  grave, ceremonious
JINGJING JANGJANG (onom.) 1. the
  sound of various types of flutes
  and pipes 2. the sound of a flock
  of birds singing in the springtime
JINGKINI 1. honest, upright, orderly,
  regular 2. chief, main, principal
    JINGKINI BEYE one's own person, in
      person
    JINGKINI CIFUN chief tax, main tax,
      regular tax
    JINGKINI DORON JAFAHA HAFAN chief
      magistrate
    JINGKINI ILHI chief and subordinate
    JINGKINI KADALARA DA (宗學
      總管) Director of the School
      for Imperial Clansmen; cf. BH 717
    JINGKINI UJU JERGI rank 1-A, chief
      rank of the first order
    JINGKINI WESIMBURE BITHE the
      original copy of a memorial
      (the one read by the emperor-- the

second copy went to the archives)

JINGNEMBI to advance by pairs at a
funeral to offer a libation of wine

JINGSE knob indicating rank on an official cap
  JINGSE I ALIGAN the support for a
  knob on an official cap
  JINGSE KIYAMNAMBI to attach a knob
  to an official hat
  JINGSE UMIYESUN BISIRENGGE possessing knob and sash--i.e., an official

JINGSITUN (井) the name of a constellation
  JINGSITUN TOKDONGGO KIRU (井宿
  旗) a banner with the constellation jingsitun depicted on it

JINJAHA testicles

JINJIBA white-eye, bird of the genus
Zosterops

JINJIMA lentil

JINJIRI JANJIRI (onom.) noise of a
group of children

JIO imperative of jimbi

JIR JIR SEME (onom.) 1. the sound of
bubbling water 2. the crying of
crickets, birds, or mice

JIRA close together, dense, thickly
spaced

JIRAHUN obstinate, stubborn

JIRAMIKAN rather thick

JIRAMILABUMBI caus. of jiramilambi

JIRAMILAMBI 1. to make thick, to
thicken 2. to treat generously 3.
to treat courteously

JIRAMILANJIMBI to come to treat generously

JIRAMIN 1. thick 2. generous, kind

JIREN see jerin

JIRGABUMBI caus. of jirgambi

JIRGACUN leisurely, at ease, comfortable

JIRGAMBI 1. to be at ease, to enjoy
leisure, to be comfortable 2. not
to be employed in an official capacity 3. to die (of the emperor)

JIRGEKU a sprayer used to put out fires

JIRGEMBI to twitter, to chirp

JIRGIO a kind of waterfowl

JIRHA CECIKE North China wren (Troglodytes troglodytes)

JIRI ten trillion

JIRIN see jeren

JIRUMTU SURU a fine white horse

JIRUN ten million

JISE a draft, rough draft
  JISE ICIHIYARA BOO (槁房)
  office for preparing drafts in
  the Court of Colonial Affairs

JISELEMBI to make a rough draft, to
draft

JISIHA hazelnut tree

JISUBUMBI caus. of jisumbi

JISUMBI to cut leather and similar
objects in a straight line

JIYA an emphatic sentence particle

JIYAN HOOŠAN a lip of paper

JIYANG WANG ASU a large fishnet used
from a boat in still water; cf.
horilaku asu

JIYANG ŽUNG velvet

JIYANGGIYUN 1. general 2. (將軍)
Manchu General-in-Chief, BH 744

JIYE an emphatic sentence particle

JIYEI 1. older sister, miss 2. a
tasseled tally used as an emblem by
princesses

JO a Chinese pint

JO BANJIMBI to belch, to regurgitate
acidy substances

JOBOBUMBI caus. of jobombi

JOBOCUKA causing concern, disquieting,
worrisome, distressing

JOBOCUN worry, affliction, grief,
sorrow

JOBOLON harm, trouble, disaster,
calamity, sorrow, mourning, funeral

JOBOMBI 1. to suffer, to be in need
2. to worry, to be distressed
  JOBOHO ARAMBI to compensate for
  trouble caused to someone
  JOBORO SUILARA worry and pain,
  suffering

JOBON distress

JOBORAKU ILHA an exotic flower that is
said to bloom when it is caressed
by a woman

JOBOSHUN 1. concerned, worried 2.
worry, concern

JOBOŠOMBI to suffer deeply, to be
greatly distressed, to worry much

JOCIBUMBI 1. caus. of jocimbi 2.
to harm, to reduce to dire straits,
a euphemism for 'to murder'

JOCIMBI 1. to be in need, to be at
the end of one's means 2. to be
murdered

JOCIN see jojin

JODOBA common plantain (Plantago major)

JODOBUMBI caus. of jodombi

JODOHUN CECIKE one name for the hoopoe;
cf. indahun cecike

JODOMBI 1. to weave 2. to come and go
unexpectedly, to be always coming
and going
  JODORO ARARA YAMUN (織造府)
  office of the Superintendent of
  the Imperial Manufactories
  JODORO FAKSI weaver
  JODORO ICERE KUWARAN (織染局)
  Imperial Weaving and Dyeing Office, BH 96
  JODORO WEILERE KUNGGERI (織造
  科) section on weaving and manu-
  facturing in the Board of Works

JODON grass linen

J

JODONGGA CECE gauze of coarse linen

JODORGAN USIHA "the weaving girl"-- the star Vega in the constellation Lyra

JODORHO a kind of aquatic plant

JOFOHO 1. point, edge 2. corner, angle 3. harpoon for spearing fish
    JOFOHO ACABUMBI to match the points

JOFOHOCI shaddock (*Citrus decumana*)

JOFOHON pomelo

JOFOHONGGO pointed, projecting

JOFOHORI citrus fruit, orange, tangerine
    JOFOHORI ŠATAN orange cake

JOFOHOTO *Citrus acida*

JOHIBUMBI caus. of *johimbi*

JOHIMBI to heal (of a boil or sore)

JOHOLIMBI (-ka) to be pudgy, to be flabby

JOHOMBI to belch, to burp

JOJIN 1. horse's bit 2. a mistaken spelling for *jorin*, q.v.
    JOJIN BE SUDAMIMBI to slacken the reins
    JOJIN I SONGGIHA crossbar

JOJINGGA pertaining to a bit

JOK SEME abruptly, suddenly (of stopping)

JOKJABUMBI caus./pass. of *jokjambi*

JOKJAMBI to thrash (as punishment), to chastise

JOKSI a wooden dipper without a handle

JOKSIKŪ a small hatchet with a curved blade

JOKSILAMBI to stuff oneself, to be a glutton

JOKSINAMBI to be overweight, to eat to excess

JOKSON 1. first stage, beginning, inception 2. at first 3. skinny (of horses)

JOKTONDA Japanese lily (*Lilium japonicum*)

JOKŪ fodder knife

JOLABUMBI see *joolabumbi*

JOLACAMBI to bow, to stoop, to be obsequious

JOLAMBI same as *joolambi*

JOLBONOMBI to get dull

JOLDOMBI to buy back things one has given or sold to someone else, to redeem one's former goods

JOLFO oyster

JOLGOCOMBI to press forward in a rage, to stampede, to rush off in a fury

JOLHOCOMBI see *jolgocombi*

JOLHOMBI to gush up, to well up

JOLI a ladle with many small holes in it used for straining

JOLIBUMBI caus. of *jolimbi*

JOLIGAN ransom money, ransom

JOLIKŪ see *joolikū*

JOLIMBI 1. to redeem, to ransom 2. to row

JOLINAMBI to go to redeem

JOLINJIMBI to come to redeem

JOLO 1. doe, female deer 2. hateful, hideous
    JOLO BUHŪ doe, female deer

JOMAN edge, seam, end
    JOMAN ACABUMBI to join (folded) edges (in sewing)

JOMBI (1) (-ho, -ro) to cut with a fodder knife

JOMBI (2) (-ngko, -ndoro, -mpi) 1. to bring to mind, to recall, to mention, to bring up 2. to move in the womb

JOMBUMBI 1. caus./pass. of *jombi* (2) 2. to remind, to suggest, to advise to

JON memory, recall

JONDOBUMBI caus. of *jondombi*

JONDOMBI to recall to mind, to mention, to bring up, to concentrate on

JONG JONG SEME grumbling, complaining
    JONG JONG SEME GASAMBI to grumble from discontent

JONGDON bright satin with gold threads woven through it

JONGGINAMBI to knit the brow from anxiety

JONI the name of the magpie in the Kanjur

JONOMBI the same as *jondombi*

JOO 1. an imperial order 2. interjection: enough! stop! it won't do!
    JOO BAI interjection: enough! stop!
    JOO ELE OHO KAI that's enough! sufficient!
    JOO SIOWAN HAFAN (招宣) commander of the military police

JOOBAI same as *joo bai*

JOOCIN see *jojin*

JOOCINA let it be!

JOOKŪ see *jokū*

JOOLABUMBI to turn over one's duty to another at the relief time

JOOLACAMBI see *jolacambi*

JOOLAMBI 1. to join the hands as greeting 2. to put the hands behind the back or into the sleeves

JOOLI a bamboo ladle for lifting things from water; cf. *hereku*

JOOLIBUMBI caus./pass. of *joolimbi*

JOOLIGAN ransom, redemption payment

JOOLIKŪ oar

JOOLIMBI 1. to ransom, to redeem 2. to row

JOOLINAMBI to go to redeem

JOOLINGGA pertaining to ransom, ransom money

JOOLINJIMBI to come to redeem

JOOMAN 1. the base of a fingernail 2. see *joman*

JOOMBI 1. see *jombi* (1) 2. to cease, to desist

JOR (onom.) the sound of many humans, dogs, chickens, or animals screaming

JOR JAR (onom.) the sound of people or birds screaming

JORAN amble (of a horse)

JORAN MORIN ambling horse

JORDABUMBI caus. of *jordambi*

JORDAMBI to amble (horses and mules)

JORGIMBI to chirp, to twitter, to hum

JORGINDUMBI to chirp, to hum (of a group of birds or insects)

JORGIRHEN lesser skylark (*Alauda arvensis*)

JORGON BIYA the twelfth month

JORGON INENGGI the eighth day of the twelfth month

JORHO a pointed arrowhead with holes on each side

JORHO CECIKE one name for the wren; cf. *jirha·cecike*

JORHO FODOHO *Salix gracilistyla*--a type of willow from which arrow shafts were made

JORHO SINGGERI mole

JORIBUMBI caus. of *jorimbi*

JORIKŪ pointer, index finger

JORILAMBI the same as *jorišambi*

JORIMBI 1. to point, to indicate, to point out 2. to aim 3. to use a pretext

JORIRE SIMHUN the index finger

JORIN 1. aim, goal 2. intent, meaning, elucidation

JORIN I GISUN words of elucidation or direction (on a document)

JORIN SAIN good shot, steady aim

JORINGGA theme (on an examination)

JORINGGA HOOŠAN examination paper

JORINGGA I ACABUN the second part of a formal essay (immediately following the *joringga i faksabun*)

JORINGGA I FAKSABUN the first two sentences of a formal essay

JORINGGA I TUCIBUN the section following the introduction (*deribume fiyentehe*) in a formal essay

JORINGGA I YARUN the part of an official essay following the opening expositon (*deribume giyangnan*)

JORISI magistrate

JORIŠAMBI to point out continually, to indicate continually, to give guidance

JORO a type of arrow with a horn head

JORON wild beans (*Lophatherum gracile*)--a straight plant with large leaves and flowers resembling the blooms of the bean plant--it is used as feed for horses

JORTAI 1. deliberately, willfully 2. pretending

JORTANGGI the same as *jortai*

JOTOMBI to be always coming and going

JU 1. imperative of *jimbi* 2. a musical instrument in the shape of a square peck measure--it was used as a signal for other musical instruments to begin

JU SY MUKE I SEKIYEN GOLMIN I MUDAN a musical piece used by the board of rites when it entertained the hereditary duke who was a descendant of Confucius

JUBEN story, tale

JUBEN ALAMBI to tell a story

JUBENGGE tale-carrier

JUBESI storyteller

JUBEŠEMBI to slander someone behind his back

JUBKI an islet in a river, a sand bar

JUBU (主 簿) clerk, recorder, registrar; cf. *dangse jafašakū*

JUBUNGGA pertaining to a clerk

JUBUNGGE see *jubengge*

JUBURAMBI see *jiberembi*

JUBURŠEMBI to get diphtheria, to get an inflammation of the throat

JUBUŠEMBI to ponder, to judge

JUCE 1. pond, pool (with clear, deep water) 2. a guard post, checkpoint, police precinct

JUCE TEMBI to stand watch, to stand guard duty

JUCELEBUMBI caus. of *jucelembi*

JUCELEMBI to stand guard, to stand a watch

JUCEN see *juce*

JUCERHEN a leather line attached to a saddle at the place where the pommel and the frame of the saddle join

JUCIBA firefly

JUCUBA see *juciba*

JUCULEMBI to sing Chinese opera, to act

JUCULESI actor, opera performer

JUCUMA a face mask worn as a protection against small insects

JUCUN play, opera, theatrical performances

JUCUN I HŪFAN a theatrical troupe

JUCUNGGE pertaining to the stage, theatrical

JUCUNGGE KARAN stage

JUDA ten Chinese feet

JUDUN the ridge of a mountain

JUDURA a domestic pig colored like a wild pig

JUDURA IHAN a cow with a white stripe down the spine

JUDURAKŪ striped silk

JUDURAME along the ridge of a mountain

JUDURAN 1. stripe, line 2. the grooves on a file 3. fold, crease

JUFELIYEBUMBI caus. of *jufeliyembi*

J

J

JUFELIYEMBI to prepare dried provi-
  sions for a long journey
JUFELIYEN dried provisions used on a
  long journey
JUGEMBI to offer sacrifice to the Big
  Dipper at night
JUGŪN 1. road, way, street 2. the
  name for a province during Sung and
  Yüan times
  JUGŪN CINGGIYA the way is short
  JUGŪN GIYAI BE KADALARA TINGGIN
  (街道廳) Roadway Office,
    BH 796A
  JUGŪN GIYAI BE KADALARA TINGGIN I
  HAFAN (街道廳) head of
    the Roadway Office
  JUGŪN I ANDALA on the way, along
    the way
  JUGŪN I YARUN a road pass carried
    by officials
  JUGŪN MALHŪN the way is unexpectedly
    long
  JUGŪN NEIMBI to open a way (by
    force)
  JUGŪN YABUMBI to travel
  JUGŪN YABURE ANDALA halfway along
    (on a trip)
 JUHE ice
  JUHE AKIYAHABI "the ice has
    dried"--i.e., has frozen solid
  JUHE DUKDUREKEBI the ice has swol-
    len up, the ice has formed a
    raised spot
  JUHE FUSEJEHE the ice has become
    brittle
  JUHE HUJUREMBI the ice grinds to-
    gether (in the spring when it
    starts to melt)
  JUHE JAFAHA the ice has frozen
    solid
  JUHE OROME GECEHEBI the ice has
    formed a thin crust (a thin crust
    of ice has formed on the surface
    of water)
  JUHE SICAKABI the ice has cracked
  JUHE SULHUMBI the ice is thawing
  JUHE ŠATAN sugar-candy
  JUHE TUHEKE the ice has fallen
    (into the water at the thaw)
 JUHEN SINGGERI mammoth frozen in the
  ice in Siberia
JUHENEMBI to form ice
JUHIYAN a precious head ornament made
  of pearls and other jewels
  JUHIYAN I DA (朱顯達) chief
    of workers who searched for fish,
    pearls, honey, ginseng, etc.
 JUI 1. child 2. son
  JUI JALAN the generation of one's
    children (including nephews and
    nieces)
  JUI JONGKO the child has moved in
    the womb

JUI TAKSIHA has become pregnant
JUINGGE pertaining to children or
  sons
JUJIN a name for the peacock; cf.
  kundujin; tojin
JUJU JAJA with a lot of useless
  chatter
JUJUMBI to mark out a line with a
  needle in sewing
JUJURAMBI to act in a petty way, to be
  small about things
JUKDEN a plant resembling the wild
  grape (Vitis labrusa) from which red
  dye is produced
JUKE a type of cake made of crumbled
  toholiyo cakes
  JUKE EFEN the same as juke
JUKEN 1. ordinary, everyday, plain
  2. just enough, just right
  JUKEN ISIKA just sufficient
  JUKEN SAIN just right
JUKIBUMBI caus. of jukimbi
JUKIDUN partridge (Perdix daurica)
JUKIMBI to stop up, to fill in, to
  plug up
JUKIMBUMBI see jukibumbi
JUKJA see jokja
JUKJAMBI see jokjambi
JUKJUHU NIYEHE a black-footed wild
  duck that is very good at diving
JUKTE long, thick piece
JUKTEHEN temple, shrine
  JUKTEHEN I SARASI (知觀)
    assistant to the priest in charge
    of a Taoist temple
JUKTELEBUMBI caus. of juktelembi
JUKTELEMBI to cut into small slices
  or pieces
JUKTEMBI to offer sacrifice to
JUKTEN sacrifice, offering
  JUKTEN BE ALIHA HAFAN (主祠)
    master of ceremonies (at a sacri-
    fice)
  JUKTEN I BOO shrine where offerings
    were made to one's ancestors or
    famous men
  JUKTEN I USIN land belonging to a
    temple
JUKTESI sacrificial attendant
JUKTU stout, developed, strong
JUKTURI a two-year-old bear
JULAN a place in a river where the fast
  current precludes freezing in winter
JULEFUN for his sake, in his stead
  (used in prayers for terei jalin)
JULEHEN see emu julehen
JULEN story, tale
  JULEN ALAMBI to tell a story
  JULEN BITHE book of stories, novel
JULERGI 1. front, in front of, before
  2. south
  JULERGI BITHEI BOO (南書房)
    the name of a study used by the

emperor

JULERGI COLHON I KIRU a banner depicting the southern holy mountain

JULERGI FISEMBUHE BOO a veranda in
front of a house

JULERGI HECEN the southern part of
a city

JULERGI ICE CALU a storehouse in
Peking belonging to the Board of
Finance

JULERGI JUWERE JEKUI KUNGGERI
(南漕科) office of grain
transport in Yunnan

JULERGI KŪWARAN I CALU (南館
倉) a storehouse in Mukden

JULERGI NAHAN a *kang* on the south
wall

JULERI front, in front

JULERI YARHŪDAN (洗馬) an
official in Supervisorate of Imperial Instruction

JULESI forward, toward the front,
southward

JULESI BUMBI to offer an animal in
sacrifice; cf. *metembi*

JULESIKEN a little bit forward

JULETUN ancient vessels and objects

JULGE antiquity, ancient times

JULGECI EBSI from antiquity until
now

JULGEI ULASI monument of antiquity

JULGEN good fortune, lucky chance

JULGEN SAIN "luck was good"--said
of a safe return from a journey
or a hunt

JULGUME short boots worn by women

JULGŪ see *julhū*

JULHUN see *julkun*

JULHŪ reins

JULHUMBI to polish an arrow shaft
with wood filings, hair, or lint

JULIBUMBI to become swollen

JULIMBI (-ka) to swel.

JULISHŪN swollen

JULIYAMBI to spit out something one
can't chew

JULKIYEMBI see *jukimbi*

JULKUN 1. the depression at the base
of the neck or throat 2. depression
on the chest of animals

JULUNGGA docile, obedient

JUMALAMBI to attach a spearhead to
a shaft

JUMAN a level area above the opening
on a stove

JUMANGGA ILHA the name of an exotic
blue flower

JUMANGGI a small bag

JUMANGGILAMBI to put in a small bag

JUMARA suslik (*Citellus dauricus*)

JUMARGAN another name for the suslik;
cf. *jumara*

JUMBALI right in

JUMBI (-nggke, -mpi) to clench the
teeth

JUN 1. stove, hearth 2. tissue,
pulp of a tree 3. vein

JUN EJEN the kitchen god, the god
of the hearth

JUN I BILHA smoke outlet of a stove

JUN I EJEN the kitchen god

JUN I NUHALIYAN a depressed area
near the opening of a stove

JUN I ŠENGGIN an area jutting out
on the front of a stove--used for
adding fuel

JUN I WECEN sacrifice to the
kitchen god

JUN TONGGO strong three-strand
thread

JUNAFI the same as *juwe nofi*

JUNARA one name for the partridge; cf.
jukidun

JUNG bell--the same as *jungken*

JUNG YUWAN the Yellow River Plain

JUNGGALA the inside of a stove--the
firebox

JUNGGE veined

JUNGGE SUJE veined silk

JUNGGE SURI veined satin

JUNGGEBUMBI caus. of *junggembi*

JUNGGEMBI to transfer a person's
possessions to another place secretly

JUNGGIDEI KIYOO a sedan chair used by
the imperial concubines that was
carried by sixteen men

JUNGGILA GASHA one name for the turkey; cf. *ildedei*

JUNGGIN brocade

JUNGGIN ABUHA ILHA a type of
swallow (*Malva sylvestris*)

JUNGGINAMBI to become like brocade--
to get furrows on the forehead, to
worry

JUNGGINGGE HOOŠAN "brocade paper"--
a strong paper with a pattern on it

JUNGGIRI COKO the golden pheasant
(*Chrysolophus pictus*)

JUNGGISUN the same as *garunggū*

JUNGGISUN COKO a type of phoenix
resembling the pheasant

JUNGGISUN ILHA *Diervilla ambiflora*

JUNGGITU an ancient name for the
pheasant

JUNGGUHE a spotted myna

JUNGKEN bell

JUNGKEN MUCIHIYANGGA FUKJINGGA HER-
GEN (鐘鼎篆) a style of
calligraphy

JUNGKENGGE 1. a measure of volume
equaling six bushels and four pecks
2. pertaining to a bell

JUNGŠU (中書) Secretary of the
Grand Secretariat, BH 137

JUNGŠUN water or wine poured in a

J

sacrificial pig's ear

JUNIHIN a type of ancient land tax

JUNINGGE a measure of volume equaling 18 pecks

JUNIRU a measure of length equaling 16 Chinese feet

JUNOFI *juwe nofi*

JUNTA an animal path

JURAMBI (-ka, -ndara) to set out, to begin a journey

JURAMBUMBI 1. caus. of *jurambi* 2. to send on one's way

JURAN point of departure, place from where a journey begins

JURANUMBI to set out together

JURCEBUMBI caus. of *jurcembi*

JURCEHEN disobedient, obstinate

JURCEMBI to disobey, to go against, to go against one's word, to turn the back on, to oppose (in battle)

JURCEN disobedience

JURCENDUMBI/JURCENUMBI to oppose one another

JURCENJEMBI to resist one another, to turn the back on one another

JURCIT Jurcen, the rulers of the Chin dynasty and ancestors of the Manchus

JURGALAMBI 1. to make lines, stripes or creases 2. to form lines or stripes 3. to mark lines on cloth (of tailors)

JURGAN 1. line, column, row 2. the right, loyalty, duty, devotedness 3. ministry, board

JURGAN BE FEKUMBI to fail in one's duty

JURGAN BE YABUBUMBI to perform one's duty

JURGAN I AMA foster father

JURGAN JORIMBI to command (an army)

JURGAN JURGAN line by line, row by row, column by column

JURGAN SINGGERI a type of short-tailed rodent--when a number of them move, they align themselves by carrying the tail of the one ahead in their mouths

JURGAN TONDO the trajectory is straight (of an arrow shot from horseback)

JURGANGGA 1. honorable, loyal, upright, righteous 2. for the public benefit

JURGANGGA GASHA one name for the wild goose

JURGANGGA HAHA a widower who has not remarried after the death of his wife

JURGANGGA HEHE a widow who has not remarried after the death of her husband; cf. *jalangga hehe, ilihangga hehe*

JURGANGGA INENGGI the day on which the sixty-day cycle begins anew

JURGANGGA SAISA an honorable man, a devoted generous person

JURGANGGA TACIKŪ a free school

JURGANGGA YABUN a proper act, an act of loyalty

JURGATU GASHA one name for the ptarmigan

JURGIMBI 1. to chop down a tree by chopping from two sides 2. see *jorgimbi*

JURGUNTU CECIKE a bird resembling the magpie with black beak and tail and striped wings

JURHA USIHA the constellations Cancer and Leo

JURHU colored coarse linen cloth

JURHU FUNGKU a towel made of colored coarse linen cloth

JURHU SURI a cloth made partly of silk and partly of colored coarse grass linen

JURHUN a Chinese inch; cf. *tsun*

JURJUN a game resembling backgammon; cf. *šuwanglu*

JURJUN CECIKE one name for the goatsucker; cf. *simari cecike*

JURSAN GIO a one-year-old roe

JURSI Borneo camphor

JURSU 1. two-layered, double, complex, complicated 2. pregnant

JURSU ETUKU padded clothing, clothing made of two layers

JURSU MULU MOO a piece of wood nailed over the foot of a ship's support

JURSU OMBI to become pregnant

JURSU OYO a felt cover for the smoke hole of a yurt

JURSU SIJIGIYAN a padded gown

JURSULEBUMBI caus. of *jursulembi*

JURSULEMBI to double, to add a layer to, to fold over, to be doubled

JURU 1. pair, doubled 2. even (number)

JURU ACABUMBI to become man and wife

JURU BIYA even-numbered months

JURU GARGAN doubled and single, even and odd

JURU GISUN a matched couplet

JURU GISUN I DENGJAN a matched couplet hung on the "myriad year lantern" in the palace during the first month

JURU HOLBON joining in pairs

JURU KOTOLI JAHŪDAI a "double-sailed ship"--the name of a large warship

JURU MUDURINGGA SUWAYAN ŠUN DALIKŪ a parasol of the escort with a pair of dragons embroidered on it

JURU NIYAMAN parents

JURU SIRHA the stars *alpha* and *beta*

J

of Ursa Minor

JURU SONGGIHA FITHEKU BERI a crossbow with a double mechanism

JURU USIHA the stars *alpha* and *beta*
of Ursa Minor

JURUCILEN a text of paired couplets
of four or six words

JURUKEN in pairs, paired

JURULEBUMBI caus. of *jurulembi*

JURULEMBI to make a pair, to pair, to
join in pairs

JURUMBI to vomit

JURUME ILIMBI to stand with head
hanging down (horses)

JURUN a rat- or mousehole

JURUNGGE GASHA one name for the mandarin duck; cf. *ijifun niyehe*

JUSE the plural of *jui*

JUSE BAYAN children are many, having many children

JUSE DASU children

JUSE DEOTE sons and younger brothers, youngsters

JUSE JIRA children are closely
spaced

JUSE OMOSI sons and grandsons--
descendants

JUSEI HALBULHA a lair where kidnap-
ped children are kept

JUSEKI childish, juvenile

JUSETU MOO *Ixora chinensis*

JUSHE the vine of cucurbitaceous plants

JUSIHUN see *jušuhun*

JUSIKŪ see *jusukū*

JUSIN see *jušen*

JUSKU see *jusukū*

JUSTALABUMBI caus. of *justalambi*

JUSTALAMBI to make into strips

JUSTAN a strip, a stripe, any elongated
object

JUSTAN I FEMPI a strip used for
sealing houses or vessels

JUSTANGGA SORO striped jujube

JUSUBUMBI caus. of *jusumbi*

JUSUKŪ a block of lead used for drawing lines on paper

JUSUMBI to draw a line (on paper)

JUŠA cinnabar

JUŠEMBI (-ke) to sour, to have a sour
stomach

JUŠEMBUMBI caus. of *jušembi*

JUŠEMPE alkekengi, Chinese lantern
plant (*Physalis alkekengi*)

JUŠEN serf of the Manchus

JUŠEN BOO serf's quarters

JUŠEN HALANGGA NIYALMA a serf of
the Manchus

JUŠUCI lemon

JUŠUHE a small wild pear the skin of
which is used as a medicine

JUŠUHUKEN rather sour

JUŠUHUN sour

JUŠUHUN JOFOHORI an orange

JUŠUHUN MUYARI an exotic sour fruit
about the size of a chestnut--
Nephelium lappaceum

JUŠUHURI an exotic sour fruit

JUŠUK a sour fruit about the size of
an egg that grows in South China

JUŠUN vinegar

JUŠUN MUKE "vinegar water"--a drink
made of cucumbers, vegetables, and
cabbage

JUŠURI fruit of the *Prunus mume*

JUŠURU a Chinese foot, ruler

JUŠUTU *Prunus tomentosa*

JUŠUTUN an exotic fruit grown in
Szechuan

JUTEO scroll

JUTUHAN a five-stringed musical instrument played with a bamboo pick

JUTUNGGA JODON a piece of coarse grass
linen sufficient for the production
of two articles of clothing

JUTURI CECIKE one of the names of the
hawfinch; cf. *yacin ūn cecike*

JUWABUMBI caus. of *juwambi*

JUWAJIRI ORHO *Pinellia tuberifera*

JUWALI a small green frog

JUWAMBI (-ngka, -mpi) to open the
mouth

JUWAN 1. ten 2. biography, account

JUWAN BIYA the tenth month, ten
months

JUWAN BOOI DA chief of ten house-
holds in a village

JUWAN CIKTEN the ten earth's stems
(地支)

JUWAN I DA (護軍校) Lieu-
tenant, BH 734

JUWAN JAKŪN SIMNERE BOO (十八
房) the eighteen examination
rooms at the national examination
hall

JUWAN JUWE GARGAN the twelve heav-
en's branches (天干)

JUWAN JUWE TUHEBUKU I MAHATU an ancient-style hat with twelve pendants

JUWAN JUWE UJU BITHE the twelve
divisions of the Manchu syllabary

JUWAN TUMEN one hundred thousand

JUWANCI tenth

JUWANDA chief of ten, decurion

JUWANGDUWAN colored satin with gold
threads inwoven

JUWANGGA preserved cucumbers

JUWANGGERI ten times

JUWANTA ten each

JUWARAN see *joran*

JUWARANTAMBI see *jordambi*

JUWARI summer

JUWARI BE BODORO HAFAN (夏官
正) Astronomer for the Summer,
BH 229

JUWARI DOSIKA one of the twenty-

J

four solar divisions of the year
falling on May 6 or 7

JUWARI GŪLDARGAN one name for the
western house swallow; cf. *gūl-*
dargan

JUWARI TEN the summer solstice

JUWARIKTEN the summer sacrifice to the
ancestors

JUWARINGGA JUNGGIDEI the mountain
pheasant with its summer plumage

JUWATA ten each

JUWE two

JUWE BIYA the second month, two
months

JUWE DUBE ŠOLONGGO pointed at both
ends

JUWE IRUNGGE MAHATUN an ancient-
style hat with two ridges on top

JUWE JEYENGGE SUHE a double-edged
ax

JUWE MURU the two regulators--yin
and yang

JUWE NOFI two persons, two people

JUWE SIDENDE between two

JUWE UJAN both ends

JUWE UJAN ŠOLONGGO the same as
juwe dube šolonggo

JUWEBUMBI caus. of *juwembi*

JUWECI second

JUWEDEMBI to lean to two sides, to be
conflicting, to contain contradic-
tion, to contradict oneself, to act
in a contradictory way

JUWEDEME ILADAME in an undecided
manner, in a vacillating manner

JUWEDERAKŪ loyal, consistent, un-
contradictory

JUWEMBI to transport, to ship, to
transfer, to move

JUWERE BIRAI ANGGA canal junction

JUWERE DATA banner chiefs

JUWERE HAFAN transport official

JUWERE HAFASI bannermen

JUWERE JEKU tribute grain

JUWERE JEKUI BAITA BE TEFI ICIHIYARA
HAFAN (坐糧廳) Supervisor

of the Government Granaries at the
Capital, BH 565

JUWERE JEKUI BAITA BE UHERI KADALARA
AMBAN (漕運總督) Dir-
ector-General of Grain Transport,
BH 834

JUWERE JEKUI CALU a granary located
in Honan

JUWERE NIYALMA grain porter

JUWEN earnings, loan

JUWEN BUMBI to lend, to give on
loan

JUWEN GAIMBI to borrow

JUWEN SINDAMBI the same as *juwen*
bumbi

JUWEN USEN loans and debts

JUWENGGERI twice

JUWENUSI porter, stevedore, one who
loads grain at a water lock

JUWERGE a two-stringed musical instrument

JUWETE two each

JUYEDUN one name for the partridge;
cf. *jukidun*

JUYEHEN YALI the meat on both sides of
the tendons on the spine

JUYEMBI (-ke) to become difficult to
open (of the jaws)

JUYEN a short padded cotton jacket

JY CUWANG NIMEKU hemorrhoids

JY GI a long-tailed pheasant; cf.
nikan ulhūma

JY JEO (知州) Department
Magistrate, BH 855

JYFU (知府) Prefect BH 848

JYHIYAN (知縣) District Magistrate, BH 856

JYJEO see *jy jeo*

JYJOO BITHE license, authorization,
pass

JYŠI (知事) 1. Archivist, BH
830A 2. Deputy Police Superintendent

JYTU the fourth note in the classic
pentatonic scale

K

KAB KIB SEME snapping at each other
  (of dogs fighting or biting)
KAB SEME snapping, biting (of a pack
  of dogs)
KABA in pairs, paired
   KABA BOJIRI ILHA a double chrysan-
     themum
   KABA JUI twin
KABALAMBI to form a pair
KABANGGA JUI twin; cf. *kaba jui*
KABARABUMBI see *kaparabumbi*
KABARI 1. a Pekingese dog 2. a growth
  on the noses of horses and donkeys
   KABARI INDAHŪN Pekingese dog
   KABARI TUWAMBI to make bubbles (of
     fish in the water)
KABCIHŪN flat, level
KABKAŠAMBI to answer impudently, to
  talk back to
KABSITAMBI to speak foolishly, to
  answer disrespectfully
KABUMBI caus./pass. of *kambi*
KACANG SEME hard (of foods), sound made
  when hitting something hard
   KACANG SEME MANGGA stiff and hard
KACAR KICIR (onom.) 1. sound of walk-
  ing on gravel 2. sound of biting
  something hard or gritty
KACAR SEME not cooked soft, hard and
  stiff, coarse and hard
KACIKI a ragged coat of deer or roe
  hide
KACILAN an arrow used for target prac-
  tice
KADALABUMBI caus./pass. of *kadalambi*
KADALACI (主管) administrator
KADALAKŪ manager, director
KADALAMBI to administer, to manage, to
  control, to rule
   KADALAME BOŠORO BA (督惟圻)
     Office of Encitement, BH 493
   KADALAME SIMNERE HAFAN (監臨
     官) Supervisor (of an examina-
     tion), BH 652F

KADALAN 1. administration, control
  2. a rectangular-shaped seal used
  by high provincial officials, BH 984
KADALANGGA (總共) Brigade Gen-
  eral, BH 751
KADALASI see *dabsun juwere kadalasi*
KADALATU (管勾) clerk of a
  Confucian temple
KADARAKŪ daring, brave
KADURAMBI to contest, to dispute with
KADURŠAMBI to be always disputing
KAFUR KIFUR 1. agile, quick 2. (onom.)
  the sound made in stepping on snow
  or ice
KAFUR SEME 1. (onom.) the sound of
  walking on ice or snow (crunching)
  2. decisive, straightforward, with-
  out further ado
   KAFUR SEME MOKCOHO broke with a
     snap
   KAFUR SEME YABUMBI to act in a
     straightforward manner
KAI sentence particle showing emphasis
KAICA a basket made of birchbark
KAICABUMBI caus. of *kaicambi*
KAICAMBI to shout, to yell
   KAICAME INJEMBI to laugh loudly, to
     guffaw
KAICAN 1. shouting, yelling 2. the
  shouting of hunters on a battue
  after roe
KAICANDUMBI/KAICANUMBI to shout to-
  gether
KAICARI see *kaiciri*
KAICI border
   KAICI ACAMBI to patrol the area
     between two guard posts
KAICIRI a box that hangs from the belt
  for holding toothpicks and ear
  cleaners
KAIDEO see *kaidu*
KAIDU lone (horse), single (horse)
   KAIDU MORIN I YABUMBI for a single
     rider to ride along on a lone

horse

KAIKADA askance

KAIKAMARI see *kaikari*

KAIKARAMBI to be slanted or crooked, to look at askance

　　KAIKARAFI TUWAMBI to look at askance

KAIKARI white mother-of-pearl used for buttons of rank

KAIKATA see *kaikada*

KAILAN a type of large river turtle

KAILARI ORHO *Leonurus sibiricus*--a medicinal herb

KAILUN a brown horse with black mane and tail

　　KAILUN NIONGNIYAHA a brown wild goose

KAIPI a covered basket made of willow branches used to hold sewing materials

KAITU see *kaidu*

KAJAMBI to break with the teeth

KAJILAN see *kacilan*

KAKA feces of children

KAKA FAKA (onom.) the sound of many people laughing

KAKA KIKI (onom.) the sound of happy laughter

KAKABUMBI caus. of *kakambi*

KAKAMBI to defecate (of children)

KAKARI FAKARI (onom.) the sound of many people laughing

KAKI 1. violent, quick-tempered, strong (of liquor) 2. small, narrow (of clothing), cramped

KAKIRI *Zanthoxylum piperitum*--an aromatic tree

KAKITU a tight-fitting sleeveless jacket

KAKSAHA one name for the magpie; cf. *saksaha*

KAKSIMBI 1. to cough up (blood or phlegm) 2. to loosen something tangled

KAKŪ water gate, lock

　　KAKŪ UNDEHEN the horizontal boards in a water gate that cut off the flow of water

KAKŪNG KIKUNG (onom.) the sound made by a heavily loaded cart or by a heavy load

KAKŪNG SEME gritting the teeth, with hate, with effort

KAKŪR (onom.) the sound of gritting the teeth

　　KAKŪR KIKŪR (onom.) the sound made by ropes and pegs when securing a load on a wagon

KALANG (onom.) the sound of metal or stone objects banging together

　　KALANG KILING (onom.) the same as *kalang*

KALAR KALAR (onom.) the sound of metal objects hitting one another

KALAR KILIR (onom.) the sound of keys or small bells jingling

KALAR SEME kindly, courteously, harmoniously

KALBI see *kalbin*

KALBIKŪ an arrow with a small head and a slender shaft used for shooting at distant targets

KALBIMBI to shoot a *kalbikū*

KALBIN the lower part of the belly

　　KALBIN TUCIKE the belly has protruded--to have a paunch

KALBIYAMBI see *kalbimbi*

KALCA see *kalja*

KALCUHŪN having a broad forehead

KALCUN spirit, energy

　　KALCUN SAIN in good spirits

KALCUNGGI high-spirited, energetic, full of vitality

KALFIMBI the same as *kalbimbi*

KALFIN 1. the distance the *kalbikū* is shot 2. see *kalbin*

KALFINI sea flounder, flatfish

　　KALFINI MUDAN ILHA bleeding-heart (*Dicentra spectabilis*)

KALFIYAMBI see *kalbimbi*

KALFIYAN see *halfiyan*

KALIBUMBI caus. of *kalimbi*

KALIMBI to soar, to glide (of hawks, etc.)

KALIMU whale

KALJA 1. a white stripe or a bare strip on the head of an animal 2. white spot on a horse's nose 3. bald head

　　KALJA SEBERI MORIN a horse with white feet and a white spot on the forehead

　　KALJA SELE the horizontal piece of iron on a bridle that goes over the nostrils

KALJAKŪ WEIJUN one name for the stork; cf. *weijun*

KALJANGGA IJIFUN NIYEHE a mandarin duck with white stripes

KALJU ski pole (the end of the pole is shaped like a spoon)

KALKA shield

　　KALKA GIDA shields and spears--metaphor for war

KALKANGGA pertaining to a shield

　　KALKANGGA COOHA troops carrying shields

　　KALKANGGA LOHO a sword carried along with a shield

KALTARA 1. a brown horse with white around the mouth and eyes 2. slick, shining (of bird's feathers)

　　KALTARA NIYEHE mallard; cf. *borjin niyehe*

KALTARABUMBI 1. caus./pass. of *kaltarambi* 2. to suffer a fall (by slipping)

K

KALTARAMBI to slip (and fall)
KALTARASHŪN slippery
KALTARŠAMBI to be slippery
 KALTARŠARA BA a slippery spot
KALTASHŪN 1. on bad terms with 2.
 adversary, opponent
KALTU MULTU just, almost, almost with-
 in reach but not quite
KALU MULU coarse, careless
KALUMIMBI to pierce the skin but not
 the flesh (of an arrow)
KAMBI 1. to surround, to lay siege
 2. to obstruct, to ward off, to stop,
 to impede
 KAME ABALAMBI to go on the winter
  hunt
 KAME GISUREMBI to hinder someone
  from speaking, to interrupt some-
  one
KAMBULJAMBI to be soft and damp (the
 earth), to be swampy
KAMCIBUMBI caus. of *kamcimbi*
KAMCIMBI to place close together, to
 be together, to be in the same place,
 to serve concurrently, to act at the
 same time, to be placed together
KAMCIN concurrent, consolidated, in
 one place
KAMKŪ a brown silk from which hats
 were made
KAMNI a narrow pass, a strategic pass
KAMNIBUMBI caus./pass. of *kamnimbi*
KAMNIMBI to sew together, to bring
 together, to put back together, to
 close (the eyelids or lips)
 KAMNIME TABUMBI to button up
KAMTU felt hat, felt liner in a helmet
KAMTUN a coarse silken cloth used for
 tying the hair in ancient times
KANAGAN pretext, pretense, excuse
 KANAGAN ARAMBI to make excuses
KANAHAN see *kanagan*
KANCAMBI see *kanjambi*
KANDA the soft skin under the neck of
 a cow, dewlap
KANDAHAN Manchurian moose (*Alces alces*)
 KANDAHAN TOHOMA a piece of moose
  hide hanging down at the sides of a
  saddle to protect the rider's legs
  from dirt and mud, saddle skirt
KANDARHAN a decoration attached to the
 bridle that hangs down from the
 horse's jaw
KANG SEME aloud, out loud
KANGGARAMBI 1. to slip slightly 2.
 to pierce the skin with an arrow
KANGGARŠAMBI to keep on slipping
KANGGASIKŪ an overbearing person,
 braggart
KANGGASITAMBI to be overbearing, to be
 a braggart
KANGGAŠAMBI to swagger, to act
 haughtily

KANGGILI slim, shapely, possessing a
 fine delicate build
KANGGILJAMBI (-ka) to become slim and
 shapely
KANGGIR (onom.) the sound of metal or
 porcelain falling
 KANGGIR KINGGIR (onom.) the sound
  of bells
 KANGGIR SEME (onom.) the sound of
  metal or porcelain falling
KANGGIRI the fitting on a box or
 cabinet into which the clasp is inserted
 KANGGIRI ILHA an exotic flower that
  grows in clusters and flutters
  even when there is no wind
KANGGŪ NIYEHE smew (*Mergellus albellus*)
KANGGŪR KINGGŪR (onom.) the sound of
 a large structure collapsing
KANGGŪR SEME 1. (onom.) the sound of a
 wall falling 2. foolhardy, reckless,
 impudent
KANGKAMBI to be thirsty
KANGNAMBI 1. to ride bareback 2. to
 leap onto (a horse)
KANGSAMBI to shave hair off a pelt
KANGSANGGI an arrogant and reckless
 person
KANGSIRI the top of the nose ridge
 just below the eyes
KANGTARAMBI 1. to rise up in the front,
 especially a cart that is loaded too
 heavily at the rear 2. to tie the
 reins of a horse to the pommel of a
 saddle to keep the horse from wandering
KANGTARŠAMBI to walk with the head
 high, to act in a proud manner
KANI related, of the same or similar
 kind
 KANI ACARAKŪ doesn't fit in the
  same category, doesn't belong to
  the same class
 KANI AKŪ eccentric, odd, uncongenial
KANIN 1. kelp, edible seaweed 2. see
 kani
 KANIN AKŪ see *kani akū*
KANINGGA having a relationship, related, of the same sort
KANIRAKŪ doesn't fit, doesn't belong
KANJAMBI to play with the *gacuha*
KANJIDU one name for the eastern great
 bustard; cf. *humudu*
KANJIHA IHAN a cow with a white nose
KANJIHA NIONGNIYAHA a small wild goose
 with a red beak and a red fleshy
 crest on the head
KANJIMBI to come to surround, to come
 to lay siege
KANUMBI to surround together, to be-
 siege together
KAPAHŪN flat, compressed, pressed down,
 small in stature

K

KAPAHŪN DEDUHEBI is lying flat
KAPARABUMBI caus./pass. of *kaparambi*
KAPARAMBI (-ka) to be pressed flat, to
  be pressed together, to be flat
KAPI a sewing basket with a cover; cf.
  kaipi
KAPIHŪN see *kapahūn*
KAR SEME defensive
KARA black (of animals)
    KARA CAI strong black tea (drunk
      with milk added)
    KARA CECIKE one name for the myna
    KARA FULAN an iron-gray horse
    KARA HŪNA a tree whose fiber is
      used to fasten arrowheads to the
      shaft
    KARA INDAHŪN a black dog
    KARA KEIRE a dark brown horse
    KARA KIONGGUHE a black myna
    KARA SAKSAHA a black magpie
    KARA YARHA a black panther
KARA FARA hot-tempered
KARABA mutual protection
KARABUMBI caus. of *karambi*
KARAHI WEIJUN a white stork with black
  feathers on the breast
KARAKI a crow
KARALJA one name for the coot; cf.
  karan kalja
KARALTU one name for the sparrow hawk;
  cf. *silmen*
KARAMBI to look down from a height, to
  gaze into the distance
    KARARA DENGJAN a lantern that shines
      very far at night, a signal lantern
KARAN 1. a lookout tower, watchtower,
  platform 2. see *kara*
    KARAN KALJA coot (*Fulica atra*)
KARANAMBI to go to look from a height
KARANDUMBI/KARANUMBI to look from a
  height together
KARANDUN see *karanidun*
KARANGGA TAKTU watchtower, sentry
  tower
KARANIDUN merlin (*Falco columbarius*)
KARANJIMBI to come to look from a
  height
KARASU one name for the cormorant; cf.
  suwan
KARCABUMBI caus./pass. of *karcambi*
KARCAMBI to run into, to collide with,
  to bump into
    KARCAME GUWEMBI to make a noise by
      rubbing the wings together (lo-
      custs, crickets, etc.)
KARCANDUMBI/KARCANUMBI to bump into
  one another, to collide, to clash
KARCIN a type of a spotted or speckled
  hawk resembling the black-eared kite
KARGAMA croup of a horse or mule
    KARGAMA HŪWALAME NIYAMNIYAMBI to
      turn around and shoot over the
      croup of a horse (archery)

KARGIBUMBI caus. of *kargimbi*
KARGIMBI to break off, to cut off
  evenly, to pluck, to pull (grass)
KARHAMA the same as *kargama*
KARIMBI see *kalimbi*
KARJAMBI see *garjambi*
KARKA CECIKE common snipe (*Cappella
  gallinago*)
KARKAKŪ "scraper"--a musical instru-
  ment made in the shape of a tiger
  with a corrugated back over which a
  bar can be run to produce a grating
  sound; cf. *ioi*
KARKALA see *karkalan*
KARKALAN wild peach (the inner bark of
  which is used for attaching arrow-
  heads to the shaft)
KARKAMBI to scrape with a wooden or
  bamboo stick
KARKAN CECIKE see *karka cecike*
KARKIMBI see *kargimbi*
KARMABUMBI caus. of *karmambi*
KARMACUN protection
KARMAKŪ protector
KARMAMBI to protect, to take care of
KARMAN the same as *karmacun*
KARMANDUMBI/KARMANUMBI to protect to-
  gether, to protect one another
KARMANGGA (衛) First Class Transport
  Station (on the Grand Canal), BH 834
KARMANI a written charm
KARMARAMBI see *karmambi*
KARMASI protector, patron
KARMATAMBI to protect continually
KARMATANGGA protective
KARMATU MAHATUN a hat worn in ancient
  times by the officers of the imperial
  bodyguard
KARU 1. retribution, recompense, re-
  ward, revenge 2. gratitude
    KARU BUMBI to repay, to recompense
    KARU GAIMBI to exact revenge
    KARU TEMGETU receipt for a document
      issued by the authorities
KARULABUMBI caus. of *karulambi*
KARULAMBI 1. to repay, to recompense
  2. to requite, to get revenge
KARULAN 1. recompense 2. karma
KARUN outpost sentry, border guard
    KARUN COOHA troops on sentry duty
    KARUN I BA an outpost, sentry post
    KARUN I CUWAN patrol boat
    KARUN I NIYALMA sentry, border
      guard
    KARUN SABUMBI to see the first
      signs of smallpox
    KARUN SINDAMBI to place a sentry
KARUŠAMBI to persist in repaying
KAS KIS swift, agile
KAS SEME 1. (onom.) sound of a grazing
  arrow 2. swift
KASARI see *kabari*
KASKAN haughtiness, arrogance

K

KASKANAMBI to become arrogant or conceited

KATA FATA in a rush, in a flurry, concerned, anxious

KATA KITI (onom.) 1. the sound of shoes
treading on a hard surface 2.
squeaking, scraping

KATABUMBI caus. of *katambi*

KATAHA FADU the name of a bird whose
call sounds like *kataha fadu*

KATAK (onom.) the sound of a lock
clicking shut
KATAK KITIK (onom.) the sound of an
object falling from a high place

KATAMBI to dry
KATAHA YALI dried meat

KATANG SEME very hard, solid

KATANGGA SORO jujubes dried in the sun

KATAR FATAR 1. affable, warm 2. with
all one's might, to the best of one's
ability

KATAR SEME dried out, dried up

KATARABUMBI caus. of *katarambi*

KATARAMBI to trot

KATI brocade embroidered in silk
KATI JONGDON grass linen with brocade embroidery work on it

KATUN 1. effort, exertion 2. queen,
princess

KATUNJAMBI to force oneself to do
something, to struggle to do something, to exert effort to do something

KATUR KITUR (onom.) the sound of eating
hard brittle things (like ice)

KATUR SEME brittly, crunching

KATURI crab, crayfish

KE 1. interjection of surprise 2.
a quarter of an hour; cf. *kemu*

KEB KAB SEME affectionate, warm,
affable, sincere

KEB SEME 1. warm, affable 2. exhausted
3. falling, dropping

KEBISU see *keibisu*

KEBSE a little bit too much
KEBSE EKIYEHE diminished a little
too much

KEBSIMBI 1. to slap the legs against
leather saddle skirts 2. to click
or snap loudly

KEBSISU see *keibisu*

KEBSU see *keibisu*

KECEMBI see *hecembi*

KECER SEME in large quantity (of very
small objects)
KECER SEME ADAMBI to fit many small
pieces together

KECU fierce, cruel

KECUDEMBI to be fierce, to act fiercely

KEDEREBUMBI caus. of *kederembi*

KEDEREMBI to patrol, to watch, to make
the rounds
KEDEREME BAICARA HAFAN (巡邏

宜) an official who patrols the
examination hall, proctor

KEDEREŠEMBI see *kederšembi*

KEDERŠEMBI to hurt with harsh words, to
attack verbally

KEFUCEN brittle, fragile

KEIBIRI ILHA an exotic flower--when
growing very close together they
resemble a brightly colored carpet

KEIBISU carpet, rug

KEIFU the name of an arrow used for
shooting tigers, bears, and buck
deer

KEIFULEMBI to pierce, to go through
(arrows)

KEIKE partial, unfair, prejudiced

KEIKEDEMBI to act in an unfair or
prejudiced manner

KEIKELJEMBI to lean to one side, to
act partially

KEIKEMBI see *keikedembi*

KEIKUHEN a kestrel

KEILEN a crocodilelike reptile

KEIRE a dark brown horse with a black
tail and mane

KEIŠEMBI 1. to implore, to beg 2. to
heal, to dry up (of a sore on a
horse)

KEJINE a while, a long time, a lot

KEK SEMBI to be pleased, to be
gratified, to be refreshed

KEKDE KAKDA not level, bumpy (of a
place where one is walking)

KEKE elder sister of husband or wife--
sister-in-law

KEKE KAKA (onom.) stuttering, stammer-
ing

KEKEREMBI to belch; cf. *jo banjimbi*,
johombi

KEKERI TATAMBI to act conceited

KEKI KAKA (onom.) laughing, cackling

KEKSEBUKU a good-luck scepter, a
scepter made in a fantastic shape

KEKSEBUMBI caus. of *keksembi*

KEKSEMBI see *kek sembi*

KEKSEN joy, gratification

KEKSENGGE GOHON a hook for hanging
curtains made in the shape of a
good-luck scepter

KEKTE KAKTA uneven, rough (surface)

KEKU the uvula; cf. *ilmaha*
KEKU UMIYAHA a type of multicolored
caterpillar that appears in large
groups on trees

KEKUHE Asiatic cuckoo (*Cuculus canorus*)

KEKUTU a variety of cuckoo

KELENG KALANG slack, loose, lax
KELENG KALANG UMESI SULA limp,
tired out (of horses and cows)

KELER KALAR 1. undone, unraveled (of
seams) 2. careless, negligent,
absent-minded 3. lax, loose

K

KELER KALAR SEME loose, lax
KELER KALAR SEME AŠŠAMBI to be
  loose (undone) and move
KELERI slack, loose
  KELERI KALARI loose, lax, slack
KELFIMBI (-ke) 1. to lean, to tilt
  2. to be about to set (the sun), to
  be past the zenith
KELFIŠEMBI 1. to lean to one side (of
  a ship in a storm) 2. to waver, to
  be irresolute, to be in doubt 3.
  to run (of wild animals)
  KELFIŠEME FEKSIMBI to run (of wild
    animals)
KELFIYEDEMBI see *kelfišembi*
KELFIYEMBI see *kelfimbi*
KELFIYEŠEMBI see *kelfišembi*
KELI men who have married sisters--
  brothers-in-law
KELMEMBI see *kemnembi*
KELTEHE golden carp; cf. *onggošon*
KELTERHEN a type of swallow--it has a
  short beak, black body, speckled
  breast, and loud cry
KEMIN marrow
KEMKI KAMKI shameless, forward, ob-
  trusive
KEMKIMBI to chase and bite (of dogs,
  geese, etc.)
KEMNEBUMBI caus. of *kemmembi*
KEMNEKU a measuring device
KEMNEMBI 1. to measure, to weigh 2.
  to moderate, to use with measure,
  to use temperately, to be frugal
  KEMNEME BODORO BOLGOBURE FIYENTEN
  (虞 衡 清 吏 司) Depart-
    ment of Weights and Measures, BH
    460A
  KEMNERE OLHOŠORO NAMUN (節 慎
    庫) the name of a silver de-
    pository of the Board of Works
KEMNEN measure, measuring
  KEMNEN AKŪ without measure, intem-
    perate
KEMŠU one name for the Chinese button
  quail; cf. *niyo mušu*
KEMU a quarter of an hour; cf. *ke*
  KEMU I TAMPIN a water clock
  KEMU TAMPIN TUWARA HAFAN (挈 壺
    正) Keeper of Clepsydra, BH 231
KEMUHEN norm, scale
KEMUN 1. measure, dimension, model,
  ruler, rule, regulation 2. a
  marker beyond which one is not al-
  lowed to step when competing in
  archery 3. a point beyond which one
  is not allowed to go
  KEMUN AKŪ without measure, without
    rule
  KEMUN DURUN dimension, scale, model,
    standard
  KEMUN I JIHA a model coin--a model
    from which other copper coins were

made
  KEMUN I SUJE silk used for offer-
    ings
  KEMUN KOOLI measure, rule, regula-
    tion
  KEMUN MIYALIN measure, dimension
  KEMUN TON reckoning, measuring
  KEMUN YANGSE manners, deportment
KEMUNGGE 1. having measure, frugal
  2. simple
KEMUNI 1. often 2. still, yet
  KEMUNI JAFAŠAMBI to practice con-
    stantly (what one has learned)
  KEMUNI UNDE not yet, still not
KEMURI COKO one name for the chicken;
  cf. *ikiri coko*
KEN 1. mad, crazy 2. willing
KENDELE NISIHA a small fish resembling
  the chum salmon
KENDERHEN the long hair under the neck
  of a camel
  KENDERHEN NIONGNIYAHA one name for
    the wild goose; cf. *jurgangga
    gasha*
  KENDERHEN NIYEHE the tufted duck
    (*Sythya fuligula*)
KENEHUNJEBUMBI caus./pass. of *kenehun-
  jembi*
KENEHUNJECUKE doubtful, suspicious
KENEHUNJEMBI to doubt, to suspect
KENEHUNJEN doubt, suspicion
KENG (onom.) the sound of coughing
  KENG KANG (onom.) the sound of many
    people coughing or clearing their
    throats
  KENG KENG (onom.) the sound of kow-
    towing
KENG SEME see *kek sembi*
KENGCEMBI to break, to collapse (of
  soft things)
KENGGEHUN 1. emaciated 2. empty,
  vacant
  KENGGEHUN KANGGAHŪN empty, vacant
KENGGERI 1. diaphragm 2. the front
  section of a slaughtered animal
  3. the clavicle of a bird
KENGGIN walrus
KENGKEMBI 1. to dry out, to be dried
  up 2. to be famished, to be very
  hungry and thirsty
KENGKEŠEMBI to crave, to desire greatly
KENGSE resolute, determined
  KENGSE LASHA decisive, resolute
KENGSEJEMBI to become worn (of ropes
  and fine objects)
KENGSELEBUMBI caus. of *kengselembi*
KENGSELEMBI to decide, to determine
KENGSIMBI 1. to call (of the cuckoo)
  2. to cough, to hack, to clear the
  throat
KENGTEHUN 1. stooped, hunched 2.
  towering above the herd
  KENGTEHUN AMBA larger than the rest

of the herd

KENJE small in stature, stunted

KENŠEMBI see *kengkešembi*

KEO KEO SEME fervent

KER (onom.) the sound of a belch

KERCIBUMBI caus. of *kercimbi*

KERCIMBI to cut up or dissect a slaughtered animal, to butcher
  KERCIHE YALI chunks of meat from a butchered animal

KEREMU rampart, walled enclosure or city, wall made of mud and bricks, citadel
  KEREMU DE AKTALAME straddling a rampart

KERKENEMBI to become severely pock-marked

KERKERI a pockmarked person; cf. *mase*

KERKIMBI 1. to bark incessantly, to yap 2. to scrape a winnowing fan with a bamboo stick during the 'snake song'

KERKIN KARKAN uneven, rough, bumpy

KERME a sea fish resembling the *tubehe*

KERMEYEN NIMAHA a sea fish similar to the *heihule*

KERSEN the skin and flesh between the breast and front legs on sheep and wild animals

KERSU the flesh from the breast of a sheep

KERU a young crow--the same as *holon gaha*

KERULEMBI to impose a reparation or compensation as a punishment

KERUN reparation, compensation

KES as if cut off with a knife, sharp, sheer
  KES SEME sharp, sheer, cut off
  KES SEME LAKCAHA severed smoothly, broke sharply
  KES SERE BA a precipitous place that looks like it has been cut off with a knife, a sheer drop

KESE MASA 1. in dire need 2. crude, unkempt, careless

KESEMBUREO idler, sluggard, scoundrel

KESEMBURU see *kesembureo*

KESER SEME (onom.) the sound of chewing hard things

KESI kind act (from above), favor, grace, kindness, graciousness
  KESI BE SELGIYERE FULEHUN BE ISIBURE TEMGETUN the name of an insignia of the imperial escort
  KESI BE TUWAKIYARA GURUN BE DALIRE GUNG (奉恩鎮國公   ) Prince of the Blood of the fifth degree, BH 20
  KESI BE TUWAKIYARA GURUN DE AISILARA GUNG (奉恩輔國公   ) Prince of the Blood of the sixth degree, BH 21

KESI BE TUWAKIYARA JANGGIN (奉恩將軍) Noble of the Imperial lineage by Imperial Favor, BH 27A

KESI BELE I CALU a granary of the Board of Finance in Peking

KESI DE HENGKILEMBI to kowtow as an act of thanksgiving for the emperor's favor

KESI ISIBUMBI to bestow favor

KESI MENGGUN I NAMUN a treasury located in every banner for rewarding the troops

KESI SIMEHE his grace has permeated (everywhere)

KESI ŠANGNAHAN I KUNGGERI (賞賜科) office of rewards and bestowals in the Board of Rites

KESI YALI meat used as offerings

KESIKE cat
  KESIKE FATHA a wild herb whose leaves resemble cat's paws

KESINGGE blessed with good fortune, blessed, favored
  KESINGGE HAFAN (恩騎尉) a hereditary rank of the ninth grade, BH 944

KESIRI MASIRI 1. coarse, unkempt, careless, worthless 2. in dire need

KESITU blessed, favored

KETE KATA 1. (onom.) the sound of horse's hoofs striking stone 2. snacks (dried fruits and biscuits) eaten by children

KETEK KATAK (onom.) the sound of cart wheels on a rough surface

KETERI 1. lip 2. vulva

KI 1. breath, vapor 2. anger 3. banner
  KI FULHAMBI to dissipate one's anger

KI KŪ (onom.) the sound of sniggering or giggling

KI PAI HAFAN (旗牌) police commissioner

KI YANG JODON a type of coarse grass linen produced in Chi-yang in Hunan

KIB SEME (onom.) the sound of hitting something with the fist

KICAN one hundred sheets of paper

KICEBE diligent, assiduous

KICEBUMBI caus. of *kicembi*

KICEMBI to strive, to exert oneself, to be diligent, to apply oneself, to concentrate on, to be intent on, to study

KICEN 1. diligence, exertion, striving 2. task, undertaking, lesson 3. vīrya, one of the six pāramitā

KICENDUMBI/KICENUMBI to strive together

KIDUBUMBI caus./pass. of *kidumbi*

KIDULAMBI see *kiyangdulambi*

K

KIDUMBI (-ha) to think about, to long
  for, to miss
KIDUN longing
  KIDUN CECIKE the Hopei crow-tit
    (*Suthora webbiana*)
KIFUR (onom.) the sound of crunching
  or gnashing
  KIFUR SEME crunching, grinding
    (of sounds)
KIJIMI 1. trepang, sea slug 2. an
  oath used toward children
KIK KIK SEME anxious, troubled, con-
  fused
KIKI KAKA (onom.) the sound of many
  people laughing
KIKŪR (onom.) the sound made by cart
  wheels, the sound of teeth gnashing
  KIKŪR SEME 1. the same as *kikūr*
    2. heavy, thick (of cloth)
KILA ILHA the name of a white wild
  flower
KILAHŪN seagull, gull, birds of the
  genus *Larus*
KILAKCI a very small cooking pot
KILANG KALANGGA (onom.) the sound of
  ringing or tingling
KILHANA bramble-bush (*Bidens bipinnata*)
KILIN a unicorn, chilin
KILTAN banner, pennant
KILTANGGA bearing a banner or pennant
KILTARI signal flag
KILUK a black-spotted horse
KIMA Szechuan hemp (*Sida ziliaefolia*)
  KIMA SUSE mortar mixed with hemp
    fibers
KIMCIBUMBI caus. of *kimcimbi*
KIMCIKŪ 1. checker, examiner 2.
  thorough, exact, careful
KIMCIMBI to examine, to check, to
  investigate, to look into carefully,
  to do carefully
  KIMCIME BAICAKŪ (檢討) Cor-
    rector, BH 200C
  KIMCIME BAICARA BA (稽察房)
    an office of the Grand Secretariat
  KIMCIME BAICARA BOO (查核房)
    inspection office of the Printing
    Office and Bookbindery
KIMCIN examination, checking
KIMCINDUMBI/KINCINUMBI to examine to-
  gether
KIMCISI (照磨) Commissary of the
  Seal or Correspondence Secretary,
  BH 826
KIMU see *kimun*
KIMULEBUMBI caus. of *kimulembi*
KIMULEMBI to harbor enmity, to harbor
  a grudge, to get revenge
KIMUN enmity, grudge, feud, revenge
  KIMUN BAITA a matter of enmity,
    feud, a matter for revenge
  KIMUN BATA enemy, bitter foe
  KIMUN BE KARULAMBI to get revenge

KIMUN JAFAMBI to harbor a grudge
KIMUNDUMBI to get revenge on one an-
  other, to have a grudge against one
  another
KIMUNGGE 1. having a grudge, harboring
  enmity 2. a personal enemy
KIN the seven-stringed lute
  KIN ŠE lute and harp
KINA ILHA garden balsam (*Impatiens
  balsamina*)
KINAMU ILHA henna (*Lawsonia inermis*)
KING 1. (onom.) the sound of a heavy
  object falling 2. a musical stone
  3. land measure equal to one hundred
  mu
KINGGIR SEME clinking, clattering
KINGGIRI one name for the hill myna
KINGGIRI SEME (onom.) the sound of
  breaking into many small pieces
KINGGUHE one name for the myna
KINGKEN musical stone
KINGKIRI SEME crashing loudly
KINTALA see *kitala*
KINUMBI to loathe, to despise
KIONGGUHE myna of South China (*Acrido-
  theres cristatellus*)
KIONGGUN firm, unshakable
KIONGGURI ILHA hydrangea
KIOR SEME (onom.) the sound of a bird
  taking off suddenly
KIRAGA attentive, observant
KIRFU sturgeon
KIRHO lettuce
KIRIBA 1. a patient person 2. patient,
  long-suffering
KIRIBUMBI caus. of *kirimbi*
KIRICA female demon (Buddhist)
KIRICUN patience, forbearance
KIRIJY demons
KIRIKŪ endurer, sufferer
KIRIMBI 1. to endure, to tolerate,
  to suffer 2. to lie still (of
  animals who sense a nearby danger)
KIRSA corsac, fox of the steppes
  (*Vulpes corsac*)
  KIRSA CABI the white breast and
    belly pelt of the corsac
KIRU a small banner (worn on the back
  by soldiers)
KIRUDA red signal flag
KIRULAMBI see *karulambi*
KIRUMBI to seek out a mare (of a stal-
  lion)
KIRUSI battle banner
KISARI a sterile mare
KIŠAN fresh, new, neat, bright
KIŠIMIŠI small green seedless grape
KITALA 1. the stock of a writing brush
  2. quill
KITARI a type of wild pig with white
  hair on its neck and legs
KITIR SEME fast (galloping)
KITUHAN the seven-stringed lute

K

KITUHAN I KUYERHEN knots on the cords of a lute
KITUHAN I MURIKŪ the pegs of a lute
KITUHAN I SUJAKŪ the base of a lute
KITUHANGGA pertaining to the seven-stringed lute
KIYA honeycomb, cell
KIYAB KIB SEME sprightly, nimbly, smartly
KIYAB SEME 1. quickly 2. snug fitting, just right 3. concentrated 4. tight
KIYAB SEME GENE go quickly
KIYAB SEME JIO come quickly
KIYADAMBI to inlay (pearls or jewels)
KIYAFUR KIFUR (onom.) 1. the sound of chewing hard objects 2. the sound of something smashing
KIYAK (onom.) the sound of dried wood breaking
KIYAK KIK (onom.) the sound of a large tree splitting
KIYAK SEME the same as *kiyak*
KIYAKIYABUMBI caus. of *kiyakiyambi*
KIYAKIYAMBI 1. to sigh 2. to click the tongue with admiration, to praise, to admire
KIYAKIYAME FERGUWEMBI to click the tongue in amazement, to sigh from admiring something
KIYAKŪ river perch
KIYAKŪHA a hawk of mixed breed--considered useless for falconry
KIYAKŪNG (onom.) the sound made by a heavily loaded wagon, with a rumbling sound
KIYAKŪNG KIKŪNG the same as *kiyakūng*
KIYAKŪNG SEME GUWEMBI to make a rumbling sound (of a heavy wagon)
KIYALABUMBI caus. of *kiyalambi*
KIYALAMBI to bind (books)
KIYALARA DOBTOLORO FALGA (裝書作) bookbindery in the Printing Office and Bookbindery; cf. BH 94
KIYALANG (onom.) 1. the sound of a single bell 2. the sound of metal colliding with another object
KIYALANG SEMBI to ring, to clang
KIYALMABUMBI caus. of *kiyalmambi*
KIYALMAGAN an inlaid ornament
KIYALMAMBI to inlay pearls, jewels, or coral in gold or silver
KIYAMBI to inlay (jewels or pearls in gold or silver)
KIYAMNAMBI to inlay--the same as *kiyalmambi*
KIYAMNAN MAHATUN an ancient-style hat adorned with golden cicadas and sable tails
KIYAN 1. a paper measure equaling twenty-five sheets, a quire 2. anything folded or bound together
KIYANGDU powerful, forceful
KIYANGDUKAN rather powerful, rather forceful
KIYANGDULABUMBI caus./pass. of *kiyangdulambi*
KIYANGDULAMBI to use force, to take by force
KIYANGKIYAN powerful, excelling
KIYANGKIYAŠABUMBI caus./pass. of *kiyangkiyašambi*
KIYANGKIYAŠAMBI to offer powerful resistance
KIYANGKIYATU MAHATUN a style of hat worn by heroes in ancient times
KIYAR (onom.) the sound made by a wild hawk
KIYAR KIR (onom.) the cry of alarm made by birds of prey and martens
KIYAR SEME shrieking fiercely (to keep someone from advancing)
KIYARIBUMBI caus. of *kiyarimbi*
KIYARIMBI 1. to chop firewood 2. to decimate, to slaughter 3. to cackle (after laying and egg)
KIYARIME WAHA totally decimated
KIYARKIYA SEME worn out, weary
KIYAS (onom.) the sound of something brittle breaking
KIYATA young sea bream
KIYATAR SEME rumbling, roaring
KIYATAR SEME INJEMBI to laugh uproariously
KIYATUBUMBI caus. of *kiyatumbi*
KIYATUMBI to be famished, to suffer hunger
KIYATUR KITUR (onom.) the sound of clods being crushed under wagon wheels
KIYEI NAN HIYANG a type of incense
KIYOB SEME (onom.) the sound of arrows striking a target
KIYOKAN a small pointed knife used by an arrow maker
KIYOKIYON the name of an edible wild plant with hollow stems
KIYOKIYON GIRANGGI the tail bone
KIYOLORJOMBI to put on airs, to behave in an affected manner
KIYOO 1. sedan chair, litter 2. bridge
KIYOO CAMBI to throw a bridge (across a stream)
KIYOO DOOMBI to cross a bridge
KIYOO NIONGNIYAHA a small black-headed wild goose
KIYOO SEJEN sedan chair
KIYOO TUKIYEMBI to carry a sedan chair
KIYOOKA kindling
KIYOOKAN see *kiyooka*
KIYOR SEME (onom.) cackling
KO 1. ditch, sewer 2. (onom.) sound of gagging
KO KA (onom.) sound made when something gets caught in the throat,

K

the sound of gagging

KO SANGGA sewer, ditch

KO MOO a species of oak

KOB SEME 1. right on the mark, right on
target 2. wholly, totally 3. without more ado, forthwith

 KOB SEME GAMAHA took it away forthwith

 KOB SEME GENEHE went without any
 ado

 KOB SEME TEHE sat down without any
 ado

KOBCIHIYADAMBI to put on airs, to strut
about

KOBCIHIYAN dandy, poser, pretentious
person

KOBCIMBI to become detached, to fall
off, to peel off

KOBDOLOMBI to keep in a *kobdon*

KOBDON a container for arrows or tools

KOBI 1. concave place, depression 2.
the depressions on both sides of
the nose

KOBKOLOMBI to remove (paper that has
been stuck to some surface)

KOBSOHON 1. long-nosed 2. something
floating on the surface of water

 KOBSOHON SABUMBI to see something
 floating on water

KOBSOLJOMBI to brag about small things,
to be a petty braggart

 KOBSOLJOME ARBUŠAMBI to behave like
 a petty braggart

KOBTO respect, awe

KOBTOLOMBI to treat respectfully

KOBTON respect, reverence

KOBTONGGO respectful, deferential

KOCO angle or corner in a house

 KOCO WAI angular, curved, crooked

KODO the third stomach of sheep and
cows that is eaten filled with blood

KOFON SUJE a type of porous silk
material

KOFOR SEME rotten or soft on the inside (of food)

KOFORI 1. bubble, pore, hollow, porous
2. the name of a fruit similar to
the pomelo

 KOFORI EFEN a type of very porous
 pastry

 KOFORI ILHA a very fragrant exotic
 white flower that blooms toward
 the end of spring

KOFORINAMBI to become hollow, to become porous

KOHODOMBI to cry (of pheasants in the
autumn)

KOHONG KOHONG (onom.) the sound of
repeated coughing

KOIKA 1. scalp 2. short plants growing thickly together that resemble
human hair 3. bricks made of clay
and plant roots

K

 KOIKA FU a wall built of adobe
 brick

 KOIKA HOTON a mud wall

KOIKALAMBI to scratch the scalp, to
hurt the scalp

KOIKAŠABUMBI caus. of *koikašambi*

KOIKAŠAMBI to scuffle, to fight, to
get in trouble

KOIKOHON floating high on the surface

KOIKOLJOMBI to behave in a reckless
or peculiar fashion

KOIKON short fine feathers that appear
on the tails of fowl--their appearance on a hen indicates the hen is
no longer willing to sit on eggs

 KOIKON DEKDEHEBI 'tail feathers
 have appeared'--said of person
 who has become fed up or obstinate

KOIMALI cunning, tricky, shifty,
deceitful

KOIMALIDAMBI to act cunningly, to act
in a tricky manner, to act deceitfully

KOIMAN tricky, cunning, deceitful

KOIMASITAMBI to act always in a tricky
manner

KOITOLOMBI to employ tricks, to act
deceitfully

KOITON trick, deceit, subterfuge

KOITONGGO cunning, tricky

KOKI tadpole

KOKIMA poverty-stricken, indigent

KOKINGGA FUKJINGGA HERGEN (蝌蚪
書) a style of calligraphy

KOKIRABUMBI caus./pass. of *kokirambi*

KOKIRAKŪ one who harms other people

KOKIRAMBI to harm, to damage, to injure, to wound

KOKIRAN damage, harm, injury

KOKIRANDUMBI to harm one another

KOKIRANGGA INENGGI a day on which the
earth's branch overcomes the heav-
en's stem

KOKO (onom.) the sound made by
chickens

KOKOLI 1. a garment without lapels
that is pulled on over the head 2.
baby's clothing 3. the name of a
small bird that resembles the woodcock

KOKOLIBUMBI caus. of *kokolimbi*

KOKOLIMBI to remove, to take off, to
strip off (clothing)

KOKSIMBI 1. to cackle 2. to cry (of
pheasants in springtime)

KOKSIN ULHŪMA "cackling pheasant"--
the cackling by a pheasant when it
senses an oncoming storm

KOLABUMBI caus. of *kolambi*

KOLAMBI to skin, to remove the tile
from a roof

KOLOI channel, furrow

KOLONGSO bad body odor, the odor of

the armpits

KOLOR SEME too large, loose fitting (shoes, boots, etc.)

KOMO a felt blanket placed under a camel's saddle

KOMOLOBUMBI caus. of *komolombi*

KOMOLOMBI to put on a felt saddle blanket, to put a felt pad on a camel
KOMOLOHG ENGGEMU a saddle with felt padding for skinny or saddle-sore horses

KOMON see *komo*

KOMSO few, little, a little

KOMSOKON rather little, rather few

KOMSOLABUMBI caus. of *komsolambi*

KOMSOLAMBI to become little or few, to decrease

KOMSOLOMBI see *komsolambi*

KOMSONGGE what is few, that which is little

KONGGIR (onom.) the sound of a small bell
KONGGIR KANGGIR (onom.) the sound of many small bells
KONGGIR SEME (onom.) ringing, tinkling

KONGGOHON 1. sunken (eyes) 2. emaciated

KONGGOLO the crop of a bird

KONGGOR (onom.) the sound of pouring water
KONGGOR SEME flowing swiftly

KONGGORO Isabella colored, an Isabella horse

KONGSIMBI to speak nonsense in a loud voice

KONJISUN see *konjosu*

KONJOSU the end of the large intestine

KONSUN hemorrhoidal swelling

KOOJIHA dolphin, porpoise

KOOLAMBI see *kolambi*

KOOLI 1. rule, norm, statute, codex, decree, law 2. custom, habit 3. document 4. method
KOOLI AKŪ without regulation, without a rule
KOOLI DURUN rule, regulation
KOOLI DURUN I BOLGOBURE FIYENTEN (儀制清吏司) Department of Ceremonies, BH 376A
KOOLI HACIN regulations and precedents
KOOLI HACIN I BITHEI KUREN (則例館) division of regulations and precedents (one in every Board and important organ of government)
KOOLI ICIHIYARA BA (辨例處) office of regulations of the Imperial Household
KOOLI OBUMBI to make into a rule, to make the norm
KOOLINGGA prescribed, ordered, ordained

KOOSA see *kūwasa*

KOR (onom.) the sound of sniffling or snoring

KORAMBI the same as *kūrambi*

KORDON a person good on skis or snowshoes

KORIBUMBI 1. caus./pass. of *korimbi* 2. to be washed away (by a river current)

KORIKŪ gouge, chisel, a small curved knife

KORIMBI to erode, to hollow out, to dig out, to cut out

KORKONG KORKONG (onom.) the sound of repeated coughing

KORO sorrow, regret, damage, injury, offense, wound
KORO ARAMBI to take offense at, to be wounded
KORO BAHA 1. was wounded, was injured 2. sustained loss
KORO BAHAMBI to suffer loss, to be at a disadvantage, to be hurt
KORO DE DAILAMBI to fight a vendetta
KORO GOSIHON sorrow and suffering
KORO ISIBUMBI to bring harm to

KOROMBI to be sorrowful, to suffer, to regret

KORSOBUMBI caus./pass. of *korsombi*

KORSOCUKA regrettable, annoying

KORSOCUN regret, annoyance

KORSOMBI 1. to regret, to miss 2. to be annoyed at, to hate

KORSONDUMBI/KORSONUMBI to be mutually annoyed, to regret mutually

KOS SEME suddenly (got away or became skinny)
KOS SEME UKCAHA suddenly got away
KOS SEME WASIKA suddenly became skinny

KOSHA globefish, swellfish

KOSIHIMBI to strive for, to aspire to

KOSKON KASKAN assiduous, busy, urgent

KOTOLI sail (of a ship)

KOTONG hard and dry
KOTONG KATANG SEME hard and dry

KOTOR (onom.) the sound of pheasants flying
KOTOR KATAR (onom.) 1. the sound of hard things rattling together or falling 2. the sound of a flock of pheasants flying
KOTOR SEME 1. in one gulp 2. (onom.) the sound of pheasants taking off

KOYORHOLOMBI to kill and skin the horse of a deceased man--after the offering at the grave the horse's skin and saddle are burnt together with paper money

KU 1. soot (from cooking) 2. storehouse, warehouse
KU IJUMBI to smear (the face) with

K

    soot

KU NAMUN storehouse

KUB SEME out of energy, exhausted, (fell) in a heap

KUBCEN see *kubcin*

KUBCIN 1. hem on a skirt 2. border at the top of boots or socks

KUBERHEN welt caused by a whip or cane

KUBERHENEMBI to raise a welt, to cause a swelling (insects)

KUBSUHUN clumsy, cumbersome, large and awkward

KUBSUHURI unwieldy, massive

KUBSUREMBI to swell

KUBUHEN border, edging, hem

KUBUMBI to edge, to add a border to, to hem

    KUBUHE FULGIYAN bordered red (banner)

    KUBUHE LAMUN bòrdered blue (banner)

    KUBUHE SUWAYAN bordered yellow (banner)

    KUBUHE ŠANYAN bordered white (banner)

KUBUN cotton

    KUBUN FOMOCI cotton stockings

    KUBUN I ETUKU cotton clothing, cotton padded clothing

KUBUNEMBI to become mushy (of melons)

KUBUNGGE HOOŠAN a type of soft thin paper

KUBUNGGE MOO a tree that grows in Szechuan with fruit resembling cotton and which can be woven into cloth

KUBURGEN scar, cicatrice

KUBURHEN grape vine

KUCIKER FULAN a horse with a dark mane and tail

KUCUNG SEME diligent, assiduous

KUDE a plaited basket for feeding cows

    KUDE ŠORO feeding basket woven from brambles

KUDEBUMBI caus. of *kudembi*

KUDEMBI to tie up (a boat)

KUDEŠEMBI to beat the back with both hands (a type of massage)

KUFAN two partitioned rooms at both sides of the main house

KUFANG see *kufan*

KUFUMBI to run aground on a sandbar

KUFUR SEME crisp, brittle

KUFUYEN crisp, brittle, the pleasant sound of someone chewing brittle things

    KUFUYEN ŠULHE a type of juicy pear

KUHEN 1. a large blood vessel in the belly of livestock that is attached to the spine 2. in traditional Chinese anatomy, a vessel along the spine that was thought to nourish the five vital organs 3. grooves on a knife, sword, or arrowhead 4. sprouts on a tree

KUHENGGE swollen up lout! (oath used toward a lazy person)

KUI HŪWA mallow

KUILEBUMBI caus. of *kuilembi*

KUILEKU a form used for maintaining the shape of quivers, shoes, boots, and hats

KUILEMBI to place on a form (*kuileku*)

KUINI spoon

KUINIHE (奎) the name of a constellation

    KUINIHE TOKDONGGO KIRU (奎 宿 旗) a banner depicting the constellation *kuinihe*

KUKDURI braggart, boaster

KUKELE ALHA a red and white spotted horse

KUKEN a horizontal piece of wood at the base of a window, window sill

KUKJI a response used in group singing

KUKJUHŪN see *kumcuhun*

KUKJUREMBI (-ke) to be bent over, to be stooped

KUKU 1. blue-gray, gray 2. a sort of incense

    KUKU FULAN a blue-gray horse

    KUKU IHAN a gray cow

    KUKU ULHŪMA a blue-gray pheasant

KUKU KAKA (onom.) the sound of many people laughing

KUKU SEME INJEMBI to laugh unintentionally, to titter, to giggle

KUKULE see *kukulu*

KUKULEMBI to foment a serious wound in the open breast of an animal

KUKULU 1. the tuft on the head of a bird 2. the hair in the ears of horses and mules

KUKUREMBI to call a mate, to call the female (of birds)

KUKURI a flat vessel for tea and milk

KUK'AN a board along the edge of an oven-bed

KULGE means of transport, vehicle

KULKURI SURU a white horse good in mountain terrain

KULU healthy, vigorous, strong

KULUK JERDE sorrel

KULUN vigor, strength

KULURI MALARI gradually

KULUTU FULAN a gray steed

KUMBI (-ke/he) to swell, to bloat

KUMCUHUN bent forward, stooped, crooked

    KUMCUHUN WASE tiles used on the roof ridge

KUMCUN MUKE TASHARI one name for the eagle; cf. *ing gasha*, *tashari*

KUMCUREMBI to have stooped posture

KUMDU empty, hollow

KUMDULEBUMBI caus. of *kumdulembi*

KUMDULEMBI to be empty or hollow

KUMDUN MOO a tree that grows in mountain valleys, six or seven (Chinese) feet tall, having light reddish bark

KUMGETU a red staff with one hundred vermilion lacquered bamboo rods and velvet tassels hanging from it--used to direct music

KUMUCI 1. master of music in antiquity 2. official of the Board of State Music
    KUMUCI DA (署 使 長) bursar of the Board of State Music

KUMUDA (司 樂) Master of Music, Director of Music; cf. BH 391

KUMUN music
    KUMUN BE ALIHA AMBAN (大 士) an official concerned with musical matters in antiquity
    KUMUN BE ALIHA HAFAN (太 師) an official of antiquity who was in charge of musical matters
    KUMUN BE KADALARA HAFAN (典 樂) an official in charge of music
    KUMUN DE BAITALARA JAKA musical instrument
    KUMUN I AHŪRA musical instrument
    KUMUN I FAIDASI (奉 鑾) director of music
    KUMUN I JURGAN (樂 部) the Board of State Music, BH 387
    KUMUN I KARMANGGA (旗 手 衛) Standard-bearers Section, BH 122
    KUMUN I NIYALMA musician

KUMUNGGE noisy, festive, exciting, lively, animated
    KUMUNGGE SIMENGGE noisy and exciting, full of bustle and excitement

KUMUSI dancer (in the palace)
    KUMUSI I DA the chief dancer (of the palace)
    KUMUSI MAHATUN a hat worn by dancers in ancient times

KUNDU respect, honor

KUNDUJIN one name for the peacock; cf. tojin

KUNDULEBUMBI caus./pass. of kundulembi

KUNDULEMBI to respect, to treat with respect, to honor
    KUNDULERE KOBTOLORO honor and respect

KUNDULEN respect, honor

KUNDUN respectful

KUNESUN provisions (for a journey)

KUNG (onom.) the sound of a large object falling to the ground

KUNG CANG (onom.) the sound of drums and cymbals
    KUNG CANG SEME BANJIMBI to live on a a grand scale

KUNGGE YAMUN a section (of an organization)

KUNGGER SEME incessantly

KUNGGERI bureau

KUNGGERI SEME see kungger seme

KUNGGUHEN see kungguhun

KUNGGUHUN having sunken eyes

KUNGGUR (onom.) 1. the sound made by empty wagons 2. the sound of heavy thunder
    KUNGGUR KANGGAR (onom.) the sound of thunder
    KUNGGUR SEME 1. the same as kunggur 2. in droves
    KUNGGUR SEME YAMULAMBI to go to the yamen in droves

KUNGGURI SEME see kunggur seme

KUNGŠUKEN a little burnt or scorched

KUNGŠUMBI to burn, to scorch, to boil (milk)

KUNGŠUN burnt, scorched, scalded
    KUNGŠUN WA the odor of something scorched or scalded

KUNUSUN see kunesun

KUR (onom.) the sound of growling

KURBU a flat ridge on an arrowhead

KURBULAMBI to turn around

KURBUMBI to turn around, to turn over, to toss and turn (while sleeping)

KURBUSEMBI 1. to turn round and round, to turn over, to toss and turn 2. to be upset, to be anxious

KURBUŠETEMBI to turn over repeatedly, to be in great anxiety

KURCE the name of a white sea fish that resembles the fu nimaha

KURCILEMBI to harden an arrow shaft by wrapping it in wood shavings and firing it
    KURCILEHE SIRDAN an arrow hardened by fire

KURCIN a scaleless short white river fish with dark spots

KURDUN a Buddhist cycle, samsara

KURE a tench

KUREHU the great black woodpecker (Dryocopus martius)

KURELEMBI to form cavalry into squadrons

KUREN 1. squadron, detachment 2. establishment, office, depository 3. chestnut-colored, dark brown

KURENE weasel

KURI 1. spotted, striped, dapple 2. a dog striped like a tiger
    KURI ALAN spotted birchbark
    KURI DAMIN a striped eagle
    KURI HIYAHALI CECIKE a striped crossbill
    KURI IHAN a spotted cow
    KURI KARA black and yellow spotted
    KURI WEIFUTU a black-spotted dog

KURINGGE spotted, striped
    KURINGGE GASHA a black-headed bird with a spotted body
    KURINGGE HOOHAN a black-striped

K

K

crane

KURKU 1. a children's toy cast from
    lead in a hollowed-out bone--used
    like dice 2. head, chief, ring-
    leader, instigator
KURNE see *kurene*
KURU height, elevation, rise
KURUKEN a somewhat elevated place
KURUME a coat or garment worn over the
    outside of one's other garments
KURUNE see *kurene*
KUS SEME INJEMBI to not be able to
    keep from laughing
KUSKUN SEME steadily, without rest,
    assiduously
KUSKUREMBI to ruffle the feathers and
    beat the dirt with the wings (of
    birds)
KUŠULEBUMBI caus./pass. of *kušulembi*
KUŠULEMBI to dislike, to find annoying,
    to be tired of, to be disgusted
KUŠUN 1. disgusted, sick of, unwell
    2. not well-fitting (clothes)
KUŠUNGGE SURI silk crepe
KUTECI a horse herder, stableboy
KUTITU LORIN a mule born from a jenny,
    a hinny
KUTULE 1. serf, banner slave 2. horse
    herder
KUTULEBUMBI caus. of *kutulembi*
KUTULEMBI to lead (animals)
KUTUNG (onom.) the sound of a large
    object falling to the ground
KUTUR FATAR 1. affectionate, friendly,
    affable 2. with all one's might, to
    the best of one's ability
KUTUR SEME (onom.) 1. the sound of
    incessant drumbeating 2. the sound
    of horses galloping 3. the sound of
    horses shaking themselves off
KUTURCEMBI to behave deferentially
    toward
KUWAI ŠEO bailiff
KUWALAR see *kūwalar, hūwalar*
KUWANG CANG SEME see *kūwang cang seme*
KUWANGGAR SEME see *hūwanggar seme*
KUWANGSE basket
KUWECEHE see *kuwecihe*
KUWECICEHE see *kuweciheri*
KUWECIHE pigeon, dove
    KUWECIHE BOCO dove-gray, light gray
KUWECIHERI dove-gray, light bluish gray
KUWEDAN see *kuweten*
KUWELEMBI to remove the skin and the
    layer of fat attached to it (from
    bears and pigs)
KUWETEN see *huweten*
KUYERHEN knot on a bowstring
KŪ CA (onom.) the sound of fighting
KŪBULIBUMBI caus. of *kūbulimbi*
KŪBULIMBI (-ka) to change, to become
    altered (in appearance), to revolt
KŪBULIN change, alteration, revolt

KŪBULIN ILENGGU CECIKE one name for
    the myna
KŪCA a male goat
KŪDARGALAMBI to grasp the crupper
    KŪDARGALAME DORIME FIYELEMBI to
        trick ride, at a gallop holding
        the crupper
KŪDARGAN crupper (on a horse)
    KŪDARGAN DABAME CASHŪN FIYELEMBI
        to ride backwards passing over the
        crupper (equestrian acrobatics)
    KŪDARGAN TATAME CASHŪN FIYELEMBI
        to ride backwards pulling on the
        crupper
    KŪDARGAN TATARALAME KURBUME FI-
        YELEMBI turn about while pulling
        on the crupper (equestrian acro-
        batics)
KŪDARHAN see *kūdargan*
KŪLAN 1. a yellow horse with black
    tail and mane 2. wild ass
KŪLIBUMBI caus. of *kūlimbi*
KŪLIMBI to be scared stiff, to be
    stunned (from fear), to lie silently
    because of fear (animals)
KŪLIN CALIN frivolous, not serious,
    inconstant, furtive
KŪLISIDAMBI see *kūlisitambi*
KŪLISITAMBI 1. to be petrified by
    fear, to be extremely frightened
    2. to be frivolous, to be irrespon-
    sible, to act furtively
KŪME see *kūwarame*
KŪNGGA deep valley, canyon
KŪR KAR (onom.) 1. sound made when
    something is caught in the throat
    2. the sound made by the intestines
KŪRAMBI to engage in sexual inter-
    course
KŪRCA black (from smoke)
KŪRCALAMBI to blacken (with smoke)
KŪRCAN eastern common crane (*Grus grus*)
KŪRCANAMBI 1. to blacken (with smoke)
    2. to cover with soot
KŪRDAMBI to stir up, to mix up
KŪRU a type of sour cake made from
    cow or mare's milk and liquor
KŪTAMBI to mix
KŪTAN pelican (*Pelecanus philippensis*)
    KŪTAN MORIN a white horse with red
        breast
KŪTHŪBUMBI caus. of *kūthūmbi*
KŪTHŪMBI to mix, to mix up, to stir,
    to stir up, to mingle, to confuse
    KŪTHŪME AFAMBI to fight a fierce
        battle
KŪTHŪRI a decorative cloud form used
    on the tops of boots, yurts, and
    other objects
    KŪTHŪRI ŠUFATU a turban decorated
        with cloud designs that was worn.
        in ancient times
KŪTKA the young of the Tibetan black

bear; cf. *mojihiyan*

KŪTU FATA hurrying, rushed

KŪTU KATA (onom.) the sound of walking feet

KŪWA light-yellow (horse)
  KŪWA DAMIN a light-yellow eagle

KŪWACA 1. an inkstone made of horn (carried on trips) 2. an ink vessel used by carpenters to draw straight lines 3. object babies can suck on, a pacifier
  KŪWACA I BERI a vessel made of horn used for holding gunpowder, powder horn
  KŪWACA YORO a large bone arrowhead used for mounted archery

KŪWACAMBI to cry (of deer)

KŪWACARABUMBI caus. of *kuwacarambi*

KŪWACARAMBI to hollow out, to clean out the inside of some object with a small knife, to scrape

KŪWAHA the name of a small bird with a thin beak that cries at night

KŪWAHALAMBI to open the mouth wide
  KŪWAHALAFI INJEMBI to laugh out loud, to rock from laughter

KŪWAI FAI SEME frivolous and talkative, shallow, empty-headed
  KŪWAI FAI SEME HŪWALIYASUN affable, friendly in a frivolous sort of way
  KŪWAI FAI SEME WEIHUKEN thoroughly frivolous

KŪWAICI 1. a fastener on the crupper 2. with the toes pointing outward

KŪWAICIDAMBI to walk with the toes pointing outward

KŪWAK CAK (onom.) the sound of fighting with poles or sticks
  KŪWAK CAK SEME 1. careless, coarse, carelessly boasting 2. (onom.) the sound of fighting with sticks
  KŪWAK CAK SEME ARBUŠAMBI to act in a careless, boastful manner

KŪWALA light yellow
  KŪWALA IHAN a light-yellow cow

KŪWALABUMBI caus. of *kuwalambi*

KŪWALACI a board over which hides are stretched to remove the hair

KŪWALAMBI to skin, to peel

KŪWALAR SEME straightforward, friendly
  KŪWALAR SEME GISUREMBI to speak in a straightforward manner

KŪWANG (onom.) 1. the sound of an explosion 2. the sound of knocking on wood
  KŪWANG CANG (onom.) the sound of drums and cymbals
  KŪWANG SEME (onom.) the sound of

many people talking

KŪWANGKAR SEME see *huwanggar seme*

KŪWANGTAHŪN 1. an area without trees or plants 2. bare, waste

KŪWAR (onom.) the sound of a seam ripping

KŪWARA MEGU a wild mushroom of a faint greenish color

KŪWARA SENCE the same as *kuwara megu*

KŪWARABUMBI caus./pass. of *kuwarambi*

KŪWARACANAMBI to look askance at

KŪWARAMBI to surround, to encircle, to circle (an erroneous word)

KŪWARAN 1. enclosure, encirclement, corral 2. camp (military), barracks 3. workshop, plant, factory 4. market place 5. yard of a monastery or temple
  KŪWARAN FAIDAN USIHA (勾 陳 星) the name of a constellation
  KŪWARAN I BOO barracks
  KŪWARAN I CALU the name of the granary of the troops of the green banner and garrison troops
  KŪWARAN I DA a commander elected by the officers of a camp
  KŪWARAN I KUNGGERI (營 料) the barracks office of the Board of War

KŪWARANAMBI to encircle, to circle

KŪWAS (onom.) 1. the sound of chopping wood 2. the sound of a falcon striking an object with its wings
  KŪWAS KIS (onom.) 1. the sound made by someone dragging his feet 2. the sound of a sickle mowing 3. the sound of dragging sacks of grain on a floor 4. the sound of a breaking stick

KŪWASA braggart, boastful

KŪWASADAMBI to brag, to boast wildly

KŪWATA KITI (onom.) the sound of a hard object striking something

KŪWATAR SEME spooked (of an excitable horse)

KŪWATIKI a one-year-old bear

KŪWATIRI a small animal resembling the bear, with scant shiny hair

K'AMDURI (亢) the name of a constellation
  K'AMDURI TOKDONGGO KIRU (亢 宿 旗) a banner depicting the constellation *k'amduri*

K'ARSI see *garša*

K'O section (of an organization)-- same as *kunggeri*

K'OSE a figured textile woven from gold and silk threads on a gauze background

K
K'

L

L

LA LI AKŪ see *la li seme akū*

LA LI SEMBI capable, adept

LA LI SEME quick-witted, sharp

    LA LI SEME AKŪ slow, slow-witted, desultory, lethargic

LA TAI a candleholder

LA ŽU YALI smoked meat

LAB SEME with the mouth packed full

LABA a horn; cf. *buleri*

LABARI 1. a large wooden cup for liquor 2. canopy over a Buddha-image

LABDAHŪN hanging down, drooping

    LABDAHŪN SUDULI I FUKJINGGA HERGEN (倒殣篆) a style of calligraphy

LABDU 1. many, much 2. wide, extensive (learning)

LABDUKAN rather a lot, rather many

LABDULAMBI to increase, to make more

LABDUNGGE much, many

LABI 1. diaper 2. protective curtain for defense against arrows on warships and battle wagons

LABSA 1. scant, rare, lacking 2. disappointed 3. considerably, rather much

    LABSA BAHARA JAKA a rare item

    LABSA EKIYEHE considerably diminished

    LABSA OHO become disappointed

LABSAMBI to fall in large flakes (snow)

LABSAN snowflake

LABSARI ILHA the name of a snow-white flower

LABSIMBI 1. to become soiled all over, to become covered with sores 2. to speak foolishly 3. to gulp down, to devour

    LABSIME JEMBI to gulp down food

LABTA LABTA in tatters, in rags

LADU a round quiver made of pigskin

LADURAMBI to drag around, to drag back and forth (as the result of a dispute)

LAFIHIYAN stupid, clumsy, awkward

LAFU SOGI Chinese cabbage (*Brassica sinensis*)

LAGU a river shrimp resembling the *hasima*

LAGU YOO a large sore on the hand

LAHA 1. straw mixed with mortar, used for making walls 2. catfish

LAHARI tarajo tree (*Ilex latifolia*)

LAHIN complicated, troublesome

    LAHIN TABUMBI to involve in a troublesome matter

    LAHIN TAHA got involved in a troublesome matter, became burdened with

LAHŪ 1. not adept, unskilled (especially at hunting and dealing with livestock) 2. scoundrel, hoodlum

LAHŪTA a type of small, rather incompetent hawk

LAHŪTAN ILGA the same as *hosan ilha*

LAI COKO bustard

LAIDABUMBI caus./pass. of *laidambi*

LAIDAKŪ 1. lapwing, peewit 2. mischievous, ill-behaved, self-willed (children)

LAIDAMBI 1. to welsh, to refuse to recognize one's debts or promises, to disavow 2. to blame someone else for one's own errors 3. to be mischievous, to be self-willed

LAIFA a type of small wild bean suitable for horse's fodder

LAIFAN see *laifa*

LAIFARAMBI (-ka) to collapse (from exhaustion), to wither and fall (of flowers)

LAIHŪ 1. a person who repudiates his debts or promises, a person who blames others for his own mistakes, shameless, unreliable 2. a self-willed child, a mischievous child

    LAIHŪ JUI profligate, undependable rascal

LAIHŪDAMBI to refuse to recognize one's debts or deeds, to be obstinate

LAIHŪN an undependable person, a good-for-nothing, a rogue

LAIHŪŠAMBI 1. to behave like a good-for-nothing, to act like a rogue 2. to be self-willed and obstinate (of children)

LAIHUTU a worthless rascal, a good-for-nothing

LAIHŪWA the same as *laihū*

LAJU clumsy, awkward, heavy, cumbersome

LAJUKAN rather clumsy, rather cumbersome

LAK AKŪ inconvenient, inappropriate, not right

LAK OHO appropriate, just right

LAK SE quickly! hurry up!

LAK SEME just right, right on the nose, it happened that . . .

LAKACAN NISIHA eelpout

LAKCA NIMAHA cod

LAKCABUMBI caus. of *lakcambi*

LAKCAMBI 1. to break off (v.i.), to snap 2. to come to an end 3. to be outstanding 4. to be remote

LAKCAN interruption, breaking off, pause
  LAKCAN AKŪ uninterrupted
  LAKCAN I SIRABUN one of the six yang tones

LAKCASHŪN broken off, interrupted

LAKDA simple, foolish; cf. *lokdo lakda*
  LAKDA LIKDI drooping, hanging down

LAKDAHŪN hanging down, drooping
  LAKDAHŪN TUHEKE fell into a drooping position

LAKDAHŪRI fully drooping, hanging all the way down

LAKDARI just then, all of a sudden (caught or grasped)
  LAKDARI NAMBUHA grabbed all of a sudden

LAKDARILAMBI to happen all of a sudden, to occur just at the right time

LAKDARŠAMBI to hang down, to droop

LAKIYABUMBI 1. caus./pass. of *lakiyambi* 2. to be in need, to be hard-pressed, to be in difficult straits

LAKIYAKŪ rod for hanging things
  LAKIYAKŪ HACUHAN a hanging pot

LAKIYAMBI to hang, to let hang, to hang up, to suspend
  LAKIYAHA ULMENGGE FUKJINGGA HERGEN (懸 針 篆) a style of calligraphy

LAKIYAN a string of cash

LAKIYANGGA hanging, suspended
  LAKIYANGGA HANGSE noodles that are hung out to dry
  LAKIYANGGA HUWEJEHEN a screen that is hung on the wall

LAKIYARI MONIO spider monkey

LAKU thick padded cotton trousers

LAKŪ see *lahū*

LALA 1. end, last, final, last throw with the *gacuha* 2. cooked glutinous millet or rice
  LALA BUDA steamed glutinous millet or rice
  LALA JUHE EFEN four-cornered dumplings made of glutinous rice wrapped in rush or bamboo leaves and boiled

LALAHA soft, weak

LALAHŪN 1. rather weak 2. faded

LALAKAI mushy, pulpy

LALANJI 1. very soft, mushy, pulpy, tender 2. exhausted, spent 3. repeatedly 4. very
  LALANJI HENDUHE said repeatedly

LALI agile, nimble, effortless; cf. *la li seme*

LALIMBI 1. to be soft, tender, pulpy 2. to be weakened from hunger

LALIN open, direct, straightforward

LALURI DUDU the name of a green turtledove with heavy plumage, same as *ilhuru dudu*

LAMA lama, monk
  LAMA NIYEHE in older Manchu used for *anngir niyehe* and later used for *ijifun niyehe*

LAMPA chaos, disorder, chaotic, disordered
  LAMPA I FON primeval chaos

LAMPALAMBI to be mixed up

LAMPANGGA desolate, primitive

LAMU indigo
  LAMU ORHO indigo plant

LAMUDAI the same as the *garunggū*

LAMUKAN light blue, bluish

LAMUKE Eastern red-spotted bluethroat (*Cyanosylvia svecica*)

LAMUN blue
  LAMUN BOJIRI ILHA China aster (*Callistephus chinensis*)
  LAMUN CECIKE ILHA an exotic blue flower that resembles a small bird
  LAMUN FUNGGALA (藍 翎 侍 衛) Junior Bodyguard (wearing the Blue Feather), BH 99
  LAMUN FUNGGALA BE BORO DE HADAMBI to attach a blue feather to the summer hat
  LAMUN GARUDAI a blue phoenix
  LAMUN GŪSAI FALGA (藍 旗 甲) office for the blue banners in the Board of War
  LAMUN GŪWASIHIYA Eastern gray heron, (*Ardea cinerea*)
  LAMUN HOOHAN the same as *lamun gūwasihiya*
  LAMUN LAHŪTA a black kite, a black vulture

L

LAMUN MUHELIYENGGE GU a flat piece of blue jade with a hole in the center used in sacrifices to heaven

LAMUN NARHŪNGGA HOLBONGGO HOOŠAN a type of blue paper used for mounting things

LAMUN SAMSU a type of fine blue linen

LAMUN ULGIYAN CECIKE black-capped kingfisher (*Halcyon pileata*)

LAMURCAN a bird that resembles the crane--it is over three Chinese feet tall and is raised in gardens

LAMURHAN one name for the heron

LAN 1. indigo; cf. *lamu* 2. Chinese orchid, see *lan ilha*

LAN DIYAN HŪWA ILGA indigo flower

LAN GAIMBI to attest, to base oneself on good evidence

LAN ILHA Chinese orchid

LAN ORHO indigo plant; cf. *lamu orho*

LANG LANG SEME (eating) with the mouth stuffed full

LANGCA garnet

LANGGABUMBI caus./pass. of *langgambi*

LANGGAMBI to detain, to hold up, to delay

LANGGAŠAMBI to be indecisive

LANGGŪ pumpkin

LANGJU one ten-millionth (of a Chinese foot)

LANGKA the flower of reeds or rushes

LANGLAI dung beetle

LANGSE dirty, unclean

LANGSE MOO the horizontal wooden supports at both ends of a wagon or sedan chair

LANGSEDAMBI to act or speak in a dirty manner, to be dirty

LANGTANAMBI to have a large head, to be thick or heavy at an extremity

LANGTANGGA see *langtungga*

LANGTU a large double-headed hammer for use on iron

LANGTULAMBI to hit with a double-headed hammer

LANGTUNGGA large-headed

LAR LIR SEME 1. profuse, abundant 2. sticky

LAR SEME 1. talkative, long-winded 2. sticky, viscous, gluey

LAR SEME DALHŪN viscous and sticky

LARBAHŪN weary, worn out

LARGIKAN rather profuse

LARGIN 1. profuse, abundant, complicated 2. annoying

LARGIN LAMPA complex, intricate

LARGIŠAMBI to act in a diffuse, complicated way

LARGIŠAME GISUREMBI to speak in a confused, complicated manner

LARHŪN sweet potato

LARIN one name for the donkey

LARSEN soggy

LARSENDA yam (*Dioscorea japonica*)

LARTURI moonseed (*Menispermum dauricum*)

LASAN a consolation toss in playing with *gacuha*

LASARI hanging down so as to form a canopy (leaves and branches)

LASARI MOO a tree with thick drooping branches

LASARI ŠUFATU an ancient-style hat with tassels hanging down in back

LASARINAMBI to hang down (of branches)

LASHA 1. asunder, into sections, in two, into pieces 2. decidedly, definitely

LASHA LASHA in sections, asunder, in two

LASHA OBUMBI to break off, to make a break with

LASHA SARKŪ don't know at all

LASHAJAMBI to break off, to break in two

LASHALABUMBI 1. caus. of *lashalambi* 2. to cut off, to terminate

LASHALAMBI 1. to break in two, to cut in two, to sever 2. to terminate 3. to make a decision, to act decisively

LASHALAME ICIHIYAMBI to manage decisively

LASHALAN cutting off, decision

LASHANGGA JAHŪDAI a boat used in rapids or shallows

LASHATAI decisively, decidedly, definitely

LASIHIBUMBI caus./pass. of *lasihimbi*

LASIHIDABUMBI caus./pass. of *lasihidambi*

LASIHIDAMBI to shake hard

LASIHIKŪ 1. thongs with balls at the end that are attached to a drum and that strike the drum when shaken 2. a weapon consisting of a pole with a shorter pole attached to its end by a chain, a flail

LASIHIKŪ TUNGKEN a hand drum with thongs attached that have balls at the end

LASIHIMBI 1. to shake, to toss around, to brandish 2. to write the cursive script

LASIHIME ARAMBI to write the cursive script

LASIHIRE HERGEN grass script--the most cursive of the Chinese scripts

LASIHIRE JANGKŪ a sword with a very long handle (more like a spear with a long curved blade)

LASIRI see *lasari*

LATA 1. slow 2. dull, not clever

LATA JATA untalented, not up to par

LATA MOYO slow, dull-witted
LATA MOYO ERDEMU AKŪ dull-witted
  and untalented
LATAI a candlestand
LATAKAN rather slow, rather dull
LATIHI torn piece of a mat
LATUBUKŪ a sticky pole used for catching birds
LATUBUMBI caus./pa s. of *latumbi*
  LATUBUHA AFAHA a page pasted to the
    back of a document
LATUKŪ SOGI a wild plant with yellow
  flowers and sticky leaves that can
  be cooked and eaten--similar to
  hūrga sogi
LATUMBI 1. to paste, to glue 2. to
  attach, to stick on 3. to have an
  illicit affair with, to commit
  adultery 4. to get dirty and sticky
  (of clothing) 5. to get (an illness)
  6. to incite, to provoke
LATUNAMBI to go to incite, to go to
  encroach, to go to commit an illicit
  sexual act
LATUNGGA fond of interfering, fond of
  causing dissension, fond of butting
  into other people's business
LATUNJIMBI to come to incite, to come
  to encroach, to come to commit an
  illicit sexual act
LAYABUMBI caus. of *layambi*
LAYAMBI (-ka) to wilt, to wither
LE LA SEME (going) all together, com-
  ing and going all together
LEB SEME unexpectedly, spontaneously
LEBDEHUN spineless, untalented, stupid
LEBDEREMBI (-ke) 1. to lack talent, to
  appear stupid 2. to be spineless,
  to go limp, to droop (of birds'
  wings)
LEBENGGI swampy, marshy, damp, muddy
  LEBENGGI BA marsh, swamp
  LEBENGGI USIN muddy field
LEBKIDEMBI see *lekidembi*
LEDEHUN see *letehun*
LEDER SEME slow (of a flying object)
  LEDER SEME DEYEMBI to fly slowly
LEDUREMBI to beat up on someone (of a
  group)
LEFU bear
  LEFU ŠAN 'bear's ears,' a creeping
    plant with leaves that are green
    on the outside and white on the
    inside (*Senecio campestris*)
LEHEBUMBI caus. of *lehembi*
LEHELE 1. prostitute, whore 2. il-
  legitimate, born of a whore
  LEHELE JUI bastard, child of a whore
  LEHELE MAMA mistress of a brothel
LEHEMBI to protest a fait accompli,
  to appeal, to complain, to regret
LEHENDUMBI/LEHENUMBI to appeal to-
  gether

LEJIRHI one name for the wildcat; cf.
  ujirhi
LEKCEHUN the same as *lekdehun*
LEKDE LAKDA 1. hanging in shreds or
  rags 2. hanging like fruit on a
  plant 3. following closely behind
LEKDEDEMBI see *lekderembi*
LEKDEHUN hanging down and screening
  something
  LEKDEHUN DALIBUMBI to hang down and
    screen something
LEKDEREMBI (-ke) to have an unkempt,
  dirty appearance
LEKDERI NIONGNIYAHA one name for the
  wild goose; cf., e.g., *jurgangga
  gasha*, *kenderhen niongniyaha*
LEKDERI NIYEHE one name for the duck
LEKE 1. a whetstone, a grinding stone
  2. a type of honey pastry made in
  the form of a whetstone
LEKEBUMBI caus. of *lekembi*
LEKEDEMBI see *lekidembi*
LEKEMBI to sharpen, to grind on a
  whetstone
LEKERHI sea otter (*Latax lutris*)
LEKERHIN a seal (animal)
LEKERI a spiral shell used as a horn
LEKETEMBI see *lekidembi*
LEKIDEMBI to wave the hands over the
  head while dancing, to wave the
  hands and feet at wrestling
LEKSEI all together, in unison
LELI 1. extensive, vast, wide 2. pro-
  tective armor for the chest
LEMBAN see *lempen*
LEMPEN 1. a tent of rush mats used as
  a shade from the sun 2. a protec-
  tive shelter of rush mats for cat-
  tle
LEMPI prematurely gray, with white
  hairs among the black
LEMPINEMBI to turn prematurely gray,
  to get white hairs among the black
LEN immense, strong and big
  LEN COKO one name for the chicken;
    cf. *kemuri coko*
LENGGERI a type of large rat
LENGGETU the name of a ceremonial hat
  of the Hsia dynasty
LENGKEN rather big and strong
LENGLEN LANGLAN SEME sloppy, careless,
  slovenly
LENGSEKI coarse, crude, clumsy, awk-
  ward
LENGSENGGI see *lengseki*
LENGTENEMBI to be crude or awkward
LEOLEBUMBI caus. of *leolembi*
LEOLEMBI to discuss, to talk over
LEOLEN discussion, disputation
LEOLENDUMBI/LEOLENUMBI to discuss
  together
LEOMBI (-ha) to perform feats of mili-
  tary prowess on horseback in front

L

of enemy troops in order to frighten
them

LEOSE multistoried building, tower,
building

LER BIYAR SEME walking slowly

LER LAR SEME the same as *ler biyar
seme*

LER SEME 1. profuse, luxuriant (vege-
tation) 2. serious, upright, solemn
3. harmonious, ordered
  LER SEME AGAMBI to rain a fine rain
  LER SEME BANJIHABI grows profusely

LERGIYEN resolute, having great determination, having great capacity

LESEREMBI to ripple, to form ripples

LESUMBI 1. to run fast (of camels and
horses) 2. to skim the earth (of
birds)
  LESUME ŠODOME galloping without
  stopping

LETE LATA 1. heavy (of a load) 2. lagging behind and trying to catch up

LETEHUN large or wide at the top

LETUHUN see *letehun*

LEYECUN ballad

LEYEMBI to sing without accompaniment

LI one-thousandth (of a Chinese foot)

LI JY litchi

LIB SEME right through, piercing (of
a spear thrown at an animal)

LIBKI 1. worn-out horse, a horse that
has been beaten with a whip 2.
scorching hot, sweltering (weather)

LIBKIMBI (-ha) to be worn-out (of
horses)

LIBU one-billionth (of a Chinese foot)

LICISE the name of an exotic fruit that
resembles a crossbow projectile

LIDU mung bean (*Phaseolus mungo*)

LIFA deep (into), penetrating
  LIFA DAHA penetrated deeply (of an
  arrow)
  LIFA DOSIKA penetrated deeply
  LIFA GIDALAHA pierced deeply

LIFABUMBI caus./pass. of *lifambi*

LIFADAMBI to sink slightly (into mud
or mire)

LIFAGAN see *lifahan*

LIFAHAN mud, muck, slime
  LIFAHAN CIFAHAN mud and slime

LIFAHANAMBI to become muddy

LIFAKŪ swamp, morass

LIFAMBI to engulf (in mud), to suck
into (mud)

LIFAN a stone or wooden vessel used to
catch oil and wine from a press

LILCI down, downward

LIMU (吏目) see *icihiyasi*

LING PAI tally with a charm written on
it--used by Taoist priests

LING SEME heavy, burdensome

LING YABUMBI to play wine-drinking
games

LINGDAN a miraculous medicine, elixir

LINGGE a shining deed, glorious deed

LINGJY a kind of auspicious fungus
(*Fomes japonicus*)

LINGSE 1. a type of thin satinlike
material, damask 2. collar

LINGSIKA one name for the tiger

LIO HŪWANG sulphur

LIO KIO GURUN I KUREN (琉球馆)
an establishment for taking care of
Ryukyuan emissaries

LIO SING USIHA meteor

LIOHO a white-striped sea fish, Siberian salmon

LIOHŪWANG the same as *lio hūwang*

LIR LIYAR SEME smooth and sticky (like
a good paste)

LIRHA (柳) the name of a constellation
  LIRHA TOKDONGGO KIRU a banner depicting the constellation *lirha*

LIẎANSE curtain

LIYAR LIYAR NASAMBI to slink

LIYAR SEME sticky, pasty

LIYASE a hanging, a curtain or drape

LIYELIYEBUMBI caus. of *liyeliyembi*

LIYELIYEHUN dizzy, faint, delirious

LIYELIYEMBI to become dizzy, to become
faint

LIYELIYEN ILHA a purple flower whose
odor causes faintness

LIYELIYENDUMBI/LIYELIYENUMBI to become
faint together

LIYELIYEŠEMBI to be (constantly) faint,
to be very dizzy

LIYOLIYO an interjection of derision
used toward untalented, worthless
people

LIYOO fodder, forage
  LIYOO ORHO fodder

LO 1. cymbal, gong 2. silk gauze,
crepe
  LO SUJE a very thin, light silk
  gauze for autumn clothing

LO CA see *rakša*

LO HAN an arhat

LO LA SEME unexpectedly, all of a
sudden

LOB SEME suddenly dark

LOBI gluttonous, ravenous
  LOBI HUTU the ghost of an evil person who can never satisfy his
  hunger or thirst, preta

LOBIN see *lobi*

LOCA see *rakša*

LODAN the anklebone of a cow or sheep
(used in a dicelike game); cf.
gacuha

LODUR SEME see *ludur seme*

LOHO sword
  LOHO USIHA see *lohū usiha*

LOHOBUMBI to cause great trouble, to
place in a difficult position, to

have difficulty, to be in difficult
   straits
LOHŪ USIHA the unlucky star Rāhu--
   Ypsilon in the constellation Pegasus
LOK SEME suddenly, unexpectedly
LOKDI dense, thick
LOKDO LAKDA clumsy, awkward
LOKDOHON sitting alone, alone and quiet
LOKDORI unexpectedly, in an unforeseen
   manner
LOKSEME see *lok seme*
LOKSIMBI to speak foolishly or crazily
LOKSIN foolishness, nonsense
LOKSINAMBI to become pudgy, obese
LOKSOBUMBI to be despondent from teas-
   ing or taunting
LOKSON vexation, annoyance (at being
   teased)
LOKTOHON see *lokdohon*
LOKTOROMBI (-ko) to sit alone
LOLI FODOHO weeping willow (*Salix
   babylonica*)
LOLI FULANA ILHA a crabapple (*Pyrus
   spectabilis*) with hanging branches
LOLO the anklebone of a pig used as a
   die
LOLO SEME boasting idly, chattering
   foolishly
LOMI rice kept in storage for a number
   of years--the same as *hukšeri bele*
LOMIKTE a light yellow gem resembling
   the cat's-eye
LONG LONG SEME see *long seme*
LONG SEME to keep on talking foolishly,
   to talk nonsense
LONGKO a cooking pot made of bronze or
   copper
LONGKON a gong or cymbal
LONGSIKŪ a person who chatters on and
   on
LONGSIMBI to chatter on and on, to
   talk foolishness
LONGTO halter, headstall
LONGTOLOBUMBI caus. of *longtolombi*
LONGTOLOMBI to wear a halter or head-
   stall
LONGTU see *longto*
LOO 1. prison 2. gong; cf. *lo* 3. see
   lomi
   LOO BE TUWAKIYARA NIYALMA see *loo
      dz*
   LOO DZ jailer
LOO LOO maternal grandmother
LOO NIYANG old lady, lady of the
   household
LOO SIYAN ŠENG old man, old gentleman
LOODAN 1. old female role in Chinese
   opera 2. see *lodan*
LOOMBI to bark or growl fiercely
LOOYE master of the household
LOR SEME speaking incessantly, talka-
   tive
LORBODO three-year-old deer

LORIN mule
LOSA the same as *lorin*
LOSE the same as *lorin*
LOSHAN a basket woven from willow
   branches used for carrying preserved
   vegetables; cf. *šangšaha*
LOSO slushy, muddy (especially refers
   to the spring when the fields are
   still too muddy to plow)
LOSTU JAHŪDAI a small, wide river boat
   with low sides
LU LU SEME see *lulu seme*
LU NIMAHA a sort of perch, see *sahamha*
LU ŠUI MUKE brine in which bean-curd
   is prepared
LUDAHŪN (旻) the name of a constel-
   lation
   LUDAHŪN TOKDONGGO KIRU a banner
      depicting the constellation
      ludahūn
LUDUN a reed basket for grain
LUDUR SEME thick and sticky (of liq-
   uids)
   LUDUR SEME HALHŪN sticky hot
LUDZ oven, stove
LUGIYA HENGKE bitter melon (*Momordica
   charantia*)
LUHU 1. a headless arrow with a dull
   point resembling a pestle--used for
   shooting sitting birds and for tar-
   get practice
   LUHU CECIKE one of the names of the
      snipe; cf. *karka cecike*
LUHULEBUMBI caus. of *luhulembi*
LUHULEMBI to shoot a headless arrow
   (*luhu*)
LUJEN an imperial coach
LUJU one hundred-millionth
LUJURI pelt of a black fox
   LUJURI DOBI black fox
LUK SEME strongly, intensely, thickly,
   in considerable quantity
   LUK SEME DUSHUN intensely dark
   LUK SEME HALHŪN hot and windless
   LUK SEME TALMAKA a thick fog has
      descended
LUKA the young of the lynx; cf. *silun*
LUKDEREMBI see *lukdurembi*
LUKDU dense
   LUKDU LAKDA wobbling, flopping
      about, flabby, pudgy
LUKDUHUN ruffled, dishevelled (of the
   feathers on sick birds)
LUKDUREMBI (-ke) to become ruffled,
   dishevelled (of the feathers on sick
   birds)
LUKSIMBI to throb (of a festered
   wound or sore)
LUKU 1. thick, dense (of hair and
   plants) 2. caterpillar
LUKUKEN rather thick, rather dense
LULU ordinary, common, average (of
   ability)

L

LULU LALA muddled, illogical
LULU SEME ordinary, average
LUMBABUMBI caus./pass. of *lumbambi*
LUMBAMBI to smear with glue or paste
LUMBANAMBI to become covered with dirt
  or mud
LUMBIMBI (-ha) see *lumbambi*
LUMBU suddenly flowing slowly (of a
  place in a stream)
  LUMBU MUKE slow-flowing water
  LUMBU OHO suddenly became slow-
    flowing
LUMBURJAMBI to be soft, not firm (of
  wet earth)
LUNG SEME see *luk seme*
LUNGGU a male sable; cf. *seke*
LUR SEME thick, viscous, concentrated
LURGIKEN rather rough (of the voice)
LURGIN rough, coarse (of the voice)

LURGIŠEMBI to change (of an adoles-
  cent's voice), to be rough (of the
  voice)
LURGIYAN see *lurgin*
LUSHUN tired, weary
LUSU ŠOBIN a pastry with a walnut
  filling
LUSUMBI to become tired, to become
  weary
LUŠI (錄事) secretary in a Board
  of the eighth or ninth rank
LUWAN the male of a colorful phoenix-
  like bird that was considered a
  symbol of concord between prince and
  minister as well as between husband
  and wife
LUWANGGON small bells on the bits of
  the horses that drew the imperial
  coach

L

M

MA here! (said when handing something to another person)

MABU a cloth for wiping off objects

MABULABUMBI caus. of *mabulambi*

MABULAKŪ mop, swab (a rag attached to a pole used for wiping the floor)

MABULAMBI to wipe, to wipe off

MACA a bitter-tasting wild plant resembling garlic

    MACA DUHA large intestine of horses, donkeys, and mules

MACI an iron ring on the crupper of beasts of burden

MACIBUMBI caus. of *macimbi*

MACIHA see *macika*

MACIHI the observation of the Buddhist commandments

    MACIHI JAFAMBI to meditate and observe the Buddhist commandments

MACIKA border or edge of a mat or net

    MACIKA ARAMBI to weave the rope border of a hunting or fishing net

MACIMBI 1. when patching a garment, to gather the edges of the patch on the inside while smoothing out the outside surface 2. to lay squares of grass to form a lawn

MACUMBI to become thin, skinny

MADABUMBI 1. caus. of *madambi* 2. to collect

MADAGA 1. interest 2. massive, large

MADAGAN interest (on money)

MADAGE an affectionate expression used while patting an old person or child on the back

MADAMBI 1. to expand, to swell, to grow (of interest) 2. to stand on end (of hair)

MADANGGA elastic, extensile

MADARI UJU an animal head made of bronze with a ring in its mouth attached to a door to facilitate opening and closing

MADASU leaven, fermenting agent

MADIYOO mah-jongg tiles; cf. *sasuri*

MAFA grandfather, ancestor, old man

MAFANGGE having a grandfather or ancestor

MAFARI plural of *mafa*

    MAFARI MIYOO ancestral temple

    MAFARI SOORIN ancestral tablets

MAFUTA 1. a buck deer 2. rope made of hemp

    MAFUTA BUHŪ a buck deer

MAGER 1. a wild plant with edible roots--the white variety is known as *šanggiyan selbete*, the red variety as *monggo sedo*

MAGI see *maki*

MAHALA hat, cap--especially the round fur winter hat of Manchu officials

    MAHALA ELBEKU a cover for a hat (used when raining)

    MAHALA GAHA a crow with a large body and white head

    MAHALA IHAN a cow with head and body of different colors--usually black and white

    MAHALA MAKTAME TUWAMBI to look upward

    MAHALA TUKIYEKU a hatrack

MAHALALAMBI to wear a hat

MAHATU 1. hat worn by high officials and nobles in ancient times 2. hat worn by the emperor, crown

MAHATUN a hat of ancient times

MAHILA stalk, stem

MAHŪ 1. a (devil) mask 2. a leather hood covering the head, neck, and shoulders

MAHŪLABUMBI caus./pass. of *mahūlambi*

MAHŪLAMBI 1. to wipe out, to strike out (errors when writing) 2. to humiliate, to disgrace 3. to wear a hood

MAHŪNTU another name for the large black monkey called *elintu*

MAIDARI Maitreya, the coming Buddha

MAIFARAHA a motherless child

MAIGU deaf; cf. *dutu*

MAIKAN tent

MAILACI krishum (*Iris ensata*)--the roots of this plant are used to make brushes

MAILAMBI to get infected

MAILAN *Iris pallasii*, or perhaps the same as *mailaci*

MAILAN I USE the seeds of *Iris palasii*

MAILARU 'won't you get infected please!'--an oath

MAILASUN arbor vitae, cypress

MAIMADAMBI to walk weaving from side to side, to stagger

MAIMAN business, trade; cf. *hūda*

MAIMAŠAMBI to do business

MAISE wheat, grain

MAISEI WEKJI SUSE wheat husk, chaff from wheat

MAISHA see *maishan*

MAISHAN 1. a decorative clasp on the crupper of beasts of burden 2. Chinese boxthorn (*Lycium chinense*)

MAISHAN HALU a meal made from the fruit of the Chinese boxthorn

MAISHAN HALU I SACIMA a pastry made from sesame and the fruit of the Chinese boxthorn

MAISIRI a club held in one hand (a type of weapon)

MAITU a pole heavier at one end than the other (a weapon), mace

MAITULAMBI to fight with a pole

MAITUN DA a pealike plant with an edible root that secretes a white juice

MAITUŠABUMBI caus./pass. of *maitušambi*

MAITUŠAMBI to beat with a pole

MAJAN a long arrow with a long narrow head used for fighting

MAJIGE 1. a little, a little bit 2. somewhat, about

MAKA an introductory particle of doubt or questioning: I wonder . . ., could it really be that . . . .

MAKAMBI to become muddled, to become confused in one's thinking

MAKARAMBI to become weak, to become decrepit

MAKARAME SAKDAKA became old and decrepit

MAKI tassel on a banner, yak-tail pendant on a banner

MAKITU a yak-tail banner

MAKJAHŪN short, dwarflike

MAKJAN short, midget, dwarf

MAKJANAMBI to be short, to be a midget

MAKSIBUMBI caus. of *maksimbi*

MAKSIKŪ dancer

MAKSIKŪ MOO a horizontal stick on a banner pole from which the banner hangs

MAKSIMBI to dance

MAKSIRE GARUDANGGA KIRU a banner on which a dancing phoenix is embroidered

MAKSIN a dance, dancing

MAKSINAMBI to go to dance

MAKSINJIMBI to come to dance

MAKSISI MAHATUN a hat worn by dancers in ancient times

MAKTABUMBI 1. caus./pass. of *maktambi* 2. to get lost, to lose one's way, to be abandoned

MAKTACUKA praiseworthy

MAKTACUN praise

MAKTAMBI 1. to throw, to toss 2. to let loose, to release (a hawk) 3. to kick (of horses, cows, etc.) 4. to praise, to extol

MAKTANDUMBI/MAKTANUMBI to praise together

MAKTANJIMBI 1. to come to throw 2. to come to praise

MAKTAŠAMBI to throw around, to toss about, to fling

MALA a wooden mallet

MALAHI a striped yellow wild cat

MALANGGŪ sesame

MALANGGŪ ABDAHA EFEN thin sesame cakes used by the Manchus at offerings in the sixth month

MALANGGŪ CAI tea with sesame added

MALANGGŪ HAKSANGGA EFEN baked wheat cakes garnished with sesame seeds

MALANGGŪ IRA FISIHE MAISE TURI sesame, glutinous millet, panicled millet, wheat, and beans-- the five grains

MALANGGŪ MISUN sesame paste

MALANGGŪ ŠOBIN baked wheat cakes covered with sesame seeds

MALARI lax, dilatory

MALAŠAMBI to beat to death fish caught under ice

MALFUN CECE transparent cloth that has holes resembling sesame seeds

MALHŪKAN rather a lot, quite a few

MALHŪN 1. economical, frugal 2. seemingly near but really far, long and dull (road) 3. thick at one end

MALHŪN YOKCINGGA modest and (still) good looking

MALHŪNGGA 1. frugal 2. sufficient for use 3. long and boring (road)

MALHŪŠABUMBI caus. of *malhūšambi*

MALHŪŠAMBI to use frugally

MALHŪŠANDUMBI/MALHŪŠANUMBI to use frugally together

MALJIHA an anklebone die (*gacuha*) polished on both sides

MALTA beluga, white whale, dolphin

MALTA BERI a bow covered with water buffalo horn

MALTAKŪ a tool for scraping dirt or mud

MALU a bottle (for liquor)

MALUKA see *malukan*

MALUKAN abundant, in large quantities

MAMA 1. grandmother, female ancestor, old lady 2. pocks, rash

MAMA ERŠEMBI for pocks to appear, to get smallpox

MAMA TUCIMBI the same as *mama eršembi*

MAMA YADAHŪN the pocks are few

MAMAN support for a rafter; cf. *bangtu*

MAMARAMBI see *namarambi*

MAMARI plural of *mama*

MAMFIN see *mampin*

MAMGIYABUMBI caus. of *mamgiyambi*

MAMGIYAKŪ extravagant person, lavish spender, squanderer

MAMGIYAMBI to be extravagant, to squander, to dissipate

MAMGIYANDUMBI/MAMGIYANUMBI to squander together, to spend lavishly together

MAMPI see *mampin*

MAMPIBUMBI caus. of *mampimbi*

MAMPILAMBI to tie a knot

MAMPIMBI to tie a knot, to knot

MAMPIN knot

MAMPINGGA ILHA the name of a light yellow flower--*Edgeworthia chry-santha*

MAMUGIYA crab apple

MAMUHAN vent, ventilation hole

MAMUHAN FA a skylight

MAMUHAN SANGGA ventilation hole in the wall of a house

MAMUHAN SIHAN bamboo air pipe inserted into grain in storage for ventilation

MAMUHAN TURA a short pillar between the upper and lower beams of the ceiling

MAMUKE one name for the rabbit

MAMUN AKŪ listless, dejected, depressed, without any enthusiasm left

MAMYARI an exotic fruit from Tonkin and South China from a tree that resembles the litchi

MAN I NIYALMA a southern aborigine

MANABUMBI caus./pass. of *manambi*

MANAGA diapers

MANAMBI 1. to be worn-out, to be tattered, to be old (not new) 2. to be dispersed (troops) 3. to come to an end, to wane, to diminish

MANAHA BIYA last month

MANAHA ŠANIYAHA torn and tattered

MANASHŪN 1. worn-out, old, tattered 2. waning, end, the month's end

MANDA slow, late

MANDAKAN rather slow, a little slow

MANDAL (Buddhist) the mandala

MANDAL BOLGOMIMBI on the day of a religious service, to purify the cult objects with incense and recite a portion of scripture

MANDAL ILHA *Datura alba*

MANDALAMBI to be slow, to be late

MANDARA (Buddhist) the tree of paradise

MANDARAWA ILHA fig bloom (*Ficus carica*)

MANDUMBI to mature, to grow up

MANG ORHO *Illicium anisatum*

MANG ORHO USENEMBI one of the divisions of the solar year falling on June 7th or 8th

MANGGA 1. hard (not soft), difficult 2. expensive 3. expert at, strong in, capable 4. expertly made, well-crafted 5. strong, fierce, a strong man

MANGGA ARAMBI to show off one's strength, to intimidate

MANGGA BUDA pastry

MANGGA CECE hard silk gauze

MANGGA CECERI a type of hard, strong silk

MANGGA DOOSE a skilled Taoist

MANGGA FILI hard and fast

MANGGA MOO oak

MANGGA MOO I USIHA acorn

MANGGA NIYECEN leather patch attached to the inner side of a boot's heel

MANGGA TANGGA tough, too hard to chew

MANGGA TUWABUNGGA HOOŠAN a type of hard, thick poster paper

MANGGABURU a daring fellow

MANGGAI merely, simply

MANGGAI OCI if worst comes to worst, if it is with difficulty, in extreme cases

MANGGAKAN rather hard, difficult, capable, etc.

MANGGALAMBI to be difficult, to be serious (of an illness), to worsen, to act in a hard or vigorous manner

MANGGASA plural of *mangga*: strong men

MANGGAŠABUMBI caus. of *manggašambi*

MANGGAŠACUKA difficult, embarrassing

MANGGAŠAMBI to have difficulties, to be shy, to be hesitant (about doing something)

MANGGI after (after the perfect participle or imperative)

MANGGICI if worst comes to worst

MANGGISU badger; cf. *dorgon*

MANGGIYAN 1. running nose (of horses and cattle) 2. a spirit that descends into a shaman who has invoked the tiger god, causing the shaman to dance

MANGGIYAN WECEKU WASIKA the spirit who causes the shaman to dance has descended

M

MANGGIYANAMBI to get a running nose
  (of livestock)
MANGGO same as *manggao*
MANGKAN sand dune
  MANGKAN GŪWARA another name for
    the *elben gūwara*
MANGKARA a horse or dog with white
  hair on the head, eyes, and muzzle
  MANGKARA GAHA 1. white-headed crow
    2. same as *mahala gaha*
MANJIHA came late, came slowly
MANJU Manchu
  MANJU BITHE Manchu writing, Manchu
    text
  MANJU DANGSE BOO (滿檔房)
    Record and Registry Office (also
    in charge of preparing Manchu
    documents), BH 379
  MANJU GŪSA Manchu banner, general
    of a Manchu banner
  MANJU HERGEN Manchu script, Manchu
    letter (of the alphabet)
  MANJU MONGGO BITHE UBALIYAMBURE BOO
    (滿洲蒙古翻譯房)
    the Manchu translation Office of
    the Court of Colonial Affairs
  MANJU WESIMBURE BITHEI BA (滿本
    堂) Manchu Copying Office, BH 138
MANJURABUMBI caus. of *manjurambi*
MANJURAMBI 1. to speak or write Manchu
  2. to act like a Manchu, to behave
  in the Manchu manner
MANJUSA plural of *manju*
  MANJUSAI MUKŪN HALA BE UHERI EJEHE
    BITHE WEILERE KUREN (滿洲民
    族通譜館) office con-
    cerned with Manchu genealogies
MANJUSIRI Mañjuśrī--the name of a
  bodhisattva
MANOO agate
MANSUI brightly colored satin with
  golden cloud and dragon designs
  MANSUI UNDURAKŪ the same as *mansui*
MANTUMBI see *mandumbi*
MAOBIN HOOŠAN a kind of paper made
  from bamboo pulp
MAOKALA a kind of hawk
MARABUMBI caus. of *marambi*
MARAKŪ one who declines or rejects
MARAMBI to decline, to reject, to turn
  down, to refuse
MARANDUMBI/MARANUMBI to refuse, to
  decline together
MARATAMBI to decline weakly, to refuse
  moderately
MARGAN the young of the roe deer
MARHAN see *margan*
MARI time, occasion (same as *jergi* and
  mudan)
MARIBUMBI caus. of *marimbi*
MARIMBI 1. to return, to go back, to
  turn around, to about-face 2. to
  fall off (of pocks)

MARIMBU WEHE agate
MARIN turning around, return, return
  trip
MARMA NISIHA a small red-spotted sea
  fish
MARU a school of fish; cf. *hingge*
MARULAMBI to form a school, to school
  (of fish)
MARUTU CECIKE spice finch (*Lonchura
  punctulata*)
MASAKŪ a swing hung from a rafter in-
  side a building
MASAMBI to swing in a *masakū*
MASAN the sediment of sesame seeds
  left after the oil has been ex-
  tracted
  MASAN DEHE a fishhook with a bait
    of sediment
MASE 1. pockmarks 2. a pockmarked
  person; cf. *kerkeri*
  MASE MUYARI litchi
  MASE USIHA walnut
  MASE USIHA I FAHA the edible part
    of the walnut
MASELAKŪ a snare for catching birds
MASIKAN weighty, robust
MASILABUMBI caus. of *masilambi*
MASILAMBI to exist in abundance, to
  strain one's powers, to do force-
  fully
  MASILAME in abundance, plentifully,
    forcefully, tightly (of tying)
MASIRI an exotic fruit that tastes
  like the walnut
MAŠA dipper, ladle
MAŠALAKŪ a piece of wood above a win-
  dow with holes in which the pivots
  of the casement turn
MAŠAN support, handle
  MAŠAN BAHAMBI to obtain support,
    to get something to hold on to
MAŠANGGA NIYALMA a person who under-
  stands how to manage affairs well
MATABUMBI caus. of *matambi*
MATALAMBI to stamp the earth with the
  hind hoof
MATAMBI to heat in order to bend
  (bone, horn, wood, bamboo, etc.)
MATAN a kind of sweet food made from
  barley, malt candy
MATANGGA caved in (cheeks), sunken
  and pursed (lips)
  MATANGGA WASE a ridge tile
MATARAKŪ a round straw pad that is
  placed on the head for carrying
  things
MATUN a watch station on a city wall
MAYA a dipper with a spout
MAYALAMBI to carry on the forearm
MAYAMBI (-ka/ha) to diminish, to sub-
  side, to go down (of swelling), to
  calm down, to be freed from a spell
MAYAMBUMBI 1. caus. of *mayambi* 2. to

M

exorcise, to break a spell

MAYAN 1. arm 2. blood from a wounded
animal, blood stuck on an arrow
MAYAN SAIN many animals were killed
on the battue

ME pulse, vein
ME JAFAMBI to take the pulse
ME TUWAMBI to check the pulse

MEDE news, information, intelligence

MEDEBUMBI to give news, to bring news
MEDEBURE DENGJAN a red lantern that
was hoisted as a signal at certain
intervals while the emperor was
traveling

MEDEGE news, information
MEDEGE GASHA seagull
MEDEGE NIYEHE the same as *medege
gasha*

MEDEGERI CECIKE 1. one name for the
seagull 2. a bird that announces the
arrival of guests by crying and flying

MEDEHE news, information

MEDERGU ILHA *Rhododendron sinicum*

MEDERI sea
MEDERI DORGON sea otter; cf. *lekerhi*
MEDERI EIHEN seal; cf. *lekerhin*
MEDERI GUBCI TAIFIN NECINGGE MUDAN
a piece of music played while tea
was brought in at great banquets
MEDERI HŪLHA pirate
MEDERI JAKA sea product
MEDERI JAKARAME along the seacoast
MEDERI JUWERE CALU a Peking granary
of the Board of Finance
MEDERI KATURI sea crab (of the North
China Sea)
MEDERI KILAHŪN seagull; cf. *medege
gasha*
MEDERI KIONGGUHE the sea myna of
Fukien
MEDERI MELKEŠEMBI the sea produces
a mirage
MEDERI SAMPA sea shrimp, prawn
MEDERI ULHŪMA a black sea bird re-
sembling the pheasant

MEDESI messenger

MEGU mushroom

MEHE a spayed cow

MEHEJEN sow

MEHELE the same as *mehejen*
MEHELE JUI piglet, shote

MEHEN a sow that has not yet farrowed

MEHETE having a short upper lip

MEHUBUMBI caus. of *mehumbi*

MEHUMBI to bow, to make a bow to, to
bow down

MEHUN see *mehen*

MEI GUI rose

MEI ILHA plum blossom (*Prunus mume*)

MEI MUKE the name of a sweet beverage

MEI YAHA (fossil) coal

MEIFEHE slope of a hill

MEIFEN neck
MEIFEN BE GIDARALAME TASIHIMBI to
press on the neck and kick the leg
from the side (in wrestling)
MEIFEN BUKTAKABI got a crick in the
neck
MEIFEN DABALI NIYAMNIYAMBI to shoot
from under the neck of a horse
MEIFEN I ŠURDEN neck-ring used during sword play

MEIHE 1. snake 2. the sixth of the
earth's branches (巳)
MEIHE BIYA the fourth month
MEIHE BULUNAMBI the snake is hibernating
MEIHE CECIKE the name of a small
bird that has a long neck and a
sharp tongue
MEIHE GELEKU Gastrodia, from which
oil is extracted
MEIHE GIRANGGI snake bones!--an
oath
MEIHE GŪN HALAMBI the snake changes
its skin
MEIHE ŠARI the name of a bitter
wild vegetable
MEIHE YOO a red eruption on the
skin

MEIHEGUWELEKU see *meihe geleku*

MEIHEN SINGGERI mongoose

MEIHENGGE pertaining to the snake
MEIHENGGE ANIYA the year of the
serpent

MEIHEREBUMBI caus. of *meiherembi*

MEIHEREMBI to carry on the shoulder,
to lift to the shoulder
MEIHEREFI MAKTAMBI to lift to the
shoulder and throw down (in
wrestling)

MEIHETU mud eel--*Apterigia immaculata*
MEIHETU HENGKE fiber melon (*Luffa
cylindrica*)

MEIJEBUMBI 1. caus. of *meijembi* 2.
to shatter, to pulverize

MEIJEMBI to shatter, to fragment, to
break, to become powder

MEILEBUMBI caus. of *meilembi*

MEILEMBI to carve up, to dissect (a
carcass), to cut off, to cut out

MEIMENI each one, every, severally,
the same as *meni meni*

MEIREN 1. shoulder 2. on a battue,
the two banners marching on both
sides of the center 3. side-, vice-,
sub- 4. the sides of a bow grip
5. the large beads on both ends of
a Buddhist rosary
MEIREN ADAME shoulder to shoulder,
side by side
MEIREN GIRANGGI shoulder bone
MEIREN I JANGGIN (副 都 統)
Lieutenant-general, BH 658

MEIRENGGE having shoulders

M

MEIRETU the shoulder piece of a suit of armor

MEISE the fruit of *Prunus mume* (Japanese apricot)

MEISILE light yellow amber

MEITEBUMBI caus. of *meitembi*

MEITEMBI to cut off, to cut in two, to excise

MEJIGE news, information

    MEJIGE ALAMBI to report news

    MEJIGE BA information point, place where news can be obtained

    MEJIGE GAIMBI to collect information, to gather news

MEJIGELEBUMBI caus. of *mejigelembi*

MEJIGELEMBI to make inquiries, to seek information, to look for news

MEJIN CECIKE a long-tailed bird with a black neck and back whose cry announces good luck

MEKCEREMBI to bend forward, to incline the shoulders forward

    MEKCEREFI ILIHABI stands bent forward

MEKCERŠEMBI to bend very far forward

MEKE the side of a *gacuha* without a hole

MEKELE in vain, vainly, emptily, merely

MEKENI a mouth harp with a metal tongue

MEKENIMBI to play the mouth harp

MEKENIYEN see *mekeni*

MEKEREBUMBI caus. of *mekerembi*

MEKEREMBI to be decrepit, to be disabled, to be beaten to a pulp

MEKTEBUMBI caus. of *mektembi*

MEKTEMBI to bet, to wager

MEKTEN bet, wager

MEKTEREMBI see *mektembi*

MELBIKU oar

    MELBIKU JAHŪDAI a short, light rowboat

MELBIMBI to row

MELBIN MOO a tree similar to the cedar (*Cedrela chinensis*)

MELE on the lookout

MELEBUMBI 1. caus. of *melembi* 2. to overlook, to neglect, to omit, to forget

MELEMBI 1. to water (livestock) 2. to sneak away, to hide

MELENDUMBI/MELENUMBI to water together

MELENEMBI to go to water

MELENJIMBI to come to water

MELERHI one name for the manul; cf. *ujirhi*

MELERJEMBI to sneak off, to shrink away

MELERŠEMBI 1. see *memeršembi* 2. see *melerjembi*

MELEŠETEMBI to shrink back, to fear to step forward

MELI jasmine

MELJEBUMBI caus. of *meljembi*

MELJEMBI to compete, to compete in, to engage in a contest, to gamble

MELKEN vapor rising from the earth

MELKEŠEMBI to rise (of vapor from the earth), to form a mirage

    MELKEŠERE DENGJAN lanterna magica

MELKETU clam

MELMEN blood clot

MELMENEMBI to clot, to coagulate

MEMBE accusative form of *be*: us

MEME wet nurse, see *meme eniye*

    MEME AMA husband of a wet nurse

    MEME ENIYE wet nurse

MEMEMA husband of a wet nurse

MEMENIYE wet nurse (of a noble family)

MEMEREKU stubborn, firm

MEMEREMBI 1. to be stubborn, to remain fixed in one's opinions 2. to be greedy for, to covet

MEMEREN stubborn, unyielding

MEMERŠEMBI to be obstinate, to insist upon, to be recalcitrant

MEN ŠEN ENDURI the gate god

MENCI ablative of *be*: from us, than us

MENDE dative of *be*: to us, for us

MENDEREMBI (-ke) to get one's speech confused (of old people)

MENDZ doorkeeper

MENE 1. indeed, actually, truly, honestly 2. see *menen*

MENEHUN stupid, not intelligent

MENEKEN rather invalid, somewhat crippled, rather stupid

MENEN 1. paralyzed, invalid, disabled 2. stupid, silly

MENEREMBI (-ke) 1. to be stupid, to be silly 2. to be numb, to be asleep (of parts of the body) 3. to be paralyzed

MENGDE a window that does not open, a blind window

MENGDELEMBI to be fixed, to be strong

MENGGE hard (of foods), hard to chew

MENGGUN silver

    MENGGUN GUILEHE the fruit of the ginkgo

    MENGGUN I NAMUN (銀庫) silver depository, treasury, Bullion Vaults, BH 7], 497

    MENGGUN INGGALI the name of a small white bird

    MENGGUN JALUNGGA NAMUN the name of a silver depository in Tatung, northern Shansi

    MENGGUN NISIHA silverfish--a tasty white fish that is taken from frozen water in the winter

    MENGGUN UREBUMBI to mine silver ore

MENGLEN vain, futile

MENGSE a curtain, drapery

MENGSEKU curtain made of cloth or felt

hung before a door

MENGSEKU I LAKIYAKŪ rod for hanging
a door curtain

MENGSEKU I NAMUN depository of door
curtains belonging to the Board of
Works

MENI genitive of *be*: our

MENI MENI each, every, severally

MENINGGE ours

MENJI turnip

MENTEHE missing a tooth, toothless

MENTEHEJEMBI to have missing teeth, to
be gap-toothed

MENTU steamed bread (usually round in
shape)

MENTUHUDEMBI to behave stupidly, to
act in a silly fashion

MENTUHUKEN rather stupid, rather silly

MENTUHUN stupid, silly

MENTUHUREMBI to speak stupidly, to
behave stupidly, to act in a silly
fashion

MENTUN see *mentu*

MERE buckwheat

MERE JEMPIN fried cakes made of
buckwheat

MERE NIMANGGI snow that has frozen
into small beads the size of a
grain of buckwheat

MEREN ILHA an exotic white flower that
resembles crushed rice

MERGEDEMBI to be an excellent hunter
or fisherman, to excel, to be outstanding

MERGEMBI see *merhembi*

MERGEN 1. a very good hunter or fisherman, an intelligent or wise man
2. outstanding, wise, worthy,
skilled, adept

MERGEN CECIKE another name for the
shrike; cf. *giyahūn*

MERGEN HEHE title of honor of the
third rank conferred upon the wife
of a meritorious official

MERGENGGE MAHATUN a hat worn by worth-
ies and scholars in ancient times

MERGESE the plural of *mergen*

MERHE a double-edged fine-toothed comb

MERHEBUMBI caus. of *merhembi*

MERHEMBI to comb with a *merhe*

MERKIMBI to recollect, to bring to
mind

MERKIHE SEME BAHARAKŪ not to be
able to recollect

MERKIN recall, memory, consciousness

MERKINGGE alert, conscious

MERPINGGE NIYEHE one name for the
common duck

MERSEN small black spots on the face

MERSENEMBI to get small black spots on
the face

MERSENGGE spotted

MERSENGGE ASHA a quail with small

spots on the wing

MERSENGGE CUSE MOO spotted bamboo

MERSENGGE DUDU a small spotted
purple dove

MERSERI betel nut; cf. *binse*

MERSETU COKO one name for the turkey;
cf. *suihetu coko*

MEŠEBUMBI caus./pass. of *mešembi*

MEŠEMBI 1. to shove in 2. to copulate, to ma'e sexual connection with
(a female)

METEKU a pole for offerings

METEMBI 1. to pay a vow to a god 2.
to offer animals in sacrifice to
heaven

METU one name for the *itu*--the partridge; cf. *jukidun*

MEYE younger sister's husband (in the
older language it also meant wife's
younger brother)

MEYELEBUMBI caus./pass. of *meyelembi*

MEYELEMBI to cut into sections

MEYEN 1. section, segment, division,
piece, chapter 2. group, squadron,
rank (of troops), row

MEYEN I AFAHA a list on which the
number of the group who was to
have an audience with the emperor
was written

MEYEN I AMBAN (領隊大臣)
Commandant of the Forces, BH 865

MEYEN MEYEN I section by section,
piece by piece, etc.

MEYENGGE CARGILAKŪ firecrackers that
explode in rapid succession

MEYETE plural of *meye*

MI ORHO see *mijiri orho*

MIBSEHE a type of insect that attacks
the rice plant

MIBSEHENEMBI to become insect infested
(rice)

MIBURI one-sextillionth

MICEO a type of fine cotton

MICIHA ARAMBI to make rope for fishing
and hunting nets

MICIHIYAN 1. shallow 2. narrow-minded

MICIHIYAN BE FETEMBI to dredge
shallows

MICIKA see *micihiyan*

MICUBUMBI 1. caus. of *micumbi* 2. to
beat someone so that he can't get up

MICUDAMBI to crawl around (of children)

MICUMBI to crawl

MICURŠEMBI to crawl continuously

MIDA see *midada*

MIDADA the name of a plant whose
sweet-tasting roots resemble the
roots of the *šari sogi*

MIDAHA leech

MIDALJAMBI 1. to move back and forth,
to move in a zigzag way, to slither
(like a snake) 2. to shake the

M

body so as to make the bells on the belt ring (of shamans)

MIGAN   see *mihan*

MIHACAN   the young of the wild pig

MIHADAMBI   to jump about, to hop

MIHAN   a young pig

MIJIREBUMBI   1. caus. of *mijirembi*   2. to beat someone until he can't move

MIJIREMBI   the same as *mijurambi*

MIJIRI ORHO   Ligusticum

MIJURABUMBI   1. caus. of *mijurambi*   2. to beat someone until he can't move

MIJURAMBI   to make a motion back and forth, to rock back and forth (while sitting), to drag the feet while walking

MIKCAN   1. one name for the musk deer; cf. *miyahū*   2. musk; cf. *jarin*

MILA   1. open, wide open   2. be off! be gone!   3. light yellow amber

MILA NEIMBI   to open wide

MILACAMBI   see *milarambi*

MILAHŪN   wide open, gaping

MILAHŪN MORO   bowl with a thick rim and wide opening

MILAMBI   to go away, to be off

MILAN   water in which rice has been rinsed

MILARABUMBI   caus. of *milarambi*

MILARAMBI (-ka)   1. to open wide   2. to shun, to dodge, to stay far away from

MILARCAMBI   see *milarambi*

MILATA   wide open, agape

MILTAHŪN   bare, vacant

MIMBE   accusative of *bi*: me

MIMI   a type of large fly

MIMIMBI   to close (the mouth)

MIMSORO   a jujubelike exotic fruit

MINCI   ablative of *bi*: from me, than me

MINDE   dative of *bi*: to me, for me

MINDZ   a brush

MINGGA   see *minggan*

MINGGACI   thousandth

MINGGADA   chiliarch

MINGGAHA   the name of an exotic fruit that grows on a vine, has up to two hundred seeds in a pod, and tastes like a chestnut

MINGGAN   one thousand

MINGGAN TUMEN   ten million

MINGGANGGERI   one thousand times

MINGGARI   one thousand square *li*

MINGGATA   one thousand each

MINGGATU   (千總) chiliarch, lieutenant, BH 752E, 796, etc.

MINGMIYAHA   a small green bug found on the mulberry

MINI   genitive of *bi*: my, of me

MINI BEYE   myself

MININGGE   mine

MIODORI MIODORI   walking with diffi- culty (because of a sore back)

MIOMIOHON   see *miyoomiyoohūn*

MIORI   see *miyori*

MIOSIHODOMBI   to act or speak in a false and heretical way

MIOSIHON   evil, false, heretical, heterodox

MIOSIHON TACIN   heretical teaching, heretical doctrine

MIOSIHŪN   the same as *miosihon*

MIOSIRI   smile

MIOSIRI MIOSIRILAMBI   to smile, to have a smile on the face

MIOSIRILAMBI   to smile

MIOŠOROMBI (-ko)   to become crooked or bent, to become askew

MISAN   tub, vat

MISE   slack, loose (of a bow with a loose string)

MISEN   a jar with a wide mouth

MISHA   see *mishan*

MISHABUMBI   caus. of *mishambi*

MISHABURE DALANGGA   a dam through which the current is regulated

MISHALABUMBI   caus. of *mishalambi*

MISHALAKŪ   vessel for holding the inked string used by carpenters for marking straight lines

MISHALAKŪ HŪRKA   snare for catching wild animals

MISHALAMBI   to mark a straight line with an inked string

MISHAMBI   to shun, to avoid, to dodge

MISHAN   an inked string used for mark- ing straight lines by a carpenter

MISJAN   mason

MISU HŪSIHA   *Schizandra chinensis*

MISUIJAN   see *misjan*

MISUN   a thick sauce, jam, fermented bean paste

MISUN BOCO   the color of fermented bean paste--brown

MISUN I KŪRDAKŪ   a wooden stirring stick for bean paste

MISURU   brown

MIŠUN   one hundred trillion

MITA   an iron ornament on the end of a crupper

MITA JAFU   a piece of red felt that hangs under the horse's tail and is attached to a crupper

MITA UŠE   a leather thong used to attach the *mita jafu*

MITABUMBI   caus. of *mitambi*

MITALJAMBI   see *midaljambi*

MITAMBI   to spring back (of a bow when the string is removed)

MITAN   1. sweet rice porridge   2. see *mita*

MITANDUMBI   to spring back together

MIYAHA   see *mihan*

MIYAHŪ   musk deer (*Moschus moschiferus*)

MIYAHŪ FUNGSAN   musk

MIYAHŪTU   the muntjac of South China

M

MIYALIBUMBI caus. of *miyalimbi*

MIYALIDA the man who measures grain in a granary

MIYALIKŪ 1. measurer, measure 2. powder measure (for guns)

MIYALIMBI to measure

MIYALIN a measure

MIYAMIBUMBI caus. of *miyamimbi*

MIYAMIGA see *miyamigan*

MIYAMIGAN 1. ornament, jewelry 2. makeup

MIYAMIHAN see *miyamigan*

MIYAMIKŪ see *miyamišakū*

MIYAMIMBI 1. to adorn, to decorate 2. to make up, to dress up

MIYAMIŠAKŪ one fond of making up, one fond of dressing up

MIYAMIŠAMBI to adorn oneself, to decorate, to dress up

MIYAMIYAHAN see *miyamigan*

MIYAN CEO a fine cotton fabric; cf. *miceo*

MIYAN DIYAN GURUN Burma

MIYAN GIN gluten

MIYANG (onom.) the sound of a child's crying

　MIYANG MING (onom.) 1. the sound of many children crying 2. the sound made by the young of deer, roe, and sheep

MIYANGGIN wheat gluten

MIYANTS HŪLHA Burmese bandits

MIYAR MIR (onom.) the sound of children crying

MIYAR MIYAR (onom.) 1. the sound made by a baby crying 2. the sound made by young deer, roe, and sheep

MIYARGA see *miyarha*

MIYARHA clitoris

MIYARIMBI to bleat, to baa

MIYARSEME 1. bleating 2. nagging

MIYASI MIYASI see *miyasihi miyasihi*

MIYASIDAMBI to walk unsteadily, to fly unsteadily (of an arrow)

MIYASIHI MIYASIHI unsteady, staggering

MIYASIHIDAMBI to walk unsteadily

MIYASIHITAMBI see *miyasihidambi*

MIYASIRILAMBI to pucker the mouth as if ready to cry

MIYASITAMBI see *miyasidambi*

MIYEGU crust

　MIYEGU EFEN a kind of pastry made of glutinous millet

　MIYEGU WECEMBI to offer *miyegu* pastry

MIYEHU see *miyegu*

MIYEHUDEMBI to jump about, to hop around (of wild animals)

MIYEHUNEMBI 1. to form a crust 2. to become decrepit

MIYEHUSU bean-curd skin

MIYEKUDEMBI see *miyehudembi*

MIYOO temple, shrine

MIYOOCALABUMBI caus. of *miyoocalambi*

MIYOOCALAMBI to fire a musket

MIYOOCALANDUMBI/MIYOOCALANUMBI to fire muskets together

MIYOOCAN musket, flintlock

　MIYOOCAN I COOHA musketeers, musket troops

MIYOOMIYOOHŪN bent outward, protruding (lips)

MIYORI a second (of time)

MIYOSIRILAMBI see *miosirilambi*

MIYOŠORI see *miosiri*

MIYOŠOROBUMBI caus. of *miyošorombi*

MIYOŠOROMBI see *miošorombi*

MO one ten-trillionth

MO LI ILHA jasmine

MO SEME right in the face, right to one's face

　MO SEME BASUMBI to make fun of someone to his face

MOBIN HOOŠAN a type of writing paper made from bamboo

MOBSEHE a small insect that attacks the roots of grain

MOCIKO askance, crooked, askew; cf. *waiku*

MOCIN a fine smooth cotton, usually dark brown or black

　MOCIN SAMSU a fine smooth brown or black cotton cloth

MOCINJI see *mojihiyan*

MOCO incompetent, unskillful, stupid, blunt, tactless

　MOCO SIMHUN the index finger

MOCODOMBI to act in an incompetent, stupid, or tactless manner

MOCOKON rather incompetent, rather stupid

MODAN ILHA peony

MODO slow-witted, dull, lacking agility, clumsy, careless

　MODO GASHA one name for the cuckoo; cf. *kekuhe*

MODOKON rather dull, rather clumsy

MOHOBUMBI caus./pass. of *mohombi*

　MOHOBUME FONJIMBI to question thoroughly

MOHOLO a hornless castrated bovine

MOHOMBI 1. to be exhausted, to be depleted 2. to be at a loss for words 3. to be in dire need

MOHON exhaustion, depletion, end, finish, need

MOHORI SOHORI rudely, impolitely, shabbily

MOHOTO hairless (a horse's tail); cf. *mokto*

MOJIHIYAN Tibetan black bear (*Euractos thibetanus*)

MOKCOMBI to break off, to break in two

MOKO (昴) the name of a constellation

　MOKO TOKDONGGO KIRU a banner depicting the constellation *moko*

MOKSO asunder, in two, in the center
  MOKSO GENEHE went asunder, broke in
  two
MOKSOLOMBI to break in two, to cleave
MOKTO 1. docked off, bobbed 2. violent
  3. bare, bald (of an animal's tail)
  MOKTO ŠOŠONGGO MAHALA an ancient-
  style hat similar to the *mahatu* but
  without a fringe
MOLHO the large intestine of the wild
  pig
MOLHŪRI a hornless bovine; cf. *moholo*
MOLI ILHA jasmine; cf. *meli*
MOLO maple tree
MOLODOMBI to glue back together
MOLOJIN the name of the peacock in
  Buddhist scriptures
MOLORI MOO *Rhododendron metternichii*
MOMOHORI sitting together silently,
  sitting still (of a group), sitting
  erect
MOMOKON silent because of shyness,
  retiring
MOMOROMBI to sit silently (of a group),
  to sit erect, to keep to one's seat
MOMORŠOMBI to sit firmly on a horse
  (when practicing archery)
MONCON knob on a cap shaped like a
  chrysanthemum
MONGGO Mongolia, Mongolian
  MONGGO AISIN HERGENGGE LOHO a sword
  with a Mongolian inscription in
  gold letters
  MONGGO BITHEI BA (蒙古堂)
  Mongolian Copying Office, BH 138
  MONGGO BOO a yurt
  MONGGO BUDA a broth made of meat
  and rice
  MONGGO BUREN a long horn used by
  Mongolian lamas
  MONGGO CIBIN the Mongolian swallow
  MONGGO COOHA Mongolian troops
  MONGGO DASHŪWAN DUBE the second
  jalan of the Mongols
  MONGGO GŪSA 1. a Mongolian banner
  2. Lieutenant-General of a Mongo-
  lian banner
  MONGGO HERGEN the Mongolian written
  language, Mongolian writing or
  letters
  MONGGO JEBELE DUBE the first *jalan*
  of the Mongols
  MONGGO JURGAN another name for the
  Tulergi golo be dasara jurgan--
  Court of Colonial Affairs, BH 491
  MONGGO SEDO the name of a wild
  plant with edible stalks--the same
  as *fulgiyan selbete*
  MONGGO TALA the Mongolian plateau,
  Mongolia
  MONGGO YORO an arrow with a square
  birch-wood head with holes in it

used for shooting rabbits on
  rocky terrain
MONGGOCON a bottle with a narrow mouth
  and long neck
MONGGOCUN see *monggocon*
MONGGOLIBUMBI caus. of *monggolimbi*
MONGGOLIKŪ 1. ornamental neckband worn
  by women 2. dog collar
MONGGOLIMBI to wear on the neck
MONGGON neck, throat
  MONGGON FAITAMBI to cut the throat
  MONGGON HUSIKŪ 1. a protective
  piece of armor for the neck 2.
  a collar around the neck
  MONGGON SOYOMBI to draw in the neck
MONGGOROBUMBI caus. of *monggorombi*
MONGGOROKŪ a bordered collar fixed to
  a jacket
  MONGGOROKŪ HŪSIKŪ neckpiece, neck-
  scarf
  MONGGOROKŪ SIJIGIYAN a gown with
  collar and cuffs trimmed in bro-
  cade
  MONGGOROKŪ ULHI WAHAN collar and
  cuffs trimmed in brocade
MONGGOROMBI 1. to act in a Mongolian
  manner 2. to speak Mongolian, to
  use Mongolian 3. to kick the shut-
  tlecock
  MONGGOROME in the Mongolian manner
  MONGGOROME TEMBI to sit in the
  Mongolian manner--i.e., with one
  foot under the buttocks
MONGGOSO plural of *monggo*
MONGGOŠUN crucian (carp)
MONGGŪ see *monggo*
MONGNIOHON gasping for breath
MONIO monkey, ape; cf. *bonio*
MONIOCILAMBI to behave like a monkey
MONJIBUMBI caus. of *monjimbi*
MONJIMBI (-he) to rub, to knead, to
  massage
MONJIRAMBI 1. to rub with the hand, to
  knead 2. to wring the hands (from
  frustration, etc.), to be in an
  agitated state
MONJIRŠAMBI 1. to rub vigorously, to
  knead vigorously 2. to sit rocking
  back and forth in anger 3. at
  wrestling, to keep pressing an opponent down
MONJIŠAMBI to massage
MOO 1. tree 2. wood 3. stick, pole
  4. a bamboo stick used for beating
  MOO GARMA an arrow with a four-
  sided wooden head with a barb
  sticking out from each side--used
  for shooting pheasants and rabbits
  MOO HENGKE quince
  MOO I BERI a wooden bow used for
  preparing cotton
  MOO I CALU I KUNGGERI (木倉科)
  office of wood storehouses in the

Board of Works
MOO I FUKTALA mistletoe
MOO I HASI persimmon
MOO I HOTON a wooden wall
MOO I JUN lumber, wood (as opposed
  to the other parts of a tree)
MOO I KEMUN set square, used for
  measuring wood
MOO I NORAN a pile of wood
MOO IHAN yak
MOO LUJEN the name of a six-horse
  imperial coach with a roof con-
  sisting of four pieces of wood
MOO MORIN a wooden horse used by
  children at play
MOO SACIMBI to chop wood, to cut
  firewood
MOO SACIRE NIYALMA a woodcutter
MOO SIKA I KEIBISU a carpet made of
  palm fiber
MOO ŠU ILHA *Magnolia liliflora*
MOO USIHA the planet Jupiter
MOO YAHA charcoal
MOOI CALU wood warehouse of the
  Board of Works
MOOI FAKSI carpenter
MOOI HASI BOCO persimmon-colored
MOOI KEMNEKU set square used for
  measuring lumber
MOODASI a person in charge of planting
  and caring for trees, a forester
MOOSITUN a type of ancient sacrificial
  vessel (豆)
MOOYEN ILHA Rose of Sharon (*Hibiscus
  syriacus*)
MORHO toothed bur clover (*Medicago
  hispida*), alfalfa
MORICI a person who watches horses at
  official establishments
MORILABUMBI caus. of *morilambi*
MORILAMBI to ride a horse, to go by
  horse
  MORILARA WEHE stones placed on both
    sides of the main gate of a house
MORIN 1. horse 2. the seventh of the
  earth's branches (午)
  MORIN BARGIYAMBI to rein in a horse,
    to round up horses
  MORIN BIYA the fifth month
  MORIN DELERI ETEHE UCUN a piece of
    music played during the greeting
    of a general
  MORIN GAJIMBI to lead one's horse
    to the target (in mounted archery)
  MORIN HŪWAITAMBI 'to tie up the
    horse'--euphemism for going to the
    toilet
  MORIN JURCEMBI to join battle on
    horseback
  MORIN I BAITA horse affairs
  MORIN I BAITAI KUNGGERI (馬 政
    科) office of horse affairs in
    the Board of War

MORIN I JALIN WECEMBI to make an
  offering to the horse god
MORIN I TORON branding iron for
  horses
MORIN JALMIN polygonum
MORIN SEJEN BELHERE BOLGOBURE FIYEN-
  TEN (車 篤 清 吏 司   )
  Remount Department, BH 415A
MORIN SILMEN a female kite
MORIN SINDAMBI to give the horse
  his head
MORIN TORHO wild ginger (*Asarum
  sieboldi*)
MORIN TURGEN the same as *morin
  torho*
MORIN WEIHE a sore in children's
  mouths
MORINGGA 1. pertaining to the horse,
  mounted 2. horseman, rider
  MORINGGA ANIYA the year of the
    horse
  MORINGGA COOHA cavalry, mounted
    troops
  MORINGGA FAIDAN the mounted impe-
    rial escort
  MORINGGA HŪLHA mounted bandit
  MORINGGA UKSIN armor for a horse
MORO 1. bowl 2. a dry quart
  MORO HIYASE a dry quart
  MOROI DOBTON covering for a bowl
MOROHON big and round (of eyes)
  MOROHON NEIMBI to open up wide
    (the eyes)
  MOROHON TUWAMBI to look at with
    wide open eyes
MOROMBI to open wide (the eyes)
MOSELABUMBI caus./pass. of *moselambi*
MOSELAKŪ a large millstone
  MOSELAKŪ I LIFAN WEHE stone trough
    for a stone roller
MOSELAMBI 1. to mill, to grind 2. to
  sit with the feet tucked under the
  body
  MOSELAME with the feet tucked under
    the body
  MOSELAME TEMBI to sit with the feet
    tucked under the body
MOSIKE the name of a small monkeylike
  animal of Tonkin that is very adept
  at catching rats
MOŠUSE an exotic purple fruit resem-
  bling the walnut
MOTON HOOŠAN a type of strong paper
  made from hemp
MOTORO a type of sour, astringent
  quince (*Cydonia japonica*)
  MOTORO GAHA a type of crow that
    nests in forests
MOYACI ILHA an exotic red flower of
  South China that blooms in spring
  and autumn--it resembles hibiscus
MOYO 1. dull 2. chicken-pox
MOYORO an exotic fruit resembling the

M

quince but somewhat larger

MU a *mu* (畝)--about one-sixth of an acre

MUCE see *mucen*

MUCEJUN one name for the stork; cf. *weijun*

MUCEN a cooking pot, caldron

MUCENGGE 1. pertaining to a cooking pot 2. a measure equaling 6 pecks and 4 quarts

MUCESI a cook

    MUCESI I KUNGGERI (廚役料) an office in charge of preparing sacrificial animals

MUCIHA 1. bamboo or rush splints for making baskets and mats 2. the center part of a grass or rush mat

    MUCIHA FUTA a bamboo rope used for hauling boats

    MUCIHA I HOSERI a container woven from thin bamboo or reed splints

    MUCIHA MAHATUN an ancient-style hat made from bamboo splints

MUCIHIYAN a tripod vessel

MUCITU MAHATUN an ancient-style hat made of bamboo splints and decorated with lacquer on the outside

MUCITUN a sacrificial vessel of antiquity woven from bamboo

MUCU grape

    MUCU BOCOI HAKSANGGA EFEN crisp grape-colored cake

    MUCU BOCOI JIYOO BING the same as *mucu bocoi haksangga efen*

    MUCU HALU I SACIMA cake made of flour, sesame oil, sesame seeds, sugar, and grapes

MUCUNGGAI GASHA one of the names of the spotted kingfisher; cf. *cunggai*

MUDACI ILHA corn poppy (*Papaver rhoeas*)

MUDAKIYAMBI to walk on a sinuous path, to turn (corners)

MUDALI see *mudari*

MUDALIMBI 1. to turn (a corner) 2. to go the long way around, to make a detour 3. to be sinuous, winding

    MUDALIME via a detour, in a round-about way

MUDALIN a round section cut out in a garment

MUDAMBI to return

MUDAN 1. curve, bend, curved, bent 2. detour, roundabout way 3. sound, tone, melody, rhyme 4. expression, tone of voice, implication 5. out of the way, remote 6. time, as in one time, two times, etc. 7. peony 8. see *mudan efen*

    MUDAN ARAMBI to knead to and fro (dough)

    MUDAN BAHA started to sweat--after the crisis in an illness

    MUDAN DARI every time

MUDAN DE ACABUMBI (諧聲) to form characters according to the phonetic principle

MUDAN EFEN a deep-fried twisted pastry made from millet, rice, and buckwheat flour

MUDAN GAIME YABUMBI to go by a roundabout way

MUDAN HŪWALIYAMBURE FALGARI (和聲署) Music Office, BH 388

MUDAN I ACABUMBI to match in sound--i.e., to form new characters by compounding a phonetic and semantic element

MUDAN I BA a remote place

MUDAN MUDAN every time

MUDAN MUDAN DE at various times, periodically

MUDAN TEBUMBI to set a trap for someone

MUDAN WAI a remote place in the mountains, a precipitous and inaccessible place

MUDAN YOHO a remote area

MUDANDARI see *mudan dari*

MUDANGGA 1. curved, bent 2. having sound or tone

    MUDANGGA DALAN a dike that follows the curves of a river

    MUDANGGA FESIN I HAKSAN BOCOI SUJE SARA a yellow silk umbrella with a crooked handle used as an insignia by the imperial concubines

    MUDANGGA JUGŪN a crooked road

    MUDANGGA NAHAN a crooked oven-bed

MUDARI there and right back

MUDUMBI to file, to file smooth

MUDUN 1. a file for working wood, horn, or bone 2. spur off the foot of a mountain

    MUDUN FUTA a snare for catching the lynx

MUDURI 1. dragon 2. the fifth of the earth's branches (辰)

    MUDURI BIYA the third month

    MUDURI DUKA the name of the ceremonial arch behind the second door of the Examination Hall

    MUDURI DUKAI DALANGGA a dam with a sluice

    MUDURI GARUDAI SUWAYAN SUJE ŠUN DALIKŪ a large fan made of yellow satin embroidered with phoenixes and dragons

    MUDURI GARUDAI TUMIN LAMUN SUJE KIRU a dark blue satin banner embroidered with phoenixes and dragons

    MUDURI MUYAME TASHA MURAME crying like a dragon and growling like a tiger

    MUDURI OŠOHONGGO FUKJINGGA HERGEN (龍爪篆) a style of calligraphy

MUDURI SOORIN DE WESIMBI to ascend
the Dragon Throne
MUDURI UJUNGGE GIRDAN the 'dragon-
headed pennant'--the name of an
insignia of the escort
MUDURIKŪ tile figures of dragons on
both ends of the ridge of the roofs
of palaces
MUDURINGGA pertaining to the dragon
MUDURINGGA ANIYA the year of the
dragon
MUDURINGGA DOYONGGO gold brocade
with inwoven walking dragons
MUDURINGGA FUKJINGGA HERGEN (龍
書) a style of calligraphy
MUDURINGGA GIYANCIHIYAN HOOŠAN let-
ter paper with a dragon design
MUDURINGGA HIYAN MOO *Dryobalanops
camphora*
MUFI ILHA flower of the tree *Magnolia
kobus*
MUFUYEN 1. blunt, rounded, having
rounded edges and corners 2. dull-
witted
MUFUYEN MODO 1. blunt and dull 2.
dull and slow-witted
MUGŪN see *mukūn*
MUHADUMBI see *muhantumbi*
MUHALIYABUMBI caus. of *muhaliyambi*
MUHALIYAMBI to pile up, to stack up
MUHALIYAN 1. ball, sphere, bead, round
projectile 2. pile, stack
MUHAN a male tiger or panther
MUHAN SEBSEHE walking stick (insect)
MUHAN TASHA a male tiger
MUHAN YARHA a male panther
MUHANTUMBI to copulate, to breed (of
cows, tigers, and cats)
MUHARI an exotic fruit about the size
of a crossbow projectile with a
taste like that of the chestnut
MUHARŠAMBI to get some foreign matter
in the eye
MUHAŠAN bull, steer
MUHELIYEKEN rather round
MUHELIYEN round
MUHELIYEN JAN a round whistling
arrow--an arrow with three holes
in the head that was used for
shooting deer and roe
MUHELIYEN MOO a wooden ball on the
end of a stick
MUHELIYEN MUHUN the round earthen
altar at the Temple of Heaven
MUHEREN 1. wheel 2. ring, earring
3. a metal ring used as a paperweight 4. the end of an axle
MUHERI ILHA *Kerria japonica*--a member
of the rose family
MUHEŠEMBI to carry mud in the beak
(of swallows)
MUHI 1. a sable (or other animal's)
tail attached to the front of a fur

jacket below the lapel 2. a curved
board on the back of a wagon to
which the ropes that hold the load
are fastened 3. wooden ring to
which the ropes of a swing are at-
tached
MUHIYAN ILHA banksia (*Rosa banksiae*)
MUHU a high ridge or mound
MUHUN a mound on which funerary of-
ferings to the nobility were made
in ancient times
MUHURU the female of the sea-fish *cime*
MUHŪLU a yellow dragonlike creature
without horns
MUHŪLU BUCIN a *bucin* without horns
MUHŪRI rounded off, leveled off
MUJAKŪ extremely, truly
MUJAN carpenter
MUJANGGA truly, indeed, actually,
true, real, correct
MUJANGGAO is it true that . . . ?
can it be that . . . ?
MUJANGGO the same as *mujanggao*
MUJI barley (*Hordeum vulgare*)
MUJILEN mind, intention, heart
MUJILEN AKŪMBUMBI to exhaust all
efforts, to do one's best
MUJILEN BAHABUKŪ (啟心郎)
an official title used at the be-
ginning of the dynasty ranking
just below *ashan i amban*
MUJILEN BAIBUMBI to be upset, to
have one's plans upset
MUJILEN DE TEBUMBI to be concerned
about, to keep in mind
MUJILEN EFUJEMBI to be distressed,
to grieve
MUJILEN FARFABUMBI to be confused
in one's mind
MUJILEN FAYABUMBI to go to a lot of
trouble
MUJILEN FEREKE fainted, lost con-
sciousness
MUJILEN FERIMBI to exert all ef-
fort, to strive
MUJILEN GIRKŪMBI to concentrate
one's efforts
MUJILEN GŪNIN thoughts, intentions
MUJILEN GŪWALIYAMBI to have a
change of heart, to alter one's
intentions
MIJILEN HUNGKEREHE repented, was
remorseful
MUJILEN ICAKŪ ill-pleasing
MUJILEN ISHELIYEN narrow-minded,
petty
MUJILEN JANCUHŪN willing, content,
pleased
MUJILEN JUWENDERAKŪ steadfast,
loyal
MUJILEN NIYAMAN feeling, sincerity
MUJILEN SESULAMBI to be startled
MUJILEN SINDAMBI to put the mind at

M

ease, not to worry

MUJILEN SIDARAMBI to be calm or tranquil in grief or difficulty

MUJILEN SITHŪMBI to concentrate one's efforts on

MUJILEN SUILAMBI to be troubled, to be upset

MUJILEN TENG SEME JAFAMBI to make a strong resolution, to have a strong intention

MUJILEN USAMBI to grieve, to be sad

MUJILEN USATALA OHO fell into grief or despair

MUJILENGGE 1. having purpose or aim 2. spirited, stout-hearted

MUJIMBI to moan (during an illness), to cry, to roar

MUJIN ambition, aim, will

MUJIN BE UJIMBI to nurture an ambition, to follow the goal that one's parents have set

MUJIN BE WESIHULERE TANGGIN name of the third hall of the east gallery of the Imperial Academy of Learning

MUJIN DE ACABUMBI to attain one's ambitions

MUJINGGA strong-willed, ambitious

MUJUHU carp; cf. *hardakū*

MUJUKU see *mujuhu*

MUK MAK SEME obstinate, stubborn

MUKCUHUN having a deformed hip that protrudes forward

MUKDAN MOO *Codium mucronatum*

MUKDEHEN root or branch of a desiccated tree, a desiccated tree

MUKDEHUN altar

MUKDEHURI an exotic sweet fruit somewhat larger than a jujube that grows in Fukien

MUKDEMBI (-ke/he) 1. to rise, to go upward 2. to flourish 3. to soar upward 4. to increase

MUKDEMBUMBI caus. of *mukdembi*

MUKDEN 1. rising, ascent, flourishing, prosperous 2. Mukden

MUKDEN I BOIGON I JURGAN (盛京 户部) the board of Finance in Mukden

MUKDEN I ILAN MUNGGAN I KADALAN JAFAHA HAFAN I YAMUN (盛京三 陵掌關防衙門) the office of the official in charge of the three mausoleums of Mukden

MUKDENDEMBI to rise

MUKE 1. water 2. river, stream

MUKE BE NECIN OBURE TAMPIN the third vessel of a water clock

MUKE DENDERE TAMPIN a vessel located behind the *muke be necin obure tampin* on a water clock

MUKE GAHA one name for the cormorant; cf. *suwan*

MUKE GAHACIN another name for the cormorant

MUKE GOCIRE BERI bow with a hollow stock through which water can be sucked

MUKE HASI sunberry (*Solanum nigrum*)

MUKE HŪSAHŪ a sort of gull that resembles the owl

MUKE IBADAN a tree whose bark resembles that of the elm

MUKE IHAN a water buffalo

MUKE MAKTAMBI to sprinkle water

MUKE NOHO BA I USIN field covered with water, field with standing water

MUKE TASHA the name of a predatory fish, the same as the *edeng*

MUKE TASHARI the Siberian white crane

MUKE TEBUKU a container for water that is used for making ink

MUKE USIHA the planet Mercury

MUKEI AISI BE YENDEBURE TINGGIN (水利廳) office of an official in charge of water conservancy, irrigation, etc.

MUKEI CIFUN water taxes

MUKEI DABABUKŪ a long tin pipe used for siphoning water

MUKEI DALIN bank of a stream

MUKEI EYEBUKU a water pipe, a drain pipe

MUKEI FEISE unfired, sun-dried brick

MUKEI FORON whirlpool, eddy

MUKEI GASHAN flood

MUKEI HUJUREKU a small water-run mill

MUKEI HŪSUN boatman

MUKEI IHAN water buffalo

MUKEI IHAN I UIHE BERI a bow made from the horn of a water buffalo

MUKEI ISIHIKŪ a pole with wet hemp attached to the end used for extinguishing fires

MUKEI JUGŪN water route

MUKEI MOSELAKŪ a large water mill

MUKEI MUDAN bend in a river

MUKEI NIOWANGGA MOO a tree that grows near water (*Xylosma racenosum*)

MUKEI NURE clear wine, wine clear as water

MUKEI SINGGERI water mouse

MUKEI ŠURDEKU a water wheel

MUKEI TALGAN the surface of water

MUKEI TEBUN a container for water

MUKEI WEILEN BE ICIHIYARA BOLGOBURE FIYENTEN (都水清吏司) an office concerned with water conservancy in the Board of Works

MUKELEMBI to water, to irrigate

MUKELU ILHA hyacinth

MUKENEMBI to turn to water, to melt
MUKERI watery, weak (of tea)
MUKIYEBUMBI caus. of *mukiyembi*
MUKIYEMBI to go out (fire), to be ex-
  tinguished, to expire, to perish, to
  cool off
MUKIYEN extinction
MUKJURI MAKJARI idle (talk), paltry,
  petty, inconsequential
MUKJURI MUKJURI running slowly (of
  short people)
MUKJURŠEMBI to bow deeply
MUKŠALABUMBI caus./pass. of *mukšalambi*
MUKŠALAMBI to beat with a stick
MUKŠAN a stick, club, cudgel
    MUKŠAN FU the name of small, round,
      quick river fish
MUKŠATU NIMAHA minnow, tench
MUKTEHEN temple, monastery
MUKTEMBI see *mektembi*
MUKTUHUN sand grouse; cf. *nuturu*
MUKTUN mole, animals of the family
  Talpidae
MUKŪMBI to hold a liquid in the mouth
MUKŪN 1. clan, extended family, kin-
  dred 2. fleet 3. herd, flock
    MUKŪN FALGA clan
    MUKŪN I AHŪN DEO all the boys of
      one generation in a clan, brothers
      and cousins of the same surname
    MUKŪN I URSE members of a clan
MULAN 1. a stool 2. an ironing board
MULDERHEN lesser skylark; cf. *guwender-*
  hen
MULFIYEN 1. round and flat 2. circles
  woven into a textile 3. a round disc
MULHŪRI a cow without horns
MULINAMBI to swallow, to gulp down
MULIYAN 1. the curve of the jawbone
  under the ear 2. the curve at the
  base of the wings of birds
MULMEN a type of fish hawk, possibly
  the same as *suksuhu*
MULTUJEMBI to come loose, to come off,
  to get free, to leave
MULTULEMBI to come loose (of knots),
  to loosen, to slacken
MULTUMBI see *multulembi*
MULU 1. ridgepole, beam 2. support
  pole of a tent or yurt 3. ridge of
  a mountain 4. the back line on a
  pelt
    MULU I FERE MOO supporting beam in
      a ship's cabin
    MULU I HETU MOO a horizontal beam
      in the ship's cabin
    MULU TUKIYEMBI to place a beam in
      position, to hoist a beam
MULUNOMBI (-ho, -ro) to form a ridge,
  to form a mound
MULUSE an exotic fruit that grows inside the bark of a tree--it is a
  four- or five-inch long sweet,

yellow fruit
MUMANAMBI to wallow in mud (of deer)
MUMIN very deep, profound, unfathom-
  able
    MUMIN WEHE lapis lazuli
MUMUHU 1. a football, often made from
  pig's bladder 2. a term of abuse
MUMUHUN see *mumuhu*
MUMUREMBI to buck, to kick (of horses
  and other livestock)
MUMURHŪN vague, indistinct, blurred
MUMURI 1. toothless, missing a tooth
  2. worn smooth
MUNAHŪN morose, surly, out of humor,
  annoyed, displeased
MUNARI a round exotic fruit that at
  first tastes bitter then turns sweet
  when eaten
MUNG MANG (onom.) sound made by cattle
  or deer
    MUNG MANG SEME lowing, bellowing,
      roaring
MUNG MUNG SEME see *mung mang seme*
MUNGGA see *munggan*
MUNGGAN 1. low hill, mound, tumulus
  2. tomb, mausoleum
MUNGGE NIONGNIYAHA one name for the
  wild goose
MUNGGIREMBI to play boisterously, to
  romp
MUNGKERI ILHA laurel magnolia
MUNGKU a fish frozen in the ice
MUNJIMBI to cry out from pain; cf.
  mujimbi
MUR MAR SEME obstinate, stubborn
MURADAMBI to roar from rage
MURAKŪ a whistle for calling deer
MURAMBI 1. to roar, to low, to bellow,
  to neigh 2. to call deer with a
  whistle
MURAN a battue held at the time of
  the deer-breeding season
    MURAN I ABA a battue for deer dur-
      ing the mating season
MURCA a wooden crossbar for making
  fast the ropes that hold down a
  load
MURCAKŪ 1. spiral, whorl, helix 2.
  snail-shaped ornament on a hat
    MURCAKŪ FARA I ILETU KIYOO an open
      sedan chair with a spiral shaft
MURCAN a small gray crane, the same
  as *ajige kūrcan*
MURFA a type of barley that grows in
  cold areas in the west
MURHU unclear, vague, blurred
    MURHU FARHŪN now clear, now un-
      clear, first blurred then dis-
      tinct, indistinct (in the mind)
MURHŪN see *murhu*
MURIBUMBI caus./pass. of *murimbi*
MURIGAN see *murihan*
    MURIGAN WECEKU a deity to whom

M

sacrifice was offered at the north
wall of a house

MURIHAN a curved place on a road or
path

MURIHAN BOO a house with a curving
front

MURIKŪ 1. obstinate, stubborn, perverse
2. peg (of stringed instruments)

MURIKŪ MOO a board on a wagon for
tying down the ropes that hold the
load

MURIMBI (-ha) 1. to twist, to wring,
to wring out, to pinch 2. to be
stubborn, to be obstinate 3. to
wrong (someone) 4. to throw side-
ways (at wrestling)

MURIME with legs tucked under the body;
cf. *moselame*

MURIN TARIN difficult to manage, awkward, recalcitrant, stubborn

MURINJAMBI to be stubborn, to act re-
calcitrantly

MURISHŪN wronged, unjustly judged,
treated unjustly

MURITAI obstinate, stubborn

MURKIBUMBI caus. of *murkimbi*

MURKIMBI to trim off the corners, to
round out, to round off

MURSA 1. radish, daikon (large white
Chinese radish) 2. an engraved
round ornament

MURTAMBI to cry out, to scream

MURTASHŪN recalcitrant, refractory,
unreasonable, pertinacious

MURU 1. form, shape, appearance, lay
(of the land), style, manner 2.
nearly, almost; cf. *amba muru*

MURU AKŪ unreasonable

MURU TUCIKE has taken form

MURUNG a spotted wildcat

MURUNGGA 1. similar in appearance 2.
exemplary, model

MURUŠEMBI 1. to do in outline, to do
only in a general way, to do in an
approximate way 2. to take form, to
obtain a shape

MURUŠEME in general, in outline,
approximately

MUSE we (inclusive)

MUSEBUMBI caus. of *musembi*

MUSEINGGE ours

MUSEMBI 1. to bend, to become bent,
to become warped 2. to become discouraged, to become disheartened

MUSEMBUMBI 1. caus. of *musembi* 2. to
bend, to make crooked or warped

MUSEN 1. bending, warping 2. an open
grave 3. outer coffin

MUSENGGE the same as *museingge*

MUSHA a short-haired tiger--one name
for the tiger; cf. *tasha*

MUSI a broth made of roasted flour,
sugar, and water

MUSI WEHE soapstone

MUSIHA MOO a type of oak (*Quercus
serrata*)

MUSIHI a wooden dipper with a long
handle

MUSIREN rattan (*Calamus rotang*)

MUŠEKU see *musihi*

MUŠU quail (*Coturnix coturnix*)

MUŠU ALGAN a snare for quail

MUŠU GIDARA ASU a net, four feet
by four feet, used by one man for
catching quail

MUŠUHU excrescence on a tree, a gnarl

MUŠUHURI just, just now, just right

MUŠURHU the 'yellow fish' that is
supposed to turn into a quail in
the ninth month

MUŠURI a type of linen produced in
Korea

MUTEBUKŪ a type of local school in
ancient times

MUTEBUMBI 1. caus. of *mutembi* 2. to
achieve, to bring about 3. to fill
(a post)

MUTEMBI 1. to be able, can, to be
possible 2. to be completed, to be
achieved

MUTEHE BE SIMNERE BOLGOBURE FIYENTEN
(考功清更司) office
for examining merit in the Board
of Civil Appointments

MUTEREI TEILE with all one can,
with all one's capabilities, to
the extent of one's power

MUTEN 1. capability, potentiality 2.
achievement, skill, art 3. material

MUTEN AKŪ without skill or talent

MUTEN ARAMBI to show off one's
abilities or talents

MUTENGGE skilled, talented

MUTULHEN a type of fish hawk possibly
identical with *suksuhu*

MUTUMBI (-ha) to grow, to grow up, to
mature

MUTUN 1. growth, maturing 2. share,
portion

MUWA coarse, crude, rough, thick

MUWA BOSO coarse cloth

MUWA DUHA the large intestine

MUWA EDUN TUWAMBI euphemism for
'to defecate'

MUWA FUNIYESUN coarse woolen fabric

MUWA HONCI the skin of a large
sheep

MUWA SUSERI HOOŠAN a type of paper
made from bamboo

MUWA UHUNGGE HOOŠAN a type of
coarse yellow wrapping paper

MUWA WEHE uncarved stone

MUWAKAN rather coarse, crude, rough

MUWARUNGGA FUKJINGGA HERGEN (大篆)
a style of calligraphy--the great
seal

MUWAŠAMBI 1. to be coarse, crude, or
  rough 2. to do or make coarsely, to
  do roughly
MUYA the broken stalks of grain, chaff,
  straw
    MUYA SUSE chaff and straw
MUYAHŪN complete, intact, unblemished

    MUYAHŪN AKŪ incomplete, not intact
MUYAMBI 1. to roar 2. to be angry
  without speaking of it
MUYARI 'dragon's eye'--longan (*Nephelium longana*)
MŪNGGU bird's nest--the edible nest of
  a type of swallow

M

N

NA 1. earth, land, field 2. background (of a design on a textile), base 3. local 4. a sentence particle of mild interrogation

NA BEŠEKEBI the earth has become saturated from rain

NA DE FEKUMBI to throw oneself to the ground

NA I ENDURI DOBON the hall where sacrifices to the earth were offered

NA I GINDANA (Buddhist) hell

NA I GIYAN the lay of the land, configurations of the land, geography

NA I HAFAN local magistrate

NA I LOO hell, the underworld

NA I MANGGA BA firm earth

NA I OILO HETU I DURUNGGA TETUN the name of an astronomical instrument in the Peking observatory

NA I OILO HETU UNDU I DURUNGGA TETUN the name of an astronomical instrument in the Peking observatory

NA I TAN the altar to earth

NA SULHUMBI the earth is spongy (at the spring thaw)

NACA wife's elder brother

NACEO a type of silk with inwoven designs

NACIHIYABUMBI caus. of *nacihiyambi*

NACIHIYAMBI to comfort, to console

NACIN the peregrine falcon (*Falco peregrinus*)

NADACI seventh

NADAJU see *nadanju*

NADAN 1. seven 2. goods, possessions 3. paper money hung on a long pole and offered at the grave on the seventh and forty-ninth day after a person's death

NADAN BIYA the seventh month

NADAN IRUNGGE MAHATUN an ancient-style hat with seven ridges on top

NADAN TUHEBUKU I MAHATU an ancient-style cap with seven tassels

NADAN USIHA the Big Dipper, Ursa Major

NADANCI seventh

NADANGGA pertaining to the number seven

NADANGGA HOOŠAN seven-layered paper

NADANGGA INENGGI the seventh day of the seventh month

NADANGGERI seven times

NADANJU seventy

NADANJUTA seventy each

NADANJUTE see *nadanjuta*

NADASE seven years (old): *nadan se*

NADATA seven each

NAGALAMBI see *nahalambi*

NAGAN see *nahan*

NAG'A ILHA the 'naga flower,' which has a white blossom surrounded by six leaves

NAHALAMBI to lie on an oven-bed, to tend the oven-bed

NAHAN *kang*, oven-bed of North China and Manchuria

NAHAN I BAITA sexual intercourse

NAHAN I HOSORI soot from an oven-bed

NAHAN I IRUN chimney of an oven-bed

NAI a large sacrificial tripod used in ancient China

NAIHŪ the same as *nadan usiha*

NAIHŪ DE SUCUNANGGA LOHO a sword that glitters when it is drawn from the scabbard

NAIHŪBUMBI caus. of *naihūmbi*

NAIHŪMBI to tilt, to lean to one side, to stagger

NAIJI ILHA spikenard

NAIMISUN the hem of the lining of a fur jacket; cf. *afin*

NAINAI housewife, mistress of a household

NAIRAHŪN gentle, kind, warm and generous

NAJIHIYAN one name for the *mojihiyan*,
the Tibetan black bear

NAKABUMBI 1. caus. of *nakambi* 2. to
dismiss, to let go, to discharge

NAKAMBI 1. to stop, to cease, to desist 2. to leave (a post) 3. to
leave a perch (chicken)
NAKA BAI stop! cease!

NAKCU mother's brother

NAKCUSE plural of *nakcu*; cf. *nakcuta*

NAKCUTA plural of *nakcu*

NAKŪ after (used after the imperative)

NAMA see *naman*
NAMA GIDA a small spear used by the
vanguard
NAMA SIRDAN a military arrow with
a head shaped like a spearhead

NAMALABUMBI caus. of *namalambi*

NAMALAMBI to stick with a needle, to
practice acupuncture

NAMAN a needle used for acupuncture

NAMARABUMBI caus./pass. of *namarambi*

NAMARAMBI to desire still more, to
take up again (a quarrel), to raise
(a price)

NAMAŠAN (used after the participles)
at the point of, just when, right
after, about to

NAMBUMBI to catch, to have fall into
one's hand
NAMBUHA NAMBUHAI at random, happen-
ing upon, by chance, unintentionally

NAMGIN a red persimmonlike fruit of
Hainan

NAMI a garment made of cured deerskin

NAMKI saddle blanket or pad

NAMKŪ the name of a famous sword kept
in the arsenal

NAMSI NAMSI at random, haphazard

NAMŠAN (used with the participles) at
the point of, just when, when about
to; cf. *namašan*

NAMŠURI an exotic fruit from a bush
over three feet tall that blooms in
winter

NAMU 1. ocean, sea 2. overseas,
foreign 3. a large-leafed green
vegetable eaten raw, lettuce
NAMU ANGGA port, harbor
NAMU COKO a peacock; see *tojin*
NAMU DENGJAN a lamp made of a
sheep's horn hung before a Buddha
image
NAMU NIYEHE a 'sea duck' or 'foreign
duck' with a white body, spotted
head and wings, and a red fleshy
growth on the bill
NAMU SIKA MOO a variety of South
Sea palm
NAMU ULGIYAN dolphin
NAMU URANGGA MOO a type of conifer

in Annam

NAMUN storehouse, granary

NAMURI name of a flaxlike plant from
which fabric can be woven

NAMUSI keeper of a warehouse or
granary

NAN MU MOO the *nanmu* tree

NANDABUMBI caus. of *nandambi*

NANDAMBI to ask for something for
nothing, to demand

NANGGIN porch, veranda, gallery, corridor

NANGGIŠAMBI to show off one's charms,
to ingratiate oneself with, to
allure with one's charms

NANGGITU COKO one name for the turkey;
cf. *junggila gasha*

NANGGŪ a trap for badger and raccoon-
dogs

NANTUHŪN dirty, filthy

NANTUHŪRABUMBI caus./pass. of *nantuhūrambi*

NANTUHŪRAMBI to dirty, to make filthy,
to soil

NARACUKA regrettable, causing feelings
of longing and attachment

NARACUN longing, attachment

NARAHŪNJAMBI to continually long for

NARAMBI (-ka) to long for, to feel
attached to, to linger over

NARANGGI finally, after all, really

NARAŠAMBI to long for continually, to
linger over a long time

NARAŠEMBI see *narašambi*

NARGA harrow, rake

NARGABUMBI caus. of *nargambi*

NARGAMBI to level with a harrow, to
rake

NARHŪDAMBI to be stingy, to be miserly

NARHŪN 1. fine, thin 2. detailed,
minute 3. secret, confidential 4.
sparing, economical, frugal 5.
grazing the target (at archery)
NARHŪN BA (窓本房) office
of secret communications in the
Board of War
NARHŪN BAITA a secret matter
NARHŪN DUHA the small intestine
NARHŪN EDUN euphemism for 'urine'
NARHŪN EDUN TUWAMBI euphemism for
'to urinate'
NARHŪN FUNIYESUN a type of fine
woolen
NARHŪN HONCI lambskin
NARHŪN MUCIHA FUTA a thin tow rope
of bamboo
NARHŪN NIMEKU 1. tuberculosis 2.
hernia
NARHŪN SELEI FUTA fine wire
NARHŪN WEHE a stone polished
smoothly

NARHŪNGGA fine, refined, detailed
NARHŪNGGA FUKJINGGA HERGEN (小

N

篆) a style of calligraphy--
the small seal

NARHŪNJAMBI see *narahūnjambi*

NARHŪŠABUMBI caus. of *narhūšambi*

NARHŪŠAMBI 1. to be fine, to be minute
2. to be sparing, to be economical
3. to do carefully, to do minutely
4. to do secretly 5. to make (an
arrow shaft) thin

NARHŪŠAME FEMPILERE BA bureau for
sealing (examination papers)

NARHŪŠAME FEMPILERE FALGANGGA (彌
封所) the same as *narhūšame
fempilere ba*

NARHŪŠAME FEMPILERE HAFAN (彌封
官) Sealer of Examinations, BH
652F

NARHŪŠEMBI see *narhūšambi*

NARI a female black bear; cf. *nasin*

NASA see *nasan*

NASABUMBI caus. of *nasambi*

NASACUKA regrettable, lamentable

NASACUN regret, lament

NASAMBI to regret, to lament

NASARA BITHE obituary, memorial
essay for a deceased person

NASAN salted cabbage, preserved vegetables

NASAN GIDAMBI to make salted cabbage

NASAN HENGKE salted cucumber, pickle

NASHŪLABUMBI caus. of *nashūlambi*

NASHŪLAMBI to meet with an opportunity,
to take advantage of an opportunity,
to seize a chance

NASHŪN opportunity, chance, happen-
stance

NASHŪN BE ACABUMBI to take advantage of an opportunity

NASIN large black bear (*Ursus arctos*)

NASUCUNGGA regrettable, pitiable

NAYA younger brother of one's wife

NE 1. now, at present, current 2.
sentence particle of mild interrogation

NE ANIYA the current year

NE BELEN ready, available

NE JE immediately, right now

NE JEN BELHEHE already prepared

NE TUŠAN current post

NECE the wife of one's wife's elder
brother

NECIBUMBI caus./pass. of *necimbi*

NECIHIYEBUMBI caus. of *necihiyembi*

NECIHIYEMBI 1. to level, to smooth out
2. to console, to calm down 3. to
subjugate, to subject, to pacify

NECIHIYEN peaceful, tranquil, serene

NECIHIYENEMBI to go to pacify, to go
to subdue

NECIKEN rather level

NECIMBI 1. to encroach on, to attack,
to raid 2. to incite, to provoke,
to stir up

N

NECIN 1. level, flat, even 2. peaceful, tranquil, calm

NECINEMBI to go to encroach or provoke, to go to attack

NECINGGE level, flat

NECINGGE KARAN watchtower, lookout
tower

NECINGGE KEMUN a level

NECINGGE MAHATUN an ancient-style
hat with a flat board on top

NECINGGE MUDAN the level tone of
Chinese

NECINGGE SAIFI a flat spoon

NECINJIMBI to come to encroach, to
come to provoke, to come to attack

NEGELEMBI to be unsteady, to wobble
(of things just placed in an erect
position)

NEHŪ (this word and the next have the
peculiar spelling of soft *h* before
ū): a slave girl

NEHŪJI a slave girl

NEHŪJI MAMA an old slave woman

NEI sweat, perspiration

NEI FUNIYEHE body hair

NEI TARAN perspiration

NEI TUCIMBI to sweat

NEI YOO heat rash

NEI YOO DEKDEMBI to get heat rash

NEIBUMBI caus. of *neimbi*

NEIGECILEBUMBI caus. of *neigecilembi*

NEIGECILEMBI to divide equally, to
even out

NEIGELEMBI to make even, to make uniform, to act uniformly, to behave
equally

NEIGEN even, uniform

NEIGENJEBUMBI caus. of *neigenjembi*

NEIGENJEMBI to make even, to make
uniform, to divide evenly

NEIKU SITHAN small hinge on a box

NEILEBUKŪ tutor of the heir-apparent
during the Three Kingdoms Period

NEILEBUMBI caus. of *neilembi*

NEILEBUN introduction, exposition (a
type of essay)

NEILEMBI to disclose, to elucidate,
to introduce to something new--
especially knowledge

NEILEN introduction, disclosure,
primer, letter (from a superior)

NEILESHŪN beginning, beginning of
spring

NEIMBI to open, to open up

NEKCU the wife of one's mother's
brothers

NEKCUTE plural of *nekcu*

NEKELIYEKEN rather thin, rather flimsy

NEKELIYELEMBI to make thin, to make
scanty, to make unimportant, to
treat as unimportant

NEKELIYELENEMBI see *nekeliyelembi*

NEKELIYEN 1. thin, flimsy, fine 2.

unimportant, trifling 3. scanty,
meager

NEKELIYEN CECERI a variety of thin
silk

NEKELIYEN HOLBONGGO HOOŠAN a variety of strong thin paper made from
bamboo

NEKELIYEN ŠOBIN a thin baked cake
made of flour, sugar, walnuts, and
lard

NEKU a woman's female friend, sworn
sister

NEKULAMBI (-ha) the same as *nekulembi*

NEKULEMBI 1. to take advantage of (a
friend's good offices, an opportunity, someone's misfortune) 2. to
rejoice over another's misfortune or
weakness

NELHE peaceful, healthy

NEMEBUMBI caus. of *nemembi*

NEMEGIN a measure equal to thirty
catties

NEMEHEN addition, increment

NEMEKU OMOLO a descendant of the fifth
generation

NEMEMBI 1. to add, to increase 2.
to remove the husks from grain

NEMEME moreover, on the contrary,
especially

NEMENDUMBI 1. to add together 2. to
hull together

NEMERGEN see *nemerhen*

NEMERHEN a raincoat made of reeds

NEMERI tender, young (of fruits and
vegetables)

NEMERKU a raincoat, rain jacket

NEMEŠEMBI to add to repeatedly

NEMEYEKEN rather tender, rather graceful

NEMEYEN tender, gentle, graceful,
docile, easygoing

NEMEYEN CECERI a soft silk used for
women's garments

NEMGIYAN see *nemgiyen*

NEMGIYEN graceful, affectionate, gentle

NEMKIBUMBI caus. of *nemkimbi*

NEMKIMBI to hem, to border

NEMKIYAMBI see *nemkimbi*

NEMSELEMBI to add more, to intensify,
to make more serious (an illness),
to aggravate (someone's anger)

NEMSURI BELE a variety of rice that is
cultivated in dry fields in the
south

NEMŠEKU insatiable

NEMŠEMBI to be insatiable, to be unsatisfied, to desire still more

NEMU a mine, mine shaft

NENDEBUMBI caus. of *nendembi*

NENDEMBI to be in front, to put first,
to come before, to be prior, to
act first

NENDEN first, beforehand, prior, pre-

mature

NENDEN BOJIRI ILHA a variety of
chrysanthemum that blooms in the
seventh month

NENDEN ILHA plum flower (*Prunus
mume*)

NENDEN ILHAI GIYEN the name of a
dark blue dye

NENDEN USIHA *Elaeagnus pungens*

NENEMBI to be first, to be ahead; cf.
nendembi

NENEHE former, prior, which went
before

NENEHE ANIYA former year, previous
year

NENEHE BIYA previous month

NENEHE ENDURINGGE SAISA former holy
sages, sages of antiquity

NENEHE INENGGI former day, previous
day

NENEHE JALAN former age, previous
age

NENEHE TUŠAN former post

NENEME formerly, previously, beforehand

NENGGE a white spot on the eye

NENGGELEBUMBI to cushion, to support,
to prop up

NENGGELEKU see *fi i nenggeleku*

NENGGEREBUMBI the same as *nenggelebumbi*

NENGGERESHUN cushioned, supported

NENGGESHUN see *nenggereshun*

NEOMBI to roam, to wander away from
home

NEORE TUGI a floating cloud, a lone
moving cloud

NERE 1. a three-legged prop for a
cooking pot 2. a hole used for
cooking purposes

NERE FETEMBI to dig a cooking hole

NERE JUN a portable stove made of
iron, used when traveling

NEREBUMBI 1. caus. of *nerembi* 2. to
shoot a wounded animal again 3. to
vilify further, to add insult to
injury

NEREKU a sleeveless rain cape made
from leather or oilskin

NEREKU NEREMBI to put on a rain
cape

NEREMBI to throw over the shoulders
(clothing)

NERGEN see *nergin*

NERGI smart, clever, sharp

NERGIN moment, short space of time,
occasion, opportunity

NERGIN DE just at this time, at
that moment, on an occasion

NERGIN I HŪSUN a temporary worker

NERGINGGE clever at grasping opportunity

NERKIMBI to open, to open out (a

N

scroll, roll of cloth, etc.)

NERKU see *nereku*

NESHUN flat

NESI 1. right now, just at this minute 2. a crack on an animal's hoof

NESIDUN one of the names of the partridge; cf. *jukidun*

NESUKEN gentle, tender, mild

    NESUKEN HEHE posthumous title of wives of officials of the sixth rank

    NESUKEN NEMEYEN gentle and easygoing

NEYE the wife of one's wife's younger brother

NI 1. genitive particle after words ending in -*ng* 2. interrogative particle at the end of a clause 3. a particle used at the caesura in archaic verse 4. an exclamation of wonder

    NI GIDAMBI to notice, to note, to record

NICANGGA TUNGKEN a large drum on a stand

NICARAMBI see *nijarambi*

NICUHE pearl

    NICUHE ŠUNGKERI ILHA a type of Chinese orchid with fragrant purple blossoms

    NICUHEI ŠURDEHEN a sphere inlaid with pearls that was used for observing the sun, moon, and stars in ancient times

NICUHERI MOO a variety of arbor vitae whose leaves resemble pearls

NICUHŪN see *nincuhūn*

NICULAMBI to wink, to blink

NICUMBI to close the eyes

NICUN ILHA *spiraea thunbergii*

NICUŠAMBI the same as *niculambi*

NIDUMBI to groan, to moan

NIJARABUMBI caus. of *nijarambi*

NIJARAKŪ a vessel for grinding hard materials into powder, mortar

NIJARAMBI to grind fine (as in a mortar)

NIJI path around a swamp or damp place

NIJIHE bran

NIKACILAMBI to act like a Chinese

    NIKACILARAKŪ non-Chinese, acting in a non-Chinese manner

NIKAI an emphatic sentence particle

NIKAN Chinese

    NIKAN BITHEI KUNGGERI BOO (漢科房) Chinese Copying Office, BH 138

    NIKAN DANGSE BOO (漢檔房) Translation Office (for Manchu and Chinese)

    NIKAN GŪLDARGAN a small type of swallow that is fond of chirping

    NIKAN HENGKE a variety of sweet-tasting melon somewhat larger than

the 'sweet melon' (*Cucumis melo*)

    NIKAN HERGEN Chinese character, Chinese writing, the Chinese written language

    NIKAN ULHŪMA the long-tailed pheasant, Reeve's pheasant (*Syrmaticus reevesii*)

    NIKAN ULI a type of sour apple that is often preserved

    NIKAN WESIMBURE BITHEI BA (漢本堂) office of Chinese memorials of the Grand Secretariat

    NIKAN YOO a pustule or boil on the skin, venereal sore

NIKARABUMBI caus. of *nikarambi*

NIKARAMBI to speak Chinese

NIKASA plural of *nikan*

NIKCABUMBI caus./pass. of *nikcambi*

NIKCAMBI 1. to shatter, to disintegrate 2. to be at a disadvantage, to suffer loss

NIKDE the part of the back that supports a saddle on horses, mules, and donkeys

NIKEBUKU a prop, support, doorstop

NIKEBUMBI 1. caus. of *nikembi* 2. to prop up, to support, to serve as a support 3. to undergo (a punishment) 4. to entrust to, to hand over to 5. to confer (on), to bestow

NIKEBUN painted representation of a deity or a plaque with a deity's name written on it

NIKEDEMBI to be just exactly enough, to manage to get by

    NIKEDEME just enough, just a little

NIKEKU a support, something to lean on

    NIKEKU MULAN a chair

    NIKEKU MULAN I DASIKŪ covering or cushion on a chair

NIKEKUNGGE SEKTEFUN cushion or padding on the back of a chair

NIKEMBI 1. to lean, to lean on, to depend on, to rely on 2. to bend over something 3. to incline, to support oneself 4. to remain abed for a month after the birth of a child

NIKEN support, reliance

NIKENDUMBI to support one another, to support together

NIKENEMBI 1. to go to lean on 2. to draw near to

NIKENJIMBI 1. to come to lean, to come to rest on 2. to draw near to

NIKEŠEMBI to limp slightly

NIKETU support, reliance

    NIKETU AKŪ without means of support

NIKSIMBI to shiver from cold

NIKTAN a divine elixir, an elixir of cinnabar that is supposed to confer immortality

    NIKTAN SIKTAN the same as *niktan*

NIKTEMBI to stamp the earth with the
  hoof
NIKTON at peace, peaceful
NIKTONGGA peaceful, tranquil
  NIKTONGGA GECUHERI a type of silk
    decorated with dragon figures
    produced in Nanking
  NIKTONGGA SURI a fine silken fabric
    from Nanking
  NIKTONGGA UNDURAKŪ a silken fabric
    from Nanking with a design of
    prancing dragons
NILABUMBI caus. of *nilambi*
NILAKŪ a small roller for crushing or
  grinding objects, crusher, grinder
NILAMBI to grind, to polish (lenses)
  NILARA YONGGAN fine sand used for
    polishing jade, glass, etc.
NILEMBI see *nilambi*
NILGIYAN shiny, glistening, slick,
  smooth, oily
  NILGIYAN SUJE a variety of shiny
    satin
NILGIYANGGA lustrous, brilliant, shin-
  ing
NILHI dysentery; cf. *ilhi*
NILHŪDAMBI to be smooth, shiny, slick
NILHŪMA one name for the pheasant
NILHŪN slippery, slick
NILHŪŠAMBI to be slick (of ice)
NILTAJABUMBI caus./pass. of *niltajambi*
NILTAJAMBI to damage a skin surface by
  rubbing
NITUBUMBI to singe hair off a skin
NILUGA see *nilukan*
NILUKAN 1. smooth, not rough 2.
  gentle, fine, tactful
NIMACI goatskin
NIMADA 1. hornless dragon 2. alliga-
  tor
NIMADAN a type of tree that grows in
  groves in valleys and produces a
  hard, fine-grained wood
NIMAHA fish
  NIMAHA BUTAMBI to fish
  NIMAHA BUTARA NIYALMA a fisherman
  NIMAHA GABTARA ŠAKA an arrow with
    a five-pronged forked head used
    for shooting fish
  NIMAHA USIHA a star in the Milky
    Way located north of the constel-
    lation *weisha*
  NIMAHA YASA a corn on the foot
NIMAHAŠAMBI to fish
NIMALA see *nimalan*
NIMALAN mulberry tree
  NIMALAN MOO the same as *nimalan*
NIMAN goat
NIMANGGI snow
  NIMANGGI ILHA snowflake, snow crys-
    tal
  NIMANGGI KIYALMAMBI (the wind)
    drives the snow in whirls

  NIMANGGI LABSAN snowflake
NIMARAMBI to snow
NIMARGAN little kingfisher (*Alcedo
  atthis*)
NIMARI 1. goatskin 2. snowlike
  NIMARI GŪWASIHIYA the eastern
    egret; cf. *gūwasihiya*
  NIMARI ILHA rose-of-China (*Hibis-
    cus rosa-sinensis*)
  NIMARI YANGGALI a small bird with
    snow-white feathers--when it
    sings it is supposed to snow
NIMASI one name for the kingfisher; cf.
  ulgiyan cecike
NIMAŠAKŪ a small two-man boat made
  from a tree trunk
NIMAŠAN 1. water from melting snow
  2. the sea eagle (*Haliaeetus albi-
  cilla*)
  NIMAŠAN MUKE water from melting snow
NIMEBUMBI caus. of *nimembi*
NIMECUKE 1. painful, excruciating 2.
  frightful, terrible 3. cruel 4.
  strong (of liquor)
  NIMECUKE HORONGGO POO the name of
    an iron cannon four feet eight
    and one-half inches long
NIMEKU 1. sickness, illness 2. pain
  3. defect, weakness
  NIMEKU DE DARUBUMBI to be prone to
    frequent illnesses
  NIMEKU DE HŪSIBUHABI is afflicted
    by a chronic illness
  NIMEKU TURGEN the illness is acute
NIMEKULEBUMBI caus. of *nimekulembi*
NIMEKULEMBI to become ill, to develop
  an illness
NIMEKUNGGE ill, sick, one who is ill
NIMEMBI to ache, to be painful, to
  suffer, to be ill
NIMENGGI oil, fat; cf. *imenggi*
  NIMENGGI NOHO covered with oil,
    full of fat
  NIMENGGI YASA the two depressions
    on the coccyx of a man
NIMENGGILEMBI to grease, to oil, to
  press oil, to produce oil
NIMETEMBI to be ill together, to
  suffer mutually
NIMHELIYEN ILHA snowball (*Viburunum
  roseum*)
NINCUHŪN smelling of fish or raw meat,
  smelly
NINDARŠAMBI to pay compliments to,
  to flirt
NINGCEO Nanking silk
NINGCU see *ningceo*
NINGDAN a growth on the neck, goiter
NINGDANGGA having a growth on the
  neck, having a goiter
NINGGE the one which . . . ,
  he who . . .
NINGGIŠAMBI see *nindaršambi*

N

NINGGIYA 1. water caltrop, horn chest-
nut (*Trapa natans*) 2. anchor 3.
a weapon used for stopping enemy
horses
  NINGGIYA BULA *Tribulus terrestris*
  NINGGIYA EFEN small meat-filled
  dumplings boiled in soup
  NINGGIYA MOO an anchor made of wood
  NINGGIYA SELE 1. an iron anchor 2.
  a horseshoe with teeth or cleats
NINGGIYAN see *ninggiya*
NINGGU top, on top
NINGGUCI sixth
NINGGUDE (postposition) on top of
NINGGULE linden tree
NINGGUN 1. six 2. same as *ninggu*
  NINGGUN ACAN the six directions:
    north, south, east, west, up, and
    down
  NINGGUN BIYA the sixth month
  NINGGUN IRUNGGE MAHATUN an ancient-
    style hat with six ridges on top
  NINGGUN MUTEN the six skills: rites,
    music, archery, chariot-driving,
    calligraphy, and arithmetic
  NINGGUN YANGSANGGA INENGGI the six
    auspicious days of the year
NINGGUNGGERI six times
NINGGUREME on top, over, upward
NINGGUSE six years old
NINGGUTE six each
NINGKABUMBI to be inflated, to
  become puffed up
NINGNIYEN see *ninggiya*
NINIYARILAMBI to get a pain in the
  back, to wrench the back
NINIYARŠAMBI to set the teeth on
  edge (by eating sour or hard things)
NINJU sixty
  NINJU DULEFUN I DURUNGGA TETUN an
    astronomical instrument of the
    Peking observatory used for ob-
    serving the variation in degrees
    among the equator, ecliptic, sun
    moon, and stars
NINJUCI sixtieth
NINJUTE sixty each
NINKIMBI 1. to search for a doe (of
  buck deer) 2. to search for fawns
  (of a mother doe); cf. *nirkimbi*
  NINKIME BAIMBI to search for fawns
    (of a mother doe)
NINTEHE ILHA a fragrant white blossom
  of Hainan that resembles jasmine
NINTUHŪ having a crooked neck, a
  crooked-necked man
  NINTUHŪ HARI a crooked-necked man
NINURI one name for the cat
NIO 1. an interrogative sentence par-
  ticle 2. an emphatic particle
NIOBOMBI to tease, to taunt with words
NIOBORO deep green
NIOCUHE see *nicuhe*

NIOHAN (牛) the name of a constel-
  lation
  NIOHAN TOKDONGGO KIRU a banner
    depicting the constellation *niohan*
NIOHE wolf
  NIOHE SUBE a wild plant whose
    leaves are used as padding for
    saddles
  NIOHE YOO small red eruptions on
    the skin
NIOHERI a type of mythical wolf
NIOHOBUMBI see *niyohobumbi*
NIOHOKON light green, greenish
NIOHOMBI the same as *niyohombi*
NIOHON 1. green 2. the second of the
  heaven's stems (乙)
  NIOHON ABKA the blue sky
  NIOHON ELBENGGE FUKJINGGA HERGEN
  (碧落篆) a style of
    calligraphy
  NIOHON JILI BANJIMBI to fly into a
    blue rage
  NIOHON TALKIYANGGA LOHO the name of
    a type of sword
  NIOHON TEMGETUNGGE GU a flat piece
    of jade with a hole in the center
    used at certain feudal investi-
    tures and at sacrifices
NIOHUBUMBI caus. of *niohumbi*
NIOHUKEN somewhat pea green
NIOHUMBI 1. to pound, to stamp 2.
  to construct a pounded earth wall
NIOHUN pea green
  NIOHUN TEIŠUN bronze
NIOHUREMBI to act fiercely, to put on
  a fierce expression
NIOHUŠULEBUMBI caus. of *niohušulembi*
NIOHUŠULEMBI to go naked, to be naked
NIOHUŠUN naked
NIOJAN NIYEHE Chinese little grebe
  (*Podiceps ruficollis*)
NIOKAN a small arrow made from a wil-
  low branch used by children for play
  NIOKAN BOLGOMBI to throw small play
    arrows or chopsticks into a pot--
    a drinking forfeit game
NIOKJI moss on stones in water; cf.
  niolmonggi
NIOKSO a stringlike form of algae
  found on the surface of water
NIOLHUCEMBI to plunge headlong, to
  rush forward
NIOLHUMBI to gallop
NIOLHUMBUMBI caus. of *niolhumbi*
NIOLHUN the sixteenth day of the first
  month, the end of the new year's
  festivities
  NIOLHUN EFEN round boiled pastries
    filled with walnut and sesame
    that are eaten on the evening of
    the fifteenth day of the first
    month
  NIOLHUN ILHA a red flower resem-

bling the quince that blooms around
the sixteenth of the first month
NIOLHUŠEMBI to slip, to lose one's
footing
NIOLHŪN see *niolhun*
NIOLMON moss
    NIOLMON BEYE without helmet and
    armor
NIOLMONGGI moss on rocks in water; cf.
    niokji
NIOLMUN see *nioron*
NIOLOCUKA too greasy, too oily, dis-
gusting
NIOLOMBI to get stuck in the throat
because of being too greasy, to gag
on something because it's disgusting
NIOMBI (-ho) to be frozen to the bones
    NIOME NIMEMBI to have the bones
    ache from cold
    NIOME ŠAHŪRUN cold that penetrates
    to the bones
NIOMERE octopus
NIOMOŠON Siberian salmon (*Brachymystax
lenok*)
NIOMŠUN see *niomošon*
NIONGGAJAMBI 1. to damage a surface
with metal, wood, stone, etc. 2.
to pierce
    NIONGGAJARA ADALI as if pierced
    (on seeing something pitiful)
    NIONGGAJARAHŪ oh that he may not be
    hurt!
NIONGGALABUMBI caus./pass. of *nionggal-
ambi*
NIONGGALAMBI to damage the surface of
some object slightly
NIONGNIO 1. the largest feather on a
bird's wing 2. outstanding, best,
superior
    NIONGNIO DETHE the largest and
    toughest feather on a bird's wing
NIONGNIYAHA goose
    NIONGNIYAHA I BE the name of a
    plant that is the same as *meihe
    šari*
NIONIO 1. pupil of the eye 2. an
expression of affection used by
adults to children
    NIONIO FAHA the pupil of the eye
NIONIORU a small basket tray
NIORI see *niowari nioweri*
NIOROMBI (-ko, -pi) 1. to turn green,
to turn blue, to turn black and
blue (after being hit) 2. to be
moved profoundly
NIOROMBUMBI 1. caus. of *niorombi*
2. to make iron shine
NIORON rainbow
    NIORON BURUBUHA the rainbow became
    covered with clouds
    NIORON GOCIKA the rainbow appeared
    NIORON GOCINGGA LOHO a sword that
    sparkles like a rainbow

NIORON SAMSIHA the rainbow has gone
NIORONGGO DABTANGGA LOHO a sword
    forged like a rainbow
NIORONGGO KILTAN a pennant of the im-
    perial escort that is colored like a
    rainbow
NIORUMBI see *niorombi*
NIOŠUMBUMBI see *nišumbumbi*
NIOWANCIHIYAN smelling of new-mown hay
    or grass, having the fragrance of
    grass
NIOWANGGA ILHA *Lychnis fulgens*
NIOWANGGA MOO *Ilex pedunculosa*
NIOWANGGIYAKAN apple-green, light
    green, greenish
NIOWANGGIYAN 1. green 2. the ninth of
    the earth's branches (申)
    NIOWANGGIYAN DERHUWE a green fly
    NIOWANGGIYAN FIYORHON green wood-
    pecker
    NIOWANGGIYAN FULAN a blue-black
    horse
    NIOWANGGIYAN FULHA a green poplar
    NIOWANGGIYAN GU turquoise
    NIOWANGGIYAN GURJEN a type of large
    green cricket of North China; cf.
    gergen
    NIOWANGGIYAN MUDURINGGA KIRU a ban-
    ner of the imperial escort em-
    broidered with a green dragon
    NIOWANGGIYAN TU I COOHA Chinese
    troops of the green banner
    NIOWANGGIYAN TURI green pea, green
    bean
    NIOWANGGIYAN TURUN the green ban-
    ner, i.e., the Chinese troops of
    the provinces
    NIOWANGGIYAN TURUN COOHA the Chi-
    nese troops of the green banner
    NIOWANGGIYAN UJU a green lacquered
    tablet on which a person granted
    an audience with the emperor wrote
    his name and rank
    NIOWANGGIYAN YENGGEHE a green par-
    rot
    NIOWANGGIYAN YENGGETU a type of
    macaw
NIOWANIORI HIYABAN light green summer
    cloth
NIOWARGI GASHA turquoise kingfisher
NIOWARI shiny green or blue
    NIOWARI BOJIRI ILHA a blue chrys-
    anthemum
    NIOWARI CECIKE siskin
    NIOWARI NIORI the same as *niowari
    nioweri*
    NIOWARI NIOWERI bright and shining
    green
NIOWARIKŪ jasper green
NIOWARIMBU WEHE emerald
NIOWARIŠAMBI to be green, to become
    green
NIRAHA see *nirga*

N

NIREHE (女) the name of a constellation

NIREHE TOKDONGGO KIRU a banner depicting the constellation *nirehe*

NIRGA short, sparse (of hair)

NIRGAKAN rather short, rather sparse (of hair)

NIRHŪWATU one name for the bamboo partridge; cf. *cuse moo i itu*

NIRKIMBI to look for a doe (of a buck deer); cf. *ninkimbi*

NIRU 1. a large arrow for shooting game and people 2. a *niru*, a banner company of a hundred men 3. (佐領) the head of a banner, Captain, BH 726

NIRU BELHERE BA (備箭處) the place where arrows for the emperor's use were made

NIRU FAKSI an arrow maker

NIRUI FALGA the meeting place of a banner company

NIRUI JANGGIN (佐領) Captain, BH 726

NIRUBUMBI caus. of *nirumbi*

NIRUGAN picture, chart, map, diagram, drawing, painting

NIRUGAN I TEMUN a round stick on which paintings are rolled

NIRUHAN see *nirugan*

NIRUMBI (-ha/ke) to draw, to paint

NIRURE CECERI silk used for painting

NIRWAN Nirvana, paradise

NIRWAN TUWABUMBI to die (of monks)

NISELEMBI to fend off

NISIHA 1. a small fish 2. the name of a card game

NISIHA EFEN flat boiled cakes made from wheat flour and eaten with cream

NISIHA UMIYAHA a bookworm

NISIHAI along with, together, with, along with so as to make a complete set

NISIKTE moss, lichen

NISUBUMBI caus. of *nisumbi*

NISUKŪ skates, shoes used for walking on ice

NISUMBI to slide, to glide, to skid, to skate (on ice)

NISUNDUMBI to skate together on the ice, to slide together

NISURI a device attached to the grip of a bow to allow it to release smoothly

NIŠA strong, heavy, solid, firm

NIŠA ACIHA a heavy load

NIŠA BUMBI to give in sufficient quantity

NIŠA GAIMBI to take in ample quantity

NIŠA GIDAMBI to press firmly

NIŠA TEBUMBI to pack in firmly

NIŠAKAN rather strong, rather heavy

NIŠALABUMBI caus. of *nišalambi*

NIŠALAMBI 1. to hit solidly 2. to pick off lice

NIŠAN an undyed spot on both ends of a piece of cloth, mark, sign

NIŠARGAN a small sore (on the head)

NIŠE one-millionth

NIŠUI FAKSI a mason

NIŠUMBUMBI to stick into, to insert, to fit into

NITAN 1. weak, diluted, insipid, light, dulled 2. without worldly desires

NITAN AISIN gold that is not 100 percent pure

NITAN MENGGUN silver that is not 100 percent pure

NITARAMBI (-ka) to become weak, diluted

NITUKŪ see *nituri*

NITUMBI to groan, to moan (from pain)

NITURI CECIKE a snipe with a white beak

NIYABUMBI caus. of *niyambi*

NIYADA late in maturing, slow in growing

NIYADA JEKU late grain

NIYADAHA a late maturing pear from the south

NIYAHAN puppy, whelp

NIYAHARA tender sprouts, tender leaves, tender buds

NIYAHARA I YARUN one of the six yang tones

NIYAHARI ILHA 'child's flower'--a small flower that grows in thick clusters

NIYAHARI NUNGGELE MOO the catalpa tree (*Catalpa Bungei*)

NIYAHARNAMBI to put forth tender shoots or buds

NIYAHAŠABUMBI caus. of *niyahašambi*

NIYAHAŠAMBI 1. to set a dog on game 2. to drive cattle 3. to limp (of horses and cattle with a damaged hoof)

NIYAJIBA shepherd's purse (*Capsella bursa pastoris*)

NIYAKI pus, nasal and bodily discharge

NIYAKI SIRIMBI to blow the nose, to wipe the nose

NIYAKINABUMBI caus. of *niyakinambi*

NIYAKINAMBI to form pus

NIYAKITU a dirty-nosed child

NIYAKŪN genuflection, kneeling

NIYAKŪRABUMBI caus. of *niyakūrambi*

NIYAKŪRAMBI to kneel

NIYALHŪNJAMBI to get dizzy from heat or hunger

NIYALMA 1. man, person 2. another person, someone else, others 3. the line or groove that goes from the bottom of the nose to the upper lip

NIYALMA DE HOLBOMBI to get married

NIYALMA HENDUHE BALAMA people say so, such is the popular opinion

NIYALMA I URKIN DE YABUMBI to go along with other people's actions, to go along with the crowd

NIYALMA NIMAHA 1. a creature half fish, half man 2. seal

NIYALMA TATARA BOO inn, hotel

NIYALMA UNCARA HŪDACI a person who deals in slaves, especially girls and children

NIYALMA USIHA the name of five stars in the Milky Way

NIYALMAI DUWALI mankind, humankind

NIYALMAI SABI hundred-year-old man, a very old man

NIYALMAINGGE belonging to someone else

NIYAMALA moss found on trees and stones

NIYAMALAMBI to honor (one's parents), to serve (one's parents)

NIYAMAN 1. heart 2. pistil of a flower 3. center, innermost part 4. relative, parent 5. trusted friend, intimate 6. wick of a candle

NIYAMAN BE UJIMBI to take care of one's parents

NIYAMAN FELIYEMBI to discuss marriage

NIYAMAN GABTAKŪ the beams that connect the ridge beam and the horizontal beams in a roof

NIYAMAN HADAHAN the iron pegs on a harness to which the reins are fastened

NIYAMAN HOLBOMBI to contract a marriage

NIYAMAN HŪNCIHIN relative, relations

NIYAMAN I BAITA marriage, match-making

NIYAMAN I JUKTEHEN shrine to one's parents

NIYAMAN ILIHA the ears appeared (on grain)

NIYAMAN JAFAMBI to marry

NIYAMAN JAKA the center of the chest

NIYAMAN JAKA NIMEMBI to have a pain in the chest, to have a pain in the heart

NIYAMAN TUKSIMBI to form a heart, to form a hard core

NIYAMAN UFUHU intimate friend

NIYAMANAMBI to form a center, to form a heart

NIYAMANGGA related (by blood), having an innermost part

NIYAMANI a term of endearment used toward young children and elderly people

NIYAMARAMBI to treat as an honored relative

NIYAMARCAMBI to be jealous of others, to envy, to be inwardly contemptuous

NIYAMAŠAMBI to live on an islet

NIYAMAŠAN 1. islet in a river 2. center, middle part

NIYAMBI to rot, to decay, to go bad

NIYAMBULU weakling

NIYAMCIRI grass and leaves placed under hides by a tanner

NIYAMNIYABUMBI caus. of *niyamniyambi*

NIYAMNIYAMBI to shoot (arrows) from horseback, to practice mounted archery

NIYAMNIYARA MAHALA a hat worn for mounted archery

NIYAMNIYAN an arrow used in mounted archery

NIYAMNIYAN GABTAN the same as *niyamniyan*

NIYAMNIYANAMBI to go to practice mounted archery

NIYAMNIYANDUMBI/NIYAMNIYANUMBI to practice mounted archery together

NIYANCAKŪ a wooden stick for beating starched clothes while washing

NIYANCAMBI to starch

NIYANCAN 1. starch 2. sharpness, courage

NIYANCAN AKŪ 1. unstarched, limp 2. lacking courage

NIYANCAN BIJAHA 1. become limp (of starched cloth) 2. lost courage

NIYANCAN BIJAMBI to grow limp

NIYANCAN BILAMBI to lose courage

NIYANCANGGA starched, strong, firm, hard, brave, long-winded

NIYANCANGGANGGE one who is brave, strong, that which is strong, firm, hard

NIYANCI HIYAN a plant that grows in the mountains with fragrant willow-like leaves that are burnt like incense at sacrifices

NIYANCIHA green grass, green plants

NIYANCIRI HAMGIYA *Artemisia capillaris*

NIYANDZ a small ball of some material that has been rolled between the fingers

NIYANG girl

NIYANG NIYANG goddess

NIYANGDZ lady, mistress (of a household)

NIYANGGU JE BELE a type of white millet

NIYANGGŪBUMBI caus. of *niyanggūmbi*

NIYANGGŪMBI 1. to chew 2. to backbite, to criticize

NIYANGNIYA clear (after clouds have dispersed)

NIYANGNIYA TUCIKE it has become clear (after clouds have parted or dispersed)

NIYANGNIYAHŪN grimacing (from pain or fatigue)

NIYANGNIYANG goddess

NIYANGNIYARAMBI (-ka) to grimace (from pain or fatigue)

N

NIYANHŪN puppy, whelp; cf. *niyahan*

NIYANINGJIJI *Polygonum filiforma*--a medicinal plant

NIYANIOMBI 1. to chew 2. to backbite

NIYANIYUN betel nut

NIYANJAN an imperial chariot

NIYANJARI ILHA an exotic bloom with purple petals, a white center, and an odor that inhibits sleep

NIYANSE see *niyandz*

NIYARA in making liquor, sweetened grain that has been allowed to ferment

NIYARAN see *niyara*

NIYARANGGA TARA a mixture of sour milk, sugar, and *niyara*

NIYARHOCA the young of the Manchurian moose; cf. *kandahan*

NIYARHŪKAN rather fresh

NIYARHŪLAMBI to remain in confinement for a month after the birth of a child

NIYARHŪN fresh

NIYARI wet land, muddy area, marsh

NIYASI YALI flesh that is between the cracks of the teeth

NIYASUBUMBI caus. of *niyasumbi*

NIYASUMBI (-ka) to come to a head (a boil), to fester, to discharge pus

NIYAŠA see *niyasi*

NIYECEBUMBI caus. of *niyecembi*

NIYECEBUN same as *niyececun*

NIYECECUN filling out, supplementing, mending

NIYECEMBI 1. to mend 2. to fill in, to fill (a post) 3. to supplement 4. to nourish (of foods and medicines)

NIYECEN a patch, a small piece of cloth

NIYECETEMBI to mend continually, fill in regularly

NIYEHE duck

    NIYEHE TATARA ASU a long net for catching wild ducks

    NIYEHE TUNGGE the name of an edible wild plant that creeps along the earth

    NIYEHE UMHAN I TOHOLIYO a pastry made of duck's eggs, sugar, honey, rice, and flour and fried in lard

NIYEKDECUKE 1. spoiled 2. hateful, loathsome, detestable

NIYEKDEMBI (-ke) to spoil, to become rancid, to become sour

NIYEKEJE the male *cime*

NIYEKSE light, thin (of clothing)

NIYEKSEMBI (-ke) to thaw on the surface (while still frozen underneath)

NIYEKSERHEN a bird of Fukien with a yellow head, black back, yellow-striped feathers, and long legs that eats fish and shrimp

NIYEKSU see *niyokso*

NIYELEBUMBI caus. of *niyelembi*

NIYELEJEMBI to abrade, to hurt the skin by rubbing against something

NIYELEKU 1. a stone roller, upper millstone 2. a stick for washing

    NIYELEKU I ALIKŪ WEHE the lower millstone

    NIYELEKU WEHE a stone roller for separating the grains from the ear, a millstone

NIYELEMBI 1. to roll, to mill (grains) 2. to roll fabrics with a stone roller 3. to read out loud

NIYEMPEREMBI to thaw on the surface (while still frozen underneath)

NIYENGCERI ILHA *Lychnis fulgens*

NIYENGGARI CECIKE one name for the myna

NIYENGGUWERI CECIKE the same as *niyenggari cecike*

NIYENGNIYELTU CECIKE the name of a bird that has a white head and neck, black wings, and sings incessantly during the spring

NIYENGNIYERI spring (season)

    NIYENGNIYERI BE BODORO HAFAN (春官正) Astronomer for Spring, BH 229

    NIYENGNIYERI DOSIMBI 'spring enters'--one of the twenty-four divisions of the solar year falling on the 4th or 5th of February

    NIYENGNIYERI DULIN the vernal equinox

    NIYENGNIYERI ENDURI the name of a god to whom sacrifice is offered on 'spring enters'

    NIYENGNIYERI FIYAN DE URGUNJERE MUDAN a piece of music played while tea was brought in to the banquet following the spring plowing ceremony

    NIYENGNIYERI MUJILEN sexual feelings

    NIYENGNIYERI ŠUNGGA ILHA a fragrant white flower with six petals and a yellow center

NIYENGNIYERIKTEN the spring offering to the ancestors

NIYENIYE 1. weak willed, lacking initiative 2. hibernation of snakes and insects

NIYENIYEDEMBI see *niyeniyeršembi*

NIYENIYEHŪDEMBI to be weak willed, to be lacking in initiative

NIYENIYEHŪN weak willed, lacking initiative

NIYENIYEHŪNJEMBI to be weak willed, to lack initiative, to be weak of character

NIYENIYEN see *niyeniye*

NIYENIYERŠEMBI to bite gently

NIYERE 1. weak, feeble, slight 2.

N

light, flimsy (of clothing)

NIYEREBUMBI caus. of *niyerembi*

NIYEREKEN rather weak, flimsy, light

NIYEREMBI 1. to wear light clothing 2. to be lacking protective garb (armor, helmet, etc.) 3. to swim (of animals)

NIYEREME lightly attired

NIYEREME BEYE without helmet and armor

NIYERENGGE one who wears light clothing

NIYO swamp, marsh, slough

NIYO COKO peewit, lapwing (*Vanellus vanellus*)

NIYO I BA marsh, slough

NIYO I HOOHAN a type of bittern

NIYO I LEFU a marsh bear

NIYO ILHA pygmy water lily (*Nymphaea tetragona*)

NIYO MUŠU Chinese button quail (*Turnix tanki*)

NIYO SAKSAHA marsh magpie

NIYOBUMBI caus. of *niyombi*

NIYOCIKI a small bird that resembles the bittern

NIYOHOMBI to have sexual intercourse

NIYOKDOKO ravine, gully, defile

NIYOKSO flosslike green algae

NIYOLMON see *niolmon*

NIYOLOCUKA see *niolocuka*

NIYOLODO hateful, detestable (in speech)

NIYOMBI to scrape meat from bones

NIYOMOŠUN drifting ice

NIYOOLOCUKA oily, greasy, fatty; cf. *niolocuka*

NIYOROMBI see *niorombi*

NO a sentence particle denoting mild interrogation

NOFI person (used after numbers larger than one)

NOHO covered, filled, all over, saturated

NOKAI very

NOKAI JA very easy

NOKCIMBI to get very angry

NOMHOKON rather tame, rather docile

NOMHON docile, quiet, tame, guileless, unobtrusive, simple minded

NOMHON MORIN I FIYENTEN (馴 馬 司) Equestrian Section, BH 118

NOMHON SUFAN I FALGANGGA (馴 象 所) Elephant-training Section, BH 122

NOMHON SUFAN UJIRE BOO (馴 象 房) elephant-training house

NOMIN 1. lapis lazuli 2. fat of fish and frogs

NOMULAMBI to preach, to expound the scriptures

NOMUN 1. classic book, classic 2. sutra, scripture 3. law, holy

teaching, religion 4. preaching

NOMUN BE KADALARA YAMUN (司 經 局) library where sutras were kept in the palace

NOMUN BITHE NADAN AFAHA ŠU FIYELEN the seven purports of the classics

NOMUN HAN Dharma king, Dharmarāja

NOMUN HŪLAMBI to recite sutras

NOMUN JIBEHUN a funeral garment with dharanis embroidered on it

NOMUN MANDAL a Buddhist or Taoist scripture reading service in a temple of private home

NOMUN TARNI KUREN (經 呪 舘) an office for the copying of dharanis in Manchu, Chinese, Mongolian, and Tibetan

NON younger sister

NONGGIBUMBI 1. caus./pass. of *nonggimbi* 2. to advance, to increase

NONGGIBURE GUCU an intimate friend

NONGGIMBI 1. to add, to add to 2. to increase (in rank)

NONGGIME FUNGNEMBI to raise to a higher rank as a sign of favor

NONGGINAMBI to go to add, to go to increase

NONGGINDUMBI to add together, to increase together

NONGGINJIMBI to come to add, to come to increase

NONO water scallion (*Allium hakeri*)

NORAMBI to pile up wood or plants

NORAN a pile of wood or plants

NOROMBI to remain still in one place, to remain at home, to remain in the nest, to remain silently in one place, to lie without moving

NOROME AMHAMBI to sleep soundly

NORON longing, attachment; cf. *naracun*

NOSIKI an excellent hunter

NOTA the plural of *non*

NOTHO skin, rind, bark of a tree

NOTHORI a sweet-tasting exotic fruit

NU a sentence particle showing mild interrogation

NU BERI a crossbow

NUHAKAN rather at ease

NUHALIYAN swamp, marsh, depression in the land, slough

NUHAN at ease, easy-going

NUHASI one name for the rhinoceros

NUHECI hide of the wild boar

NUHEN a one-year-old wild pig

NUHERE a puppy seven or eight months old

NUHERE DAFAHA the female chum salmon; cf. *dafaha*

NUHERE MAFA JIHE 'puppy grandfather came'--said to small children by old people who want to keep them awake to play

NUHERI see *nuhere*

N

NUHU a high place, an area higher than a surrounding depression

NUJALAMBI to beat with the fist

NUJAN fist

NUJAN AŠŠARAKŪ the fist is not moving (at archery)

NUJAN BARGIYAMBI to clench the fist

NUJANGGA MAITU a red-lacquered pole with a golden fist on the end

NUJAŠAMBI to beat all over with the fists

NUKABUMBI caus./pass. of *nukambi*

NUKACUKA sharp, pointed

NUKAJAMBI to get sick, to have a sharp pain in the eye

NUKAMBI to stick, to prick

NUKCIBUMBI caus. of *nukcimbi*

NUKCIMBI (-ke) 1. to act in a rage, to advance valiantly 2. to make a desperate retreat (of bandits)

NUKCIME YABUMBI to advance valiantly or fiercely

NUKCISHUN 1. raging, violent, fierce 2. coarse, rude, rash

NUKIBUMBI caus./pass. of *nukimbi*

NUKIMBI 1. to stir up, to incite 2. to be agitated, to act rashly

NUKTE 1. an area in which nomads lead their flocks and herds following water and grass 2. baggage carried on pack animals

NUKTEBUMBI caus. of *nuktembi*

NUKTEMBI to lead a nomadic life, to wander with one's flocks or herds, to be nomadic

NUKTENDUMBI/NUKTENUMBI to lead the nomadic life together

NUKTENEMBI to go to lead a nomadic life

NUKTENJIMBI to come to lead a nomadic life

NUNGGALAMBI to stew slowly

NUNGGALAHA YALI stewed meat

NUNGGARI down, fuzz

NUNGGARI FATHANGGA KUWECIHE sand grouse (*Syrrhaptes paradoxus*)

NUNGGARI FUNGGAHA one name for the quail; cf. *mušu*

NUNGGARI FUNIYESUN a type of woolen

NUNGGARI JAFU fuzzy felt

NUNGGASUN a fine material woven from down

NUNGGASUN SUJE a satinlike material woven from down

NUNGGELE linden tree

NUNGGEMBI to swallow

NUNGGILE see *nunggele*

NUNGGIMBI see *nunggembi*

NUNGNEBUMBI 1. caus./pass. of *nungnembi* 2. (euphemistic) to be murdered

NUNGNECUN harm, injury

NUNGNEKU injurer, provoker

NUNGNEMBI 1. to tease, to provoke, to incite 2. to bother, to annoy, 3. to harm, to wrong, to oppress 4. (euphemism) to murder

NUNGNENJIMBI to come to provoke, to come to harm

NUNGNERI MONIO one name for the monkey

NUNJIBUMBI to be lulled to sleep (by storytelling, singing, etc.)

NURAN a wooden vat with holes used for pressing out wine

NURE undistilled liquor, (rice) wine; cf. *arki*

NURE BELHERE FALGARI (良醞署) the wine section of the Court of Banqueting

NURE DE SOKTOMBI to get drunk on wine

NURE HUHU leaven for making wine

NURE JUŠUN I BOO (酒醋房) wine, vinegar, and soya-sauce factory for the palace

NURE TARGAMBI to abstain from wine

NURE TEBUMBI to make undistilled spirits

NUREI EKŠUN sediment from undistilled spirits (sometimes used in cooking)

NURHŪMBI to be connected, to be in series

NURHŪME connected, in a row, in a series

NUSHUMBI to rush (toward), to charge, to storm, to assail

NUTURU sand grouse (*Syrrhaptes paradoxus*)

N

O

O 1. an interjection of reply 2. armpit; cf. *oho* 3. the depression of a mortar; cf. *ogo* 4. sentence particle of interrogation

O MAYAN armpit; see *ogū*, *oho*

O A (onom.) the sound made by small children trying to talk

O GUWA pumpkin

O NIMAHA alligator

O ŠO SEME coddling, fondling

O UMIYAHA moth

OBDOMBI (-ko) to become tasteless

    OBDOKO YALI meat of game that has been exhausted and has thereby become tasteless

OBGIYA a hook on a long pole used to catch birds on water

OBIHIYA YALI the meat from the shoulder blade of an animal

OBOBUMBI caus. of *obombi*

OBOKO see *obokū*

OBOKŪ a basin used for washing the face

    OBOKŪ EFEN cake made of egg yolks, flour, sugar, and wine--a filling made of jujubes was sometimes added

OBOMBI to wash

OBONGGI bubble, foam

    OBONGGI ARKI a bubbling distilled liquor made by the Manchus

OBONGGINAMBI to form foam, to foam, to bubble

OBONGGO HIYAN dragon spittle incense

OBONOMBI to go to wash

OBUBUMBI caus. of *obumbi*

OBUMBI 1. caus. of *ombi* 2. to make, to make into, to cause to become, to consider as

OCA see *ooca*

OCAN 1. seam 2. loop for a button

OCI (conditional of *ombi*) a particle used to set off the subject: 'as for'

OCIR the head of a Buddhist rosary

ODODON one name for the crested lark; cf. *wenderhen*

ODOLI an ornamental iron hook attached to the ring of a horse's bit

ODONTU KAILUN a horse that has spots resembling stars

OFI 1. a snare for catching pheasants 2. (perfect converb of *ombi*) because

OFOHO a plowshare

OFORDOMBI see *oforodombi*

OFORO 1. nose 2. outcropping on a mountain

    OFORO ACABUMBI to tell tales, to gossip about, to backbite, to incite by slander

    OFORO FETERI FETERILEMBI to move the sides of the nose

    OFORO I DUBE the end of the nose

    OFORO I SANGGA the nostrils

    OFORO NIYAKI nasal discharge, nasal mucous

    OFORO SANGGA nostril

    OFORO TURA the small ridge that separates the two nostrils

OFORODOMBI to incite by slander, to engage in malicious gossip

OFORONGGO slanderer, gossip

OGO 1. the depression of a mortar 2. the holes on the iron plate that is used for making the heads of nails

OGŪ see *oho*

OHA 1. obedient, docile, agreeable 2. see *ooha*

OHAKŪ disobedient, perverse

OHO armpit; cf. *o*, *o mayan*, *ogū*

    OHO DA the top of the sleeve

OHODOMBI to support by holding under the arms

OHOLIYO a handful: ten *oholiyo* is the equivalent of one *moro*, ten *sefere* comprise one *oholiyo*

OHOLIYOMBI to hold in both hands, to take in both hands

221

O

OHOLJI see *oholjon*

OHOLJOMBI to make a loose knot
  OHOLJOME HŪWAITAMBI to tie a loose knot

OHOLJON 1. a loose knot 2. a loose snare for catching pheasants

OHOLJUN see *oholjon*

OHORŠOMBI to feel nauseated, to be disgusted

OHOTONO mole, an animal of the *Talpidae* family

OI 1. exclamation used to call people's attention 2. sound used to call animals

OIBOBUMBI caus. of *oibombi*

OIBOMBI (-ko) to become decrepit, to become old and unable to move steadily

OIFO frivolous, thoughtless, superficial

OIHORI 1. careless, superficial 2. fine, splendid 3. exceedingly, very
  OIHORI SAIN exceedingly good, how splendid!
  OIHORIO isn't it wonderful? wouldn't it be nice?

OIHORILABUMBI caus./pass. of *oihorilambi*

OIHORILAMBI to take lightly, to slight, to insult, to neglect, to behave carelessly

OILO surface, outside

OILOHODOMBI to act frivolously, to be frivolous

OILOHON frivolous, superficial, not serious

OILOKON rather superficial, frivolous

OILON surface
  OILON I BELE the top layer of grain in a granary

OILORGI surface, outside

OILORI 1. on the surface, on the outside 2. suddenly, without reason
  OILORI DELERI superficial, trivial, frivolous

OITOBUMBI to be in dire straits, to be hard pressed

OJIN a long sleeveless court garment worn by women

OJIRAKŪ the same as *ojorakū*

OJOJO an interjection of derision

OJOMBI to kiss

OJORAKŪ it won't do (to), one may not . . . ; cf. *ombi*

OJORO imperfect participle of *ombi*

OJORONGGE that which is, that which is permissible

OK (onom.) 1. the sound made when frightened 2. the sound of gagging and vomiting

OKCILABUMBI caus. of *okcilambi*

OKCILAMBI to cover, to put on a cover

OKCIN 1. a cover, covering 2. shell (of a crab)

OKCINGGA MORO a bowl or cup with a cover

OKDOBUMBI caus. of *okdombi*

OKDOJIMBI see *okdonjimbi*

OKDOMBI (-ko/ho) 1. to go to meet, to meet halfway, to greet, to welcome 2. to engage (an enemy)
  OKDORO KUMUN a piece of music played during the return of the emperor from sacrifices

OKDOMO one of two leather straps on the left side of the saddle that are put through the clasps of the saddle girth

OKDONAMBI see *okdonombi*

OKDONJIMBI to come to meet

OKDONOMBI to go out to meet, to go to greet

OKE the wife of father's younger brother

OKETE plural of *oke*

OKI YORO a large wooden arrowhead

OKJIHA 1. reed, rush 2. calamus, sweet-flag
  OKJIHA SEKTEFUN a cushion made of rushes
  OKJIHA UHURI a container woven from rushes

OKJIHADA the roots of the calamus

OKJOSLAMBI 1. to speak or handle carelessly 2. to act hastily or rashly, to act irreverently
  OKJOSLAME KORO BAHAMBI to suffer loss due to a careless action

OKSIBUMBI 1. caus./pass. of *oksimbi* 2. to come out of a scabbard, to fall out of a quiver

OKSIMBI to spit out, to spit up

OKSOBUMBI caus. of *oksombi*

OKSOMBI to step, to go step by step

OKSON step, pace

OKSONJOMBI to make small steps (of children learning to walk)

OKTALAMBI to cut off the nose--an ancient punishment

OKTO 1. drug, medicine 2. gunpowder 3. dye 4. poison
  OKTO ACABUMBI to mix medicine
  OKTO FANGDZ drug prescription
  OKTO FUSHUBUMBI to set off gunpowder
  OKTO I BOO apothecary
  OKTO I DASARHAN the same as *okto fangdz*
  OKTO I SIREN fuse
  OKTO NIRU a poisoned arrow
  OKTO OMIMBI to take medicine
  OKTOI AFAHA ointment, salve, plaster
  OKTOI HORON action of a poison
  OKTOI PUSELI drugstore, apothecary
  OKTOI ŠUGI salve, ointment

OKTOI WAMBI to poison

OKTOLOMBI 1. to treat with medicine
2. to poison

OKTOLOME WAMBI to murder with poison

OKTOROHON overly hungry, so hungry that
one is incapable of eating

  OKTOROHON BANJIHA became overly
  hungry

OKTOSI doctor, physician; cf. *daifu*

  OKTOSI BE KADALARA YAMUN (太醫
  院) The Imperial Medical Department, BH 233

  OKTOSI BE KADALARA YAMUN I ALIHA
  HAFAN (太醫院院使)
    Commissioner of the Imperial Medi-
    cal Department, BH 235

  OKTOSI BE KADALARA YAMUN I ILHI HAFAN
  (太醫院院判) Vice-
    commissioner of the Imperial Medi-
    cal Department, BH 236

OKTOSILABUMBI caus. of *oktosilambi*

OKTOSILAMBI to treat (sickness), to
cure

OLBIHIYAN see *olfihiyan*

OLBO 1. a short padded jacket worn on
the outside 2. (敖爾布)
Manchurian Orbo, Private of the 2nd
Class (in the Chinese banners), BH
731

OLBORO YALI meat from the cheeks of
a bear

OLFIHIYAN impatient, negligent,
frivolous

OLGOCUKA see *olhocuka*

OLGOMBI see *olhombi*

OLGON see *olhon*

OLGOŠOMBI see *olhošombi*

OLHOBA careful, attentive

OLHOBUMBI caus. of *olhombi*

OLHOCUKA frightful, scary

OLHOCUN fear

OLHOKON rather dry, rather thirsty,
rather afraid

OLHOMBI 1. to fear 2. to dry, to dry
up

OLHON 1. dry, dried up 2. dry land

  OLHON BE YABUMBI to go by land

  OLHON BUDA dry rice (as opposed to
  gruel or porridge made from rice)

  OLHON FEYE a surface wound, contu-
  sion

  OLHON JUGŪN land route

  OLHON MONGGON the windpipe, trachea

OLHOŠOMBI 1. to be cautious, to be
careful 2. to respect, to revere

OLHOŠON cautious, careful, respectful

OLHOTUN alimentary canal

OLIHA cowardly, shy

  OLIHA NIYALMA a coward

OLIHADAMBI to be cowardly, to be shy

OLIMBI to avoid the road, to veer to
the side, to wind

  OLIME MUDALIME twisting and turning

OLIME YABUMBI to go avoiding the
road

OLJI 1. captive, prisoner of war 2.
booty, loot, plunder

OLJILABUMBI caus./pass. of *oljilambi*

OLJILAMBI to capture (a prisoner during wartime)

OLO flax

  OLO FOYO a plant that resembles
  shredded flax and is used as
  padding in boots

OLOBUMBI caus. of *olombi*

OLOHOI interjection of surprise

OLOMBI to wade, to cross a stream,
to wade across, to ford

OLON girth of a horse

OLONGDO long boots used for mountain
climbing

OLOSI a wader, i.e., one who fishes
standing in shallow water wearing
leather trousers

OLOŠON long leather trousers used for
wading in shallow streams

OMBI (imperfect participle -*joro*, imperative -*so*) 1. to become, to
change into 2. to be, to exist
3. to be proper, to be permissible

OMCOKO harelip, having a harelip

OMI SANGGA a hole used by rats and
squirrels for storing food

OMIBUMBI caus. of *omimbi*

OMICAMBI to drink together

OMIHOLOBUMBI caus. of *omiholombi*

OMIHOLOMBI to suffer hunger, to starve

OMIHON hunger, starvation

OMILABUMBI caus. of *omilambi*

OMILAMBI to ford a stream

OMIMBI 1. to drink 2. to smoke (tobacco) 3. to take (medicine)

OMIN famine, year of famine

OMINAMBI to go to drink

OMINGGA drink, beverage

OMINJIMBI to come to drink

OMKIYA flying squirrel, an animal of
the genus *Sciuropterus*

OMO lake, pond

  OMO DABSUN salt taken from a lake
  by distillation

OMOKTU KONGGORO a yellow horse

OMOLO grandson

  OMOLOI OMOLO great-grandson

OMOSI plural of *omolo*

  OMOSI MAMA Manchu goddess of good
  fortune and fecundity

OMŠOKO harelipped

OMŠON BIYA the eleventh month

ON stage of a journey, distance

  ON DOSOMBI to be able to travel a
  long distance (of horses, camels,
  etc.)

  ON GAIMBI to travel hard, to travel
  double the usual rate

  ON GAIME YABUMBI to make a forced

O

O

march

ON TEMŠEMBI to travel hard

ONASU giraffe

ONCO broad, wide, generous

ONCO UMIYESUN the leather belt on
which the quiver hangs

ONCODOMBI to forgive, to grant amnesty

ONCODOME GAMAMBI to forgive

ONCOHON 1. lying on the back, facing
upward 2. overbearing, arrogant

ONCOHON TUWAMBI to look upward

ONCOHON UMUŠUHUN on the back and
on the stomach

ONCOHOŠOMBI to be arrogant, to be overbearing

ONCOKON rather wide, broad

ONDOBUMBI caus./pass. of ondombi

ONDOMBI to be mischievous, to fool
around, to perform sexual intercourse

ONDONUMBI to engage in sexual intercourse together

ONG SEME (onom.) the sound made by an
arrowhead called oki yoro

ONGGOBUMBI caus./pass. of onggombi

ONGGOCON a short two-stringed musical
instrument

ONGGOLO 1. before, previous, ago 2.
in front 3. a river port

ONGGOLOKON a little before

ONGGOMBI to forget

ONGGORO CECIKE jay

ONGGORO ILHA the bloom of Hemerocallis graminea--the flower of
forgetfulness

ONGGORO MANGGA the same as onggotai

ONGGORO ORHO Hemerocallis graminea

ONGGON the space between the saddle
and the animal's back, bare back of
a horse

ONGGORO 1. the hammer bone of the inner ear (worn by children as a
charm against forgetfulness) 2.
forgetful; cf. onggombi

ONGGOSU an absent-minded person

ONGGOŠON golden carp, Carassius aura-
tus

ONGGOTAI forgetful

ONGKIMBI to flee (of animals when they
see or smell an approaching person)

ONGKO pasture, pastureland

ONGNIKA wolverine

ONGTON boorish, rustic, unsophisti-
cated

ONGTORI boorish, ignorant

ONON the male zeren; cf. jeren

OO NIMAHA the great sea turtle

OOCA the name of small river fish with
red eyes and a big mouth

OOHA river perch

OOLAMBI to step aside, to make way

OOLOŠOMBI to move out of the way

OOME used for ome (imperfect converb

of ombi)

OORI 1. semen 2. essence, spirit,
energy

OORI SIMEN spirit, energy, essence

OORI SUKDUN energy, essence, basic
principle

OORON see oron

OR (onom.) 1. sound made by tigers
2. sound of vomiting

OR IR (onom.) sound of chanting sutras

ORA a long sleeveless jacket made of
satin with a dragon design

ORCUN see orhoco

ORDO 1. palace, palace in the form of
a pavilion 2. pavilion

OREN see ūren

ORGI the sharp edges of an arrowhead

ORGILAMBI to graze (of an arrow)

ORGON see orhon

ORHO grass, plant

ORHO DA ginseng; cf. orhoda

ORHO I KŪWARAN a place for the
storage of hay in Mukden

ORHO JODON coarse grass linen

ORHO LIYOO fodder

ORHO MUKE AMCARAKŪ 'can't reach
grass and water'--said of ill
horses and cattle

ORHO ŠOFOROKŪ the name of two
feathers on the right wing of
hawks and other birds of prey

ORHOCO a very small newborn baby

ORHODA ginseng

ORHODA GURURE TEMGETU BITHE a
license issued for the gathering
of ginseng

ORHODA ICIHIYARA KŪWARAN bureau in
charge of matters relating to
ginseng

ORHON white and black feathers on the
tails of falcons

ORHONGGO KILTARI signal flag with
feathers attached to it

ORI 1. a rosary of glass beads worn
about the neck 2. see oori

ORICI twentieth

ORIMA the name of a sea fish that
resembles the can nimaha

ORIMBI to walk in one's sleep

ORIN twenty

ORINCI twentieth

ORINTA twenty each

ORITA see orinta

OROBUHANGGE various foods made from
curdled milk

OROBUMBI caus. of orombi

OROLOKŪ substitute, one who fills in

OROLOMBI to fill in, to put a substitute in, to fill a vacancy, to
fill in for, to substitute for

OROLOME SIMNEMBI to sit in for
someone else at an examination

OROMBI (-ko) to form a layer on the

surface (gruel or other liquids)

OROKO NIOWARIKŪ verdigris

OROMU cream

ORON 1. vacant post, vacancy 2. a section of the sky without stars 3. the physical or earthly soul, vitality, animation 4. a negative intensifier, (not) at all, altogether (not) 5. domesticated reindeer

  ORON AKŪ 1. altogether lacking, completely without 2. without a vacancy

  ORON BUHŪ a tame reindeer

  ORON DE at a post, in a position

  ORON EJELESI incumbent who puts his position up for sale

  ORON I KUNGGERI (缺科) office concerned with vacant posts--part of the Board of Civil Appointments

  ORON I ŠUSI (天文生) the name of an official of the Imperial Board of Astronomy

  ORON SOORIN point of the compass, bearing

ORONCO I NIYALMA a reindeer herder

ORONDE see *oron de*

ORONGGO Przewalski's gazelle

OROS Russia, Russian, foreign

  OROS BITHEI KUREN (俄羅斯文館) the name of an institution for the study of Russian

  OROS KUREN (俄羅斯館) hostel for Russian emissaries and merchants in Peking

  OROS NIRU a company of the Peking banner troops made up of captured Russians

  OROS TACIKŪ (俄羅斯學) the Russian school in Peking

ORSON NIMEMBI to have pains in the abdomen after child delivery

OSE Japanese

OSHODOMBI to be cruel, to be brutal, to mistreat

OSHON 1. cruel, brutal, tyrannical 2. see *osohon*

OSO the imperative of *ombi*

  OSO NAKŪ not yet, still hasn't

OSOHOKON rather small

OSOHON small, little

OŠO a leather glove with three fingers used for holding falcons

OŠOHO claw, talon

OŠOHOLOMBI to catch in the claws

OŠOHONGGO having claws

OŠONGGO ILHA an exotic flower whose petals resemble falcon's claws

OTALA see *odoli*

OTGO a drake's tail that flares frontward

OTHO the same as *otgo*

OTOLO until (terminal converb of *ombi*)

OTON a wooden tub without handles or feet

OTORI a small scale battue in springtime

OTORILAMBI to hunt (on a battue) in springtime

OYO 1. roof (of a house, tent, or sedan chair), top of a grave 2. crown of a hat 3. sandfly, gnat

  OYO GAIMBI to perform a Manchu sacrifice that involves throwing pieces of meat onto the roof

  OYO JAFARA ALIKŪ a vessel used for making offerings to deities

  OYO OYO (onom.) sound used for calling small dogs

OYOBUMBI caus. of *oyombi*

OYOKI hasty, hurried

OYOLOMBI see *oyombi*

OYOMBI (1) (-ho) to bend, to curve, to arch, to roll up, to coil up, to rock

  OYOME SAHAMBI 1. to build an enceinte before a city gate 2. to build a bridge arch

OYOMBI (2) (-ko/ho) 1. to go more than halfway (on a trip) 2. to be more than half finished, to be almost done 3. to be very exhausted

OYOMBUMBI to hurry, to hasten, to do more than half

  OYOMBURAKŪ not urgent, unimportant

  OYOMBURE BAITA WAKA it is not an urgent matter

OYON peak

  OYONDE ISINAHA to have arrived at the peak (of destitution)

OYONGGO important, urgent, essential

  OYONGGO BAITA urgent or important matter

  OYONGGO JECEN an important border area

OYONGGON important matter, important point

OYOTONGGO MAHATUN a hat of Ch'in and Han times with an arched top

OYOYO an expression of derision

PUSA bodhisattva
PUSE insignia of rank on the official
    and court clothing of officials and
    nobles
    PUSE KURUME a court garment with
        the insignia of rank on it
    PUSE NOHO CECE silken gauze with
        insignias of rank on it
    PUSE NOHO NIKTONGGA SURI Nanking
        silk bearing insignia of rank
    PUSE NOHO SUJE silk with a design

of dragons in golden circles
PUSELI store, shop
    PUSELI EJEN proprietor, store owner
    PUSELI SINDAMBI to open up a store
PUTU PATA (onom.) 1. the sound of many
    small things falling in succession
    2. hurried, pressed, in haste
PUTUR (onom.) the sound of a large
    bird taking off
PUTUR SEME drop by drop, bit by bit,
    gradually, unevenly

R

RAKCA see *rakša*
RAKŠA 1. a man-eating demon, ogre

2. Russian
RIDI magic, supernatural power

P
R

S

SA 1. shaft or thill of an oxcart 2. feather grass from which the outside surface of summer hats are made 3. plural suffix (sometimes written separately)

SABARAMBI 1. to drip, to trickle 2. to scatter, to disperse

SABCIRAMBI to rear (of horses)

SABDABUMBI caus. of *sabdambi*

SABDAMBI to leak, to drip, to trickle, to fall in drops

SABDARA SILENGGINGGE FUKJINGGA HERGEN (垂露篆) a style of calligraphy

SABDAN 1. drop 2. leaking

SABDAN I ALIGAN rain drain under the projection of a roof

SABDAN SABDAN drop by drop

SABDANGGA WASE roof tile that permits water to drip down

SABE the plural suffix -*sa* plus the accusative particle -*be*

SABI 1. omen, sign, portent 2. propitious

SABI FERGUWECUN the omen is wondrous, wonderful

SABIBUMBI to give a sign

SABINGGA propitious, pertaining to a good omen

SABINGGA CECIKE a dark gray bird with a strong wide red beak--the male and female are always found together

SABINGGA DARUDAI one name for the phoenix

SABINGGA HOOŠAN good-luck paper money hung on doors and gates at New Year's

SABINGGA MOO the name of a mythical tree in which the Chinese characters for 'universal peace' are supposed to appear

SABINGGA ORHO the fungus *Fomes japonicus* before it forms its cap

SABINGGA SENCE the fungus *Fomes japonicus*

SABINGGA SENCE I FUKJINGGA HERGEN (芝英篆) a style of calligraphy

SABINGGA SENCE I ŠUŠUNGGE SARACAN a purple parasol of the imperial escort embroidered with a figure of the auspicious fungus *Fomes japonicus*

SABINTU a female unicorn

SABINTUNGGA FUKJINGGA HERGEN (麟書) a style of calligraphy

SABIRGAN CECIKE a small black bird with a white forehead

SABIRGAN ORHO a perennial plant with violet flowers that open when happy events occur--*Reineckia carnea*

SABIRGI an insignia of rank worn on the official and ceremonial clothing of officials and nobles; cf. *puse*

SABIRGI KURUME the same as *puse kurume*

SABIRGI NOHO CECE the same as *puse noho cece*

SABIRGI NOHO NIKTONGGA SURI the same as *puse noho niktongga suri*

SABIRGI NOHO SUJE the same as *puse noho suje*

SABIRI ILHA *Daphne odora*

SABITUN the (male) unicorn

SABKA chopstick

SABKA SELE 1. linchpin 2. iron pin used on a loom

SABKALAMBI to pick up with the chopsticks, to eat with chopsticks

SABSIBUMBI caus. of *sabsimbi*

SABSIKŪ garment, religious habit

SABSIMBI 1. to sew tightly (boots and saddle pads) 2. to brand characters on the face and arms of criminals 3. to trim a horse's mane

SABTA 1. a stick used for spreading glue 2. a small bone or piece of

S

cartilage in the knee, elbow, or shoulder joint

SABTARAMBI to mark with an ax, to incise slightly

SABTARI WASIKA the area above the hoof has swollen (causing the horse to be lame)

SABU shoe

SABUBUMBI caus./pass. of *sabumbi*

SABUGAN experience, perception

    SABUGAN AKŪ inexperienced, easily impressed by trifling matters

    SABUGAN BE SABUHAKŪ hasn't seen much of the world

SABUHŪ see *ebuhu sabuhū*

SABULA pubic hair

SABUMBI to see, to perceive

SABUN 1. sight, vision 2. visage, appearance

SABUNAMBI to go to see

SABUNDUMBI/SABUNUMBI to see together

SABUNJIMBI to come to see

SACA helmet

    SACA I TEMGETU an insignia of the color of the wearer's banner that was attached to the back of the helmet and on which the name and rank of the banner chief was written

SACALABUMBI caus. of *sacalambi*

SACALAMBI to wear a helmet

SACALANDUMBI/SACALANUMBI to wear helmets (of a group)

SACIBUMBI caus./pass. of *sacimbi*

SACIKŪ hoe, mattock, chisel

    SACIKŪ SIRDAN a flat-headed arrow

    SACIKŪ UMIYAHA a type of beetle

SACIMA a small pastry made of noodles, sugar, and sesame seeds and cooked in sesame oil

SACIMBI 1. to chop, to hack, to chop off 2. to hoe 3. to chisel 4. to clip (a horse's hooves)

    SACIME WAMBI to behead

SACIMRI LOHO a large sword used for chopping the legs of horses during battle

SACINDUMBI/SACINUMBI to chop together, to hoe together

SACIRAMBI to hack, to chop at, to chop into pieces

SACU grains of buckwheat

    SACU FUNGSE I UFA strained buckwheat flour

    SACU UFA buckwheat flour

SACURAMBI 1. to grind buckwheat 2. to fall in grainlike flakes (of snow)

SADA pine needle, any needlelike leaf from a plant

SADE the plural suffix plus *-de*

SADULAMBI to form an in-law relationship, to betroth

SADUN related by marriage, a relative by marriage

    SADUN HALA relative by marriage

    SADUN JAFAMBI to form an in-law relationship, to betroth

SADUSA plural of *sadun*

SAGAMBI see *sahambi*

SAGIN an exotic sour-sweet fruit about the size of the fruit of the lacquer tree

SAHA hunting, a small-scale battue

SAHABUMBI caus. of *sahambi*

SAHADABUMBI caus. of *sahadambi*

SAHADAMBI 1. to hold a small-scale battue 2. to hunt in autumn

SAHAHŪKAN the color of (Chinese) ink

SAHAHŪN 1. blackish, rather black 2. the tenth of the heaven's stems (癸)

    SAHAHŪN MUKE TASHARI a type of crane

SAHAHŪRI jet black

SAHALCA pelt of a black sable

SAHALDAI a black gibbon

    SAHALDAI MONIO the same as *sahaldai*

SAHALIYAKAN rather black, blackish

SAHALIYAN 1. black 2. the ninth of the heaven's stems (壬)

    SAHALIYAN BONIO a black monkey

    SAHALIYAN DOBIHI a black fox pelt

    SAHALIYAN FAHA black pupil, black eye

    SAHALIYAN FATHA a type of quail with black feet

    SAHALIYAN GIRANGGI COKO a type of chicken with fuzzy white feathers and black bones and skin

    SAHALIYAN GU a type of black gem

    SAHALIYAN IHAN black cow

    SAHALIYAN KEKUHE a black pigeon or dove

    SAHALIYAN MALANGGŪ black sesame

    SAHALIYAN MOO ebony

    SAHALIYAN NILGIYAN HOOŠAN paper made from bamboo fiber and coated with gold

    SAHALIYAN TURI small black beans

    SAHALIYAN TUYEKU YONGGAN a black sand used in casting bronze

    SAHALIYAN UJUNGGA 'the black-headed ones'--the common people

    SAHALIYAN YARHA black panther

SAHALJA a black coot

SAHALTU having a black face

    SAHALTU CECIKE the name of a black-headed bird somewhat larger than a sparrow with a white neck, back, and dark yellow wings with white spots

SAHAMBI 1. to pile up, to stack 2. to build a wall or other structure by laying bricks

    SAHAME WEILEMBI to build up, to

S

erect

SAHAMHA sea perch (*Labrax luyu*)

SAHAN pile, stack, a stack of *gacuha* piled up by a winner

SAHARABUMBI caus. of *saharambi*

SAHARAMBI (-ka) to turn black

SAHARI into a heap
 SAHARI TUHEMBI to be thrown in wrestling

SAHIBA obsequious, fawning, groveling

SAIBIGAN birthmark

SAIBIHAN spoonbill pelican; cf. *halbahan*

SAIBUMBI caus./pass. of *saimbi*

SAIBURU canter (of a horse)

SAICUNGGA FENGŠEN the Chia-ch'ing (嘉慶) reign period, 1796--1820

SAIFA WEIHE the molars, the back teeth

SAIFATU a four-year-old horse

SAIFI a spoon; cf. *kuini*

SAIFILAMBI to scoop out with a spoon

SAIHA 1. anklebone 2. see *alin i saiha*
 SAIHA I DOKO the inside of the anklebone
 SAIHA I TUKU the outside of the anklebone

SAIHADA shinbone, tibia

SAIHŪWA a bramble plant with round leaves and a red blossom used for weaving baskets and as an implement for beating criminals

SAIHŪWADA the light rod, a bamboo rod used for flogging; cf. *cy*

SAIHŪWADALABUMBI caus./pass. of *saihūwadalambi*

SAIHŪWADALAMBI to flog with the light bamboo rod

SAIKA see *saikan*

SAIKAN 1. pretty, good-looking, beautiful 2. rather well, nicely, properly
 SAIKAN ARBUNGGA ILHA *Rosa semperflorens*
 SAIKAN ARBUNGGA ILHA I SUWAYAN SUJE SARA a silver parasol of the escort embroidered with yellow, red, and black rosae semperflorentes
 SAIKAN EJE keep well in mind

SAIKŪ snacks to go with liquor

SAIKŪNGGE pertaining to snacks

SAIMBE the same as *sain be*

SAIMBI to bite, to chew

SAIMENGGE worth tasting, good to eat

SAIN 1. good, well 2. auspicious, favorable
 SAIN ACABUN good omen
 SAIN BE FONJIMBI to ask after someone's health
 SAIN BE IBEBURE TEMGETUN a banner of the escort bearing the inscription *sain be ibebure*
 SAIN DE AISILAKŪ (贊善) a court title just below that of

giyan be jorikū
 SAIN DOROLON wedding
 SAIN I YABU have a good trip!
 SAIN INENGGI an auspicious day, a clear day
 SAIN IRGEN common people
 SAIN SABI a good or auspicious omen

SAINAMBI to go to bite

SAINTU good, excellent

SAISA a man proficient in letters and good in his speech and conduct, scholar, gentleman
 SAISA BE BAIRE KUNGGERI (求賢 科) Office for the recruiting of candidates for official service

SAISAHA basket with a wide handle

SAISE small cake, cracker, biscuit

SAISHA CECIKE one name for the sparrow

SAISHAN a basket with a handle that can be carried in the hand at one's side

SAIŠABUKŪ praise, flattery

SAIŠABUMBI caus./pass. of *saišambi*

SAIŠACUKA praiseworthy, worthy of commendation

SAIŠAKŪSAMBI to look for praise, to seek praise

SAIŠAMBI to praise, to commend

SAIŠANDUMBI/SAIŠANUMBI to praise or commend together

SAIŠANGGA famous, renowned

SAITU minister, man of high rank

SAIYŪN interrogative form of *sain: si saiyūn*? 'How are you?'

SAJA a million

SAJINGGA DEO younger (in respect to speaker) student of the same teacher

SAKA 1. fish or meat cut up finely, mixed with seasonings and eaten raw 2. clause particle used after the imperfect converb: just, as soon as-- the same as *jaka* 3. an adjectival suffix: as if, like, somewhat, rather: *necikesaka* 'rather level'; *hocikon saka* 'rather nice'

SAKDA 1. old (of people) 2. old man 3. a four-year-old wild sow

SAKDABUMBI caus. of *sakdambi*

SAKDAKI having the aspect of old age-- said of children who are quiet and composed

SAKDAMBI (-ka, -pi) to get old, to age

SAKDANDALA until old age, until old

SAKDANDAMBI to near old age

SAKDANTALA until old, till old age

SAKDANUMBI to revere as old

SAKDASA plural of *sakda*

SAKDATALA see *sakdantala*

SAKIDUN one name for the partridge; cf. *jukidun*

SAKSAHA magpie (*Pica pica*)
 SAKSAHA DAMIN a one to two-year-old eagle

S

SAKSAHŪN support, prop, rack for pil-
 ing wood and like things
SAKSALABUMBI to get stuck (of an arrow
 in a tree)
SAKSALIBUMBI caus./pass. of *saksalimbi*
SAKSALIKŪ a frame for setting off
 fireworks
SAKSALIMBI to prop up, to make (branches, brush, etc.) into a rack or
 frame
SAKSAN 1. a pole with a hook or branch
 on the end used for hanging things
 up 2. a cake used in sacrifices
 SAKSAN GOLBON a clothing rack
 SAKSAN JUHE a number of ice floes
  frozen together
SAKSARI onto one's back (of falling)
 SAKSARI KEKUHE the name of a bird
  that resembles the Asiatic blue
  magpie but is smaller
SAKSIME see *ekšeme saksime*
SAKSIN Chinese juniper--*Juniperus
 chinensis*
SAKSU 1. a basket made from brambles
 for holding grain 2. a small bamboo
 basket for holding tea, paper, etc.
SAKSULABUMBI caus. of *saksulambi*
SAKSULAMBI to place in a basket
SAKŪRA a three-legged wooden support
 for hanging a pot over a fire
SALA MOO a large Indian tree--*Shorea
 robusta*
SALABA pineapple
SALABUMBI caus. of *salambi*
SALAMBI to distribute, to pass out
SALAMBUMBI see *salabumbi*
SALANAMBI to go to distribute
SALANDUMBI/SALANUMBI to distribute
 together
SALANJIMBI to come to distribute
SALGABUHANGGE that which was ordained
 by heaven, that which was preor-
 dained
SALGABUMBI to be fixed by fate, to be
 preordained, to be ordained by heaven
 SALGABUHA ABKAI BANIN nature, in-
  born quality
 SALGABUHA BABI it is fixed by fate
SALGABUN fate, decree of heaven, prov-
 idence
SALGANGGA MUJILEN conscience
SALGATU HOOHAN one of the names of the
 heron; cf. *hoohan*
SALHŪ 1. a piece of iron fastened to
 the end of the plow, the plowshare
 2. the wooden frame of a comb on a
 loom
SALHŪMA pheasant of the north
SALIBUMBI 1. caus. of *salimbi* 2. to
 set the price, to estimate a price
 3. to discount 4. to reduce the
 number of strokes in flogging, to
 commute

SALIBUME BODOMBI to estimate
SALIGAN 1. autonomy, independence,
 sense of responsibility 2. estimate, calculation 3. in small
 quantity, meagerly, judiciously
 4. control over the senses
 SALIGAN AKŪ lacking a sense of
  responsibility, lacking initiative
 SALIGAN I BA estate of a noble in
  ancient times
 SALIGAN I BUMBI to give in small
  quantity, to give scarcely any
SALIMBAHARAKŪ not able to undertake
 responsibility, unable to show
 initiative
SALIMBI 1. to be worth, to be valued
 at 2. to undertake, to take the
 responsibility oneself, to do by
 oneself, to monopolize 3. to in-
 herit
 SALIRAKŪ you're welcome (response
  to being thanked for a favor or
  gift)
SALINGGA assertive (person), prone to
 usurp authority, self-reliant
SALIYAHAN just enough, just barely
 enough
SALIYAN the same as *saliyahan*
SALJA a fork in a road
 SALJA JUGŪN a forking road
SALMANDARA salamander
SALU beard, whiskers
 SALU FUSIMBI to shave (one's
  whiskers)
SALUNGGA bearded
SAMA see *saman*
SAMADAMBI to perform shamanistic rites
SAMADI meditation
 SAMADI BOO meditation room
 SAMADI DE TOKTOMBI to remain fixed
  in meditation, to meditate
 SAMADI HŪWA monastery, meditation
  hall
 SAMADI TEMBI to sit in meditation,
  to meditate
 SAMADI TERE BOO hall of meditation
  (in a monastery)
SAMAN shaman
 SAMAN CECIKE North China crested
  lark (*Galerida cristata*); cf.
  wenderhen
 SAMAN HEHE shamaness
SAMANGGA NIYALMA shaman, one who
 practices shamanism
SAMARA a large wooden bowl
SAMARABUMBI caus. of *samarambi*
SAMARAMBI to mix tea or soup by re-
 peatedly ladling out a quantity
 with a spoon and pouring it back
SAMARAN the name of an ancient sacri-
 ficial vessel (盨)
SAMAŠAMBI to perform a shamanistic
 rite

S

SAMBARŠAMBI see *sambiršambi*

SAMBI (1) to know, to understand

SAMBI (2) (-ngka) 1. to stretch, to extend 2. to milk 3. to be distant, to be far away

SAMBIRŠAMBI to stretch, to stick out, to extend

SAMDAMBI to perform a shamanistic rite; cf. *samadambi, samašambi*

> SAMDAME TARIMBI to plant another type of seed between the furrows of a field

SAMHA mole or birthmark on the face or body

SAMINA one ten-sextillion

SAMPA shrimp, prawn

SAMSIBUMBI caus. of *samsimbi*

SAMSIMBI to disperse, to scatter, to adjourn

SAMSU a type of fine blue linen

SAMSULABUMBI caus. of *samsulambi*

SAMSULAMBI to engrave designs on metal

SAMURI one sextillion

SANAT senate (from French)

SANCA Jew's ear, wood-ear, the edible fungus *Auricularia auricula-judae*

SANCIHA 1. nose ring or hook for cows and camels 2. an iron wire fastening device on a bird trap

SANDAHŪN distant from, separated from

SANDALABUMBI 1. caus. of *sandalambi* 2. to lie in between, to be separated from, to be distant from

> SANDALABUHA SIDEN the interval in between

SANDALAMBI 1. to have the legs spread apart (when sitting or standing) 2. to be apart, to have a space in between

SANDARŠAMBI to walk with the legs spread

SANDUMBI/SANUMBI to know one another, to know together

SANGGA hole, opening

> SANGGA TŪMBI to knock a hole in

SANGGATA having holes or openings

SANGGATANAMBI to form holes or openings

SANGGATANGGA having holes, riddled with holes

SANGGUHE one name for the myna

SANGGUJI jellyfish

SANGGŪ right, just right, just as one wished

SANGGŪŠABUMBI caus./pass. of *sanggū-šambi*

SANGGŪŠAMBI to be pleased, to have matters turn out according to one's wishes

SANGKA (perfect participle of *sambi* [2]) distant, distantly related

> SANGKA AHŪN DEO great-grandfather's brother

SANGKANGGA JALAHI JUI son of a second or third cousin

SANGKANGGE very distant

SANGSARABUMBI caus. of *sangsarambi*

SANGSARAMBI (-ka) to fall into disrepair, to fall into ruins

SANGSE 1. a finger wringer (a type of torture instrument) 2. manacles

> SANGSE GUWANGSE manacles

SANGSELABUMBI caus. of *sangselambi*

SANGSELAMBI 1. to press the fingers (as a punishment) 2. to manacle

SANIYABUMBI caus. of *saniyambi*

SANIYAMBI 1. to stretch out, to extend, to stretch 2. to give an extension, to extend a deadline

SANIYAN extension, stretching out

SANIYANGGA extensive

SANIYASHŪN somewhat extended

SAR SAR (onom.) the sound of grasshoppers flying

SAR SAR SEME (onom.) 1. the sound of insects chirping 2. the sound of leaves falling 3. the sound of washing rice 4. without delay

SAR SEME 1. pouring out (tears) 2. without delay, quickly 3. (onom.) the sound of washing

SAR SIR (onom.) the sound of leaves falling

SAR SIR SEME 1. (onom.) the sound of washing rice 2. without delay

SARA 1. umbrella, parasol 2. general term for the seven iron pieces fixed to a quiver and bow case

> SARA BELHERE BA (備 傘 處) the imperial umbrella chamber where the ceremonial parasols and umbrellas were kept

SARABUMBI caus. of *sarambi*

SARACA mountain barberry

SARACI magistrate; cf. *hiyan i saraci*

SARAHŪN loosely woven, elastic

SARAMBI 1. to open (out), to unfold, to expand, to rub smooth 2. to fan, to winnow

SARASU knowledge

SARAŠAMBI to go on an excursion, to go strolling, to go on an outing, to take pleasure in viewing scenery

SARAŠAN excursion, outing, pleasure in viewing scenery

SARAŠANJIMBI to come on an excursion

SARATAI KEIRE a sorrel with a white crescent-shaped spot on the forehead

SARBA a shuttle used for weaving nets; cf. *sarfu*

SARBACAN 1. visor on a helmet 2. a veil attached to the brim of a woman's summer hat

SARBAHŪN 1. lying spread-eagled on the back 2. sparse, scraggly

S

SARBAŠAMBI 1. to rock back and forth, to writhe, to struggle 2. to become agitated when some matter cannot be settled

SARBATALA writhing, struggling

SARCA GUWEJIHE the third stomach of ruminants

SARCAN see *sarca*

SARFU a shuttle used in net weaving

SARGA NIMAHA Siberian salmon

SARGAJI CECIKE one name for the titmouse; cf. *jirha cecike*

SARGAMBI see *saraŝambi*

SARGAN wife, woman, female

    SARGAN GAIHA ICE NIYALMA bridegroom

    SARGAN GAIMBI to get married (of men)

    SARGAN JUI girl, daughter

    SARGAN JUI BUMBI to give a daughter in marriage

    SARGAN JUSE girls, daughters

SARGANJI NIMAHA the name of a river fish with a long mouth--white fish

SARGAŠAMBI the same as *saraŝambi*

SARGATA plural of *sargan*

SARGIYA groin, pubic region, crotch

SARGIYAKAN rather sparse, rather wide-meshed

SARGIYALAKŪ ASU a wide-meshed fish net thrown by hand

SARGIYAN sparse, wide-meshed

SARHŪ a rack or shelf for dishes

SARHŪN MOO the name of a tree with sparse fine branches that grew on the grave of Confucius

SARILABUMBI caus. of *sarilambi*

SARILAMBI to feast, to hold a banquet

SARIN 1. feast, banquet 2. skin from the hind section of a horse, mule, or donkey from which boots are made

    SARIN BE DAGILARA BOLGOBURE FIYENTEN (精膳清吏司) banquet-department, BH 376A

    SARIN BE DAGILARA YAMUN (光祿寺) Court of Banqueting, BH 376B, 934

    SARIN DAGILAMBI to hold a banquet, to throw a feast

    SARIN GŪLHA boots made from the skin from the hind part of a quadruped

SARINGGIYAMBI to pour hot and cold tea together

SARKI see *sarkiyan*

    SARKI SALIBURAKŪ to do upon one's own initiative, not to take others into account (in handling some matter)

SARKIYABUMBI caus. of *sarkiyambi*

SARKIYAMBI 1. to copy, to make a clean copy 2. to thin (out), to sort out, to strip off

    SARKIYAFI SELGIYERE BOO (報房) Printing Office, BH 435C

SARKIYAME ARAMBI to copy over, to make a clean copy of

SARKIYAME ARARA BA office for copying

SARKIYAME ARARA FALGANGGA (謄錄所) office where examination papers were recopied before being read by the examiners

SARKIYAME ARARA HAFAN (謄錄官) an official charged with copying examination papers

SARKIYAME ARARA NIYALMA a copyist

SARKIYAN copy, clean copy

    SARKIYAN SALIBURAKŪ the same as *sarki saliburakū*

SARKIYANGGA BITHE copies of imperial edicts kept in the archives of the six ministries

SARKIYANUMBI 1. to thin out together 2. to copy together

SARKŪ don't know, doesn't know--contraction of *sara akū*

SARLA a gray-colored horse

SARNI BOIHON yellow earth, ochre

SARPA grasshopper

SARPAHŪN dragonfly

SARSEN DOLI the overripe meat in a melon that has a rough, sandlike texture

SARŠAMBI see *saraŝambi*

SARTA MORO large wooden or pottery bowl

SARTABUMBI 1. caus. of *sartambi* 2. to put at ease, to comfort, to calm (someone) down 3. to take up (a person's time), to procrastinate, to postpone, to put off

SARTABUN 1. postponement, delay 2. comfort

SARTACUN delay, postponement

SARTAMBI 1. to delay, to postpone, to put off 2. to act at one's leisure, to be free and easy, to idle

SARTASHŪN slow, delayed, postponed

SARU see *abka saru*

SASA together

SASAMBI 1. to shuffle (mah-jongg tiles or cards) 2. to grow up (of children)

SASARI together

SASE a pastry eaten in summer--made from buckwheat flour, honey, and sesame

SASUKŪ mah-jongg tiles, cards

SASULIN CECIKE one name for the oriole; cf. *gūlin cecike*

SASUMBI the same as *sasambi*

SASURI mah-jongg tiles

SATA pine needles

SATANGGA COKO hazel grouse (*Tetrastes bonasia*)

SATI male of the large black bear; cf. *nasin*

SAYA a very small cooking pot; cf.

S

kilakci

SE 1. year (of age), age 2. raw silk,
unprocessed silk 3. the juncture of
the stem and root on the ginseng
plant 4. horse's teeth 5. plural
suffix
SE ASIGAN young, youthful
SE BAHA aged
SE BARU OMBI to become old
SE BE BODOME according to age
SE CIKSIN mature, grown-up
SE DE GOCIMBUMBI to grow decrepit
SE DE OMBI to age, to get old
SE ELEN TELEN AKŪ of almost the
   same age
SE I BARU OMBI the same as *se baru
   ombi*
SE I ONGGOLO SAKDAKABI became old
   before his time
SE JEKE became old, old (of horses)
SE KOMSO young
SE MULAN BAHA became old
SE SAKDAKABI has aged
SE SELAHA content, pleased, happy
SE SIRGE raw silk, unprocessed silk
SE TUCIKE is above age, superannu-
   ated
SEB SAB dripping, in scattered drops
   SEB SAB AGAMBI to rain in scattered
      drops
SEBCELEMBI to taste, to try (food)
SEBDEMBI (-ke) to rust
SEBDEN rust
SEBDENEMBI (-ke) the same as *sebdembi*
SEBDERI shady
   SEBDERI BA shady place, shade
   SEBDERI EYE an ice hole used for
      cold storage
SEBDERIBUMBI to rest in the shade
SEBDERILEBUMBI caus. of *sebderilembi*
SEBDERILEMBI to take advantage of the
   shade, to rest in the shade
SEBE the plural suffix *se* and the ac-
   cusative particle *be*
SEBE SABA AGAMBI to rain in scattered
   drops
SEBEDERI see *seberi*
SEBERI a horse or mule with white
   hoofs
SEBERŠEMBI to drip
SEBIMBI to recover, to come around, to
   feel refreshed after being tired; cf.
   sebkimbi
SEBJELEBUMBI caus. of *sebjelembi*
SEBJELEMBI to rejoice, to be glad
SEBJELENDUMBI/SEBJELENUMBI to rejoice
   together
SEBJEN joy, gladness
SEBJENGGE joyful, glad
SEBJENGGE BAIBULA one name for the
   paradise flycatcher; cf. *baibula*
SEBJENGGE ILHA the name of an exotic
   purple flower that blooms for long

periods without withering
SEBJENGGE YENGGUHE another name for
   the 'phoenix parrot'--*garudangga
   yengguhe*
SEBKE SAKA just, just now
SEBKELEMBI to eat at intervals, to eat
   between meals
SEBKEMBI to spring (of tigers, wild-
   cats, and leopards)
SEBKEN the same as *sebke saka*
SEBKESAKA the same as *sebke saka*
SEBKIMBI to recover, to be refreshed
   after being fatigued, to regain
   one's strength
SEBSEHE grasshopper
SEBSEHENEMBI to become infested, to
   have locusts
   SEBSEHERI locust
SEBSIBUMBI caus. of *sebsimbi*
SEBSIHIYEN affable, pleasant
SEBSIMBI to shake someone who has
   passed out
SEBSINGGE affable, pleasant, friendly
SEBTEMBI see *sektembi*
SECEN part in the hair
SECIBUMBI caus. of *secimbi*
SECIMBI 1. to cut off, to cut away 2.
   to make furrows in a field
SECINDUMBI/SECINUMBI 1. to cut off
   together 2. to make furrows to-
   gether
SECIREMBI to stab wildly, to cut at
SECU a type of sturgeon
SEDEHENGGE one who has been killed--
   an oath
SEDEHERI clever, bright child
SEDEMBI to kill
SEDU bean meal
SEDZ dice
SEFERE 1. a handful, a bundle 2.
   twenty strips of meat tied together
   3. a unit of measure--a pint
   SEFERE YALI meat tied together in
      strips
SEFEREMBI to take a handful, to grab
   with the hand
SEFEREŠEMBI to keep on taking handsful,
   to keep on grabbing
SEFERŠEMBI see *seferešembi*
SEFU teacher, master
SEFUSE plural of *sefu*
SEHEHUN standing on end, erect, verti-
   cal
   SEHEHUN ILIHABI is standing erect
      (of someone's hair when he is
      angry)
SEHEHURI 1. towering high (of many
   mountain peaks) 2. straight, erect
   (of sitting and standing)
   SEHEHURI DEN high and towering (of
      many peaks)
   SEHEHURI HADA towering cliffs, pre-
      cipitous peaks

S

SEHEHURI ILICAHABI standing tall (of a group of able-bodied men)

SEHERCEMBI to·roll up the sleeves and get ready to fight

SEHEREMBI 1. to arch the eyebrows in anger 2. to bristle (of the beard) 3. to be enraged to the point of violence

SEHERI towering, precipitous
SEHERI HADA sheer, precipitous, peak

SEHERI SAHARI 1. uneven (of mountain peaks) 2. uneven or flickering in the distance
SEHERI SAHARI SABUMBI to see one or two things flickering in the distance

SEHERI SEHERI see *seheri sahari*

SEHERŠEMBI to be agitated to the point of action

SEHIYEN see *sesheri*

SEHUJI one-tenth to the twentieth power

SEHULEMBI to step forth, to step to the front
SEHULEME ILIMBI to stand in front (of the ranks)

SEI *se* plus the genitive particle *i*

SEIBENI formerly, once, in the past
SEIBENI FONDE in the past, formerly

SEILEBUMBI caus. of *seilembi*

SEILEMBI to boil meat that has been cut up

SEIRE 1. hipbone 2. spine (of animals)

SEJECI wagoner, person in charge of official vehicles, wagonmaker

SEJEN wagon, cart, vehicle
SEJEN BAŠAMBI to drive a vehicle
SEJEN BOŠOMBI the same as *sejen bašambi*
SEJEN CI EBUMBI to get off a vehicle
SEJEN DE TAFAMBI to get on a vehicle
SEJEN DE TEMBI to ride in a vehicle
SEJEN I DOBTON canopy over a sedan chair
SEJEN I FAKSI wagonmaker, cartwright
SEJEN JAFAMBI to drive a vehicle
SEJEN KIYOO I FIYENTEN (鑾 輿 司) Carriage Section, BH 118
SEJEN TOHORO ENGGEMU saddle for attaching a cart

SEJESI driver, wagoner

SEJILEMBI to sigh

SEJILENDUMBI/SEJILENUMBI to sigh together

SEJULEN wild garlic; cf. *suduli*

SEK SEME suddenly, with a start (of awaking)

SEKE sable (*Martes zibellina*)

SEKEJEMBI to get worn thin, to become tattered

SEKEMBI to take the bait (of fish)

SEKIMBI see *sekiyembi*

SEKIYEBUMBI caus. of *sekiyembi*

SEKIYEKU a straw hat, a rain hat made of reeds or leaves

SEKIYEMBI to let drip, to let drip dry, to filter, to strain through

SEKIYEN spring (of water), source, origin

SEKJI straw, straw bed (especially the one used by women during childbirth)

SEKJINGGE not rich but can still manage

SEKSE SAKSA 1. untalented, of little ability 2. uneven, jagged, of unequal height
SEKSE SAKSA TEKSIN AKŪ jagged and uneven

SEKSEHE 1. the back of the head 2. front part of the head of a horse

SEKSEHUN 1. withered, pining, emaciated, haggard 2. frozen from the cold (the face)

SEKSELIBUHA see *seksen lifabuha*

SEKSEN see *seksen i yali*
SEKSEN BANJIHABI literally: 'meat frozen in a pitfall has been formed'--used to describe a lucky find or good opportunity
SEKSEN I YALI meat of an animal that has fallen into a hole and subsequently frozen solid
SEKSEN LIFABUHA slipped into a pitfall

SEKSEREMBI (-ke/he) to stand on end (of hair)

SEKSERI firm, fixed (of an arrow)

SEKSERŠEMBI see *sengseršembi*

SEKSU a basket lined with paper treated with oil used for carrying liquids

SEKTEBUMBI caus. of *sektembi*

SEKTEFUN cushion, pad used for sitting
SEKTEFUN I JIBSIGAN a pad of skin or felt spread under a cushion or sitting pad

SEKTEMBI to spread, to make (a bed), to spread out, to cover
SEKTERE MOO boards covering the deck of a ship

SEKTU 1. clever, agile, alert, sharp, quick (of intelligence) 2. light (of sleep)

SEKTUKEN rather clever, rather agile

SEKTUSI talented and superior, refined

SELABUMBI caus. of *selambi*

SELACUKA happy, content, pleased

SELAMBI to be content, to be pleased, to be happy

SELBETE *Artemisia lactiflora*

SELBI oar
SELBI NOHO JAHŪDAI a galley ship

SELBIBUMBI caus. of *selbimbi*

SELBIMBI 1. to row 2. to tread water

SELBIN GORO with wide steps (of trotting horses)

SELE iron

SELE FAKSI blacksmith, ironworker

SELE FUTA iron cable

SELE GARMA an arrow with an iron head surrounded by four barbs-- used for hunting pheasants and rabbits

SELE I HOSORI iron shavings or splinters

SELE I SIRGE iron wire

SELEI EJEN magnet

SELEI HOLBOKŪ iron clamp, iron fastener

SELEI ILHANGGA MOO veined ironwood

SELEI JUŠURU an iron self-defense weapon in the shape of a measuring stick

SELEI MALA an iron hammer

SELEI TAIMIN an iron poker

SELEI YONGGAN birdshot

SELEKJE an imaginary animal that supposedly resembles a bear, has an elephantlike trunk, a lion's head, and a cow's tail

SELEKTEN red water found under piles of earth and grass, rusty water

SELEME a dagger carried at the belt, somewhat larger than a *dabcilakū*

SELENGGE MOO 'iron tree'--a tree with black trunk and leaves, and a light purple flower that blooms for months without withering

SELFEN a slit in clothing

SELGIYEBUKŪ an interpreter in ancient times

SELGIYEBUMBI caus. of *selgiyembi*

SELGIYEMBI to promulgate, to announce, to issue, to disseminate, to circulate, to inform, to advertise (for)

SELGIYERE HESE imperial edict, imperial decree

SELGIYEN order, command, announcement, promulgation, advertisement

SELGIYESI promulgator, announcer, herald

SELHE the pendulous fold of skin under a cow's neck, dewlap

SELHEN a cangue

SELHEN ETUBUMBI to have the cangue put on, to cause to wear the cangue

SELMIN 1. mechanism, spring 2. a trap for animals by which an animal steps on a trip cord and gets shot by a crossbow mechanism

SELMIYEN see *selmin*

SEMBI (1) to say, to call, to mean

SERE ANGGALA instead of, not only (but also)

SEMBI (2) (-ngke) to melt, to dissolve, to run (of colors)

SEMBUMBI caus. of *sembi* (2)

SEMECEN see *semejen*

SEMEHUKEN rather coarse, rather coarsely woven, rather loose

SEMEHUN coarse, coarsely woven, loose, sparse

SEMEHUN BOSO coarsely woven summer cloth

SEMEJEN the fat covering the intestines and inner organs

SEMEMBI to melt, to soak through, to saturate

SEMEO the imperfect converb *seme* plus the interrogative particle *o*: used to form rhetorical questions

SEMERHEN a curtain or mat hung over a wooden frame, cover for a sedan chair, a small tent used for sleeping

SEMERHEN I YABUMBI to act in earnest, to act with sincerity

SEMEYEN see *semehun*

SEMIBUMBI caus. of *semimbi*

SEMIKU the end of a thread that has been tapered to pass through the eye of a needle more easily

SEMIMBI to thread (a needle)

SEMIYEKU see *semiku*

SEMKELE see *sengkule*

SEMKEN bracelet

SEMKIMBI to mistrust, to suspect

SEMNIO (觜) the name of a constellation

SEMNIO TOKDONGGO KIRU a banner depicting the constellation *semnio*

SEMSU the fat covering of intestines; cf. *semejen*

SEMSU NIMENGGI the same as *semsu*

SEN eye of a needle, small hole (as in the ears for earrings), any small opening

SENDE GENEHE formed a hole, formed a breach

SENCE mushroom

SENCE JINGGERI a nail made in the shape of a mushroom (with a large, wide head)

SENCEHE 1. the chin 2. a wooden or bamboo hook in the nose of a cow or camel; cf. *sanciha* 3. a bamboo hook that is part of a bird trap

SENCEHE SIBSIHŪN the chin is narrow

SENCEHELEKU a part of the bridle that hangs under the chin of a horse

SENCETU one name for the bamboo partridge; cf. *cuse moo i itu*

SENCI see *senji*

SENCIHE see *sencehe*

SENCIKU leather catches on boots through which the laces are threaded

SENDEHEN a board on which offerings to deities are placed

S

SENDEJEMBI to break (of a levee), to
  form a breach, to get washed out, to
  form a hole, to form a notch or gap
  (in a blade)
  SENDEJEHE ANGGA a breach
SENDELEBUMBI caus. of *sendelembi*
SENDELEMBI to make a breach (in a
  levee)
SENDEMBI see *sendejembi*
SENEMBI to be saturated, to expand
  (of a wet spot), to leak (of a brush
  too saturated with ink)
SENGGE 1. elder, old 2. (Chinese)
  hedgehog (*Erinaceus europaeus*)
  SENGGE ŠUFATU a head covering used
    by old men in ancient times
SENGGEDA calamus
SENGGELE 1. rooster's comb 2. gill
  (of a fish) 3. reed (of a musical
  instrument) 4. spring of a lock
  5. the opening of a bow case
  SENGGELE ILHA cockscomb (*Celosia
    cristata*)
SENGGELENGGE having a comb (like a
  rooster)
  SENGGELENGGE COKO one name for the
    gray partridge; cf. *itu*
  SENGGELENGGE GASHA the name of a
    black-headed bird with a brown
    beak and a comb on the top of the
    head
SENGGETE 1. plural of *sengge*: old men
  2. *Xanthium japonica*
SENGGI blood
  SENGGI BILJAKA there was a blood
    bath
  SENGGI DUHA blood sausage
  SENGGI HEFELIYENERE NIMEKU typhus
  SENGGI JUGŪN blood vessel
  SENGGI JUN artery, blood vessel
  SENGGI KAKSIMBI to cough up blood
  SENGGI SOSOMBI to have bloody diar-
    rhea
  SENGGI SUDALA the same as *senggi
    jugūn*
  SENGGI TEBUMBI to shed blood
SENGGILEMBI to act in a bloody manner
  SENGGILEME AFAMBI to fight a bloody
    battle
SENGGIME intimate, friendly, on good
  terms, devoted
SENGGIRI HIYAN rue, a sort of incense
  burned at sacrifices
SENGGIRI ILHA rhododendron
SENGGUWEBUMBI caus./pass. of *senggu-
  wembi*
SENGGUWECEMBI to be prone to fear, to
  be fearful
SENGGUWECUKE dreadful, frightening
SENGGUWEMBI to fear, to dread
SENGGUWENDEMBI the same as *sengguwembi*
SENGGUWENDUMBI/SENGGUWENUMBI to fear
  together, to dread together

SENGKEN 1. small loop in which a
  button is fastened 2. a rope or
  similar object attached to a basket
  to facilitate carrying 3. ring on
  which a bell is hung 4. small knob
  on the end of a seal
SENGKIRI HIYAN the name of a plant
  burned at sacrifices--rue; cf.
  senggiri hiyan
SENGKULE a thin-bladed variety of leek
  (*Allium odorum*)
  SENGKULE I ARSUN the sprouts of
    the leek that have been protected
    from the sun and are of a yellow
    tint
SENGSE a lazy woman
SENGSEBUMBI caus. of *sengsembi*
SENGSEMBI (-ke) to dry, to become dry
SENGSEREBUMBI caus. of *sengserembi*
  SENGSEREBUME WAMBI to kill by
    drowning
SENGSEREMBI 1. to choke by getting
  food or water in the windpipe 2.
  to drown, to suffocate
SENGSERŠEMBI to like very much
SENGSU loose rocks on a mountain
SENIHUN rare (of meat)
SENIYEHUKEN rather rare
SENIYEHUN see *senihun*
SENJI back sight on a rifle
SENTEHE chipped, having a piece broken
  off, notched
SEO lacking pupils in the eyes
SEOLEBUMBI caus. of *seolembi*
SEOLEKU small-minded, petty, vindic-
  tive, vengeful
SEOLEMBI to consider, to think over,
  to reflect
SEOLEN consideration, reflection,
  thought
  SEOLEN BE GOROMILA banish the
    thought
SEOLTEI goral; cf. *imahū*
SER SEME small, tiny
  SER SEME AGAMBI to rain lightly
  SER SEME AJIGE tiny, minute
  SER SEME DAMBI to blow gently (of
    the wind)
  SER SERE tiny, small, minute
SERBEN SARBAN 1. in a swarm, swarming
  2. in torrents
SERE fly's eggs, maggot
  SERE WALIYAMBI to lay eggs (of
    flies)
SEREBE careful, painstaking, meticu-
  lous
SEREBUMBI 1. caus./pass. of *serembi*
  2. to feel 3. to come to light, to
  become known, to be discovered 4.
  to reveal
SEREBUN feeling, experience
SERECUN a feeling for what is right,
  sensitivity

S

SERECUN AKŪ insensitive

SERECUNGGE one who is sensitive, one whose feelings are right

SEREHUN half-awake, half conscious

SEREMBI (-he/ke) to feel, to perceive, to find out, to experience, to have a presentiment

SEREME yellow hair five or six inches long from the tail of a deer sewn onto shoes and socks as decoration

SEREMŠEBUMBI caus./pass. of *seremšembi*

SEREMŠEMBI to defend, to guard (against), to prevent

SEREMŠEME TENEMBI to go to do garrison duty

SEREMŠEN defense, prevention

SERGE ŠU ILHA the name of a flower similar to the Tibetan lotus, the filaments of which are like iron wires

SERGUWEN cool

SERGUWEN CIRKU a pillow used in summertime

SERGUWEN EDUN a cool wind

SERGUWEŠEBUMBI caus. of *serguwešembi*

SERGUWEŠEMBI to cool off, to take advantage of a cool place or time

SERI sparse, scanty, diluted, infrequent

SERIKEN rather sparse or thin

SERKI scout, spy, a messenger who carries military intelligence, a messenger who goes by the post stations

SERKI FEKSIBUMBI to send a messenger with military intelligence

SERKIN report, intelligence, report sent to the emperor by the post stations

SERKINGGE TEMEN a fast camel

SERKUWEN see *serguwen*

SERSEN SARSAN shaking, trembling

SERSEN SEME the same as *sersen sarsan*

SERTEI harelipped

SERUKEN 1. cool 2. rather sparse or thin

SESE 1. gold thread 2. a small silver or copper wire that was tied on the tails of falcons 3. die, dice

SESE GECUHERI silk brocade

SESE I MORO cup for dice

SESE TABUMBI to sew with gold thread, to decorate with gold thread

SESE SASA frivolous, shallow, superficial

SESEME very little

SESENGGE BONIO a type of yellow monkey whose hair resembles gold threads

SESHE EFEN steamed bread; cf. *feshen efen*

SESHEBUMBI 1. caus. of *seshembi* 2. to disgust (someone with something)

SESHECUKE disgusting, unappetizing (because one has had too much already), loathsome

SESHEMBI 1. to be tired of, to be disgusted with, to be fed up with, to find loathsome 2. to shake, to shiver, to shake out 3. to sprinkle (flour, salt, sugar), to scatter, to spread (over)

SESHERI vulgar, common, lacking elegance

SESHETEBUMBI pass. of *seshetembi*

SESHETEMBI to shake vigorously

SESHUN disgusting, loathsome

SESI a curved deep-fried pastry made from millet and bean meal

SESILEMBI to form a herd (of deer)

SESIRI one-trillionth

SESUKIYEMBI to shiver from the cold

SESUKU die, dice

SESUKU MAKTAMBI to cast dice

SESULABUMBI caus. of *sesulambi*

SESULAMBI to be surprised, to be startled

SESULEMBI see *sesulambi*

SETERINEMBI to form holes (in ice at the spring thaw)

SEYEBUMBI caus./pass. of *seyembi*

SEYECUKE regrettable, vexing, hateful

SEYEMBI to regret, to find vexing, to dislike, to hate

SEYENDUMBI/SEYENUMBI to hate together

SI 1. you (singular) 2. space (in writing); cf. *siden* 3. a file of five men 4. obstruction, blocking

SI AKŪ without obstruction, without interruption

SI AKŪ TALKIYAMBI to lighten without interruption

SI BI SEME ILGARAKŪ without making a distinction of 'you' and 'me'

SI SINDAME YABUMBI to walk in files of five

SI IHAN buffalo, rhinoceros

SI YANG the West, Europe

SIBCAMBI 1. to slip down, to slide off 2. to come back after finding one isn't needed (for some rotating duty)

SIBDAN see *sabdan*

SIBE *Equisetum hiemale*--a plant whose stems are used for polishing wood and bone

SIBEDEMBI to polish with the stem of the plant *Equisetum hiemale*

SIBEHE the short ribs of the chest cavity

SIBEREBUMBI caus. of *siberembi*

SIBEREMBI 1. to knead 2. to spin thread in the fingers, to make a small ball (of felt, lint, or thread) by rolling in the fingers 3. to massage

S

SIBERHEN 1. wick 2. some substance like paper or hemp that has been rolled into a string between the fingers

SIBERI sweat of the hands and feet
  SIBERI DAHA 1. something held in the hand constantly 2. a man who has been sent on errands often 3. something left behind by a dead person

SIBIBUMBI caus. of *sibimbi*

SIBIDA NASAN the pickled stem of celery cabbage (*Brassica pekinensis*)

SIBIMBI 1. to grasp in the hand and pull through the fingers (of various long slender objects), to pull something long and slender 2. to pound into a long strip (gold or silver)

SIBIRGAN a type of speckled swallow

SIBIŠAMBI 1. to pull through the hand continually 2. to look at furtively

SIBIYA 1. counter, tally stick, tally used in fortune-telling, yarrow stalks 2. a patch running diagonally downward under the arm on a garment
  SIBIYA ALIBUMBI to hand over a tally (of guards)
  SIBIYA BAIMBI to consult the tallies (a kind of fortunetelling)
  SIBIYA TATAMBI to draw lots, to draw the tallies

SIBIYALAKŪ a clasp or fastener for books and paintings

SIBIYALAMBI 1. to cast the tallies, to cast lots 2. to split with a wedge 3. to fasten or nail with a wooden or bamboo wedge

SIBIYAMBI short and sparse (of a person's hair)

SIBKE 1. a wooden or metal peg placed in the hasp of a lock 2. pin, rivet, peg 3. bar, lever
  SIBKE MOO a two-man carrying pole
  SIBKE SELE iron pin on a loom

SIBKELEBUMBI caus. of *sibkelembi*

SIBKELEMBI to carry on a pole between two men
  SIBKELERE HŪSUN bearer, coolie

SIBKIBUMBI caus. of *sibkimbi*

SIBKIMBI to pursue (a problem, a grudge, etc.), to investigate, to be persistent
  SIBKIME FUHAŠAMBI to do research on

SIBKURI a hole at the bottom of a city wall used as a passage for water

SIBSIHŪN 1. wide at the top and narrow at the bottom 2. having a face that is narrow at the bottom, having a narrow chin
  SIBSIHŪN FURGI a weir that is pointed at one end

SIBSIKA a switch

SIBSIKALAMBI to beat (hides and rugs)

SIBŠA suddenly, precipitously, quickly
  SIBŠA EBEREKE suddenly dropped in price
  SIBŠA GENEHE suddenly finished
  SIBŠA TUTAHA suddenly left behind

SIBŠALAMBI to exclude, to shut out

SIBUMBI 1. caus./pass. of *simbi* 2. to be stopped up, to be obstructed

SIBUSHŪN stopped up, obstructed

SICAMBI (-ka) 1. to crack, to form a crack (of porcelain, jade, etc.) 2. to make an ear-shattering noise

SICING celadonite

SIDAHIYAMBI to roll back the sleeves, to bare the arms

SIDAMBI (-ka) to begin lactation, see *huhun sidakabi*

SIDAMBUMBI caus. of *sidambi*

SIDAN 1. young, immature 2. unadorned, unspoiled 3. see *si*
  SIDAN JEKU the scattered grain left behind on the threshing floor
  SIDAN JUSE juveniles, youths
  SIDAN MOO a small, immature tree

SIDARABUMBI caus. of *sidarambi*

SIDARAMBI (-ka) 1. to unfold (the fist), to release, to spread out 2. to stretch out (of distances), to become distant 3. to become calm, relieved

SIDARAMBUMBI the same as *sidarabumbi*

SIDEHEN see *sidehun*

SIDEHULEBUMBI caus. of *sidehulembi*

SIDEHULEMBI 1. to leave a space 2. to bar a door

SIDEHUN 1. a horizontal wooden bar for a door 2. the horizontal pieces of window frames 3. the horizontal supports on the bottom of wagons and sedan chairs 4. the steps on a ladder

SIDEHUNJEMBI to leave a space, to make a pause, to do alternatively

SIDEN 1. space, interval, interstice 2. a while 3. measure word for rooms 4. witness 5. official, public
  SIDEN BAKCIN corroborative evidence
  SIDEN DE in between
  SIDEN I BAIBUNGGA official expenditures
  SIDEN I BAITA official matter, official business
  SIDEN I BAITALAN official use, official employment
  SIDEN I BITHE official document
  SIDEN I HACIN public property
  SIDEN I HAHA extra-quota man
  SIDEN I NIYALMA 1. middleman 2. witness
  SIDEN NIRU a company formed from the bannermen of the imperial

S

household who serve on court duty

SIDEN OBUMBI to let serve as a witness

SIDEN TEMGETU 1. official credential
or certificate 2. witness to an
agreement

SIDEN WALIYAMBI to leave a space,
to make a pause

SIDENGGE HERGEN (祿書) a style
of calligraphy--the clerical style

SIDEREBUMBI caus. of *siderembi*

SIDEREKU an iron decoration on the side
of a horse's bridle

SIDEREMBI to hobble, to tie up, to
trip, to encumber

SIDEREME ACILAMBI to throw by entangling the feet (in wrestling)

SIDERI 1. hobbling device, foot fetters, a hobble for animals 2. anklet

SIDERILENGGE pertaining to foot fetters

SIDERSHUN hobbled, lame, stiff-legged

SIDU WEIHE canine teeth (of a man)

SIDUMBI to scrape, to scrape off; cf.
šudumbi

SIFA MACA wild leek; cf. *sumpa maca*

SIFIBUMBI caus. of *sifimbi*

SIFIKŪ a hairpin

SIFIMBI to wear a hairpin, to stick in
the hair

SIFIRI ILHA an exotic flower with very
thin stems and a bloom resembling a
hairpin

SIFU FULANA ILHA the blossom of a variety of cherry-apple

SIFULU the bladder; cf. *sike fulhū*

SIGAMBI see *sihambi*

SIGAN 1. mist, heavy fog 2. see *sihan*
SIGAN TEMBI a mist settles

SIHABUMBI caus. of *sihambi*

SIHAKŪ a short bamboo flute with nine
holes

SIHALI the area where the buttocks and
waist join

SIHAMBI 1. to fall (of leaves), to
fall out (of hair) 2. to wither
3. to give hot pursuit, to follow on
the heels of 4. to examine in detail, to examine carefully

SIHAN 1. tube, pipe 2. a cylindrical
container, cask, keg, pail 3. the
inner barrel of a 'mother-child'
cannon 4. see *sigan*
SIHAN SIRABURE POO a 'mother-child'
cannon

SIHARAKŪ MOO a nondeciduous tree

SIHELEBUMBI caus./pass. of *sihelembi*

SIHELEMBI to hinder (because of envy
or spite), to thwart, to get in the
way

SIHERI EBCI floating rib

SIHEŠEMBI 1. to act frisky, to wag the
tail 2. to fawn, to act obsequi-
ously

SIHETE sparse and short

SIHIN 1. eaves (of a house) 2. the
canopy of a tree, treetop
SIHIN DEN the top of the tree is
high
SIHIN I EYEBUKU a drain at the
junction of two eaves
SIHIN I KANGGIRI a thin piece of
metal hung from the eaves that
hums when the wind blows
SIHIN I SELE a piece of iron on a
saddle used for attaching the
stirrups
SIHIN I ULHUN a board that connects
the eaves to the structure of the
roof
SIHIN SELE the same as *sihin i sele*

SIHINGGE SON support for the eaves

SIHIYA roots and other inedible parts
of grass left uneaten by cattle,
sheep, etc.

SIHIYAKŪ 1. a hole in the footboard
(*cirku moo*) of a door 2. a horizontal piece of wood on a pestle

SIHIYAN porch, pavilion

SIJA meat that has been cooked very
soft in its own juice; cf. *silja*

SIJIBUMBI caus. of *sijimbi*

SIJIGIYAN a long gown

SIJIHŪN erect, straight
SIJIHŪN ILIHABI is standing erect
(and still)

SIJILEMBI to shoot an arrow with a
line attached to it, to throw an
object with a line attached

SIJIMBI to sew with very fine stitches

SIJIN 1. line, string, fishline 2.
line tied to the foot of a falcon
3. broken grain from which the chaff
has been removed (especially rice
and millet)
SIJIN BELE broken grain from which
the chaff has been removed

SIJIRAHŪN see *sijirhūn*

SIJIRAMBI to make straight, to be
straight

SIJIRHŪN straight, not crooked

SIKA 1. the hair of the mane or tail
of an animal 2. a tassel for a hat
made from the mane or tail of a cow
SIKA FOYO 'red sand grass'--a type
of red-colored grass that is used
for cushioning in shoes and boots
SIKA HADAHAN a peg on the rim of a
wagon to which the load can be
fixed
SIKA MOO the windmill palm--*Tra-
chycarpus excelsus*
SIKA SORSON a tassel for a hat made
from the hairs of a cow's tail

SIKARI one name for the wild pig, the
same as *kitari*

SIKE urine

S

SIKE FULHŪ   the bladder
SIKE ONGGOHO   'forgot urine'--said
  of horses that can't urinate
SIKE SEN   the opening of the urethra
SIKSE   yesterday
SIKSERGAN   a lizard
SIKSERI   dusk, twilight
SIKTAN   elixir, elixir of immortality
SIKŪ   see *sikū*
SIKŪ   pieces of leather or felt in a
  quiver used to hold the arrows in
  place
SILAN   a type of fine blue cloth
SILBA   having the same name or surname;
  cf. *cilba*
SILDA YALI   meat from the neck
SILE   meat soup, broth
SILEHEN   one name for the crane; cf.
  bulehen
SILEMI   see *silemin*
SILEMIDEMBI   to act in a lazy, indolent
  manner
SILEMIN   1. tough, tenacious, resilient
  2. lasting, long-winded, untiring 3.
  reluctant, hard to move
SILENGGI   1. dew 2. saliva that runs
  from the corners of the mouth--drivel
  SILENGGI FUHEŠEMBI   the dew rolls
    (in abundance)
  SILENGGI GEBKELJEMBI   the dew glis-
    tens (in the sunlight)
  SILENGGI SABDAN   dewdrop
  SILENGGI TOKTOHOBI   the dew has
    settled
  SILENGGI WASIKA   the dew has fallen
SILENGGINEMBI   to form dew
SILENGGIŠEMBI   to drool, to slaver
SILGABUMBI   caus. of *silgambi*
SILGABUN   selection
SILGAMBI   to sort out, to select, to
  hand-pick
SILGASI (貢生)   Senior Licentiate,
  BH 629A
SILGIMBI   1. to slip through an opening
  (as a fly through a crack, or a fish
  through a net) 2. euphemism for 'to
  slaughter' in sacrificial language
SILGIYABUMBI   caus. of *silgiyambi*
SILGIYAMBI   to rinse out
SILHAMBI   see *silgambi*
SILHATA   alone, friendless, lone
SILHI   1. gall bladder 2. envy
SILHIDABUMBI   pass. of *silhidambi*
SILHIDAMBI   to envy, to be jealous
SILHIMBI   1. to penetrate, to slip
  through; cf. *silgimbi* 2. to place
  an arrowhead on a shaft
SILHINGGA   envious, jealous
SILIHI   one name for the weasel; cf.
  solohi
SILIMBI   to select, to pick out; cf.
  silgambi
  SILIHA COOHA   crack troops, hand-

picked troops
SILIN   topnotch, elite, crack (troops)
  SILIN DACUNGGA KŪWARAN I SIDEN YAMUN
  (健 銳 營 街 門)   office
    of the Light Division, BH 733, 738
SILJA   meat that has been cooked to
  pieces in it own juices--the same as
  sija
SILKA   see *silkan*
SILKADA   a crafty or shrewd person,
  a slippery person
SILKAN   1. crafty, cautious, shrewd
  2. a type of small oak, the wood of
  which was used for bow grips and
  axles
SILKARI MOO   *Quercus sclerophylla*, a
  sort of oak tree
SILMELEMBI   to dry in the shade
  SILMELEHE YALI   meat that has been
    dried in the shade
SILMEN   1. shady, sunless 2. sparrow
  hawk (*Accipiter nisus*)
SILMENGGE SARA   a parasol
SILTABUMBI   caus. of *siltambi*
SILTAKŪ   a shirker
SILTAMBI   1. to shirk, to get out of
  doing something, to refuse respon-
  sibility 2. to make excuses, to put
  someone off
SILTAN   mast, flagpole used in a tem-
  ple, pole
  SILTAN I HAFIRAKŪ MOO   wooden holder
    for a mast
  SILTAN I ŠURDEBUKU   hoist for a sail
    (attached to the mast)
  SILTAN MOO   a sacred tree erected in
    the shamanistic shrine of the
    palace
SILUN   lynx (*Felis lynx*)
SIMACUKA   1. lonely 2. desolate,
  mournful 3. meager, scant
SIMAGA   see *šumgan*
SIMARI CECIKE   one name for the goat-
  sucker (*Caprimulgus indicus*)
SIMATUN CECIKE   one name for the goat-
  sucker, the same as *simari cecike*
SIMBE   accusative form of *si* 'you'
SIMBI (-he)   1. to stop up, to plug up,
  to fill in 2. to stand in for, to
  substitute for 3. to bribe, to
  employ as bribery
  SIME BUMBI   to give as a bribe
SIMEBUMBI   caus./pass. of *simembi*
SIMELEMBI   to be muddy, to be marshlike
SIMELEN   marsh, mire
  SIMELEN COKO   marsh hen
  SIMELEN ŠUNGKERI ILHA   marsh orchid--
    Arethusa chinensis
SIMELI   1. poor and forlorn, miserable,
  wretched 2. poverty-stricken
SIMELJE   a gull-like bird with a white
  growth on its black head
SIMEMBI (-ke, -he)   1. to soak, to

S

moisten, to seep into 2. to favor
SIMEN 1. moisture, juice, secretion,
   vital fluids, fluids 2. favor,
   beneficence
   SIMEN AKŪ 1. uninteresting, dull,
      unexciting 2. lonely, desolate,
      not prospering
   SIMEN ARAMBI to keep company, to
      pass the time, to be friendly with
   SIMEN GOCIMBUMBI the liquids
      freeze--said to describe an unbear-
      able cold
   SIMEN NIYOLOCUKA saturated with fat,
      fatty
SIMENGGE bustling, exciting, prosper-
   ing, thriving, animated
SIMENGGI tung oil
   SIMENGGI URANGGA MOO tung tree
      (*Aleurites fordii*)
SIMENGGILEBUMBI caus. of *simenggilembi*
SIMENGGILEMBI to apply (tung) oil, to
   paint
   SIMENGGILEHE WADAN an oil cloth
SIMGAN see *šungan*
SIMHULEMBI to play the finger game
   SIMHULERE EFIN the finger guessing
      game
SIMHUN finger, toe
   SIMHUN BUHIYEMBUMBI the same as
      simhulembi
   SIMHUN FATAME TOLOMBI to count on
      the fingers
   SIMHUN GIDAME TOLOMBI the same as
      simhun fatame tolombi
   SIMHUN HEFELI palm of the hand,
      sole of the foot
   SIMHUN SEHEI SIHERI EBCI BE JAFAHA
      'saying he would take only a fin-
      ger, he took a rib'--proverb
SIMHURI the name of a wild finger-
   shaped fruit that ripens in the
   sixth month
SIMIBUMBI caus./pass. of *simimbi*
SIMIKTE a cat's-eye
SIMIMBI to suck
SIMINUMBI to suck together, to suck
   one another
SIMNEBUMBI caus./pass. of *simnembi*
SIMNEMBI to examine, to take an exam-
   ination, to test
   SIMNEHE SILGASI (拔貢) desig-
      nation of superior students chosen
      every twelve years for the court
      examination, imperial student by
      special selection
   SIMNEME DOSIMBI to pass an examina-
      tion
   SIMNERE BAITAI KUNGGERI (學政
      科) board of affairs relating to
      examinations in the Board of Rites
   SIMNERE BE KADALARA KUNGGERI (督
      學 科) examination office of
      the Metropolitan Prefecture

SIMNERE BOO (號房) the place
   where the examinees were lodged
   during an examination
SIMNERE BUKDARUN examination paper
SIMNERE HAFAN (考試官)
   examination officer
SIMNERE KŪWARAN (貢院) examination hall
   SIMNERE KŪWARAN I BAITA BE UHERI
   KADALARA HAFAN (知貢舉)
   official in charge at the metropolitan examination
SIMNEN examination, testing
SIMNENDUMBI/SIMNENUMBI to take an
   examination together, to examine
   together
SIMNENEMBI to go to take an examina-
   tion, to go to examine
SIMNENJIMBI to come to take an exam-
   ination, to come to examine
SIMNESI examinee, student--a person
   who had passed the examination given
   by the district magistrate
SIMORI (星) the name of a constel-
   lation
   SIMORI TOKDONGGO KIRU a banner de-
      picting the constellation *simori*
SIMTEN taste, tasty
SIMTU a large iron cooking pot
SIN a measure equaling one Chinese
   bushel and eight pecks
   SIN I HIYASE the same as *sin*
   SIN JEKU JETERE AHA a slave as-
      signed to the imperial household
SINAGALAMBI to keep the mourning
   period, to mourn
SINAGAN mourning
   SINAGAN DE ACANJIMBI to come to a
      funeral
   SINAGAN I BAITA funeral
SINAHI mourning garment (of sackcloth)
   SINAHI HŪWAITAMBI to don mourning
      garments
SINAHILAMBI to wear mourning clothes
SINCI ablative form of *si*
SINDABUMBI caus./pass. of *sindambi*
SINDAMBI 1. to put, to place, to set
   2. to let go, to let out, to re-
   lease, to dissipate 3. to dissipate,
   to be unrestrained 4. to play
   (chess) 5. to appoint (an official)
   6. to bury 7. to fire (a gun) 8.
   to give head to (a horse) 9. to
   give off (rays of light) 10. to
   remit, to forgive
SINDARALAMBI to free, to release, to
   let go
SINDE dative/locative of *si*
SINDU ILHA the bloom of the *Opuntia
   cactus*
SINDUBI (心) the name of a constellation
   SINDUBI TOKDONGGO KIRU a banner

S

depicting the constellation *sindubi*

SING SING an ape; *cf. sirsing*

SING SING JAN see *singsingjan*

SINGGEBUMBI caus./pass. of *singgembi*
  SINGGEBUME TEBUMBI to sink to the bottom, to fall all the way to the bottom
  SINGGEBUME ULHIBUMBI to instruct or inform thoroughly

SINGGEKU the internal organs

SINGGEMBI 1. to soak into, to permeate, to saturate, to soak through, to become thoroughly wet 2. to be digested 3. to suck (into) 4. to dissolve 5. to appropriate, to take for one's own use, to take on the sly

SINGGERI 1. rat, mouse 2. the first of the earth's branches (子)
  SINGGERI BIYA the eleventh month
  SINGGERI HUHUN a small tumor on the skin
  SINGGERI ŠAN 'rat's ears'--*Gnaphalium multiceps*
  SINGGERI YOO a growth on the neck

SINGGERINGGE pertaining to the rat
  SINGGERINGGE ANIYA the year of the rat

SINGGEŠU one name for the large quail (*ihan mušu*)

SINGGETEI soaked, saturated

SINGGIRAMBI to be envious

SINGGIYAMBI 1. to ache, to be numb, to be sore 2. to stick in the belt (an arrow)

SINGGIYAN aching, numb

SINGKEYEN cloudy and cold

SINGSILAMBI see *cincilambi*

SINGSIN physiognomy

SINGSINGJAN red felt

SINI genitive of *si*

SININGGE yours

SIOI foreword, preface (to a book); cf. *šutucin*

SIOJAN embroiderer

SIOJUWAN (修 撰) a secretary in the Hanlin Academy

SIOLEMBI to embroider

SIOWAN a ocarinalike musical instrument with five holes

SIR SEME somewhat numb, rather numb, asleep (of a limb)
  SIR SEME FUNGKE gone to sleep (of the limbs)

SIR SIYAR (onom.) 1. the sound of grass and leaves moving slightly 2. palpitating (of the heart)

SIR ŠAR SEME 1. walking slowly 2. see *sir siyar*

SIRA 1. yellow 2. the bone of the leg below the knee, the tibia
  SIRA DEN long-legged
  SIRA MOO mountain barberry--a vine

that grows in thickets and can be woven into walking canes

SIRABUMBI caus. of *sirambi*

SIRACA 1. Chinese boxthorn--*Lycium chinensis* 2. a yellow dye made from the rotten bark of the tree *Quercus bungeana*

SIRAKŪ false hair

SIRAMBI 1. to continue, to follow 2. to connect, to tie together 3. to inherit
  SIRARA HAFAN hereditary official
  SIRARA HAFAN I TACIKŪ (幼 官 學) a school for the sons of worthy officials

SIRAME 1. next (in sequence) 2. step-
  SIRAME AMA stepfather
  SIRAME ENIYE stepmother
  SIRAME HAFAN (監 丞) Proctor, BH 412A
  SIRAME HAFAN I TINGGIN (寺 丞 廳) the name of a hall in the Court of Sacrificial Worship
  SIRAME JALAHI JUI the son of a cousin on the father's side
  SIRAME KADALARA AMBAN (宗 正) Controller of the Imperial Clan Court, BH 58, 59

SIRAMENGGE continuing, connecting

SIRAN continuation, succession, sequence, order
  SIRAN SIRAN I continually, one after another

SIRANDUHAI one after another, in succession

SIRANDUMBI/SIRANUMBI to follow after one another, to follow in succession

SIRANUHAI the same as *siranduhai*

SIRASHA an exotic fruit that resembles a clam and tastes like a walnut

SIRATA SAKSAHA the same as *niyo saksaha*

SIRATA UKSIN net armor; cf. *asu uksin*

SIRBAŠAMBI 1. to wag the tail 2. to get agitated, to become flustered

SIRBE WEHE CINUHŪN a cinnabar mined in the mountains of Yunnan that is used both as a medicine and a dye

SIRDAN a military arrow with a two-edged iron arrowhead
  SIRDAN JUHE icicle
  SIRDAN SELE a piece of iron with two holes that was attached to the top of a sword's scabbard

SIRDANGGA pertaining to an arrow

SIREBUMBI caus. of *sirembi*

SIREBUN the name of a form of Chinese verse (行)

SIRECU an exotic fruit that grows on a vine and resembles small grapes

SIREMBI to twist (thread or rope), to spin

SIREMI see *sirembi*

SIREN 1. string, line, thread 2. run-
ner, tendril, creeper (all of plants)
3. fuse 4. vein, capillary 5. a
paper figure used for exorcisms
SIREN FAITAMBI to cut the 'thread
of life' on a paper figure used in
shamanistic exorcism
SIREN FUTA 1. pieces of colored
paper and cloth attached to a rope
on a willow pole and then tied to
the altar 2. string used to bind
books between boards 3. rope
used to hold a plowshare tight 4.
fuse
SIREN SIREN continually, uninterruptedly
SIREN SUDALA the part of the pulse
nearest the wristbone
SIREN TATAMBI a rainbow has formed
SIREN WALIYAME ASU ARAMBI to spin a
web (of spiders)
SIRENDUMBI to be joined together, to
ask secretly for a favor
SIRENEMBI 1. to be connected, to be
joined, to be in rows 2. to send
out tendrils, to send forth runners
3. to keep on sounding, to continue
singing (of birds)
SIRENEHE MAILAN dodder--*Cuscuta
chinensis*
SIRENEME BANJIMBI to grow in rows
SIRENERE DALAN a type of levee
longer and narrower than the usual
kind
SIRENEN ILHA bignonia
SIRENGGE MUDAN ILHA a flower resembling
the peony that grows in shallow
water; the red and pink blossoms are
smaller than the peony
SIRENTU MOO the banyan tree
SIRENTUMBI to enter into a secret
agreement with, to plot with
SIRENTUSI secret agent, plotter
SIRESI 1. puller, one who pulls a rope
2. agent, middleman
SIRGA 1. a light bay (horse) 2. roe
deer; cf. *gio*
SIRGA KUWARAN a park for keeping
wild animals
SIRGACIN see *sirhacin*
SIRGAHUN the name of a deep yellow
pigment
SIRGATU muntjac, Hydropotes (a variety
of deer); cf. *gi buhū*
SIRGE 1. silk thread, silk floss
(from a cocoon) 2. string (of a
musical instrument) 3. a strip
(of dried meat) 4. measure word for
a rib
SIRGE FOLONGGO a type of silk fabric on which the designs resemble
carving
SIRGELEMBI to cut apart the ribs (of

a slaughtered animal)
SIRGEMBI to be anxious, to worry
SIRGENGGE COKO a variety of chicken
whose feathers resemble silk threads
SIRGERI spun silk, pongee, silken
yarn; cf. *fangse*
SIRGERI FISA a type of quail with
white feathers on its back
SIRGERI UJU a type of quail with
white feathers on its head
SIRGETU GASHA one name for the egret;
cf. *gūwasihiya*
SIRHACIN a female zeren; cf. *jeren,
onon*
SIRHE see *sirge*
SIRI a young carp
SIRI FUCIHI Mañjuśrī
SIRIBUMBI caus./pass. of *sirimbi*
SIRIKU squeezer
SIRIMBI 1. to wring, to squeeze out
(a liquid) 2. to milk 3. to blow
the nose
SIRIN raw copper
SIRIN MORO a copper bowl
SIRIN SAIFI a copper spoon
SIRKE long lasting, protracted, end-
less
SIRKEDEMBI to go on endlessly, to
last for a long time
SIRKEDEME AGAMBI to rain for a
long time
SIRKEDERI persisting, endless
SIRKEMBI see *sirgembi*
SIRSING an ape
SISA bean, pea
SISA DO a filling made of beans
SISA UFA bean flour
SISA WEHE a weak stone that can be
easily crushed
SISABUMBI caus. of *sisambi*
SISALAMBI to sprinkle; cf. *sisambi*
SISAMBI to sprinkle, to strew
SISEBUMBI caus. of *sisembi*
SISEHEN braid, piping, edging
SISEKU a sieve
SISEMBI 1. to sift 2. to baste
(sewing)
SISEME ARAMBI to make a rough draft
SISETEMBI 1. to write a rough draft,
to make a general plan 2. to manage
in a rough or general manner
SISETEME BODOMBI to make a rough
estimate
SISETEME BODORO FALGANGGA (料
估所) Department of Esti-
mates, BH 460A
SISETEME GISUREMBI to speak in gen-
eral terms, to speak in outline
form
SISHE a mattress
SISI hazelnut
SISI JAN an arrow with a hazelnut-
shaped head made of horn with

S

three holes in it--used for shooting wild game

SISI MEGU 'hazelnut mushroom'--a
small yellow mushroom found in
areas where hazelnuts grow

SISI NIRU an arrow similar to the
sisi jan except that it has an
iron head and is used for shooting
deer

SISI SENCE the same as *sisi megu*

SISI ŠAŠA shivering (from cold)

SISIBUMBI caus./pass. of *sisimbi*

SISIKU 1. a vessel filled with ashes
or sand in which one can insert incense sticks, candles, etc. 2. a
vase for flowers

SISIMBI (-ha) to insert, to stick into
SISIHA GESE 'as if stuck in,' said
of someone who eats with gusto

SISIN insertion, sticking in, intake
SISIN AMBA 'intake is great'--said
of someone who eats a lot

SISINAMBI to stick into (there)

SISINGGA having a large intake, glutton
SISINGGA HUWEJEHEN a small screen
placed in a stand, which may be
decorated with a picture or calligraphy

SISIRI pistachio nut

SISUHU one name for the fish hawk; cf.
suksuhu

SIŠA 1. bells worn on a shaman's belt
2. peacock feather worn on the hat
by officials
SIŠA ARKI the last of the liquor
distilled from kumiss
SIŠA SELE an ornament with red
tassels that hangs from a horse's
breast

SIŠABUMBI caus. of *sišambi*

SIŠAMBI to worm into (of maggots)

SIŠANAMBI to hang down (of icicles)

SIŠANTUMBI to offer a small amount of
food to a dead person on the eighth
day after burial; cf. *boohalambi*

SIŠARGAN a small bird resembling the
fiyabkū with a blue breast and black
markings on the back

SIŠARI hemp gathered after a frost
from which grass-linen can be woven
SIŠARI CECIKE a small bird with a
pink and yellow beak, pink and
yellow tail and wings, and white
tufts on the cheeks

SITA matter, affair; cf. *baita*

SITABUMBI 1. caus. of *sitambi* 2. to
be delayed

SITAHŪN few, scarce, deficient, sparse
SITAHŪN NIYALMA term used by rulers
in antiquity to refer to themselves

SITAMBI to fall behind, to be deficient, to lag, to be slow, to be

late (for an appointment)

SITASHŪN 1. behind, lagging behind,
late, deficient 2. poor, wretched

SITEKU a bed-wetter, one who urinates
frequently
SITEKU UMIYAHA a winged black bug
that bites and causes blisters

SITEMBI to urinate
SITERE TAMPIN a chamber pot, night
pan

SITENEMBI to go to urinate

SITHEN box, a box for documents

SITHŪMBI to apply oneself, to be
diligent, to exert oneself, to concentrate on

SITHŪN application, diligence

SITUHŪMBI 1. to rinse 2. to grind, to
whet

SITUMBI to grow up, to mature
SITUME GENEMBI to grow up gradually

SIYAL mister, gentleman

SIYAN one one-hundred-millionth

SIYAN EL see *siyal*

SIYAN FUNG vanguard

SIYAN JANG Taoist abbot

SIYAN LO GURUN Thailand, Siam

SIYAN ŠENG mister, gentleman, sir

SIYANCEO a type of silk fabric

SIYANG GUNG see *siyanggung*

SIYANGCI chess

SIYANGGUNG 1. your honor, respected
sir 2. young man of a good family

SIYANGKI the same as *siyangci*

SIYOO 1. saltpeter 2. flute

SIYOO JIYEI young lady

SIYOO ŠENG a young man's role in
opera

SIYŪN AN HAFAN (巡 按) provincial
censor (Ming)

SIYŪN FU (巡 撫) provincial governor

SIYŪN GIYAN (巡 檢) see *giyarimsi*

SO 1. a bad omen 2. vinegar 3. dewlap
SO JORIMBI to point out a bad omen

SOBONIO a type of monkey with long
light yellow hair

SOBORI a horse or cow with one hoof
that is a different color from the
other three

SOBORO light yellowish green

SOCA rice that is strewn as an offering to a deity

SOCILI NIYEHE pintail duck (*Dafila
acuta*)

SOCO ORHO fodder that is gathered in
the mountains or on the steppe

SODZ rice that has turned red from
long storage

SOFIDAMBI to mill around, to be jittery (of livestock)

SOFIN restless, jittery (of livestock)
SOFIN AKŪ restless, unsettled,

S

unrestrained

SOFORO saddle cushion--small square pieces of leather at both sides of the saddle covering the upper part of the stirrup straps

SOGI vegetable, edible plant

SOGIMBI see *sohimbi*

SOGIYA pock, pustule (especially on a child)

SOHIMBI to become dimmed (the eyes when some foreign object gets in them), to get something in the eye

SOHIN a piece of ice in a river in the autumn

SOHIN GŪLHA a boot with a round toe

SOHO the name of a wild plant with long white leaves, yellow flowers, and a sweet taste

SOHOCI the name of a small yellow exotic fruit

SOHOCO the name of a variety of sea fish

SOHOHORI bright yellow--the same as *sohohūri*

SOHOHŪRI bright yellow--the same as *sohohori*

SOHOKOLIYAN deep yellow

SOHOKON yellowish, rather yellow

SOHON 1. deep yellow (the color of the sunflower) 2. the sixth of the heaven's stems (己)

SOHON CECIKE one name for the oriole; cf. *gūlin cecike*

SOHON HIONGHIOI CECIKE one name for the oriole; cf. *gūlin cecike*

SOHON HOOHAN one name for the heron; cf. *hoohan*

SOHON MOO boxwood

SOHON NIMEKU jaundice

SOHON SAKSAHA DAMIN a light yellow young eagle

SOHON TASHARI a yellow eagle

SOHON TEMGETUNGGE GU the name of a square jade tablet used at sacrifices to the earth

SOIHO the end of a bird's tail

SOIHON see *suihon*

SOIKARA WEIJUN one name for the stork; cf. *weijun*

SOILO hair of the fetlock of horses, mules, and donkeys

SOILOMBI 1. to soar, to fly up 2. to fly up after hitting the target, to ricochet (of an arrow)

SOISON squirrel

SOKJI plants that grow underwater in rivers

SOKO the earth god

SOKSIMBI to sob

SOKSO SAKSA galloping wildly, galloping madly

SOKSOHON pouting, sulking

SOKSOHORI sitting idly, sitting quietly (of a group)

SOKSORI suddenly (of standing up and leaving)

SOKSORJAMBI see *sosorcombi*

SOKSOROMBI see *sosorombi*

SOKTOBUMBI caus. of *soktombi*

SOKTOKŪ a good drinker, one who likes to drink

SOKTOMBI to be drunk, to get drunk

SOKŪ see *soko*

SOLAMBI to give one's daughter in marriage

SOLBIBUMBI caus. of *solbimbi*

SOLBIMBI to put an arrow on a bowstring

SOLBIN estimation, guessing; cf. *tulbin*

SOLHA a covered vessel for holding food and soup

SOLHI see *solohi*

SOLHO Korea, Korean

SOLHO BING 'Korean cake'--a cake made of honey, flour, and sesame oil

SOLHO BOSO cloth produced in Korea

SOLHO EFEN the same as *solho bing*

SOLHO GURUN Korea

SOLHO GURUN I KUREN the hostel for Korean emissaries

SOLHO HARA a type of sage--*Salvia japonica*

SOLHO HENGKE Korean muskmelon

SOLHO HOOŠAN a type of durable paper from Korea

SOLHO LEKE flat cakes made of honey, flour, and sesame oil

SOLHO NIRU the banner-chief of the Koreans who surrendered to the Manchus at the beginnning of the dynasty

SOLHO YEYE HANDU BELE Korean glutinous rice

SOLIBUMBI caus./pass. of *solimbi*

SOLIMBI to invite, to summon, to hire, to engage

SOLIN CECIKE one name for the oriole; cf. *gūlin cecike*

SOLINABUMBI caus. of *solinambi*

SOLINAMBI to go to invite

SOLINDUMBI/SOLINUMBI to invite together, to invite one another

SOLINGGIMBI to send to invite

SOLINJIMBI to come to invite

SOLMIN 1. eyelash 2. the end of a hair

SOLO the fine hairlike roots of ginseng

SOLOHI weasel (*Mustela sibirica*)

SOLOMBI to go against the current, to go upstream

SOLON Solon (a tribe in northern Manchuria)

SOLON JAN an arrow with a narrow steel head used in war and for hunting bears and wild boar

S

SOLON MAJAN a long Solon arrow

SOMBI (-ha) to strew, to scatter

SOME GABTAMBI to shoot arrows in all directions

SOMIBUMBI caus./pass. of *somimbi*

SOMIMBI 1. to hide, to store away, to conceal 2. to bury (a coffin), to inter

SOMIHA SAISA a hermit, one who has retired to the country from public life

SOMIME TEMBI to live in retirement, to live as a hermit

SOMINA ORHO sedge

SOMINDUMBI/SOMINUMBI to hide together

SQMINJIMBI to come to hide

SOMISHŪN hidden, secret, concealed

SOMISHŪN COOHA concealed troops

SOMITAMBI to stay hidden, to go into hiding

SOMO the votive or spirit pole erected by Manchu families

SOMOO see *somo*

SON rafter, roof support of a tent

SON SON I fragmentary, scattered, in every direction, in disarray

SONAMBI to form a callus

SONCOHO 1. pigtail, braid 2. a holder for the bowstring that is made from cow's horn and attached to the ends of the bow 3. odd numbered; cf. *sonio*

SONCOHO BIYA an odd-numbered month

SONCOHO CECIKE one name for the hoopoe; cf. *indahūn cecike*

SONCOHO FUTA a rope fastened to the middle of a dragnet

SONCOHO HŪWALAMBI 1. 'to cut the braid'--said of girls who get married 2. to deflower a virgin

SONCOHO HŪWALAME HOLBOHO 'parted the braid and made a chignon'-- i.e., got married

SONCOHO ISAMBI to plait a braid

SONCOHO MUTUKŪ the name of a plant that grows on rocks and on roofs (*Cotyledon japonica*)

SONCOHO ŠUKUMBI to glue on the holders for the bowstring

SONCOHOLOMBI 1. to plait a braid 2. to be odd

SONDA see *suwanda*

SONDURI a type of flowered yellow silk

SONGGIHA 1. the tip of the nose 2. a wooden nose hook for camels and cows 3. hook on a quiver to which a strap can be attached 4. catch on a bird trap

SONGGIN see *songgiha*

SONGGOBUMBI caus. of *songgombi*

SONGGOCOMBI to weep together

SONGGOCONOMBI to go to weep together

SONGGOMBI 1. to weep, to cry 2. to

cry loudly (of birds before rain)

SONGGOME FAMBI to weep bitterly (when parting)

SONGGOME FANCAMBI the same as *songgome fambi*

SONGGOTU a crybaby, a person who cries frequently

SONGKIYABUMBI see *suwangkiyabumbi*

SONGKO 1. trace, track, footprint 2. see also *songkoi*

SONGKO AKŪ without a trace

SONGKO BE BURUBUMBI to blot out one's tracks, to destroy the traces

SONGKO BENEMBI to reveal one's presence to the enemy hoping that they will retreat

SONGKO DE SONGKO first here then there, changeable

SONGKO FAITAMBI to follow the tracks (of a wounded animal)

SONGKO FULU good at seeking advantages for oneself

SONGKO I FAITAMBI the same as *songko faitambi*

SONGKO WALIYAMBI to leave tracks (in order to deceive the enemy)

SONGKOI (postposition) according to, in accordance with

SONGKOLOBUMBI caus. of *songkolombi*

SONGKOLOMBI to follow the tracks of, to follow in the tracks of, to imitate, to act in accordance with

SONGKŪ see *songko*

SONIHON odd (of numbers)

SONIHON MUDURINGGA SUWAYAN ŠUN DALIKŪ a round yellow parasol of the imperial escort

SONINGGA new, fresh

SONIO 1. odd (number) 2. odd numbered line of a hexagram of the *Book of Changes*

SONIO JURU odd and even

SONIO SABU a single shoe

SONIOHON see *sonihon*

SONJOBUMBI caus. of *sonjombi*

SONJOKU vulnerable (because of error), objectionable, criticizable

SONJOMBI to choose, to select for an official post after having passed the state examination

SONJOME ABALAMBI to select and kill the animals that have no young in springtime

SONJONDUMBI/SONJONUMBI to select together

SONJOSI (貢士) one who passed the Metropolitan examination (*acalame simnembi*)

SONOKDUN see *sonokton*

SONOKTON tassel on a helmet

SONOMBI to protrude the buttocks

SONTAMBI to fling away

S

SONTU CECIKE a small yellow bird with yellow lines over its eyes, a long tail, and yellowish feet

SOORILAMBI to enthrone

SOORIN throne, seat of honor

SOR SAR SEME in quantity, in profusion
SOR SAR SEME NIMARAMBI to snow in great quantity

SOR SEME many, in great quantity

SOR SIR SEME see *sor sar seme*

SORBO braid or string on the top of a hat

SORI SAHAMBI during a sacrifice, to make piles of nine flat round cakes on the altar

SORI YALI small pieces of meat used in sacrifices

SORIGANJAMBI to be shaken, to waver (in the face of power or authority)

SORIHA strips of cloth tied to a horse's mane and tail during a sacrifice

SORIHALAMBI to tie strips of cloth to a horse's mane and tail for a religious rite

SORIHANJAMBI see *soriganjambi*

SORIMBI 1. to kick (of horses), to paw the ground, to jump around 2. to be in disorder, to be confused
SORIHA SIRDAN arrows shot wildly

SORIN DEN running with the chest high (horses)

SORINDUMBI to be in total disarray, to be crisscrossed

SORKO thimble

SORO jujube

SOROBUMBI caus. of *sorombi*

SOROCOMBI 1. to be very sensitive and painful (of the skin and of embarrassing situations) 2. to be embarrassed

SOROKI taboo, tabooed
SOROKI AMBA strictly tabooed

SOROKIYA a wasp; cf. *dondoba*

SOROKU FUTA multicolored strings hung on a child's neck during a shamanistic rite

SOROMBI (-ho/-ko, -fi/-pi) 1. to turn yellow 2. to avoid as taboo, to shun
SOROME NIMERE NIMEKU jaundice; cf. *sohon nimeku*

SOROMBUMBI caus. of *sorombi*

SOROSU a variety of Chinese olive-- *Canarium Pimela*

SOROTU an exotic fruit resembling the sour jujube that is produced at a temple in Kansu

SORSON 1. tassel on a hat 2. the flowers of onions, scallions, and leeks

SORSONGGO pertaining to a tassel

SOSAMBI to capture (prisoners of war)

SOSANDUMBI/SOSANUMBI to capture together

SOSE see *sodz*

SOSOMBI to have a case of watery diarrhea

SOSORCOMBI to back up, to shrink back, to withdraw

SOSOROBUMBI caus. of *sosorombi*

SOSOROMBI (-ko) 1. to back up, to withdraw, to retreat 2. to wither, to become senile 3. to rake (grass)

SOTAMBI to strew about, to scatter around

SOTI one name for the parrot

SOTKI sea carp

SOYOMBI 1. to tie up livestock to allow them to dry off after having sweated from running 2. to draw in, to shrink 3. to train a riding horse

SOYON fed to a certain standard, fattened to a certain standard
SOYON ACABUHA the same as *soyon*
SOYON ACABUMBI to fatten to a certain standard, to feed a special diet in preparation for a race
SOYON ACAHA the same as *soyon*

SOYONGGŪ a sweating horse tied up so that it can dry off

SOYORI an exotic fruit about the size of a yellow plum

SU whirlwind
SU EDUN whirlwind
SU ORHO see *surho*

SUBADABUMBI caus. of *subadambi*

SUBADAMBI to jump about waving the hands and shouting

SUBARGAN see *subarhan*

SUBARHAN pagoda; cf. *sumarhan*

SUBARI a wooden tool for digging ginseng and other herbs

SUBCALU uneven in height (plants)

SUBDUNGGA see *sultungga*

SUBE tendon, nerve, muscle; cf. *ca*
SUBE HŪSIMBI to wrap with sinew (an arrow)
SUBE MAKTAMBI to wrap sinew (around a bow shaft)

SUBEHE 1. the end of a branch 2. the end of a hair from the beard 3. sash, girdle, cord, band, ribbon, mourning sash 4. cord for holding pearls or beads (for a ceremonial garment)

SUBELIYEN silk floss, silk fiber
SUBELIYEN HŪSIMBI to wrap with silk fiber
SUBELIYEN SORSON a tassel of silk floss

SUBERHE a bird used as bait in catching falcons

SUBERI a thin silken fabric with a glossy finish, damask

S

SUBETU sinewy, muscular
SUBETUNGGE one who is sinewy, muscular
SUBKEJEMBI to unravel (of silk)
SUBKELEMBI to unravel, to take silk floss from a spindle
SUBKERI a mourning garment with unsewn hems
SUBSI 1. chronic, persistent (of an illness) 2. trifling, insignificant, small
SUBSIN ILHA the name of a small fragrant exotic flower that grows on the end of small branches
SUBUHŪN sober, not drunk
SUBUMBI 1. caus. of *sumbi* 2. to put off, to remove 3. to absolve from guilt or blame 4. to explain, to comment on 5. to become sober, to recover from a drinking bout 6. to abort, to miscarry 7. to slake (one's thirst) 8. to soothe, to calm
SUBUN explanation, discussion, elucidation
SUBURI a sweet-tasting exotic fruit the size of a hen egg that is supposed to sober up a person who is drunk
SUCI fetus of an animal
SUCI SUMBI to miscarry (of an animal)
SUCILEMBI 1. to become pregnant (of animals) 2. to form ears (of grain)
SUCUMBI (-ha) to storm (the enemy's lines), to charge, to attack suddenly
SUCUN WEIHE the incisors
SUCUNAMBI to go to storm, to fly up, to soar upward
SUCUNGGA the first, initial, beginning
SUCUNGGA NADAN the first seven days after death
SUCUNJIMBI to come to storm, to come to charge
SUCUNUMBI to charge together, to storm together
SUCUTU a two-year-old horse
SUDALA 1. vein, artery, blood vessel 2. the geomantic veins of the earth
SUDALA JAFAMBI to take the pulse
SUDALAMBI to wear short hanging hair
SUDAMIMBI to remove the bit, to take out the bit (of livestock)
SUDAMU the temples
SUDAN 1. the hair at the temples of a woman 2. curly hair
SUDARA sutra
SUDERHEN a type of rice-colored skylark
SUDU shin, shinbone
SUDU NIRU an arrow without holes in its head
SUDULI 1. *Allium victorialis* 2. wild garlic

SUDULI ABDAHA FUKJINGGA HERGEN (蕊葉篆) a style of calligraphy
SUDURI history, chronicle, annal
SUDURI AMBAN annalist, historian
SUDURI BE ALIHA AMBAN (大史) historiographer
SUFAN elephant
SUFAN I WEIHE ivory
SUFAN I WEIHE SABKA ivory chopstick
SUFAN ILERI ILHA an exotic flower from Indochina that blooms at the end of winter whose leaves resemble the leaves of the jujube tree
SUFANGGA LUJEN an imperial ceremonial coach with a dome decorated with ivory that is drawn by eight horses
SUFEN Indian rhinoceros
SUHAI MOO the tamarisk--*Tamarix juniperus*
SUHARAMBI (-ka) to hang (of the head), to droop
SUHE 1. ax, halberd 2. gold and silver bars made of paper used as offerings for the dead
SUHE ARGACAN I FIYENTEN (斧鉞司) Halberd Section, BH 121
SUHE HOOŠAN gold and silver bars made of paper used as offerings for the dead
SUHE JURUTU an ancient official garment with axes depicted on it
SUHECEN small ax, hatchet
SUHELEMBI to split with an ax
SUHEN commentary on a classic
SUHENGGE pertaining to an ax, decorated with ax designs
SUHERI NIMENGGI the fragrant resin from the bark of the tree *Liquidambar orientalis*
SUHEŠEMBI to chop repeatedly with an ax
SUHUKEN ivory-colored
SUHUN very light yellow, cream-colored
SUHUN WENDERHEN an ivory-colored skylark
SUI 1. crime, transgression, sin, guilt 2. malevolent influence, evil
SUI AKŪ innocent, without guilt
SUI BOCO olive-green
SUI CECIKE kingfisher; cf. *ulgiyan cecike*
SUI ISIFI EHE DE ISINAME MAILAKINI an oath with the same meaning as *mailaru*
SUI ISIKA met with misfortune
SUI ISIRU an oath--may you meet with misfortune! miscreant!
SUI MANGGA guilt-ridden
SUI GUNG yearly tribute
SUIBUMBI caus. of *suimbi*

SUIFULEBUMBI caus. of *suifulembi*
SUIFULEMBI to bore (with an awl)
SUIFUN awl
SUIGA see *suiha*
SUIHA 1. artemisia, moxa 2. brush,
    overgrowth
    SUIHA CECIKE 'moxa bird'--the name
        of a small bird with brown back
        and sides and a white breast
    SUIHA FULAN a light gray horse
    SUIHA SINDAMBI to apply moxa, to
        cauterize with moxa
SUIHANA resembling artemisia
    SUIHANA WEHE a type of green stone
        with spots resembling the artemi-
        sia plant
    SUIHANA YARHA a leopard with spots
        resembling the leaves of the ar-
        temisia plant
SUIHE 1. an ear of grain 2. tassel,
    crest 3. end of a whip
    SUIHE ILHA the flower of knotweed
SUIHEN see *emu suihen i banjimbi*
SUIHENEMBI to put forth ears (grain)
SUIHETU having a tassel or crest
    SUIHETU COKO one name for the tur-
        key; cf. *nanggitu coko*
    SUIHETU FUKJINGGA HERGEN (穗書)
        the name of a style of calligraphy
    SUIHETU GASHA the same as *suihetu
        coko*
    SUIHETU GŪWASIHIYA one name for the
        egret; cf. *gūwasihiya*
SUIHON a deer-horn awl worn on the belt
    and used for untying knots
    SUIHON I UNCEHEN a final stroke in
        cursive Manchu script
SUIHUMBI to be rowdy when drunk
    SUIHUME LAIHŪDAME YABUMBI to behave
        offensively while intoxicated
SUIHUN a large earring used by men
SUIHUTU a rowdy drunk
SUIHŪN unnatural sexual act, sodomy
SUILABUMBI caus. of *suilambi*
SUILACUKA distressing, laborious, dif-
    ficult, agonizing
SUILACUN distress, labor, agony, hard-
    ship
SUILAMBI to be in distress, to suffer
    hardship, to be in agony, to be ex-
    hausted
SUILAN hornet
SUILASHŪN 1. burdensome, onerous, en-
    cumbering 2. distressed, afflicted
SUIMANGGA see *sui mangga*
SUIMBI (-he) 1. to grind ink 2. to
    mix (dough)
SUINGGA harmful, grievous, wicked, il-
    legal
    SUINGGA JUI son of a concubine
SUISIMBI (-ka) to suffer hardship or
    distress
SUISIRU the same as *sui isiru*: mis-

creant!
SUISIRUSA plural of *suisiru*
SUITABUMBI caus. of *suitambi*
SUITAKŪ a long vessel used for pouring
    libations
SUITAMBI to pour, to water (plants),
    to spill, to splash
SUJABUMBI caus. of *sujambi*
SUJAGAN see *sujahan*
SUJAHAN supporting pole, prop, support
SUJAKŪ a support, a grip
SUJAMBI 1. to prop up, to support 2.
    to push against, to resist, to be a
    match for
SUJANAMBI to push upward (of sprouts),
    to sprout while still underground
SUJANDUMBI to support one another, to
    resist one another
SUJE silk, silk material
    SUJE I NAMUN (緞疋庫) Silk
        Store, BH 77
SUJIKDE a sort of willow from which
    arrow shafts were made--*Salix
    gracilistyla*
SUJUBUMBI caus. of *sujumbi*
SUJUMBI (-ha) to run, to hasten, to
    rush
SUJUNAMBI to run thither
SUJUTEMBI to run together
SUK SEME INJEMBI to laugh while trying
    to remain serious, to laugh through
    the nose while trying to hold a
    straight face
SUKDEN MOO *Rhus cotinus*--a tree that
    grows in Szechuan whose leaves are
    used for making yellow dye
SUKDUHEN one name for the crane; cf.
    bulehen
SUKDUN 1. vapor, air, breath, gas
    2. vital fluid, spirit 3. air, as-
    pect, manner
    SUKDUN BE GIDAMBI to hold the
        breath
    SUKDUN CIRGABUMBI to hold the
        breath
    SUKDUN HŪWALIYASUN NESUKEN I MUDAN
        a piece of music played during
        a banquet given by the Board of
        War to a new military metropolitan
        graduate
    SUKDUN NIYECEBUMBI to nourish the
        vital vapors (of the body)
    SUKDUN TON fate
SUKDUNGGA pertaining to vapor, breath,
    etc.
SUKDUNGGI see *sukdungga*
SUKIYABUMBI caus. of *sukiyambi*
SUKIYAMBI to drain, to pour out com-
    pletely
    SUKIYAME OMIMBI to drink dry, to
        drink 'bottoms up'
SUKIYANGGA ILHA a carved or decorated
    piece of wood suspended in a gate;

S

cf. *bongko sukiyara duka*

SUKIYARI CECIKE loricula, the green lovebird of Taiwan

SUKJI the edible seed pods of the elm tree

SUKJIBUMBI caus. of *sukjimbi*

SUKJIBURE HIYAN a variety of fragrant purple incense

SUKJIMBI to offer, to present

SUKJINGGE BA the southwest corner of a house

SUKSAHA 1. thigh 2. hind leg of livestock

SUKSALABUMBI caus. of *suksalambi*

SUKSALAMBI to open up (new land), to open to cultivation, to clear (virgin land)

SUKSALANAMBI to go to open up for cultivation

SUKSALANDUMBI/SUKSALANUMBI to open to cultivation together

SUKSALANJIMBI to come to open to cultivation

SUKSAN newly opened land, land newly opened to cultivation

SUKSUBUMBI caus. of *suksumbi*

SUKSUHU fish hawk, osprey (*Pandion haliaetus*)

SUKSUHUN bristling (mad)

SUKSUKU see *suksuhu*

SUKSUMBI (-he) to winnow

SUKSUREKU a winnowing fan

SUKSUREMBI (-ke) 1. to swell, to become swollen 2. to shake out (a bird, of its feathers) 3. to strike prey (of birds of prey)

SUKU 1. tumbleweed 2. bushy, thick (of growth)

SUKU HAMGIYA overgrowth, brush, weeds

SUKŪ skin, hide, pelt

SUKŪ I JAKA WEILERE HAFAN (獸工) an official who was in charge of making leather goods in antiquity

SUKŪ I SOŠONGGO MAHALA an ancient-style hat made from deerskin

SUKŪ SOFORO a leather saddle cushion; cf. *soforo*

SUKŪNAMBI to form a skin, to develop a layer of skin

SUKŪNGGE LUJEN the name of a ceremonial carriage with a leather-covered dome

SULA 1. loose 2. idle, unoccupied, at leisure, free 3. incomplete 4. unemployed in an official capacity

SULA AMBAN (散秩大臣) Junior Assistant Chamberlain of the Imperial Bodyguard, BH 98

SULA BA empty land, wasteland

SULA BAISIN unemployed, at leisure

SULA BITHE novel, storybook, frivolous literature

SULA BOIHON loose soil

SULA GISUN idle talk, gossip

SULA HAFAN I USIN government land

SULA HAHA an idle laborer, non-quota man

SULA HEHE a household slave girl, female servant

SULA INENGGI a free day

SULA JANGGIN (散騎郎) the name of an officer in the Palace of a Prince of the Blood

SULA NIYALMA an idle person, man of leisure

SULA SAISA a scholar in private life

SULA SINDAMBI to put at ease

SULA UMIYESUN a loose belt without a clasp

SULABUMBI 1. caus. of *sulambi* 2. to leave free, to leave a little bit over, to leave remaining 3. to let hang 4. to let grow (the hair)

SULAHŪN one name for the river gull; cf. *ula kilahūn*

SULAKA see *sulakan*

SULAKAN 1. rather loose 2. rather free 3. rather idle 4. somewhat better (of an illness) 5. relieved, at ease

SULAMBI 1. to be left over, to remain behind, to be handed down 2. to be loose, to be free 3. to be idle 4. to awake from a cat nap

SULAHA DURSUN traditional character

SULAHA TACIN traditional custom

SULDARGAN one name for the kestrel; cf. *baldargan*

SULFA at leisure, leisurely, idle, free, at ease, without cares, loose

SULFAKAN rather leisurely, rather loose

SULFAMBI to be loose, to be slack

SULFANGGA relaxed, at ease, peaceful

SULHUMBI to be damp (of the earth)

SULKU a wooden or bamboo flower stand

SULTAHA the river gull; cf. *ula kilahūn*

SULTEI goral; cf. *imahū*

SULTUNGGA wise, sagacious

SUMALA a small bag

SUMALTU an Ethiopian marsupial

SUMAMBI (-ka) to spread out (of vapors and mist)

SUMAN vapors, mist

SUMARHAN pagoda--the same as *subargan*

SUMARI ALIN see *sumiri alin*

SUMARI CECIKE the name of the goatsucker in Szechuan; cf. *simari cecike*

SUMBI (1) (-he) 1. to take off, to remove 2. to shed (horns, of a deer) 3. to untie, to unhitch 4. to abort 5. to explain, to annotate

SUME ALAMBI to report giving an explanation

SUME BODOMBI to compute for report

SUME BODORO BOO (銷算房) Expenditure Section, BH 425

SUME EFULERE KUNGGERI (註鋪科) accounting department of the Court of Colonial Affairs

SUMBI (2) (-ngke, -mpi) 1. to freeze, to congeal 2. to whirl

SUMBULJAMBI to be soft (of wet ground)

SUMBUR SAMBAR SEME ragged, tattered

SUMBUR SEME the same as *sumbur sambar seme*

SUMBURŠAMBI to be in disarray (of troops)

SUMIRI ALIN Mount Sumeru (Buddhist)

SUMPA 1. having gray hair at the temples, graying 2. the name of a small plant that resembles artemisia SUMPA MACA wild leek

SUMPANAMBI to turn gray at the temples

SUMU see *jukden*

SUMUSU rice broth with a few kernels of rice left in it

SUN milk
SUN I CAI tea mixed with milk
SUN NIMENGGI butter
SUN SAMBI to milk

SUNA a leather leash for a dog; cf. *sūna*

SUNDALABUMBI caus. of *sundalambi*

SUNDALAMBI 1. to ride double on a horse 2. to give hot pursuit, to pursue 3. to take up a matter again after it has already passed

SUNEMBI to drip down, to fall (of rain), to condense (of clouds before the onset of rain)

SUNG EL the male sparrow hawk; the same as *ajige hiya silmen*

SUNGGADA the name of a freshwater fish with a red tail and red fins

SUNGGALI CECIKE North China nutcracker (*Nucifraga caryocatactes*)

SUNGGARI BIRA the Milky Way

SUNGGARI ULA the Sunggari River

SUNGGARTU USIHA the name of a star located south of the Milky Way

SUNGGELJEMBI to shake, to tremble

SUNGGELSON a red tassel that was attached to certain ancient-style hats

SUNGGEMBI to waste away, to grow skinny and pale

SUNGGILJAMBI see *sunggeljembi*

SUNGGIMBI see *sunggembi*

SUNGGINA a type of wild onion that grows in cold spots and on cliffs

SUNGGIYEN wise, enlightened

SUNGGUHE one name for the myna

SUNGKE congealed, shriveled up; cf. *sumbi* (2)

SUNGNIYAHA see *songgiha*

SUNJA five
SUNJA AKJANGGA KIRU a banner on which five symbols representing thunder appeared
SUNJA BAKTAKŪ the five organs-- liver, heart, spleen, lungs, and kidney

SUNJA BIYA the fifth month

SUNJA COLHON the five sacred mountains of China

SUNJA DOBON the five offerings that sit on the altar--an incense boat, two candlesticks, and two flower vases

SUNJA DZANG same as *sunja baktakū*

SUNJA ENTEHEME the five constants-- humaneness, loyalty, propriety, knowledge, and trust

SUNJA FETEN the five elements-- fire, water, wood, metal, and earth

SUNJA FETEN BE BODORO HAFAN (五官正) Astronomer, BH 229

SUNJA FETEN BE BODORO HAFAN I TINGGIN (五官廳) hall of the astronomers

SUNJA HACIN I JEKU the five grains-- rice, glutinous millet, common millet, wheat, and beans

SUNJA HACIN I OROBUHANGGE a sweet food made from dried pears, dried berries, barberry juice, cream, and honey

SUNJA HERGIN the five ordering principles--year, moon, sun, fixed stars, and planets

SUNJA IRUNGGE MAHATUN an ancient-style hat with five ridges on top

SUNJA JALAN GENGGIYESU a house slave of the fifth generation

SUNJA JILGAN the five notes of the Chinese pentatonic scale

SUNJA TUGINGGE KIRU a triangular shaped banner of the imperial escort in five colors embroidered with a cloud design

SUNJA TUHEBUKU I MAHATU a crown of ancient times that had five tassels hanging down from it

SUNJA YAMUN I KUNGGERI (五府科) an establishment charged with producing weapons and casting cannon for the provinces

SUNJACI fifth
SUNJACI JALAN I OMOLO a descendant of the fifth generation

SUNJANGGA pertaining to five
SUNJANGGA FAIDAN a battle rank of five men in antiquity
SUNJANGGA INENGGI the fifth day of the fifth month--the Dragon Boat Festival

SUNJANGGERI five times

SUNJARI comprised of five elements
SUNJARI ILHA an exotic flower that resembles the bloom of the pomegranate
SUNJARI SUJE satin woven in strips each consisting of five threads

SUNJATA five each

SUNJI one hundred-thousandth

S

SUNTA 1. a very small bag 2. a small
   net bag of meat tied to the waist of
   falconers--used for feeding falcons
SUNTAHA snowshoe, ski
SUNTALAMBI see *sundalambi*
SUNTAMBI see *suntembi*
SUNTANAMBI to be stuffed full, to be
   paunchy
SUNTEBUMBI caus./pass. of *suntembi*
SUNTEMBI to exterminate, to wipe out,
   to annihilate
SUNTO a measure equaling five small
   pecks
SUR SEME 1. sharp, fragrant, stimulat-
   ing to the olfactory nerves 2.
   gently (of laughing)
SURA see *suran*
SURABUMBI caus. of *surambi*
SURAFU an awl with a round handle
S'JRAFUN see *surafu*
SURAHA water in which rice has been
   rinsed--used as pig feed
SURAKŪ a pig trough
SURAMBI 1. to rinse (rice), to wash
   (rice) 2. to hawk goods in a loud
   voice
SURAN 1. water in which rice has been
   rinsed 2. flea
SURBEJEN the cutting edge of a knife
   or arrowhead
SURBU a cord for holding a hat on
SURE 1. wise, intelligent 2. prajna,
   wisdom (Buddhism) 3. chilled (of
   fruit)
   SURE HIYAN a variety of light brown
      incense
   SURE MAMA the goddess of smallpox
SUREKEN rather wise, intelligent
SUREMBI (1) (-he) to yell, to shout
SUREMBI (2) (-ke) to be wide awake,
   to wake up refreshed
SUREN wisdom, mind; cf. *sure*
SURENDUMBI to yell together
SURGI a smallpox pustule
   SURGI WERIHE left behind smallpox
      pustules
SURGIN damp, humid, warm and humid
SURHO goosefoot, pigweed
SURHŪN intelligence, understanding
   SURHŪN AKŪ lacking intelligence,
      lacking understanding, not bright
SURI silk cloth; cf. *cuse*
SURIHA withered up, dead (of trees)
SURSAN SURSAN intermittent (snow or
   rain)
SURSEN ORHO the name of a plant (排
   草)
SURSERI 'Buddha's hand,' a variety of
   citrus fruit that has the shape of
   five fingers held together--*Citrus
   medica*
SURTEBUMBI caus. of *surtembi*
SURTEMBI to race, to run
SURTENUMBI 1. to race together, to run
   a race together 2. to run in all

directions (of a group)
   SURTENUME BAIMBI to ask for without
      shame, to seek shamelessly
SURU white (horse)
   SURU MORIN a white horse
SURUDAI the phoenix of the west
SURUHŪN see *surhūn*
SURUMBI (-ke) to quiet down, to calm
   down
SURUMBUMBI caus. of *surumbi*
SUSAI fifty
   SUSAI NADAN GŪSA the fifty-seven
      Mongolian banners of Outer Mongo-
      lia
SUSAICI fiftieth
SUSAITA fifty each
SUSAKANGGE dead thing!--an oath
SUSAMBI (-ha/-ka) to die, to perish
SUSE 1. straw, hemp stalks, paper cord,
   etc. that is mixed into mortar or
   adobe 2. crude, coarse 3. trash
SUSEDEMBI to do crudely, to make
   coarsely
SUSERI 1. fennel (*Foeniculum vulgare*)
   2. coarse, worn down
   SUSERI HOOŠAN coarse paper
   SUSERI JIHA a worn-down copper coin
   SUSERI NENDEN ILHA the name of a
      yellow flower with long petals
      that wave in the wind and resemble
      butterflies
SUSU 1. home, birthplace 2. desolate,
   bleak, barren
SUSUBUMBI 1. caus. of *susumbi* 2. to
   lay waste, to ruin
SUSUKIYEMBI to shiver from the cold
SUSULTUNGGA intelligent, highly gifted,
   outstanding
SUSUMBI (-ha) to become desolate,
   bleak
SUSUNGGIYAMBI to ruin, to lay waste
SUTHA see *suntaha*
SUTUHŪN CECIKE one of the names of the
   hoopoe; cf. *indahūn cecike*
SUWA the North China sika, spotted
   deer (*Cervus nippon*)
   SUWA BUHŪ the same as *suwa*
   SUWA NASIN a large brown bear
      (*Ursus arctos*), especially one
      with a light yellow tinge
SUWABIRGAN 'yellow swallow'--the name
   of a bird
SUWAFINTU CECIKE Bohemian waxwing, the
   same as *taifintu cecike*
SUWAKIDUN CECIKE the name given by the
   people of Kiangnan to the crow-tit;
   cf. *kidun cecike*
SUWALIN CECIKE one name for the oriole;
   cf. *gūlin cecike*
SUWALIYA see *suwaliyan*
SUWALIYABUMBI caus./pass. of *suwali-
   yambi*
SUWALIYAGANJAMBI to mix up, to mix
   together
SUWALIYAHANJAMBI see *suwaliyaganjambi*

SUWALIYAMBI 1. to mix, to mix up, to blend together 2. to implicate, to mix up in an affair 3. to confuse, to get mixed up 4. to combine, to put together, to connect
  SUWALIYAME altogether, together with, jointly, mixed together, with, all at once, including . . .
SUWALIYAN mixing, mixture
SUWALIYASUN seasoning
  SUWALIYASUN ACABUMBI to add seasoning
SUWALIYATA mixed, blended
SUWALIYATAMBI to be mixed or blended
SUWAMPAN abacus; cf. *bodokū*
SUWAN 1. the inside of an oven-bed 2. cormorant (*Pholocrocorax carbo*)
SUWANDA garlic
SUWANDARA a type of wild cat with a yellow back, which in spite of its small size can catch tigers, cows, and deer
SUWANGKIYABUMBI caus. of *suwangkiyambi*
SUWANGKIYAMBI to graze (of cattle)
SUWANGKIYANDUMBI/SUWANGKIYANUMBI to graze together
SUWANPAN see *suwampan*
SUWASHA NIMAHA 'siskin fish'--so-called because in the tenth month the siskin is supposed to fly to the sea and there turn into this fish
SUWAYAKAN rather yellow, somewhat yellow
SUWAYAN 1. yellow 2. the fifth of the heaven's stems (戊)
  SUWAYAN BUMBI to make an offering of 'flour pigs' (a kind of yellow cake)
  SUWAYAN CECIKE the siskin
  SUWAYAN CESE BOO (黃 冊 房) office of census records
  SUWAYAN CIBIRGAN the same as *suwabirgan*
  SUWAYAN DANGSE BOO (黃 檔 房) Genealogical Record Office of the Imperial Clan Court, BH 74
  SUWAYAN ENGGE CECIKE hawfinch (*Eophona personata*)
  SUWAYAN FAITAN a type of quail with yellow stripes over the eyes
  SUWAYAN FAITANGGA CECIKE pseudo goldcrest (*Phylloscopus inornatus*)
  SUWAYAN GARUDAI a yellow phoenix
  SUWAYAN GIYAHŪN CECIKE chicken hawk
  SUWAYAN GŪSAI FALGA (黃 旗 甲) bureau of the yellow banner
  SUWAYAN GŪSAI FIYENTEN (黃 旗 司) section of the yellow banner
  SUWAYAN GŪSAI KUNGGERI (黃 旗 科) office of the yellow banner
  SUWAYAN HOŠONGGO GU a square jade tablet used during sacrifices to the earth
  SUWAYAN JUGŪN the ecliptic
  SUWAYAN JUGŪN I HETU UNDU I DURUNGGA

TETUN (黃 道 經 緯 儀) the name of an astronomical instrument in the observatory in Peking used for observing the discrepancies in the ecliptics of the sun, moon, and planets
  SUWAYAN KILTARI a yellow pennant of the imperial escort
  SUWAYAN KURINGGE GASHA a type of yellow speckled bird
  SUWAYAN MEIHETU yellow eel
  SUWAYAN NASINGGA KIRU (黃 羆 旗) a banner of the imperial escort embroidered with the figure of a bear
  SUWAYAN NENDEN ILHA 'wax plum'-- *Chimonanthus fragrans*
  SUWAYAN NOTHORI *Clausena Wampi*
  SUWAYAN OKTO medicine made from the root of *Coptis japonica*
  SUWAYAN SENGGIRI ILHA yellow azalea
  SUWAYAN SIŠARGAN golden linnet
  SUWAYAN SOLOHI weasel; cf. *solohi*
  SUWAYAN ŠERI 'the yellow springs'-- the underworld, Hades
  SUWAYAN TURI soybean
  SUWAYAN UHUMI yellow winding band used for wrapping the *niowanggiyan uju*
  SUWAYAN USERI an exotic yellow fruit that resembles a small pomegranate
  SUWAYAN YADANA a yellow swan
  SUWAYAN YADANANGGA KIRU (黃 鵠 旗) a banner of the escort embroidered with the figure of a yellow swan
  SUWAYAN YENGGEHE a yellow parrot
  SUWAYAN YENGGETU a small green parrot with a yellow neck and breast
SUWE you (plural)
SUWELEBUMBI caus. of *suwelembi*
SUWELEMBI 1. to search (for), to look for 2. see *seolembi*
  SUWELEME BAICARA HAFAN (搜 檢 官) an inspection officer, inspector
SUWELENDUMBI to search together
SUWELENEMBI to go to search
SUWELENJIMBI to come to search
SUWEMBE accusative form of *suwe*
SUWENCI ablative form of *suwe*
SUWENDE dative/locative form of *suwe*
SUWENI genitive of *suwe*
SUWENINGGE yours
SUYA kindling
SUYAMU a reed wrapped around the iron needle of a spinning wheel
SUYEN 1. shoe or boot strings 2. water that has been filtered through ashes, water that has been filtered through the malt used for making liquor
SŪNA see *suna*
SY (寺) a Buddhist temple
SYCUWAN (四 川) Szechuan

S

Š

ŠA 1. silk gauze, tulle; cf. *cece* 2.
a dense forest on the north side of
a mountain; cf. *šuwa* 3. one-bil-
lionth; cf. *libu*
   ŠA GECUHERI silk gauze decorated
      with figures of dragons
   ŠA JUWANGDUWAN gauze material that
      has gold threads worked into it
   ŠA MI a Buddhist novice
   ŠA MOO the common Chinese fir
   ŠA MOO MAHALA official's hat
   ŠA UNDURAKŪ silk gauze decorated
      with figures of prancing dragons
ŠAB SEME (onom.) the sound of an arrow
   grazing some object
ŠAB SIB SEME (onom.) the sound of many
   arrows being shot
ŠABAN a piece of leather with attached
   iron cleat that was tied to boots or
   shoes to assist in mountain climbing
   or walking on ice
ŠABARGAN GIDAMBI to cure a child's
   sickness by pressing a container of
   uncooked rice covered with a handkerchief against his body
ŠABI disciple, student
ŠABTUN a protective ear and cheek covering (military)
ŠABTUNGGA MAHALA a hat with ear flaps
ŠABURAMBI 1. to wait upon, to serve
   (a guest) 2. to take care of, to
   look after, to manage 3. to get
   sleepy; cf. *amu šaburambi*
ŠABURU AISIN white gold
ŠACAMBI to look in every direction, to
   be always looking to the side (of
   horses and cattle)
ŠACUN NIONGNIYAHA one name for the wild
   goose
ŠACUNGGA JAHŪDAI a flat-bottomed boat
ŠADA ILHA a fragrant flower that re-
   sembles the Mandala flower and is
   usually found in Buddhist monasteries
ŠADABUMBI caus. of *šadambi*
ŠADACUKA tiring
ŠADALI CECIKE the name of a small
   bird-- the same as the *wehe yadali*

cecike except that it has white
   stripes over the eyes
ŠADAMBI to become tired, to get weary
ŠADASHŪN rather tired
ŠADU FOYO *Cyperus rotundus*--a sedge
ŠAGU crabapple
ŠAHASI one name for the rhinoceros
ŠAHŪKAN having a whitish cast
ŠAHŪN 1. whitish, pale, dull white
   2. the eighth of the heaven's stems
   (辛)
   ŠAHŪN GŪWASIHIYA a white crane
   ŠAHŪN HORONGGO GU a round white
      jade tablet used during sacrifices
      to the moon
   ŠAHŪN HURUNGGE ALHACAN NIYEHE a
      speckled duck with a white back
   ŠAHŪN SAKSAHA a white magpie
ŠAHŪRABUMBI caus. of *šahūrambi*
ŠAHŪRAMBI (-ka, -pi) 1. to become cold
   2. to catch cold
ŠAHŪRUKAN somewhat cold, rather cold
ŠAHŪRUN cold
   ŠAHŪRUN EDUN a cold wind
   ŠAHŪRUN HALHŪN BULUKAN NECIN cold,
      hot, warm, normal--the four tem-
      peratures of traditional medicine
   ŠAHŪRUN INJEMBI to laugh sarcasti-
      cally
   ŠAHŪRUN SILENGGI 'cold dew'--one of
      the twenty-four divisions of the
      solar year falling on October
      eighth or ninth
   ŠAHŪRUN ŠERI a cold spring
ŠAJILAMBI to prohibit, to forbid
ŠAJILAN 1. birch wood 2. the name of
   a green worm with a hornlike pro-
   tuberance on its head
   ŠAJILAN I SIRDAN an arrow made from
      birch wood
ŠAJIN 1. prohibition, law 2. religion,
   dharma
   ŠAJIN I MUHEREN the wheel of the
      Law--sāṃsāra
   ŠAJIN YOO a red eruption on the
      skin that resembles a small straw-
      berry

SAJINGGA pertaining to prohibition,
   religious
   ŠAJINGGA AHŪN brother in a Buddhist
      or Taoist monastery
   ŠAJINGGA BELHESI see *belhesi*
   ŠAJINGGA DEO a young brother in a
      monastery
   ŠAJINGGA GASHA the Buddha bird,
      so called because its call re-
      sembles the word *mito* (Amitābha)
   ŠAJINGGA KARAN a platform used for
      Buddhist and Taoist services
ŠAJINTU another name for the mythical
   beast *tontu*
   ŠAJINTU MAHATUN an ancient-style
      hat with the figure of the *šajintu*
      depicted on it
ŠAJIRI GASHA Buddha bird--the same as
   šajingga gasha
ŠAJULAN see *šajilan*
ŠAK SEME tall and rank, towering and
   dense (trees)
ŠAK SIK 1. (onom.) rattling, tingling
   2. strong, vigorous (horses)
ŠAKA 1. a spear with a forked head, a
   fork 2. a leftward oblique stroke
   in writing
   ŠAKA BELHERE BA (備 杈 處)
      a place where punting poles, oars,
      and forked spears were prepared for
      imperial use
   ŠAKA I TOKOMBI to stick with a *šaka*
ŠAKALABUMBI caus./pass. of *šakalambi*
ŠAKALAMBI 1. to fork, to spear with a
   fork, to stick with a fork 2. to
   cut off (enemy troops) 3. to inter-
   rupt
ŠAKANAMBI to crack (of ice)
ŠAKARI a fork for fruit
ŠAKAŠABUMBI caus. of *šakašambi*
ŠAKAŠAMBI 1. to come in a very con-
   fused, mixed-up manner 2. to bom-
   bard a person with questions (of a
   group)
ŠAKŠAHA the cheek
   ŠAKŠAHA I GIRANGGI the cheekbone of
      a fish
   ŠAKŠAHA MAKTAMBI to lose face, to
      be embarrassed
   ŠAKŠAHA MEYEN wing (of an army)
   ŠAKŠAHA SELE two pieces of iron on
      a bridle that cover the cheeks of
      the animal
ŠAKŠAHALAMBI to attack from the flanks,
   to outflank
ŠAKŠAHŪN with the teeth showing
ŠAKŠALAMBI see *šakalambi* and *šakšaha-
   lambi*
ŠAKŠALJAMBI to smile showing the teeth
ŠAKŠAN crafty, cunning, wily
ŠAKŠARI smiling with the teeth showing
ŠAKŠARJAMBI the same as *šakšaljambi*
ŠAKTALAMBI to cut off the ears (as a
   punishment)
ŠALA 1. edge, end, extremity 2. flank,

side 3. remnant, scrap (of cloth);
   cf. *ujan šala* 4. corner, oblique
   angle, a lapel
ŠALA I NIYALMA a man in the wings
   (of an army)
ŠALANGTU a fat ox
ŠALAR SEME in good order, lined up
   evenly
ŠALHŪMA the white pheasant of the west
ŠALIBUMBI to become pale
ŠALU heated, hot
ŠAMBI (1) to look, to look at
ŠAMBI (2) (-ngka, -mpi) to cook dry,
   to drain dry
ŠAMPI breeching on a harness (the part
   of harness that runs under the tail)
   ŠAMPI MOO a horizontal piece of
      wood that hangs under the tail of
      a harnessed mule or donkey
   ŠAMPI UŠE a line connected to the
      breeching of a harness
ŠAMPILABUMBI caus. of *šampilambi*
ŠAMPILAMBI to put on the breeching of
   a harness
ŠAMTULAMBI to let down the protective
   ear flaps on a hat; cf. *šabtun*
ŠAN 1. ear 2. rowlock 3. pan of a
   flintlock or flash-vent of a cannon
   4. handle 5. shoehorn
   ŠAN DABUMBI to apportion a share
   ŠAN DASAKŪ an ear cleaner consist-
      ing of cotton or down on the end
      of a small stick
   ŠAN DERDEHUN the ears are curved
      forward
   ŠAN FETEKU an earpick
   ŠAN GABTAKŪ a support with holes
      on both sides that is attached to
      the main beam
   ŠAN I ABDAHA the outer part of the
      ear
   ŠAN I AFAHA the same as *šan i
      abdaha*
   ŠAN I DA the root of the ear
   ŠAN I DELBI the back of the ear
   ŠAN I FERE eardrum
   ŠAN I FETEKU the same as *šan feteku*
   ŠAN I HEŠEN the circumference of
      the ear
   ŠAN I OKTO gunpowder
   ŠAN I OKTOI KŪWACA a powderhorn
   ŠAN I SEN 1. a hole in the earlobe
      for an earring 2. hole for powder
      on a gun
   ŠAN I SUIHE earlobe
   ŠAN I UNGGALA the opening of the
      ear
   ŠAN KAMCIME BANJIHABI the ears grow
      flat against the head
   ŠAN MILA sharp-eared
   ŠAN SICAMBI the ears shake (from
      hearing a loud noise)
   ŠAN SULHUMBI the ear runs
   ŠAN WALIYAME listening attentively
ŠANCIN fortress, small fortress on a

Š

mountain, small town on a mountain

ŠANCIN FEKUMBI to storm a fortress

ŠANDUMBI to look at one another

ŠANG 1. bestowal, reward 2. see *šangsin*

ŠANG KORO reward and punishment

ŠANGGA endowed with ears

ŠANGGA CIRKU a pillow with earlike projections on the side

ŠANGGABUDA dried cooked rice

ŠANGGABUMBI caus. of *šanggambi*

ŠANGGAMBI 1. to come to an end, to terminate successfully, to finish 2. to be accomplished

ŠANGGAHA BITHEI NIYALMA an accomplished scholar

ŠANGGAHA DORO success

ŠANGGAHA GEBU honor, well-deserved renown

ŠANGGAHA GUNGGE merit, feats

ŠANGGAME JABDUHA succeeded, successfully terminated

ŠANGGAN completion, accomplishment, accomplished

ŠANGGAN I ELIOI one of the six minor pipes (music)

ŠANGGATAI 1. finally, indeed, actually 2. fully at an end, thoroughly completed

ŠANGGIN the silver pheasant; cf. *šunggin gasha*

ŠANGGIYAKAN rather white, somewhat white

ŠANGGIYAKŪ 1. smoke from a signal fire, smoke signal 2. see *šanggiyari*

ŠANGGIYAKŪ DABUMBI 1. to send up signal smoke 2. to make smoke to ward off insects

ŠANGGIYAMBI to smoke

ŠANGGIYAN 1. (white) smoke 2. white 3. the seventh of the heaven's stems (庚); cf. *šanyan*

ŠANGGIYAN ALAN white birchbark

ŠANGGIYAN BULEHEN white crane

ŠANGGIYAN CAISE deep-fried vermicelli made from salt water and flour

ŠANGGIYAN FAHA the white part of the eyeball

ŠANGGIYAN FEKŠUN alum

ŠANGGIYAN FULHA white poplar

ŠANGGIYAN HALU I SACIMA a deep-fried cake made from sesame oil, fine flour, sugar, and sesame seeds

ŠANGGIYAN IJA a variety of small white gnat, sandfly

ŠANGGIYAN JIYOO BING a baked cake made from sugar and flour

ŠANGGIYAN MURSA Chinese radish, daikon

ŠANGGIYAN NIONGNIYAHA a wild goose that appears white in flight

ŠANGGIYAN NISIHA a small whitefish

ŠANGGIYAN SELBETE white mugwort-- *Artemisia lactiflora*

ŠANGGIYAN SILENGGI 'white dew'-- one of the twenty-four divisions of the solar year occurring on about the eighth of September

ŠANGGIYAN SUIHA white artemisia

ŠANGGIYAN TEIŠUN zinc; cf. *šanyan teišun*

ŠANGGIYAN ULHU ermine; cf. *šanyan ulhu*

ŠANGGIYARI smoke used for warding off insects

ŠANGGUHE one name for the myna

ŠANGKA 1. silk gauze flaps on both sides on an ancient-style hat 2. halo around the sun 3. thinly sliced dried meat; cf. *šangkan*

ŠANGKA ŠOMBI to rub vigorously with a copper coin that has been moistened--a method of treating certain diseases

ŠANGKA ŠUFATU an ancient-style hat with gauze flaps on either side

ŠANGKAN dried meat, some dried product

ŠANGKAN NIMAHA the same as *can nimaha*

ŠANGKŪRA NIONGNIYAHA graylag goose (*Anser anser*)

ŠANGNABUMBI caus./pass. of *šangnambi*

ŠANGNAHAN reward, prize

ŠANGNAMBI to reward, to bestow

ŠANGNAN reward, bestowal

ŠANGSI ENDURI the name of a deity sacrificed to in the shamanic shrine

ŠANGSIN one of the notes of the classical pentatonic scale, sounding like *re*

ŠANGŠAHA a basket made from willow branches

ŠANGŠANGDEO the bird kalavinka (*Cuculus melandoicus*)

ŠANIORI ILHA an exotic flower that blooms in autumn and resembles a wild goose in flight

ŠANIRI ILHA 'white caltrop flower'

ŠANIYA hempen floss, used for padding

ŠANIYALAMBI to pad (with hempen floss)

ŠANIYAMBI see *šaniyalambi*

ŠANIYAHA HUBTU a long gown padded with hempen floss

ŠANIYANGGA made from hempen floss, padded

ŠANIYANGGA ETUKU clothing padded with hempen floss, clothing made from linen

ŠANIYANGGA MAHATU an ancient-style hat made from black grass linen

ŠANJIN tradesman, merchant

ŠANTU 1. heelbone of cows 2. zinc; cf. *šanyan teišun*

ŠANTU GIRANGGI the same as *šantu*

ŠANUMBI to look at one another; cf. *šandumbi*

ŠANYAKAN rather white, somewhat white

ŠANYAN 1. white 2. the seventh of the heaven's stems (庚) 3. the hottest period of the summer; cf.

Š

šanggiyan
ŠANYAN ALAN   white birchbark
ŠANYAN BULEHEN   white crane; cf.
  šeyelhen
ŠANYAN CAISE   the same as *šanggiyan*
  caise
ŠANYAN DOSIMBI   to enter the hottest
  period of summer
ŠANYAN FAITAN   a quail with a white
  stripe over the eyes
ŠANYAN FATHA   one name for the quail;
  cf. *mušu*
ŠANYAN GAHA   a white raven
ŠANYAN GARUDAI   a white phoenix
ŠANYAN GINCIHIYAN ŠUGIN   white lac-
  quer
ŠANYAN GŪSAI FALGA (白旗甲)
  bureau of the white banner in the
  Board of War
ŠANYAN GŪSAI FIYENTEN (白旗司)
  section of the white banner
ŠANYAN HAKSANGGA EFEN   a baked cake
  covered with sugar; cf. *šanggiyan*
  jiyoo bing
ŠANYAN HALU I SACIMA   the same as
  šanggiyan halu i sacima
ŠANYAN IJA   a small white gnat, a
  sandfly
ŠANYAN KONGGOLO   one name for the
  quail
ŠANYAN KUWECIHE   a white dove
ŠANYAN MEIHETU   white eel
ŠANYAN MURSA   Chinese radish, daikon
ŠANYAN NISIHA   a small freshwater
  fish with white belly whose oil is
  used in lamps
ŠANYAN SAMSU   a fine white linen
ŠANYAN SELBETE   white mugwort--
  Artemisia lactiflora
ŠANYAN SENCEHE   one name for the
  quail
ŠANYAN SILENGGI   the same as *šang-*
  giyan silenggi
ŠANYAN SIŠARGAN   the name of a small
  black bird with white spots
ŠANYAN SUIHA   white artemisia, wild
  artemisia
ŠANYAN SUKSUHU   a white sea swallow
ŠANYAN ŠAHŪN   the Milky Way
ŠANYAN ŠONGKON   a white gyrfalcon;
  cf. *šongkon*
ŠANYAN ŠOŠONTU   an ancient-style
  head covering made from white silk
ŠANYAN ŠUNGKERI BAIBULA   the name of
  the paradise flycatcher in Kiang-
  nan
ŠANYAN TASHA   a white tiger
ŠANYAN TASHANGGA KIRU   a banner of
  the imperial escort depicting the
  figure of a white tiger
ŠANYAN TEIŠUN   zinc
ŠANYAN ULHU   ermine, stoat (*Mustela*
  erminea)
ŠANYAN ULHŪMA   a white pheasant
ŠANYAN ULHŪMANGGA KIRU   a banner of

the imperial escort depicting the
  figure of a white pheasant
ŠANYAN UMIYAHA   a tapeworm
ŠANYAN WEIFUTU   a white heron
ŠANYAN YARHA   a white panther
ŠANYANGGA CECE   a white silk gauze
ŠANYO   yam; cf. *larsenda*
ŠAR SEME   sympathetic, moved with
  sympathy, compassionate
  ŠAR SEME GOSIRE MUJILEN   a sympathet-
    ic, loving heart, compassionate
    heart
ŠARA   exceedingly
  ŠARA FANCAHA   exceedingly annoyed
  ŠARA NIMEMBI   to ache exceedingly
ŠARA YOO   a red eruption on the skin
ŠARAMBI (-ka, -pi)   to become white
ŠARHŪMBI   to snow while the sun is
  shining dimly
ŠARI   1. a kind of wild lettuce with
  edible leaves and roots   2. bright,
  shining
  ŠARI GARI   bright, snowy white
  ŠARI SELE   red-hot iron
  ŠARI SIRI   gorgeous, splendid,
    brilliant (of blossoms)
  ŠARI SOGI   see *šari*
  ŠARI ŠARI   bright, fresh and bright,
    glowing
ŠARIBUDARI   Šāriputra
ŠARIBUMBI   caus. of *šarimbi*
ŠARIL   Buddhist relics
ŠARIMBI   to smelt (iron), to refine
ŠARINGGA DABTANGGA LOHO   a steel sword
ŠARINGGIYABUMBI   caus. of *šaringgiyambi*
ŠARINGGIYAMBI   1. to clean, to scrape
  clean (arrow-shaft)   2. to expiate,
  to atone, to wipe out (a wrong or
  shame)
ŠARINJAMBI   to squint, to look while
  rolling the eyeballs
ŠARIŠAMBI   to flash white, to light up
ŠARTAN   a tall tree with few branches
ŠARU   strips of dried raw meat
ŠARUK   the name of the myna in Buddhist
  scriptures
ŠASIGAN   see *šasihan*
ŠASIHALABUMBI   caus./pass. of *sasiha-*
  lambi
ŠASIHALAMBI   to slap, to clap
ŠASIHAN   soup, seasoned soup, broth
ŠASIHAŠAMBI   to slap repeatedly
ŠASINJIMBI   see *šašanjambi*
ŠASIŠAME DAMBI   to blow from the side
  (of the wind), to cut (of the wind)
ŠAŠABUMBI   caus./pass. of *šašambi*
ŠAŠAJAMBI   see *šašanjambi*
ŠAŠAMBI   to be mixed up, to be in a
  mess
ŠAŠAN   a sour soup made from bean
  paste and mixed vegetables
ŠAŠANJAMBI   to be confused, to be criss-
  crossed, to skirmish
  ŠAŠANJAME LEOLEMBI   to carry on a
    verbal skirmish, to debate

Š

ŠAŠUN 1. tinder, small pieces of wood used to start a fire 2. shred, piece 3. meat or fish paste
  ŠAŠUN AKŪ soft, soggy, in shreds, in tatters, in pieces, in a pulp
  ŠAŠUN AKŪ MEIJEBUHE shattered to pieces
ŠAŠUNAKŪ see *šašun aku*
ŠATAN sugar
  ŠATAN UFA CAI tea mixed with sugar and flour
ŠATUBUMBI caus. of *šatumbi*
ŠATUMBI to polish, to scour
  ŠATURE OKTO a polishing compound
ŠATURNAMBI to form an icy crust (on snow)
ŠAYO vegetarian, a Buddhist, a Taoist
ŠAYOLAMBI to abstain from meat, to keep a vegetarian diet
ŠAYU see *šayo*
  ŠAYU BUDA vegetarian food
ŠE 1. amnesty 2. the earth god 3. a Chinese psaltery, an instrument of twenty-five strings 4. a name for the black-eared kite; cf. *hiyebele*
ŠEBEN a snare for lynx
ŠEBNIO (參) the constellation Orion
  ŠEBNIO TOKDONGGO KIRU a banner depicting the constellation Orion
ŠEBTEMBI to be soaked through, to become soaked
ŠEHUKEN rather barren
ŠEHUN barren, empty, forsaken
  ŠEHUN ŠAHŪN barren and desolate
ŠEJILEBUMBI caus. of *šejilembi*
ŠEJILEMBI to recite, to repeat by heart
ŠEKEBUMBI caus./pass. of *šekembi*
ŠEKEMBI 1. to drench, to get soaked 2. to become stiff
ŠELBORI ORHO hellebore
ŠELEMBI 1. to part with, to give up 2. to give (alms), to distribute
ŠELEN the continually wet area around a small spring
ŠELETEI without regard to life, disregarding danger
ŠEMPI green grained leather
ŠEMPILEBUMBI caus. of *šempilembi*
ŠEMPILEMBI to hem with (green) grained leather
ŠENG 1. a wind instrument consisting of a number of small pipes with metallic reeds 2. a Chinese pint (升) 3. nephew
ŠENGGE 1. divine, prophetic 2. prophet, seer
  ŠENGGE SAKSAHA prophetic magpie that announces joyful events beforehand by its cry
ŠENGGECI ILHA the name of a beautiful exotic flower that blooms from spring to autumn
ŠENGGEHEN one name for the crane; cf.

bulehen
ŠENGGEN MOO a five-hundred-year-old tree
ŠENGGETU the name of a divine beast that foresees the future
ŠENGGETUNGGE KIRU a banner of the imperial escort that depicts the figure of a *šenggetu*
ŠENGGIN 1. forehead 2. the place where the foot of a mountain and a river meet 3. a brick that projects forward above the door of a stove
  ŠENGGIN GAIMBI to hit lightly on the forehead, to tap on the forehead
  ŠENGGIN HETEREMBI to knit the brow
ŠENGGINTU an ancient-style headband, square in shape and decorated with lacquer and gold
ŠENGGIYEN BOSO undyed cloth
ŠENGKIRI yarrow
ŠENGKITU one of the names of the fabulous beast called *tontu*
ŠENGSIN geomancy
  ŠENGSIN I SIREN a geomantic vein
  ŠENGSIN TUWAMBI to practice geomancy
  ŠENGSIN TUWARA NIYALMA a geomancer
ŠENTU a wide cloth belt, a strip of cloth
ŠENTUHEN see *šetuhen*
ŠEO BEN a name card presented by inferiors to superiors
ŠEO GIOWAN a scroll
ŠEO SEME DAMBI to blow in sharp gusts
ŠEO SING ENDURI the god of the star of long life
ŠEO ŠA (onom.) the sound made by the wind blowing
ŠEO ŠEO in gusts
ŠEO TEO a mask in the shape of an animal's head
ŠEOBEI (守備) Second Captain; cf. *tuwakiyara hafan*
ŠEOLEBUMBI caus. of *šeolembi*
ŠEOLEHUN see *šulehen*
ŠEOLEMBI 1. to embroider 2. to collect
ŠEOLEN BOJIRI ILHA the name of a ragged purple chrysanthemum
ŠEOTEO see *šeo teo*
ŠERCEMBI to feel dizzy on a height, to feel frightened on a high place
ŠEREBUMBI caus. of *šerembi*
ŠEREMBI (-ke) 1. to glow, to be red-hot 2. to be white, to be pale
ŠEREMBUMBI caus. of *šerembi*
ŠERENTUMBI to suffer labor pains before childbirth
ŠERHE a dog sled
ŠERI spring, source
ŠERIBUMBI caus./pass. of *šerimbi*
ŠERIKULEBUMBI to be intimidated, to

Š

be coerced

ŠERIMBI to extort, to blackmail, to
    threaten, to coerce

ŠERIN 1. a protective piece for the
    forehead on a helmet 2. a golden
    figure of a Buddha on the front of
    a prince's hat

ŠERINGGIYEMBI to heat until red-hot

ŠERINJU a blackmailer, intimidator

ŠERSEN INGGALI the name of a small bird
    that has white spots on its tail

ŠERTU a die made of copper or tin, a
    copper or tin *gacuha*

ŠESIMBI see *šešembi*

ŠESIMPE see *šešempe*

ŠESIMPU see *šešempe*

ŠEŠEBUMBI caus. of *šešembi*

ŠEŠEMBI to sting (of insects)

ŠEŠEMPE a wasp

ŠEŠERI UMIYAHA a centipede

ŠETEHURI dense, solid, thick

ŠETEREMBI (-ke) to come to life (of
    drooping plants after a rain)

ŠETERŠEMBI to reel under a heavy load

ŠETUHEN a twenty-five stringed zither-
    like instrument, a Chinese psaltery;
    cf. *še*

ŠETUMBI to swim (of snakes)

ŠEYEHEN ULHŪMA silver pheasant; cf.
    šunggin gasha

ŠEYEKE female rubythroat (*Luscina cal-
    liope*)

ŠEYEKEN rather white, somewhat white

ŠEYELHEN a type of small white crane

ŠEYEN snow-white
    ŠEYEN GU white jade
    ŠEYEN HIYABAN white coarse linen

ŠI 1. a measure equaling one hundred
    twenty catties 2. poem, verse 3.
    army 4. examination 5. scholar,
    official

ŠICING celadonite

ŠIDU (侍讀) see *adaha hūlara
    hafan*

ŠIDZ 1. the heir to a feudal lord
    2. the eldest son of a Manchu prince
    of the first rank

ŠIFU see *sefu*

ŠIGIYAMUNI Śākyamuni

ŠIGIYANG (侍講) a Hanlin official
    of the fifth rank second class

ŠILGIYAN (室) the name of a constel-
    lation
    ŠILGIYAN TOKDONGGO KIRU a banner
        depicting the constellation
        šilgiyan

ŠILIO pomegranate; cf. *useri*
    ŠILIO MOO pomegranate tree

ŠO bureau, office

ŠO NIYECEN the crotch of trousers

ŠOBIN a baked sesame cake

ŠOBKOŠOMBI 1. to eat with the hands
    2. to behave uncouthly, to act

meanly or basely

ŠOBKOŠOME DERAKŪ shameless

ŠOBKOŠOME JEMBI to eat with the
    fingers

ŠOBUMBI caus. of *šombi*

ŠODAN ILHA Chinese peony (*Paeonia
    albiflora*)

ŠODOBUMBI caus. of *šodombi*

ŠODOKŪ 1. a person who likes to stroll
    2. a small fishnet

ŠODOMBI 1. to stroll, to stroll about
    at one's leisure 2. to catch fish
    in a small hand net 3. to go at a
    full gallop 4. to pan (gold)

ŠOFOR SEME in great haste, flustered,
    agitated

ŠOFORO 1. five fingers full, a pinch
    2. one ten-thousandth of a bushel
    ŠOFORO AKŪ not sure-footed (of
        horses)
    ŠOFORO CECIKE one name for the
        kingfisher; cf. *ulgiyan cecike*
    ŠOFORO SAIN sure-footed (of a
        horse)

ŠOFOROBUMBI caus. of *šoforombi*

ŠOFOROKŪ SELE an anchor

ŠOFOROMBI 1. to pick up with the fin-
    gers, to pinch, to take a pinch of
    2. to seize in the claws (of birds)
    3. to scratch

ŠOFORONJIMBI to come to take a pinch
    of, to come to seize

ŠOFORŠOMBI to scratch all over, to
    take random pinches of

ŠOFOYON narrow-minded, quick-tempered

ŠOGE ingot of gold or silver

ŠOHADAMBI 1. to hitch up, to harness
    2. to depend on others to do one's
    work

ŠOHAN I MORIN a team of (four) horses

ŠOHO the white of an egg

ŠOKIN NIYEHE one name for the wild
    duck

ŠOKISILAMBI see *šokšolimbi*

ŠOKŠOHON 1. sharp (of a mountain peak),
    prominent (of a peak) 2. pursed
    (the lips, when angry), pouting

ŠOKŠOLIMBI to heap up, to fill up
    completely

ŠOKŪ a currycomb
    ŠOKŪ AMDUN glue made into squares
        used for erasing or scraping

ŠOLEN see *šošon*

ŠOLI falling short, short of the mark

ŠOLO 1. free time, leisure, vacation,
    leave 2. opportunity 3. empty
    space
    ŠOLO AKŪ without leisure, lacking
        free time, busy
    ŠOLO AMCAMBI to take advantage of
        an opportunity
    ŠOLO BAIMBI to ask for leave, to
        seek free time

Š

ŠOLO BE TUWAME as time permits
ŠOLO JABDURAKŪ not to have time
ŠOLO TUCIBURAKŪ without giving a
   pause
ŠOLOBUMBI caus. of *Šolombi*
ŠOLOMBI to roast
ŠOLON fork, skewer, small forklike
   projection on a knife
ŠOLONGGO 1. pointed, forked 2. point,
   tip 3. adept (at war, hunting,
   archery), out in front (of one's
   competitors at war, hunting, etc.)
ŠOLONGGO MAFUTA a two-year-old deer
ŠOLONGGO SACIKŪ a pickax used for
   digging in frozen or very hard soil
ŠOLONTU a small-horned dragon
ŠOLONTU COHORO a spotted horse with
   pointed ears
ŠOMBI (-ha) 1. to scrape, to scrape
   off, to level off 2. to curry (live-
   stock)
ŠONGGE INENGGI the first day of the
   month (lunar)
ŠONGGON see *Šongkon*
ŠONGKON the peregrine falcon (*Falco
   peregrinus*)
   ŠONGKON GASHA another name of the
      Šongkon
   ŠONGKON IJA a thin-waisted insect
      somewhat longer than a sandfly
      that catches flies
ŠONGKORO another name for the *Šongkon*
ŠONUMBI to scrape together, to curry
   together
ŠOO KUMUN a piece of music of eight
   strophes that was played while the
   emperor returned to the palace or
   went to the throne room
ŠOOBOO (少保) Junior Guardian,
   BH 943
ŠOOFU (少傳) Junior Tutor--an
   honorary title bestowed on merito-
   rious officials, BH 943
ŠOOGE hard feathers at the tips of the
   wings
ŠOOHA heavy rope, hawser; cf. *gūsu*
ŠOOŠI (少師) Junior Preceptor--
   an honorary title bestowed on merito-
   rious officials, BH 943
ŠOR SEME briskly, lively, noisily
   ŠOR SEME AGAMBI to rain noisily
ŠOR ŠAR (onom.) the sound of a storm,
   the sound of wind and rain
ŠOR ŠOR SEME (onom.) rushing, roaring
ŠORDAI the concave side of a *gacuha*
ŠORGIBUMBI caus./pass. of *Šorgimbi*
ŠORGIKŪ a drill
ŠORGIMBI 1. to urge, to press 2. to
   drill, to bore 3. to strike in one
   place (of arrows) 4. to wash out,
   to wash away
   ŠORGIME GAIMBI to exact payment (of
      a debt)

ŠORGINAMBI to go to urge
ŠORGINDUMBI/ŠORGINUMBI to urge to-
   gether
ŠORGINJIMBI to come to urge
ŠORHO chick
ŠORI a straw container for holding
   rice
ŠORIMBI to oppress (of heat)
   ŠORIME HALHŪN oppressively hot
ŠORO a basket made of bamboo or small
   branches
   ŠORO SELE a small knife without a
      scabbard worn at the belt
ŠORON the young of pheasants, ducks,
   and geese
ŠORONGGO DALANGGA a dam consisting
   of rock-filled baskets
ŠOSIHI see *Šosiki*
ŠOSIKI 1. quick-tempered, irascible
   2. chipmunk (*Eutamius sibiricus*)
ŠOSIN 1. a door catch 2. catch on a
   fodder knife
ŠOSITUN the North China mole
ŠOŠOBUMBI caus. of *Šošombi*
ŠOŠOHON 1. total, sum 2. summa, com-
   pilation, outline
   ŠOŠOHON TON total number
ŠOŠOKŪ knots of hair worn by children
   on both sides of the head, the
   chignon worn by women that was often
   adorned with gold and silver orna-
   ments
ŠOŠOMBI 1. to add together, to add up,
   to pull together 2. to make a chignon 3. to defecate (of falcons,
   eagles, etc.)
ŠOŠON 1. chignon, bun 2. falcon or
   eagle feces
   ŠOŠON I WEREN an ornament made of
      wire worn by Manchu women in their
      hair
ŠOŠONGGO MAHALA an ancient-style hat
   worn to keep a hairdo in order
ŠOŠOSI petty officer in charge of a
   depository or warehouse
ŠOYOBUMBI caus. of *Šoyombi*
ŠOYOMBI to shrink, to wrinkle
ŠOYOSHŪN rather wrinkled, rather
   shrunken
ŠU 1. literature, culture, education,
   learning 2. office, bureau 3.
   younger brother of one's father 4.
   experienced, adept 5. splendid,
   magnificent, well-ordered, beautiful
   6. edible plants 7. saltpeter 8.
   lotus; cf. *Šu ilha*
   ŠU AKŪ uncultured, uneducated
   ŠU BE BADARAMBURE TEMGETU a stand-
      ard of the imperial escort with
      words *Šu be badarambure* written on
      it
   ŠU BITHE a vow written on yellow
      paper that was read before a deity

Š

and then burned

ŠU ERDEMU education, enlightenment

ŠU FIYELEN essay, article

ŠU GENGGIYEN cultured and enlightened

ŠU GI ŠI (庶 吉 士) see
geren giltusi

ŠU I BELHEKU writing materials--
paper, brush, and ink

ŠU I ICIHIYAKŪ (署 正) President of the Court of Banqueting

ŠU I SUHEN commentary

ŠU I SUIHON I BITHE ICIHIYARA KUREN
(文 穎 館) an office in
charge of compiling literary anthologies

ŠU I TEMGETU a private seal

ŠU ILHA lotus (Nelumbo nucifera)

ŠU ILHAI DA lotus root (edible)

ŠU ILHAI HITHA seed pod of a lotus

ŠU ILHAI OMO lotus pond

ŠU IMIYAHA TANGGIN (聚 奎 堂)
the name of a two-storied hall in
the Examination Halls

ŠU JAMURI ILHA a type of hedgerose
that resembles the lotus

ŠU TACIN cultured ways or habits,
culture, education

ŠU YANGSANGGA well-ordered and
beautiful

ŠU YANGSE elegant, comely

ŠU YANGSE GEMUN HECEN DE WESIHUN
OJORO MUDAN musical composition
played while the emperor attended
a banquet for the Hanlin academy

ŠU ŽIN (碩 人) beautiful woman

ŠUBAN petty clerk, scribe

ŠUBASA plural of šuban

ŠUBEREMBI see siberembi

ŠUBUREMBI (-ke) 1. to wilt in the sun
2. to go bad (of a horse's hoof)

ŠUBURI timid, retiring

ŠUBURŠEMBI 1. to be timid, to fear to
put oneself forward, to be shrinking,
to be docile 2. to be solicitous
about children

ŠUCERI ILHA an exotic purple flower
that blooms in the fourth month

ŠUCI one who pretends to know what he
in fact doesn't

ŠUCILEMBI to pretend to know something
that in fact one doesn't, to feign
knowledge

ŠUDACAN YALI pieces of meat and fat
roasted together on a skewer

ŠUDANGGA COKO one name for the chicken

ŠUDEHEN see sidehun

ŠUDEMBI to slander, to calumniate

ŠUDESI a scribe, a secretary, a clerk

ŠUDESI BE BAICARA KUNGGERI (典
史 科) section of clerks in
the Board of Civil Appointments

ŠUDESI BE KADALARA KUNGGERI (都

吏 科) section in charge of
clerks in the Boards of Civil Appointments, Works, and War

ŠUDESI ORON I KUNGGERI (書 缺 科)
section of clerks in the Board of
Works

ŠUDU 1. fodder bean 2. see šudun

ŠUDU ERIKU broom

ŠUDUBUMBI caus./pass. of šudumbi

ŠUDUKŪ a weeding hoe

ŠUDUMBI (-ha) 1. to shovel 2. to
scrape smooth, to level off 3. to
scratch, to abrade 4. to weed

ŠUDURE JAHŪDAI a boat used for
carrying off sludge from dredging

ŠUDUN scraping, shoveling

ŠUDUN I WEIHE the front teeth

ŠUDURAN ILHA a small exotic yellow
flower that blooms at the end of
spring

ŠUDZ (庶 子) Deputy Supervisor of
Instruction, BH 929

ŠUFA 1. handkerchief (sometimes with a
fringe on two sides) 2. in the
older language, šufa meant head covering, turban; cf. šufari, šufatu

ŠUFABUMBI caus./pass. of šufambi

ŠUFAMBI 1. to bite, to sting (of insects) 2. to take an equal portion,
to take an equal share, to put in an
equal share

ŠUFAN wrinkle, crease, fold

ŠUFAN JAFAMBI to get creased, to
get wrinkled

ŠUFANAMBI to crease, to fold, to be
wrinkled

ŠUFANGGA SALU a full beard

ŠUFARI a head wrapping used by women

ŠUFASU a hairnet worn under a hat
(ancient style)

ŠUFATU a cloth head covering, a turban

ŠUFIN flour made from lotus root

ŠUFUR SEME (onom.) hissing, whizzing

ŠUFURŠEMBI see fusur seme

ŠUFUYEN see šofoyon

ŠUGI fluid, clear juice, clear discharge, vital fluid of the body,
extract

ŠUGILEBUMBI caus. of šugilembi

ŠUGILEMBI to apply lacquer

ŠUGIN 1. (liquid) lacquer, paint 2.
hand towel

ŠUGIN DOSIMBUHA ILETU KIYOO a gold-lacquered open sedan chair

ŠUGIN MOO the lacquer tree--Rhus
vernicifera

ŠUGINGGE HASI a variety of wild persimmon

ŠUGIRI HIYAN the tree Pistacia lentisens from which a type of pseudo-lacquer is made

ŠUGURI see šuhuri

ŠUHI see šugi

Š

ŠUHUDU 1. a variety of pink hawthorn 2. a variety of *dalbergia*

ŠUHURI buckwheat husks
  ŠUHURI SIHAMBI to lose a scab (of one who has smallpox)

ŠUI GIOI CUWAN a flat barge used for hauling goods

ŠUI JING crystal

ŠUIJIN crystal

ŠUJIN one name for the peacock; cf. *tojin*

ŠUKDUN see *siden*

ŠUKIBUMBI caus. of *šukimbi*

ŠUKILABUMBI caus. of *šukilambi*

ŠUKILAMBI 1. to beat with the fist 2. to strike with the horns (cows, sheep, etc.), to knock against, to butt

ŠUKIMBI (-he) to bring to a bad end, to ensnare, to harm

ŠUKIŠAMBI 1. to strike at random with the fists, to strike one another with the fists 2. to butt repeatedly 3. to butt one another

ŠUKŠUHUN the same as *šokšohon*

ŠUKUMBI to sit with the legs stretched out

ŠUKUN the two notches on the end of a bow

ŠULA 1. juice (of fruit) 2. pus, discharge

ŠULABURU YENGGUHE a type of parrot with a red head and reddish brown shoulders and breast

ŠULDERI TUBIHE a figlike fruit that ripens in the fifth month and tastes like a sweet chestnut

ŠULEBUMBI caus. of *šulembi*

ŠULEHELEMBI to gather, to collect (taxes)

ŠULEHEN collection, taxation

ŠULEMBI 1. to collect (taxes) 2. see *šeolembi*

ŠULER see *šošon*

ŠULGE see *šulhe*

ŠULHE pear
  ŠULHE I BELGE a pear core

ŠULHERI an exotic pearlike fruit of yellow color having a somewhat sour taste

ŠULHUMBI to escape from a net

ŠULHŪ a box made from willow branches used for storing clothes

ŠULIHUN 1. pointed 2. a point
  ŠULIHUN ENGGEMU a saddle with a pointed bow
  ŠULIHUN GŪLHA pointed boots
  ŠULIHUN YORO an arrow having a five-sided bone and horn head that contains five holes

ŠULIMBI to twitter

ŠULIN CECIKE one of the names of the oriole; cf. *gulin cecike*

Š

ŠULMEN rolled strips of meat

ŠULU hair on the temples

ŠULUBUMBI caus./pass. of *šulumbi*

ŠULUMBI to mistreat, to harass (subordinates)

ŠULUN see *silun*

ŠUMA see *šuman*

ŠUMACUKA see *simacuka*

ŠUMAN the male sexual organs of livestock

ŠUMBI (-ngke, -mpi) to be thoroughly acquainted with, to be well-versed in, to know thoroughly

ŠUMCI sunken, sunken out of sight, underwater, submerged
  ŠUMCI DOSIMBI to sink out of sight
  ŠUMCI GENEMBI to sink, to fall

ŠUMGA see *šumgan*

ŠUMGAN 1. crucible for precious metals 2. a container for gunpowder
  ŠUMGAN GOCIMBI to set a small crucible containing fire over a sore spot

ŠUMGIYA GASHA one name for the spotted kingfisher; cf. *cunggai*

ŠUMHUN see *simhun*

ŠUMIKAN rather deep, somewhat deep

ŠUMILAMBI to do in a profound way, to become deep

ŠUMIN deep
  ŠUMIN MICIHIYAN deep and shallow, depth

ŠUMPULU powerless, without support

ŠUN 1. sun 2. day
  ŠUN BE AITUBUMBI to pray for deliverance from harm during a solar eclipse (a Chinese rite)
  ŠUN BE JEMBI there is an eclipse of the sun
  ŠUN BE TUWARA KEMNEKU the name of a gnomon in the Peking observatory
  ŠUN BUNCUHŪN the sunlight is weak
  ŠUN DABSIHA the sun is on the (western) horizon
  ŠUN DALIKŪ a (ceremonial) parasol
  ŠUN DALIKŪ I FIYENTEN (扇手司) Fan Section (of the Equipage Department)
  ŠUN DEKDEKE the sun has risen
  ŠUN DEKDERE ERGI the east
  ŠUN DOSIKA the sun has set
  ŠUN DOSITALA all day (until the sun sets)
  ŠUN DULIMBA ABKA DE ELDERE MUDAN a piece of music performed during banquets for meritorious generals and officials
  ŠUN HALANGGA 'of the sun clan'-- epithet of the Buddha
  ŠUN HELMEN TUWARA TANGGIN (晷影堂) hall of the gnomon near the observatory
  ŠUN HŪCIHINGGA related to the sun--

epithet of the Buddha

ŠUN IBKAKA   the days have become shorter (after midsummer)

ŠUN I KEMUN   a sundial

ŠUN I KIRU   a blue banner of the imperial escort embroidered with a representation of the sun

ŠUN JEMBI   to have an eclipse of the sun

ŠUN KELFIKE   the sun has begun to decline

ŠUN KŪWARAHA   the sun has a ring around it

ŠUN MUKDEHUN   altar to the sun

ŠUN MUKDEKE   the sun came up

ŠUN NIYANCAMBI   the sun shines warmly

ŠUN SANGKA   the days have lengthened (after midwinter)

ŠUN SIDARAKA   see *šun sangka*

ŠUN SIMEN   power or influence of the sun

ŠUN ŠANGGA   'the sun is eared'--i.e., the sun has a rainbow near it

ŠUN TOB   directly opposite the sun-- the south

ŠUN TUCIKE   the sun came out

ŠUN TUHEKE   the sun set

ŠUN TUHERE ERGI   the west

ŠUN TUHETELE   all day--until the sun sets

ŠUN URHUHE   the sun is about to set, the sun is low on the horizon

ŠUNEMBI   to go wild, to become overgrown (with weeds)

ŠUNG ŠANG   (onom.) the sound of the breathing of a sleeping person

ŠUNGGA HIYAN   a fragrance made of osmanthus

ŠUNGGA ILHA   osmanthus, a fragrant small white flower

ŠUNGGACI ILHA   spring osmanthus--an osmanthuslike flower that blooms in the third month

ŠUNGGAYA   see *šunggayan*

ŠUNGGAYAN   tall and slender, lank

ŠUNGGE   1. learned, educated, enlightened, wise   2. fine-grained

ŠUNGGE MOO   a type of tree that grows in the mountains and produces a fine-grained, shiny, yellow wood

ŠUNGGE TUBIHE   an exotic fruit that tastes like lotus seed--one pod contains many kernels

ŠUNGGERI   elegant, fine, graceful, in good taste

ŠUNGGIDEI   one name for the golden pheasant; cf. *junggiri coko*

ŠUNGGIN GASHA   one name for the silver pheasant (*Lophura nycthemera*); cf. *be hiyan*

ŠUNGGIYA   exemplary, fine, in good taste

ŠUNGGIYADA ILHA   narcissus

ŠUNGGIYAMBI   to throw all about

ŠUNGKE   1. perfect participle of *šumbi*   2. enlightened, knowledgeable, well-versed; cf. *šungge*

ŠUNGKECI ILHA   a very fragrant jasmine-like flower of Szechuan

ŠUNGKEN   enlightenment, education, refinement

ŠUNGKENEMBI   to be enlightened, to be well-versed

ŠUNGKERI   refined, elegant

ŠUNGKERI GŪWARA   one name for the eared owl; cf. *fu gūwara*

ŠUNGKERI HIYAN   *Eupatorium Chinense*

ŠUNGKERI ILHA   Chinese orchid (*Cymbidium virens*)

ŠUNGKON   see *šongkon*

ŠUNGKU   the depression just below the lips on a man's face

ŠUNGKUBUMBI   caus./pass. of *šungkumbi*

ŠUNGKULU   the beard that grows below the lips

ŠUNGKUMBI   (-he) to get dented, to form a depression

ŠUNGKUTU   having deep-set eyes, having cavernous eyes

ŠUNGŠUN ŠANGŠAN   speaking through the nose, having a strong nasal quality to one's speech

ŠUNTUHULE   all day, until the sun goes down

ŠUNTUHUNI   the same as *šuntuhule*

ŠUO   see *šuwe*

ŠURDEBUKU   windlass

ŠURDEBUMBI   caus./pass. of *šurdembi*

ŠURDEBURE TATAKŪ   a large water wheel used for bringing water from a low place to a higher place

ŠURDEHEN   circumference, circuit, circular course

ŠURDEHEN CINCILAN I USIHA BE ACABURE DURUNGGA TETUN   an armillary sphere of the Peking observatory

ŠURDEJEN   see *abkai šurdejen usiha*

ŠURDEKU   1. circumference   2. ring, circle   3. axle, axis, pivot   4. vortex   5. a ring attached to the feet of falcons to keep the foot fetters from getting knotted   6. ring clasp on a belt

ŠURDEKU MUKE   a whirlpool, vortex

ŠURDEMBI   to go around, to rotate, to encompass, to wind around, to spin

ŠURDEME   (postposition) around

ŠURDERE DANGSE I BA (循還處)   control office for coinage in the Board of Finance

ŠURDERE DANGSE I BOO (循還房)   office in charge of making alloys of copper, tin, and zinc in the Board of Works

ŠURDERE NANGGIN   a winding corridor

Š

(in a garden or around a pavilion)

ŠURDEHE ŠUSIHE a tally passed on to a relief on some rotating function

ŠURDERE USIHA I FUKJINGGA HERGEN (轉宿篆) a style of Chinese calligraphy

ŠURDEN 1. rotation, spinning, swirling 2. a ring

ŠURDENUMBI to encompass one another, to go around one another

ŠURGA 1. snow blown by the wind 2. blowing sand

ŠURGABUMBI caus. of *šurgambi*

ŠURGAMBI to blow (of snow or sand in a heavy wind)

ŠURGAN a three-year-old tiger

ŠURGAN TASHA the same as *šurgan*

ŠURGEBUMBI caus. of *šurgembi*

ŠURGECEMBI to tremble all over, to shiver from cold

ŠURGEMBI to shake, to tremble

ŠURGEME DARGIMBI to shake and tremble

ŠURGEME GELEME trembling with fright

ŠURHA a two-year-old wild pig

ŠURHŪ a chick

ŠURHŪN one name for the chicken, a half-grown chicken

ŠURTEKU copper or tin forks held between the fingers when playing with the *gacuha*; cf. *cohoto*

ŠURTUKU YOO a running sore

ŠURU 1. the distance between the thumb and the index finger, a span 2. coral 3. paper strips tied to the end of a pole that were offered to the gods at the beginning of a child's studies 4. heavy (of a child's weight)

ŠURU CECIKE the 'coral bird' that resembles the myna

ŠURUBUMBI caus. of *šurumbi*

ŠURUBUHA SELE twisted iron nailed onto armor

ŠURUCI boatman, sailor

ŠURUKŪ 1. a punting pole 2. a lathe

ŠURUMBI 1. to spin, to peel off the skin of fruit in a spiral 2. to make on a lathe 3. to punt (a boat) 4. to cut the meat of game into strips

ŠURUN a young quail

ŠUSAI 1. (秀才, 生員) Licentiate--the first literary degree, BH 629A 2. student, young scholar

ŠUSEBUKU 1. a border or horizontal strip hanging down from the top of a curtain, drapery, or parasol 2. fringe, border, edging 3. a bedspread

ŠUSEMBI 1. to slide down, to slip down 2. to grab from underneath

ŠUSEME TATAMBI to pull out from

underneath (an arrow from a quiver)

ŠUSEME WASIBUMBI to lower from a high place to a lower place

ŠUSEME WASIMBI to slide down, to lower oneself from a high place to a lower place, to shinny down a rope

ŠUSHA a tiger with five claws

ŠUSI ILHA a yellow flower resembling the iris that blooms in the summer

ŠUSIGE the same as *šusihe*

ŠUSIHA a whip

ŠUSIHA GUWEMBUMBI to make a whip sing

ŠUSIHALABUMBI caus. of *šusihalambi*

ŠUSIHALAMBI to whip, to flog, to beat with a whip

ŠUSIHANGGA USIHA the name of a constellation (策)

ŠUSIHAŠAMBI to beat repeatedly with a whip

ŠUSIHE 1. a square piece of wood used for writing, a piece of wood with writing on it 2. a sign, voucher, attestation

ŠUSIHE BAICAMBI to check a certificate of merit (certificates given to soldiers for meritorious service)

ŠUSIHE TEMGETU BITHE imperial patent

ŠUSIHIYEBUMBI caus./pass. of *šusihiyembi*

ŠUSIHIYEMBI to incite others to discord, to agitate

ŠUSILABUMBI caus. of *šusilambi*

ŠUSILAMBI to whip, to flog

ŠUSILEBUMBI caus. of *šusilembi*

ŠUSILEMBI to chisel, to make holes with a chisel

ŠUSIN a chisel

ŠUSINTU a type of ancient chisel

ŠUSU provisions, supplies

ŠUSUNCAMBI to whisper, to hum

ŠUŠAN a small hoe-shaped implement for scraping the sides of pots

ŠUŠEMBI to look all over for, to rummage through, to ransack

ŠUŠU 1. purple 2. sorghum, kaoliang-- *Andropogon Sorghum*

ŠUŠU BAIBULA the male paradise fly-catcher

ŠUŠU CALIHŪN the name of a small red bird--the 'kaoliang bird'

ŠUŠU JILHANGGA ILHA the name of an exotic purple flower that grows on a plant with long stalks and pointed leaves

ŠUŠU ORHO sorghum

ŠUŠU SOGI edible seaweed, laver, sea lettuce

ŠUŠU SUKDUNGGA USIHA (紫氣星) the name of a constellation

Š

ŠUŠU ŠAKŠAHA a purple-colored quail
ŠUŠU ŠAŠA (onom.) whispering, speaking softly
ŠUŠU UJUNGGA ALHACAN NIYEHE a speckled duck with a purple head
ŠUŠU YARUKŪ a lure for crayfish consisting of a rope with sorghum ears attached to it
ŠUŠUN ILHA purple bindweed
ŠUŠUNGGE KILTAN a purple pennant of the imperial escort
ŠUŠUNGGIYAMBI to whisper, to hum
ŠUŠUNIYEMBI see *šušunggiyambi*
ŠUŠUNJAMBI to whisper
ŠUŠURGAN ILHA the bloom of the Chinese redbud (*Cercis chinensis*)
ŠUŠURI the name of a sweet purple fruit
ŠUŠURI MAŠARI meticulous, fussy
ŠUTUCIN preface; cf. *sioi*
ŠUTUGI ILHA an exotic purple flower with five petals and long pointed leaves
ŠUTUHUTELE see *šuntuhule*
ŠUTUMBI to grow up gradually; cf. *situmbi*
    ŠUTUHA FULHUN one of the six minor pipes
ŠUWA dense forest on the north side of a mountain; cf. *ša*
ŠUWAI FU (帥府) commander
ŠUWAI SEME tall and slender, lank, long and slender
ŠUWAK (onom.) the sound of hitting with a whip
    ŠUWAK SIK (onom.) the sound of several whips striking
ŠUWANG LU see *šuwanglu*
ŠUWANGLIO see *šuwang lu*
ŠUWANGLU 'double six'--a board game at which thirty-two pieces were used
ŠUWANGLULAMBI to play the game *šuwanglu*
ŠUWANGŠUWANGDEO see *šangšangdeo*

ŠUWAR (onom.) the sound of a sword being drawn from a scabbard, a snake moving rapidly, or an arrow passing through the air
ŠUWAR SIR SEME agile (in climbing trees)
ŠUWARANG SEME long and thin
ŠUWARKIYALABUMBI caus./pass. of *šuwarkiyalambi*
ŠUWARKIYALAMBI to beat with the heavy staff (an official punishment), the same as *janglambi*
ŠUWARKIYAN 1. bramble branches that were used for weaving baskets 2. a dried-up branch, twig 3. a heavy staff used for flogging
    ŠUWARKIYAN UNUMBI to ask for forgiveness
ŠUWARŠAGIYAMBI see *šuwarkiyalambi*
ŠUWASE 1. brush 2. fringe
ŠUWASELABUMBI caus. of *šuwaselambi*
ŠUWASELAMBI 1. to print 2. to brush
ŠUWASELEMBI to brush
ŠUWASILEMBI see *šusilembi*
ŠUWE 1. direct, straight, totally 2. (with negatives) not at all, not in the least
    ŠUWE HAFU thoroughly versed in, having a comprehensive knowledge of
    ŠUWE UIHE BERI a bow made from one horn
ŠUWEFUN thorough realization, clear understanding
ŠUYEN 1. a hole made in the ice of a river or lake that is used for watering livestock and procuring water for household use 2. a small hole at the foot of a riverbank
ŠŪNGGE see *šungge*
ŠŪRGEKU reel, spool

Š

T

TA a lamb

TA SEME often, continually, uninterruptedly

TA TI SEME (onom.) the sound of a group working energetically

TAB upright, regular

TAB SEME 1. (onom.) the sound of a bowstring hitting the back of the bow 2. (onom.) the sound of water dripping 3. (jumped) right over

TAB TIB (onom.) the sound of dripping water

TABA the smooth side of a *gacuha*

TABARAMBI to err, to make an error, to go astray

TABCILABUMBI 1. caus./pass. of *tabcilambi* 2. to have the bowstring graze the hand or face when shooting

TABCILAMBI to plunder, to capture, to seize

TABCILANAMBI to go to plunder or capture

TABCILANDUMBI/TABCILANUMBI to plunder or capture together

TABCILANJIMBI to come to plunder or capture

TABCIN plunder, booty

TABSITAMBI 1. to talk foolishly, to talk too much, to prattle 2. to talk back to

TABTAŠAMBI to speak coarsely

TABUKŪ hook, hanger, hasp, catch, fastener
  TABUKŪ UMIYESUN a leather belt with a fastener

TABUMBI 1. caus./pass. of *tambi* 2. to hook, to catch, to engage 3. to patch up, to darn 4. to attach a string to a bow, to string a bow 5. to trap, to ensnare 6. to tie up (with), to lasso 7. to trip someone (in wrestling) 8. to implicate someone, to involve someone in a conversation or lawsuit

TABUME GOHOLOME GISUREMBI to involve someone in one's conversation

TABURE ASU the same as *eyebuku asu*

TABURI one ten-quintillionth

TABUSITAMBI the same as *tabušambi*
  TABUSITARA GISUN excuse, pretext, subterfuge

TABUŠAMBI 1. to make excuses, to give a pretext 2. to mend, to sew back together

TACIBUBUMBI caus. of *tacibumbi*

TACIBUKŪ teacher, instructor
  TACIBUKŪ HAFAN (教官，學官) instructional officer

TACIBUMBI to teach, to instruct
  TACIBURE FUNGNEHEN a document of enfeoffment for ranks below the sixth degree
  TACIBURE HESE an imperial decree, an imperial instruction

TACIHIYABUMBI caus. of *tacihiyambi*

TACIHIYAKŪ educational institution, school

TACIHIYAMBI to instruct, to train

TACIHIYAN 1. teaching, training 2. religion
  TACIHIYAN WEN teaching and culture, culture, civilization

TACIKŪ 1. school 2. learning
  TACIKŪ DE ENGGELEMBI to go to the Imperial Academy of Learning to lecture on a text (said of the emperor)
  TACIKŪ TACIHIYAKŪ schools, educational institutions
  TACIKŪI BAITA BE KADALARA HAFAN (提督學政) Superintendent of Provincial Education, BH 827A
  TACIKŪI BAITA BE KADALARA HAFAN I YAMUN (學政衙門) Office of the Provincial Director of Education BH 827A

TACIKŪI BOO schoolhouse, school
TACIKŪI JUSE students, pupils
TACIKŪI YAMUN (學院) an office in every province in charge
of the examination for the Licentiate
TACIMBI 1. to learn, to study 2. to
become accustomed to, to get used to
TACIHA HAFAN (博士) the name
of an official in the Hanlin Acad-
emy, Bureau of Sacrificial Worship,
etc.
TACIHA HAFAN I TINGGIN the office
of the above official
TACIRE URSE students
TACIMSI a student of the Imperial Acad-
emy of Learning
TACIN 1. learning, science, skill 2.
religion 3. custom, habit
TACIN BE BADARAMBURE TANGGIN (廣
業堂) a third hall of the west
gallery of the Imperial Academy of
Learning
TACIN FONJIN learning, scholarship
TACINAMBI to go to learn
TACINDUMBI/TACINUMBI to learn together
TACINJIMBI to come to learn
TACINUN 1. custom 2. air, folk melody
TADUMBI to tear apart, to rip in two
TADURAMBI to scuffle, to fight
TADURANUMBI to scuffle together
TAFABUMBI caus. of *tafambi*
TAFAKŪ see *tafukū*
TAFAMBI (-ka/ha) to ascend, to go up
TAFAMBUMBI caus. of *tafambi*
TAFANAMBI to go to ascend, to go up
TAFANDUMBI/TAFANUMBI to ascend to-
gether
TAFANJIMBI to come to ascend, to come
up
TAFITU a unicorn that is supposed to
appear when the world is unified
TAFUKŪ steps, stages, flight of stairs
TAFUKŪ I DAIBIHAN the stone ledge
on both sides of a flight of stairs
TAFULABUMBI caus./pass. of *tafulambi*
TAFULAMBI to advise, to counsel
TAFULAN advice, counsel
TAFUMBI the same as *tafambi*
TAFURŠAMBI to act vigorously, to act
ferociously or vehemently
TAGIRI CECIKE one name for the goat-
sucker; cf. *simari cecike*
TAHALABUMBI caus. of *tahalambi*
TAHALAMA a horseshoe
TAHALAMBI to nail on a horseshoe, to
shoe (a horse)
TAHAN 1. clog, wooden shoe 2. horse-
shoe 3. a stepping stone 4. a
piece of wood attached to the bottom
of a shoe, a wooden sole
TAHI a wild horse (*Equus przewalski*)
TAHŪRA shellfish, mussel, clam

TAHŪRA EFEN a meat-filled pastry
made in the shape of a mussel
TAHŪRA NOTHO mussel shell, mother-
of-pearl
TAHŪRANGGA FIYEN a powder made from
mussel shells
TAI platform, terrace, stage
TAI TEBUMBI to erect a (signal)
platform
TAI SUI ENDURI the god of misfortune
TAI ŠI see *taiši*
TAI TAI lady, mistress
TAIBOO (太保) Grand Guardian--
an honorary title
TAIBU the main beam of a roof or a
bridge
TAICANGSY I YAMUN see *wecen i baita be
aliha yamun*
TAIDZ the Heir Apparent, BH 12
TAIDZ ŠOOBOO (太子少保)
Junior Guardian of the Heir Ap-
parent--an honorary title
TAIDZ ŠOOFU (太子少傅)
Junior Tutor of the Heir Ap-
parent--an honorary title
TAIDZ ŠOOŠI (太子少師)
Junior Preceptor of the Heir Ap-
parent--an honorary title
TAIDZ TAIBOO (太子太保)
Grand Guardian of the Heir Ap-
parent--an honorary title
TAIDZ TAIFU (太子太傅)
Grand Tutor of the Heir Apparent--
an honorary title
TAIDZ TAIŠI (太子太師)
Grand Preceptor of the Heir Ap-
parent-- an honorary title
TAIDZ USIHA the first star in Ursa
Minor
TAIFIN peace, tranquillity
TAIFIN YENDEBURE CALU a granary of
the Board of Finance that was
located in the capital
TAIFINGGA pertaining to peace, peace-
ful
TAIFINGGA ILHA a blossom resembling
the flower of the peach that
blooms in autumn
TAIFINTU CECIKE the name of a small
white bird with a crest on its head,
a hooked beak and a black tail that
is golden at the end--Bohemian wax-
wing (*Bombycilla garrulus*)
TAIFU (太傅) Grand Tutor--an
honorary title
TAIGIYAN eunuch
TAIGIYASA plural of *taigiyan*
TAIHA a hunting dog with long hair on
the ears and tail
TAIHEO widow of an emperor
TAIHŪWA sea-bream
TAIJI a Mongolian title
TAIJINGGA ILHA the name of a water

flower from Kwangtung

TAILI a saucer for a wine cup

TAIMIN a stick for stirring a fire

TAIMIYOO the imperial ancestral temple

TAIMPA a type of edible river snail or mussel

TAIMPARI NIYEHE one name for the teal; cf. *borboki niyehe*

TAIPUSY YAMUN see *adun be kadalara yamun*

TAIRAN a slash cut on a tree--used by hunters as a guide or landmark
  TAIRAN GAIMBI to ascend by a winding path
  TAIRAN GAIME SACIMBI to make a slash on a tree as a landmark

TAISUI ENDURI 1. the first of the year gods--the planet Jupiter 2. the god of misfortune

TAISI (太 師) Grand Preceptor-- an honorary title

TAITAI lady, mistress

TAIYUN the name of a sea fish that resembles the bream

TAJI naughty, mischievous

TAJIHŪN ill-bred, naughty

TAJIRAMBI to act naughtily

TAK SEME (onom.) the sound made by hitting something solid

TAK TIK (onom.) 1. the sound made when chopping wood 2. the sound made when moving chessmen

TAKA temporarily, provisionally, for the time being, for a short time

TAKABUMBI caus./pass. of *takambi*

TAKAMBI to know (a person), to recognize, to be familiar with

TAKAN the name of an edible mustard-like wild plant that grows along streams

TAKANAMBI to go to recognize

TAKANDUMBI/TAKANUMBI to know or recognize together, to recognize one another

TAKANJIMBI to come to recognize, to come to know

TAKASU 1. wait a moment, just a moment 2. for the time being

TAKCIHA FILAN a wooden bow without a horn covering

TAKDAMBI (-ka/ha) to be happy over some success, to be in high spirits, to be elated to the point of haughtiness

TAKDANGGA happy, in a good mood, in high spirits, elated to the point of haughtiness

TAKITU a protective knee covering made from leather

TAKIYA the knee of animals

TAKSIBUMBI 1. caus./pass. of *taksimbi* 2. to conceive (a child)
  TAKSIBURAKŪ BERI the name of a fa-

mous bow of antiquity

TAKSIMBI 1. to survive, to remain, to last 2. to be there, to exist, to be living 3. to preserve 4. to be conceived (of a child)

TAKTA MOO yew (*Taxus cuspidata*)

TAKTAN MOO plane tree, sycamore tree

TAKTU 1. a storied building, tower 2. upstairs
  TAKTU AMBAN (武 備 院 卿) Director of the Imperial Armory, BH 89

TAKŪ tench (fish)

TAKŪLEO see *takūlu*

TAKŪLU wait a moment, just a moment; cf. *takasu*

TAKŪRABUMBI caus./pass. of *takūrambi*
  TAKŪRABURE HAFAN (司 務) Chancery Chief, BH 296
    TAKŪRABURE HAFAN I TINGGIN (司 務 廳) Chancery (in various ministries), BH 296

TAKŪRAKŪ overseer, inspector, etc.-- the name of officials in various bureaus of the government

TAKŪRAMBI 1. to send on a mission, to delegate, to commission 2. to appoint (to a post) 3. to employ, to have in one's service
  TAKŪRAHA HAFAN (差 官) official for special duty, deputy, BH 436, 778 ff.

TAKŪRAN commission, duty, mission
  TAKŪRAN BE ALIHA FIYENTEN (行 人 司) a section of the Bureau of Rites concerned with caring for foreign emissaries
  TAKŪRAN BE ALIHA HAFAN (行 人) in ancient times, the name of an official who was in charge of caring for foreign emissaries

TAKŪRANDUMBI to send to one another (on a mission)

TAKŪRANGGE official summons or invitation

TAKŪRSI beadle, bailiff

TAKŪRŠABUMBI pass. of *takūršambi*

TAKŪRŠAKŪ servant

TAKŪRŠAMBI to employ as a (personal) servant
  TAKŪRŠARA DAHALJI personal servant, valet
  TAKŪRŠARA HAFAN (供 用 官) an official charged with making preparations for official business, commissions, etc.
  TAKŪRŠARA HŪSUN a coolie, a laborer
  TAKŪRŠARA NIYALMA servant, valet
  TAKŪRŠARA SARGAN JUI servant girl

TALA 1. plain, steppe (transversed by caravan roads) 2. the space between lines of writing

TALABUMBI caus./pass. of *talambi*

TALAMBI 1. to spread out (wares for sale) 2. to confiscate, to seize (property as a legal punishment) 3. to make griddle cakes, to fry flat bread; cf. *jempilembi*
TALAME DURIMBI to rob in plain daylight
TALAME TUKIYEMBI to lift by placing the leg between the thighs (at wrestling)
TALBI IHAN a cow that hasn't been used
TALBU shuttle
TALFA a shallow place in a stream, shallow water
TALFARI a shallow place where the bottom of a boat may touch bottom
TALGAN the surface of a flat, round, or square object
TALGARI 1. the surface of a table 2. the outside surface of a memorial or examination paper
TALGIBUMBI caus. of *talgimbi*
TALGIKŪ a wooden scraper for leather
TALGIMBI 1. to scrape dressed leather 2. to act stupidly, to speak foolishly
TALIHŪN undecided, vacillating
TALIHŪNJAMBI to vacillate, to be undecided
TALIŠAMBI 1. to flicker, to shimmer 2. to blink
TALKAMBI to cook fish half-done
TALKIMBI to console, to comfort
TALKIYAMBI to lighten, to flash
TALKIYAN lightning, electricity
TALKIYAN FULARILAMBI to flash in the distance when no clouds are visible (lightning)
TALKIYAN MEJIGE telegram
TALMAHAN the white strips of hanging mist toward the end of autumn
TALMAMBI (-ka) to be foggy
TALMAN fog, mist
TALTAN 1. raised decorations around the edge of a table 2. the side of a canoe
TALTAN TATAMBI to make raised decorations on the edge of a table
TALU by chance, accidentally, perchance
TALU DE 1. by chance, accidentally, perchance, in case . . . 2. here and there, sometimes
TALU JUGŪN shortcut
TALUDE see *talu de*
TAMA sole (fish)
TAMABUMBI caus. of *tamambi*
TAMALIMBI to struggle (to keep from falling, etc.)
TAMAMBI 1. to collect scattered things into one place 2. to fill (a vessel) with 3. to tighten up the sagging portion of a battue line
TAMAN castrated swine, hog

TAMBI 1. to get caught on something, to get entangled and trip over something 2. to get caught in a trap or net
TAME AFAME YABUMBI to walk dragging the feet
TAMIN the end of an animal's hair
TAMIN ACABUMBI to arrange the hairs of a pelt naturally and in the proper direction
TAMIN ACANAHA the hairs (of a pelt) are running in the proper direction
TAMIŠAMBI to taste with the lips
TAMLIMBI see *tamalimbi*
TAMPA see *taimpa*
TAMPIN vessel, pot, container (for tea or liquor)
TAMPIN EFEN small rice cakes with a filling
TAMPIN I BOO (壺室) the room where the water clock was kept under the observatory
TAMSE a small container, jug, jar
TAMSU see *tamse*
TAMTAN a carplike sea fish with red fins
TAN 1. a sandbar, a small island in a river 2. altar 3. saliva
TANA 1. a precious freshwater pearl found in the rivers of eastern Manchuria 2. a type of wild leek that grows near salty marshes
TANANGGA ILHA the name of an exotic flower with five petals whose filaments resemble tiny pearls
TANDAMBI see *tantambi*
TANG 1. a hall 2. a praying mantis
TANG SEME 1. hard, firm 2. fluent, with ease (of speaking)
TANG SEME GECEHE frozen solid
TANG SEME GISUREMBI to speak fluently
TANG TANG (onom.) the sound of a bell
TANG TING (onom.) the sound of hitting iron or of chopping a tree
TANG U LI BOO see *tanggūli*
TANGGA see *mangga tangga*
TANGGAMBI to wrap the weak part of a bow with sinew
TANGGIBUMBI to put something under an object to cushion or support it
TANGGIKŪ a bamboo device placed in a relaxed bow to preserve its shape
TANGGIKŪ I BUKDAMBI to bend (a bow) with a *tanggikū*
TANGGILAKŪ crossbow
TANGGILAMBI 1. to fire a crossbow 2. to flick the forehead with a finger
TANGGIME GISUREMBI to correct oneself in speaking, to cover up an error or faux pas in speaking
TANGGIMELIYAN bent backward, arched,

T

bow-shaped

TANGGIN hall, chamber, office of a
high official
    TANGGIN I ALIBUN a matter presented
    to a superior for consideration by
    a subordinate, petition presented
    to a high ministry official
    TANGGIN I TEMGETU EJERE BOO (堂號
    房) registry of the Ministry
    of Works
TANGGINGGE BOO (堂房) an office
of the Board of Finance concerned
with draft documents
TANGGIRI 1. a small finger cymbal 2.
an anvil for making nails with large
heads
    TANGGIRI ILHA the name of a color-
    ful flower that blooms in the
    springtime
TANGGIYABUMBI caus. of *tanggiyambi*
TANGGIYAMBI to repaint, to relacquer
TANGGIYAN repainting, relacquering
TANGGŪ one hundred
    TANGGŪ BETHE UMIYAHA centipede
    TANGGŪ GING the last night watch
    TANGGU HALA the common people
    TANGGŪ TUMEN one million
TANGGŪCI hundredth
TANGGŪDA hereditary head of a hundred
families
TANGGŪHA white-necked crow (*Corvus tor-
quatus*)
TANGGŪLI 1. the central hall of a house
2. the central section of a tent
TANGGŪNGGERI one hundred times
TANGGŪRI ILHA the name of a red flower
that blooms for a hundred days
TANGGŪT 1. Tibet, Tibetan 2. Tangut
    TANGGŪT HERGENEHE SUJE silk with
    Tibetan writing on it
    TANGGŪT TACIKŪ Tibetan language
    school
TANGGŪTA one hundred each
TANGGŪTE see *tanggūta*
TANGKA see *tangkan*
    TANGKA AKŪ without steps or rank
    TANGKA FEJILE your majesty
TANGKAMBI to kill small fish in shal-
low water with stones
TANGKAN step, rank, grade, class
    TANGKAN TANGKAN I   step by step
    TANGKAN TANGKAN I WESIMBI to ascend
    step by step
TANGKI bump, excrescence
TANGSE the imperial shamanic shrines
in Peking and Mukden
TANGSIMBI to drum continually
    TANGSIME GISUREMBI to speak fluently
TANGSU 1. darling, dear (children)
2. delicate, tender
TANGSULAMBI to fondle, to hug (chil-
dren)
TANGSULAN fondling, tender care

TANGSUN see *tangsu*
TANI a measure equaling one hundred-
thousandth of a dry quart
TANJAMBI to stutter, to stammer
TANJI one ten-quadrillionth
TANJURAMBI to pray, to pray for bless-
ings (of shamans)
TANTABUMBI caus./pass. of *tantambi*
TANTALAMBI to thrash, to beat
TANTAMBI to hit, to beat, to strike
TANTANUMBI to beat one another, to
fight
TANTU a cultivating tool with a forked
head
TAR SEME startled, suddenly afraid
TAR TAR SEME timorous, afraid
TARA 1. clabbered milk, curd 2. chil-
dren of father's sisters or mother's
brothers 3. relative of a different
surname
    TARA AHŪN DEO cousins (see *tara*)
    TARA EYUN NON female cousins (see
    tara)
TARAK see *tara* (1)
TARAN (heavy) sweat
    TARAN WALIYAMBI to sweat (profusely)
TARANI a dharani, magic formula
TARANILAMBI the same as *tarnilambi*
TARBAHI marmot (*Marmota bobak*)
TARBALJI one of the general names of
the eagle
TARBIHI see *tarbahi*
TARCAN lead (the metal)
    TARCAN I IRUKŪ lead weight on a
    fishing net
TARFU one name for the tiger; cf.
tasha
TARGA 1. a square piece of cloth
worn on the shoulder by children
during shamanistic ceremonies 2.
a tuft of straw hung on a door in
order to forbid entrance
    TARGA I FUTA a rope hung on a door
    at midsummer to keep evil spirits
    from entering
    TARGA INENGGI the day on which an
    emperor or empress died
TARGABUMBI 1. caus./pass. of *targambi*
2. to forbid troops to plunder, to
enjoin not to . . . , to admonish
TARGABUN prohibition, admonition
TARGACUN 1. abstinence, avoidance,
prohibition 2. precept
    TARGACUN BE TUWAKIYAMBI to observe
    the Buddhist precepts
TARGAMBI 1. to abstain from, to refrain
from, to give up, to swear off 2. to
be on guard against 3. to avoid as
taboo
TARGAN small tiger
TARGANGGA 1. religious vows 2. an
oath
    TARGANGGA BE EFULEMBI to break a

T

vow

TARGANGGA GAIMBI   to take monastic
  vows
TARGIKŪ UMIYAHA a poisonous green cat-
  erpillar
TARGIMPA see *targikū umiyaha*
TARGŪ fat, see *tarhūn*
TARHŪKAN rather fat, somewhat fat
TARHŪLAMBI to make fat
  TARHŪLAHA FAHŪN deer or sheep liver
  wrapped in fat and cooked
TARHŪMBI to get fat
TARHŪN 1. fat 2. a mussel that is
  supposed to be a transformed bird
  TARHŪN EFEN small cakes soaked in
  fat
  TARHŪN YALI fat meat, fat
TARIBUMBI caus. of *tarimbi*
TARIMBI to cultivate, to farm, to plow
TARINAMBI to go to cultivate
TARINDUMBI/TARINUMBI to cultivate to-
  gether
TARINJIMBI to come to cultivate
TARMIN NIYEHE mallard; cf. *borjin
  niyehe*
TARNI dharani, magic formula, charm;
  cf. *tarani*
TARNILABUMBI caus./pass. of *tarnilambi*
TARNILAMBI to recite a dharani
TARSI cousin of a different surname
  TARSI NIYAMAN children of father's
  sisters or of mother's brothers
  TARSI OMOLO the children of father's
  sister's children and mother's
  brother's children
TARSILAMBI to marry a cousin of a dif-
  ferent surname
TARUDAMBI to chatter, to talk nonsense
TARUN a person who talks nonsense
TAS SEME (onom.) the sound of an arrow
  grazing an object
  TAS SEME TATAME GAMAMBI to jerk from
  the hand suddenly
TAS TIS SEME (onom.) the sound of a
  number of arrows grazing an object
TASGABUMBI caus. of *tasgambi*
TASGAMBI to sauté quickly
TASHA 1. tiger, the Manchurian sub-
  species is *Felis tigris amurensis*
  2. the third of the earth's branches
  (寅)
  TASHA BIYA the first month
  TASHA GABTARA NIRU an arrow with a
  short iron head for shooting lying
  tigers
  TASHA GABTARA SELMIN NIRU an arrow
  with a long iron head for a crossbow
  TASHA GABTARA YORO an arrow with a
  head of birch wood with four holes
  in it that was used for rousing
  recumbent tigers
  TASHA GIDA a spear for hunting

tigers

  TASHA I ORON I DOGON the name of a
  constellation
  TASHA ORHO 'tiger grass' (*Arisaema
  thunbergii*)
  TASHA OSOHONGGO FUKJINGGA HERGEN
  (虎爪篆) the name of a
  style of Chinese calligraphy
TASHACI a tiger skin
TASHANGGA pertaining to the tiger,
  tigerlike
  TASHANGGA ANIYA the year of the
  tiger
  TASHANGGA DOBTOLON striped over-
  pants worn by troops of the green
  banner
  TASHANGGA DUSIHI a striped skirt
  worn by troops of the green banner
  TASHANGGA ETUKU a striped uniform
  worn by the troops of the green
  banner
  TASHANGGA MAHALA a hat made in the
  form of a tiger's head that was
  worn by the troops of the green
  banner
TASHARI eagle, vulture
TASHŪ 1. a yarn or thread separator
  used in weaving 2. the bottom of
  the crop of a bird, gizzard
TASHŪMBI to go back and forth continually
  TASHŪME YABUMBI the same as *tashūmbi*
TASIHIMBI to step against one's opponent from the side in wrestling
TASIMA EFEN a somewhat larger variety
  of *toholiyo*
TASMA leather thong made of deer or
  antelope skin
TAŠAN 1. false, spurious 2. error,
  mistake
TAŠARABUMBI caus. of *tašarambi*
TAŠARAMBI to err, to make an error, to
  go astray
TAŠUN is it false?
TATABUMBI 1. caus./pass. of *tatambi*
  2. to be too tight (of clothing)
  3. to act affected, to behave in a
  ridiculous manner
TATAKŪ 1. drawer 2. a wooden bucket,
  a bucket made of willow branches
  used for sprinkling water
  TATAKŪ DERE a table with drawers
  TATAKŪ I ŠURGEKU pulley on a well
TATALA many; cf. *tutala*
TATAMBI 1. to pull, to pull at, to
  tear, to draw, to pull out, to
  extract 2. to strangle (a criminal
  as a form of capital punishment) 3.
  to stop on a journey, to halt, to
  lodge, to make camp 4. to open wide
  (the eyes) 5. to deduct 6. to chat

T

informally 7. to pull apart, to rip

TATAME NIRU an arrow with a short
roundish iron head used for hunting
wild beasts

TATAME WAMBI to strangle (one of
the two forms of capital punishment)

TATAME WARA WEILE a crime punishable
by strangulation

TATARA BOO inn, hotel; cf. *diyan*

TATARA BOOI NIYALMA innkeeper

TATARA EDUN whirlwind

TATARA GURUNG a palace used by the
emperor on his travels

TATARA YAMUN office, public hall

TATAN 1. a camp, a stopping place 2.
territory of a tribe

TATAN I DA chief of a camp

TATANAMBI 1. to go to pull 2. to go to
stop on a journey

TATANDUMBI/TATANUMBI to stop on a
journey together, to rest together

TATANGGA HANGSE noodles that are pulled
by hand

TATANJIMBI 1. to come to stop on a
journey 2. to come to pull

TATARABUMBI caus. of *tatarambi*

TATARAMBI 1. to cut meat, specifically
to slice mutton very finely with
two small knives 2. to rip to
pieces, to rip apart 3. to pull at
one another (at wrestling)

TATAŠAMBI 1. to keep pulling, to pull
continually 2. to be agitated, to
be concerned

TATHŪNJACUKA hesitant, vacillating

TATHŪNJAMBI to hesitate, to vacillate

TATHŪNJAME GŪNINJAMBI to vacillate

TATUHAN the name of a two-stringed
musical instrument, a two-stringed
fiddle

TAYAMBI to break out (of fire)

TAYAME YABUMBI to suddenly dart
across the surface of a pond (of
water striders)

TAYUNGGA NIMAHA the name of a sea fish
that resembles the carp

TE now, at present

TE BICIBE at present, presently

TE ELE OHO KAI that's enough now

TE I JALAN the present world

TEBCIMBI to endure, to suffer

TEBELIYEBUMBI caus. of *tebeliyembi*

TEBELIYEKU a piece of metal around the
middle of a scabbard

TEBELIYEKU AFAHARI a piece of yellow
paper stuck on the outside of a
family genealogy that gives the
reasons for obtaining hereditary
official positions

TEBELIYEMBI 1. to hug, to embrace, to
hold in the arms 2. to adopt a child

TEBELIYEME ACAMBI to embrace upon

meeting (upon returning from a
journey a junior embraced the legs
of his senior, a senior embraced
the back of a junior, and equals
embraced one another about the
shoulders)

TEBELIYEN 1. embrace, hug 2. an arm-
load

TEBEN MOO a support timber on a ship

TEBKE a bone or wooden bridge or plate
at both ends of a bow placed under
the knots of the bowstring

TEBKE LATUBUMBI to glue on bridges
for a bowstring's knots

TEBKE TABKA tottering and babbling
(of children learning to walk and
speak)

TEBKEJEMBI to catch a shuttlecock that
has been thrown up in the air while
holding a *gacuha* in the hand, to
hold a *gacuha* in the hand

TEBKELEMBI to cut (meat) into small
chunks

TEBKU 1. afterbirth, placenta 2. a
bow case

TEBSEHE a type of locust that eats
crops

TEBUBUMBI caus. of *tebumbi* in the
sense of to pour, to set out
(plants), to fill (a vessel), to
distill, to fill (a pipe)

TEBUMBI 1. caus. of *tembi* 2. to pour
3. to set out, to plant 4. to fill
a vessel, to fill a pipe 5. to pack,
to put in 6. to install (an official) 7. to make (liquor), to
distill 8. to place a corpse in a
coffin

TEBUNEBUMBI caus. of *tebunembi*

TEBUNEMBI to do garrison duty, to be
stationed at a border garrison

TEBUNUMBI to pack together, to plant
together, etc.; cf. *tebumbi*

TEBURELAMBI to place in a grave, to
inter

TECEBUMBI caus. of *tecembi*

TECEMBI to sit together, to sit down
together

TECENDUMBI/TECENUMBI to sit in a group,
to sit together, to sit facing one
another

TEDE 1. dative/locative of *tere* 2.
there, in that place 3. up till now

TEDERI fron there, by there, from that,
from him, from her

TEFEMBI to burn up

TEHE 1. frame, framework, rack 2.
lathe, loom 3. Siberian ibex (*Capra
sibirica*)

TEHE UJU a piece of wood over a
loom that regulates the thread

TEHE WAN scaffold

TEHEN 1. a stick-horse 2. see *tehe*

TEHEN MORIN a stick-horse

TEHENI TUNGKEN a large drum that
  sits on a stand

TEHEREBUBUMBI caus. of *teherebumbi*

TEHEREBUKU balance, scales; cf. *pingse*

TEHEREBUMBI 1. to weigh on a balance
  2. to make even, to balance out, to
  make match

  TEHEREBURE BOO (兌 房) the
    weighing office of the Peking mint

TEHEREMBI 1. to be even, to be equal
  2. to match 3. to be of the same
  generation 4. to counterbalance 5.
  to be worth the price (or exchange)

  TEHEREHE NIYALMA a person of the
    same generation

TEHEREN equal, even, matching, balanced

  TEHEREN TEHEREN balanced, in balance

TEHERENDUMBI to counterbalance one another, to be equal to one another

TEHERŠEMBI 1. to be a match for 2.
  to be the same price 3. to correspond to

TEIFULEMBI to use as a staff, to lean
  on as a staff

TEIFUN cane, staff

TEIFUNGGE one who walks with a cane--
  an old man

TEIFUŠEMBI to walk with a cane or a
  staff

TEIKE just now, a moment ago, just

TEILE 1. only, just, alone 2. (after
  participles) to the extent of . . . ;
  cf. *muterei teile*, *jabduhai teile*

  TEILE AKŪ not only

TEISU 1. assigned place, designated
  place, responsibility, one's part
  2. corresponding, matching, facing,
  opposite

  TEISU AKŪ incongruous, not matching

  TEISU B. DUMBI to follow one's
    own calling, to be content with
    one's lot

  TEISU TEISU one by one, severally,
    all together, in busy confusion,
    on every occasion

  TEISU TEMBI to sit opposite

TEISULEBUMBI 1. caus. of *teisulembi*
  2. to adapt, to fit 3. to encounter,
  to come up against 4. to fit, to
  correspond, to be suited to, to coincide with 5. to face, to be relative to 6. to inflict the proper
  punishment

  TEISULEBUME BODOMBI to settle ac-
    counts

  TEISULEBUME WECEMBI to sacrifice to
    the earth spirits

TEISULEMBI 1. to meet, to encounter, to
  happen upon 2. to correspond, to
  match

  TEISULEHE DARI in any case, each
    time that . . .

TEISULEHE ORON a suitable vacancy

TEISULEN correspondence, encounter,
  mode

TEISUNGGE corresponding, fitting

TEISUTU sergeant of the green banner

TEIŠUN copper, bronze, brass

  TEIŠUN FAKSI coppersmith

  TEIŠUN NIOWARIKŪ patina

TEJIHEN one name for the crane; cf.
  bulehen

TEK TAK SEME (onom.) the sound of
  shouting or quarreling

TEKDEBUMBI 1. caus. of *tekdembi* 2.
  to burn sacrificial money

  TEKDEBURE HOOŠAN yellow paper that
    is burnt before Buddhist images
    as an offering

TEKDEMBI (-ke) 1. to creep up (of
  sleeves) 2. to ascend, to fly upward 3. to die (a euphemism)

TEKEMBI to be soft due to warm moisture (of leather)

TEKSI see *teksin*

TEKSIKEN rather even

TEKSILEBUMBI caus. of *teksilembi*

TEKSILEMBI to put in a row, to set out
  evenly

TEKSILGAN the rhythmic shouting of
  workers at a hard job

TEKSIN 1. even, equal, straight (not
  curved), of equal length or height
  2. the tamarisk, see *suhai moo*

  TEKSIN JAN a whistling arrow with
    a bone arrowhead that has a flat
    point

  TEKSIN NIRU an arrow with an arrow-
    head that has a flat point

  TEKSIN YORO an arrow with a bone
    head that has a flat point

TEKSINGGA in a rank, in a row, in an
  orderly arrangement

TEKU 1. a seat, a place to sit, a
  perch, a place where one can settle
  2. measure word for a banquet

  TEKU UNDEHEN seat in a rowboat

TELAMBI to give way, to collapse
  suddenly (of the hind leg of livestock)

TELEBUMBI caus./pass. of *telembi*

TELEJEMBI to be raised, to be embossed

  TELEJEME JODOMBI to weave with an
    embossed or raised design

TELEJEN 1. embossment, raised design,
  a protuberance 2. a courtyard with
  walls

TELEMBI to stretch taut, to truss

  TELEME WAMBI to kill by trussing

TELEN trussing

TELERI a woman's satin ceremonial
  garment decorated with a design of
  standing dragons

TELGIN belt (for trousers)

TELGIYEN see *telgin*

T

TELIMBI see *teliyembi*

TELIYEBUMBI caus./pass. of *teliyembi*

TELIYEKU a steamer--usually made in tiers from bamboo

TELIYEMBI to steam

TELŠEMBI see *delišembi*

TEMBI 1. to sit 2. to reside, to live 3. to occupy (a post)

    TEHE MUKE standing water, stagnant water

    TEHE UIHE BERI a bow made with ibex horn

    TEHEI MONJIRŠAMBI to move back and forth while sitting

    TERE BA place of residence

TEMCIKU a sampan

TEMEGE COKO ostrich

TEMEN 1. camel 2. see *temun*

    TEMEN CECIKE bittern, birds of the genus *Botaurus*

    TEMEN GURGU wild camel

    TEMEN SELE the peg that holds the two parts of fire tongs together

TEMENE ULME a needle with three edges that is used for sewing leather and other thick or dense materials

TEMENEMBI to get insects or worms (grain or leaves), to become insect-infested

TEMERI camel-colored, tan, brown

TEMGETU 1. sign, signal, mark, brand, badge, stamp, emblem 2. (personal) seal, a seal used by low ranking provincial officials and clerks, BH 984 3. evidence, proof, verification 4. certificate, receipt, written verification 5. license, permit, manifest

    TEMGETU ARAMBI to sign one's signature, to affix one's seal

    TEMGETU BITHE license, certificate, receipt, contract, manifest

    TEMGETU BITHE ICIHIYARA BA (辨照處) office of the certificate in the Imperial Academy of Learning

    TEMGETU EJEHE DANGSE a book in which the receipt of documents already acted on by the emperor was recorded

    TEMGETU ETUKU a jacket with the emblem of a military unit on it

    TEMGETU MAHALA a hat with the emblem of a military unit on it

    TEMGETU NIRU a signal arrow (used by a commander)

    TEMGETU ŠUSIHE a written order given to a subordinate by a superior

    TEMGETU TUWA ŠANGGIYAKŪ signal fire, beacon

    TEMGETU WEHE monument, memorial tablet

TEMGETULEBUMBI caus./pass. of *temgetulembi*

TEMGETULEMBI 1. to signal, to make a sign 2. to confer a mark of distinction on

TEMGETUN pennon, pennant

    TEMGETUN JALASU I FIYENTEN (旌節司) Pennons Section, BH 120

TEMGETUNGGE 1. exhibiting a sign, mark or emblem 2. distinguished, outstanding

TEMIMBI to treat with consideration, to treat indulgently, to consider another's reputation out of affection

TEMNEMBI see *temenembi*

TEMPIN a flower vase

TEMŠEBUMBI caus. of *temšembi*

TEMŠEKU opponent, competitor

TEMŠEMBI to compete, to vie, to contend, to quarrel

TEMŠEN contention, strife

TEMŠENDUMBI/TEMŠENUMBI to vie with one another, to quarrel with one another

TEMUHEN a rod around which pictures or scrolls of calligraphy are wrapped, a spool

TEMUN axle

    TEMUN I SIBIYA a peg on the axle to keep the wheels from slipping

TEMURTU KARA an iron-colored horse

TEN 1. foundation, base 2. extreme point, highest point, peak, extreme end 3. litter, sedan chair (carried by men, camel, horse, or mule) 4. small horizontal dragons woven into dragon satin 5. exalted, lofty, noble

    TEN GAIMBI to speak factually, to require the facts

    TEN I ŠANYAN USIHA the planet Venus

    TEN I TONDO TANGGIN (至公堂) the name of a hall in the examination compound

    TEN I WECEN the suburban sacrifice--made to heaven at the winter solstice and to earth at the summer solstice

TENAKŪ see *tengneku*

TENEMBI 1. to go to sit 2. to go to reside

TENG SEME hard, firm, fast, solid, resolute

TENG TANG SEME 1. equally matched 2. straightforward

TENGGELJEKU marshy ground (which vibrates when one stands on it)

TENGGELJEMBI to vibrate, to shake (of earth that is dry on top but still wet underneath)

TENGGERI a three-stringed lute

TENGGIN lake, inland sea

TENGKI TANGKI stumbling along; cf. *tungki tangki*

TENGKIBUMBI caus./pass. of *tengkimbi*

TENGKICUKE solid, real, certain
TENGKIMBI to throw down
  TENGKIME clearly, really, solidly
  TENGKIME SAMBI to know clearly
TENGNEBUMBI to make equal, to equalize
TENGNEKU a sedan chair carried by two
  men that was used for traveling in
  mountains
TENGNEMBI 1. to weigh, to balance 2.
  to jump from one horse to another
TENGPAI 1. a rattan shield 2. a
  soldier outfitted with a rattan
  shield
TENGSE 1. rattan 2. vine
  TENGSE I SIRGE 1. creepers of a
    vine, branches of a vine 2.
    strands of rattan
TENGTEMBI to step on stones (in a
  stream)
  TENGTEME YABUMBI to go across a
    stream by stepping on stones
TENI just, then and only then, not
  until, for the first time
  TENI JUSE mere children, small chil-
    dren
TENIKEN just, for the first time, only
  then
  TENIKEN JUSE small children
TENJIMBI 1. to come to sit 2. to come
  to reside 3. to come to occupy a
  post
TENJU 1. the imperative of tenjimbi
  2. keel of a ship
TENTEKE like that, that kind, such a,
  the one in question
TENTEKENGGE one like that, such a one
  as that
TENUMBI to sit together
TEO TO mendicant monk
TEODEBUMBI caus. of teodembi
TEODEMBI to trade, to exchange, to
  barter, to transfer
TEODENJEMBI 1. to trade with one an-
  other 2. to move, to transfer
  TEODENJEME BOŠORO NIRU (輪萱佐
    頒) a banner captain trans-
    ferred from one company to another
TER SEME in good order, even, splen-
  didly arrayed (of an army or hunting
  party)
TER TAR SEME the same as ter seme
TERBUN billion
TERE 1. that 2. he, she, it 3. (post-
  position) a certain
  TERE ANGGALA moreover, all the more
  TERE DADE the same as tere anggala
  TERE ONGGOLO before that, before-
    hand
  TEREI AMALA after that, subsequently
  TEREI BAILI DE thanks to him, due to
    him
  TEREI DADE moreover, in addition
TERECI 1. after that, then 2. than

  that, from that, than him
TEREINGGE his, hers, its
TERENI thereby, thus, with that
TERESE plural of tere; cf. tese
TERGECI driver, coachman
TERGIMBI to insert an arrowshaft snugly
  into the iron base of the arrowhead
TERIN TARIN staggering
TERKEN see erken terken
TERKI see terkin
TERKIMBI to jump high, to jump over, to
  jump across
TERKIN 1. steps, staircase 2. steps
  (and terrace) before a palace build-
  ing or before a yamen
  TERKIN I JERGI steps, staircase
  TERKIN I JERGI WESIMBI to ascend
    steps, to ascend step by step
TERME LORIN a mule purportedly born
  from a cow
TERSE see tese
TERTEN TARTAN shivering, trembling
  (from an illness)
TERU 1. base of the colon, rectum 2.
  pivot pin on a spindle
  TERU YOO hemorrhoids
TES (onom.) the sound of rope, thread,
  or a leather thong breaking under
  stress
TESE plural of tere: those, they
TESEINGGE theirs
TESEREMBI see deserembi
TESU original, local
  TESU BA local area, indigenous
    place, native place
  TESU BA I COOHA indigenous troops,
    native troops
  TESU BA I EJELETU local chief,
    local ruler
  TESU BA I IRGEN local people, na-
    tive people
  TESU BA I JAKA local products
  TESU BA I NIYALMA local person
  TESU BA I NIYALMAI USIN native
    owned land
  TESU BACI TUCIRE JAKA products pro-
    duced locally
TESUBUMBI caus. of tesumbi
TESUMBI to be enough, to suffice
TESUN sufficient, satisfactory
TETE TATA unsettled, unstable, flighty
TETEKEN rather unsettled, unstable
TETELE up till now
TETEN frivolous, unstable
TETENDERE (after conditional converb)
  since, provided that, assuming that,
  in case that
TETUN 1. tool, implement 2. vessel,
  container, dishes 3. coffin
  TETUN AGŪRA implements, tools,
    vessels
  TETUN DEIJIRE SELE WENIYERE KUNGGERI
    (蜜冶科) bureau of kilns

T

and smelting

TETUN DOOLAMBI to divide the things brought by a new daughter-in-law among the relatives

TETUN JAKA I CALU storehouse for household implements in the imperial household

TETUN ŠUŠEMBI the same as *tetun doolambi*

TETUŠEMBI 1. to use as a tool 2. to employ a person in a position for which he is fitted

TEYEBUMBI caus. of *teyembi*

TEYEHUN 1. relaxation, rest, leisure 2. at ease

TEYEMBI to be at ease, to relax, to rest

TEYEMBUMBI see *teyebumbi*

TEYEN rest, pause, relaxation

TEYEN AKŪ without rest, ceaselessly

TEYENDERAKŪ without resting, without pausing

TEYENDUMBI/TEYENUMBI to rest together, to relax together

TEYENEMBI to go to rest, to go to relax

TEYENJIMBI to come to rest, to come to relax

TIDU see *fideme kadalara amban*

TILDARGAN one name for the kestrel; cf. *baldargan*

TILHŪTAN one name for the pelican; cf. *kūtan*

TIMU topic, theme

TING 1. pavilion 2. office, bureau; cf. *tinggin*

TINGDZ pavilion; cf. *tingse*

TINGGIN 1. office, bureau, section 2. hall

TINGGIN I KUNGGERI BOO (廳 科 房) a section of the yamen of the Provincial Commander-in-Chief

TINGGU CECIKE a small black bird with white spots on the back and wings

TINGGURI CECIKE one name for the goatsucker; cf. *simari cecike*

TINGSE pavilion

TITANG (提 塘) Superintendent of Military Posts, BH 435

TIYAN JU GURUN India

TIYAN JU TANG MIYOO a Catholic or Orthodox church

TIYELIN a short, sharp-pointed arrow used for bird hunting

TIYOO cicada; see *biyangsikū*

TO 1. a span, the distance between the outstretched thumb and the middle finger 2. a grain measure made from willow branches that equals five dry quarts 3. the last bead on rosaries and strings of cash 4. alligator

TO GI ostrich

TOB straight, upright, serious, right, just

TOB DULIMBA the very middle, right in the middle

TOB SEMBI to be serious, to be earnest

TOB SEME just, exactly, is just so

TOB SERE NIYALMA a serious, upright man

TOB TAB honest, forthright

TOBCILAMBI to knot, to knit together, to plait; cf. *gokjimbi*

TOBCONGGO MOO a miraculous tree that grew on the grave of Chou Kung--the colors of the leaves corresponded to the different seasons, green in spring, red in summer, white in autumn, and black in winter

TOBGIYA knee

TOBGIYA DALIKŪ knee guard, protective covering for the knee

TOBGIYA HŪWAITAKŪ knee guard

TOBGIYA MURIMBI to fell an opponent in wrestling by twisting the knee

TOBGIYALAMBI to press together with the knees

TOBO a simple hut made from willow branches or other like material

TOBOO see *tobo*

TOBTELEMBI to cut off the knees--a punishment of antiquity

TOBTOKO a horse spotted like a panther

TOBTOKO YANGGALI a speckled water wagtail

TODAI see *todo*

TODO bustard

TODOLO omen, portent

TODOLOMBI to be a good omen, to portend well

TOFOHOCI fifteenth

TOFOHON fifteen

TOFOHONGGERI fifteen times

TOFOHOTO fifteen each

TOFOROME around the fifteenth of the month

TOGIYA a piece of a broken wooden object

TOHIN a pointed peg stuck in the crossboard on the back of a wagon to which ropes holding down the load were attached

TOHIŠAMBI to beg obtrusively

TOHO a half-grown moose

TOHOBUMBI caus. of *tohombi*

TOHOLI see *toholiyo*

TOHOLIYO small flat cakes made in the shape of cash

TOHOLON tin

TOHOLON HOOŠAN paper pasted to a very thin sheet of tin, tinfoil

TOHOLON MUKE quicksilver

TOHOMA a leather covering that hangs down on both sides of the saddle for the protection of the rider's legs

TOHOMA I DALDAKŪ a leather border
  on the *tohoma* at the place where
  the stirrups rub against it

TOHOMBI 1. to weave rope from bamboo
  or reed splints 2. to attach the
  rope to a net 3. to saddle (a
  horse) 4. to hitch up (a wagon)

TOHOME see *tohoma*

TOHOMIMBI to button, to button up

TOHON a (Chinese-style) button

  TOHON I FESIN eye for a Chinese-
    style button

  TOHON I SENCIKU loop for a button

TOHORO wagon wheel

TOHORO DUHA the small intestine of a
  pig

TOHOROKŪ a stone roller used for level-
  ing cultivated earth

TOHOROMBI (-ko) to calm down, to set
  one's mind at ease

TOHOROMBUMBI 1. caus. of *tohorombi*
  2. to calm down, to put at ease
  3. to pacify, to comfort

TOILOKOŠOMBI to gaze around indeci-
  sively

TOITON 1. one name for the cuckoo; cf.
  kekuhe 2. a crafty person--so-
  called because, like the cuckoo, he
  is hard to catch

TOITONGGO crafty, wily

TOJIN peafowl, peacock; cf. *kundujin*

  TOJIN FUNGGAHA KIRU a light blue
    banner of the imperial escort with
    the figures of peacock feathers
    embroidered on it

  TOJIN FUNGGAHA SARACAN a tiered
    parasol with figures of peacock
    feathers embroidered on it

  TOJIN GASHA see *tojin*

  TOJIN I FUNGGALA peacock feather

  TOJIN I FUNGGALA HADAMBI to stick a
    peacock feather in a hat

  TOJIN KIRU a banner of the imperial
    escort embroidered with a figure
    of a peacock

TOJINGGA ŠUN DALIKŪ a large round fan
  of the imperial escort made of silk
  in the form of peacock tail feathers

TOK (onom.) the sound of striking a
  hollow wooden object

  TOK TOK (onom.) the sound of re-
    peatedly striking a hollow wooden
    object

TOKAI the flat side of a *gacuha*; cf.
  taba

TOKDON constellation

TOKDONGGO pertaining to a constellation

TOKOBUMBI 1. caus./pass. of *tokombi*
  2. to have a sharp pain in the belly

TOKOMBI to stab, to stick

TOKOŠOKŪ an implement for pricking or
  stabbing

TOKOŠOMBI to prick, to stab continually

TOKSIBUMBI caus. of *toksimbi*

TOKSIKŪ 1. a small hammer 2. a hollow
  wooden fish beaten by Buddhist monks

TOKSIMBI to knock, to strike, to beat

TOKSIN a wooden percussion instrument
  made in the shape of a square peck
  measure

TOKSITU a 'wooden fish'--a hollow
  wooden fish that is struck rhyth-
  mically during Buddhist ceremonies

TOKSO village

  TOKSO BE KADALARA BA (管莊房)
    office of village administration
    in the Board of Finance in Mukden

  TOKSO TULI village

  TOKSOI BOŠOKŪ village chief, one
    in charge in a village

TOKSOROME toward the village, to the
  village

  TOKSOROME GENEMBI to go to the
    village

TOKTO see *tokton*

TOKTOBA ILHA balloonflower (*Platyco-
  don grandiflorum*)

TOKTOBUMBI 1. caus./pass. of *toktombi*
  2. to fix, to solidify, to make sure
  3. to inlay 4. to pacify, to put
  down (a revolt), to bring under control

  TOKTOBURE GISUN oral agreement

TOKTOFI (perfect converb of *toktombi*)
  certainly, surely, without fail

TOKTOHON determination, certainty,
  fixedness

  TOKTOHON AKŪ uncertain, without
    certainty, undependable

TOKTOMBI to fix, to settle, to determine, to decide

  TOKTOHO GISUN phrase, proverb

  TOKTOHO KOOLI an established rule

TOKTON resolution, determination

TOKTONOMBI 1. to go to fix 2. to get
  backed up (of water)

TOKTOSI broker, middleman, agent

TOLBOTU a gray horse with circular
  markings on its side

TOLDOHON hilt (of a sword)

TOLGIMBI (-ka) to dream

TOLGIMBUMBI 1. caus. of *tolgimbi* 2.
  to appear in a dream

TOLGIN dream

TOLGIŠAMBI to dream about crazy
  things, to have wild dreams

TOLHIMBI see *tolgimbi*

TOLHOLOMBI to cover with birchbark

TOLHON birchbark

  TOLHON I FICAKŪ a deer lure (a type
    of whistle) made of birchbark

  TOLHON WEIHU a birchbark canoe

TOLI 1. a small mirror used by shamans
  2. a belt for holding up the trousers used by children

T

TOLOBUMBI caus. of *tolombi*

TOLOMBI 1. to count 2. to light a torch

TOLON torch

    TOLON TOLOMBI to light a torch

TOLTOHON see *toldohon*

TOMBI see *toombi*

TOME (postposition) every, each

TOMGIYAMBI see *tuwangiyambi*

TOMHIYAN see *tuwancihiyan*

TOMIKA CECIKE one name for the wren; cf. *jirha cecike*

TOMILABUMBI caus./pass. of *tomilambi*

TOMILAMBI to dispatch, to delegate, to assign, to appoint, to give a commission to

    TOMILAME SONJOMBI to select by roll call

    TOMILAME TUCIBUMBI to send out on a commission, to assign

TOMILANDUMBI to dispatch together

TOMOBUMBI caus. of *tomombi*

TOMOHONGGO constant, persevering, determined

TOMOMBI 1. to nest 2. to rest, to stand still

TOMON 1. nesting, resting 2. grave

    TOMON I BA a burial vault

    TOMON MUSEN grave

TOMONJIMBI 1. to come to nest 2. to come to rest

TOMOO frame used for weaving nets

TOMORHAN hood for a falcon

TOMORHON clear, lucid

TOMORO a rather large bowl

TOMOROHON see *tomorhon*

TOMORON a bronze sacrificial vessel used for holding soups

TOMORTAI right in the bull's-eye, right on the mark

TOMOTU LORIN offspring of a donkey and a cow

TOMSOBUMBI caus. of *tomsombi*

TOMSOMBI 1. to pick up (something dropped), to collect, to gather up, to recover 2. to collect the remains of a cremated corpse on the third or fifth day after the cremation

    TOMSOME YALUMBI to remount after a horse has reared

TON 1. number 2. counting, reckoning 3. fate 4. one of the twenty-four divisions of the solar year

    TON ARAMBI to fill out the number, to make up the number, to meet a quota, to fulfill a duty

    TON I KEMUN a weight

    TON I SUCUNGGA INENGGI the first day of one of the twenty solar divisions of the year

TONDO straight, upright, loyal, fair, public

TONDO AKDUN loyalty and trust

TONDO AMBAN 1. a loyal subject 2. a loyal minister

TONDOI HŪDAŠAMBI to do business fairly

TONDOKON 1. rather straight 2. rather loyal, upright

    TONDOKON NIYALMA an upright man

TONDOLOMBI to go straight

TONDONGGE upright, honest, loyal

TONG SEME hard, tough

TONG TONG (onom.) the sound of a shaman's drum

TONGGA limited, rare, few

TONGGALU ILHA the common day lily-- a plant that deer like to eat

TONGGIME clearly and in detail, in toto

    TONGGIME ALAMBI to relate clearly and in detail

TONGGO thread, string

    TONGGO BOSO calico, chintz

    TONGGO MIDAHA a long thin cricket

    TONGGO SUJE satin woven from yarn

    TONGGO SURI silk woven from yarn

    TONGGO TABUMBI to hang yarn

TONGGOLIBUMBI caus. of *tonggolimbi*

TONGGOLIKŪ somersault

TONGGOLIMBI to turn a somersault

    TONGGOLIME MIYOOCALAMBI to fire salvos

TONGKI dot, point

    TONGKI FUKA dots and circles (of the Manchu alphabet)

    TONGKI FUKA AKŪ HERGEN the old Manchu script (before 1641) that lacked dots and circles

    TONGKI GIDAMBI to place dots

TONGKIMBI 1. to make a dot, to write a dot 2. to box on the ear

TONGKIN a gong used when opening and closing the city gates

TONGKIŠAKŪ a type of small cymbal

TONGKIŠAMBI 1. to beat a small cymbal 2. to give repeated blows to the head, to box the ears repeatedly

TONGSIMBI 1. to chirp, to cry (of the cuckoo) 2. to recite incantations

TONGSIRAMBI to tell a story

TONIKŪ chessboard

TONIO *go*, encirclement chess

    TONIO SINDAMBI to play *go*

TONJIMBI to chase fish in a certain direction by beating the water

TONJU see *tono jinggeri*

TONO 1. knob, barb, round head 2. barbs on a *garma* arrow 3. knob on the top of a tent

    TONO JINGGERI knoblike decorations on the top of palace buildings and on city gates

TONTU a fabulous goatlike beast with only one horn that is said to attack the unjust party to a quarrel

TONTU MAHATUN   an ancient-style hat

TOO   a hand drum

TOOBUMBI   caus./pass. of *toombi*

TOODABUMBI   caus. of *toodambi*

TOODAMBI   to return (a debt or loan), to repay, to recompense

TOODANJIMBI   to bring back, to return to the owner

TOODZ   pad, support

TOOHAN   small metal ornaments attached to both sides of the belt

TOOHANJAMBI   to vacillate, to be hesitant, to be slow in deciding

TOOKABUMBI   1. caus. of *tookambi* 2. to postpone, to delay, to waste (someone's time) 3. to drive away, to banish (sadness, melancholy) 4. to miss, to neglect 5. to leave a place

TOOKAMBI   to procrastinate, to delay, to postpone, to waste (time)

TOOKAN AKŪ   1. without procrastination 2. unrestrained

TOOKANJAMBI   to procrastinate, to drag out, to delay, to be delayed

TOOMBI   to scold, to rail at, to abuse, to curse

TOOME   see *tome*

TOONUMBI   to quarrel, to abuse one another

TOOSE   1. weight (for a balance) 2. power, authority, right 3. spindle
TOOSE AKŪ   lacking authority, without power

TOOSELAMBI   1. to weight on a balance 2. to wind on a spindle 3. to exercise authority, to exercise one's power 4. to ponder, to discuss

TOOSENGGE   powerful, mighty

TOR SEME   winding, whirling, spinning

TORGIKŪ   a top
TORGIKŪ TUNGKEN   a drum, narrow at the top and bottom, which is beaten on horseback

TORGIMBI   1. to spin, to circle 2. to write a circle of the Manchu script, to make a circle

TORHIKŪ MAHALA   a hat with a straight fur-trimmed brim

TORHO CECIKE   one name for the wren; cf. *jirha cecike*

TORHO MOO   a long pole at both ends of a dragnet used for fishing in a river

TORHOMBI   to turn, to circle, to revolve, to rotate, to spin
TORHOME   in a circle, around

TORHON   one name for the woodpecker; cf. *fiyorhon*

TORHONOMBI   to form circles, to form rings

TORIBUMBI   to wander, to roam, to have no fixed abode

TORIBUHANGGE   'wanderer, one without a fixed home' a bad name applied to women who have had more than one husband, or a slave who has served more than one master

TORIMBI   to wander, to roam

TORO   peach
TORO EFEN   peach cake--a symbol of longevity
TORO MOO   peach tree

TOROCI   the name of a sour peachlike fruit from Anhui that is eaten salted

TOROMBI   (-ko) to calm down, to settle down, to put one's mind at ease

TOROMBUMBI   1. caus. of *torombi* 2. to put at ease, to comfort, to console

TORON   1. flying dust, a dust storm 2. footprint, trail 3. trace (evidence of a former illness)

TOS SEME   (onom.) the sound made by an arrow or other like implement piercing some object cleanly
TOS SEME TUCIKE   came right through (an arrow)

TOSE   see *toose*

TOSI   white spot on the forehead of an animal

TOSINGGA   having a white spot on the forehead

TOSOBUMBI   caus. of *tosombi*

TOSOMBI   1. to guard against, to prepare for in advance 2. to intercept, to cut off, to ambush on the way, to lie in wait for

TOTAN   one name for the pelican; cf. *kūtan*

TOTOROMBI   to be mischievous, to fool around

TOYON   aim
TOYON BAHA   hit the target, aim was accurate

TOYONGGO   correct (of watches and clocks)

TU   1. a large military standard 2. banner cavalry, banner guard
TU I JANGGIN (護軍統領) Captain-General, BH 734
TU I JANGGIN I SIDEN YAMUN (護軍統領衙門) headquarters of a *tu i janggin*
TU KIRU   standards and banners
TU WECEMBI   to make a sacrifice to the standard

TUB   esteemed, earnest

TUBA   there, that place
TUBACI   thence, from there
TUBADE   there, at that place

TUBAINGGE   that which is there

TUBEHE   the name of a reddish, coarse-finned, carplike river fish that has thick lips

TUBET   Tibet, Tibetan

T

TUBET ABUHA ILHA Tibetan sunflower
TUBET KIONGGUHE Tibetan myna
TUBET MOOI HASI Tibetan persimmon
TUBET ŠU ILHA dahlia
TUBI 1. half, piece, fragment 2. a basket that is placed upside down on chickens 3. a weir basket for fish, a weel
TUBIHE fruit
TUBIHE BELHERE FALGARI (掌醞署) section in charge of fruit in the Court of Banqueting
TUBIHENEMBI to form fruit, to bear fruit
TUBILEMBI 1. to catch in a weir basket, to place a basket over chickens
TUBINGGA MOO a tall tree of Kiangsi with thick, red, bitter bark and a chestnutlike fruit
TUBIŠEMBI to surmise, to estimate
TUBITU another name for the *tontu*
TUCIBUBUMBI caus. of *tucibumbi*
TUCIBUMBI 1. caus. of *tucimbi* 2. to take out, to bring out, to remove (from inside something) 3. to take a coffin to the place of burial 4. to recommend 5. to reveal, to discover 6. to appoint, to delegate, to send out (on a mission) 7. to publish 8. to save, to rescue
TUCIBURE BITHE copy of a memorial sent from the provinces
TUCIBUNJIMBI to come to take out, etc.
TUCIBUNUMBI to take out together, etc.
TUCIBUSI publisher
TUCIMBI (-ke) 1. to come out, to come forth 2. to exit, to go out, to leave 3. to rise (of the sun) 4. to sprout, to spring forth, to originate from
TUCIRE DE SELGIYEBURE KIRU a yellow banner of the escort embroidered with the words *tucire de selgiyebure*
TUCIN beginning, source, origin
TUCINE red center of a target, bull's-eye
TUCINEMBI 1. to go out (there) 2. to appear
TUCINJIMBI to come forth, to appear
TUCINUMBI to come out together, to exit together
TUDI ENDURI the earth god; cf. *banaji*
TUFULEMBI to put one's foot in a stirrup
TUFULEME DABALI FIYELEMBI to vault over a horse after putting the foot in the stirrup
TUFUN stirrup
TUFUN DE GAIFI NIYAMNIYAMBI to shoot from close range from a horse
TUFUN FESHELEME KURBUME FIYELEMBI

to turn around by kicking in the stirrup
TUFUN I FATAN the bottom or footrest of the stirrup
TUFUN I SENGKEN hole on the stirrup through which the thong that connects the stirrup to the saddle is passed
TUFUN I TURA the iron (or bronze) support for the base of the stirrup
TUFUN JAFAFI KURBUME FIYELEMBI to turn around by taking the line that holds up the stirrup in the hand
TUFUN TATAME CASHŪN FIYELEMBI to lean backwards by pulling back on the stirrups
TUFUN TEMŠEMBI to quarrel over the stirrup--i.e., the horse tries to prevent the rider from mounting
TUGI 1. cloud 2. a cloud-shaped ornament
TUGI AGA sexual intercourse
TUGI ALHATA with scattered clouds
TUGI HETEHE the clouds dispersed
TUGI NEIGEN clouds cover the sky
TUGI NOHO SUJE satin covered with cloud designs
TUGI WAN a ladder used for scaling walls
TUGI YUR SEMBI clouds billow upward
TUGIDEI one name for the golden pheasant; cf. *junggiri coko*
TUGINGGA OMOLO a descendant of the eighth generation
TUGINGGE FAN a tablet for imperial edicts of favor
TUGIRI sword bean
TUGITU a small sparrowlike bird that nests in the sand
TUGITU ILHA the name of a tall lotuslike flower
TUGITUN a gong that was beat at T'ien-an gate when imperial edicts of favor were issued
TUHAN 1. a tree that has fallen over, roots and all 2. a single tree that serves as a bridge across a stream 3. a long pole
TUHAŠAMBI to go across a bridge that is made of a single tree
TUHE 1. lid for a pot 2. a trap for weasels made from willow branches in the shape of a pot lid
TUHE EFEN a flat thin cake made of wheat flour and oil and fried on a skillet smeared with fat
TUHEBUKU 1. curtain 2. watergate, sluice 3. portcullis 4. a tassel of coral or gems hanging from a ceremonial hat
TUHEBUKU DOOHAN suspension bridge,

drawbridge

TUHEBUKU HORHO   a bird trap with a falling door

TUHEBUMBI   1. caus. of *tuhembi*   2. to bring to ruin, to drag into a crime, to implicate in a crime   3. to sentence   4. to lower (taxes)   5. to let flow (tears)   6. to let the hair hang freely

TUHEMBI (-ke)   1. to fall, to collapse, to fall down   2. to sink, to set (of the sun)

TUHERE FERE   chicory

TUHEN   fall, conclusion

TUHENEMBI   to fall in, to fall behind, to go to fall

TUHENJIMBI   to fall down from above, to fall towards the speaker, to come to fall

TUHENUMBI   to fall together

TUHERI EBCI   the short ribs of the chest cavity

TUHETE   hanging down, dangling

TUHI   see *tugi*

TUI JANGGIN   see *tu i janggin*

TUI TUI   from mouth to mouth, from hand to hand

TUIBALABUMBI   caus. of *tuibalambi*

TUIBALAKŪ   carpenter's plane

TUIBALAMBI   to plane

TUIBAN   see *tuibalakū*

TUIBUMBI   to blow out the lamp and once again sacrifice to the gods after a shamanistic rite in the home

TUIHŪLU   short-lived

TUIKŪLU   see *tuihūlu*

TUILAMBI   to stampede, to run wildly

TUILEBUMBI   caus. of *tuilembi*

TUILEMBI   to scrape the hair of a slaughtered animal after scalding

TUILENDUMBI/TUILENUMBI   to scrape the hair from a slaughtered beast together

TUIPAN   see *tuibalakū*

TUK TUK SEME   pounding (of the heart)

TUKDA   four wooden sticks in a cooking vessel on which a grill is placed

TUKDEN MOO   the name of a tree similar to *fiyatarakū*

TUKIYA DA   a variety of wild onion

TUKIYEBUMBI   1. caus./pass. of *tukiyembi*   2. to be elegantly attired, to have a striking appearance (after having made up)

TUKIYECEKU   boastful, proud, arrogant

TUKIYECEMBI   1. to lift or raise together   2. to praise, to extol   3. to boast, to be conceited, to be self-satisfied   4. to take boiling water off the fire, to cool hot water by pouring it from one vessel to another

TUKIYECENUMBI   to extol one another

TUKIYECUN   hymn of praise, panegyric

TUKIYEKU   a square fishing net that is thrown from the shore and lifted out of the water from time to time

TUKIYEMBI   1. to lift, to raise, to hold up, to hold high, to carry   2. to offer, to offer in both hands   3. to hoist   4. to recommend, to praise, to laud   5. to promote, to advance   6. to call (honorific)

TUKIYEHE AFAHA   a slip of paper with a resumé of a memorial on it

TUKIYEHE GEBU   honorary name, courtesy name, style

TUKIYEHE GISUN   memorandum, synopsis

TUKIYEHE SILGASI (優 貢)   Senior Licentiate of the second class, BH 522A, 631

TUKIYEHE ŠOŠOHON   a summary of the important points of a memorial attached to the original with a yellow strip of paper

TUKIYEHE ŠOŠOHONGGO KUNGGERI (貼 黃 科)   an office in the Board of Civil Appointments concerned with preparing summaries of memorials

TUKIYEME GAIHA HEHE   midwife

TUKIYENJIMBI   to come to lift, etc.

TUKIYENUMBI   to lift together, etc.

TUKIYERI CECIKE   meadow bunting (*Emberiza godlewski*)

TUKIYESHUN   looking up, facing upwards

TUKIYESHŪN   written for *tukiyeshun*

TUKIYESI (舉人)   Provincial Graduate, BH 629B

TUKSA BOO   a house made of birchbark-- the same as *jeofi*

TUKSAKA   bastard, son of a whore; cf. *lehele*

TUKSICUKE   1. dangerous, in danger   2. frightful, startling

TUKSIMBI (-ke)   1. to pound, to throb, (of the heart)   2. to be alarmed, to be anxious, to be afraid   3. to be exhausted (of livestock)

TUKSIN   throbbing, alarm, anxiety

TUKSITEMBI   to be alarmed, to be greatly anxious

TUKSAN   calf

TUKTAN   at first, originally, beginning

TUKTARHAN   a ladder made from a single tree

TUKTUMA   armor used by cavalry

TUKU   1. the outside surface, the outside   2. the outside of a garment

TUKU JODON   grass linen with designs of wax on it

TUKULEMBI   to put an outside part on something, to surface (v.t.), to add an outer covering

TULBIMBI   to estimate, to surmise, to ponder, to plan beforehand, to guess

T

TULBIN estimation, guessing
TULE outside
  TULE BENJIRE KUNGGERI (外 解 科) a section of the Board of Works
  TULE GENEMBI to go to relieve oneself
  TULE GENERE BA privy, toilet
  TULE GENERE HORHO the same as *tule genere ba*
TULEBUMBI caus. of *tulembi*
TULEJEMBI to put on weight, to become portly
TULEMBI 1. to set (a snare) 2. to cast (a net) 3. to attach (a handle or frame)
TULERGI 1. outside 2. outer, foreign
  TULERGI AMSU I BOO (外 膳 房) foreign kitchen in the palace
  TULERGI EFEN I BOO (外 餑 餑 房) foreign bakery in the palace
  TULERGI GOLO BE DASARA JURGAN (理 藩 院) Court of Colonial Affairs, BH 491
  TULERGI GOLOI BOLORI BEIDEMBI to review the death sentences from the provinces in the autumn
  TULERGI GOLOI HAFAN I KUNGGERI (外 官 科) office in charge of enfeoffments and honorary titles for provincial officials
  TULERGI GURUN foreign country
  TULERGI HERGEN the letters of the Manchu alphabet used for transcribing foreign sounds
  TULERGI JIJUHAN the three upper lines of a hexagram
  TULERGI KŪWARAN I SIMNERE BAITA BE BAICARA HAFAN (外 簾 監 試 官) the examination inspector of the outer hall
  TULERGI SIMNENGGE KUNGGERI (外 考 科) an office in charge of successful examination candidates from the outer provinces
  TULERGI TANGGINGGE BOO (外 堂 房) the name of an office in the Board of Civil Appointments
TULERI the outside, the outer edge, outside
TULESI 1. outward, toward the outside 2. inside out
  TULESI ETUMBI to wear inside out
TULFAMBI to ricochet, to bounce off
TULGIRI NIYEHE the name of a variety of duck--the same as *aka niyehe*
TULGIYEN besides, otherwise, other (the word preceding is followed by the ablative suffix -*ci*)
  TULGIYEN ARAMBI to act differently
  TULGIYEN GŪNIMBI to consider an outsider
  TULGIYEN OBUMBI to consider an outsider, to consider a special case

TULGIYEN SARGAN concubine
TULGUN see *tulhun*
TULHU lambskin
TULHUN cloudy, dark
TULHUŠEMBI to become cloudy
TULIBUMBI caus. of *tulimbi*
TULIMBI (-ke) to run over a deadline, to be overdue, to expire, to run out
TULIMBUMBI see *tulibumbi*
TULIN CECIKE the name of the oriole in Shantung; cf. *gūlin cecike*
TULJEMBI see *tulejembi*
TULU the breast of livestock
TULULAMBI to promote, to advance, to push forward
TULUM a cow- or sheepskin filled with air that is used to support the body across a river
TULUME a belt made of lacquered rattan, filled with air to aid a person crossing a river
TUMBI to hunt, to pursue
TUMEHE ILHA a white flower whose petals resemble butterfly wings
TUMEN ten thousand, a myriad
  TUMEN ARBUN BOLGO NIKTONGGA MUDAN the name of a piece of music played while the food was brought in at a palace banquet
  TUMEN DE in case, should it be that
  TUMEN DE EMGERI in case, should it happen that . . .
  TUMEN JALAFUN DENGJAN a lantern placed on a stand in the inner court at New Year's
  TUMEN JALAFUN JECEN AKŪ 'a myriad lives without limit'--a birthday wish
  TUMEN MUKEI TAMPIN the fourth vessel of the clepsydra of the observatory
  TUMEN SE ten thousand years--long live . . . !
  TUMEN SE OKINI long live . . . !
  TUMEN TUMEN one hundred million
TUMENCI ten-thousandth
TUMENE ILHA the name of a flower whose leaves resemble birds' wings. There are two varieties: one is red with purple spots, and the other is green with brown spots
TUMENGGE MOO *Ligustrum sinense*
TUMENGGERI ten thousand times
TUMENLEME forming a myriad
TUMETE ten thousand each
TUMGETU a certificate given to an official going out on a new assignment
TUMIHA teat
TUMIKAN rather thick, rather viscous, rather deep (colored)
TUMIN 1. thick (of soup, paste, etc.), viscous 2. close, dense, concentrated 3. on close terms, intimate

4. deep (of colors)
TUMIN LAMUN GU lapis lazuli
TUMIN LAMUN SUJE DE AISIN DAMBUHA
  AJIGE KIRU a blue banner of the
  imperial escort depicting a golden
  dragon
TUMIN LAMUN SUJE DE AISIN DAMBUHA
  MUDURINGGA TURUN a blue standard of
  the imperial escort depicting a
  golden dragon
TUMIN NIOWANGGIYAN deep green
TUMIN SOBORO olive green
TUMIN ŠUŠU deep purple
TUMIN TEMERI dark brown
TUMPANAMBI to have a large face, to
  have a pudgy face
TUMSORO a variety of jujube from Suma-
  tra
TUN island
TUN GIOWAN see *mangga ceceri*
TUNG IO tung oil
TUNG MOO the tung tree
TUNG ŠENG (童生) see *sinnesi*
TUNG TANG (onom.) the sound of bells
  and drums
TUNG TUNG (onom.) the sound of a drum
TUNGDZ young lad, boy
TUNGGALABUMBI to run into unexpectedly
TUNGGALAMBI 1. to run into, to en-
  counter 2. to experience
TUNGGALANAMBI to go to encounter
TUNGGEL young boy
TUNGGEN breast, chest, bosom
  TUNGGEN BOKŠON breastbone of cattle
  TUNGGEN DE NIKEBUMBI to take to
    heart, to treat respectfully
  TUNGGEN NEKELIYEN smart, bright
TUNGGI 1. bent over, curved, crooked
  2. too taut (of a bow when the
  string is too short)
TUNGGIOWAN see *mangga ceceri*
TUNGGIYEBUMBI caus. of *tunggiyembi*
TUNGGIYEMBI 1. to pick up 2. to col-
  lect the remains after a cremation
TUNGGU a deep pool, deep part of a
  river, lake or pond
TUNGGULEMBI to treat a wound or bite
  with the fluid obtained from burning
  willow branches
TUNGIO see *tung io*
TUNGJEO I CALU a granary in T'ung-chou
  near Peking
TUNGJY see *uhei saraci*
TUNGKEN 1. drum 2. archery target
  TUNGKEN CAN I KIRU a yellow banner
    of the imperial escort with the
    words *tungken can* written on it in
    gold thread
  TUNGKEN I KEMUN the round hole in
    the middle of a target
  TUNGKEN LAKIYARA KEMUN a hanging
    archery target made of felt
  TUNGKEN TINGGIN I YAMUN (鼓廳

衙門) complaint section of
  the Transmission Office; cf. BH
  928
  TUNGKEN YORO a small bone-headed
    arrow used for target shooting
TUNGKESI drummer
TUNGKI TANGKI staggering, reeling
TUNGKU a small dragnet used for fish-
  ing under ice
  TUNGKU TEMBI to fish with a *tungku*
TUNGLU patina, verdigris
TUNGNIBUMBI caus. of *tungnimbi*
TUNGNIMBI to treat a wound or bite
  with the fluid obtained from burning
  willow branches
TUNGSE translator, interpreter; cf.
  hafumbukū
  TUNGSE KAMCIMBI to bring along an
    interpreter
TUNGSEREBUMBI caus. of *tungserembi*
TUNGSEREMBI to translate, to interpret
TUNGSIKA GURGU jackal
TUNGTUNG TANGTANG (onom.) the sound of
  bells and drums together
TUNIYELTU CECIKE another name for the
  bird *niyengniyeltu cecike*
TUNIYEME FEKUMBI to jump with the aid
  of a pole, to pole-vault
TUNUHŪ crown daisy (*Chrysanthemum
  coronarium*)
TUR (onom.) 1. the sound of a horse
  clearing its nose 2. at a gallop
TUR SEME at a gallop, fast
TUR TAR 1. (onom.) the sound of muskets
  firing 2. anxious, frightened 3.
  crackling, like frying beans
TUR TAR SEME 1. crackling, sputtering
  2. anxious, fearful
TURA pillar, supporting pole in a tent
TURABUMBI caus. of *turambi*
TURAKI jackdaw
TURAKŪ waterfall
TURAMBI 1. to pour, to pour off, to
  pour the water off rice or meat
  2. to stand firm (like a pillar)
  TURAME AGAMBI to rain cats and dogs
  TURAME ILIMBI to stand firmly
TURBELJI one name for the eagle; cf.
  tashari
TURE the leg of a boot
TUREMIMBI to attach the leg of a boot
  or a shoe
TURGA 1. thin, skinny, lean 2. a
  round piece of cloth over the tassel
  of a hat
  TURGA EFEN round cakes made of bean
    meal without the addition of oil
TURGATU a skinny person
TURGEN 1. fast, swift 2. urgent,
  acute, serious (illness)
TURGIMBI to clear the nose (of horses),
  to snort
TURGUN reason, motive, circumstances

T

TURGUN ARBUN circumstances, situation

TURGUN BE ANAMBI to put forth as a reason

TURGUNDE (after a participle) because, since

TURGŪT Torgot, Oirat

TURHA 1. a round piece of cloth on the tassel of a cap 2. a dab (of rouge)

TURHUN see *turgun*

TURI bean, pea

TURI ARSUN bean sprout

TURI CAI a variety of wild tea whose leaves resemble the leaves of the pea plant

TURI CECIKE hawfinch (*Euphonia personata*)

TURI HOHO pea pod, bean pod

TURI MIYEHU bean curd

TURIBUMBI 1. caus./pass. of *turimbi* 2. to come loose, to come untied 3. to let go, to lose 4. to emit (semen)

TURIBUHE EJEN loser, one who has lost something

TURIGEN 1. rent 2. wages

TURIMBI to rent, to lease, to hire

TURIHE HŪSUN a hired worker

TURIHE NIYALMA a hired man

TURITU soy bean paste

TURŠUL scout, spy

TURTUN a type of thin silk yarn

TURTUN CECE a very light silk gauze

TURU 1. a belt for carrying a sword 2. sayings of holy or wise men, traditional methods handed down by the disciples of a wise man

TURULABUMBI caus. of *turulambi*

TURULAMBI to be first, to be at the head of, to be the leader

TURUN a large standard

TURUN I WECEN sacrifice to the standard (performed before battle)

TURUN WECEMBI to sacrifice to the standard

TURUNGGE JUNGKEN a musical instrument consisting of twelve bells on a frame, each one of which corresponds to one of the twelve earth's branches

TUS SEME UKCAMBI to come loose (of something tied)

TUSA profit, gain, benefit, advantage

TUSA AKŪ of no benefit, profitless

TUSA ARAMBI to do something of profit, to do something to benefit someone

TUSALAMBI to be advantageous, to be profitable

TUSANGGA beneficial, profitable

TUSANGGA CALU a government granary in which surplus grain was stored to be sold to the people in famine years

TUSERGEN a tall table on which cups and plates were placed at banquets

TUSHŪ a cup given to guests to drink from at the door

TUSIHIYA a net for catching falcons

TUSIHIYALAMBI 1. to catch falcons with a net 2. to catch in the claws (of panthers, tigers)

TUSU BIYA a month propitious for marriage

TUSULAMBI see *teisulembi*

TUSUMBI 1. to give a girl in marriage 2. to be married (of a woman)

TUSY chieftain of a native tribe

TUSY IRGEN subjects of a native chieftain

TUŠABUMBI caus. of *tušambi*

TUŠAHŪ one name for the owl; cf. *hūšahū*

TUŠAMBI 1. to encounter, to meet with (something undesirable) 2. to pass through, to experience 3. to happen, to occur 4. to commission, to charge with

TUŠAN 1. duty 2. office, official post 3. commission

TUŠAN BE AKŪMBUMBI to fulfill a duty to the best of one's ability

TUŠAN DE AFAHA HAFAN (登 仕 佐 郎) honorary title for officials of the ninth rank second degree, BH 945

TUŠAN DE AKŪMBUHA HAFAN (儒 林 郎) honorary title for officials of the sixth rank second degree, BH 945

TUŠAN DE BAITALABUHA DAIFAN (奉 直 大 夫) honorary title given to officials of the fifth rank second degree, BH 945

TUŠAN DE BAITALABUHA HAFAN (修 職 佐 郎) honorary title given to officials of the eighth rank second degree, BH 945

TUŠAN DE DOSIKA HAFAN (登 仕 郎) honorary title given to officials of the ninth rank first degree, BH 945

TUŠAN DE FAŠŠAHA DAIFAN (朝 議 大 夫) honorary title given to officials of the fourth rank second degree, BH 945

TUŠAN DE FAŠŠAHA HAFAN (徵 仕 郎) honorary title given to officials of the seventh rank second degree, BH 945

TUŠAN DE GINGGULEHE DAIFAN (奉 政 大 夫) honorary title given to officials of the fifth rank first degree, BH 945

TUŠAN DE GINGGULEHE HAFAN (修 職 郎) honorary title given to officials of the eighth rank first

T

degree, BH 945

TUŠAN DE KICEHE DAIFAN (中憲大夫) honorary title given to officials of the fourth rank first degree, BH 945

TUŠAN DE KICEHE HAFAN (文林郎) honorary title given to officials of the seventh rank first degree, BH 945

TUŠAN DE MUTEBUHE HAFAN (承德郎) honorary title given to officials of the sixth rank first degree, BH 945

TUŠAN JERGI   official rank

TUŠANAMBI   to happen upon something

TUŠANGGA MAHATUN   a hat worn by officials in ancient times

TUŠANJIMBI   to come to meet, to come to experience

TUŠU   a private seal

TUTABUMBI   1. caus. of *tutambi*   2. to leave behind

TUTALA   so many (as that), those several

TUTAMBI   1. to fall behind, to lag behind   2. to remain behind   3. to survive (from antiquity)   4. to be overdue, to expire (of a deadline)

TUTTU   like that, thus, so
   TUTTU BIME   nevertheless, however, yet
   TUTTU OCI   if like that, if thus, in that case
   TUTTU OFI   therefore, so
   TUTTU OSO   so be it
   TUTTU OTOLO   even thus, even to the point of being like that
   TUTTU SEME   but, however, yet, although it is so

TUTTUSI   in that direction, thither
   TUTTUSI OSO   a little more in that direction

TUWA   fire
   TUWA FILEKU   brazier
   TUWA I AGŪRA   firearms
   TUWA I FITHEN   sparks that fly out from a fire
   TUWA I OKTO   gunpowder
   TUWA IBERE SABKA   fire tongs
   TUWA SINDAMBI   to set a fire
   TUWA TURIBUMBI   to catch fire
   TUWA USIHA   the planet Mars
   TUWA YAHA   charcoal
   TUWAI AGŪRAI KŪWARAN I SIDEN YAMUN (火器營衙門) Headquarters of the Artillery and Musket Division, BH 733
   TUWAI BUJAN USIHAI DOOHAN I MUDAN a piece of music played at court on New Year's evening when the lanterns were hung
   TUWAI BULEKU   burning glass, lens
   TUWAI EFIN   fireworks
   TUWAI EYE   a fire pit

TUWAI OKTO   gunpowder
TUWAI OKTO I NAMUN (火藥庫) ammunition-store of the palace
TUWAI POO   a cannon
TUWAI SEYE   hole in an oven-bed
TUWAI SIBERHEN   fuse
TUWAI SIREN   fuse

TUWABUMBI   1. caus./pass. of *tuwambi*   2. to introduce into an audience   3. to divine   4. to show, to exhibit
   TUWABURE AFAHA   a slip of paper on which the names of those appearing in an audience appeared

TUWABUN   1. survey, review   2. view, prospect, situation

TUWABUNAMBI   to go to be seen, to go to be examined, to go to show or exhibit

TUWABUNGGA   the published name list of successful candidates in an examination
   TUWABUNGGA HOOŠAN   the paper on which examination results were written

TUWABUNJIMBI   to come to show or exhibit

TUWAKIYABUMBI   caus. of *tuwakiyambi*

TUWAKIYAKŪ   guard, watchman

TUWAKIYAMBI   to watch, to guard, to watch over, to observe
   TUWAKIYARA COOHA   garrison troops, guard troops
   TUWAKIYARA HAFAN (守備) Second Captain, BH 752D

TUWAKIYACAMBI   see *tuwamgiyambi*

TUWAKIYAN   discretion in conduct

TUWAKIYANAMBI   to go to watch, watchfulness

TUWAKIYANDUMBI   to watch together

TUWAKIYANGGA   inspecting, supervising

TUWAKIYANJIMBI   to come to watch together, to watch one another

TUWAKIYANTU ENDURI   the guardian deity of city walls

TUWAKIYASI   guard, watchman
   TUWAKIYASI DA (守史尉) chief of the watch

TUWAKŪ   1. aspect, appearance   2. exemplary behavior, model, example

TUWAMBI   1. to look, to look at   2. to observe, to examine, to oversee   3. to consult (the yarrow stalks), to divine   4. to visit
   TUWAME   (postposition with the accusative) in accordance with, depending on
   TUWAME KADALARA HAFAN (監督) supervisor, director, superintendent
   TUWAME WEILEBURE UHERI TUWARA HAFAN (監修總裁官) director-general

TUWARA GISUN   reference to a case

T

in the statutes

TUWARA NIYALMA a fortuneteller

TUWAMCIN circumspect, prudent

TUWAMEHANGGA nice to look at, attractive

TUWAMGIYABUMBI caus. of *tuwamgiyambi*

TUWAMGIYAMBI to straighten out, to correct (an error), to correct (something one has said)

TUWAMGIYATAMBI to correct, to make straight

TUWANABUMBI caus. of *tuwanambi*

TUWANAMBI to go and look, to go to visit

TUWANCIHIYABUMBI caus. of *tuwancihiyambi*

TUWANCIHIYABUN cultivation, rectification

TUWANCIHIYAKŪ 1. corrector 2. (庶子) supervisor of instruction in the Supervisorate of Imperial Instruction 3. rudder, helm

TUWANCIHIYAKŪ .E GIDARA MOO a piece of wood holding the rudder on the stern of a ship

TUWANCIHIYAMBI to straighten, to put in order, to correct, to rectify, to guide a horse

TUWANCIHIYARA YAMUN (春坊) a subsection of the Supervisorate of Imperial Instruction

TUWANCIHIYARA YAMUN DE BAITALAMBI to be promoted to the Supervisorate of Imperial Instruction from the Hanlin Academy

TUWANCIHIYAN correction, ordering, putting into order

TUWANCIHIYAN DAILAN a punitive war, a just war against an unrighteous enemy

TUWANCIHIYANGGA rectifying, cultivating

TUWANGGIBUMBI caus. of *tuwanggimbi*

TUWANGGIMBI to send to look, to send to examine

TUWANGGIYAKŪ inspector

TUWANGGIYAMBI to inspect, to look over

TUWANJIMBI to come to look, to come to visit

TUWANUMBI to look together, to observe together

TUWARAN Taoist temple

TUWAŠABUMBI caus. of *tuwašambi*

TUWAŠAMBI 1. to watch, to guard 2. to keep close watch on, to supervise, to take care of, to watch over

TUWAŠARA HAFAN (雲騎尉)

an honorary title of the eighth degree

TUWAŠARA HAFAN I JERGI JANGGIN (防禦) Captain, BH 97E, 746, 748

TUWAŠATABUMBI caus. of *tuwašatambi*

TUWAŠATAMBI 1. to take care of, to supervise, to look after 2. to look at, to gaze upon

TUWELEBUMBI caus. of *tuwelembi*

TUWELEMBI to buy at one place and sell in another, to deal in, to trade in, to peddle

TUWELESI peddler, small tradesman

TUWERI winter

TUWERI BE BODORO HAFAN (冬官正) Astronomer for the Winter, BH 229

TUWERI DOSIMBI 1. winter comes 2. one of the twenty-four divisions of the solar year, falling on November seventh or eighth

TUWERI HETUMBI to pass the winter, to spend the winter

TUWERI TEN the winter solstice

TUWERI WECEN the winter ancestral sacrifice

TUWERIKTEN the winter sacrifice to the ancestors

TUWERIMU ILHA the name of a fragrant red flower with long thorny stems and a yellow center

TUWETURI CECIKE another name for the *turi cecike*

TUYABUMBI 1. caus./pass. of *tuyambi*

TUYAMBI 1. to bend, to curve, to bow, to make crooked 2. to bend backward (in wrestling)

TUYEBUMBI caus./pass. of *tuyembi*

TUYEKTE the name of a sour red fruit

TUYEKU drill for making holes in metal

TUYEKU YONGGAN impure ammonia salts

TUYEMBI 1. to drill, to bore, to pierce 2. to make a concentrated attack against one point

TUYEMBUBUMBI caus. of *tuyembumbi*

TUYEMBUMBI 1. to appear, to be revealed, to be exposed 2. to have one's poverty or difficult circumstances become known at large

TŪBUMBI caus. of *tūmbi*

TŪKU 1. a wooden mallet 2. a pestle for pounding grain

TŪMBI to hit, to beat, to pound; cf. *dumbi*

TŪME EFEN a type of steamed millet cake

TS

TSAI FUNG tailor

TSAI ŠEN ENDURI the god of wealth

TSAIDZ festoon of colored thread or paper

TSAIFUNG see *tsai fung*

TSANDZAN (參贊) advisor, consultant

TSANG 1. granary 2. cabin on a boat

|TSANJENG (參政) councillor to a provincial treasurer, see *aliha hafan*

TSANJIYANG (參將) Lieutenant Colonel; cf. *adaha kadalara da*

TSOO BA DALAN dam made of grass

TSU vinegar

TSUI CECIKE kingfisher; cf. *ulgiyan cecike*

TSUI GASHA see *ulgiyari*

TSUI ILGA an ornament made of kingfisher feathers

TSUN a Chinese inch; cf. *jurhun*

TS

U

U 1. thorn 2. (onom.) noise made by
ghosts and demons 3. elder; cf.
ungga

U DA elders, the senior generation

U DZO coroner

U SEME wailing, howling

U TUNG MOO Chinese parasol tree (*Firmiana simplex*)

U U (onom.) the sound of weeping

UBA 1. here, this place 2. this
(thing)
    UBA ADARAME what is this all about?
    what is going on here?
    UBACI hence, from here
    UBADE at this place, here
    UBADE AINAMBI what is wrong here?

UBAINGGE that which belongs here, one
who is from here

UBAKA TUBAKA SEME evasively

UBALIYAMBI (-ka) 1. to turn over (v.i.)
2. to be inside out 3. to change,
to have a change of heart, to turn
against, to revolt
    UBALIYAME ETUMBI to wear wrong side
    out
    UBALIYAME FAHAMBI to overturn (at
    wrestling)

UBALIYAMBUBUMBI caus. of *ubaliyambumbi*

UBALIYAMBUMBI 1. caus. of *ubaliyambi*
2. to translate 3. to turn over

UBAMBI (-ka) to go bad, to get moldy,
to decompose

UBAŠABUMBI caus. of *ubašambi*

UBAŠAKŪ 1. inconstant, fickle, changeable 2. a type of deep-fried turn-
over

UBAŠAMBI 1. to turn over, to turn up
(soil) 2. to revolt

UBAŠATAMBI 1. to turn over and over
2. to be devious, to be fickle

UBIHIYA YALI the meat from the cavities
of the shoulder bone of an animal

UBISE gallnuts

UBIYABUMBI caus./pass. of *ubiyambi*

UBIYABURU monster, horrid creature

UBIYACUKA detestable, hateful, disgusting

UBIYACUN disgust, abomination, loathing

UBIYADA detestable, hateful, execrable

UBIYAMBI to detest, to loathe

UBIYOO a type of edible seaweed, agar-
agar

UBU 1. portion, share, part, responsibility 2. times, -fold
    UBU AKŪ hopeless
    UBU BANJIBUMBI to apportion duties
    UBU GOIBUMBI to divide into portions
    UBU SIBIYA portions and shares,
    shares
    UBUI UBU many times more, manifold

UBUNGGE pertaining to portions or
shares

UCA tail bone

UCALAMBI to dry meat in the open air
    UCALAHA YALI meat dried in the air

UCARABUMBI caus./pass. of *ucarambi*

UCARABUN the same as *ucaran*

UCARAMBI to meet, to encounter

UCARAN meeting, encounter

UCE door
    UCE BE COBALAME NEIMBI to force a
    door open

UCIKA 1. waterproof case for a bow
2. the front fin of a fish; cf.
fethe

UCIKALAMBI to put a bow in a case

UCILEN Central Asiatic hazel

UCUBUMBI caus. of *ucumbi*

UCUBUN mixing

UCUDAMBI to keep on mixing, to mix
steadily

UCULEBUMBI caus. of *uculembi*

UCULEMBI 1. to sing 2. to mix
    UCULEME HŪLAMBI 'to sing and
    shout'--said of troops after a
    victorious battle when one person
    sings a line and is then joined by

all the troops in chorus
UCULEN 1. song 2. *tz'u* (詞)--a
  genre of Chinese poetry 3. see
  ucilen
UCULENJIMBI to come to sing
UCULESI a singer, a boy singer
UCUMBI to mix, to mix together, to
  blend
UCUN song, ballad
UCURI 1. time, opportunity 2. see
  ere ucuri
  UCURI NASHŪN opportunity, chance
UDA see *uta*
UDABUMBI caus. of *udambi*
UDALA bridle bit
UDAMBI to buy
  UDAME ICIHIYARA BA (買 辦 處)
    purchasing section of the Board of
    Banqueting
UDANABUMBI caus. of *udanambi*
UDANAMBI to go to buy
UDANJIMBI to come to buy
UDANUMBI to buy together, for each one
  to buy
UDELEMBI to take a midday rest
UDEN rest at midday (especially on a
  journey)
UDU 1. how many? how much? 2. several
  3. although
  UDU GORO how far?
  UDU JUWAN several tens
  UDU URSU several layers
UDUCI what . . . -th? *si uduci de bi?*
  'what rank are you (among your broth-
  ers)?' *bi jakūci de bi* 'I am the
  eighth.'
UDUDU several, a number of, many
UDUMBARA fig
UDUNGGERI how many times
UDURSU several layers
UDUTE how many each
UDUWEN a Tibetan black bear (*Euarc-
  tos thibetanus*); *f. jaira*
UFA flour, meal
  UFA CAI tea with flour mixed in it
  UFA I DA wheat from which the flour
    has been removed
  UFA I ŠUGI gluten of wheat
UFABUMBI caus. of *ufambi*
UFAMBI to mill flour
UFARABUMBI caus. of *ufarambi*
UFARACUN loss, failure, error
UFARAKI a slight error
UFARAMBI 1. to err, to make a mistake
  about something, to fail, to miss,
  to lose (interest) 2. to perish, to
  die
UFARAN lack, loss
UFARŠAMBI see *ufarambi*
UFIBUMBI caus. of *ufimbi*
UFIHI see *ufuhi*
UFIMBI to sew; cf. *ifimbi*
  UFIRE TABURE SAIN gifted in sewing

UFUHI part, share, portion
UFUHU lung
  UFUHU EFEN small deep-fried pastries
    made of honey, egg, and flour
  UFUHU WEHE a very porous stone found
    in streams that can be used for
    dressing sable hides, pumice
UFUHUNEMBI 1. to form a soft, porous
  core 2. to form a red, porous ap-
  pearance on the face
UGINGGE COKO one name for the chicken;
  cf. *ikiri coko*
UGUNG centipede
UHALA testicles
UHE 1. community, mutuality, general-
  ity, unity 2. common, mutual, gen-
  eral, united, uniform, of one kind
  UHE DAKŪ common assent, mutual
    agreement
  UHE HŪWALIYAN mutual harmony
  UHEI united, together, mutual,
    cooperative
  UHEI SARACI (同 知) subprefect
UHELEMBI 1. to act together, to be to-
  gether, to act cooperatively 2. to
  unite, to make general
UHELENJIMBI to come to unite
UHEN younger brother's wife
UHEREME altogether, in toto
UHERI 1. altogether, jointly, in com-
  mon, in general, taken as a whole
  2. chief, main, head 3. general,
  outline, summary
  UHERI BE BAICARA YAMUN (都 察
    院) the Censorate, BH 206
  UHERI BE BAICARA YAMUN I EJEKU (都
    事) Official of the Censorate
    Chancery, BH 211
  UHERI DA (總 管) director,
    superintendent, commandant, con-
    troller-general, etc., BH 87A,
    97E, 570, etc.
  UHERI DA YAMUN (總 管 衙 門)
    office of the director, etc.
  UHERI DANGSE ASARARA KUNGGERI (櫃
    總 科) the central chancery of
    the Board of War
  UHERI DANGSE BOO (總 檔 房)
    archives at the western and
    eastern imperial tombs
  UHERI IKTAMBURE CALU the name of a
    granary in the city of Mergen in
    Heilungkiang
  UHERI KADALARA AMBAN (總 督)
    Governor-General, BH 820
  UHERI KADALARA DA (總 兵)
    Brigade General, BH 751
  UHERI KOOLI (會 典) the as-
    sembled statutes of a dynasty
  UHERI KOOLI BITHEI KUREN (會 典
    館) office charged with compila-
    tion of the *uheri kooli bithe*
    (會 典)

U

UHERI KUNGGERI (總 科) central chancellery

UHERI SARACI a subprefect

UHERI TUKIYEN general name, general designation

UHERI TUSANGGA CALU the name of granaries of the Board of Finance in Mukden and Canton

UHERI TUWAME SIMNERE HAFAN examination proctor

UHERI TUWARA AMBAN (掌 衛 事 大 臣) Superintendent of the Imperial Equipage Department

UHERILEMBI to unite, to compile, to put together, to do in a general way

UHERILEME EJEHE BITHE (一 統 志) the general dynastic geographical gazetteer

UHERILEME EJEHE BITHEI KUREN (一 統 志 館) office charged with the compilation of the above work

UHERITAI altogether, as a whole

UHESU learned, highly educated

UHETE plural of *uhen*

UHETUN harmony

UHUBUMBI caus. of *uhumbi*

UHUKEDEMBI to be weak, to be soft

UHUKELIYAN rather weak, soft

UHUKEN 1. soft, weak 2. gentle

UHUKEN TUWABUNGGA HOOŠAN white announcement paper

UHUMBI to wrap, to roll, to roll up

UHUME father's younger brother's wife

UHUMETE plural of *uhume*

UHUN bundle, package

UHUN BUHELIYEN a bundle made of grass or reeds

UHUN I HŪSUN packer, bundler--a man who puts rice into bundles at a granary

UHUNGGE HOOŠAN wrapping paper

UHUTU a scroll

UHŪBUMBI caus. of *uhūmbi*

UHŪKŪ a knife used for gouging or scooping--especially the knife used for making holes in bone and horn arrowheads

UHŪLJA wild sheep, argali, Darwin's sheep (*Ovis ammon*)

UHŪLJI see *uhūlja*

UHŪMA NIRU the name of an arrow with a head curved on the end like a crescent moon--used for hunting

UHŪMBI to gouge, to scoop out

UHŪYAN a hole that has been gouged out

UI NIMAHA flying fish

UIHE horn; cf. *weihe*

UIHE HADAMBI to nail on the horn facing of a bow

UIHENGGE horned, having horns

UIHERIN rhinoceros

UIHETON a fabulous piglike beast with one horn on its nose that can walk ten thousand miles in one day and can understand the language of the barbarians

UIHETONGGE KIRU a banner of the imperial escort depicting the figure of a horn

UILE see *weile*

UILEBUMBI caus. of *uilembi*

UILEMBI to serve, to wait on, to attend

UILEN service, attendance

UJAN 1. boundary of a field 2. the end point, the end, extremity

UJAN I BOO a building built near the side wings of a large house

UJAN ŠALA odds and ends, patches, remnants, trifles

UJAN YALU paths between cultivated fields

UJEKEN rather heavy

UJELEBUMBI caus./pass. of *ujelembi*

UJELEMBI 1. to be heavy 2. to act respectfully, to treat respectfully 3. to be serious, to act in a serious manner 4. to act generously 5. to value highly

UJEN 1. heavy 2. serious 3. valuable 4. worthy of respect

UJEN BE ETERE MORIN a horse that can carry heavy loads

UJEN COOHA the Chinese troops of the eight banners

UJEN COOHAI GŪSA (漢 軍 部 統) a banner general of the Chinese troops

UJEN JINGJI heavy and firm

UJIBUMBI caus./pass. of *ujimbi*

UJIBURE TACIHIYAN I MUDAN a piece of music played during the wine-drinking ceremony of the Metropolitan Prefecture

UJIMA livestock, domestic animal

UJIMA ERIKU a broom made from old wild broomstraw

UJIMA I HORIGAN a corral for livestock

UJIMBI (-he) 1. to raise, to nurture, to nourish 2. to give birth to

UJIHE AMA foster father

UJIHE EME foster mother

UJIHE ENIYE the same as *ujihe eme*

UJIHE JUI foster son

UJIRE EME nurse, wet nurse

UJIRE HAFAN (牧 夫) an official title of the Chou dynasty

UJIRE KŪWARAN a shelter or asylum for the destitute

UJIME see *ujima*

UJIN 1. child of a household slave 2. colt of a family horse

UJIN DAHAN colt born of a family mare

UJINAMBI to go to raise, to go to nourish

UJINDUMBI/UJINUMBI to raise together, to nurture together

UJINGGA NIONGNIYAHA one name for the goose; cf. *niongniyaha*

UJINGGA NIYEHE one name for the duck

UJIRHI manul, cat of the steppes (*Felis manul*)

UJU 1. head 2. first 3. the first month of one of the four seasons 4. a large bead at the beginning of a rosary 5. beginning

  UJU CI ANAME UNCEHEN DE ISITALA from head to tail

  UJU DE ACAMJAFI BAHAMBI to make it on the first try

  UJU DE TEBUMBI to seat in the place of honor

  UJU ETERAKŪ without being able to lift the head

  UJU GIDAMBI to bow the head

  UJU FUSIMBI to get a haircut

  UJU JAI first and second

  UJU JERGI first class, first rank

  UJU JERGI HIYA attendant of the first class

  UJU JERGI UNENGGI HEHE the wife of an official of the first rank

  UJU LIYELIYEMBI 'the head is dizzy'--to be dizzy

  UJU NIMEMBI the head aches, to have a headache

  UJU SENCEHE the chin of edible animals

  UJU TENGKIBUMBI to let the head hang

  UJU TUWANCIHIYAKŪ a rudder at the bow of a boat used for turning the boat around

UJUCI first, from the beginning

UJUDE at the beginning, first

UJUI MUDAN the first time

UJUI UJU first of all, paramount

UJULABUMBI caus. of *ujulambi*

UJULAMBI to head, to head up, to be in charge, to be head

  UJULAHA AMBAN (首輔大臣) chief minister

UJUNGGA first, leading

  UJUNGGA DANGGA leader, headman

  UJUNGGA JUI first son

UJUNGGE the first one

UKACAMBI to steal away, to sneak off, to run away together

UKADA a mound with grass growing on it

UKADAMBI to run away

UKAMBI (-ha/ka, -ra/ndara) to flee, to run away, to desert

UKAMBUMBI 1. caus. of *ukambi* 2. to bury (a coffin)

UKAN CECIKE the name of a small black-headed bird that resembles the sparrow

UKANDUMBI/UKANUMBI to flee together

UKANJU fugitive

  UKANJU BE KADALAME JAFARA BOLGOBURE FIYENTEN (督捕清吏司) section of the Board of Punishments concerned with deserters from the banner troops

UKARALAMBI to be in flight

UKATAN one name for the pelican; cf. *kūtan*

UKCABUMBI caus. of *ukcambi*

UKCAMBI to come loose, to fall off, to get free, to escape from, to elude

UKDU see *ukdun*

UKDUN a hole in the earth in which people live

  UKDUN BOO a cave dwelling, hole dwelling

UKECI a type of monkey resembling a black dog without a tail

UKI a female otter; cf. *hailun*

UKIYAKA CECIKE one name for the common snipe; cf. *karka cecike*

UKIYEBUMBI caus. of *ukiyembi*

UKIYEMBI to drink gruel or some other thin substance

UKSA unexpectedly, suddenly

  UKSA FAKSA totally unexpected

UKSAJAMBI to come loose, to slacken

UKSALABUMBI caus. of *uksalambi*

UKSALAMBI 1. to come loose, to come apart, to slacken 2. to leave, to depart from 3. to run away from, to escape from 4. to free oneself from

UKSAN see *uksa*

UKSEN a small woven belt or band

UKSILEBUMBI caus. of *uksilembi*

UKSILEMBI to put on armor

UKSILENDUMBI/UKSILENUMBI to put on armor together

UKSIN 1. armor 2. a soldier wearing armor

UKSINGGA wearing armor, armored

UKSUN 1. clan, family, kin 2. members of the imperial family descended from Nurgaci

  UKSUN BE KADALARA YAMUN (宗人府) the Imperial Clan Court, BH 56

  UKSUN I HERGEN the rank or position of a member of the imperial clan

  UKSUN I TACIKŪ (宗室學) imperial clan school

UKSUNGGA consisting of many kin, having many relations

UKSURA 1. branch of a clan 2. a people, a tribe

UKTU plaintive, sad

UKTUN quiet, possessing character, able to hold one's temper

UKU 1. a falcon trap made of a net and cage that contains a live bird bait 2. a fish weir, a cage used for

U

catching fish, a weel

UKUHU   Chinese lantern plant (*Physalis alkekengi*)

   UKUHU YOO   the same as *ukuhe yoo*

UKULEBUMBI   caus. of *ukulembi*

UKULEMBI   1. to turn down the brim (or ear flaps) of a hat   2. to surround

UKUMBI   1. to surround, to form around (someone), to form a circle, to crowd around   2. to form the retinue of an official

   UKUHE YOO   small pustules on a horse's body

UKUNDUMBI   to form a circle together, to form around together

UKUNJIMBI   1. to come to form a circle, to come to surround   2. to come with a retinue to pay homage at court   3. to turn toward   4. to surround

UKUNU   a surrounding crowd or retinue

UKURI   the name of a fine-scaled sea fish that resembles the *yabsa*

UKUDA   see *ukada*

ULA   1. a (large) river   2. relay post

   ULA KILAHUN   the Yangtze gull

   ULA ŠUŠU   provisions taken on a trip by relay posts

   ULA YALURE ŠUŠU JETERE   post mount and provisions

ULABUMBI   caus. of *ulambi*

ULABUN   1. tradition, what is handed down   2. biography

ULACI   postrider, relay rider

ULADAMBI   to be lame because of a damaged hoof

ULAHUN   another name for the Yangtze gull

ULAMBI   to hand down, to pass on, to hand on, to pass to

   ULAME BENERE KUNGGERI (遞送科) transmission office of the Board of War

   ULAME SARKIYAHA BITHE   a copy of a document issued by a board for distribution outside

ULAMBUMBI   caus. of *ulambi*

ULAN   1. traditional teaching, something handed down   2. ditch, moat   3. furrow, groove, indentation

   ULAN HAT   fruit of the flowering cherry

   ULAN ULAN I   1. by tradition, in unbroken tradition   2. from mouth to mouth, from hand to hand

   ULAN YOHORON   ditches and canals

ULANA   *Prunus humilis*--a kind of small, red, sour cherry common in Manchuria and Northern China

ULANAMBI   to go to pass on to someone

ULANDUMBI   to hand down from one person to another, to pass on from one person to another

   ULANDUME JUWERE FALGANGGA (遞運

所) freight transfer point on a river or canal

ULANDUSI (提塘)   Superintendent of a Military Post, BH 435

   ULANDUSI TINGGIN (塘務廳) office of a *ulandusi*

ULANGGA KIRU   a banner of the imperial escort with waves of the Yangtze depicted on it

ULBIMBI   to jump from branch to branch (of squirrels, sable, etc.)

ULCEN   see *ulcin*

ULCILEMBI   to string (cash)

ULCIN   string (of cash)

ULDEFUN   a large hoe made of wood

ULDEMBI   (-ke)   to become light, to dawn

ULDEN   light, rays (of the sun)

ULDENGGE   shining, lit up

   ULDENGGE USIHA   a bright star of good foreboding

ULDERHEN   one name for the lark; cf. *wenderhen*

ULE   orache, atriplex (a plant)

   ULE UMIYAHA   a long yellowish insect with narrow wings that is used as fish bait

ULEBUBUMBI   caus. of *ulebumbi*

ULEBUMBI   1. caus. of *ulembi*   2. to feed, to raise (domestic animals)   3. to dip a writing brush in ink, to saturate a brush with ink

ULEBUSI   a man who fed animals destined for sacrifice

ULEJEKU   collapse, landslide

ULEJEMBI   to collapse, to fall down

ULEMBI   to sew (a straight seam)

ULEN   irrigation ditch, small ditch between fields

ULENGGU   1. navel   2. large bead at the end of a rosary

ULERI   see *uluri*

ULGA   see *ulha*

ULGABUMBI   caus. of *ulgambi*

ULGAKU   inkwell, well for ink on an inkstone

ULGAMBI   to wet, to dampen, to dip in a liquid

ULGAN   pliant, flexible (bows that hold the string well)

ULGIMBI   see *ulhimbi*

ULGITUN   see *ulhitun*

ULGIYACI   pigskin

ULGIYADA NISIHA   the name of a speckled river fish

ULGIYAN   1. swine, pig   2. the twelfth of the earth's branches (亥)

   ULGIYAN BIYA   the tenth month

   ULGIYAN CECIKE   kingfisher (*Alcedo atthis*)

   ULGIYAN MANGGISU   one name for the badger; cf. *dorgon*

   ULGIYAN ORHO   'pig grass'--the name of a plant with fine stems, green

U

leaves, and many branches
ULGIYAN TUMBI to hunt pigs in winter
ULGIYANGGA pertaining to the twelfth
cyclical sign, pertaining to the pig
ULGIYANGGA ANIYA the year of the pig
ULGIYARI CECIKE one name for the king-
fisher; cf. *ulgiyan cecike*
ULGŪ see *ulhū*
ULHA livestock, domestic animal
ULHA TUWAKIYARA NIYALMA someone
hired to watch livestock, herdsman
ULHAI OKTOSI veterinarian
ULHAMBI see *ulgambi*
ULHI sleeve
ULHI ASU a net with sleevelike
appendages for catching fish
ULHIBUKŪ in antiquity, an interpreter
for the eastern languages
ULHIBUMBI 1. caus. of *ulhimbi* 2. to
explain to, to make clear to
ULHIBUME SELGIYERE BITHE proclama-
tion, announcement
ULHIBURE FUNGNEHEN a letter of ap-
pointment for an official position
of the fifth rank and above
ULHIBURE HESE the same as *ulhibun*
ULHIBUN proclamation
ULHICUKE understandable
ULHICUN understanding, insight, knowl-
edge
ULHICUNGGA possessing understanding or
insight
ULHILEMBI to put something in the
sleeve
ULHIMBI to understand, to comprehend
ULHINGGE understanding, comprehending
ULHINGGE AKŪ lacking in understand-
ing
ULHINJEMBI to begin to understand
ULHISU quick to grasp, sensitive, keen,
clever
ULHITUN a protective sleeve, oversleeve
ULHIYEN gradual
ULHIYEN ULHIYEN I gradually
ULHU 1. squirrel, ermine 2. ermine
pelt
ULHUN 1. dewlap 2. collar of a jacket,
fur collar on a court garment 3.
mouth of a scabbard 4. border of a
quilt 5. foundation of a battlement
of a city wall
ULHŪ reed
ULHŪ I HAŠAHAN a reed basket for
grain
ULHŪ I HIDA a curtain of reeds
ULHŪMA pheasant--in particular the
ring-necked pheasant (*Phasianus
colchicus*)
ULHŪMA ALGAN a large net for catching pheasants
ULHŪMA KŪTHŪRI the name of a plant
the fine stems of which are used
to make baskets and bird traps

ULHŪMA UNCEHENGGE ŠUN DALIKŪ a
parasol of the imperial escort
decorated with pheasant's tail
feathers
ULHŪMANGGA decorated with pheasant
designs
ULHŪRI GŪWARA one name for the eared
owl
ULI 1. bowstring 2. fruit of the
flowering cherry (*Prunus sinensis*)
ULI ACABUMBI to attach a bowstring
ULI ILGIN thong of tawed leather
ULI MOO the flowering cherry
ULIBUMBI caus. of *ulimbi*
ULIKŪ a hole used for stringing (like
the hole in a cash)
ULIMBI 1. to run a string or rope
through a hole, to string (cash)
2. to make an offering to a deity
ULIN goods, property, possessions,
wealth
ULIN BAYAN riches, wealth
ULIN DE DOSIMBI to be covetous
ULIN DOSIMBI to get rich
ULIN FUSEMBUMBI to become rich
ULIN GIDAMBI to offer riches (silk,
cows, horses, etc.) to a deity
and after kowtowing, to sell them
and offer the money
ULIN I DA (司庫) Treasurer,
Inspector, BH 77, 298, 384A, etc.
ULIN I NIYALMA (庫便) Inspec-
tor, Treasury Overseer, BH 77, 298,
384A, etc.
ULIN MADAMBI to get rich
ULIN NADAN riches, goods, posses-
sions
ULIN SIMBI to bribe
ULINTUMBI to bribe
ULIYEN a container made from birchbark
ULKILUN one name for the partridge;
cf. *jukidun*
ULKU GIRANGGI collarbone, clavicle
ULKUME breast strap of a harness
ULME needle
ULME HŪLHATU dragonfly
ULME I SEN eye of a needle
ULME JIBCI cushion for needles
(especially of nuts and seeds)
ULU 1. empty, unfertilized (of eggs)
2. white-spotted (horse)
ULU UMGAN unfertilized egg
ULU WALA unclear, muddled (of
speech)
ULUKEN rather empty
ULUMBI to collapse, to fall down
ULUME roach
ULUME BUTARA SE SIRGE ASU a small-
meshed net made of silk used for
catching roach in a swift current
ULUN GIDAMBI in summer, to hunt wild
animals that are lying in high grass
to escape insects, to go on the sum-

U

mer hunt

ULUNCU sorrel

ULUNEMBI to wither on the stalk (grain)

ULURI 1. Chinese gooseberry, carambola (*Averrhoa carambola*) 2. a type of soft jujube

ULUSU entire, whole

ULUSUN olive (tree)

UMAI (not) at all, totally, entirely
  UMAI SARKŪ totally ignorant, doesn't know at all

UMAINAMBI see below
  UMAINACI OJORAKŪ there is no way out, there is no other choice, unavoidable, inevitable
  UMAINAHAKŪ there was no way to avoid it, nothing happened
  UMAINAME MUTERAKŪ there is nothing that can be done (about it)

UMAISERAKŪ say (said) nothing

UMAN 1. gums 2. the inner side of a hoof
  UMAN DABAMBI to have a sore hoof (of camels)
  UMAN SINDAMBI to thaw out frozen ground by building a fire on it

UMBUCI CUMBUCI see *umburi cumburi*

UMBUMBI (-ha) to bury, to inter

UMBURI CUMBURI uneven, of uneven height (plants)

UME verb used for negating imperatives (stands before the imperfect participle)

UMEHEN the bone of the upper part of the front leg of animals, humerus

UMERLEMBI to become fat without conceiving (sows)

UMESI very, to a high degree
  UMESI TEKI let it be so

UMESIHUN see *umusihun*

UMESILEBUMBI caus. of *umesilembi*

UMESILEMBI to be in a high degree, to do to a high degree

UMGA see *umgan*

UMGAN 1. marrow 2. egg; cf. *umhan*
  UMGAN BANJIMBI to lay eggs
  UMGAN GIRANGGI thighbone, femur
  UMGAN ŠUGI the innermost marrow

UMHAN 1. egg 2. see *umgan*
  UMHAN DURUN cake (made with eggs)
  UMHAN HAKSANGGA EFEN baked cakes made from wheat flour, eggs, and sugar

UMHANAMBI to lay eggs, to form eggs

UMHANGGA TUBIHE 'egg fruit'--a plant that grows wild, blooms in the second month, and has mature fruit in the eighth

UMIYAHA insect, bug, worm; cf. *imiyaha*
  UMIYAHA AŠŠAMBI one of the divisions of the solar year that occurs on the fifth or sixth of March

UMIYAHALAMBI to plait with colored thread

UMIYAHANAMBI to get worms (of fruit)

UMIYAHANGGA FUKJINGGA HERGEN (蟲 篆) the name of a style of Chinese calligraphy

UMIYELEBUMBI caus. of *umiyelembi*

UMIYELEMBI to tie (a belt), to gird oneself

UMIYESU ILHA the name of an exotic red bloom with supple stems

UMIYESULEMBI to put on a girth, girdle, or sash

UMIYESUN girdle, girth, belt, sash

UMPU hawthorn (*Crataegus cuneata*)
  UMPU DEBSE hawthorn jelly
  UMPU ERHE a small black frog with a red belly that lives in very cold springs

UMRIHA membrane

UMUDU orphan

UMUHUN the upper surface of the foot, the instep
  UMUHUN BE FEHUME MURIMBI in wrestling, to throw one's opponent by stepping on his instep
  UMUHUN TUHEKE to be paralyzed by fear

UMURI a string for pulling the mouth of a bag closed, drawstring

UMURSU see *emursu*

UMUSIHUN see *umušuhun*

UMUŠUHUN on the stomach, prone, prostrate

UN a place for pigs to sleep

UNA Chinese boxthorn (*Lycium chinense*)

UNAGAN see *unahan*

UNAHAN colt, foal
  UNAHAN SUMBI to foal, to have a colt

UNCABUMBI caus. of *uncambi*

UNCAMBI to sell

UNCANAMBI to go to sell

UNCANJIMBI to come to sell

UNCANUMBI to sell together

UNCEHEN tail, tail end, tail (in Manchu writing)
  UNCEHEN BOŠORO AGA a sudden short shower
  UNCEHEN GIRANGGI tail bone
  UNCEHEN GOLMIN BUHŪ Père David's deer, *milu* (*Elaphurus davidianus*)
  UNCEHEN HETEMBI to surround suddenly and attack the rear of an enemy army
  UNCEHEN I DA the base of the tail
  UNCEHEN ŠOLONGGO ALHACAN NIYLHE the name of a speckled duck with a pointed tail
  UNCEHEN TUWANCIHIYAKŪ rudder
  UNCEHEN TUWANCIHIYAKŪ JAFAMBI to steer the rudder

UNDA YALI flesh or meat on both sides of the backbone

U

UNDAN   spring snow that has frozen on the surface for which snowshoes are required

UNDANAMBI   to freeze on the surface (of spring snow)

UNDARAMBI (-ka)   to creep, to spread, to get worse (of an illness)

UNDAŠAMBI   to hunt on the frozen spring snow

UNDE   not yet (particle used after the imperfect participle)

UNDECI   underling, bailiff (who administered floggings)

UNDEHELEMBI   to beat with a bamboo rod

UNDEHEN   1. rod, staff, board, plank 2. wooden printing block

   UNDEHEN FALAN   1. floor board   2. a low legless wooden frame on which the throne sat

   UNDEHEN ŠUSIHE   boards and bamboo strips used for writing

UNDEO   not yet?

UNDU   vertical, upright

UNDURAKŪ   satin with a design of large standing dragons without smaller horizontal dragon designs interspersed

UNDURAMBI   see *undarambi*

UNDURI   on (the way), along (the road)

UNDUSTAN   Hindustan

   UNDUSTAN SUJE   a type of red Indian silk with golden designs on it that was brought as tribute from Hami

UNENGGI   1. truly, really, honestly   2. true, honest, genuine

   UNENGGI HEHE   title of a wife of an official of the second rank

   UNENGGI YALANGGI   true and genuine

UNENGGILEMBI   1. to deem true, to treat as genuine   2. to be true, to be genuine

UNENGGINGGE   that which is true, genuine

UNESI   objects handed down for several generations in a family, heirloom

UNG   (onom.) the sound of a bell

UNG ANG   (onom.) sound made by deer and cattle

UNG WANG   (onom.) a nasal sound

UNGGA   elder generation, elders

   UNGGA DANGGA   elders, the older generation

UNGGALA   1. flash vent of a musket, hole, cavity   2. cavity of the ear, hole in a tree

   UNGGALA I ULENGGU   the part of a musket that holds the powder, flash vent

UNGGALAMBI   to respect (one's elders), treat as an elder

UNGGALANGGA MOO   a wooden clapper

UNGGAN   see *ungga*

UNGGANUMBI   to treat as an elder, to respect (as an elder)

UNGGAŠAMBI   to revere (one's elders)

UNGGATA   plural of *ungga*

UNGGE   a type of very fine, small wild onion

UNGGIBUMBI   caus. of *unggimbi*

UNGGILAKŪ   the covering of a pig's kidney

UNGGILJEMBI   to wag

UNGGIMBI   to send, to dispatch, to send off

UNGGIN   the hole in a spade, hammer, or axhead used for attaching the handle

UNGGINDUMBI   to send together, to dispatch together

UNGGU   1. first, original   2. the first player at the *gacuha* game

   UNGGU GING   the first watch (of the night)

   UNGGU MAFA   great-grandfather (paternal)

   UNGGU MAMA   great-grandmother (paternal)

UNGKAN   frozen snow on the top of grass

UNGKEBUMBI   caus. of *ungkembi*

UNGKEMBI   1. to turn over, to tip over 2. to turn one's cup upside down to show that one has drained it completely

UNGKEN ILHA   the name of a flower that resembles an overturned cup

UNGKESHŪN   tipped over, awry

UNI NIMAHA   a spotted white seafish that reaches a length of four spans

UNIKA   a young locust

UNIYEHE   one name for the duck

UNIYELE   the yellow hair that grows at the base of a deer's tail

UNIYEN   female of certain animals, a milk cow

   UNIYEN HONIN   a female sheep--ewe

   UNIYEN IHASI   a female rhinoceros

UNIYERI   strings of raw silk

UNTUHUKEN   empty, vacant

UNTUHUKESAKA   empty

UNTUHULEBUMBI   caus. of *untuhulembi*

UNTUHULEMBI   1. to be empty   2. to be idle

UNTUHUN   1. empty, vacant   2. hollow 3. idle   4. vain   5. emptiness, space

   UNTUHUN ACILAMBI   in wrestling, to grasp an opponent by the shoulders and fling him from side to side

   UNTUHUN ANGGAI NIYALMA   idle prattler

   UNTUHUN DE   in the air, in midair, in space

   UNTUHUN FIYELEMBI   to leap through the air and mount a horse from behind

   UNTUHUN FORGOŠOME FIYELEMBI   in

U

trick riding, to do a somersault on the horse

UNTUHUN JERGI   a sinecure

UNTUHURI   in vain

UNTUHURILAMBI   to act in vain

UNTUN   a small drum used by female shamans during rites in the home

UNTUŠEMBI   to beat a small drum (of female shamans)

UNUBUMBI   1. caus. of *unumbi*   2. to put the blame on someone else

UNUCUN   a child born after the death of his father

UNUJUN   one name for the stork; cf. *weijun*

UNUMBI   to carry (on the back), to bear, to shoulder

UNUN   a load (that can be carried on the back), burden

UNUN FIYANA   a frame used for carrying things on the back

UNUN USE   a strap used for carrying a gun on the back

UNURTU   opossum

UPI JAHŪDAI   a warship with black painted sides

URA   buttocks

URA FAJUHŪ   anus

URA FULCIN   the cheeks of the buttocks

URA TEBUMBI   to pursue an animal from the rear (after its escape route has been cut off)

URA TŪMBI   to whip (the buttocks)

URAHILABUMBI   caus. of *urahilambi*

URAHILAMBI   to make inquiries, to seek information

URAMBI (-ka)   1. to echo, to peal   2. to be bloodshot, to be bruised (with blood extravasated under the skin)

URAN   echo, resonance, peal

URANDAMBI   to reverberate, to re-echo, peal

URANGGA MOO   Chinese parasol tree (*Firmiana simplex*)

URDEBUMBI   caus. of *urdembi*

URDEMBI   to race a horse; cf. *uruldembi*

UREBUKŪ   1. a home school   2. driller, reviewer

UREBUMBI   1. caus. of *urembi*   2. to cure (silk floss)   3. to practice, to review, to drill, to rehearse

UREMBI   1. to be sad   2. to get ripe, to be ripe, to be done (of food)   3. to be acquainted with, to be familiar with

UREHE BANJIHA   alike by nature

UREHE USIN   a ripe field

UREŠHŪN   familiar, acquainted with

URGALABUMBI   caus. of *urgalambi*

URGALAMBI   to lasso (a horse)

URGAN   a lasso (either a rope or a noose on the end of a pole)

URGE   a paper figure of a person used by shamans against baneful spirits

URGE FAITAMBI   to cut out a paper figure; cf. *urge*

URGEDEMBI   to turn one's back on, to be ungrateful for

URGEN   length, extension

URGEŠEN   a one-year-old deer

URGETU   a wooden funerary figure

URGUMBI   see *urhumbi*

URGUN   1. joy, felicity, happiness   2. auspicious sign, good portent   3. congratulations

URGUN ARAMBI   to congratulate, to wish well

URGUN I BAITA   joyous event, pregnancy

URGUN I DORO   congratulations

URGUN I DOROI HENGKILEMBI   to congratulate (by kowtowing)

URGUN I SARIN   wedding feast

URGUN SEBJEN   joy and pleasure

URGUN ŠANGGAHA DENGJAN   lanterns used at court to celebrate New Year's

URGUNGGA   blessed, fortunate

URGUNGGE   joyous

URGUNGGE ABKA   Tuṣita heaven

URGUNGGE DERENGTU   a portrait

URGUNJEBUMBI   caus. of *urgunjembi*

URGUNJEMBI   to rejoice, to be glad

URGUNJENDUMBI/URGUNJENUMBI   to rejoice together

URGUNTU   joyful, happy

URGURI   see *urhuri*

URGUTU   see *urhutu*

URGŪMBI   see *urhumbi*

URHU   tilting, one-sided, prejudiced, partial

URHU AKŪ   impartial, unprejudiced

URHU HAIHŪ   leaning to one side (of walking), staggering

URHU HARŠAKŪ   partial to one side

URHUBUMBI   caus. of *urhumbi*

URHUMBI   to lean to one side, to be lopsided, to be partial, to be prejudiced to one side

URHUN   a unit of measure equaling half a (Chinese) inch

URHURI HAIHARI   leaning to one side, staggering, poking along, weaving, fluttering to and fro

URHUŠEMBI   to tilt toward one side, to stagger, to incline greatly to one side, to be very partial

URHUTU   leaning to one side, having one leg shorter than the other

URHŪMBI   to shy (of livestock)

URHŪN   shyness (of livestock)

URHŪTU   easily frightened (of horses and other livestock)

URI   1. a round straw container used

U

for storing grain 2. see *urui*

URIHA membrane, inner bark of trees, the skin on walnuts and hazelnuts; cf. *unriha*

URILEMBI to get so fat that motion becomes difficult (pheasants), to be packed full (of rat's nests)

URIMBI (-he) to collapse (of a mountain), to die (of the emperor)

URKA CECIKE common snipe, the same as *karka cecike*

URKI a horizontal support for a sail on a small boat

URKILAMBI 1. to make a big noise deliberately, to cause a commotion 2. to follow the lead of one horse in shying or urinating

URKIN big noise, commotion, tumult, the sound made by horses before they stampede

URKINGGA the same as *urkingge*

URKINGGE noisy, tumultuous, mighty
    URKINGGE TEIŠUN a kind of brass out of which gongs were made

URKUJI often, continuously, steadily, uninterruptedly

URKULJI the same as *urkuji*

URLEMBI the same as *urilembi*

URLU MORIN a black horse with white spots

URSAN new shoots that sprout from old roots, new branches that appear on a tree that has been cut away
    URSAN SINDAMBI to leave a sentence half finished, to pause in speaking
    URSAN SURSAN sprouts, new shoots

URSANAMBI to sprout from old roots or an old stock

URSE 1. people, men, persons (plural of *niyalma*) 2. others, other people

URSEINGGE somebody else's

URSU layer, level, -fold

URSUNGGA consisting of layers
    URSUNGGA HOSERI five or ten boxes, one smaller than the next, placed one in another
    URSUNGGA HŪNTAHAN cups, one smaller than the next, placed one in another
    URSUNGGA POLORI baskets, one smaller than the next, placed one in another

URU right, correct
    URU WAKA right and wrong

URUBUMBI caus. of *urumbi*

URUI 1. just, only 2. steadily, consistently, always

URULDEBUMBI caus. of *uruldembi*

URULDEMBI to race a horse, to test a horse for speed

URULEMBI 1. to deem right, to consider correct 2. the same as *urilembi*

URUMBI (-he/ke, -re/ndere) to get hungry, to be hungry

URUN 1. daughter-in-law 2. wife
    URUN GAIJAMBI to get married (of a man)
    URUN HENGKILEMBI to get engaged

URUNAKŪ certainly, surely, for sure, necessarily, must, under any circumstances

URUNEMBI to go about hungry

URUSA plural of *urun*

URUŠAMBI to fulfill the duties of a daughter-in-law

URUŠEMBI to deem right, to consider correct

USA exclamation used to get someone's attention

USABUMBI caus. of *usambi*

USACUKA 1. regrettable, deplorable, too bad 2. pitiful, sad

USACUMBI (-ka) to be grieved or distressed

USACUN sorrow, grief, sadness

USACUNGGA sorrowful, afflicted

USAMBI (-ka) to be without hope, to be disappointed in

USAMBUMBI caus. of *usambi*

USANDUMBI/USANUMBI to be without hope together, to give up hope together

USARI CECIKE one name for the goatsucker, the same as *simari cecike*

USATA the white portion of a fish's stomach

USE seed, egg (of an insect)
    USE FAHA grain
    USE FAHA CIFUN grain tax
    USE WALIYAMBI to lay eggs (of insects)
    USEI HITHEN a large box for holding seed

USEBUMBI caus. of *usembi*

USEKU a seeder, an implement for planting seed

USELEMBI see *usembi*

USEMBI to plant, to seed

USEN see *juwen usen*

USENE ILHA the name of a species of ranunculus

USENEMBI to go to plant seeds, to go to plant

USENGGE seedlike, grainlike

USENUMBI to seed together, to plant together

USERCI a sour pomegranatelike fruit

USEREMBI see *usuršembi*

USERI pomegranate; cf. *šilio*
    USERI CUSE MOO a bamboolike plant that forms red seed pods

USHABUMBI 1. caus./pass. of *ushambi* 2. to be blamed or rejected (by spirits or demons)

USHACUN anger, resentment

USHAMBI to be angry at, to resent, to

U

be disappointed

USHANDUMBI/USHANUMBI to be angry together, to resent together

USHATAMBI to sulk, to pout

USHE semen

USI UMIYAHA intestinal worm

USIHA 1. star 2. acorn 3. front sight of a gun
  USIHA BE ALIHA HAFAN court astronomer in ancient times
  USIHA GERI GARI stars are dim (at dawn when they begin to disappear from sight)
  USIHA KEMUN sight of a cannon
  USIHA MOO sweet (edible) chestnut
  USIHA ORON constellation
  USIHA ORON BE CINCILARA KARAN (觀 察 臺) the observatory in Peking
  USIHA TUWARA HAFAN (監 候) astronomer of the Peking observatory
  USIHA YOO scrofula

USIHANGGA clairvoyant, prophet, sensitive (in a psychic way)
  USIHANGGA GURGU sensitive animals--tigers and wolves
  USIHANGGA MAITU a staff of the imperial escort topped by a carved wooden star

USIHIBUMBI caus. of *usihimbi*

USIHIKEN rather wet

USIHIMBI to moisten, to dampen, to wet, to get wet or soaked

USIHIN wet, damp

USIHIYEBUMBI caus. of *usihiyembi*

USIHIYEMBI to drink (gruel or other such liquids)

USILEMBI to release (the bowstring)

USIMA thick padded cotton armor

USIMANGGA 1. skilled astrologer 2. under favorable astrological signs

USIN field (for cultivation)
  USIN BOŠOKŪ a type of gray grasshopper
  USIN BUTA cultivated field
  USIN DEHEN border of a field
  USIN I FIYENTEN (農 田 司) an office of the Board of Finance in charge of agricultural affairs
  USIN I HAFAN the name of an official of antiquity who was in charge of cultivation and animal husbandry
  USIN I HAHA tenant farmer
  USIN I JALIN ABALAMBI to hunt animals detrimental to crops in summer
  USIN I NARHŪN CESE register of land boundaries, land-register
  USIN I UJAN boundary of a field
  USIN WECEMBI to make offerings of cakes and small paper flags when crops were threatened by insects or drought

USIN YALU fields (collectively)

USINGGA alone, forlorn, orphaned

USISI farmer, cultivator of the land

USITAMBI see *ušatambi*

USITEN HAILAN mountain elm

USNIKA a fleshy outgrowth on the head of the Buddha

USUCILEMBI to be fussy, to be bothersome

USUKAN rather fussy

USUMBI to go downstream, to go with the current

USUN fussy, bothersome, overly talkative

USURŠEBUMBI caus. of *usuršembi*

USURŠECUKE 1. hateful, unpleasant 2. unsavory, not good to eat

USURŠEMBI to detest, to find unpleasant

UŠABUMBI caus./pass. of *ušambi*

UŠABUN implication (in a crime or plot)

UŠAKŪ hard to control, hard to rein in (of horses)

UŠAMBI 1. to pull, to drag, to haul 2. to scratch 3. to implicate, to hold back, to burden with

UŠAN FAŠAN confused, entangled, muddled, without conclusion

UŠARKI hawthorn (*Crataegus pinnatifida*)
  UŠARKI MOO hawthorn

UŠATABUMBI caus. of *ušatambi*

UŠATAMBI 1. to pull with force, to yank at 2. to vex, to plague, to afflict, to distress

UŠE cord, band, belt, thong, strap, tape
  UŠE ŠABAN a strong cord with four knots tied in it that is attached to the bottom of boots or shoes to prevent slipping
  UŠE TATAKŪ SELE a small iron fastener on a quiver strap
  UŠE UMIYAHA tapeworm

UŠEBUMBI caus. of *ušembi*

UŠEMBI to stitch the soles of cloth shoes

UŠENGGE tough, stringy

UŠIHA acorn

UTA cake made from milk, sugar, and oil
  UTA BELE a cake consisting of rice fried with oil and sugar

UTALA so many (much) as this

UTAN one name for the pelican; cf. *kūtan*

UTBALA ILHA (from Sanskrit *utpala*) a red lotuslike bloom

UTHAI then, thereupon, at once, and then, immediately

UTTU thus, like this, so
  UTTU AKŪ OCI otherwise
  UTTU DABALA only like this
  UTTU OCI if it is like this, if so
  UTTU OTOLO even like this

UTTU SEME   although it is thus,
  nevertheless
UTTU TUTTU SEME   now like this now
  like that
UTTUMBARA ILHA   (from Sanskrit *udumbara*)
  a white lotuslike flower
UTTUSI   in this direction, over here
  UTTUSI OSO   so it's like this!
UTU   one name for the tiger; cf. *tasha*
UTULIMBI   to pay attention, to notice,
  to be conscious of
UTUN WEIJUN   one name for the stork;
  cf. *weijun*
UTUNG   see *urangga moo*
UTURI   the end of a battue line
  UTURI ACAMBI   to join both ends of
    the battue line to form a circle
  UTURI FEKSIMBI   to run from both
    ends of the battue line to form a
    circle
UYA   a male Indian antelope
UYAKAN   rather thin, rather diluted
UYALJAMBI   to move winding like a snake,
  to slither
UYAN   1. thin, diluted, weak, feeble
  2. the meeting point of the two
  halves of a canoe   3. keel
  UYAN BUDA   gruel, rice broth
  UYAN I ALIGAN   keel retainer
  UYAN LALA   rice gruel eaten on the
    eighth day of the twelfth month
  UYAN MATAN ŠATAN   thin sugar cakes
UYAŠAMBI   to chew the cud
UYAŠAN   loach (fish)
  UYAŠAN DEKDEMBI   the same as *uyaša-*
    nambi
UYAŠANAMBI   to have a pain in the liga-
  ments of the hand or feet
UYAŠANGGA JAHŪDAI   the name of a small,
  long boat used on the Yangtze that
  was thought to resemble the loach
UYE   the name of a white sea fish
UYEBUMBI   caus. of *uyembi*
UYEMBI   1. to soften   2. to knead   3.
  to cure, to tan (leather)   4. to
  break in (a horse)
  UYERE FAKSI   a tanner
  UYERE ŠU   saltpeter used in the
    curing of leather
UYU   1. the name of a sea fish   2. tur-
  quoise
UYUCI   ninth
UYULEMBI   1. to punish an offense by a
  fine of nine head of cattle (a Mon-
  golian punishment)   2. to climb to a
  high place on the ninth day of the
  ninth month
UYUN   nine
  UYUN BIYA   the ninth month
  UYUN DABKŪRI   the imperial palace
  UYUN EYEN   the nine philosophical
    schools
  UYUN GARUDAI MUDANGGA FESIN I SUWA-

YAN SUJE SARA   a yellow parasol of
  the imperial escort with a crooked
  handle and nine phoenixes depicted
  on the cover
UYUN GARUDANGGA TUMIN LAMUN SUJE
SARA   a blue parasol of the imperial
  escort with nine phoenixes depicted on it
UYUN HENGKIN   nine kowtows (three
  genuflections with three kowtows
  per genuflection)
UYUN JAFAMBI   before a big sacrifice, to make smaller offerings
  on the two previous days
UYUN JUBKI   deep place in a body of
  water
UYUN MUDANGGA JIJUN (九疊文)
  the name of a style of seal writing (in Chinese calligraphy)
UYUN MUDURI DUIN GARUDAI MAHATUN
  the name of a hat worn by emperors
  in antiquity with nine dragons,
  four phoenixes, and a string of
  pearls attached to it
UYUN MUDURI MUDANGGA FESIN I SUWAYAN
SARA   the name of a yellow parasol
  of the imperial escort with a
  crooked handle and nine dragons
  depicted on it
UYUN MUDURINGGA SUWAYAN SARA   a
  yellow parasol of the imperial
  escort with nine dragons depicted
  on it
UYUN SAITU   the nine ministers (the
  heads of the six boards plus the
  heads of the Censorate, the Court
  of Judicature and Revision, and
  the Transmission Office)
UYUN SIHANGGA SUNTA   a cartridge
  pouch for nine cartridges
UYUN TUHEBUKU I MAHATU   a ceremonial
  hat of antiquity with nine tassels
UYUN UNCEHENGGE DOBI   a nine-tailed
  fox
UYUNGGE   pertaining to the ninth day
  of the ninth month (a festival)
  UYUNGGE EFEN   the name of cakes
    baked on the ninth day of the
    ninth month
  UYUNGGE INENGGI   the ninth day of
    the ninth month
UYUNGGERI   nine times
UYUNJU   ninety
  UYUNJU DULEFUN I DURUNGGA TETUN
    an armillary sphere of the Peking
    observatory
UYUNJUCI   ninetieth
UYUNJUTE   ninety each
UYURI   a black cat
UYURSU   ninefold, consisting of nine
  layers
  UYURSU MUHEREN   a toy consisting of
    a piece of brass with nine brass

U

rings attached to it--a puzzle ring

UYURŠEMBI to laugh pleasantly, to laugh prettily

UYUTE nine each

UYUTU JOFOHORI an orange containing nine sections

UYUTUNGGE GASHA one name for the owl; cf. *yabula*

ŪLEN house

ŪLET Oirat, Elut

ŪN CECIKE bullfinch, birds of the genus *Pyrrhula*

ŪREN 1. an image, doll, a Buddhist image, a religious image 2. tablet of a deceased person

ŪREN I PAI tablet of a deceased person

ŪREN TUIBUMBI to burn the clothes and hat of a deceased person at the grave together with a paper image

U
Ū
Ū

W

WA   WAINAMBI

WA odor, smell
  WA EHE having a foul odor
  WA SAIN having a pleasant odor,
    fragrant
  WA TUCIKE YADARANGGE in dire need,
    like a polecat that passes foul-
    smelling gas when it is in distress
  WA USUN having an obnoxious odor
WABUMBI caus./pass. of *wambi*
WABURU deserving of death!--a curse
WACAN a protective covering for the
  armpits on armor
WACIHIYABUMBI caus. of *wacihiyambi*
WACIHIYAMBI to complete, to conclude,
  to finish
  WACIHIYAME completely, totally
  WACIHIYAME OMI bottoms up!
  WACIHIYAME OMIMBI to drink up
WACIR thunderbolt of Indra, sacred
  instrument used in Lamaist rites as
  a symbol of the 'indestructible'
WADABUMBI to set a dog on a scent
WADAMBI to sniff, to follow a scent
  (of dogs)
WADAN 1. a cloth wrapping 2. curtain
  around a sedan chair 3. an unpadded
  bed cover 4. cloth of a flag, flag,
  banner
WADANAMBI to become distended (of live-
  stock's bellies when they have over-
  eaten)
WAHAI extremely, very, to a great de-
  gree
WAHAN 1. hoof 2. end of a sleeve on
  a gown in the form of a hoof
  WAHAN DABAMBI to stumble (of hoofed
    animals)
WAHIYABUMBI caus. of *wahiyambi*
WAHIYAMBI to support by holding under
  the arms, to help up in this way
WAHŪN stinking
  WAHŪN JALGANGGA MOO tree of heaven
    (*Ailanthus glandulosa*)
  WAHŪN JALGASU MOO the same as *wahūn*

jalgangga moo
WAHŪN NIŠARGAN diphtheria eruption
  in the throat
WAHŪN UMIYAHA bedbug
WAHŪN URANGGA MOO stinking plane
  tree
WAHŪN YASA bare spot on the front
  leg of a horse
WAHŪNDA a stinking wild plant that
  resembles garlic
WAHŪTU CECIKE one name for the myna
WAI askew, tilted, crooked, curved
  WAI SEME exhausted, tired out
WAIDABUMBI caus. of *waidambi*
WAIDAKŪ a dipper
WAIDAMBI to scoop out, to dip out
  (with a ladle or large spoon)
  WAIDARA HOTO gourd used as a dipper
WAIDANAMBI to go to scoop out
WAIDANJIMBI to come to scoop out
WAIDANUMBI to scoop out together
WAIHŪ 1. askew, tilted, off-center;
  cf. *waiku* 2. unreasonable
WAIHŪDAMBI to act unreasonably
WAIHŪNGGA a person who acts unreason-
  ably
WAIKIYAMBI see *wangkiyambi*
WAIKU askew, crooked
  WAIKU DAIKŪ askew, tilted, crooked
WAIKURABUMBI caus. of *waikurambi*
WAIKURAMBI to be askew, to be tilted,
  to be crooked
WAIKURŠAMBI to walk leaning to one
  side
WAILAN 1. in antiquity, an official
  who was in charge of a city 2.
  a petty official
  WAILAN HAFAN (委 更) a minor
    official in charge of revenue and
    grain
  WAILAN ŠUDESI (更 典) secre-
    tary in a prefecture
WAINAMBI to be crooked (of part of a
  battue line)

303

WAITUKŪ a large, handled, water dipper
WAJIBUMBI caus. of *wajimbi*
WAJIMA end, termination
WAJIMBI to finish
WAJIN the finish, the end
WAKA 1. sentence particle that negates
  nominal predicates--is not, are not
  2. mistake, error, guilt, blame
  WAKA ALIMBI to accept blame, to
    apologize
  WAKA BAHAMBI to commit an error
  WAKA SABUBUMBI to commit an offense,
    to offend
  WAKA WAKAI muddled, fouled up, con-
    fused
  WAKAI ERUN unlawful punishment
WAKALABUMBI caus./pass. of *wakalambi*
WAKALAMBI 1. to blame, to fault, to
  accuse, to impeach, to deem wrong
  2. to upbraid, to bawl out
WAKALAN error, transgression
WAKAN night heron (*Nycticorax nycti-
  corax*)
WAKAO *waka* + *o*--isn't it? n'est-ce pas?
WAKAŠABUMBI caus. of *wakašambi*
WAKAŠAMBI 1. to blame, to accuse 2.
  to deem wrong, to consider an error
WAKJAHŪN having a big belly, having
  a distended belly (of livestock that
  have overeaten)
WAKJANAMBI to form a big belly
WAKŠAN toad, frog
  WAKŠAN BURGA 'toad willow'--a vari-
    ety of willow tree
WALA 1. underneath, under, low 2. the
  west side of a Manchu house--the
  place of honor
WALDA base, vile--a term of contempt
WALGIYABUMBI caus. of *walgiyambi*
WALGIYAMBI 1. to sun, to expose to the
  sun 2. to heat
WALI trick
  WALI EFIMBI to play tricks
  WALI MAMA a goddess represented by
    a piece of cloth hung on the back
    of the door to which all food
    brought into the house must be
    presented for inspection
WALINGGA a device used for playing
  tricks
WALIYABUMBI 1. caus./pass. of *waliyambi* 2. to be lost, to get lost,
  to be left behind, to be abandoned
WALIYAMBI 1. to throw away, to throw
  down, to get rid of, to abandon 2.
  to spit out 3. to lay eggs (of insects) 4. to make an offering at a
  grave 5. to produce silk (of silk-
  worms)
  WALIYAHA 1. (interjection) alas! woe
    is me! 2. now we're in trouble!
    now we've had it!
  WALIYAHA JUI orphan

WALIYAHA USIN abandoned land, land
  unfit for cultivation
WALIYAME GAMAMBI to treat leniently,
  to excuse, to forgive
WALIYAME GAMARAO please excuse me
WALIYAN abandonment
  WALIYAN GEMIN generous, unstinting
WALIYANAMBI to go to make an offering
  at a grave
WALIYATAI to the death, without re-
  gard for one's own safety
WALIYATAMBI 1. to fling about, to
  throw around 2. to lose (face)
WALU boil, furuncle
WAMBI to kill, to slay
  WAHA INENGGI day of execution
  WAME ABALAMBI to go on the autumn
    hunt
  WAME MUKIYEBUMBI to annihilate,
    to exterminate
  WAME ŠUSIHAŠAMBI to flog severely
  WAME TANTAMBI to administer a
    severe beating
  WARA BA execution ground
  WARA WEILE capital crime
WAN ladder
WANCARAMBI to ridicule, to make fun of
  someone behind his back
WANCI an area on a pond that doesn't
  freeze in the winter
WANDUMBI/WANUMBI to kill together, to
  kill one another
  WANDURE SUKDUN violent aspect,
    venomous appearance or mood
WANDZ pill, small ball
WANG 1. prince 2. (in antiquity)
  king, monarch
  WANG NI DUKAI HIYA (護衛)
    Officer of a Prince's Bodyguard,
    BH 45
  WANG SAI BAITAI KUNGGERI (王府
    科) office concerned with the
    affairs of princes in the Board of
    Rites
WANG GIN a hair net
WANGGA 1. fragrant 2. crested heron
  3. pertaining to the new moon
  WANGGA GIYANCIHIYAN HOOŠAN perfumed
    letter paper
  WANGGA INENGGI the fifteenth day of
    a lunar month
  WANGGA JALGASU MOO *Cedrela sinensis*
  WANGGA SINGGERI muskrat
  WANGGA SOGI coriander, Chinese
    parsley
  WANGGA ŠANGGA unconscious, in a
    coma
  WANGGA ŠULHE Chinese pear (*Pyrus
    sinensis*)
WANGGARI citron (*Citrus medica*)
WANGGIYANAMBI to have a runny nose, to
  have a head cold
  WANGGIYANAHABI has a head cold

W

WANGKIYABUMBI caus. of *wangkiyambi*

WANGKIYAMBI to smell (v.t.)

WANGNAMBI to embroider (designs on shoes)

  WANGNAHA SABU embroidered shoes

WANSE pill, small ball

WANTAHA Japanese cedar (*Cryptomeria japonica*)

WAR (onom.) the sound made by toads and frogs

WAR IR (onom.) the sound of toads and frogs croaking together

WARABUMBI caus. of *warambi*

WARAMBI to fish out, to remove from a pot (things that have been cooked)

WARDABUMBI caus. of *wardambi*

WARDAMBI 1. to tread water 2. to dig up (dirt)

WARDAŠAMBI to work with the hands and feet, to exert great effort

WARGI 1. under, underneath 2. west 3. right (side)

  WARGI ASHAN (西廂) an office of the Imperial Academy of Learning

  WARGI ASHAN I BAITA HACIN I BOO (西廂案房) archives in the Imperial Academy of Learning

  WARGI BA the Western Regions--Sinkiang

  WARGI DZANG Tibet

  WARGI ERGI MUNGGAN the imperial tombs of Mukden

  WARGI ERGI SIMNERE BITHEI KŪWARAN (西文場) the rooms for examinees just to the right of the Ming-yüan tower in the Examination Compound

  WARGI FIYENTEN (西司) an office in the Imperial Equipage Department

  WARGI NAHAN the oven-bed on the western wall

  WARGI NAMU the West

WARGINGGE western, pertaining to the west

WARUMBI (-ka) to have a bad odor

WASE 1. tile 2. socks, stockings

  WASE BOO house with a tile roof

  WASEI FAKSI a tilemaker, roofer

  WASEI HOLBOKŪ a timber that holds the tiles on the roof

  WASEI JAIDA mason's trowel

WASELABUMBI caus. of *waselambi*

WASELAMBI to tile (a roof)

WASERI WEIJUN stork; cf. *weijun*

WASHA CECIKE one name for the sparrow

WASIBUMBI 1. caus. of *wasimbi* 2. to degrade, to demote

WASIHA claw, talon

WASIHALABUMBI caus. of *wasihalambi*

WASIHALAMBI to grasp in the claws, to snatch, to scratch, to claw

WASIHAŠAMBI 1. to scratch wildly

  2. to dig in the earth (of domestic animals)

WASIHI awkward, clumsy

WASIHŪN 1. downward, down 2. westward, to the west

  WASIHŪN BETHE GAIHA slipped down, fell down

  WASIHŪN I HONTOHO the last quarter of the moon

WASIHŪRAME in the last ten days of the month

WASIMBI (-ka) 1. to descend, to go down, to sink 2. to fall (of rulers) 3. to decline (of value) 4. to become skinny 5. to die (of birds)

  WASIFI GENGGEHUN OMBI to become thin and pale

WASIMBUMBI 1. caus. of *wasimbi* 2. to issue (an order), to send down (an edict) 3. to demote, to degrade; cf. *wasibumbi*

WASINAMBI to go down (there)

WASINGGA MUDAN the departing tone of classical Chinese phonology

WASINJIMBI to come down

WASURI MONIO one name for the monkey

WAŠAKTA BURGA a type of red willow whose leaves are wider and longer than those of the common willow

WAŠAKŪ an iron ladle-shaped instrument used for scraping hides

WAŠAMBI to scratch, to scrape; cf. *ušambi*

WATAI 1. to the death, fiercely 2. exceedingly

  WATAI TANTAMBI to beat to death

WATAN a fishhook with barbs

WATANGGA barbed

  WATANGGA GIDA a spear with barbs

WE who?

WEBE whom?

WECEBUMBI caus. of *wecembi*

WECEKU household god

  WECEKU I SENDEHEN altar to the household god, a board on which offerings were made to the household god

  WECEKU SOKO household god and earth god, the gods in general

WECEMBI 1. to make an offering to a deity, to sacrifice 2. to shamanize

  WECERE BITHE book containing the rites of certain sacrifices

  WECERE JAKA sacrificial vessel or object

  WECERE JUKTERE BOLGOBURE FIYENTEN (祠祝清吏司) the name of an office concerned with sacrifice in the Board of Rites

  WECERE JUKTERE KUNGGERI (祭祀科) section on sacrifice in the Board of Rites and the Court of Sacri-

W

ficial Worship

WECERE USIN a field set aside for growing grain used in sacrifices

WECEN offering, sacrifice, shamanistic rite

WECEN BITHE book containing the rites of certain sacrifices

WECEN I BAITA BE ALIHA FALGARI (祠祭署) the name of various offices concerned with sacrifices

WECEN I BAITA BE ALIHA YAMUN (太常寺) Court of Sacrificial Worship, BH 933

WECEN I KUMUN UREBURE FALGARI (神樂署) Office of Sacred Music, BH 390

WECEN I ULHA UJIRE FALGANGGA (犧牲所) office of sacrificial animals in the Court of Sacrificial Worship

WECEN JUKTEN offerings and sacrifices

WECENEMBI to go to sacrifice

WECENJIMBI to come to sacrifice

WECI ablative form of we

WECU ILHA rainbow pink (Dianthus chinensis)

WEDE dative of we: to whom, for whom

WEHE stone, rock

WEHE ALIKŪ the lower millstone

WEHE BEI a stele

WEHE BIYANGSIRI ILHA the name of a purple flower with five petals that resembles a cicada

WEHE CINUHŪN cinnabar

WEHE DABSUN rock salt

WEHE DALAN a stone dam

WEHE FIYELEN purslane

WEHE FUNGKŪ a stone roller

WEHE GIYEN smalt blue

WEHE HENGKE 'stone melon'--the name of a very hard melonlike fruit that grows on a tree in the vicinity of Mt. Omei in Szechuan

WEHE HŪWAISE hard coal

WEHE HŪWANGSE hartite

WEHE I KING a musical stone hanging from a frame

WEHE LAMUN cobalt blue

WEHE LEFU the name of a medium-sized bear with a white spot on its neck that hibernates in a cave in the winter, the same as mojihiyan

WEHE MUHALIYAN a stone ball

WEHE SELMIN 1. a stone drill 2. a crossbow for shooting stones

WEHE ŠU ILHA cotyledon

WEHE TUYEKU YONGGAN impure ammonia salts

WEHE YADALI CECIKE 'stone thrush'

WEHE YAHA coal

WEHE YAHA I NEMURI coal mine

W

WEHEI FUNGKŪ stone drum, stone cylinder

WEHEI NIKEBUKU a stone used for holding a door open

WEHENGGE stone, made of stone

WEHENGGE USIHA 'stone chestnut'--a nut tasting like a walnut that is grown in the mountains of Tonkin

WEHETU COKO the name of a chicken from Southeast Asia that is supposed to cackle when the tide comes in

WEHIYEBUMBI caus. of wehiyembi

WEHIYEMBI to support, to aid, to watch after

WEHIYENDUMBI/WEHIYENUMBI to support together, to support one another

WEHIYETEMBI to support continually

WEI 1. whose?--genitive of we 2. minute, very small 3. sort of fish

WEI PING a screen

WEIBIN (危) the name of a constellation

WEIBIN TOKDONGGO KIRU a banner depicting the constellation weibin

WEIFUTU see kuri weifutu

WEIHE 1. tooth 2. horn; cf. uihe

WEIHE DASAKŪ toothpick

WEIHE HADAMBI to attach the horn facing to a new bow

WEIHE ILHA gums

WEIHE JAKA space between the teeth

WEIHE JUYEMBI to clench the teeth

WEIHE SILGIYAKŪ toothbrush

WEIHEDE leftover pieces of brick or tile

WEIHEN one name for the donkey

WEIHENGGE having teeth or horns

WEIHU boat made from a single tree, a hollowed-out canoe

WEIHUKELEBUMBI caus./pass. of weihukelembi

WEIHUKELEMBI to treat disrespectfully, to slight, to treat lightly

WEIHUKEN 1. light (in weight) 2. not serious, frivolous

WEIHUKEN FURDEHE a light fur coat

WEIHUN alive

WEIHUN JAFAMBI to capture alive

WEIHUN NINGGE a living creature

WEIHUNGGE living thing

WEIJUBUMBI 1. caus. of weijumbi 2. to revive, to bring back to life

WEIJUHEN one name for the stork; cf. weijun

WEIJUMBI to be alive, to live

WEIJUN 1. pliers, pincers, nippers, fire tongs 2. stork (Ciconia ciconia)

WEIJUN GASHA stork; cf. weijun

WEILE 1. crime, offense, guilt 2. punishment, sentence 3. matter, affair, work, deed; cf. weilen

WEILE ALIMBI to take the guilt upon one's self, to admit guilt

WEILE ARAMBI to sentence, to accuse of, to punish

WEILE BEIDEMBI to judge a case

WEILE BEIDERE BOLGOBURE FIYENTEN (理 刑 清 吏司) Judicial Department, BH 495

WEILE BEIDERE KUNGGERI (理 刑 科) judicial section of the headquarters of a Provincial Commander-in-chief

WEILE BEIDERE TINGGIN (理 事 廳) a court dealing with matters between Manchu garrison troops and local Mongolians in Mongolia

WEILE DAKSA crimes and misdeeds, misdeeds in general

WEILE DE TAHA fell into crime

WEILE DE TANAHA see *weile de taha*

WEILE DE TUHENEHE see *weile de taha*

WEILEBUMBI 1. caus. of *weilembi* 2. to sentence to forced labor

WEILEBURE WEILE a crime carrying a penalty of forced labor

WEILEMBI 1. to work 2. to make, to construct 3. to serve

WEILERE ARARA BA (造 辦 處) Workshop of the Imperial Household, BH 86

WEILERE ARARA FIYENTEN (營 造 司) Department of Works, BH 82

WEILERE ARARA KUNGGERI (營 造 科) construction section of the Board of Works

WEILERE ARARA NAMUN (製 造 庫) warehouse for building materials in the Board of Works

WEILERE BOO (工 房) a department of the Court of Colonial Affairs

WEILERE DASARA BOLGOBURE FIYENTEN (營 繕 清 吏 司) Building Department, BH 345

WEILERE FALGA workshop, place of work

WEILERE FIYENTEN (工 司) the office concerned with construction matters in the headquarters of the Manchu General-in-Chief in Mukden

WEILERE JAKAI BOO (材 料 房) storage room for materials in the palace printing shop

WEILERE JURGAN (工 部) the Board of Works, BH 460

WEILERE JURGAN I KUNGGE YAMUN (工 科) office of the Board of Works in the Grand Secretariat

WEILEN work, construction

WEILEN BE ALIHA AMBAN (司 空) minister of works (in Chou China)

WEILENDUMBI/WEILENUMBI to work together

WEILENEMBI to go to work

WEILENGGE guilty, a criminal

WEILENGGE NIYALMA criminal, guilty man

WEILENGGE NIYALMA BE KADALARA TINGGIN (司 獄 廳) office of the Jail Warden

WEILENGGE NIYALMA KADALARA HAFAN (司 獄) Jail Warden, BH 850A

WEILUMBI 1. to do secretly, to act deceptively 2. to desert, to turn away from

WEINGGE whose

WEIPING a screen; cf. *huwejehen*

WEISHA (尾) the name of a constellation

WEISHA TOKDONGGO KIRU a banner depicting the constellation *weisha*

WEJI (dense) forest

WEJI BA a (densely) forested area

WEJI UNA the fruit of a wild plant that has small yellow leaves and stems resembling artemisia

WEKCE weaver's beam

WEKE hey you! (word used for calling people whose name is unknown or forgotten)

WEKJI husk of any sort of grain

WEKJI ARA husks and chaff

WEKJIBUMBI caus. of *wekjimbi*

WEKJIMBI to move the shuttle across horizontally, to weave in the woof threads

WEKJIME DASARA AMBAN (經 略) a high officer in charge of military affairs in border regions

WEKJIRE SIRGE woof threads

WEKJIN woof

WELDERHEN one name for the Eastern house swallow (*Hirundo rustica*)

WELHUME (胃) the name of a constellation

WELHUME TOKDONGGO KIRU a banner depicting the constellation *welhume*

WELMIYEBUMBI caus. of *welmiyembi*

WELMIYEKU fishing pole

WELMIYEMBI to fish

WEMBI (-ngke, -re/ndere, -mpi) 1. to melt 2. to be transformed, to be converted, to become cultured or civilized, to be reformed, to be influenced

WEMBUMBI 1. caus. of *wembi* 2. to make cultured, to transform (to something better), to convert, to educate, to civilize, to improve, to reform, to influence

WEMBURI a species of edible hawthorn (*Crataegus pinnatifida*)

WEMPI (perfect converb of *wembi*) improved, converted, reformed

WEN 1. influence, reform, education 2. culture, civilization, cultural

W

pursuits   3. notch (for the string
   on an arrow)
   WEN FETEMBI   to make a notch
   WEN JANG   essay--the same as *šu
      fiyelen*
   WEN TEBUMBI   to put the notch of an
      arrow to the bowstring
WENCE   the name of a plant whose leaves
   are used to make dye
   WENCE MOO   same as *wence*
WENCEN   see *wence*
WENCEO   a cloth made partly of silk and
   partly of coarse grass linen--the
   same as *jurhu suri*
WENDEDEN   one name for the lark; cf.
   wenderhen
WENDERGEN   see *wenderhen*
WENDERHEN   North China crested lark
   (*Galerida cristata*)
WENEMBI   to melt away, to go to be re-
   formed
WENGGE   highly educated, cultured
WENIYEBUMBI   caus. of *weniyembi*
WENIYEMBI   to smelt, to refine; cf.
   šarimbi
WENJE   Chinese aster (*Callistephus
   chinensis*)
   WENJE NIMEKU   consumption
WENJEBUMBI   caus. of *wenjembi*
WENJEHU   see *wenjehun*
WENJEHUN   abundant, prosperous
WENJEMBI   1. to warm up, to heat   2.
   to be warm, to have a fever   3. to
   be tipsy
WENJEN DOHOLON   expression used to de-
   scribe a horse or other beast of
   burden that limps when one first
   begins to ride it and then becomes
   normal after it has gone a little
   way
WENJENDUMBI/WENJENUMBI   to become tipsy
   together
WENJENGGE   heated
   WENJENGGE GIYALAKŪ   heated part of a
      house
   WENJENGGE KIYOO   a heated sedan chair
   WENJENGGE YUWAN   an inkstone heated
      with charcoal in the winter
WENŠU   document
WER WER   the sound used to call a dog
WERDEMBI   to climb hand over hand on a
   rope
WERE   see *banjire were*
WEREBUMBI   caus. of *werembi*
WEREMBI   1. to wash (rice), to rinse
   2. to pan (gold or other mineral)
   3. to preserve on ice in the summer
WEREN   1. ripples on water   2. hoop
   (on a barrel, tub, etc.), a wire
   circle inside a hat
WERENEMBI   to eat, to bore (of insects
   in the tender bark of trees)
WEREŠEBUMBI   caus. of *werešembi*

WEREŠEMBI   to investigate thoroughly,
   to get to the bottom of
WERI   another, other, somebody else
   WERI NIYALMA   someone else
WERIBUMBI   caus. of *werimbi*
WERIMBI   1. to leave behind, to leave
   (v.t.)   2. to retain in one's pos-
   session
WERINGGE   somebody else's
WERINJEMBI   see *werešembi*
WERIŠEMBI   see *wereŝembi*
WERIYANGGE   belonging to someone else
WERUMBI (-ke)   to melt, to thaw out
   (of frozen meat)
WESIBUMBI   1. caus. of *wesimbi*   2. to
   lift, to raise   3. to promote, to
   advance   4. see *wesimbumbi*
   WESIBUME FUNGNEMBI   to give a higher
      title
WESIBUN   advancement, lifting up
WESIHULEBUMBI   caus. of *wesihulembi*
WESIHULEMBI   to honor, to revere
WESIHULEN   posthumous respect paid to
   one's parents
WESIHUN   1. upward, up   2. eastward,
   east   3. honorable, revered, re-
   spected   4. your (honorific)
   WESIHUN BEYE   you (honorific)
   WESIHUN ERDEMUNGGE   the Ch'ung-te
      (崇德) reign period, 1627--
      1635
   WESIHUN I HONTOHO   first quarter of
      the moon--the eighth and ninth
      days of the lunar month
   WESIHUN JALAN   a brilliant age
   WESIHUN MUKDEMBURE POO   the name of
      a large iron cannon
   WESIHUN SE   how old are you? (re-
      spectful)
   WESIHUN TEMBI   to sit in the place
      of honor
WESIKU   steps provided with a railing
   used to ascend an imperial sedan
   chair or coach
WESIMBI (-ke)   1. to ascend, to go up,
   to raise   2. to advance (in rank)
   WESIRE FORGOŠORO KUNGGERI (陞調
      科) bureau of promotions and
      transfers in the Board of War
WESIMBUMBI   1. caus. of *wesimbi*   2. to
   raise, to lift   3. to advance, to
   promote; cf. *wesimbi*   4. to submit,
   to present (to the emperor), to re-
   port to the throne
   WESIMBU SEME ARAMBI   to write '*wesim-
      bu*'--i.e., to write on a document
      or memorial that it should be pre-
      sented for the personal attention
      of the emperor
   WESIMBURE AFAHA   a memorial presented
      to the throne without a cover
   WESIMBURE BITHE   a memorial presented
      to the throne

W

WESIMBURE BITHE ARARA BA (本房) Copying Office, BH 138

WESIMBURE BITHE ICIHIYARA BOO (本房) an office charged with copying Chinese memorials

WESIMBURE BITHE PILERE BA (批本處) Office for copying the Emperor's endorsements of documents, BH 138

WESIMBURE BITHEI BENESI (奉差) a messenger for memorials

WESIMBURE BITHEI JISE ICIHIYARA BOO (題槁房) an office of the Board of Civil Appointments in charge of drafting documents

WESIMBURE BITHEI TEBELIYEKU a strip of paper on the outside of a memorial that keeps it from coming apart

WESIMBURE BITHEI TON a list of the memorials to be presented to the throne

WESIMBURE BUKDARI a memorial written on folded paper

WESIMBURE KUNGGERI (啟素科) memorial office

WESINEMBI to go up

WESINGGE ILHA Chinese trumpet-creeper (*Tecoma grandiflora*)

WEŠELEMBI to catch with a *wešen*

WEŠEN a net for catching deer, roe, rabbits, etc.

Y

YA 1. which? what? 2. a clause particle expressing doubt 3. evening vapors that arise right after sunset

YA BA what place? what kind of place?

YA DE where? whither?

YA GESE how much? how many?

YA HACIN what sort of? what kind of?

YA JAKA what sort of thing?

YA ME LI GIYA JEO America

YA SI YA JEO Asia

YA SI YA JEO I ALIN I HONIN the Asian goat

YABA where?

YABE *ya* plus the accusative particle *be*

YABI boards or reeds laid on the rafters before tiles are put on a roof

YABILABUMBI caus. of *yabilambi*

YABILAMBI to lay the boards or reeds (*yabi*) on which the tiles rest

YABSA Siberian whitefish

YABSI how very . . .

YABSI BALAI YABUHA how very carelessly he acted

YABŠAHŪ eagle owl

YABUBUMBI 1. caus. of *yabumbi* 2. to put into effect, to carry out 3. to approve

YABUBUFI BURE KUNGGERI (准支科) an office of the Board of Works in charge of supplies

YABUBUME AFABURE KUNGGERI (承發科) Transmission Office, BH 212B

YABULAN a type of owl

YABUMBI 1. to go, to walk, to leave 2. to act, to perform, to carry out, to put into effect 3. to serve (at a post)

YABUHA BA a curriculum vitae

YABUHA BAITA something that has occurred

YABURE FELIYERE imperial tours away from the capital

YABURE KŪWARAN field camp, military unit on the march

YABUN act, action, performance

YABUN FACUHŪN actions are in a confused state, in a confused condition

YABUN HALAI FUDASI perverse and rebellious in his actions

YABUNDUMBI/YABUNUMBI to go together, to have comings and goings with one another

YABURELAME 1. on the way 2. walking a while, resting a while

YACI *ya* plus the ablative particle *ci*, from where?

YACI JAKA where did all these things come from?

YACIHA the name of a black fruit about the size of a finger that comes from Annam--when dried it can be made into a kind of liquor

YACIHIYABUMBI caus. of *yacihiyambi*

YACIHIYAMBI to sneeze

YACIKAN blackish, rather black

YACIKE a small sparrow-sized bird with black cheeks

YACIN black, dark

YACIN BOSOI MAHATUN an ancient-style hat made from black cloth

YACIN BULEHEN a dark gray crane

YACIN DOBI a black fox

YACIN FEKŠUN a dye concocted from the leaves and stems of the plant *wence moo*

YACIN GARUDAI a black phoenix

YACIN GARUNGGŪ ILHA a deep blue exotic flower the buds of which resemble the *garunggū* bird

YACIN HONTOHONGGO GU a dark blue gem used during sacrifices in ancient times

YACIN SAMSU a type of fine dark

blue cloth
YACIN ŠEMPI black grained leather
YACIN ŠOŠONTU an ancient-style
  scarf for the hair made from black
  cloth
YACIN ULHU a dark gray squirrel
YACIN ŪN CECIKE black hawfinch
  (*Euphona migratoria*)
YACIN WEIJUN a pure black crow
YACIN YARHA a black panther
YACINGGA dark, somber
YACISU one name for the cormorant; cf.
  suwan
YADAHŪN 1. poor, wretched 2. sparse
  (of pocks)
  YADAHŪN FUSIHŪN poor and humble
YADAHŪŠAMBI to be hungry
YADALI CECIKE song thrush (*Garrulax
  canorus*)
YADALINGGE weak, feeble
YADALINGGŪ weak, soft, feeble
YADAMBI 1. to be poor, to be wretched,
  to suffer want 2. to be weak on one
  end (of a bow)
YADAN sapped of enthusiasm, lacking
  in confidence
  YADAN CECIKE a type of small light-
    brown bird
  YADAN OLIHA shy and retiring
YADANA whooper swan (*Cygnus cygnus*)
  YADANA ILHA the name of a flower
    that blooms at the beginning of
    spring and resembles a swan
  YADANA UJUNGGA FUKJINGGA HERGEN
    (鵠頭書) a style of Chinese
    calligraphy
YADARAKŪ undetermined, unforeseeable
YADE where? whither? to whom?
YAFAGAN see *yafahan*
YAFAHA same as *yafahan*
YAFAHALABUMBI caus. of *yafahalambi*
YAFAHALAMBI to walk, to go by foot
YAFAHAN pedestrian, on foot
  YAFAHAN COOHA infantry
  YAFAHAN COOHAI UHERI DA (步軍
    統領) General Commandant of
    the Gendarmerie, GH 797
  YAFAHAN GENEMBI to go by foot
  YAFAHAN GŪSAI DA (步軍參領)
    commander of the banner infantry
  YAFAHAN ISIBURE HŪSUN an errand boy
    at a post station
  YAFAHAN ISIBURE KUNGGERI (脚力料)
    a section of the Board of War
  YAFAHAN KŪWARAN I FIYENTEN (步營
    司) office of police affairs at
    the headquarters of the Manchu
    General-in-Chief at Mukden
  YAFAHAN UKSIN armored infantry
YAFAN garden, orchard
  YAFAN I DA chief gardener
YAFASI gardener
YAGI see *yahi*

YAHA 1. charcoal, coal 2. smoldering
  embers, charcoal fire
  YAHAI TEBUN an iron container for
    burning charcoal that can be hung
    from a chain
YAHANA sorghum ears that do not de-
  velop grains and turn black
  YAHANA COKO turkey; cf. *hogi*
  YAHANA MOO a wood from the South
    Seas that leaves no ash when it
    burns
YAHANAMBI 1. to become coal, to become
  charcoal 2. to turn black and not
  develop grain (of ears of grain)
YAHARI 'charcoal fruit'--the name of
  an exotic fruit
YAHI embezzlement, fraud
YAHILAMBI to swindle, to embezzle
YAI one one hundred-billionth
YAK (onom.) the sound made by a whip
YAK SEME 1. hard, painful (of falling
  or tripping) 2. choked off (of the
  voice) 3. hard, heavy (of things
  striking)
  YAK SEME SIBUHA choked up (of the
    voice)
  YAK SEME ŠUSIHALAHA beat hard with
    a whip
YAKA someone, who?
YAKAJAMBI to become dull (the teeth
  when chewing)
YAKCA demon, yaksha
YAKI case for a quiver
YAKILAMBI to put a case or cover on a
  quiver
YAKSA a place on a riverbank where
  the earth has caved in
  YAKSA HOTON Nerchinsk
YAKSARGAN woodcock (*Scopolax rusticola*)
YAKSIBUMBI caus. of *yaksimbi*
YAKSIGAN a thin board that is placed
  vertically on the main beam of a
  roof
YAKSIKŪ bolt of a door
YAKSIMBI to close, to shut, to bolt
YAKSITAI bluntly, decisively, defi-
  nitely
YAKŪNGGA peculiar, bizarre, out of the
  ordinary
  YAKŪNGGA MUDAN a peculiar sound,
    a strange melody or intonation
YAKŪNGGALAMBI 1. to act in a peculiar
  manner 2. to sing; cf. *yangkūng-
  galambi*
YALA truly, indeed
YALAKE truly, indeed, in fact
YALANGGI true, genuine
YALDARGAN one name for the kestrel;
  cf. *baldargan*
YALGA see *yalgan*
YALGAN a type of a crow that nests in
  wild areas and has speckled wings
YALHŪ a large wooden tub with four

Y

handles and four legs

YALI meat, flesh

YALI BELHERE FALGARI (大官署)
meat department of the Court of
Banqueting

YALI HAFIRAKŪ the flexible part of
the elephant's nose

YALI I BOO (肉房) meat section of the palace kitchen

YALI JOKSON thin, skinny (of livestock)

YALI JUN NARHŪN the wood fiber is
fine

YALI MISUN meat paste, meat condi-
ment

YALI MONGGON esophagus, food pipe

YALIHANGGA fleshy, fat, adipose

YALINAMBI to form flesh

YALINAHA DOLI the meat of a melon

YALINGGA fleshy, fat

YALITU a fat person

YALMANGGI soot

YALU the boundary between two fields

YALUBUMBI caus. of *yalumbi*

YALUKŪ 1. rider 2. an animal for
riding 3. a boundary

YALUMBI to ride (an animal)

YALUME ETEMBI to overcome the resistance of a horse by riding,
break (a horse)

YALUNABUMBI caus. of *yalunambi*

YALUNAMBI to go to ride

YALUNDUMBI/YALUNUMBI to ride together

YALUNJIMBI to come to ride

YAMAKA 1. seemingly, apparently,
probably 2. some, any

YAMAKAMBIO is someone there?

YAMARI GAHA one name for the raven

YAMBI to rise (of the evening vapors
that come during the still period
right after sunset)

YAMBURAKŪ 1. doesn't fit; cf. *yum-
burakū* 2. unclear, vague

YAMJI evening

YAMJI BUDA supper, the evening meal

YAMJI TOME every evening

YAMJIDARI every evening

YAMJIMBI to become evening

YAMJIŠUN late in the day, late, toward twilight

YAMJITALA until late, until evening

YAMKA 1. probably, seemingly 2. some

YAMKA INENGGI some day or other

YAMTARI the name of a quadruped with
very tasty flesh

YAMTUN a respiratory ailment, asthma

YAMTUNGGA afflicted with a respiratory
ailment

YAMULABUMBI caus. of *yamulambi*

YAMULAMBI 1. to go to a yamen, to go
to a government office 2. to go to
court

YAMULANJIMBI 1. to come to a yamen

2. to come to court

YAMUN 1. a government office, yamen,
headquarters 2. the court, palace

YAMUN I WAILAN yamen attendant

YAN (Chinese) ounce, tael

YAN HO fireworks

YAN SIYOO saltpeter

YANDACI a young badger; cf. *dorgon*

YANDUBUMBI caus. of *yandumbi*

YANDUGAN request, entreaty

YANDUMBI to request, to trouble someone to do something, to beg

YANDUNJIMBI to come to request

YANG yang, the male or positive principle

YANG ING (onom.) the sound of insects
flying

YANG SEME see *yang ing*

YANG YANG (onom.) the sound of bells
ringing

YANGDUWAN foreign satin

YANGGA 1. pine pitch 2. a torch made
with pine pitch

YANGGAHA carrion crow

YANGGALI a type of dark wagtail

YANGGAR SEME sounding for a long time,
re-echoing

YANGGIDEI one name for the golden
pheasant; cf. *junggiri coko*

YANGGILABUMBI caus. of *yanggilambi*

YANGGILAMBI to tease, to incite, to
flirt with

YANGGILANDUMBI to tease one another

YANGGIR IMAN a wild sheep of Shensi
that resembles the female argali

YANGGON bells attached to a horse's
forehead

YANGGŪHA see *yanggaha*

YANGGŪWAN gravel

YANGKAMBI to throw to the ground (in
wrestling)

YANGKŪNGGALAMBI to sing; cf. *yakūnggalambi*

YANGMEI 1. fruit of the plant *Myrica
rubra* 2. a small red sore on the
skin

YANGSABUMBI caus. of *yangsambi*

YANGSAMBI to weed, to chop weeds

YANGSAN weeding

YANGSANAMBI to go to weed

YANGSANGGA splendid, comely, beautiful

YANGSANUMBI to weed together

YANGSE 1. form, kind, appearance,
model, style 2. beauty, comeliness
3. beautiful, splendid, comely 4.
yoke for an ox

YANGSELABUMBI caus. of *yangselambi*

YANGSELAMBI to make up, to decorate

YANGSEMBI see *yangselambi*

YANGSIMU NIYEHE shelldrake (*Tadorna
tadorna*)

YANGŠAN 1. sickly, weak (of children)
2. noisy, talkative

Y

YANGŠANGGA noisy, overtalkative

YANGŠARAMBI 1. to be sickly and whiny
(of children) 2. to be overtalkative, to be clamorous

YANGTURI ambarella (*Spondias dulcis*)

YAR SEME 1. flowing in a fine line,
trickling 2. talking on and on

YARDU one name for the bustard; cf.
hwmudu

YARFUN a long leather cord attached to
the headstall or bridle, tether
 YARFUN TEMBI the tether hangs down
 (said of a horse that can't remain
 still)

YARGA see *yarha*

YARGICAN NIYEHE the name of a variety
of duck

YARGIYAKAN rather true, rather genuine

YARGIYÁLABUMBI 1. caus./pass. of *yargiyalambi* 2. to be wounded in battle

YARGIYALAMBI 1. to ascertain the truth,
to verify 2. to be wounded in battle

YARGIYAN 1. true, real, genuine, fac-
tual 2. truth, reality
 YARGIYAN TAŠAN the real and imaginary, the true and false, the full
 and empty

YARGIYANGGA true, honest

YARGIYŪN is it true?

YARHA leopard (*Felis pardus*)
 YARHA UNCEHENGGE GIRDAN a pennant
 made from a leopard's tail

YARHŪDABUMBI caus. of *yarhūdambi*

YARHŪDAMBI to lead, to guide

YARHŪDAN introduction, guidance

YARIBUMBI to have the face and ears
freeze

YARJU CECIKE one name for the hawfinch,
the same as *yacin ūn cecike*

YARKIYABUMBI caus./pass. of *yarkiyambi*

YARKIYAMBI to entice, to lure, to dally
with
 YARKIYARA COOHA decoy troops

YARKIYAN luring, enticement, dalliance

YARKIYANDUMBI to entice one another

YARSI DAMBAGU opium; cf. *afiun*

YARTAN ILHA the name of a blue flower
that faces the sun when it blooms

YARU 1. a soup made from a type of
frog found in Kirin 2. brook char
3. see *yarun*

YARUBUMBI caus./pass. of *yarumbi*

YARUDAI 'jade phoenix'--the phoenix of
the center

YARUGAN leading
 YARUGAN I FANGSE a banner carried
 in front of the coffin in a funeral
 procession
 YARUGAN SEJEN the wagon on which a
 coffin was carried

YARUKŪ ASU a large-meshed fish net that
one lets flow with the current

YARUMBI 1. to lead, to guide 2. to be
connected together, to be close together in a row
 YARUME continually, next to one
 another, successively
 YARUME BARGIYARA EDUN the name of
 the wind that blows from the west
 after the vernal equinox
 YARUME JURUME continually
 YARUME OKDORO KUMUN a piece of
 music of two strophes that was
 played while the emperor returned
 to the palace after a sacrifice
 YARURE MORIN a lead horse
 YARURE OKDORO KUMUN the same as
 yarume okdoro kumun

YARUN 1. introduction (to a book)
2. citation 3. leading, guiding 4.
a measure equaling one hundred
Chinese feet

YARUNGGA MUKŠAN a gold-lacquered staff
of the imperial escort

YASA 1. eye 2. a round hole, mesh of
a net
 YASA ARAMBI to wink, to signal
 with the eye
 YASA DARAMBI to look closely at,
 to scrutinize
 YASA EFEBUMBI to lose one's sight
 YASA FAHA eyeball
 YASA FETEMBI to make a round hole
 in an arrowhead
 YASA GADAHŪN NEIMBI to open the
 eyes very wide, to bulge the eyes
 YASA GEDEHUN NEIMBI to open the
 eyes wide, to gape
 YASA GEHUN HOLTOMBI to lie bla-
 tantly
 YASA GEHUN OMBI to be reduced to
 dire need
 YASA HABTAŠARA SIDENDE to wink,
 in the twinkling of an eye
 YASA HADAHAI TUWAMBI to stare at
 intently
 YASA MOROHON TUWAMBI to look with
 gaping eyes
 YASA NIOWANGGIYAN having covetous
 eyes
 YASA SELE pieces of iron attached
 to the three holes on the bottom
 of a quiver
 YASA ŠAHŪN GOLOMBI to be frightened
 till the eyes turn white
 YASA TATAMBI to open the eyes wide
 YASA TUWAHAI in an instant, right
 before one's eyes
 YASAI BULEKU eyeglasses
 YASAI HOŠO the corner of the eye
 YASAI HŪNTAHAN the eye socket
 YASAI JERIN the edge of the eye
 YASAI MUKE tear
 YASAI SIDEN between the eyes
 YASAI SILENGGI tears caused by the

Y

wind or by emotion

YASAHANGGE provided with small holes or openings

YASALABUMBI caus./pass. of *yasalambi*

YASALAMBI to glance at, to look at

YASATABUMBI to keep a hawk from closing its eyes during a whole night

YASATU HAFAN an ancient designation for censors

YASATU HIYAN a type of incense

YASE middleman, agent

YASHA 1. netting, screen, grating 2. a net woven from the hair of a horse's tail for catching small birds and animals 3. a screen placed on the eaves of the palace to keep birds from nesting there

YASHA FA a window covered with a criss-crossed netlike screen

YASHLABUMBI caus. of *yashalambi*

YASHALAMBI 1. to make netting or screen 2. to make lanterns 3. to place in a net bag

YASHALAHA DALANGGA a dam with filters

YASHANGGA provided with grillwork

YASHANGGA GIYALAKŪ a grillwork partition

YASHANGGA LOHO a sword with grillwork designs on the blade

YASHANGGA UCE a grillwork door

YASUKA an eagle resembling the *isuka* that is found in Liaotung

YATARABUMBI caus. of *yatarambi*

YATARAKŪ an instrument for striking a fire, a flint

YATARAKŪ FADU a bag for flint

YATARAKŪ MIYOOCAN a flintlock

YATARAMBI to strike a fire (with a flint)

YATUGAN see *yatuhan*

YATUHAN a zitherlike instrument having fourteen strings

YAYA every, each, any

YAYA DEMUN I OCI OKINI let it be as it may

YAYA HACIN every kind, every sort

YAYADAMBI to lisp, to speak unclearly

YAYAMBI to mumble (an incantation)

YE the secondary beams of a roof, a small beam

YE CA demon, yaksha

YEBCUKE see *yebcungge*

YEBCUNGGE pretty, likable, attractive

YEBCUNGGE BAITA affair of the heart

YEBE better, improved (of an illness)

YEBECUNGGE one who has gotten better, convalescent

YEBELEMBI to find amusing, to find pleasure in, to esteem (generally used only in the negative)

YEBEŠEMBI see *yebelembi*

YEBEŠEO bailiff, constable

YEBIHEN a ceiling cover made from paper

YEBKELEMBI to be capable

YEBKEN 1. capable, efficient 2. sharp, fine

YEBKEN HAHA a capable man

YEBKEN MORIN a fine horse

YECA see *yakca*

YECE a ghost with white hair and bloody wounds

YECE HUTU the same as *yece*

YECUHE 1. the name of a small black fly 2. flying ant

YEDUN a deer-head mask worn by hunters who are trying to lure deer

YEHE 1. a tube on the top of a helmet used for attaching a tassel 2. the surface of an arrowhead 3. white hemp that has been treated in lime water

YEHENGGE made of bleached linen

YEHENGGE ETUKU a mourning garment

YEHENGGE MAHALA a mourning hat

YEHERE porcelain, chinaware

YEHERE FENGSE a porcelain tray

YEHERENGGE made of porcelain

YEHETUN a kiln (for making porcelain)

YEISE coconut

YEKEMBI to sing erotic songs

YEKEN AKŪ lowly, debased, not upright

YEKENGGE noble, grand

YEKENGGE HAHA a noble man

YEKERAKŪ not upright, ignoble

YEKERŠEBUMBI caus./pass. of *yekeršembi*

YEKERŠEMBI to taunt, to incite

YEKSE a shaman's cap

YEKSEHE see *yekse*

YEKSERHEN a house lizard

YELMEN one name for the sparrowhawk; cf. *silmen*

YELU a boar, a male pig

YELU BAIMBI to seek a boar (of a sow)

YEMCEN 1. see *imcin* 2. see *yemji*

YEMJI 1. apparition, ghost 2. a deity of lakes and rivers--it takes the form of a three-year-old child with long ears, red eyes, and beautiful hair

YEMJIRI GASHA one name for the owl

YEMJITU DOBI the name of a mythical reptile on the Yangtze

YEN 1. a mountain path, an animal trail 2. yin--the female principle; cf. *e*

YENDEBUMBI caus. of *yendembi*

YENDEBUN (興) the name of one of the parts of the *Classic of Poetry*

YENDEMBI to rise, to flourish, to be prosperous

YENDEHE flourishing, prosperous

YENDEN ascent, rise

YENDENGGE MUDAN the rising tone of

Y

classical Chinese phonology

YENGGE bird-cherry (*Prunus padus*)

YENGGEHE small parrot

YENGGEHERI bright green, parrot-green

YENGGUHE large parrot

YENGGŪHE see *yengguhe*

YENGHUHE a female parrot

YENGKE MENGGUN small silver bars of about five ounces weight

YENGSI a banquet, a bridal banquet

YENJU a mountain path

YENMANGGI soot on the bottom of a pot

YENTU 1. a narrow woven belt 2. new feathers that grow next to the large wing feathers on a bird 3. an iron for ironing clothes

YENTU CECIKE the name of a small bird with brown eyes, blackish beak, white stripes over the eyes, speckled feathers, and yellow legs

YERHUWE ant

YERTEBUMBI caus./pass. of *yertembi*

YERTECUKE shameful

YERTECUN shame

YERTECUN GIRUCUN shame and disgrace

YERTEMBI to be ashamed, to be embarrassed

YERTEŠEMBI to be mortified from shame

YERU hole, pit, den (of tigers, panthers, leopards, wildcats, etc.)

YERUTU a stone house used by various aboriginal peoples of South China

YESORO an exotic apricotlike fruit

YEYE 1. maggot 2. glutinous, sticky 3. sticky mud 4. annoying, obtrusive 5. (paternal) grandfather

YEYE BELE glutinous rice

YEYE BOIHON sticky mud

YEYE HANDU the same as *yeye bele*

YEYE IRA glutinous millet

YEYE SESHUN annoying and loathsome

YEYE ŠUŠU glutinous kaoliang

YEYEDEMBI to speak in a long-winded, annoying manner

YO 1. a handful; cf. *sefere* 2. see *yoo*

YOBO 1. fun, play, joking 2. a person who likes to play, a merrymaker, mischievous person

YOBO MAKTAMBI to make someone laugh by amusing-talk, to joke

YOBO NIYALMA a mischievous person, a practical joker

YOBODOBUMBI caus./pass. of *yobodombi*

YOBODOMBI to have fun, to joke, to make sport of

YOCAMBI to itch, to be bitten by bugs

YODAMBI to carry suspended

YODAN raincoat, rain cape

YOGE a food offering (see below)

YOGE SINDAMBI to perform a service for the dead, to perform the *ullambana* service during which a

miniature pagoda made of fruit is scattered by monks

YOGE SINDARA ISAN a gathering for the *ullambana* service

YOGE SINDARA KARAN a miniature pagoda made from cakes (a type of offering)

YOGE SINDARA MANDAL the place where the *ullambana* service was performed, a service for the dead

YOHAN cotton

YOHAN SURI a type of thin cotton material

YOHAN UKSIN padded armor

YOHI 1. complete, intact, without gaps 2. a (complete) set

YOHIBUN a collection of documents or writings

YOHIMBI (-ka, -ra/ndara) 1. to form a scab 2. to pay heed to, to mind, to pay attention to

YOHINGGA whole, entire

YOHO yolk

YOHON water ditch in a field

YOHORON 1. a waterway in the mountains 2. small stream or canal

YOHORON GOCIMBI to expand like a dammed stream (said of fattening horses)

YOHORONOMBI to form a groove or furrow

YOJIN one name for the peacock; cf. *tojin*

YOJOHO itching

YOJOHOŠOMBI to itch to the point where one can't bear it any longer

YOJOMBI to itch; cf. *yocambi*

YOKCIN imposing, impressive

YOKCIN AKŪ small and pale, petty, unimpressive

YOKCINGGA having a good appearance, impressive

YOKIDUN the (Cantonese) partridge; cf. *jukidun*

YOKTAKŪ see *yokto akū*

YOKTO 1. proper, suitable, meet 2. meaningful 3. see also *ai yokto*

YOKTO AKŪ 1. improper, unsuitable, embarrassing 2. meaningless, depressed, without enthusiasm

YOKTOKŪ see *yokto akū*

YOLO cinereous vulture (*Vultur monachus*)

YOLO INDAHŪN the name of a dog with a thick head and tail, hanging lips, and big ears

YOLO JAHŪDAI the name of a boat propelled by a scull at the stern

YOLO YOKTO AKŪ thoroughly improper, thoroughly embarrassing

YOLOKTO pied woodpecker (*Dryobates cabanisi*)

YOLONGGI sparks or cinders that fly out from a fire

Y

YOLONGGO JAHŪDAI see *yolo jahūdai*
YOMBI (-ha) to go, to walk, to leave
YOMBUMBI see *yumbumbi*
YON walking, going
YONAMBI to go there
YONDOMBI to hold (of containers), to
  contain, fit
YONG SEME stupid, foolish
YONGGADUN HOOŠAN sandpaper
YONGGAJI NIYEHE a type of small gray
  wild duck
YONGGAN sand
  YONGGAN AISIN low-grade gold
  YONGGAN CIBIN sand martin (*Riparia
    riparia*)
  YONGGAN FETEKU the name of a small
    fish that burrows into the sand
YONGGARI crabapple
YONGGOR SEME continually, ceaselessly
YONGGŪWAN see *yonggan*
YONGKIRI COKO one name for the peewit;
  cf. *niyo coko*
YONGKIRI INGGALI one name for the pee-
  wit; cf. *niyo coko*
YONGKIYABUMBI caus. of *yongkiyambi*
YONGKIYAMBI to be complete, to do com-
  pletely, to complete
YONGKIYAN 1. completion, perfection
  2. complete, perfect
YONGKIYANGGA complete, perfect
YONGSIKŪ a person who talks foolishly
YONGSOMBI to lose (at gambling)
YONGSU ceremony, rite, custom, usage
YOO 1. sore, skin ulcer 2. a kiln
  3. name of a South Chinese aborig-
  inal people, Yao
YOOHAN see *yohan*
YOOMBI see *yombi*
YOONAMBI to form a sore or skin ulcer
YOONI complete, entire, all together,
  all
  YOONI BEYE the entire body
YOONINGGA complete, perfect
  YOONINGGA DASAN the T'ung-chih (同
    治) reign period, 1862--1875
YOOSE lock
YOOSELABUMBI caus. of *yooselambi*
YOOSELAMBI to lock, to lock up
  YOOSELARAKŪ UMIYESUN a leather belt
    with a lock
YOR SEME in a row, in a file
YORDOBUMBI caus./pass. of *yordombi*
YORDOMBI to shoot a horn or bone-tipped
  arrow; cf. *yoro*
YORO a horn-, bone-, or wood-tipped
  arrow
  YORO BAITA useless matter
  YORO GISUN rumor

YOSO principle, rule, way
YOSU see *yoso*
YOTO 1. fool, moron 2. foolish, stupid
YOYO an interjection of derision
YOYOMBI (-ho/ko) to be in dire need, to
  suffer dire poverty
YUBURŠEMBI to crawl (of worms and in-
  sects), to crawl away, to sneak off
YUMBI (-ngke, -pi/mpi, -ndere) 1. to
  have a preference for, to have an
  inclination toward 2. to be ad-
  dicted to, to become entranced 3.
  to absorb (a dye), to soak in 4. to
  fit, to contain, to hold
YUMBU SEME peacefully flowing
YUMBU YUMBU SEME swarming
YUMBUMBI caus./pass. of *yumbi*
YUMK'A one of the five notes of the
  classical pentatonic scale sounding
  like *la*
YUN rut, track
YUNGGE harmonious, peaceful
YUNGGIOI GASHA the emu
YUNGTURU fearless, dauntless
  YUNGTURU JANGKŪ a very sharp large
    sword with a thick back
YUR SEME flowing ceaselessly, billowing
  (of clouds)
YURUDAI the phoenix of the center; cf.
  yarudai
YURUN see *irun*
YUTU one-quadrillionth
YUWAMBOO a large bar of silver weighing
  fifty taels
YUWAN 1. an inkstone 2. an ape 3. a
  type of large turtle
  YUWAN AIHŪMA a type of large turtle
  YUWAN BOO see *yuwamboo*
YUWAN PAN (院判) an official in
  the Board of Colonial Affairs
YUWAN SIYOO the lantern festival
YUWANŠUWAI commander, marshal
YUWEI TAI a platform
YUYUMBI to starve, to go hungry
  YUYURE BEYERE hunger and cold,
    starving and freezing
YUYUN 1. hunger, starvation 2. poor
  harvest
YŪN BAN a sort of a cymbal or gong
YŪN FU (運副) Deputy Assistant
  Salt Controller, BH 835A
YŪN PAN (運判) Sub-Assistant
  Salt Controller, BH 835A
YŪN SY YAMUN I YŪN ŠI (鹽運司運
  使) Salt Controller, BH 835
YŪN TUNG (運同) Assistant Salt
  Controller, BH 835A

Y

Ž

ŽAN   see *sahaldai*

ŽI BEN GURUN   Japan

ŽU LAI   Tathāgata, epithet of Buddha
used by Buddha when speaking of
himself

Ž

Appendix

Ch'ing Reign Titles

1616-1626	Abkai Fulingga	天	命
1627-1635	Abkai Sure	天	聰
1636-1643	Wesihun Erdemungge	崇	德
1644-1661	Ljishūn Dasan	順	治
1662-1722	Elhe Taifin	康	熙
1723-1735	Hūwaliyasun Tob	雍	正
1736-1795	Abkai Wehiyehe	乾	隆
1796-1820	Saicungga Fengšen	嘉	慶
1821-1850	Doro Eldengge	道	光
1851-1861	Gubci Elgiyengge	咸	豐
1862-1874	Yooningga Dasan	同	治
1875-1908	Badarangga Doro	光	緒
1909-1911	Gehungge Yoso	宣	統

Common Weights and Measures

The system of weights and measures was standardized during the early Ch'ing period by the Board of Works (*Weilere arara fiyenten* 營造司).

MEASURES OF LENGTH
   Scale: 1 *jušuru* = .32 meters

   1 *juda*   (丈) = 10 *jušuru*

   1 *jušuru* (尺) = 10 *jurhun* -- one Chinese foot

   1 *jurhun* (寸) = 10 *fuwen* -- one Chinese inch (1/10th of a foot)

   1 *fuwen* (分) = 10 *eli* -- 1/100th of a foot

   1 *eli*   (釐) = 10 *hina* -- 1/1000th of a foot

319

MEASURES OF QUANTITY
  Scale: 1 *hiyase* = approximately 1 1/5 English pecks

  1 *hule*   (石) = 2 *sunto* -- a Chinese bushel

  1 *sunto*   (斛) = 5 *hiyase* -- 1/2 bushel

  1 *hiyase*   (斗) = 10 *moro hiyase* -- one Chinese peck

  1 *moro hiyase* (升) = 10 *oholiyo* -- 1/10th of a peck; a dry quart

MEASURES OF DISTANCE
  Scale: 1 *ba* = 576 meters

  1 *ba*   (里) = 360 *okson* -- one Chinese mile

  1 *okson* (步) = 5 *jušuru* -- see Measures of Length above

MEASURES OF AREA
  Scale: 1 *delhe* = 66,980.2 square meters

  1 *delhe* (頃) = 100 *mu*

  1 *mu*   (畝) = 240 square *okson* -- one Chinese acre; about 1/16 of
                                       an English acre

  1 *fuwen* (分) = 24 square *okson* -- 1/10th of a Chinese acre

MEASURES OF WEIGHT
  Scale: 1 *gingge* [catty] = 596.82 grams

  1 *ginggen* (斤) = 16 *yan* -- one catty

  1 *yan*   (兩) = 10 *jiha* -- one Chinese ounce

  1 *jiha*   (錢) = 10 *fuwen* -- 1/10th of an ounce

  1 *fuwen*   (分) = 10 *eli* -- 1/100th of an ounce

Smaller units of weight correspond to those for measures of length.

PUBLICATIONS ON ASIA OF THE SCHOOL OF INTERNATIONAL STUDIES (formerly the Institute for Comparative and Foreign Area Studies)

1. Boyd, Compton, trans. and ed. *Mao's China: Party Reform Documents, 1942-44.* 1952. Reissued 1966. Washington Paperback-4, 1966. 330 pp., map.
2. Siang-tseh Chiang. *The Nien Rebellion.* 1954. 177 pp., bibliog., index, maps.
3. Chung-li Chang. *The Chinese Gentry: Studies on Their Role in Nineteenth-Century Chinese Society.* Introduction by Franz Michael. 1955. Reissued 1967. Washington Paperback on Russia and Asia-4. 277 pp., bibliog., index, tables.
4. *Guide to the Memorials of Seven Leading Officials of Nineteenth-Century China.* Summaries and indexes of memorials to Hu Lin-i, Tseng Kuo-fan, Tso Tsung-tang, Kuo Sung-tao, Tseng Kuo-ch'üan, Li Hung-chang, Chang Chih-tung. 1955. 457 pp., mimeographed. Out of print.
5. Marc Raeff. *Siberia and the Reforms of 1822.* 1956. 228 pp., maps, bibliog., index. Out of print.
6. Li Chi. *The Beginnings of Chinese Civilization: Three Lectures Illustrated with Finds at Anyang.* 1957. Reissued 1968. Washington Paperback on Russia and Asia-6. 141 pp., illus., bibliog., index.
7. Pedro Carrasco. *Land and Polity in Tibet.* 1959. 318 pp., maps, bibliog., index.
8. Kung-chuan Hsiao. *Rural China: Imperial Control in the Nineteenth Century.* 1960. Reissued 1967. Washington Paperback on Russia and Asia-3. 797 pp., tables, bibliog., index.
9. Tso-liang Hsiao. *Power Relations within the Chinese Communist Movement, 1930-34.* Vol. 1: *A Study of Documents.* 1961. 416 pp., bibliog., index, glossary. Vol. 2: *The Chinese Documents.* 1967. 856 pp.
10. Chung-li Chang. *The Income of the Chinese Gentry.* Introduction by Franz Michael. 1962. 387 pp., tables, bibliog., index.
11. John M. Maki. *Court and Constitution in Japan: Selected Supreme Court Decisions, 1948-60.* 1964. 491 pp., bibliog., index.
12. Nicholas Poppe, Leon Hurvitz, and Hidehiro Okada. *Catalogue of the Manchu-Mongol Section of the Toyo Bunko.* 1964. 391 pp., index.
13. Stanley Spector. *Li Hung-chang and the Huai Army: A Study in Nineteenth-Century Chinese Regionalism.* Introduction by Franz Michael. 1964. 399 pp., maps, tables, bibliog., glossary, index.
14. Franz Michael and Chung-li Chang. *The Taiping Rebellion: History*

32. Jerry Norman. *A Manchu-English Lexicon*. 1978. 320 pp., appendix, bibliog.
33. James Brow. *Vedda Villages of Anuradhupura: The Historical Anthropology of a Community in Sri Lanka*. 1978. 268 pp., tables, figures, bibliog., index.